MASTER THE GRE® 2014

PETERSON'S
Publishing

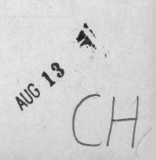

PETERSON'S
Publishing

About Peterson's Publishing

Peterson's Publishing provides the accurate, dependable, high-quality education content and guidance you need to succeed. No matter where you are on your academic or professional path, you can rely on Peterson's print and digital publications for the most up-to-date education exploration data, expert test-prep tools, and top-notch career success resources—everything you need to achieve your goals.

For more information, contact Peterson's, 3 Columbia Circle, Suite 205, Albany, NY 12203-5158; 800-338-3282 Ext. 54229; or find us online at www.petersonspublishing.com.

Bernadette Webster, Managing Editor; Jill C. Schwartz, Editor; Ray Golaszewski, Publishing Operations Manager; Linda M. Williams, Composition Manager; Kim Marcelliano, Project Manager; Jim Holsinger, Product Manager; Practical Strategies, CCG: Contributing Writers, Carol Domblewski, Demetrios Bonaros, Christopher F. Ryan, Reyna Eisenstark, Margaret C. Moran

ISBN-13: 978-0-7689-3748-0
ISBN-10: 0-7689-3748-5

Printed in the United States of America

10 9 8 7 6 5 4 3 2 1   15 14 13

By printing this book on recycled paper (40% post-consumer waste) 234 trees were saved.

Petersonspublishing.com/publishingupdates

Check out our Web site at www.petersonspublishing.com/publishingupdates to see if there is any new information regarding the test and any revisions or corrections to the content of this book. We've made sure the information in this book is accurate and up-to-date; however, the test format or content may have changed since the time of publication.

Certified Chain of Custody

60% Certified Fiber Sourcing and
40% Post-Consumer Recycled

www.sfiprogram.org

*This label applies to the text stock.

Sustainability—Its Importance to Peterson's Publishing

What does sustainability mean to Peterson's? As a leading publisher, we are aware that our business has a direct impact on vital resources—most especially the trees that are used to make our books. Peterson's Publishing is proud that its products are certified by the Sustainable Forestry Initiative (SFI) chain-of-custody standard and that all of its books are printed on paper that is 40% post-consumer waste using vegetable-based ink.

Being a part of the Sustainable Forestry Initiative (SFI) means that all of our vendors—from paper suppliers to printers—have undergone rigorous audits to demonstrate that they are maintaining a sustainable environment.

Peterson's Publishing continuously strives to find new ways to incorporate sustainability throughout all aspects of its business.

ANOTHER RECOMMENDED TITLE

Peterson's GRE®/GMAT® Math Review

OUR PROMISE
SCORE HIGHER. GUARANTEED.

Peterson's Publishing, a Nelnet company, focuses on providing individuals and schools with the best test-prep products—books and electronic components that are complete, accurate, and up-to-date. In fact, we're so sure this book will help you improve your score on this test that we're guaranteeing you'll get a higher score. If you feel your score hasn't improved as a result of using this book, we'll refund the price you paid.

Guarantee Details:

If you don't think this book helped you get a higher score, just return the book with your original sales receipt for a full refund of the purchase price (excluding taxes or shipping costs or any other charges). Please underline the book price and title on the sales receipt. Be sure to include your name and mailing address. This offer is restricted to U.S. residents and to purchases made in U.S. dollars. All requests for refunds must be received by Peterson's within 120 days of the purchase date. Refunds are restricted to one book per person and one book per address.

Send to:

Peterson's Publishing, a Nelnet company
3 Columbia Circle, Suite 205
Albany, NY 12203-5158

This guarantee gives you the limited right to have your purchase price refunded only if you are not satisfied that this book has improved your ability to score higher on the applicable test. If you are not satisfied, your sole remedy is to return this book to us with your sales receipt (within 120 days) so that we may refund the amount you paid for the book. Your refund is limited to the manufacturer's suggested retail price listed on the back of the book. This offer is void where restricted or prohibited.

Contents

PART III: ANALYTICAL WRITING

PART IV: VERBAL REASONING

PART V: QUANTITATIVE REASONING

PART VI: THREE PRACTICE TESTS

Contents

APPENDIXES

Before You Begin

Master the GRE® is your guidebook for navigating the GRE® revised General Test. In 2011, the test changed dramatically from the previous version. The biggest news was probably the removal of analogy and antonym questions. The test-makers finally woke up to the fact that in real life, a person is unlikely to be asked for the antonym of a word—unless the person is a crossword or Scrabble® aficionado. The new version of the GRE is designed to better predict test-takers' overall performance in graduate school.

The emphasis is on the test-takers' ability to think. You'll see that in the design of questions. You'll find reading comprehension questions that ask you to critique the validity of an author's argument or ask you to identify information that supports an author's argument. Other questions in the Verbal Reasoning section ask you to select the best word choice based on analyzing the context of a sentence or passage. In the Analytical Writing section, you'll be asked to evaluate someone else's argument and to develop an argument of your own. In the Quantitative Reasoning section, an on-screen calculator has been added for those taking the computer-based version of the test (those taking the paper-and-pencil test will be given a calculator at the testing site to use) to de-emphasize computation and emphasize the thought process used to arrive at answers.

You needn't begin to hyperventilate at this information. *Master the GRE®* will

- walk you through the parts of the test.
- give you strategies to use for each type of question.
- explain how to avoid some common writing problems.
- review basic arithmetic, algebra, geometry, and data analysis.
- help you develop your vocabulary for word-choice questions.
- provide simulated practice with four practice tests.

HOW THIS BOOK IS ORGANIZED

Master the GRE® is divided into six parts to facilitate your study:

- **Part I** explains basic information about the GRE revised General Test and provides an overview with examples of the different question types you'll find on the test.
- **Part II** offers a diagnostic test to help you identify your areas of strength and those areas where you will need to spend more time in your review sessions.
- **Part III** explores the Analytical Writing section of the test and offers strategies for developing well-supported and coherent responses to the types of tasks that you will be required to answer.
- **Part IV** goes into detail about the different question formats that you will find in the Verbal Reasoning section and offers strategies for answering each type.

- **Part V** describes the different question formats in the Quantitative Reasoning section of the test and offers strategies to help you figure out answers to the math questions.

- **Part VI** has three more tests that provide you with simulated practice in taking the GRE exam under timed conditions.

- The **Appendixes** offer two additional chapters to help you improve your writing. "Appendix A: Common Errors in Grammar and Mechanics," can help you avoid such mistakes as sentence faults, misplaced modifiers, subject-verb agreement, and pronoun problems. If misspelled words are a problem for you, check out "Appendix B: Often Confused and Confusing Words." Here you'll find a list of commonly misspelled words—words that sound somewhat similar but have completely different meanings and when used incorrectly could lower your score.

Each chapter in Parts IV and V contains practice sections to help you review what you have just learned.

SPECIAL STUDY FEATURES

Master the GRE® has several features that will help you get the most from your study time.

Overview

Each chapter begins with a listing of the major topics in that chapter followed by an introduction that explains what you will be reviewing.

Summing It Up

Each chapter ends with a point-by-point summary of the main points of the chapter. It can be a handy last-minute guide to review before the test.

Bonus Information

You will find three types of notes in the margin of the *Master the GRE®* to alert you to important information.

Note

Margin notes marked "Note" highlight information about the test structure itself.

Tip

A note marked "Tip" points out valuable advice for taking the GRE revised General Test.

Alert

An "Alert" identifies pitfalls in the testing format or question types that can cause mistakes in selecting answers.

USING THIS BOOK TO PREPARE FOR THE COMPUTER-BASED GRE

Important things to remember as you work through this book: When taking the computer-based version of the GRE, you'll be entering answers by typing on a keyboard or using a mouse. The Analytical Writing section requires that you compose short essays by typing in words, sentences, and paragraphs. The numeric entry questions from the Quantitative Reasoning section require that you type numbers into boxes. Other sections require that you pick choices by clicking on them with your mouse. Since you can't answer in this fashion in a book, you'll have to fill in your answers by hand when taking the tests and completing the exercises. Also, bear in mind that some questions may appear in a slightly different fashion due to the limitations of print. For instance, answer options will appear as letters with parentheses around them [(A), (B), (C), etc.] in this guide. On the actual exam, the answer options may appear as ovals or squares. But rest assured that all of the question content is similar to that found on the GRE revised General Test.

ACCESS THREE NEW GRE TESTS ONLINE

Peterson's is providing you with access to three additional GRE practice tests. The testing content on these three practice tests was created by the test-prep experts at Peterson's. The Peterson's online testing experience resembles the testing experience you will find on the actual GRE exam. You can access these three practice tests at http://www.petersonspublishing.com/gre. You will be asked to enter your e-mail address, and Peterson's will e-mail you an activation code and the link needed to access the GRE online practice tests.

YOU ARE WELL ON YOUR WAY TO SUCCESS

You have made the decision to apply to graduate school and have taken a very important step in that process. *Master the GRE®* will help you score high on the exam and prepare you for everything you'll need to know on the day of your exam. Good luck!

FIND US ON FACEBOOK®

Join the GRE conversation on Facebook® at www.facebook.com/petersonspublishing and receive additional test-prep tips and advice. Peterson's resources are available to help you do your best on these important exams—and others in your future.

GIVE US YOUR FEEDBACK

Peterson's publishes a full line of books— test prep, career preparation, education exploration, and financial aid. Peterson's publications can be found at high school guidance offices, college libraries and career centers, and your local bookstore and library. Peterson's books are now also available as eBooks.

We welcome any comments or suggestions you may have about this publication. Your feedback will help us make educational dreams possible for you—and others like you.

PART I

ABOUT THE GRE REVISED GENERAL TEST

The Basics of the GRE revised General Test

chapter 1

OVERVIEW

- **Test organization**
- **Test time limits**
- **Test tools**
- **Scoring the test**
- **Test day**
- **General test-taking strategies to remember**
- **International test-takers: paper-and-pencil version**
- **Summing it up**

Can a standardized test be "test-taker friendly"? That's the claim of the Graduate Record Exam revised General Test that launched in 2011. In addition, the General Test claims to be a better predictor of success in graduate school than the old version of the exam. All GRE test-takers began using the GRE revised General Test as of August 1, 2011.

Educational Testing Service (ETS), the creator and administrator of the GRE, notes that there is increased maneuverability and functionality in the computer-based version. Test-takers can now edit and change their work and even skip questions within a section to return to before timing out of that section. In other words, the General Test is not as computer adaptive and so more closely resembles a paper test in which you can go back and forth within sections and "erase" and change answers. However, the Quantitative Reasoning and Verbal Reasoning sections are section-level adaptive; that is, the questions for the second Quantitative reasoning and Verbal Reasoning sections are based on how well you perform on the first sections of questions. (The test also has an on-screen calculator for use in doing computations and a word processing program for the two Analytical Writing tasks.)

According to ETS, the new question types better mirror the types of reasoning skills that test-takers are called on to use in graduate and business school. The topics in the Analytical Writing section, the problems in the Quantitative Reasoning sections, and the passages used as the basis for questions in the Verbal Reasoning sections simulate the real-world issues and situations that students encounter in their course work for advanced degrees. The scores that result from the revised GRE are considered by ETS to be "more reliable" than the previous test.

TEST ORGANIZATION

The GRE revised General Test is divided into three areas of assessment: Analytical Writing, Verbal Reasoning, and Quantitative Reasoning. The first section will always be Analytical Writing. The other sections may appear in any order.

Analytical Writing

Analytical Writing assesses your ability to think critically and transfer your ideas into well-developed, well-reasoned, and well-supported writing. There are two tasks for this section of the test: an Argument Task and an Issue Task. The first requires that you analyze someone else's argument and the second that you build your own argument either in support of or in disagreement with an opinion, policy, recommendation, or claim. Thus, the GRE assesses your ability to develop and support your own ideas and your ability to analyze another's argument and his or her supporting evidence. In addition, you will also be expected to sustain well-focused and coherent writing and control the elements of Standard Written English.

You won't have a choice of tasks in either section; there will only be one prompt to answer for each task. In addition, the tasks are more specific and completing them will rely on your ability to think critically and write analytically.

Verbal Reasoning

NOTE
According to ETS, more than 800 MBA programs worldwide now accept the revised GRE® as an alternative to the Graduate Management Admissions Test (GMAT®). In the last four years, the number of business schools accepting the GRE revised General Test for MBA admissions has quadrupled.

The Verbal Reasoning sections of the GRE revised General Test assess your ability to understand, analyze, and apply information found in the types of reading you'll be doing in graduate school. According to ETS, the questions "better measure your ability to understand what you read and how you apply your reasoning skills." Among the questions you'll find are ones that ask you to reason from incomplete data; analyze and draw conclusions; identify authors' assumptions and perspectives; distinguish major and minor points; understand the structure of a text; understand the meaning of words, sentences, and passages; and understand multiple levels of meaning.

Three types of questions appear in the Verbal Reasoning section:

1. Reading comprehension
2. Text completion
3. Sentence equivalence

The reading comprehension questions are further divided into multiple-choice questions—select one answer choice; multiple-choice questions—select one or more answer choices; and select-in-passage questions. The text completion questions may require one, two, or three answers, whereas each sentence equivalence question requires two answers.

Quantitative Reasoning

According to the GRE, Quantitative Reasoning sections measure your ability to understand, interpret, and analyze quantitative information; use mathematical models to solve problems; and apply basic mathematical knowledge and skills. The Quantitative Reasoning section requires basic knowledge in arithmetic, algebra, geometry, and data analysis. On the GRE revised General Test, the subject matter of the questions will emphasize real-world scenarios and data interpretation.

The purpose of the on-screen calculator is to de-emphasize computation and emphasize the thought processes used to determine what the question is asking and how to go about finding the answer. While you'll find that the traditional multiple-choice question is the format used for the majority of questions, some multiple-choice questions will ask you to select one or more answers and the numeric entry questions provide no answer options from which to choose.

The Quantitative Reasoning section consists of four types of questions:

1. Multiple-choice questions—select one answer choice
2. Multiple-choice questions—select one or more answer choices
3. Quantitative comparison questions
4. Numeric entry questions

With the exception of quantitative comparison questions, the questions in the Quantitative Reasoning sections may also appear as part of a data interpretation set: a group of questions that refer to the same tables, graphs, or other data presentation.

Number of Questions

The computer version of the GRE revised General Test is divided into five scored sections and one additional section that may be an unidentified unscored section or an identified research section. The unidentified unscored section may be either a Verbal Reasoning or a Quantitative Reasoning section and may come in any order after the Analytical Writing section, which always comes first. The research section is always the last section and may be either Verbal Reasoning or Quantitative Reasoning. You won't have both unscored sections in any given test.

The breakdown of scored sections by question is:

Section	Number of Sections	Number of Questions
Analytical Writing	One	Two writing tasks
Verbal Reasoning	Two	Approximately 20 questions
Quantitative Reasoning	Two	Approximately 20 questions

Within the Verbal Reasoning and Quantitative Reasoning sections, you will find the different types of question formats mixed together. For example, you may find a sequence of three reading comprehension passages (with several different question formats), a sentence equivalence question, two text completion questions, two reading comprehension passages, and so on. The same is true of Quantitative Reasoning sections, which will mix the two types of multiple-choice questions, numeric entry, and quantitative comparison questions.

TEST TIME LIMITS

The GRE revised General Test will take approximately 3 hours and 45 minutes. You will also have time for several short breaks, which are not included in the actual testing time. There will be a 10-minute break after you finish the third section. Between the other test sections, you'll be allotted breaks of 1 minute each.

NOTE

The time allotments and number of questions differ for test-takers outside the United States who will be taking the paper-and-pencil version of the revised GRE. This information can be found in the International Test-Takers: Paper-and-Pencil Version section of this chapter.

The breakdown of time allotments for each section is as follows:

Section	Number of Sections	Number of Questions	Time Per Section
Analytical Writing	One	Two writing tasks	30 minutes for each writing task
Verbal Reasoning	Two	Approximately 20 questions	30 minutes per section
Quantitative Reasoning	Two	Approximately 20 questions	35 minutes per section

The unscored sections will have the same number of questions and the same time allotments as the scored sections.

TEST TOOLS

Test-takers at computer testing sites will find two on-screen tools as well as increased maneuverability and functionality. For the Quantitative Reasoning sections, you'll find an on-screen calculator with the four basic functions—addition, subtraction, multiplication, division—and a square root. You'll also be able to enter some of the answers directly from the calculator into the answer boxes using a transfer function. The calculator was added, according to ETS, in order to place more emphasis on test-takers' reasoning skills than on their computational skills.

For the Analytical Writing tasks, you'll be working in an ETS-designed word processing program that will allow you to write, insert and delete text, cut and paste, and undo actions. However, the program doesn't have a spell checker or a grammar checker.

The increased functionality of the revised GRE enables you to move back and forth within a section so you can

- preview a section.
- mark questions within a section to return to later.
- change and edit answers within a section.

The testing experience mirrors much of the paper-and-pencil testing process that you've been familiar with since taking your first standardized test. As a result, many of the same strategies such as "skip and return" that you've honed through years of testing can be used with the computerized GRE.

SCORING THE TEST

For the Verbal Reasoning and Quantitative Reasoning sections of the GRE revised General Test, the scoring has changed. Instead of the familiar 200 to 800 range with a 10-point increment, the scales for both sections changed to a 130 to 170 range. Perhaps the biggest change is the use of 1-point increments in reporting scores. No longer will scores be reported in jumps of 10 points, but in small increments of 1 point. (So, the score scale has moved from a 61-point scale to a 41-point scale.) ETS states that the reason for the change in increments is "to produce scores that don't exaggerate small performance differences between examinees." A 2-point difference looks a great deal smaller than a 20-point difference.

Analytical Writing hasn't substantially changed, so it continues to be reported in half-point increments using a 0-to-6 range. Each writing task is evaluated separately, and an average is taken and used as the reported score based on the 0–6 scale.

TEST DAY

There are several rules and restrictions to be aware of on test day. The following bulleted lists are from the ETS Web site (http://www.ets.org/gre/revised_general/test_day/). You should check the Web site for more updates as test day approaches.

Test Center Procedures and Regulations for Both Computer-Based and Paper-Based Tests

- Dress so that you can adapt to any room temperature.

- Visitors are not permitted in the testing room while testing is in progress.

- ID verification at the test center may include thumbprinting, photographing, videotaping, or some other form of electronic ID confirmation. If you refuse to participate, you will not be permitted to test and you will forfeit your registration and test fees. This is in addition to the requirement that you must present acceptable and valid identification.

- Food, drinks, and tobacco are not allowed in the testing room.

- If you have health-related needs that require you to bring equipment, beverages, or snacks into the testing room or to take extra or extended breaks, you need to follow the accommodations request procedures described in the *Bulletin Supplement for Test Takers with Disabilities or Health-related Needs* available at http://www.ets.org/s/gre/pdf/bulletin_supplement_test_takers_with_disabilities_health_needs.pdf.

- Do not bring cell phones, smartphones (e.g., BlackBerry® devices, iPhones), PDAs, and other electronic or photographic devices into the test center.

- Personal items other than identification documents are not allowed in the testing room. Neither ETS nor the test centers assume any responsibility whatsoever for personal items or devices that you choose to bring into the test center.

- The test administrator will assign you a seat.

- On occasion, weather conditions or other circumstances beyond the test administrator or ETS's control may require a delayed start or the rescheduling of your test appointment. In the event that a technical problem at the test center makes it necessary to cancel your test session, or if it is later determined that your scores could not be reported, you will be offered the opportunity to schedule another test appointment free of charge or receive a full refund of the original test fee.

- You will be asked to designate your score recipients at the test center on the test day. If an institution is not listed, ask the test center administrator for the appropriate form to indicate unlisted institutions. Complete the form and turn it in before you leave the test center. The form will not be accepted after you leave the test center.

- If you do not select score recipients on the test day, or you would like to send your scores to more than four score recipients, you will need to submit an Additional Score Report request for a fee of $25 per score recipient.

For Computer-Based Tests Only

The following procedures and regulations apply during the entire test session, which begins at sign-in, ends at sign-out, and includes breaks.

- If you requested and received an authorization voucher from ETS, you must take it with you to the test center.

- You will be required to write (not print) and sign a confidentiality statement at the test center. If you do not complete and sign the statement, you cannot test and your test fees will not be refunded.

- You may be required to sign the test center log before and after the test session and any time you leave or enter the testing room.

- You may be asked to remove your watch and to store it during the test administration.

- The test administrator will provide you with scratch paper that may be replenished after you have used all pages of the scratch paper initially given to you. You may not take your own scratch paper to the test, nor may you remove scratch paper from the testing room at any time.

- If at any time during the test you have a problem with your computer, or for any reason need the administrator, raise your hand.

- Testing premises are subject to videotaping.

- The GRE revised General Test includes an optional 10-minute break after the third section and 1-minute breaks between the remaining sections of the test. These break times cannot be exceeded. You are required to remain in the test center building or in the immediate area.

- If you need to leave your seat at any time other than the break, raise your hand; timing of the section will not stop.

- You will have access to an on-screen calculator during the Quantitative Reasoning sections.

- Personal calculators are not permitted in the testing room.

- Because of the essay scoring process, you will not be able to view your Analytical Writing scores at the time you test.

- Test centers cannot provide printed copies of unofficial score reports.

For Paper-Based Tests Only

The following procedures and regulations apply during the entire test session, which begins when you are admitted to the test center, ends when you leave the test center, and includes breaks.

- Test administrators will not honor requests for schedule changes.

- Take your admission ticket and identification document(s) to the test center.

- Take three or four sharpened soft-lead (No. 2 or HB) pencils and a good eraser. Pencils and erasers will not be supplied at the center. Mechanical pencils and pens are not permitted.

- No test-taker will be admitted after test materials have been distributed.

- With the exception of your admission ticket, paper of any kind is not permitted in the testing room.

- You must have the test administrator's permission to leave the room during the test. Any time lost cannot be made up. You are required to remain in the test center building or in the immediate area.

- You may wish to pace yourself with your own watch, but the test administrator is the official timekeeper. *Watch alarms are not permitted to track time.*

- You may work only on the test section designated by the test center supervisor and only for the time allowed. You will not be permitted to continue the test or any part of it beyond the established time limit.

- You will write your essay responses and enter your answers to test questions in the test book, rather than on a separate answer sheet.

- You will be provided with an ETS calculator to use during the Quantitative Reasoning sections.

- You may not use your own personal calculator.

- At the end of the test you will be required to return your test book to the test administrator. This material is the property of ETS.

- The GRE revised General Test includes a 10-minute break after the second Analytical Writing section. This break time cannot be exceeded.

- At the end of the test, you will be given the option to cancel your scores.

GENERAL TEST-TAKING STRATEGIES TO REMEMBER

Not all strategies will work for all questions. But there are some strategies that will work for most, if not all, questions:

- Anticipate and use the clock.
- Skip and return to questions.
- Eliminate answer choices that you know are incorrect.
- Use educated guessing.

The more you practice these and the strategies described for particular kinds of question formats described in this book, the easier the strategies will be to remember, to figure out which are appropriate to use with which questions, and to apply on test day.

Anticipate and Use the Clock

When you take the GRE revised General Test, a clock icon will appear on your screen to show elapsing time. That is, at all moments, you will know exactly how much time you have remaining. To take full advantage of this on-screen device, time yourself using the practice tests in this book and figure out how much time you have per question.

Suppose you typically do the easier text completion and sentence equivalence items at the rate of 30 seconds per item, whereas the harder ones take you about a minute. Given that approximately half the questions on the Verbal Reasoning sections consist of those two types, and the total number of questions on a Verbal Reasoning section is 20 questions, you might budget about 10 minutes for those two types of questions, adding in a minute or so for review, extra-hard questions, or other issues. For the 30-minute test, that leaves approximately 20 minutes for the reading comprehension questions, or about 2 minutes a question.

If you find at the halfway point for time that you're working significantly faster than is necessary, you may want to slow down and take more time with each question. If, on the other hand, you find at the halfway point you're working slower than you need to be, you may want to speed up and take less time with each question. Keep in mind, however, that you cannot speed-read passages and questions, so speed up only a bit.

Skip and Return to Questions

If at first you don't see how to answer a certain question in a reasonable amount of time, don't hesitate to skip it. If you do skip a question, make sure you click the "Mark" button so that you can find that question quickly on the "Review" screen at a later point. After you've answered all the other questions—and before your time for the section has run out—go back to any question you've left unanswered and try to solve it. Remember: There's no wrong-answer penalty, so don't leave any questions unanswered!

Eliminate Answer Choices You Know Are Incorrect

Don't overlook this time-honored strategy! It will not only help you arrive at the answer, but it can also help calm test jitters as you come closer and closer to the correct answer.

Educated Guessing

Educated guessing builds on the strategy of eliminating answer choices that you know are incorrect, but you have to know something about the question for educated guessing to be effective. The process works this way:

- Eliminate answer choices you know are incorrect.
- Discard any choices in which part of the answer is incorrect.
- Reread the remaining answer choices against each other and against the question again.
- Choose the answer that seems correct to you. More often than not, you'll be right.

INTERNATIONAL TEST-TAKERS: PAPER-AND-PENCIL VERSION

Test-takers outside the United States without access to a computer testing site will have a slightly different paper-and-pencil GRE test from the paper-and-pencil test given to test-takers in the United States. The test will not have an unidentified unscored or identified unscored research section. The test will be composed of the following sections, number of questions, and time per section:

Section	Number of Sections	Number of Questions	Time Per Section
Analytical Writing	One	Two writing tasks	30 minutes for each writing task
Verbal Reasoning	Two	25 questions	35 minutes per section
Quantitative Reasoning	Two	25 questions	40 minutes per section

You'll be given a calculator to use for the Quantitative Reasoning sections of the GRE.

The test will be given in October, November, and February, and scores will be reported six weeks after the test date.

ALERT!

The paper-and-pencil version has a multiple-choice adaptation of the select-in-passage question. All other question formats are the same.

SUMMING IT UP

- The GRE revised General Test launched in 2011 is considered by ETS to be a better measure of a test-taker's success in graduate or business school than the previous test.

- The GRE revised General Test is not computer-adaptive. It allows test-takers to move back and forth within sections to return to skipped questions and to change and edit answers. An on-screen calculator and word processing program are included.

- The GRE has three sections: Analytical Writing, Quantitative Reasoning, and Verbal Reasoning. Analytical Writing is always first.

- Quantitative Reasoning and Verbal Reasoning have two scored sections each, which may come in any order. The computer version of the test may have an unidentified, unscored Quantitative Reasoning or Verbal Reasoning section or an identified, unscored research section of either type.

- The Analytical Writing section has two tasks: an Argument Task and an Issue Task. You'll be given one prompt for each task and will not have a choice from which to select.

- Verbal Reasoning sections have a mix of reading comprehension, text completion, and sentence equivalence questions. Each has its own question format. Questions based on reading passages may be multiple-choice—select one answer; multiple-choice—select one or more answers; or select-in-passage questions. Text completion questions may require one, two, or three responses selected from lists of multiple-choice answers. Sentence equivalence questions require two answers selected from a single list of multiple-choice options.

- Quantitative Reasoning sections have multiple-choice, quantitative comparisons, and numeric entry question formats. The last does not offer a list of potential answers from which to choose.

- The test takes 3 hours and 45 minutes and has the following time limits and questions:

Section	Number of Sections	Number of Questions	Time Per Section
Analytical Writing	One	Two writing tasks	30 minutes for each writing task
Verbal Reasoning	Two	Approximately 20 questions	30 minutes per section
Quantitative Reasoning	Two	Approximately 20 questions	35 minutes per section

- The scores for the Quantitative and Verbal Reasoning sections are reported on a score scale of 130 to 170 with 1-point increments. The Analytical Writing score is reported on a scale of 0 to 6 with half-point increments.

- Four general test-taking strategies will help in most situations: (1) anticipate and use the clock, (2) skip and return to questions, (3) eliminate answer choices that you know are incorrect, and (4) use educated guessing.

- In some places outside the United States, test-takers will take a paper-and-pencil version of the General Test incorporating the new philosophy of the test items and the new question formats. The number of questions and time allotments per section are slightly different.

A Quick Look at GRE Question Formats

chapter 2

OVERVIEW

- Analytical Writing
- Answer Option Differences
- Verbal Reasoning
- Quantitative Reasoning
- Summing it up

The GRE assesses three areas: (1) Analytical Writing, (2) Verbal Reasoning, and (3) Quantitative Reasoning. You'll have to write two types of essays for the Analytical Writing section: an essay to support an argument and an essay discussing an issue. While you'll find the majority of test items are in the multiple-choice format that you're familiar with from other standardized tests, the GRE presents several additional test-item formats both in the Verbal Reasoning and Quantitative Reasoning sections. This chapter introduces each test-item formats with examples and also discusses the differences between the two types of writing tasks and their requirements.

ANALYTICAL WRITING

The Analytical Writing section of the GRE tests both your ability to think critically and your ability to write analytically. The section has two writing tasks: one is called the argument task and the other is the issue task. You'll be given a prompt and a set of directions for each task; you won't have a choice of tasks from which to select.

The argument task prompt will ask you to evaluate an argument and the evidence to support it, not to give your opinion about it. The issue task essay is your opportunity to opine about an issue. In this way, the GRE assesses both your ability to state a position and to support it as well as your ability to assess another person's position and the evidence supporting it. As you will see below, both types of essay prompts are accompanied by specific instructions about how to respond to the prompt.

Time Limits

If you're taking the computer version, you'll have 30 minutes to read each prompt, gather your ideas, and write your response. In allotting your 30 minutes, take about 5 minutes to read the prompt, decide on your point of view, and marshal your ideas; take about 20 minutes to write your essay; and leave about 5 minutes to reread and edit your essay. Points are not deducted for spelling and grammar mistakes, but as ETS points out: "severe and persistent errors will detract from the overall effectiveness of your writing and lower your score accordingly."

Software

The computer you'll be taking your test on will be equipped with a word processing program developed by ETS. According to ETS, you'll be able to insert and delete text, cut and paste, and undo actions. However, the program doesn't include either a spell checker or a grammar checker, so using a few minutes at the end of the writing period to edit for grammar, usage, and spelling errors can be helpful in ensuring that your essay is clearly expressed.

The Scoring Rubric

Your argument task and issue task essays will be scored on a 6-point scale by two readers. These readers are your audience, and your purpose in writing this essay is to earn the best score that you can. Six is the maximum score your response can earn. The scale ranges in 1-point increments from 6 to 0.

Rubric for the Issue Task

6 Points

To earn 6 points, your response should exhibit these characteristics:

- A clear, focused position on the issue, and an overall response to the specific writing task that is thorough, cogent, and sophisticated.
- Fully developed, persuasive support for the position, including, but not limited to, particularly apt or well-chosen examples, facts, and other illustrations, as well as an explanation that clearly and effectively links the support to the specific requirements of the writing task.
- A rhetorically effective method of organization, such as one that organizes support by order of importance and saves the most effective reasons for last. Connections between and among ideas are logical and may also be as subtle as they are effective.
- A formal grace that is a product primarily of well-constructed, varied sentences and exact and rhetorically effective word choices.
- Adherence to almost all the conventions of Standard Written English, including grammar, usage, and mechanics. If there are any errors, they are minor.

5 Points

To earn 5 points, your response will likely have these characteristics, though it may exceed one or more of them yet fall short on another:

- A clear, focused position on the issue, and a thoughtful, complete response to the specific writing task.
- Persuasive support for the position, including, but not limited to, examples, facts, and other illustrations, as well as an explanation that clearly links the support to the specific requirements of the writing task.
- An effective method of organization with logical connections between and among all ideas.
- Well-constructed, varied sentences and appropriate word choices that help create clarity as well as interest.

- Adherence to almost all the conventions of Standard Written English, including grammar, usage, and mechanics. If there are any errors, they should be minor.

4 Points

To earn 4 points, a response will have these characteristics:

- A clear position on the issue, and a generally complete response to the specific writing task.
- Support for the position, as well as an explanation that links the support to the specific requirements of the writing task.
- A logical method of organization.
- Sentences and word choices that generally create clarity.
- General adherence to the conventions of Standard Written English. Some errors may occur.

3 Points

Your response will earn only 3 points if it has *one or more* of the following characteristics:

- A generally clear position and a response to the specific writing task that may be limited in scope or marred by occasional vagueness, extraneous detail, repetition, or other flaws.
- Limited or inadequate support for the position or a limited or inadequate explanation that links the support to the specific requirements of the writing task.
- Lapses in organization or confusing organization, and/or lack or misuse of transitional words and phrases.
- Sentences and word choices that occasionally interfere with clarity.
- One or more errors in the conventions of Standard Written English that are so significant that they obstruct meaning.

2 Points

Your response will earn only 2 points if it has *one or more* of the following characteristics:

- A wandering, unclear, or limited response characterized by an unclear or not fully articulated position and a response to the specific writing task that is limited or inadequate in scope or marred by vagueness, extraneous detail, repetition, or other flaws.
- Inadequate support and explanation.
- Confusing organization, and/or general lack or misuse of transitional words and phrases.
- Sentences and word choices that interfere with clarity.
- Repeated errors in the conventions of Standard Written English that are so significant that they obstruct meaning.

1 Point

Your response will earn only 1 point if it has *one or more* of the following characteristics:

- An unclear position and almost no response to, or minimal understanding of, the specific task.
- A total lack of support or only illogical or flawed support for the main point or points; a total lack of explanation or only an illogical or flawed explanation of the main points of your argument in relation to the specific details of the task.

- No pattern of organization or confusing organization.
- Sentences and word choices that interfere with clarity.
- So many errors in the conventions of Standard Written English that they obstruct meaning throughout the response.

0 Points

This score is possible under the following circumstances:

- The response does not answer the task in any way.
- The response is written in a foreign language.
- The response simply copies the argument.
- The response is not legible.
- The response is nonverbal.

Rubric for the Argument Task

6 Points

To earn 6 points, your response should exhibit these characteristics:

- A logically sound, well-focused answer to the specific task that is particularly insightful, thoughtful, deep, or sophisticated.
- Fully developed, persuasive support for the main point or points of your response. At this high level of response, examples and other illustrations are particularly apt or well chosen, and their relationship to the focus of your analysis is extremely clear and/or well articulated.
- A method of organization that complements the main ideas of the analysis by effectively creating a flow of well-organized paragraphs and easing the reader's progress through the paper from first word to last. Connections between and among ideas are logical and may also be as subtle as they are effective.
- A formal grace that is a product primarily of well-constructed, varied sentences and exact and rhetorically effective word choices.
- Adherence to almost all the conventions of Standard Written English, including grammar, usage, and mechanics. If there are any errors, they are minor.

5 Points

To earn 5 points, your response will likely have these characteristics, though it may exceed one or more of them yet fall short on another:

- A logically sound, focused answer to the specific task that reflects insight and evidences some deep thought.
- Well-developed, persuasive support for the main point or points of your response. Examples and other illustrations are well chosen, and their relationship to your argument is clear.
- A method of organization that complements main ideas and connects ideas clearly and in a logical order.

- Well-constructed, varied sentences and appropriate word choices that help create clarity as well as interest.
- Adherence to almost all the conventions of Standard Written English, including grammar, usage, and mechanics. If there are any errors, they are minor.

4 Points

To earn 4 points, a response will have these characteristics:

- A generally focused answer to the specific task.
- Varying degrees of adequate and inadequate support.
- A logical method of organization, although some linkages may be missing or unclear.
- Sentences and word choices that generally create clarity, though some problems may exist with structure or usage.
- General adherence to the conventions of Standard Written English. Some errors may occur.

3 Points

Your response will earn only 3 points if it has *one or more* of the following characteristics:

- An inadequate answer to the specific task. It may not quite respond to the task or all aspects of it; it may be limited in its scope or number of points; or it may be vague or confusing in places.
- Inadequate support for the main point or points of your response or support that is illogical.
- A pattern of organization that does not complement the main ideas or causes confusion for the reader.
- Sentences and word choices that occasionally interfere with clarity.
- One or more errors in the conventions of Standard Written English that are so significant that they obstruct meaning, or very frequent minor errors.

2 Points

Your response will earn only 2 points if it has *one or more* of the following characteristics:

- An inadequate or unclear answer to the specific task. It may not quite respond to the task or all aspects of it; or it may be too vague or confusing to answer the task adequately.
- Little, if any, support, or support that is illogical.
- Confusing or inadequate organization.
- Sentences and word choices that interfere with clarity.
- Repeated errors in the conventions of Standard Written English that are so significant that they obstruct meaning.

1 Point

Your response will earn only 1 point if it has *one or more* of the following characteristics:

- Almost no response to, or minimal understanding of, the specific task.
- A total lack of support or only illogical or flawed support.
- No pattern of organization or confusing organization.
- Many sentences and word choices that interfere with clarity.

- So many errors in the conventions of Standard Written English that they obstruct meaning throughout the response.

0 Points

This score is possible under the following circumstances:

- The response does not answer the task in any way.
- The response is written in a foreign language.
- The response simply copies the argument.
- The response is not legible.
- The response is nonverbal.

Understanding Scoring

Both the issue task and the argument task have their own scoring rubrics. As you can see from the previous rubrics, the emphasis in evaluating your response will be placed on your ability to put together a cogent and coherent piece of writing. The position that you take is not important. What is important is that you state your position effectively and demonstrate in your response an ability to state, develop, and support your position clearly and with pertinent evidence.

Note also that the rubrics include an assessment of writing style. Varying your sentence structure and using a precise, appropriate, and effective vocabulary can make your response clearer and more interesting and forceful. Lack of sentence variety and vague, imprecise language can pull down your score. While adherence to Standard Written English conventions is part of each rubric, it's less important (according to the test-makers) than your ability to craft a well-developed, well-reasoned, and well-supported piece of writing. However, remember that sloppy and incorrect grammar and spelling can get in the way of coherence.

Each essay is evaluated and scored separately, but a single combined score is reported for Analytical Writing. The combined, or reported, score is an average of the scores for the two essays. The range for the reported score is 0 to 6 with half-point increments, that is, 6 and 5.5, 5 and 4.5, 4 and 3.5, 3 and 2.5, 2 and 1.5, and 1 and 0.5. The evaluation instrument is similar to the rubrics at each level.

The Issue Task

The prompt for the issue task presents you with a very brief statement, recommendation, claim, viewpoint, or policy and asks you to agree or disagree with it. The issue will be of a general nature to which anyone could respond. No special knowledge is required. You can choose to agree or disagree with the issue as long as you follow the set of instructions that accompany the premise that is set up in the prompt. For example, you might find the following prompt and a set of instructions similar to the following wording:

> A nation should require all its citizens between the ages of 18 and 30 to serve one year in national service.
>
> Write a response in which you discuss your viewpoint on the proposed policy and the reasons for your point of view. Take into consideration the potential consequences of implementing the policy and the extent to which these consequences influence your viewpoint in developing and supporting your response.

There are six different sets of instructions that the item writers may choose from to state how you should respond to an issue task. These instructions specify the degree or conditions of your agreement or disagreement. For example, you may be asked to respond using instructions similar to the following wording:

1. Discuss how much you agree or disagree with the statement and why, as well as considering how the statement might or might not always be true and how these considerations affect your point of view.

2. Discuss how much you agree or disagree with the recommendation and why. Using specific examples, explain how the circumstances under which the recommendation could be adopted would or would not be advantageous. In developing and supporting your viewpoint, explain how these specific circumstances affect your point of view.

3. Discuss how much you agree or disagree with the claim and include the most compelling reasons and/or examples that someone could use to dispute your point of view.

4. While addressing both viewpoints provided, discuss which more closely aligns with your own. Explain your reasons for holding this position when providing evidence for your response.

5. Discuss how much you agree or disagree with the claim and the reasoning used to support that claim.

6. Discuss your viewpoint on the proposed policy and the reasons for your point of view. Take into consideration the potential consequences of implementing the policy and the extent to which these consequences influence your viewpoint in developing and supporting your response.

The Argument Task

The prompt for the argument task essay presents you with a brief argument and then states your task: to analyze the argument for its logic or reasonableness and express your analysis in a well-developed, well-reasoned, and well-supported response. To do so, you'll have to identify problems in the argument's reasoning, its evidence, the assumptions (stated or implied) on which the argument's claim is based, the conclusions drawn from the argument, or the predictions based on the argument. You may also have to point out a lack of evidence, raise questions, present alternative explanations, and consider other implications. You will not have to—nor should you—agree or disagree with the argument. Save your own views for the issue task essay.

Like the issue task, the argument task provides a prompt and a set of instructions telling you how to craft your response. The prompt—the argument—and instructions might look like the following:

In an effort to save money and be environmentally conscious, Philadelphia replaced all its traffic lights with red, green, and amber LED lights. The move was estimated to save the city $1 million. However, the first heavy snowfall showed a flaw in the plan. The LED lights did not throw off as much heat as the old-style bulb, so the snow did not melt from the traffic lights, causing disruptions at major intersections. A city council member put forward a motion to replace immediately all the LED lights with the older bulbs.

Write a response in which you discuss the questions that need to be asked and answered to determine if the recommendation and the argument on which it is based are reasonable. As part of your response, describe how the answers would help in the evaluation process.

There are eight different sets of instructions for writing your response. For example, you may have wording similar to the following:

1. Discuss the evidence needed to assess the argument. Include specific examples and an explanation of how the evidence might weaken or strengthen the argument.

2. Discuss the stated and/or unstated assumptions and explain how the argument is based on these assumptions and the implications for the argument if the assumptions are shown to be unjustified.

3. Discuss the questions that need to be asked and answered to determine if the recommendation and its argument are reasonable. As part of your response, describe how the answers would help in the evaluation process.

4. Discuss the questions that need to be asked and answered to determine if the advice and its argument are reasonable. As part of your response, explain how the answers would help in the evaluation process.

5. Discuss the questions that need to be asked and answered to determine if the recommendation is likely to result in the outcome that is projected. As part of your response, explain how the answers would help in the evaluation process.

6. Discuss the questions that need to be asked and answered to determine if the prediction and its argument are reasonable. As part of your response, explain how the answers would help in the evaluation process.

7. Presented with an explanation, discuss one or more alternative explanations that could reasonably compete with the proposed explanation. Explain how your explanation(s) account for the facts in the argument that is proposed.

8. Discuss the questions that need to be asked and answered to determine if the conclusion and the argument it is derived from are reasonable. As part of your response, explain how the answers would help in the evaluation process.

A Word About Numbers in Argument Prompts

The GRE cautions test-takers not to be confused by the purpose of any numbers, percentages, or statistics in the prompts used for the argument task. They are present as evidence and should be evaluated in terms of whether they support the argument that is presented, show flaws in the argument, or are extraneous. Such information may also be evidence that you can use to buttress your own points. The following is an example similar to what you might find on the GRE:

> A recent study showed that fatal crashes were reduced by 24 percent in intersections where traffic safety cameras had been installed. The data was collected between 1996 and 2004 in fourteen large cities that instituted the program during that period. The conclusion was that people were paying more attention to the lights as they got close to them because running a red light meant getting a ticket. The tickets averaged as much as $100. As a result, every major city and medium-sized city should install traffic cameras at busy intersections.

As you think through ideas to write a response, you might turn these pieces of data into questions to ask yourself such as: 24 percent seems like a lot, but is that number cumulative or an average of the fourteen cities? How many fatalities in real numbers does this represent? For how many years was each city actually in the program? Is the percentage skewed downward because the majority of cities were only in it two years, three years, and so on? The data is not meant to provide you with a math problem to solve, but as a source of questions to help you shape your response.

ANSWER OPTION DIFFERENCES

All multiple-choice questions in the computer-based test will have answer options preceded by either blank ovals or blank squares depending on the question type. You will use your mouse to select one or more of these options. The paper-and-pencil test will follow the same format of answer choices, but it will use letters instead of ovals or squares for answer choices.

For your convenience in answering questions and checking answers in this book, we use (A), (B), (C), etc. By using letters with parentheses, you will find it easy to check your answers against the answer key and explanation sections.

Numeric entry questions will have to be typed in, and Analytical Writing essays will need to be composed using a keyboard and mouse in the computer-based test. For this guide and the paper-and-pencil exam, you will have to handwrite all of your answers and essays.

VERBAL REASONING

The Verbal Reasoning section has three components and several question formats. The components are (1) Reading Comprehension, (2) Text Completion, and (3) Sentence Equivalence. While the majority of questions on the Verbal Reasoning sections will be multiple-choice and the majority of those will require choosing a single answer, you will find some nontraditional question formats.

Reading Comprehension Question Formats

The Reading Comprehension questions may be multiple-choice—select one answer choice; multiple-choice—select one or more answer choices; and a select-in-passage format. The multiple-choice questions may refer back to the passage using line or sentence numbers or highlighting text with bold type.

NOTE

For your convenience in answering questions and checking answers, this book uses (A), (B), (C), etc., instead of the blank ovals and squares that appear on the computer-based test.

ALERT!

The computer version will have two verbal reasoning sections of approximately 20 questions each to be completed in 30 minutes, and the paper-and-pencil version for test-takers outside the United States will have 25 questions to be completed in 35 minutes.

Multiple-Choice—Select One Answer Choice

You are undoubtedly familiar with this question format from all the other standardized tests you've ever taken. For the GRE, you'll have a list of five answer choices from which to choose for the majority of reading comprehension questions. On the actual computer-based exam, instead of capital letters in parentheses, you'll see blank ovals. The format will look something like this:

FOR THIS QUESTION, CHOOSE ONLY <u>ONE</u> ANSWER CHOICE.

The author of the passage would most likely agree with which of the following statements?

- ○ Professor Bates did not take into consideration the number of voters who said they would vote, but didn't.
- ○ Professor Bates did not consider the problems with accuracy inherent in exit polls.
- ● Professor Bates's sample was neither large enough nor random enough.
- ○ Professor Bates should have known that plus or minus 10 points was too large a range to be valid.
- ○ Professor Bates should not have stopped sampling 10 days before the election, considering how volatile the race was.

Multiple-Choice—Select One or More Answer Choices

The list of multiple-choice options for this question format is limited to three. The answer choices for multiple-choice—select one or more answer choices are preceded by blank squares, not ovals. (But again, we use letters in parentheses to indicate answer options in our guide, which allows for easy checking against the answer key and explanation sections.) The question will indicate that you should select all answer choices that apply. You may find that only one of the answers is correct, or you may find that two are, or even all three. The format will look something like this:

FOR THIS QUESTION, CONSIDER EACH ANSWER INDIVIDUALLY AND CHOOSE <u>ALL</u> THAT APPLY.

According to the critic, what qualities were more evident in her later novels than in her earlier ones?

- ■ less social satire
- ☐ more stereotypically drawn characters
- ■ more dialogue and less description of characters' motivations

A Variation on the Standard Multiple-Choice Question

Within the multiple-choice format—either select one answer choice or select one or more answer choices—you may find questions that use line numbers to refer to a particular line. Questions with line numbers are usually vocabulary questions such as "In line 4, the word 'sterling' most nearly means" followed by a list of possible answers. You're probably familiar with this question type if you have taken the SAT Subject Test on Literature or the AP English Literature and Composition Exam.

A Variation on the Standard Multiple-Choice Passage

You may find a passage with bold type highlighting two parts of the passage and a question that asks you about the two parts. The arrangement might look something like the following:

> ...**Jones's ultimate mistake in the eyes of historians was his disregard of Turner's thesis on the closing of the frontier.** However, Jones's own theory was found to be no more penetrating nor half as well supported as he claimed Turner's was. For one thing, Jones's argument was considered weak because he had not consulted the territorial records. His articles tended to lack
> 5 statistical support, and his conclusions overly generalized from the spotty data that he had used.
>
> Jones's response centered on the fact that he considered his function in life to be popularizing dull and boring history for a popular audience. This won him no friends in academia, but his books about the colorful frontier made him pots of money—like the pot of gold at the end of a rainbow on a rain-soaked prairie—to satirize Jones's florid prose. **Jones claimed his wealth**
> 10 **evoked jealousy in his peers.**
>
> How does the author of the passage use the two sentences in bold to make his point that Jones was an egotist?

Select-in-Passage Questions

Select-in-passage questions appear on the computer version of the GRE in one format and on the paper-and-pencil version in another format. On the latter test, select-in-passage questions will be in the form of traditional multiple-choice questions. On the computer version, test-takers will be asked to highlight a sentence within the passage itself.

If the passage is a single paragraph, the entire passage may be the source of the answer. If the passage has several paragraphs, only a certain portion of the passage will be relevant to the question. That portion will be called out between arrows ($\rightarrow$). To answer the question, you will need to click on the sentence that is your answer choice. If you try to click on a sentence outside the selected area, the sentence will not be highlighted. The question and directions will be set up similarly to the following arrangement:

> ... rather than allow for a vote on the bill, the senator chose to begin a filibuster that would last for 24 hours and 18 minutes. $\leftarrow$ Senator Thurmond was speaking against the passage of the Civil Rights Act of 1957. Because of the strong emotionalism of the opposition to civil rights for African Americans, the Senate saw another record-breaking filibuster in 1964. Senator
> 5 Robert Byrd and his colleagues held the Senate floor for 75 hours. Senator Byrd who came in time to renounce his opposition to civil rights legislation spoke for 14 hours and 13 minutes. $\rightarrow$
>
> Filibusters against civil rights legislation continued during the 1960s as Southern senators fought to keep the status quo in place. However, the Civil Rights Movement had gained momentum and would not be silenced. ...
>
> 10 Select the sentence that explains the causal relationship between filibusters and proposed civil rights legislation.

Note the arrows within the passage. The portion of the passage that is the subject of the question begins within the paragraph and ends at the end of the same paragraph.

Text Completion Questions

Text completion questions are based on a single passage. The passage may have from one to three blanks. If the passage has one blank to fill in, there is a list of five answer choices from which to select set up in a column. If the passage has two or three blanks, there will be a list of three answer choices for each blank set up in two to three columns. Once you have decided on your answer, you click on the cell with that answer. In our guide, there will be letter next to the word choices. The format will look something like the following:

> **FOR THIS QUESTION, CHOOSE ONE ANSWER FOR EACH BLANK. SELECT FROM THE APPROPRIATE COLUMN FOR EACH BLANK. CHOOSE THE ANSWER THAT BEST COMPLETES THE SENSE OF THE TEXT.**

A major issue that may slow the (i) _____ of electric cars is the difficulty of charging the engines. Until or unless local (ii) _____ legislate the installation of charging stations in new construction, at train stations, and in parking lots, (iii) _____ of electric cars say that the general public will not embrace these environmentally friendly vehicles.

Blank (i)	Blank (ii)	Blank (iii)
(A) manufacturing	(D) municipalities	(G) opponents
(B) proliferation	(E) companies	(H) advocates
(C) building	(F) people	(I) lovers

Sentence Equivalence Questions

Sentence equivalence questions differ from traditional multiple-choice questions in two significant ways. First, there are six answer choices rather than the usual five. Second, you have to choose two answers from the list to complete the one answer blank. That is, sentence equivalence questions ask you to complete a sentence using two different words that are similar, or equivalent, in meaning. Both completed versions of the sentence must convey a similar meaning. To receive credit for your answer, both answer choices must be correct. The answer choices are preceded by blank squares, not ovals. No partial credit is given if only one of the words is correct.

The direction line for all sentence equivalence questions is the same and is worded something like the following:

FOR THIS QUESTION, CHOOSE <u>TWO</u> ANSWERS THAT BEST FIT THE MEANING OF EACH SENTENCE AND THAT RESULT IN COMPLETED SENTENCES WITH THE SAME OR NEARLY THE SAME MEANING.

The art expert, hired by the potential buyer, was unable to _____ the painting as being from the school of Rembrandt.

- ■ authenticate
- ☐ place
- ☐ authorize
- ■ verify
- ☐ depose
- ☐ approve

Some Advice About Checking Answers

As you work through the practice test, you should get an idea of how long a text completion item takes you. As you increase your proficiency with these items, you may find that a simple text completion, or a text completion with just one blank, takes perhaps twenty to thirty seconds, while the longer two-blank and three-blank text completion items may run 45 seconds to a minute or more to complete.

For this reason, if you come to the end of a Verbal Reasoning section, and you have a minute or two left, your wisest use of time might be to double-check text completion or sentence equivalence items. Every one of them counts just as much as a reading comprehension answer. So, with a remaining 60 seconds, you may be able to skim and, conceivably, correct two text completion items, or 8 percent of the test, whereas 60 seconds spent on a reading comprehension question might not get you through a rereading of a passage and question.

QUANTITATIVE REASONING

The Quantitative Reasoning sections of the test intersperse multiple-choice, quantitative comparison, and numeric entry questions. The multiple-choice questions will be in two formats: the traditional "select one answer choice" and the newer "select one or more answer choices." The majority of questions will be the multiple-choice format, and the majority of those will be the traditional "select one answer choice."

Those taking the computer version of the GRE will have an on-screen calculator to use. It will allow you to add, subtract, multiply, divide, and find square roots. It will look something like this:

Those taking the paper-and-pencil test outside the United States will be given a calculator at the test site. Don't bring your own because you won't be allowed to use it.

Multiple-Choice—Select One Answer Choice

All questions using the multiple-choice—select one answer choice format list five possible answer choices, only one of which is correct. The choices are preceded by an oval to click to select your answer. The question will look something like the following:

FOR THIS QUESTION, CHOOSE ONE ANSWER CHOICE.

If $y = (x + 8)^2$, then $(-3x - 24)^2$ must equal which of the following?

○ $-9y^2$

○ $-3y^2$

○ $-9y$

○ $3y$

● $9y$

Multiple-Choice—Select One or More Answer Choices

This format may have, as the name states, one, two, three, or more correct answers. Unlike reading comprehension test items that use the multiple-choice—select one or more answers format, questions using this format in the Quantitative Reasoning section may have up to eight answer options. However, there will always be at least three answer choices listed and they will all have blank squares in front of them.

In most instances, the direction line with one of these questions will tell you to "indicate all that apply." However, the direction line may specify the number that you should choose. The following example provides a typical direction line for such a question:

> **FOR THIS QUESTION, INDICATE <u>ALL</u> THE ANSWERS THAT APPLY.**

Which two of the following integers give you a product of less than −54?

- ■ −9
- ☐ −5
- ☐ 6
- ■ 9
- ☐ 4
- ☐ −6
- ☐ 5
- ☐ 1

NOTE

The correct answers are −9 and 9. You need to look at numbers that when multiplied together result in a negative number. So, −9 × 6 = −54, which is not less than −54. Next, look at −9 × 9 = −81, which is less, so there is no need to do more.

In order to gain credit for multiple-choice—select one or more answer questions, you need to select the correct number of answers and the answers you choose must all be correct. There is no partial credit for partially correct answers.

Quantitative Comparison Questions

Quantitative comparison questions present you with two quantities, A and B. The objective is to compare the two quantities and choose one of the following answers, which always appear in this order:

Quantity A is greater.
Quantity B is greater.
The two quantities are equal.
The relationship cannot be determined from the information given.

Some quantitative comparison questions will have additional information centered above the two columns. This information will help you determine the relationship between the two quantities. Any symbol that appears more than once in a question has the same meaning throughout the question; for example, a symbol in the centered information and in Quantity A.

TIP

To save time on the test, memorize the answers so that you don't have to read them each time you come across a quantitative comparison question.

A quantitative comparison question will look like the following:

> **FOR THIS QUESTION, COMPARE QUANTITY A AND QUANTITY B. THIS QUESTION HAS ADDITIONAL INFORMATION ABOVE THE TWO QUANTITIES TO USE IN DETERMINING YOUR ANSWER.**

1 kilo = 2.2 pounds

Quantity A	Quantity B
1 kilo of gold	2.2 pounds of flour

○ Quantity A is greater.

○ Quantity B is greater.

● The two quantities are equal.

○ The relationship cannot be determined from the information given.

NOTE

The two quantities are equal. Since it's stated that a kilo is equal to 2.2 pounds, Quantity A and Quantity B are equal.

Numeric Entry Questions

Unlike the other Quantitative Reasoning question formats, numeric entry questions don't have a list of answer choices from which to choose your answer. Instead, you're given a question and one or two answer boxes. If the answer is an integer or decimal, there will be one answer box. If the answer is a fraction, you'll see two answer boxes, one over the other with a line between them. You'll enter the numerator in the top box and the denominator in the bottom box.

To solve the problem, you'll use the onscreen calculator. If the answer is an integer or decimal, you can use the "Transfer Display" function to enter your answer in the box. If the answer is a fraction, you'll need to type your answer into the two boxes using the keypad.

A numeric entry question will look like the following:

> **FOR THIS QUESTION, ENTER YOUR ANSWER IN THE BOX.**

If x and y are integers, what is the absolute value of y if $y = -6x + 32$ and $x = -4$?

NOTE

The correct answer is 56. Solve the equation for y using the value –4 for x, so

$y = -6(-4) + 32$

$y = 24 + 32$

$y = 56$

Data Interpretation Sets

In addition to the different types of question formats, you'll probably also find at least one group of questions revolving around the same table, graph, or other data representation. These are known as data interpretation sets. All that means is that to answer the two or three questions related to the data on the graphic, you will need to reference the graphic.

SUMMING IT UP

- The GRE assesses three areas: (1) Analytical Writing, (2) Verbal Reasoning, and (3) Quantitative Reasoning.

- The Analytical Writing section requires two writing assignments: an issue task and an argument task. The issue task asks you to give your opinion about an issue, whereas the argument task asks you to evaluate an argument and the evidence used to support it.

- Each writing prompt is accompanied by a set of instructions indicating how you should respond to the issue or argument. Finished writing tasks are evaluated against a 6-point rubric. The rubrics are different for the two kinds of writing.

- The Verbal Reasoning section has three components: (1) reading comprehension, (2) text completion, and (3) sentence equivalence.

- Reading comprehension questions may be multiple-choice—select one answer choice; multiple-choice—select one or more answer choices; and select-in-passage questions. The last requires test-takers using the computer version to highlight a sentence within the subject passage as the answer. For the paper-and-pencil test, this format has been converted to a multiple-choice—select one answer choice question.

- Reading comprehension questions that use the traditional one-answer multiple-choice format present a list of five answer choices preceded by ovals. The multiple-choice—select one or more answer choices format presents only three possible answers preceded by squares. All three options may be correct, or only one, or only two.

- Text completion questions present a passage with from one to three blanks that must be completed by choosing from a list of possible answers. If the question has only one blank, then five possible choices are provided. If the question has two or three blanks to fill in, there will be a list of only three possible answers for each blank.

- Sentence equivalence questions provide six possible answers, but only one blank to complete. To answer the question, you must use two words from the list that will complete the sentence so that both versions are similar, or equivalent, in meaning.

- Quantitative Reasoning questions may take the form of multiple-choice—select one answer choice; multiple-choice—select one or more answer choices; quantitative comparison; and numeric entry formats.

- Multiple-choice—select one answer choice is the traditional multiple-choice format and lists five possible answer choices preceded by ovals.

- Multiple-choice—select one or more answer choices lists at least three answer choices, but may have as many as eight possible answers. The direction line usually says simply to "indicate all that apply." However, some questions may indicate an exact number to select.

- Quantitative comparison questions are set up as two columns, Quantity A and Quantity B, which you must compare and decide if one is greater than the other, they are equal, or the relationship can't be determined from the information. Some questions may provide additional information above the quantities to help you determine your answer.

- Numeric entry questions don't list answer choices. You must calculate your answer using the on-screen calculator and enter it on-screen. If you're taking the paper-and-pencil test because you're outside the United States, you'll be given a calculator at the test site to use.

- For questions that require more than one answer, credit is given only if all answer choices are correct.

PART II

DIAGNOSING STRENGTHS AND WEAKNESSES

CHAPTER 3   Practice Test 1: Diagnostic

PRACTICE TEST 1: DIAGNOSTIC ANSWER SHEETS

Section 1: Analytical Writing

Analyze an Issue

FOR PLANNING

ANALYZE AN ISSUE RESPONSE

_____
_____
_____
_____
_____
_____
_____
_____
_____
_____
_____
_____
_____
_____
_____
_____
_____
_____
_____
_____
_____
_____
_____
_____
_____
_____
_____
_____
_____
_____
_____
_____
_____
_____
_____
_____
_____
_____

ANALYZE AN ISSUE RESPONSE

_____

_____

_____

_____

_____

_____

_____

_____

_____

_____

_____

_____

_____

_____

_____

_____

_____

_____

_____

_____

_____

_____

_____

_____

_____

_____

_____

_____

_____

_____

_____

_____

_____

answer sheet

ANALYZE AN ISSUE RESPONSE

_____
_____
_____
_____
_____
_____
_____
_____
_____
_____
_____
_____
_____
_____
_____
_____
_____
_____
_____
_____
_____
_____
_____
_____
_____
_____
_____
_____
_____
_____
_____
_____
_____
_____
_____
_____
_____
_____
_____
_____
_____
_____

ANALYZE AN ISSUE RESPONSE

_____

_____

_____

_____

_____

_____

_____

_____

_____

_____

_____

_____

_____

_____

_____

_____

_____

_____

_____

_____

_____

_____

_____

_____

_____

_____

_____

_____

_____

_____

answer sheet

Analyze an Argument

FOR PLANNING

ANALYZE AN ARGUMENT RESPONSE

answer sheet

ANALYZE AN ARGUMENT RESPONSE

ANALYZE AN ARGUMENT RESPONSE

_____

_____

_____

_____

_____

_____

_____

_____

_____

_____

_____

_____

_____

_____

_____

_____

_____

_____

_____

_____

_____

_____

_____

_____

_____

_____

_____

_____

_____

_____

_____

_____

answer sheet

ANALYZE AN ARGUMENT RESPONSE

Section 2: Quantitative Reasoning

1. Ⓐ Ⓑ Ⓒ Ⓓ
2. Ⓐ Ⓑ Ⓒ Ⓓ
3. Ⓐ Ⓑ Ⓒ Ⓓ
4. Ⓐ Ⓑ Ⓒ Ⓓ
5. Ⓐ Ⓑ Ⓒ Ⓓ
6. Ⓐ Ⓑ Ⓒ Ⓓ
7. Ⓐ Ⓑ Ⓒ Ⓓ
8. Ⓐ Ⓑ Ⓒ Ⓓ
9. Ⓐ Ⓑ Ⓒ Ⓓ Ⓔ
10. Ⓐ Ⓑ Ⓒ Ⓓ Ⓔ

11. Ⓐ Ⓑ Ⓒ Ⓓ Ⓔ Ⓕ Ⓖ Ⓗ
12. Ⓐ Ⓑ Ⓒ Ⓓ Ⓔ
13. Ⓐ Ⓑ Ⓒ Ⓓ Ⓔ
14. Ⓐ Ⓑ Ⓒ Ⓓ Ⓔ
15. Ⓐ Ⓑ Ⓒ Ⓓ Ⓔ Ⓕ Ⓖ Ⓗ

16. Ⓐ Ⓑ Ⓒ Ⓓ Ⓔ
17. Ⓐ Ⓑ Ⓒ Ⓓ Ⓔ
18. Ⓐ Ⓑ Ⓒ Ⓓ Ⓔ
19. ☐
20. ☐
     ☐

Section 3: Verbal Reasoning

1. Ⓐ Ⓑ Ⓒ Ⓓ Ⓔ
2. Ⓐ Ⓑ Ⓒ Ⓓ Ⓔ Ⓕ
3. Ⓐ Ⓑ Ⓒ Ⓓ Ⓔ Ⓕ
4. Ⓐ Ⓑ Ⓒ Ⓓ Ⓔ Ⓕ Ⓖ Ⓗ Ⓘ
5. Ⓐ Ⓑ Ⓒ
6. Ⓐ Ⓑ Ⓒ Ⓓ Ⓔ
7. Ⓐ Ⓑ Ⓒ Ⓓ Ⓔ
8. Ⓐ Ⓑ Ⓒ Ⓓ Ⓔ
9. Ⓐ Ⓑ Ⓒ Ⓓ Ⓔ
10. Ⓐ Ⓑ Ⓒ

11. Ⓐ Ⓑ Ⓒ Ⓓ Ⓔ
12. Ⓐ Ⓑ Ⓒ Ⓓ Ⓔ
13. Ⓐ Ⓑ Ⓒ
14. Ⓐ Ⓑ Ⓒ
15. Ⓐ Ⓑ Ⓒ Ⓓ Ⓔ

16. Ⓐ Ⓑ Ⓒ Ⓓ Ⓔ Ⓕ
17. Ⓐ Ⓑ Ⓒ Ⓓ Ⓔ Ⓕ
18. Ⓐ Ⓑ Ⓒ Ⓓ Ⓔ Ⓕ
19. Ⓐ Ⓑ Ⓒ Ⓓ Ⓔ Ⓕ
20. Ⓐ Ⓑ Ⓒ Ⓓ Ⓔ

Section 4: Verbal Reasoning

1. Ⓐ Ⓑ Ⓒ Ⓓ Ⓔ
2. Ⓐ Ⓑ Ⓒ Ⓓ Ⓔ
3. Ⓐ Ⓑ Ⓒ Ⓓ Ⓔ Ⓕ
4. Ⓐ Ⓑ Ⓒ Ⓓ Ⓔ Ⓕ Ⓖ Ⓗ Ⓘ
5. Ⓐ Ⓑ Ⓒ Ⓓ Ⓔ Ⓕ Ⓖ Ⓗ Ⓘ
6. Ⓐ Ⓑ Ⓒ Ⓓ Ⓔ
7. Ⓐ Ⓑ Ⓒ
8. Ⓐ Ⓑ Ⓒ Ⓓ Ⓔ
9. Ⓐ Ⓑ Ⓒ
10. Ⓐ Ⓑ Ⓒ Ⓓ Ⓔ

11. Ⓐ Ⓑ Ⓒ Ⓓ Ⓔ
12. Ⓐ Ⓑ Ⓒ Ⓓ Ⓔ
13. Ⓐ Ⓑ Ⓒ Ⓓ Ⓔ Ⓕ
14. Ⓐ Ⓑ Ⓒ Ⓓ Ⓔ Ⓕ
15. Ⓐ Ⓑ Ⓒ Ⓓ Ⓔ Ⓕ

16. Ⓐ Ⓑ Ⓒ Ⓓ Ⓔ
17. Ⓐ Ⓑ Ⓒ Ⓓ Ⓔ
18. Ⓐ Ⓑ Ⓒ
19. Ⓐ Ⓑ Ⓒ Ⓓ Ⓔ
20. Ⓐ Ⓑ Ⓒ Ⓓ Ⓔ

answer sheet

Section 5: Quantitative Reasoning

1. (A) (B) (C) (D)
2. (A) (B) (C) (D)
3. (A) (B) (C) (D)
4. (A) (B) (C) (D)
5. (A) (B) (C) (D)
6. (A) (B) (C) (D)
7. (A) (B) (C) (D)
8. (A) (B) (C) (D)
9. (A) (B) (C) (D) (E)
10. (A) (B) (C) (D) (E)

11. (A) (B) (C) (D) (E)
12. (A) (B) (C) (D) (E)
13. ☐
14. (A) (B) (C) (D) (E)
15. (A) (B) (C) (D) (E)

16. (A) (B) (C) (D) (E)
17. (A) (B) (C) (D) (E)
18. (A) (B) (C) (D) (E) (F) (G) (H)
19. (A) (B) (C) (D) (E) (F)
20. ☐
    ☐

Practice Test 1: Diagnostic

The test begins with general information about the number of sections on the test (six for the computer version, including the unidentified unscored section or an identified research section, and five for the paper-and-pencil version) and the timing of the test (approximately 3 hours and 45 minutes, including one 10-minute break after Section 3, 1-minute breaks after the other sections for the computer version, and 3 hours and 30 minutes for the paper-and-pencil version with similar breaks). The following practice test contains the five scored sections.

Each section has its own time allocation and during that time period, you may work on only that section.

Next, you will read ETS's policy on scoring the Analytical Writing responses. Each essay is read by experienced readers, and ETS may cancel any test scores that show evidence of unacknowledged use of sources, unacknowledged collaboration with others, preparation of the response by another person, and language that is "substantially" similar to the language in one or more other test responses.

Each section has specific instructions for that section.

You will be told when to begin.

chapter 3

SECTION 1: ANALYTICAL WRITING

Analyze an Issue
30 minutes

The time for this task is 30 minutes. You must plan and draft a response that evaluates the issue given below. If you do not respond to the specific issue, your score will be zero. Your response must be based on the accompanying instructions, and you must provide evidence for your position. You may use support from reading, experience, observations, and/or course work.

> To be informed citizens, all students should know the U.S. Constitution. As part of the national social studies standards, all U.S. students should read and learn the U.S. Constitution well enough to be able to pass an exam with specific questions on any or all of the Constitution's articles. Passing such an exam should be a graduation requirement.
>
> Write an essay that expresses the degree to which you agree or disagree with the claim and the reason or reasons that underlie the claim.

Your response will be read by experienced readers who will assess your ability to do the following:

- Follow the set of task instructions.
- Analyze the complexities involved.
- Organize, develop, and explain ideas.
- Use pertinent reasons and/or illustrations to support ideas.
- Adhere to the conventions of Standard Written English.

You will be advised to take some time to plan your response and to leave time to reread it before the time is over. Those taking the paper-and-pencil version of the GRE will find a blank page in their answer booklet for making notes and then four ruled pages for writing their actual response. Those taking the computer version will be given scrap paper for making notes.

STOP

> If you finish before the time is up, you may check your work in this section only.

Analyze an Argument

30 minutes

The time for this task is 30 minutes. You must plan and draft a response that evaluates the argument given below. If you do not respond to the given argument, your score will be zero. Your response must be based on the accompanying instructions, and you must provide evidence in support of your analysis.

You should not present your views on the subject of the argument, but on the strength or weakness of the argument.

> Skybold and Associates has seen a remarkable surge in productivity since it instituted its policy of allowing its creative staff to work from home for as many as two workdays (16 hours) per week. Results of this policy have included employees taking fewer sick and personal days as well as greater employee satisfaction and enhanced employee loyalty. In addition, Skybold envisions in the not so distant future a reduced need for office space as fewer offices and cubicles will be needed to accommodate a smaller in-house staff. This will result in dramatic savings for the company. Skybold's new telecommunicating policy is clearly a win-win situation.
>
> Write an essay that identifies questions to be answered before deciding whether the conclusion and the argument on which it is based are reasonable. Explain how the answers would help you determine whether the argument's conclusion is logical.

Your response will be read by experienced readers who will assess your ability to do the following:

- Follow the set of task instructions.
- Analyze the complexities involved.
- Organize, develop, and explain ideas.
- Use pertinent reasons and/or illustrations to support ideas.
- Adhere to the conventions of Standard Written English.

You will be advised to take some time to plan your response and to leave time to reread it before the time is over. Those taking the paper-and-pencil version of the GRE will find a blank page in their answer booklet for making notes and then four ruled pages for writing their actual response. Those taking the computer version will be given scrap paper for making notes.

STOP

> If you finish before the time is up, you may check your work in this section only.

INSTRUCTIONS FOR THE VERBAL REASONING AND QUANTITATIVE REASONING SECTIONS

You will find information here on the question formats for the Verbal Reasoning and Quantitative Reasoning sections as well as information about how to use the software program, or, if you're taking the paper-and-pencil version, how to mark your answers in the answer booklet.

Perhaps the most important information is a reminder about how these two sections are scored. Every correct answer earns a point, but wrong answers don't subtract any points. The advice from ETS is to guess if you aren't sure of an answer. ETS says that this is better than not answering a question.

All multiple-choice questions in the computer-based test will have answer options preceded by either blank ovals or blank squares depending on the question type. The paper-and-pencil test will follow the same format of answer choices, but it will use letters instead of ovals or squares for answer choices.

For your convenience in answering questions and checking answers in this book, we use (A), (B), (C), etc. By using letters with parentheses, you will find it easy to check your answers against the answer key and explanation sections.

SECTION 2: QUANTITATIVE REASONING

35 minutes • 20 questions

(The paper-and-pencil version will have 25 questions to be completed in 40 minutes.)

For each question, follow the specific directions and choose the best answer.

The test-maker provides the following information that applies to all questions in the Quantitative Reasoning section of the GRE:

- All numbers used are real numbers.

- All figures are assumed to lie in a plane unless otherwise indicated.

- Geometric figures, such as lines, circles, triangles, and quadrilaterals, *are not necessarily* drawn to scale. That is, you should *not* assume that quantities such as lengths and angle measures are as they appear in a figure. You should assume, however, that lines shown as straight are actually straight, points on a line are in the order shown, and more generally, all geometric objects are in the relative positions shown. For questions with geometric figures, you should base your answers on geometric reasoning, not on estimating or comparing quantities by sight or by measurement.

- Coordinate systems, such as *xy*-planes and number lines, *are* drawn to scale. Therefore, you can read, estimate, or compare quantities in such figures by sight or by measurement.

- Graphical data presentations, such as bar graphs, circle graphs, and line graphs, *are* drawn to scale. Therefore, you can read, estimate, or compare data values by sight or by measurement.

FOR QUESTIONS 1–8, COMPARE QUANTITY A AND QUANTITY B. SOME QUESTIONS WILL HAVE ADDITIONAL INFORMATION ABOVE THE TWO QUANTITIES TO USE IN DETERMINING YOUR ANSWER.

1.

Quantity A	Quantity B
$6\dfrac{7}{8}$	$3.42(2)$

- (A) Quantity A is greater.
- (B) Quantity B is greater.
- (C) The two quantities are equal.
- (D) The relationship cannot be determined from the information given.

QUESTIONS 2–4 REFER TO THE DIAGRAM BELOW.

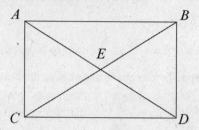

ABCD is a rectangle.

E is the intersection of *AD* and *BC*.

2.   Quantity A   Quantity B
              the area of △*CED*   the area of △*AEC*

(A) Quantity A is greater.

(B) Quantity B is greater.

(C) The two quantities are equal.

(D) The relationship cannot be determined from the information given.

3.   Quantity A   Quantity B
         m∠*ACD* + m∠*CDB*   *m*∠*AEC* + m∠*CED*

(A) Quantity A is greater.

(B) Quantity B is greater.

(C) The two quantities are equal.

(D) The relationship cannot be determined from the information given.

4.   Quantity A   Quantity B
             $(AB)^2 + (BD)^2$ *AD*

(A) Quantity A is greater.

(B) Quantity B is greater.

(C) The two quantities are equal.

(D) The relationship cannot be determined from the information given.

$$y < x < 0$$

5.   Quantity A   Quantity B
                       $|x|$ $|y|$

(A) Quantity A is greater.

(B) Quantity B is greater.

(C) The two quantities are equal.

(D) The relationship cannot be determined from the information given.

$$a > b > 0$$

6.   Quantity A   Quantity B
                     $a^2 - b^2$ $(3a + 3b)(-2a + 2b)$

(A) Quantity A is greater.

(B) Quantity B is greater.

(C) The two quantities are equal.

(D) The relationship cannot be determined from the information given.

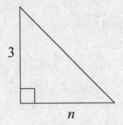

The area of the triangle is 15.

7.   Quantity A   Quantity B
                         n 12

(A) Quantity A is greater.

(B) Quantity B is greater.

(C) The two quantities are equal.

(D) The relationship cannot be determined from the information given.

$$x^2 = 9$$

8.   Quantity A   Quantity B
                         x -3

(A) Quantity A is greater.

(B) Quantity B is greater.

(C) The two quantities are equal.

(D) The relationship cannot be determined from the information given.

Questions 9–20 have several formats. Unless the directions state otherwise, choose one answer choice. For Numeric Entry questions, follow the instructions below.

Numeric Entry Questions

The following items are the same for both the computer-based version of the test and the paper-and-pencil version. However, those taking the computer-based version will have additional information about entering answers in decimal and fraction boxes on the computer screen. Those taking the paper-and-pencil version will have information about entering answers on answer grids.

- Your answer may be an integer, a decimal, or a fraction, and it may be negative.

- If a question asks for a fraction, there will be two boxes. One box will be for the numerator and one will be for the denominator.

- Equivalent forms of the correct answer, such as 2.5 and 2.50, are all correct.

- Enter the exact answer unless the question asks you to round your answers.

9. The local pastry shop sells its doughnuts for $1.90 each, and the shop owner makes an 8% profit on each. How much profit would the owner make if she sold 15 doughnuts?
    (A) $0.15
    (B) $2.28
    (C) $28.50
    (D) $1.12
    (E) $3.45

10. Evaluate $\dfrac{13(0.2)}{4}$
    (A) 0.0065
    (B) 0.065
    (C) 65
    (D) 6.5
    (E) 0.65

FOR QUESTION 11, INDICATE <u>ALL</u> THE ANSWERS THAT APPLY.

---

11. Find the next 3 numbers in the sequence. 1, 1, 2, 3, 5, 8, ...
    (A) 12
    (B) 13
    (C) 14
    (D) 21
    (E) 22
    (F) 33
    (G) 34
    (H) 55

12. Let $f(x) = 2x^3 - x^2 + 7$. Find $f(3)$.

   (A) 25

   (B) 19

   (C) 16

   (D) 52

   (E) 54

13. Solve for x: $4(3x - 5) = x + 3$

   (A) $x = \dfrac{23}{11}$

   (B) $x = \dfrac{8}{11}$

   (C) $x = \dfrac{2}{3}$

   (D) $x = -4$

   (E) $x = 23$

14. Find the value of x.

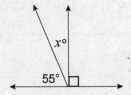

   (A) $55°$

   (B) $35°$

   (C) $90°$

   (D) $145°$

   (E) $125°$

FOR QUESTION 15, INDICATE <u>ALL</u> THE ANSWERS THAT APPLY.

15. List all the factors of 51.

   (A) 1

   (B) 2

   (C) 3

   (D) 7

   (E) 16

   (F) 17

   (G) 48

   (H) 51

QUESTIONS 16–18 ARE BASED ON THE FOLLOWING DATA.

Annual State Budgets (in millions of dollars)

	2007	2008	2009	2010	2011	2012, est
State A	53.0	75.9	85.5	101.6	131.2	142.1
State B	14.4	14.5	20.0	19.0	39.2	43.5

16. What is the ratio of the total (State A + State B) estimated budget of 2012 to 2007's budget?

    (A) 33.7 : 92.8
    (B) 142.1 : 53.0
    (C) 43.5 : 14.4
    (D) 14.4 : 43.5
    (E) 92.8 : 33.7

17. What is the total budget for State A for 2007, 2008, and 2011?

    (A) 68.1
    (B) 260.1
    (C) 268
    (D) 276.4
    (E) 308.7

18. What year had the biggest percentage increase from the previous year in State B and what was the percentage increase?

    (A) 2009, 138%
    (B) 2011, 206%
    (C) 2009, 37%
    (D) 2011, 106%
    (E) 2012, 11%

FOR QUESTIONS 19–20, ENTER YOUR ANSWERS IN THE BOXES.

---

19. Mary went to the convenience store with $20. She wanted to buy a newspaper for $1.25, a magazine for $6.50, a soda for $1.75, and then spend the rest of her $20 on dime candy. How many pieces would she get?

    [ ]

20. Using the information from the question above, find the ratio of the amount of money spent for the magazine to the total amount of money spent.

    Give your answer as a fraction.

STOP

If you finish before the time is up, you may check your work in this section only.

SECTION 3: VERBAL REASONING
30 minutes • 20 questions

(The paper-and-pencil version will have 25 questions to be completed in 35 minutes.)

For each question, follow the specific directions and choose the best answer.

> FOR QUESTIONS 1–4, CHOOSE <u>ONE</u> ANSWER FOR EACH BLANK. SELECT FROM THE APPROPRIATE COLUMN FOR EACH BLANK. CHOOSE THE ANSWER THAT BEST COMPLETES THE SENSE OF THE TEXT.

1. The unsophisticated nature of research tools affects the _____ and validity of market research into the potential market for products and programs.

(A) accountability
(B) acceptability
(C) reliability
(D) liability
(E) approval

2. That Jane Austen's satiric wit is lost on some readers is (i) _____ because it is so (ii) _____ as to become caricature; for example, consider the Rev. Collins in *Pride and Prejudice*.

Blank (i)	Blank (ii)
(A) logical	(D) flashy
(B) understandable	(E) showy
(C) inexplicable	(F) overdrawn

3. As a result of overconfidence and a number of (i) _____ errors in judgment to employ a(n) (ii) _____, the majority party in the state legislature became the minority party in the last election.

Blank (i)	Blank (ii)
(A) embarrassing	(D) paradox
(B) inconvenient	(E) aphorism
(C) upsetting	(F) euphemism

4. One consequence of the desire among modern playwrights to bring (i) _____ to the theater has been the diminution of poetry as a dramatic language. On the other hand, realism in language has brought a (ii) _____ end to rant and rhetoric upon the stage. As one critic wrote, modern playwrights have been pushed to develop plays that are (iii) _____ and convincing when they could no longer rely on "verbal pyrotechnics."

Blank (i)	Blank (ii)	Blank (iii)
(A) vibrancy	(D) welcome	(G) more forceful
(B) verisimilitude	(E) final	(H) more cerebral
(C) resemblance	(F) limited	(I) more believable

FOR QUESTIONS 5–20, CHOOSE ONLY <u>ONE</u> ANSWER CHOICE UNLESS OTHERWISE INDICATED.

QUESTIONS 5–7 ARE BASED ON THE FOLLOWING PASSAGE.

In a 1983 speech, President Ronald Reagan announced his plans to create a shield against nuclear missile attacks by the Soviet Union. This would consist of a system of lasers or rockets, deployed in space that could destroy any missile launched at the United States by the Soviet Union. The news media quickly dubbed Reagan's proposal for this Strategic Defense
5 Initiative, or SDI, as "Star Wars," a recently released science fiction movie. The Soviets, however, took it seriously. Mikhail Gorbachev, the leader of the Soviet Union, pointed out to Reagan that a missile shield would enable the United States to easily launch a first strike against the Soviet Union, knowing the Soviets could not retaliate. In response, Reagan offered to share SDI technology with the Soviets, but they refused.
10 The Soviets were also concerned about a new arms race: the United States would have to spend billions of dollars developing SDI technology, while the Russians would have to increase their spending on their own offensive technologies in the hope of defeating SDI. This reallocation of spending could severely set back Gorbachev's own plans for improving the Soviet economy and the standard of living of Soviet citizens. Ultimately, the Intermediate
15 Nuclear Force (INF) treaty of December 1987 was proposed, in which the Americans and Russians agreed to eliminate all intermediate-range nuclear missiles from Europe.

FOR QUESTION 5, CONSIDER EACH ANSWER INDIVIDUALLY AND CHOOSE <u>ALL</u> THAT APPLY.

---

5. The passage suggests that the creation of SDI could have resulted in which of the following?
   (A) A nuclear war between the United States and the Soviet Union
   (B) A first strike against the Soviet Union by the United States
   (C) The sharing of missile technology between the United States and the Soviet Union

6. It can be inferred from the passage that the U.S. news media called the SDI "Star Wars" because it
   (A) seemed likely that it would start a nuclear war between the Americans and the Soviets.
   (B) would cost the United States billions of dollars, taking money away from other programs.
   (C) was based on technology that science fiction writers had developed.
   (D) was seen as the beginning of the end of the Cold War.
   (E) seemed to be an impossible idea straight out of science fiction.

7. In the final paragraph, the author is primarily concerned with describing
   (A) reasons that persuaded the Soviets to entertain the possibility of an INF treaty.
   (B) the U.S.'s refusal to halt the SDI program.
   (C) a potential arms race between the United States and the Soviet Union.
   (D) Gorbachev's concerns with the potential impact of SDI on Soviet domestic policy.
   (E) Gorbachev's concerns over possible war with the United States.

QUESTIONS 8–9 ARE BASED ON THE FOLLOWING PASSAGE.

Obesity results when a person consumes significantly more calories than energy burned over a long period of time, though at this point scientists cannot point to a single cause of obesity. In a large majority of obesity cases, the causes are related to genetic factors that influence the metabolism of fat and that regulate the hormones and proteins that control appetite. A
5 person's appetite is determined by different processes that occur both in the brain and the digestive system. **During digestion, carbohydrates break down into different types of sugar molecules, including glucose.** Immediately after eating, blood glucose levels rise, which triggers the release of insulin, a hormone that helps change glucose into energy. As the insulin pours into the bloodstream, it pushes the glucose into cells. Insulin is a significant
10 factor in terms of obesity because it helps determine which nutrients will be burned for energy and which will be stored in cells for future use. Recent studies have found that the faster a cell processes insulin, the more fat it stores. This might be one cause of obesity, though there may be other factors to consider, and to date no one theory has been determined to be conclusive.

8. This passage suggests that obesity is caused by which of the following?
   (A) The breakdown of carbohydrates into different types of sugar molecules
   (B) The consumption of too many calories
   (C) The inability of the body to process glucose
   (D) The inefficiency of insulin to process fat during digestion
   (E) The inability of a person to feel full after eating

9. Which of the following best characterizes the function of the boldfaced sentence in lines 6–7 of the passage?
   (A) It provides evidence on which a theory is based.
   (B) It summarizes a theory with which the author agrees.
   (C) It restates a point made earlier in the passage.
   (D) It disproves a commonly accepted theory.
   (E) It presents a specific application of a general concept.

QUESTIONS 10–12 ARE BASED ON THE FOLLOWING PASSAGE.

Dutch artist M.C. Escher's work covers a variety of subjects, though he is probably best known for the pieces that he drew from unusual perspectives, which result in enigmatic effects. During the course of his life, Escher adopted a highly mathematical approach, using special notations that he invented himself, including a system for categorizing shapes, colors,
5 and symmetrical properties. Looking at his work, you can see clearly that mathematics played an important role in the development of his distinctive style, yet though he studied and admired various mathematical theories over the years, Escher did not consider himself a mathematician. However, this lack of formal training allowed him to explore mathematics in a unique way, without having to adhere to any set rules or restrictions. In 1958, he wrote:
10 "In mathematical quarters, the regular division of the plane has been considered theoretically . . . . [Mathematicians] have opened the gate leading to an extensive domain, but they have not entered this domain themselves. By their very nature they are more interested in the way in which the gate is opened than in the garden lying behind it."

FOR QUESTION 10, CONSIDER EACH ANSWER INDIVIDUALLY AND CHOOSE ALL THAT APPLY.

---

10. What material would help to support the intersection of art and mathematics in Escher's work?

    (A) Escher's notebooks containing his mathematical notations

    (B) A painting of Escher's demonstrating his use of mathematical principles in his art

    (C) Art criticism of Escher's works

11. From the passage, what is Escher's view of mathematicians?

    (A) They do not grasp how mathematics and art are interconnected.

    (B) They will never have the ability to appreciate Escher's art.

    (C) They cannot translate their theories into their own personalized notations.

    (D) They will never be able to translate their theories into art.

    (E) They cannot see the beauty that is inherent in their theories.

12. In the passage, "enigmatic" (line 2) means

    (A) rational.

    (B) inscrutable.

    (C) comprehensible.

    (D) decipherable.

    (E) theoretical.

QUESTIONS 13–15 ARE BASED ON THE FOLLOWING PASSAGE.

The fire at the Triangle Shirtwaist Factory in New York City in 1911 was one of the worst industrial disasters in U.S. history. The fire killed 146 people, many of them young immigrant women. The Triangle Shirtwaist Factory produced women's blouses, or "shirtwaists," and took up the eighth, ninth, and tenth floors of a building in New York's Greenwich Village.
5 The fire started near closing time on March 25, 1911, on the eighth floor of the building. Most of the workers could not escape because the supervisors had locked the doors to the stairwells and exits from the outside to prevent the workers from leaving early or removing materials. Many women died from being trapped inside the building or jumped to their deaths from the top floors because ladders could not reach them. This devastating tragedy
10 brought to light for many Americans the inhumane working conditions of sweatshops and it had a huge impact on U.S. workers. It galvanized many to push for improved factory safety standards and led to the rapid growth of the International Ladies' Garment Workers' Union, which fought for better and safer working conditions in the garment industry. New York State created a commission to investigate factory conditions and in 1915 the state legislature
15 enacted new measures to protect factory workers from just such tragedies as the Triangle Shirtwaist Factory fire.

FOR QUESTIONS 13–14, CONSIDER EACH ANSWER INDIVIDUALLY AND CHOOSE <u>ALL</u> THAT APPLY.

---

13. According to the passage, what was it about the Triangle Shirtwaist fire that evidently caused so great an impact on public opinion?
    (A) The fire killed so many people, many of whom were young women.
    (B) The workers could not escape during the fire because supervisors had locked the doors to the stairwells and exits.
    (C) The fire resulted in a strengthened labor movement and new labor laws.

14. Select the sentence in the passage that does NOT add to the support for the main idea of the passage.
    (A) This devastating tragedy brought to light for many Americans the inhumane working conditions of sweatshops and it had a huge impact on U.S. workers.
    (B) The fire started near closing time on March 25, 1911, on the eighth floor of the building.
    (C) Many women died from being trapped inside the building or jumped to their deaths from the top floors because ladders could not reach them.

15. In the passage, "galvanized" (line 11) most nearly means
    (A) impeded.
    (B) increased.
    (C) hurtled.
    (D) angered.
    (E) incited.

FOR QUESTIONS 16–19, CHOOSE THE TWO ANSWERS THAT BEST FIT THE
MEANING OF THE SENTENCE AS A WHOLE AND RESULT IN TWO COMPLETED
SENTENCES THAT ARE ALIKE IN MEANING.

16. In shuttering programs to reduce costs, the new CFO was _____ toward employees and refused to listen to their concerns and alternative suggestions.

(A) arrogant
(B) unkind
(C) uncharitable
(D) dismissive
(E) contentious
(F) confrontational

17. Green building, that is, the construction of new buildings and the renovation of existing ones to make them eco-friendly, is a fast-growing segment of the construction industry and one that ALLIED Builders hopes to _____ according to its five-year business plan.

(A) promote
(B) advance
(C) capitalize on
(D) upgrade
(E) exploit
(F) endorse

18. The original intention in creating NASA was to explore space, but many of the products people take for granted today such as cordless power tools and sunglasses with polarized lenses resulted from _____ research that NASA conducted for the space program.

(A) far-reaching
(B) wide-ranging
(C) innovative
(D) unusual
(E) cutting-edge
(F) conventional

19. Many researchers believe that _____ bacteria keep harmful bacteria from invading humans by using the material that harmful bacteria need to live.

(A) helpful
(B) malignant
(C) pathogenic
(D) benign
(E) benevolent
(F) beneficial

QUESTION 20 IS BASED ON THE FOLLOWING PASSAGE.

Emily Dickinson, a poet virtually unknown in her lifetime, wrote some of the most memorable lines in American poetry. Her poems are instantly recognizable for their brevity (they are often no longer than 20 lines) and their quirky punctuation and capitalization. Her frequent and often idiosyncratic use of the dash serves to emphasize many of her recurrent topics. A great

5 number of Dickinson's almost 1,800 poems deal with the themes of death and immortality, though her poems are also filled with joy and hope. Because of its unusual syntax and use of figurative language—imagery, metaphor, personification—Dickinson's poetry can seem to the uninitiated reader something of a puzzle. Present-day readers would do well to renounce a literal way of reading in order to truly appreciate Dickinson's poetry.

20. What does the author imply by the last statement in the passage?

(A) Readers should not try to find literal meaning in Dickinson's poetry.

(B) Readers of poetry today are not used to so much figurative language.

(C) Readers should try to figure out what themes were most important to Dickinson.

(D) Readers who try to unlock the mysteries of Dickinson's figurative language are doing themselves a disservice.

(E) Readers of poetry today need to consider the context in which Dickinson's poetry was written.

STOP

> If you finish before the time is up, you may check your work in this section only.

SECTION 4: VERBAL REASONING

30 minutes • 20 questions

(The paper-and-pencil version will have 25 questions to be completed in 35 minutes.)

For each question, follow the specific directions and choose the best answer.

FOR QUESTIONS 1–5, CHOOSE <u>ONE</u> ANSWER FOR EACH BLANK. SELECT FROM THE APPROPRIATE COLUMN FOR EACH BLANK. CHOOSE THE ANSWER THAT BEST COMPLETES THE SENSE OF THE TEXT.

---

1. Social networking is a marketing tool that many companies are harnessing to sell their products; however, it must be used _____ because the hard sell risks offending potential customers.

(A) with ease
(B) actively
(C) judiciously
(D) expeditiously
(E) efficiently

2. In composing "Scheherazade," Rimsky-Korsakov hoped to _____ the "magical spirit" of *One Thousand and One Nights*, a collection of exotic folk tales from the Middle East and South Asia.

(A) motivate
(B) induce
(C) inspire
(D) evoke
(E) provoke

3. Garraty states that the problems faced by private colleges in the 1820s and 1830s were of their own making to a degree. Many cities and towns wanted the (i) _____ of hosting a college, but the supply of colleges soon (ii) _____ the demand, that is, the number of potential students.

Blank (i)	Blank (ii)
(A) honor	(D) outperformed
(B) admiration	(E) outstripped
(C) character	(F) outshone

4. The nation-states of early modern Europe guarded their sovereignty (i) _____, finding countless reasons—real and (ii) _____—for wars. Peace (iii) _____ only when one nation managed to subdue its neighbors.

Blank (i)	Blank (ii)	Blank (iii)
(A) jealously	(D) feigned	(G) occurred
(B) intolerantly	(E) facetious	(H) mediated
(C) liberally	(F) deceptive	(I) intervened

5. The speaker, a former prosecutor turned politician, remains direct, candid, and (i) _____ in her assessment of policy, but she can also be (ii) _____ and offhand toward her colleagues. She is considered a/n (iii) _____ legislator.

Blank (i)	Blank (ii)	Blank (iii)
(A) frank	(D) rough	(G) very ambitious
(B) pragmatic	(E) brusque	(H) really approachable
(C) rigid	(F) brisk	(I) no-nonsense

FOR QUESTIONS 6–20, CHOOSE ONLY <u>ONE</u> ANSWER CHOICE UNLESS OTHERWISE INDICATED.

QUESTIONS 6–7 ARE BASED ON THE FOLLOWING PASSAGE.

A 2007 study by the United Nations University reported that desertification, or desert encroachment, was "the greatest environmental challenge of our times." About two out of five African countries on the edges of the Sahara are under the threat of desertification. The UN study reported that "[d]esertification has emerged as an environmental crisis of global
5 proportions, currently affecting an estimated 100 to 200 million people, and threatening the lives and livelihoods of a much larger number." The study explained that although climate change has caused major degradation of Africa's soil, overgrazing, deforestation, and unsustainable irrigation practices are also contributing factors. The study added that people who are displaced by desertification put additional strains on local natural resources and nearby
10 communities as conflicts arise over competition for farmland. The UN report suggests that new farming practices, such as planting forests in dryland areas, could help prevent the spread of deserts.

6. Based on the passage, which of the following is NOT a cause of desertification?

(A) climatic change
(B) competition for farmland
(C) overgrazing
(D) poor irrigation practices
(E) cutting down trees

7. Select the sentence in the passage that is NOT a major detail supporting the thesis.

   (A) A 2007 study by the United Nations University reported that desertification, or desert encroachment, was "the greatest environmental challenge of our times."

   (B) The study added that people who are displaced by desertification put additional strains on local natural resources and nearby communities as conflicts arise over competition for farmland.

   (C) About two out of five African countries on the edges of the Sahara are under the threat of desertification.

QUESTIONS 8–9 ARE BASED ON THE FOLLOWING PASSAGE.

During World War II, the U.S. system of rationing did not work as planned not only because it conflicted with personal needs and wants (which had grown during the previous years of deprivation because of the Great Depression and its aftermath), but because it went against the national character of the American people. This was a nation based on the principle that
5 as long as you have money to spend, nothing is off limits. By limiting each individual's purchasing power, the government had imposed a new economic system that attacked this principle. The emergence of the illegal black market, on the other hand, supported this basic principle of acquisition, or consumerism, for Americans. This is not to deny that many who ran or even patronized the black market were actually motivated by greed, but it does suggest
10 that the individualistic (and frontier) spirit of Americans had not been lost.

8. Select the statement that restates the premise of the author's argument.

   (A) Normally law-abiding citizens will break the law to satisfy what they consider to be their basic needs and wants.

   (B) Americans during World War II acted unlawfully due to circumstances out of their control.

   (C) The American system of rationing did not work because Americans circumvented its principles through the practice of the black market.

   (D) As long as Americans have enough money to spend, they will spend it however they can.

   (E) If the Great Depression had not deprived so many Americans of basic needs and wants, they would not have patronized the black market during World War II.

9. Which of the following, if it were true, would weaken the author's argument?

   (A) During the Great Depression, many Americans found ways to circumvent the law in order to provide for their families.

   (B) The majority of American citizens are law abiding and will not break the law under any circumstances.

   (C) Many Americans continued to patronize the black market after rationing ended.

The increasing awareness of lighting inefficiency and the billions of dollars of potential annual energy savings that can be achieved by switching to LED lighting has resulted in many government-funded research initiatives around the world. In addition, governments in the United States, Canada, Europe, and Australia have responded to the growing need for energy
5   conservation by passing legislation that regulates or eliminates the sale of incandescent and halogen light bulbs by a certain date. However, though increasing consumers' awareness of the inefficiency of other light sources can help increase the adoption of LED lighting, regulations that focus on enforcing energy-efficient lighting are likely to work better. One example is California's Energy Efficiency Standards for Residential and Nonresidential Buildings, or
10   Title 24, that provides a set of mandatory regulations covering all aspects of new building construction. The Residential Lighting section of Title 24 requires that a high-efficiency light source be used in several areas of the home, including the kitchen and bathrooms, and that all outdoor light fixtures must either use energy-efficient bulbs, or must be controlled by light and motion sensors.

10. This passage achieves all of the following purposes EXCEPT it

   (A) implies that LED lighting will become a necessity of the future.

   (B) explains one way governments are forcing people to switch to LED lighting.

   (C) cites a regulation that enforces the use of high-efficiency light sources.

   (D) describes how LED lighting is more energy efficient than incandescent lighting.

   (E) implies that government-funded research on energy efficiency is essential.

11. The author introduces California's Title 24 in order to

   (A) support the concept that the government needs to set rules to increase the adoption of LED lighting.

   (B) provide a possible explanation for why more Americans have adopted LED lighting.

   (C) reinforce the concept that other methods of lighting are less efficient than LED lighting.

   (D) introduce the idea that governments need to enforce rules about high-efficiency lighting in residential buildings.

   (E) cast doubt on studies that show that Americans are not eager to switch to LED lighting.

12. "Mandatory" (line 10) most nearly means

   (A) provisional.

   (B) permanent.

   (C) predetermined.

   (D) discretionary.

   (E) obligatory.

FOR QUESTIONS 13–15, CHOOSE THE <u>TWO</u> ANSWERS THAT BEST FIT THE MEANING OF THE SENTENCE AS A WHOLE AND RESULT IN TWO COMPLETED SENTENCES THAT ARE ALIKE IN MEANING.

13. If life did exist on other planets, scientists theorize that it would not _____ life on Earth. For example, depending on the wavelengths of life given off by the plant, plants could be red, yellow, or green.

   (A) epitomize
   (B) mimic
   (C) illustrate
   (D) typify
   (E) imitate
   (F) reflect

14. Scientists believe that unlocking the genome is _____; it will forever change the way we diagnose, treat, and someday even prevent disease.

   (A) modernization
   (B) reforming
   (C) revolutionary
   (D) transformative
   (E) huge
   (F) corrective

15. Many of his critics complain that once they finish reading his books with their convoluted plot lines, they are no wiser and their brains perhaps even more _____.

   (A) befogged
   (B) taxed
   (C) muddled
   (D) weakened
   (E) wary
   (F) heedful

QUESTIONS 16–17 ARE BASED ON THE FOLLOWING PASSAGE.

Among people who want to make informed choices about what they eat, the issue of whether to buy local or organic food is often debated. The most popular reasons cited for buying organic are to avoid pesticides that harm your health and damage ecosystems, to support a system of agriculture that uses natural fertilizers, and to support more humane animal husbandry
5 practices. The reasons cited for buying local food include supporting the local economy, and also buying food that is fresher, has less packaging, and has fewer "food miles," or the distance food has to travel from source to end user. It turns out to be a complicated question, one that can sometimes lead to additional questions that must be answered in order to make a choice. Sometimes the questions are personal ones, such as: What food tastes better? But
10 larger questions can arise, too, such as: How do the choices we make about our food affect the planet?

16. What is the author's opinion about whether to buy organic or local food?

    (A) We can never really know which is better.

    (B) We should try to answer important questions before trying to make that decision.

    (C) We should figure out which food tastes better.

    (D) We should try to find other ways to support the local economy.

    (E) We should buy the food that has the fewest "food miles."

17. Which of the following statements does the passage most clearly support?

    (A) Buying local or organic food is better than buying food from a big chain supermarket.

    (B) Buying organic food does not support the local economy.

    (C) The distance food has to travel is an important consideration to make when deciding where to buy your food.

    (D) Animals raised on organic farms are treated more humanely.

    (E) Food from local farms may have been sprayed with pesticides.

FOR QUESTION 18, CONSIDER EACH OF THE THREE CHOICES INDIVIDUALLY AND CHOOSE <u>ALL</u> THAT APPLY.

---

18. What function does "the distance food has to travel from source to end user" (lines 6–7) serve in the passage?

    (A) It is support for the argument for buying local food.

    (B) It defines the term "food miles."

    (C) It is support for the larger question about how food choices affect the planet.

QUESTIONS 19–20 ARE BASED ON THE FOLLOWING PASSAGE.

Voter opinion polls are often disparaged because they are seen as inaccurate or misused by network news shows eager to boost ratings. However, those who want to discredit voter opinion polling for elections overlook a few facts. First, the last week or two before an election is notoriously volatile. Voters finally decide whether or not to vote and undecided
5 voters make up their minds about the candidates for whom they will vote. This means that polls taken too far in advance of an election cannot possibly forecast with precision the outcome of that election. Second, exit polls differ from most other types of scientific polling, mainly because dispersed polling places preclude exit pollsters from using normal sampling methods. However, debating whether voter polls are accurate or not misses the point. Voter
10 polls are not intended to forecast winners and losers. They are designed to describe the broad spectrum of public opinion and to elucidate what voters are really thinking and what policies are most important to them. In fact, most of what we know about voter behavior and policy preferences comes from past opinion polls about elections. Understood in this context, we should not dismiss polling outright, but instead consider how to improve polling and to use
15 it to its best advantage.

19. "Elucidate" (line 11) most nearly means

    (A) confound.

    (B) elevate.

    (C) vanquish.

    (D) illuminate.

    (E) predict.

20. Which of the following expresses the author's thesis about voter opinion polls?

    (A) They can never predict the results of an election.

    (B) They can help us get a sense of the general trend in an election.

    (C) They can help undecided voters make up their minds.

    (D) They are misused by the news media.

    (E) They are highly unpredictable.

STOP

> If you finish before the time is up, you may check your work in this section only.

SECTION 5: QUANTITATIVE REASONING

35 minutes • 20 questions

(The paper-and-pencil version will have 25 questions to be completed in 40 minutes.)

For each question, follow the specific directions and choose the best answer.

The test-maker provides the following information that applies to all questions in the Quantitative Reasoning section of the GRE:

- All numbers used are real numbers.

- All figures are assumed to lie in a plane unless otherwise indicated.

- Geometric figures, such as lines, circles, triangles, and quadrilaterals, *are not necessarily* drawn to scale. That is, you should *not* assume that quantities such as lengths and angle measures are as they appear in a figure. You should assume, however, that lines shown as straight are actually straight, points on a line are in the order shown, and more generally, all geometric objects are in the relative positions shown. For questions with geometric figures, you should base your answers on geometric reasoning, not on estimating or comparing quantities by sight or by measurement.

- Coordinate systems, such as *xy*-planes and number lines, *are* drawn to scale. Therefore, you can read, estimate, or compare quantities in such figures by sight or by measurement.

- Graphical data presentations, such as bar graphs, circle graphs, and line graphs, *are* drawn to scale. Therefore, you can read, estimate, or compare data values by sight or by measurement.

FOR QUESTIONS 1–8, COMPARE QUANTITY A AND QUANTITY B. SOME QUESTIONS WILL HAVE ADDITIONAL INFORMATION ABOVE THE TWO QUANTITIES TO USE IN DETERMINING YOUR ANSWER.

1.

Quantity A	Quantity B
0.324875	$\dfrac{10}{31}$

(A) Quantity A is greater.

(B) Quantity B is greater.

(C) The two quantities are equal.

(D) The relationship cannot be determined from the information given.

2.

Quantity A	Quantity B
$\lvert x \rvert$	$\lvert y \rvert$

(A) Quantity A is greater.

(B) Quantity B is greater.

(C) The two quantities are equal.

(D) The relationship cannot be determined from the information given.

Mary is twice as old as Stephen. Stephen is 5 years older than Joe. Joe is $\frac{3}{4}$ of Mary's age. All three were born in the twenty-first century.

3.

Quantity A	Quantity B
Mary's birth year	Joe's birth year

(A) Quantity A is greater.

(B) Quantity B is greater.

(C) The two quantities are equal.

(D) The relationship cannot be determined from the information given.

A try is worth 5 points. A conversion is worth 2 points. A penalty goal is worth 3 points.

4.

Quantity A	Quantity B
3 tries, 2 conversions, 1 penalty	24

(A) Quantity A is greater.

(B) Quantity B is greater.

(C) The two quantities are equal.

(D) The relationship cannot be determined from the information given.

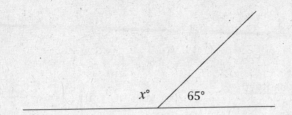

5.   Quantity A   Quantity B
           x   115

(A) Quantity A is greater.
(B) Quantity B is greater.
(C) The two quantities are equal.
(D) The relationship cannot be determined from the information given.

6.   Quantity A   Quantity B
        $-\dfrac{15}{16}$ $-\dfrac{16}{15}$

(A) Quantity A is greater.
(B) Quantity B is greater.
(C) The two quantities are equal.
(D) The relationship cannot be determined from the information given.

There are 15 players on Team 1. There are 22 players on Team 2.

There are more offensive players than defensive players on each team.

7.   Quantity A   Quantity B

   Number of goalies on Team 1   Number of goalies on Team 2

(A) Quantity A is greater.
(B) Quantity B is greater.
(C) The two quantities are equal.
(D) The relationship cannot be determined from the information given.

$$\frac{y}{x} = 3$$
$$x, y \neq 0$$

8.

Quantity A	Quantity B
x	y

(A) Quantity A is greater.

(B) Quantity B is greater.

(C) The two quantities are equal.

(D) The relationship cannot be determined from the information given.

Questions 9–20 have several formats. Unless the directions state otherwise, choose one answer choice. For Numeric Entry questions, follow the instructions below.

Numeric Entry Questions

The following items are the same for both the computer-based version of the test and the paper-and-pencil version. However, those taking the computer-based version will have additional information about entering answers in decimal and fraction boxes on the computer screen. Those taking the paper-and-pencil version will have information about entering answers on answer grids.

- Your answer may be an integer, a decimal, or a fraction, and it may be negative.

- If a question asks for a fraction, there will be two boxes. One box will be for the numerator and one will be for the denominator.

- Equivalent forms of the correct answer, such as 2.5 and 2.50, are all correct.

- Enter the exact answer unless the question asks you to round your answers.

---

9. Evaluate the function $f(x) = 5x^3 + 4x^2 + 8x + 1$, when $x = 2$.

(A) 73

(B) –11

(C) 183

(D) 117

(E) –73

10. Solve the equation $4xy + 8y = 128$ for x, when $y = 4$.

(A) $x = 10$

(B) $x = 6$

(C) $x = 1$

(D) $x = 12$

(E) $x = 32$

11. If $\dfrac{3}{x-1} = \dfrac{6}{3x+6}$, then $x =$

(A) −8

(B) −1

(C) 0

(D) 1

(E) 8

12. A new model hybrid car gets 45 miles per gallon for city driving and 20% more for highway driving. How many miles per gallon does the hybrid get for highway driving?

(A) 34

(B) 46

(C) 51

(D) 54

(E) 58

FOR QUESTION 13, ENTER YOUR ANSWER IN THE BOX.

13. Find the area of the trapezoid.

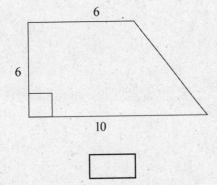

QUESTIONS 14–16 REFER TO THE TABLE BELOW.

Number of Children per Family in a Neighborhood

Number of Children	Number of Families
1	19
2	36
3	21
4+	9
0	15

14. What is the total number of families that have no more than two children?
    (A) 19
    (B) 36
    (C) 55
    (D) 70
    (E) 81

15. What is the percentage of families who have no children?
    (A) 9%
    (B) 12%
    (C) 15%
    (D) 18%
    (E) 21%

16. What percentage of the families has 6 children?
    (A) 19
    (B) 9
    (C) 15
    (D) 12
    (E) unknown

17. The angle x and the angle that measures 115, are what type of angles?

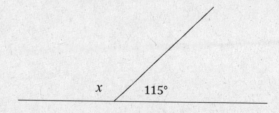

    (A) complementary
    (B) obtuse
    (C) acute
    (D) supplementary
    (E) paired

FOR QUESTION 18–19, CHOOSE __ALL__ THE ANSWERS THAT APPLY.

18. Find the four even factors of 28.
    - (A) 0
    - (B) 1
    - (C) 2
    - (D) 3
    - (E) 4
    - (F) 7
    - (G) 14
    - (H) 28

19. When multiplied in pairs, which of the following numbers will give you a product less than −43?
    - (A) −8
    - (B) −6
    - (C) 0
    - (D) 4
    - (E) 5
    - (F) 9

FOR QUESTION 20, ENTER YOUR ANSWER IN THE BOXES.

20. If *AB* and *BD* are equal lengths and *ABDC* is a rectangle, what is the ratio of the area of triangle *CED* to the area of rectangle *ABDC*?

    Give your answer as a fraction.

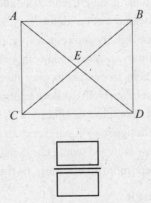

STOP

If you finish before the time is up, you may check your work in this section only.

ANSWER KEY AND EXPLANATIONS

Section 1: Analytical Writing

Analyze an Issue

Model: 6 points out of 6

It no doubt sounds ideal that every citizen of the United States know and understand the fundamental document on which our nation is based. After all, the U.S. Constitution is the principle document from which we derive our rights and freedoms as citizens. The Constitution encapsulates the workings of a great democracy that has become a beacon and a model to many other countries. Its words represent the wisdom of our founders and the ideals of our leaders and citizens.

Yet, is it really necessary to informed citizenship to know every article of the Constitution so well and pass a test on it? Does informed citizenship rely on this and this alone? It seems to me that anyone can Google and read the Constitution at any time. Whatever the issue may be, whether it is the right to bear arms, the meaning of due process, or the history of prohibition, the exact words of the Constitution on that topic are just a few clicks away. With the tendency to carry mobile devices for accessing information becoming ever more common, there is less and less need to know information about the Constitution or any other topic just for the sake of knowing it; all one really needs to know is how to find and interpret information. Furthermore, if we spend time in our schools on memorizing documents, even very important ones, that is less time we have to spend on more important skills such as finding information, and analyzing, interpreting, and evaluating it. Knowing and spitting back information on a test is not enough; a student must process and draw his or her own conclusions. An exam based on the Constitution with specific questions on each article is highly unlikely to require or foster such skills.

Moreover, is informed citizenship necessarily good citizenship or the best citizenship? I would argue that engaged, active citizenship is just as important as informed citizenship, and that one can engage in cleaning up one's community or other good-citizen tasks quite effectively without knowing even one article or word of the central document of our democracy. In addition, all citizens can exercise their duties as citizens by voting thoughtfully and responsibly; performing jury duty; paying taxes; and serving one's country in the military if called upon without knowing every article—or perhaps any article—of the Constitution. There are, naturally, exceptions, and those who seek a career in public service should know the Constitution well. But does a person who designs landscape, performs physical therapy, or creates apps need complete familiarity with the Constitution? It would scarcely seem so. And even if that landscape designer, physical therapist, or app creator could rattle off every article on command, just exactly how enriched would our democracy be by that? If we want more informed and better citizens, let's spend more time, not less, on the thinking skills that actually matter.

This essay scores 6 out of 6 because it

- **answers the task.** It clearly tells the extent to which it disagrees with the claim (that all U.S. students should read and learn the U.S. Constitution well enough to be able to pass an exam), and it competently disputes the reason on which it is based (that such an exam would produce better informed citizens or that being better informed about the Constitution makes a better citizen).

- **is well supported.** The essay offers specific, accurate examples of what one might know about the Constitution, as well as persuasive examples of what a citizen might do well without knowing about the Constitution. Throughout the essay, support and development are abundant, clear, and convincing.

- **is well organized.** Paragraph 1 leads smoothly into the main attack on the claim; paragraphs 2 and 3 effectively refute the reason for the claims, thereby refuting the claim itself. Each paragraph is a well organized, discrete, and unified unit, with the third paragraph leading smoothly to closure. Several transitional words and phrases help create coherence.

- **is fluid, precise, and graceful.** Sentences are varied throughout, with many effective uses of questions. Words are precise and varied.

- **observes the conventions of Standard Written English.**

Model: 1 point out of 6

It is very important to know and understand the constitution, it is the most important document of our nation and a very important document in the world. It is very wrong when some politicians do not know about the constitution. They do not know what freedoms it gives us. They do not know about freedom of speech and religion and so on.

I would be proud of a study of the constitution and know about the constitution and to answer questions about every article. I think this should be the part of the education of every student because it will make all better informed. I think it would make all proud to know the constitution and it's articles, too.

We will know more about the jobs in goverment of the differant people at the voting, so we will be able to chose better people for the jobs. We will also understand the news better when the supreme court decides constitutional or unconstitutional. We will also better understand what is happening when congress makes laws or the President takes actions.

This essay scores 1 out of 6 because it

- **answers only part of the task and reflects little or no insight.** It conveys the extent to which it disagrees with the claim (that all U.S. students should read and learn the U.S. Constitution well enough to be able to pass an exam), but it offers little or no meaningful insight into how that would make people better informed.

- **is poorly supported.** The essay is seriously limited and flawed in terms of support. In fact, it does not support claims. Rather, it basically repeats the prompt and supplies simple, illogical, or unsubstantiated support. For example, it suggests that being able to pass a test on the Constitution would make people able to vote in a more informed matter (why would that be so? and would it apply to state and local elections?) and able to understand the constitutionality of issues before the Supreme Court (would that necessarily be the case? why?). Its claims go unanswered.

- **is not organized well.** While paragraphs 1 and 2 exhibit some unity and coherence, the information in paragraph 3 consists of examples that should be used to support sentence 2 of paragraph 2. Both the opening and closing lack the sophistication and focus of a higher-scoring essay.

- **has poorly constructed sentences.** There is little variety in sentence structure and many sentences begin with "I" and "We."

- **has some major and minor errors in the conventions of Standard Written English.** Despite these problems, the low score does not result mainly from problems with conventions; rather, it results mainly from lack of insight and development; most fundamentally, the essay lacks content.

Analyze an Argument

Model: 6 points out of 6

Upbeat and affirmative, Skybold (or its representative) appears to want to sound as visionary, decisive, and forward-looking in this argument as its name suggests. Certainly, it presents and "envisions" ideas that many readers could wish were true. What company would not want to institute a policy with such desirable and money-saving benefits? Yet, many questions must be answered in order to evaluate the conclusion that "Skybold's new telecommunicating policy is clearly a win-win situation."

First among questions to be addressed are those that probe the exact statistics about fewer sick days and personal days. By what precise number or percent have the number of sick and personal days diminished? Could that diminishment be due to factors other than the new work-at-home policy? Furthermore, over what span of time has this diminishment been measured? For example, if the policy has been in place for three months, and the absenteeism rate has truly dropped significantly over that period of time, could that not be accounted for by the fact that the policy is new? Once it is in place for a year or several years, will the same rates hold true? For the claims to have logical weight, the results surely should have held true for some long span of time, such as a year or more. These answers would help evaluate the conclusion that the policy is a "win" for Skybold.

Specific questions must also be asked in order to interpret the fabulous, though unsubstantiated, claims of greater employee satisfaction and enhanced employee loyalty. Have employees completed questionnaires about greater satisfaction? How many employees are actually more satisfied? Exactly how was the assertion of greater employee loyalty arrived at? Or does Skybold just assume this to be true? Is there any quantifiable data that exists to substantiate these claims? Finally, even if the claims are true, one must consider the dampening effects on satisfaction and loyalty should an employee have his or her desk removed at work and, consequently, be forced to share a space, or use someone else's space, on those days when he or she does not telecommute. Would he or she experience "greater employee satisfaction" then? The answers to all the questions raised in this paragraph would help evaluate the conclusion that the policy is a "win" for employees.

Perhaps the most important questions of all have to do with the writer's motivation and point of view. Was this argument written by the person who instituted the policy, perhaps as a bit of self-aggrandizement? What is the purpose, and just exactly who is the audience for this seeming self-congratulation? The answers to these questions might help peel away the outer layers of argument to expose a propagandistic core.

This essay scores 6 out of 6 because it

- **answers the task.** With sophistication and perceptiveness, the response raises questions that would have to be answered in order to evaluate the conclusion and the reasons on which it is based. The questions are not only apt, but they are offered in abundance.

- **is well supported.** In this case, the support is the questions, as well as the way in which they are introduced, explained, and related back to the writer's evaluative purpose. Although there are many other questions that could be asked, the ones that appear here are logically sound and presented with clarity and rhetorical effect.

- **is well organized.** The essay is a tour de force of good organization, with its attention-provoking opening that not only draws the reader in, but clearly states the claim of the argument. The three remaining paragraphs offer discrete, well-developed analyses of major points and concerns, and lead skillfully to the final "most important" issues of author, purpose, and audience.

- **is fluid, precise, and graceful.** Sentences are varied throughout, with many effective uses of questions. The essay is a trove of particularly well-chosen words and phrases, from "visionary," "institute," and "probe" to the "propagandistic core" and its accompanying metaphor.

- **observes the conventions of Standard Written English.**

Model: 2 points out of 6

Many questions must be asked about the many claims made in this argument. The first about if there was a remarkable surge in productivity. This being an interesting claim that is not explained. In order to evaluate if there was a remarkable surge in productivity, you should ask how much the production of the creative staff people had went up and basing that on the before and after figures of production of those workers, so that you would know if productivity doubled, or if it went up by 50% or if it went up by .05%, the exact amount being crucial to knowing if the policy resulted in a remarkable surge in productivity. Other questions you must ask and answer being about why Skybold brought about its new policy, after all, if the employees were upset that they couldn't ever telecommute, as so many employees do these days, then it only stands to reason that they were happier when they could finally get to telecommute. This would also help you evaluate the claim that there was a remarkable surge in productivity because the telecommuters now felt better about getting to telecommute after not being let to work from there homes before.

This essay scores 2 out of 6 because it

- **does not fully answer the task.** This essay never evaluates the conclusion that Skybold's new telecommuting policy is a win-win situation. While it does begin to raise and support interesting and logical questions about the reasons on which that conclusion is based, it falls well short of presenting a full analysis.

- **lacks organization.** This single paragraph lacks one clear focus. The response fails to divide main ideas into separate, cogent units of discourse.

- **has poorly constructed sentences.** Sentences are convoluted, lacking punctuation and subordination that result in meaningless jumbles of words.

- **contains major errors in the conventions of Standard Written English.** Some of these errors are serious enough to obstruct meaning.

Section 2: Quantitative Reasoning

1. A	11. B, D, G	16. E
2. C	12. D	17. B
3. C	13. A	18. D
4. D	14. B	19. 105
5. B	15. A, C, F, H	20. $\dfrac{6.5}{20.00}$
6. A		
7. B		
8. D		
9. B		
10. E		

Question

1.   <u>Quantity A</u>   <u>Quantity B</u>

$6\dfrac{7}{8}$ 3.42(2)

(A) Quantity A is greater.

(B) Quantity B is greater.

(C) The two quantities are equal.

(D) The relationship cannot be determined from the information given.

Answer Explanation

The correct answer is (A).

$6\dfrac{7}{8} = 6.875$

$3.42(2) = 6.84$

Quantity A is greater.

QUESTIONS 2–4 REFER TO THE DIAGRAM BELOW.

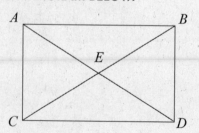

Question

ABCD is a rectangle.

E is the intersection of AD and BC.

2.   Quantity A   Quantity B

     the area of $\triangle CED$ the area of $\triangle AEC$

(A) Quantity A is greater.

(B) Quantity B is greater.

(C) The two quantities are equal.

(D) The relationship cannot be determined from the information given.

Answer Explanation

The correct answer is (C). Any values that are assigned to the side lengths of the figure will result in the two areas being equal. This is true for both whole and fractional values.

Question

3.   Quantity A   Quantity B

     m$\angle ACD$ + m$\angle CDB$ m$\angle AEC$ + m$\angle CED$

(A) Quantity A is greater.

(B) Quantity B is greater.

(C) The two quantities are equal.

(D) The relationship cannot be determined from the information given.

Answer Explanation

The correct answer is (C). Angles in the corners of rectangles are equal to 90°, so any two added together will equal 180°. Angles formed by the bisection of a line by another line equal 180°; so Quantity A is equal to Quantity B.

Question

4.   Quantity A   Quantity B

$(AB)^2 + (BD)^2$ AD

(A) Quantity A is greater.

(B) Quantity B is greater.

(C) The two quantities are equal.

(D) The relationship cannot be determined from the information given.

Answer Explanation

The correct answer is (D). If whole number values are assigned to the side lengths of this right triangle, then answer choice (A) would be correct. If fractional or decimal values (less than 1) are assigned to the side lengths of this right triangle, then answer choice (B) would be correct. Therefore the correct answer is (D).

Question

$$y < x < 0$$

5.   Quantity A   Quantity B

$|x|$ $|y|$

(A) Quantity A is greater.

(B) Quantity B is greater.

(C) The two quantities are equal.

(D) The relationship cannot be determined from the information given.

Answer Explanation

The correct answer is (B). Since y is less than x which is less than 0, when we take the absolute value of x and y, y will always be greater than x.

Question

$$a > b > 0$$

6.   Quantity A   Quantity B

$a^2 - b^2$ $(3a + 3b)(-2a + 2b)$

(A) Quantity A is greater.

(B) Quantity B is greater.

(C) The two quantities are equal.

(D) The relationship cannot be determined from the information given.

Answer Explanation

The correct answer is (A). Factor Quantity A and multiply Quantity B to find the comparison:

$$a^2 - b^2 = (a + b)(a - b)$$

$$(3a + 3b)(-2a + 2b) = -6(a + b)(a - b) = -6(a^2 - b^2)$$

Since $a > b > 0$, $a^2 - b^2$ will always be positive, and $-6(a^2 - b^2)$ will always be negative.

Question

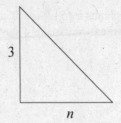

The area of the triangle is 15.

7.   Quantity A   Quantity B

                     n 12

(A) Quantity A is greater.

(B) Quantity B is greater.

(C) The two quantities are equal.

(D) The relationship cannot be determined from the information given.

Answer Explanation

The correct answer is (B). The area of a triangle is $\frac{1}{2} b \times h$ so using the working backwards strategy:

$\frac{1}{2}(3)(n) = 15$, so $n = 10$

Question

$$x^2 = 9$$

8.   Quantity A   Quantity B

                     x -3

(A) Quantity A is greater.

(B) Quantity B is greater.

(C) The two quantities are equal.

(D) The relationship cannot be determined from the information given.

Answer Explanation

The correct answers is (D).

$$x^2 = 9$$

$$x^2 - 9 = 0$$

$$(x + 3)(x - 3) = 0$$

$$x = 3, -3$$

Since x can be either 3 or -3, Quantity A can be both equal to and less than Quantity B.

Question

9. The local pastry shop sells its doughnuts for $1.90 each, and the shop owner makes an 8% profit on each. How much profit would the owner make if she sold 15 doughnuts?

    (A) $0.15
    (B) $2.28
    (C) $28.50
    (D) $1.12
    (E) $3.45

Answer Explanation

The correct answer is (B). This is a question where turning verbose or abstract language into something concise and concrete will help you.

$15 \times \$1.90 \times 0.08 = \$2.28$

Question

10. Evaluate $\dfrac{13(0.2)}{4}$

    (A) 0.0065
    (B) 0.065
    (C) 65
    (D) 6.5
    (E) 0.65

Answer Explanation

The correct answer is (E). Use your calculator.

$$\frac{13(0.2)}{4} = \frac{2.6}{4} = 0.65$$

Question

11. Find the next 3 numbers in the sequence. 1, 1, 2, 3, 5, 8, ...

    (A) 12
    (B) 13
    (C) 14
    (D) 21
    (E) 22
    (F) 33
    (G) 34
    (H) 55

Answer Explanation

The correct answers are (B), (D), and (G). You can find the next number by adding the last two numbers in the sequence.

$5 + 8 = 13$

$8 + 13 = 21$

$13 + 21 = 34$

Question

12. Let $f(x) = 2x^3 - x^2 + 7$. Find $f(3)$.
    (A) 25
    (B) 19
    (C) 16
    (D) 52
    (E) 54

Answer Explanation

The correct answer is (D). To evaluate the function $f(x) = 2x^3 - x^2 + 7$ for $f(3)$:

$$f(3) = 2x^3 - x^2 + 7$$
$$= 2(27) - 9 + 7$$
$$= 54 - 9 + 7$$
$$= 52$$

Question

13. Solve: $4(3x - 5) = x + 3$

    (A) $x = \dfrac{23}{11}$

    (B) $x = \dfrac{8}{11}$

    (C) $x = \dfrac{2}{3}$

    (D) $x = -4$

    (E) $x = 23$

Answer Explanation

The correct answer is (A). Solve the equation $4(3x - 5) = x + 3$.

$$12x - 20 = x + 3$$
$$11x = 23$$
$$x = \frac{23}{11}$$

Question

14. Find the value of x.

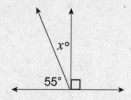

(A) 55°
(B) 35°
(C) 90°
(D) 145°
(E) 125°

Answer Explanation

The correct answer is (B).

$$90 = 55 + x$$
$$35 = x$$

Question

15. List all the factors of 51.

(A) 1
(B) 2
(C) 3
(D) 7
(E) 16
(F) 17
(G) 48
(H) 51

Answer Explanation

The correct answers are (A), (C), (F), and (H). 51 is odd, so eliminate answers (B), (E), and (G). That leaves 1, 3, 7, 17, and 51. Divide 51 by each:

$51 \div 1 = 51$, so 1, 51 are factors.

$51 \div 3 = 17$, so 3, 17 are factors.

$51 \div 7 = 7.3$, not a factor.

QUESTIONS 16–18 ARE BASED ON THE FOLLOWING DATA.

Annual State Budgets (in millions of dollars)

	2007	2008	2009	2010	2011	2012, est
State A	53.0	75.9	85.5	101.6	131.2	142.1
State B	14.4	14.5	20.0	19.0	39.2	43.5

Question

16. What is the ratio of the total (State A and State B) estimated budget of 2012 to 2007's budget?
    - (A) 33.7 : 92.8
    - (B) 142.1 : 53.0
    - (C) 43.5 : 14.4
    - (D) 14.4 : 43.5
    - (E) 92.8 : 33.7

Answer Explanation

The correct answer is (E).

$142.1 + 43.5 = 185.6$

$53.0 + 14.4 = 67.4$

$\dfrac{185.6}{67.4} = \dfrac{92.8}{33.7} = 92.8 : 33.7$

Question

17. What is the total budget for State A for 2007, 2008, and 2011?
    - (A) 68.1
    - (B) 260.1
    - (C) 268
    - (D) 276.4
    - (E) 308.7

Answer Explanation

The correct answer is (B).

$53.0 + 75.9 + 131.2 = 260.1$

Question

18. What year had the biggest percentage increase from the previous year in State B and what was the percentage increase?

    (A) 2009, 138%
    (B) 2011, 206%
    (C) 2009, 37%
    (D) 2011, 106%
    (E) 2012, 11%

Answer Explanation

The correct answer is (D). Estimate the difference from year to year, and then calculate the percentage. The difference between 2010 and 2011 is more than double and none of the other amounts is even close, so 2011 is the year.

$39.2 - 19.0 = 20.2$
$20.2 \div 19.0 = 106\%$

Question

19. Mary went to the convenience store with $20. She wanted to buy a newspaper for $1.25, a magazine for $6.50, a soda for $1.75, and then spend the rest of her $20 on dime candy. How many pieces would she get?

Answer Explanation

The correct answer is 105.

$20 - (1.25 + 6.50 + 1.75) = $ amount spent on candy

$20 - (9.50) = 10.50$

$10.50 \div 0.10 = 105$

Question

20. Using the information from question 19, find the ratio of the amount of money spent for the magazine in relation to the total amount of money spent.

Give your answer as a fraction.

Answer Explanation

The correct answer is $\dfrac{6.50}{20.00}$.

$$\frac{magazine}{total} = \frac{6.50}{20.00}$$

Section 3: Verbal Reasoning

1. C	11. E	16. A, D
2. B, F	12. B	17. C, E
3. A, F	13. A, B	18. C, E
4. B, D, G	14. B	19. A, F
5. B, C	15. E	20. B
6. E		
7. A		
8. D		
9. A		
10. B		

Question

1. The unsophisticated nature of research tools affects the _____ and validity of market research into the potential market for products and programs.

(A) accountability
(B) acceptability
(C) reliability
(D) liability
(E) approval

Answer Explanation

The correct answer is (C). "Reliability" means "dependability and consistency," both characteristics required for sound, or valid, market research data. Choice (A), "accountability," means "capable of being accountable" as a person is for her/his actions. It doesn't fit the context, nor does choice (B), "acceptability," which means "satisfactory or merely adequate." The meaning is not strong enough to balance "valid." Choice (D), "liability," makes no sense because it means either "an obligation" or "a handicap." Choice (E), "approval," is also incorrect; it means "the formal agreement" of something. Substituting the answer choices in the blanks can help you determine the correct answer.

Question

2. That Jane Austen's satiric wit is lost on some readers is (i) _____ because it is so (ii) _____ as to become caricature; for example, consider the Rev. Collins in *Pride and Prejudice*.

Blank (i)
(A) logical
(B) understandable
(C) inexplicable

Blank (ii)
(D) flashy
(E) showy
(F) overdrawn

Answer Explanation

The correct answers are (B) and (F). Answer Blank (i): Choice (A), "logical," means "capable of reasoning in a clear and consistent manner" and may seem correct. But choice (B), "understandable," is a better choice between the two because it means "capable of being understood." In the context of the sentence, the writer is not reasoning something out, but stating his/her opinion. Choice (C), "inexplicable," means "impossible to explain, incomprehensible." It is the opposite of "understandable." In the context of the entire sentence, the word does not fit the meaning, and so, is incorrect.

Answer Blank (ii): In choosing answers for text completion items, consider the style and tone of the text. Choices (D) and (E), "flashy" and "showy," don't fit either. Only choice (F), "overdrawn," meaning "exaggerated" fits the meaning.

Question

3. As a result of overconfidence and a number of (i) _____ errors in judgment to employ a(n) (ii) _____, the majority party in the state legislature became the minority party in the last election.

Blank (i)
(A) embarrassing
(B) inconvenient
(C) upsetting

Blank (ii)
(D) paradox
(E) aphorism
(F) euphemism

Answer Explanation

The correct answers are (A) and (F). Answer Blank (i): Choice (B), "inconvenient," means "hard to reach" in one sense and "troublesome or difficult" in another sense. In this instance, it would be a euphemism for a stronger qualifier. The same is true of "upsetting," choice (C). Neither are strong enough descriptors based on the information in the sentence.

Answer Blank (ii): Choice (D), "paradox," means "something that is contradictory." It doesn't fit the context. An aphorism, choice (E), is a saying or adage, so it's incorrect because "error in judgment" isn't an aphorism, but it is a euphemism, substituting a mild or inoffensive term for a harsh or blunt term.

Question

4. One consequence of the desire among modern playwrights to bring (i) _____ to the theater has been the diminution of poetry as a dramatic language. On the other hand, realism in language has brought a (ii) _____ end to rant and rhetoric upon the stage. As one critic wrote, modern playwrights have been pushed to develop plays that are (iii) _____ and convincing when they could no longer rely on "verbal pyrotechnics."

Blank (i)	Blank (ii)	Blank (iii)
(A) vibrancy	(D) welcome	(G) more forceful
(B) verisimilitude	(E) final	(H) more cerebral
(C) resemblance	(F) limited	(I) more believable

Answer Explanation

The correct answers are (B), (D), and (G). Answer Blank (i): Context will help you complete this blank. This is also an instance when you might find it easier to begin by filling in one of the other blanks. Choice (A) doesn't make sense in the context because poetry would add vibrancy to the theater, but the sentence says that the position of poetry has been diminished in modern plays. Choices (B) and (C) are somewhat similar in meaning, but choice (C), "resemblance," doesn't make sense if you read it in the sentence. Choice (B), "verisimilitude," meaning "something that has the appearance of being real," is the answer by the process of elimination.

Answer Blank (ii): Choice (E), "final," is redundant; an end is final. Choice (F), "limited," doesn't make sense; how can you have a limited end? Choice (D), "welcome," is the correct answer by the process of elimination, but more importantly because it means "giving pleasure."

Answer Blank (iii): The word that you're looking for has to balance "convincing." Choice (I), "more believable," is similar to "more convincing," so choosing it would be redundant. There is nothing in the passage to indicate that modern plays should be "more cerebral" [choice (H)] because playwrights can't use rant and rhetoric. Choice (G), "more forceful," meaning "effective," is the best choice.

QUESTIONS 5–7 ARE BASED ON THE FOLLOWING PASSAGE.

In a 1983 speech, President Ronald Reagan announced his plans to create a shield against nuclear missile attacks by the Soviet Union. This would consist of a system of lasers or rockets, deployed in space, that could destroy any missile launched at the United States by the Soviet Union. The news media quickly dubbed Reagan's proposal for this Strategic Defense
5   Initiative, or SDI, as "Star Wars," a recently released science fiction movie. The Soviets, however, took it seriously. Mikhail Gorbachev, the leader of the Soviet Union, pointed out to Reagan that a missile shield would enable the United States to easily launch a first strike against the Soviet Union, knowing the Soviets could not retaliate. In response, Reagan offered to share SDI technology with the Soviets, but they refused.
10   The Soviets were also concerned about a new arms race: the United States would have to spend billions of dollars developing SDI technology, while the Russians would have to increase their spending on their own offensive technologies in the hope of defeating SDI. This reallocation of spending could severely set back Gorbachev's own plans for improving the Soviet economy and the standard of living of Soviet citizens. Ultimately, the Intermediate
15   Nuclear Force (INF) treaty of December 1987 was proposed, in which the Americans and Russians agreed to eliminate all intermediate-range nuclear missiles from Europe.

Question

5. The passage suggests that the creation of SDI could have resulted in which of the following?

   (A) A nuclear war between the United States and the Soviet Union
   (B) A first strike against the Soviet Union by the United States
   (C) The sharing of missile technology between the United States and the Soviet Union

Answer Explanation

The correct answers are (B) and (C). The Soviets feared that having SDI technology would enable the United States to launch a first strike against them, so choice (B) is correct, and Reagan suggested that the United States share the technology with the Soviets, so choice (C) is also correct. Answer choice (A) is incorrect because the passage does not suggest that a nuclear war would have resulted from the creation of SDI.

Question

6. It can be inferred from the passage that the U.S. news media called the SDI "Star Wars" because it

   (A) seemed likely that it would start a nuclear war between the Americans and the Soviets.
   (B) would cost the United States billions of dollars, taking money away from other programs.
   (C) was based on technology that science fiction writers had developed.
   (D) was seen as the beginning of the end of the Cold War.
   (E) seemed to be an impossible idea straight out of science fiction.

Answer Explanation

The correct answer is (E). *Star Wars* was a popular science fiction movie of the period and the technology that was being proposed seemed something impossible, hence the use of a science fiction nickname by the press. Choice (A) is incorrect because the technology was suggested in order to *prevent* a nuclear war. Choice (B) is true, but this was not the reason the news media called SDI "Star Wars." Choice (C) is related to the correct answer, but is not entirely true, so eliminate it. Choice (D) is incorrect because there is no mention of the Cold War in the passage.

Question

7. In the final paragraph, the author is primarily concerned with describing

   (A) reasons that persuaded the Soviets to entertain the possibility of an INF treaty.
   (B) the U.S.'s refusal to halt the SDI program.
   (C) a potential arms race between the United States and the Soviet Union.
   (D) Gorbachev's concerns with the potential impact of SDI on Soviet domestic policy.
   (E) Gorbachev's concerns over possible war with the United States.

Answer Explanation

The correct answer is (A). The author describes some of the reasons that led the Soviets to consider the INF treaty, choice (A). Choice (B) is incorrect because a refusal to halt SDI is not mentioned in the passage. Choice (C) is incorrect because although the arms race is mentioned, it's not the focus of the paragraph. Choice (D), Gorbachev's domestic policy concerns, is described in the paragraph, but it's not the main idea of the paragraph. Choice (E) is implied in the mention of the concern over an arms race, but it's only one aspect of Gorbachev's concerns. Taken together, his concerns make up choice (A).

QUESTIONS 8–9 ARE BASED ON THE FOLLOWING PASSAGE.

Obesity results when a person consumes significantly more calories than energy burned over a long period of time, though at this point scientists cannot point to a single cause of obesity. In a large majority of obesity cases, the causes are related to genetic factors that influence the metabolism of fat and that regulate the hormones and proteins that control appetite. A
5   person's appetite is determined by different processes that occur both in the brain and the digestive system. **During digestion, carbohydrates break down into different types of sugar molecules, including glucose.** Immediately after eating, blood glucose levels rise, which triggers the release of insulin, a hormone that helps change glucose into energy. As the insulin pours into the bloodstream, it pushes the glucose into cells. Insulin is a significant
10 factor in terms of obesity because it helps determine which nutrients will be burned for energy and which will be stored in cells for future use. Recent studies have found that the faster a cell processes insulin, the more fat it stores. This might be one cause of obesity, though there may be other factors to consider, and to date no one theory has been determined to be conclusive.

Question

8. This passage suggests that obesity is caused by which of the following?
   (A) The breakdown of carbohydrates into different types of sugar molecules
   (B) The consumption of too many calories
   (C) The inability of the body to process glucose
   (D) The inefficiency of insulin to process fat during digestion
   (E) The inability of a person to feel full after eating

Answer Explanation

The correct answer is (D). The statement that insulin helps determine which nutrients are burned for energy and which are stored for future use means that if the insulin release is inefficient, more nutrients will be stored as fat, thus causing obesity. Choice (A) simply describes what happens during digestion. Choices (B) and (E) may seem correct, but each is only partially true. Consuming too many calories would not cause obesity if the body was able to burn them for energy. If a person did not feel full after eating, he or she might eat more and, therefore, consume too many calories, but this is neither stated nor implied in the passage. Choice (C) is incorrect because the passage never suggests that the inability to process glucose causes obesity; instead obesity is related to how insulin processes glucose.

Question

9. Which of the following best characterizes the function of the boldfaced sentence in lines 6–7 of the passage?

(A) It provides evidence on which a theory is based.

(B) It summarizes a theory with which the author agrees.

(C) It restates a point made earlier in the passage.

(D) It disproves a commonly accepted theory.

(E) It presents a specific application of a general concept.

Answer Explanation

The correct answer is (A). This statement provides evidence for the theory that obesity may be caused by the inability of insulin to process glucose properly. Choice (B) is incorrect because the statement is not a summary of a theory, but a detail related to the theory. Choice (C) is incorrect because the information in the sentence was not made earlier in the passage. Choice (D) is incorrect because instead of disproving a theory, the statement supports a theory. Choice (E) is incorrect because a general concept is not involved.

QUESTIONS 10–12 ARE BASED ON THE FOLLOWING PASSAGE.

Dutch artist M.C. Escher's work covers a variety of subjects, though he is probably best known for the pieces that he drew from unusual perspectives, which result in enigmatic effects. During the course of his life, Escher adopted a highly mathematical approach, using special notations that he invented himself, including a system for categorizing shapes, colors,
5 and symmetrical properties. Looking at his work, you can see clearly that mathematics played an important role in the development of his distinctive style, yet though he studied and admired various mathematical theories over the years, Escher did not consider himself a mathematician. However, this lack of formal training allowed him to explore mathematics in a unique way, without having to adhere to any set rules or restrictions. In 1958, he wrote:
10 "In mathematical quarters, the regular division of the plane has been considered theoretically . . . . [Mathematicians] have opened the gate leading to an extensive domain, but they have not entered this domain themselves. By their very nature they are more interested in the way in which the gate is opened than in the garden lying behind it."

Question

10. What material would help to support the intersection of art and mathematics in Escher's work?

(A) Escher's notebooks containing his mathematical notations

(B) A painting of Escher's demonstrating his use of mathematical principles in his art

(C) Art criticism of Escher's works

Answer Explanation

The correct answer is (B). One of Escher's paintings would prove that his art went beyond the theories of mathematics and actually expressed the beauty of it. Choice (A) is incorrect because they would not demonstrate how Escher created art from theories of mathematics. Choice (C) might or might not indicate an awareness of the mathematical underpinnings of Escher's work and, therefore, is not a viable answer.

Question

11. From the passage, what is Escher's view of mathematicians?

(A) They do not grasp how mathematics and art are interconnected.

(B) They will never have the ability to appreciate Escher's art.

(C) They cannot translate their theories into their own personalized notations.

(D) They will never be able to translate their theories into art.

(E) They cannot see the beauty that is inherent in their theories.

Answer Explanation

The correct answer is (E). By saying that mathematicians are only interested in the way the gate is opened but not the garden lying behind it, Escher is pointing out that they are only interested in how their theories work but not in how their theories can be expressed artistically. Choices (A) and (B) are incorrect because even if they might be true about some mathematicians, Escher does not imply this in the quote. Choice (C) is incorrect because Escher never addresses the personalized notations of other mathematicians. Choice (D) is incorrect because although Escher believes that mathematical theories can be expressed artistically, he does not imply that mathematicians need to do this, just that they are not interested in doing so.

Question

12. In the passage, "enigmatic" (line 2) means

(A) rational.

(B) inscrutable.

(C) comprehensible.

(D) decipherable.

(E) theoretical.

Answer Explanation

The correct answer is (B). "Enigmatic" in this passage means "inscrutable, or mysterious." Choice (A) is incorrect because something can be enigmatic without being rational. Choices (C) and (D) are incorrect because if something is comprehensible or decipherable, it is easy to read and not mysterious. Choice (E) is incorrect because "theoretical" means "hypothetical or speculative," which is not the same as inscrutable.

QUESTIONS 13-15 ARE BASED ON THE FOLLOWING PASSAGE.

The fire at the Triangle Shirtwaist Factory in New York City in 1911 was one of the worst industrial disasters in U.S. history. The fire killed 146 people, many of them young immigrant women. The Triangle Shirtwaist Factory produced women's blouses, or "shirtwaists," and took up the eighth, ninth, and tenth floors of a building in New York's Greenwich Village.

5 The fire started near closing time on March 25, 1911, on the eighth floor of the building. Most of the workers could not escape because the supervisors had locked the doors to the stairwells and exits from the outside to prevent the workers from leaving early or removing materials. Many women died from being trapped inside the building or jumped to their deaths from the top floors because ladders could not reach them. This devastating tragedy

10 brought to light for many Americans the inhumane working conditions of sweatshops, and it had a huge impact on U.S. workers. It galvanized many to push for improved factory safety standards and led to the rapid growth of the International Ladies' Garment Workers' Union, which fought for better and safer working conditions in the garment industry. New York State created a commission to investigate factory conditions and in 1915 the state legislature

15 enacted new measures to protect factory workers from just such tragedies as the Triangle Shirtwaist Factory fire.

Question

13. According to the passage, what was it about the Triangle Shirtwaist fire that evidently caused so great an impact on public opinion?

    (A) The fire killed so many people, many of whom were young women.

    (B) The workers could not escape during the fire because supervisors had locked the doors to the stairwells and exits.

    (C) The fire resulted in a strengthened labor movement and new labor laws.

Answer Explanation

The correct answers are (A) and (B). The fire had a huge impact on public opinion because of the tragic death of so many young people, mostly women, and the exposure of the unsafe working conditions in the factory, implied in choice (B). Choice (C) is incorrect because the strengthening of the labor movement and the passage of new labor laws were both results of heightened public opinion, not causes.

Question

14. Select the sentence in the passage that does NOT add to the support for the main idea of the passage.

    (A) This devastating tragedy brought to light for many Americans the inhumane working conditions of sweatshops, and it had a huge impact on U.S. workers.

    (B) The fire started near closing time on March 25, 1911, on the eighth floor of the building.

    (C) Many women died from being trapped inside the building or jumped to their deaths from the top floors because ladders could not reach them.

Answer Explanation

The correct answer is (B). The time and place of the fire are minor details that aren't absolutely necessary to understand the main idea. Choices (A) and (C) are true, but they are incorrect answers because these are important details that clearly support the main idea of the passage. Remember that to answer a "NOT" question, like an "EXCEPT" question, you need to find the answer that doesn't match the information.

Question

15. In the passage, "galvanized" (line 11) most nearly means

    (A) impeded.

    (B) increased.

(C) hurtled.

(D) angered.

(E) incited.

Answer Explanation

The correct answer is (E). In this passage, "galvanized" means "incited or spurred on." Choice (A) is incorrect because "impeded" means "hindered," which is the opposite of what occurred. Choice (B) is incorrect because, though "increased" may seem correct, it doesn't match the strong quality implied in "galvanized." Choice (C) is incorrect because "hurdled" means "jumped over," which doesn't make sense. Choice (D) is incorrect because "angered," while likely true, doesn't mean the same as "incited."

Question

16. In shuttering programs to reduce costs, the new CFO was _____ toward employees and refused to listen to their concerns and alternative suggestions.

    (A) arrogant

    (B) unkind

    (C) uncharitable

    (D) dismissive

    (E) contentious

    (F) confrontational

Answer Explanation

The correct answers are (A) and (D). Choice A, "arrogant," means "displaying an exaggerated opinion of one's self-worth; being self-important" and choice (D), "dismissive," means "showing disregard, being disdainful of others." Both fit the context of the sentence. Choices (B) and (C) are also synonym pairs, and while the new CFO was undoubtedly "unkind" and "uncharitable" toward employees, the word "refused" in the sentence indicates that these two words are not strong enough; they also aren't typically used to describe business dealings. Choices (E) and (F) are also synonym pairs, but the word "refused" indicates that the CFO cut off communication so that there was no occasion for being either "contentious" or "confrontational," both of which mean "argumentative and quarrelsome."

Question

17. Green building, that is, the construction of new buildings and the renovation of existing ones to make them eco-friendly, is a fast-growing segment of the construction industry and one that ALLIED Builders hopes to _____ according to its five-year business plan.

    (A) promote

    (B) advance

    (C) capitalize on

    (D) upgrade

    (E) exploit

    (F) endorse

Answer Explanation

The correct answers are (C) and (E). "Capitalize on" and "exploit," choices (C) and (E), mean "take advantage of, make the most of." Choices (A) and (B), "promote" and "advance," both mean "to put forward, to aid the growth of." In the context of a business plan, the pair don't fit the sense. Choices (D) and (E) are not synonyms, and neither is a synonym of the other words in the list. "Upgrade" means "to improve," and "endorse" means "to approve."

Question

18. The original intention in creating NASA was to explore space, but many of the products people take for granted today, such as cordless power tools and sunglasses with polarized lenses, resulted from _____ research that NASA conducted for the space program.

    (A) far-reaching
    (B) wide-ranging
    (C) innovative
    (D) unusual
    (E) cutting-edge
    (F) conventional

Answer Explanation

The correct answers are (C) and (E). Although you may be confused that the answer choices contain three synonyms: innovative, unusual, and cutting-edge, choices (C), (D), and (E), you can eliminate choice (D) because the characteristic of being unusual is not so strong as being either innovative or cutting edge, the correct answers. Choice (A), "far-reaching," and choice (B), "wide-ranging," are synonyms, but the implication from the first part of the sentence is that NASA conducted research related to the space program, so that it wasn't doing research over a wide number of fields of study. You can eliminate choice (F) because NASA by the nature of its program wouldn't be conducting conventional research.

Question

19. Many researchers believe that _____ bacteria keep harmful bacteria from invading humans by using the material that harmful bacteria need to live.

    (A) helpful
    (B) malignant
    (C) pathogenic
    (D) benign
    (E) benevolent
    (F) beneficial

Answer Explanation

The correct answers are (A) and (F). From the context of the sentence, you can tell that choices (B) and (C), "malignant" and "pathogenic," are incorrect. The blank that you need to complete must be the opposite of the word "harmful," and both "malignant" and "pathogenic" are harmful. Choice

(D), "benign," is incorrect because it means "harmless, having little or no effect, showing mildness." Choice (E) is incorrect because "benevolent" means "doing good, showing goodwill" and refers to people and organizations. The context requires two words that have a good effect, choices (A) and (F), "helpful" and "beneficial."

QUESTION 20 IS BASED ON THE FOLLOWING PASSAGE.

Emily Dickinson, a poet virtually unknown in her lifetime, wrote some of the most memorable lines in American poetry. Her poems are instantly recognizable for their brevity (they are often no longer than 20 lines) and their quirky punctuation and capitalization. Her frequent and often idiosyncratic use of the dash serves to emphasize many of her recurrent topics. A great
5 number of Dickinson's almost 1,800 poems deal with the themes of death and immortality, though her poems are also filled with joy and hope. Because of its unusual syntax and use of figurative language—imagery, metaphor, personification—Dickinson's poetry can seem to the uninitiated reader something of a puzzle. Present-day readers would do well to renounce a literal way of reading in order to truly appreciate Dickinson's poetry.

Question

20. What does the author imply by the last statement in the passage?
    (A) Readers should not try to find literal meaning in Dickinson's poetry.
    (B) Readers of poetry today are not used to so much figurative language.
    (C) Readers should try to figure out what themes were most important to Dickinson.
    (D) Readers who try to unlock the mysteries of Dickinson's figurative language are doing themselves a disservice.
    (E) Readers of poetry today need to consider the context in which Dickinson's poetry was written.

Answer Explanation

The correct answer is (B). Choice (B) most closely describes what the author implies: modern readers are not used to figurative language and could have a difficult time making sense of Dickinson's work. Choice (A) is incorrect because the author doesn't suggest that modern readers should not look for literal meaning in Dickinson's work, just that it might be a little difficult to do so. The author would likely agree with choice (C), but it doesn't reflect the last statement in the passage. Choice (D) contradicts what the author is implying in the last sentence. Choice (E) doesn't relate to anything in the passage.

Section 4: Verbal Reasoning

1. C	11. A	16. B
2. D	12. E	17. C
3. A, E	13. B, E	18. B
4. A, D, I	14. C, D	19. D
5. B, E, I	15. A, C	20. B
6. B		
7. C		
8. A		
9. C		
10. D		

Question

1. Social networking is a marketing tool that many companies are harnessing to sell their products; however, it must be used _____ because the hard sell risks offending potential customers.

(A) with ease
(B) actively
(C) judiciously
(D) expeditiously
(E) efficiently

Answer Explanation

The correct answer is (C). The clue to the correct answer is the phrase "hard sell"; the context of the sentence indicates that you need to find the word that indicates some opposite action. Choice (C), "judiciously," means "showing good judgment, being prudent," and matches the sense. Choice (A), "with ease," doesn't quite fit the sense; you can do a hard sell easily. The same problem occurs with choice (B), "actively." Choice (D), "expeditiously," means "efficiently and quickly," and is incorrect because doing a hard sell efficiently and quickly doesn't make it any more palatable to the consumer. Nor does being simply efficient, choice (E).

Question

2. In composing "Scheherazade," Rimsky-Korsakov hoped to _____ the "magical spirit" of *One Thousand and One Nights*, a collection of exotic folk tales from the Middle East and South Asia.

(A) motivate
(B) induce
(C) inspire
(D) evoke
(E) provoke

Answer Explanation

The correct answer is (D). To evoke, choice (D), means "to bring to mind or suggest," in this case metaphorically. Choice (A), "motivate," which means "to provide an incentive," doesn't make sense in the context of the sentence. Nor does choice (B), "induce," meaning "to lead or cause to happen." Inspiring the spirit doesn't make sense either, so eliminate choice (C). To provoke, choice (E), means "to incite or irritate," which doesn't make sense.

Question

3. Garraty states that the problems faced by private colleges in the 1820s and 1830s were of their own making to a degree. Many cities and towns wanted the (i) _____ of hosting a college, but the supply of colleges soon (ii) _____ the demand, that is, the number of potential students.

Blank (i)	Blank (ii)
(A) honor	(D) outperformed
(B) admiration	(E) outstripped
(C) character	(F) outshone

Answer Explanation

The correct answers are (A) and (E). Answer Blank (i): "Honor" means "respect, distinction, privilege" and fits the sense of the sentence. Choice (B), "admiration," means "a feeling of pleasure or approval," but doesn't fit in the sentence because the context usually references the source of the admiration, that is, "towns wanted the admiration of other cities for hosting a college." In the sentence, however, it's the college that admires the town, which makes no sense. Choice (C) is incorrect because none of the many meanings of "character" fits the sense.

Answer Blank (ii): Choice (E), "outstripped," means "to surpass, to grow greater or faster and leave behind," which fits the sense. Choice (D) is incorrect because "outperform" means "to perform better" and the sense of the discussion of supply and demand requires a quantitative response. The same reason makes choice (F), "outshone," incorrect.

Question

4. The nation-states of early modern Europe guarded their sovereignty (i) _____, finding countless reasons—real and (ii) _____—for wars. Peace (iii) _____ only when one nation managed to subdue its neighbors.

Blank (i)	Blank (ii)	Blank (iii)
(A) jealously	(D) feigned	(G) occurred
(B) intolerantly	(E) facetious	(H) mediated
(C) liberally	(F) deceptive	(I) intervened

Answer Explanation

The correct answers are (A), (D), and (I). Answer Blank (i): Choice (A), "jealously," meaning in this case "vigilantly," fits the sense of fighting to keep one's authority and territory. Choice (B) is incorrect because "intolerantly" means "unwilling to tolerate, that is, allow or respect, differences" and is not strong enough to match the context of warfare, though intolerance led to warfare. Choice (C) can mean "freely" in the sense of giving freely or generous and so doesn't match the context.

Answer Blank (ii): Choice (D), "feigned," means "fake, made up, fictitious" and counterbalances "real" in the parenthetical expression. Choice (E), "facetious," means "humorous, playful" and is a distractor for "fictitious." Choice (F), "deceptive," though meaning "capable of deceiving" doesn't necessarily mean fake.

Answer Blank (iii): This set of answers is a good example of why you should read all the answers. You might jump at choice (G), "occurred," because it does make sense in the context that peace occurred, but choice (I), "intervened," is a better choice because it identifies peace as happening in between bouts of warfare. Choice (H) is incorrect because "mediate" means "to resolve differences or bring about a settlement between two parties."

Question

5. The speaker, a former prosecutor turned politician, remains direct, candid, and (i) _____ in her assessment of policy, but she can also be (ii) _____ and offhand toward her colleagues. She is considered a/n (iii) _____ legislator.

Blank (i)	Blank (ii)	Blank (iii)
(A) frank	(D) rough	(G) very ambitious
(B) pragmatic	(E) brusque	(H) really approachable
(C) rigid	(F) brisk	(I) no-nonsense

Answer Explanation

The correct answers are (B), (E), and (I). Answer Blank (i): You're looking for a word that logically completes the description of the speaker. Eliminate choice (A) because "frank" means the same as "candid." Choice (C), "rigid," doesn't have the same sense as "direct" and "candid," which leave "pragmatic," meaning "practical, guided by experience and observation." One synonym is "hard-nosed."

Answer Blank (ii): In this set of descriptors, you need one that fits with "offhand." Choice (D), "rough," in this sense means "coarse, rude, inconsiderate" which may seem to fit, but choice (E), "brusque," meaning "abrupt or blunt in manner or speech," fits better with the earlier description and with "offhand," which it is meant to balance. Choice (F), "brisk," means "lively, quick" and doesn't fit the context.

Answer Blank (iii): The speaker may be very ambitious, choice (G), but there is nothing in the passage to support this, so eliminate it. Everything about the description, especially the second set of descriptors, indicates that the speaker is not approachable, choice (H). That leaves choice (I), "no-nonsense," that completes the passage logically.

QUESTIONS 6–7 ARE BASED ON THE FOLLOWING PASSAGE.

A 2007 study by the United Nations University reported that desertification, or desert encroachment, was "the greatest environmental challenge of our times." About two out of five African countries on the edges of the Sahara are under the threat of desertification. The UN study reported that "[d]esertification has emerged as an environmental crisis of global
5 proportions, currently affecting an estimated 100 to 200 million people, and threatening the lives and livelihoods of a much larger number." The study explained that although climate change has caused major degradation of Africa's soil, overgrazing, deforestation, and unsustainable irrigation practices are also contributing factors. The study added that people who are displaced by desertification put additional strains on local natural resources and nearby
10 communities as conflicts arise over competition for farmland. The UN report suggests that new farming practices, such as planting forests in dryland areas, could help prevent the spread of deserts.

Question

6. Based on the passage, which of the following is NOT a cause of desertification?
   (A) climatic change
   (B) competition for farmland
   (C) overgrazing
   (D) poor irrigation practices
   (E) cutting down trees

Answer Explanation

The correct answer is (B). Choices (A), (C), (D), and (E) are mentioned in the passage as causes of desertification, including cutting down trees, or deforestation, choice (E). The passage mentions that competition for farmland is a *result* of desertification, but not that it is a cause. Remember for "NOT" questions, you're looking for the answer choice that doesn't fit.

Question

7. Select the sentence in the passage that is NOT a major detail supporting the thesis.

(A) A 2007 study by the United Nations University reported that desertification, or desert encroachment, was "the greatest environmental challenge of our times."

(B) The study added that people who are displaced by desertification put additional strains on local natural resources and nearby communities as conflicts arise over competition for farmland.

(C) About two out of five African countries on the edges of the Sahara are under the threat of desertification.

Answer Explanation

The correct answer is (C). This information, while important, does not directly support the thesis of what causes desertification and what has happened as a result. Choices (A) and (B) are both important points that support the thesis of the passage.

QUESTIONS 8–9 ARE BASED ON THE FOLLOWING PASSAGE.

During World War II, the U.S. system of rationing did not work as planned not only because it conflicted with personal needs and wants (which had grown during the previous years of deprivation because of the Great Depression and its aftermath), but because it went against the national character of the American people. This was a nation based on the principle that
5 as long as you have money to spend, nothing is off limits. By limiting each individual's purchasing power, the government had imposed a new economic system that attacked this principle. The emergence of the illegal black market, on the other hand, supported this basic principle of acquisition, or consumerism, for Americans. This is not to deny that many who ran or even patronized the black market were actually motivated by greed, but it does suggest
10 that the individualistic (and frontier) spirit of Americans had not been lost.

Question

8. Select the statement that restates the premise of the author's argument.

(A) Normally law-abiding citizens will break the law to satisfy what they consider to be their basic needs and wants.

(B) Americans during World War II acted unlawfully due to circumstances out of their control.

(C) The American system of rationing did not work because Americans circumvented its principles through the practice of the black market.

(D) As long as Americans have enough money to spend, they will spend it however they can.

(E) If the Great Depression had not deprived so many Americans of basic needs and wants, they would not have patronized the black market during World War II.

Answer Explanation

The correct answer is (A). The author's argument is that during the time of rationing, people who wouldn't ordinarily have broken the law did so out of the frustration of not being able to have the goods they believed they deserved. The author never states choice (B) in the passage. Choice (C) restates the facts of what happened, but doesn't address the author's argument of why it happened.

Choice (D) might seem to be true, but it is not so close a reading of the author's argument as choice (A). Choice (E) might be true, but this is a conclusion based on the facts, and the author never draws this conclusion in the passage.

Question

9. Which of the following, if it were true, would weaken the author's argument?

   (A) During the Great Depression, many Americans found ways to circumvent the law in order to provide for their families.

   (B) The majority of American citizens are law abiding and will not break the law under any circumstances.

   (C) Many Americans continued to patronize the black market after rationing ended.

Answer Explanation

The correct answer is (C). If most Americans patronized the black market after rationing ended, choice (C) weakens the argument that Americans only did it as a direct response to rationing. Choice (A) is incorrect because it would strengthen the argument that Americans will break the law if special circumstances leave them no choice. If most Americans would not break the law under any circumstances, choice (B) doesn't affect the author's argument that Americans as a generalized category were willing to break the law once rationing was implemented.

QUESTIONS 10–12 ARE BASED ON THE FOLLOWING PASSAGE.

The increasing awareness of lighting inefficiency and the billions of dollars of potential annual energy savings that can be achieved by switching to LED lighting has resulted in many government-funded research initiatives around the world. In addition, governments in the United States, Canada, Europe, and Australia have responded to the growing need for energy
5 conservation by passing legislation that regulates or eliminates the sale of incandescent and halogen light bulbs by a certain date. However, though increasing consumers' awareness of the inefficiency of other light sources can help increase the adoption of LED lighting, regulations that focus on enforcing energy-efficient lighting are likely to work better. One example is California's Energy Efficiency Standards for Residential and Nonresidential Buildings, or
10 Title 24, that provides a set of mandatory regulations covering all aspects of new building construction. The Residential Lighting section of Title 24 requires that a high-efficiency light source be used in several areas of the home, including the kitchen and bathrooms, and that all outdoor light fixtures must either use energy-efficient bulbs, or must be controlled by light and motion sensors.

Question

10. This passage achieves all of the following purposes EXCEPT it

   (A) implies that LED lighting will become a necessity of the future.

   (B) explains one way governments are forcing people to switch to LED lighting.

   (C) cites a regulation that enforces the use of high-efficiency light sources.

   (D) describes how LED lighting is more energy efficient than incandescent lighting.

   (E) implies that government-funded research on energy efficiency is essential.

Answer Explanation

The correct answer is (D). The passage doesn't describes how LED lighting works and what makes it more energy efficient than incandescent lighting, so choice (D) is the correct answer. Choices (A), (B), (C), and (E) are all achieved in the passage.

Question

11. The author introduces California's Title 24 in order to
    (A) support the concept that the government needs to set rules to increase the adoption of LED lighting.
    (B) provide a possible explanation for why more Americans have adopted LED lighting.
    (C) reinforce the concept that other methods of lighting are less efficient than LED lighting.
    (D) introduce the idea that governments need to enforce rules about high efficiency lighting in residential buildings.
    (E) cast doubt on studies that show that Americans are not eager to switch to LED lighting.

Answer Explanation

The correct answer is (A). The author's point is that government needs to set rules to increase the adoption of LED lighting and uses Title 24 as an example of states' doing this. Choice (B) is incorrect because Title 24 doesn't explain why more Americans have adopted LED lighting; instead it illustrates how it can be done. Choice (C) is incorrect because although LED lighting is more efficient, this is not why the author specifically introduces Title 24. Choice (D) is incorrect because the author never specifically states anything about the importance of high efficiency lighting in residential buildings; this is merely described by Title 24. Choice (E) is incorrect because studies showing Americans are not eager to switch to LED lighting are not introduced in this passage.

Question

12. "Mandatory" (line 10) most nearly means
    (A) provisional.
    (B) permanent.
    (C) predetermined.
    (D) discretionary.
    (E) obligatory.

Answer Explanation

The correct answer is (E). "Mandatory" means about the same as "obligatory," meaning "compulsory or required." Choice (A) is incorrect because "provisional" means "temporary," which is not the same as "required." Choice (B) is incorrect because "permanent" means "fixed," which is also not the same as "required." Choice (C) is incorrect because "predetermined" means "determine in advance or to influence in a certain way," which doesn't fit the context. Choice (D) is incorrect because "discretionary" means "optional," which is the opposite of mandatory.

Question

13. If life did exist on other planets, scientists theorize that it would not _____ life on Earth. For example, depending on the wavelengths of life given off by the plant, plants could be red, yellow, or green.

    (A) epitomize
    (B) mimic
    (C) illustrate
    (D) typify
    (E) imitate
    (F) reflect

Answer Explanation

The correct answers are (B) and (E). Choices (B) and (E), the synonyms "mimic" and "imitate," mean "to copy, to resemble." Choices (A) and (D) are a synonym pair, meaning "to be a typical example of," which is not exactly the same as imitating, which fits the sense better. Choice (C), "illustrate," means "to clarify, to present an example" and doesn't fit the sense, nor does it have a synonym among the answer choices. Choice (F), "reflect," meaning "to make apparent or show an image of," has neither a synonym in the list nor fits the sense.

Question

14. Scientists believe that unlocking the genome is _____; it will forever change the way we diagnose, treat, and someday even prevent disease.

    (A) modernization
    (B) reforming
    (C) revolutionary
    (D) transformative
    (E) huge
    (F) corrective

Answer Explanation

The correct answers are (C) and (D). The phrase "forever change" in the second part of the sentence is the clue that identifies "revolutionary" and "transformative," choices (C) and (D). Both indicate radical change. Choice (A), "modernization," is also a form of change, but it doesn't fit the context. Choice (B), "reforming," may seem correct because it means "to change for the better," but it doesn't have the connotation of radical change that is implied in the sentence. Choice (E), "huge," is a vague word that doesn't indicate the nature of the change. Choice (F) is incorrect because "corrective" implies that something was wrong and needed to be fixed, and that's not what is implied in the sentence.

Question

15. Many of his critics complain that once they finish reading his books with their convoluted plot lines, they are no wiser and their brains perhaps even more _____.

    (A) befogged

    (B) taxed

    (C) muddled

    (D) weakened

    (E) wary

    (F) heedful

Answer Explanation

The correct answers are (A) and (C). The sense of the sentence is that reading convoluted books doesn't make the reader any more intelligent, but it does make his/her brain tired or confused. Choices (A) and (C), "befogged" and "muddled," fit the sense of confused. Choice (B), "taxed," fits the idea of tired, but there is no synonym for it in the list of answer choices, so eliminate it. Don't be fooled by choice (E), "wary," which on a fast read might look like "weary"; "wary" means "cautious." "Heedful" is a loose synonym of "wary," but neither makes sense. Choice (D), "weakened," might work, but there is no synonym for it in the list.

QUESTIONS 16–17 ARE BASED ON THE FOLLOWING PASSAGE.

Among people who want to make informed choices about what they eat, the issue of whether to buy local or organic food is often debated. The most popular reasons cited for buying organic are to avoid pesticides that harm your health and damage ecosystems, to support a system of agriculture that uses natural fertilizers, and to support more humane animal husbandry
5   practices. The reasons cited for buying local food include supporting the local economy, and also buying food that is fresher, has less packaging, and has fewer "food miles," or the distance food has to travel from source to end user. It turns out to be a complicated question, one that can sometimes lead to additional questions that must be answered in order to make a choice. Sometimes the questions are personal ones, such as: What food tastes better? But
10 larger questions can arise, too, such as: How do the choices we make about our food affect the planet?

Question

16. What is the author's opinion about whether to buy organic or local food?

    (A) We can never really know which is better.

    (B) We should try to answer important questions before trying to make that decision.

    (C) We should figure out which food tastes better.

    (D) We should try to find other ways to support the local economy.

    (E) We should buy the food that has the fewest "food miles."

Answer Explanation

The correct answer is (B). The author suggests at the end of the passage that the answer is not simple, but that we should ask ourselves questions that could help us make the decision. Choice (A) seems like the correct choice, except that the fact of asking ourselves questions is a closer reading of what the author seems to be implying. Choices (C) and (E) are incorrect because according to the author there are more than just these factors we should consider. Choice (D) is incorrect because this statement is neither stated nor implied in the passage.

Question

17. Which of the following statements does the passage most clearly support?

(A) Buying local or organic food is better than buying food from a big chain supermarket.

(B) Buying organic food does not support the local economy.

(C) The distance food has to travel is an important consideration to make when deciding where to buy your food.

(D) Animals raised on organic farms are treated more humanely.

(E) Food from local farms may have been sprayed with pesticides.

Answer Explanation

The correct answer is (C). Distance is clearly stated in the passage as one of the considerations to make when deciding whether to buy organic or local food (assuming they are not one and the same). Choice (A) might seem correct, but it is possible to buy organic and local food at big chain supermarkets; therefore, this statement isn't entirely supported by the passage. Choice (B) makes an assumption that is not necessarily true and is never addressed in the passage. Choice (D) might be correct in some cases, but animals raised on local nonorganic farms might be treated more humanely than those raised on organic farms, and thus the passage does not support this. Choice (E) might also be correct in some cases, but once again, the passage does not support this entirely.

Question

18. What function does "the distance food has to travel from source to end user" (lines 6–7) serve in the passage?

(A) It is support for the argument for buying local food.

(B) It defines the term "food miles."

(C) It is support for the larger question about how food choices affect the planet.

Answer Explanation

The correct answer is (B). The parenthetical clause defines the term "food miles" and this is its only function in the sentence. The discussion of food miles is one piece of evidence used to support buying locally grown food, choice (A), but that's not the function of the definitional clause. Choice (C) is incorrect for the same reason.

QUESTIONS 19–20 ARE BASED ON THE FOLLOWING PASSAGE.

Voter opinion polls are often disparaged because they are seen as inaccurate or misused by network news shows eager to boost ratings. However, those who want to discredit voter opinion polling for elections overlook a few facts. First, the last week or two before an election is notoriously volatile. Voters finally decide whether or not to vote and undecided
5 voters make up their minds about the candidates for whom they will vote. This means that polls taken too far in advance of an election cannot possibly forecast with precision the outcome of that election. Second, exit polls differ from most other types of scientific polling, mainly because dispersed polling places preclude exit pollsters from using normal sampling methods. However, debating whether voter polls are accurate or not misses the point. Voter
10 polls are not intended to forecast winners and losers. They are designed to describe the broad spectrum of public opinion and to elucidate what voters are really thinking and what policies are most important to them. In fact, most of what we know about voter behavior and policy preferences comes from past opinion polls about elections. Understood in this context, we should not dismiss polling outright, but instead consider how to improve polling and to use
15 it to its best advantage.

Question

19. "Elucidate" (line 11) most nearly means

(A) confound.

(B) elevate.

(C) vanquish.

(D) illuminate.

(E) predict.

Answer Explanation

The correct answer is (D). "Elucidate" means about the same as "illuminate," or "to make clear." Choice (A) is incorrect because "confound" means "to mystify," which is the opposite of elucidate. Choice (B) is incorrect because "elevate" means "to raise," which has nothing to do with making clear. Choice (C) is incorrect because "vanquish" means "to conquer," which also has nothing to do with making clear. Choice (E) is incorrect because "predict" means "to forecast," which is not the same as making clear.

Question

20. Which of the following expresses the author's thesis about voter opinion polls?

(A) They can never predict the results of an election.

(B) They can help us get a sense of the general trend in an election.

(C) They can help undecided voters make up their minds.

(D) They are misused by the news media.

(E) They are highly unpredictable.

Answer Explanation

The correct answers is (B). The author clearly states that voter opinion polls help us identify what voters are thinking about issues. Choice (A) may seem correct because the author states that polls can be inaccurate, but the author doesn't explicitly state that polling can never predict the results of an election, and so this cannot be assumed. Choice (C) is incorrect because although the author states that undecided voters make up their minds during the last week or two before an election, the author doesn't imply that polls help these voters make up their minds. Choice (D) is true in that the author states this, but this is not his thesis in the passage. Choice (E) is incorrect because the unpredictability of polls is neither stated nor implied.

Section 5: Quantitative Reasoning

1. A	11. A	16. E
2. D	12. D	17. D
3. B	13. 48	18. C, E, G, H
4. B	14. D	19. A, B, F
5. C	15. C	20. $\frac{1}{4}$
6. A		
7. D		
8. D		
9. A		
10. B		

Question

1.

Quantity A	Quantity B
0.324875	$\frac{10}{31}$

(A) Quantity A is greater.

(B) Quantity B is greater.

(C) The two quantities are equal.

(D) The relationship cannot be determined from the information given.

Answer Explanation

The correct answer is (A). Change $\frac{10}{31}$ into a decimal: 0.32258, which is less than 0.324875.

Question

2.

Quantity A	Quantity B
$|x|$	$|y|$

(A) Quantity A is greater.

(B) Quantity B is greater.

(C) The two quantities are equal.

(D) The relationship cannot be determined from the information given.

Answer Explanation

The correct answer is (D). With no parameters set for x or y, there is no way to determine a relationship between the two.

Question

Mary is twice as old as Stephen. Stephen is 5 years older than Joe. Joe is $\frac{3}{4}$ of Mary's age. All three were born in the twenty-first century.

3.   Quantity A   Quantity B
          Mary's birth year   Joe's birth year

(A) Quantity A is greater.

(B) Quantity B is greater.

(C) The two quantities are equal.

(D) The relationship cannot be determined from the information given.

Answer Explanation

The correct answer is (B). Because Mary is the oldest, she will have a birth year that is less than either Joe or Stephen.

Question

A try is worth 5 points. A conversion is worth 2 points. A penalty goal is worth 3 points.

4.   Quantity A   Quantity B
     3 tries, 2 conversions, 1 penalty   24

(A) Quantity A is greater.

(B) Quantity B is greater.

(C) The two quantities are equal.

(D) The relationship cannot be determined from the information given.

Answer Explanation

The correct answer is (B). Evaluate each quantity:

$3(5) + 2(2) + 3 = 15 + 4 + 3 = 22$

22 is less than 24.

Question

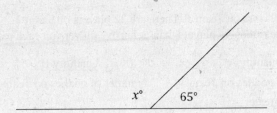

5.   Quantity A   Quantity B

                       x 115

  (A) Quantity A is greater.

  (B) Quantity B is greater.

  (C) The two quantities are equal.

  (D) The relationship cannot be determined from the information given.

Answer Explanation

The correct answer is (C). Supplementary angles equal 180°.

$180° = 65° + x$

$115° = x$

Question

6.   Quantity A   Quantity B

                  $-\dfrac{15}{16}$ $-\dfrac{16}{15}$

  (A) Quantity A is greater.

  (B) Quantity B is greater.

  (C) The two quantities are equal.

  (D) The relationship cannot be determined from the information given.

Answer Explanation

The correct answer is (A). $-\dfrac{15}{16}$ is greater than -1 and $-\dfrac{16}{15}$ is less than -1.

Question

There are 15 players on Team 1. There are 22 players on Team 2. There are more offensive players than defensive players on each team.

7.

Quantity A	Quantity B
Number of goalies on Team 1	Number of goalies on Team 2

(A) Quantity A is greater.

(B) Quantity B is greater.

(C) The two quantities are equal.

(D) The relationship cannot be determined from the information given.

Answer Explanation

The correct answer is (D). There is no way to know the number of goalies on each team.

Question

$$\frac{y}{x} = 3$$

$$x, y \neq 0$$

8.

Quantity A	Quantity B
x	y

(A) Quantity A is greater.

(B) Quantity B is greater.

(C) The two quantities are equal.

(D) The relationship cannot be determined from the information given.

Answer Explanation

The correct answer is (D). Pick some numbers and evaluate:

If $y = 12$, then $x = 4$. If $y = -12$, then $x = -4$

Question

9. Evaluate the function $f(x) = 5x^3 + 4x^2 + 8x + 1$, when $x = 2$.

(A) 73

(B) −11

(C) 183

(D) 117

(E) −73

Answer Explanation

The correct answer is (A). Evaluate the function:

$$f(x) = 5x^3 + 4x^2 + 8x + 1$$
$$f(2) = 5(8) + 4(4) + 8(2) + 1$$
$$f(2) = 40 + 16 + 16 + 1$$
$$f(2) = 73$$

Question

10. Solve the equation $4xy + 8y = 128$ for x, when $y = 4$.

(A) $x = 10$
(B) $x = 6$
(C) $x = 1$
(D) $x = 12$
(E) $x = 32$

Answer Explanation

The correct answer is (B). Solve for x:

$$4xy + 8y = 128$$
$$4x(4) + 8(4) = 128$$
$$16x + 32 = 128$$
$$16x = 96$$
$$x = 6$$

Question

11. If $\dfrac{3}{x-1} = \dfrac{6}{3x+6}$, then $x =$

(A) -8
(B) -1
(C) 0
(D) 1
(E) 8

Answer Explanation

The correct answer is (A). Solve for x:

$$\frac{3}{x-1} = \frac{6}{3x+6}$$
$$3(3x+6) = 6(x-1)$$
$$9x + 18 = 6x - 6$$
$$3x = -24$$
$$x = -8$$

Or, work backwards from the answer choices:

$$\frac{3}{x-1} = \frac{6}{3x+6}$$
$$\frac{3}{-8-1} = \frac{6}{-24+6}$$
$$\frac{3}{-9} = \frac{6}{-18}$$
$$-\frac{1}{3} = -\frac{1}{3}$$

Question

12. A new model hybrid car gets 45 miles per gallon for city driving and 20% more for highway driving. How many miles per gallon does the hybrid get for highway driving?
    (A) 34
    (B) 46
    (C) 51
    (D) 54
    (E) 58

Answer Explanation

The correct answer is (D). Turn the verbose language into concise and concrete terms to help you solve this problem.

$$45(0.20) = 9$$
$$45 + 9 = 54$$

Question

13. Find the area of the trapezoid.

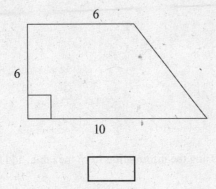

Answer Explanation

The correct answer is 48. Redraw the diagram to show all the information that you need.

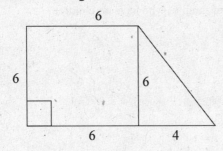

$$6 \times 6 = 36$$
$$\frac{1}{2} 6 \times 4 = 12$$
$$36 + 12 = 48$$

QUESTIONS 14–16 REFER TO THE TABLE BELOW.

Number of Children per Family in a Neighborhood

Number of Children	Number of Families
1	19
2	36
3	21
4+	9
0	15

Question

14. What is the total number of families that have no more than two children?

    (A) 19

    (B) 36

    (C) 55

    (D) 70

    (E) 81

Answer Explanation

The correct answer is (D). Using the information from the table, add the families having 0, 1, and 2 children:

$19 + 36 + 15 = 70$

Question

15. What is the percentage of families who have no children?

    (A) 9%

    (B) 12%

    (C) 15%

    (D) 18%

    (E) 21%

Answer Explanation

The correct answer is (C). Using the information from the table, there are $19 + 36 + 21 + 9 + 15 = 100$ total families and there are 15 families with no children, so $\frac{15}{100} = 0.15$, or 15%.

Question

16. What percentage of the families has 6 children?

    (A) 19

    (B) 9

    (C) 15

    (D) 12

    (E) unknown

Answer Explanation

The correct answer is (E). There is no information given on the number of families with 6 children.

Question

17. The angle x and the angle that measures 115, are what type of angles?

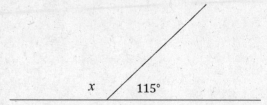

(A) complementary

(B) obtuse

(C) acute

(D) supplementary

(E) paired

Answer Explanation

The correct answer is (D). Two angles that equal 180° are supplementary angles.

Question

18. Find the four even factors of 28.

(A) 0

(B) 1

(C) 2

(D) 3

(E) 4

(F) 7

(G) 14

(H) 28

Answer Explanation

The correct answers are (C), (E), (G), and (H). Find the factors of 28, and choose the even ones to answer the question.

28 ÷		
1	28	yes
2	14	yes
3	9.33	no
4	7	yes
5	5.6	no
6	4.6	no

All the factors are 1, 2, 4, 7, 14, 28, and the even factors are 2, 4, 14, 28.

Question

19. When multiplied in pairs, which of the following numbers will give you a product less than −43?

    (A) −8
    (B) −6
    (C) 0
    (D) 4
    (E) 5
    (F) 9

Answer Explanation

The correct answers are (A), (B), and (F). Estimate and work backwards:

$$-8(\geq 6) \leq -43$$
$$-6(\geq 8) \leq -43$$
$$0(x) = 0$$

$$-8, -6, 9$$

Question

20. If AB and BD are equal lengths and $ABDC$ is a rectangle, what is the ratio of the area of triangle CED to the area of rectangle $ABDC$?

    Give your answer as a fraction.

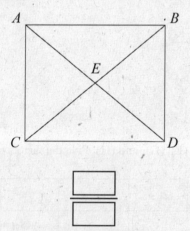

Answer Explanation

The correct answer is $\dfrac{1}{4}$. Since $ABDC$ is a rectangle and sides AB and BD are equal, $ABDC$ is a square. The diagonals of a square form 4 equivalent triangles, so the ratio of triangle CED to the rectangle $ABDC$ is $\dfrac{1}{4}$.

PART III

ANALYTICAL WRITING

The Issue Task

chapter 4

OVERVIEW

- Basic information about the issue task
- Understand the prompt: the issue
- Understand the prompt: the writing instructions
- Understand the scoring rubric
- Review the anatomy of an issue essay
- Create your writing plan
- A final note of caution
- Issue prompt with six model responses, scoring, and analyses
- Summing it up

The Analytical Writing section of the GRE revised General Test measures both your ability to think and your ability to write in response to two kinds of prompts: the Issue Task and the Argument Task. The Issue Task assesses how well you can develop and support your own position on an issue, and the Argument Task evaluates how well you can analyze someone else's argument. This chapter will focus on the Issue Task.

To respond to the Issue Task, you will need to take a position either agreeing or disagreeing with an issue and defend your position with evidence. As part of that defense, you may be required to counter potential arguments of others. The issue prompt presents you with a brief statement of a general issue and sets the conditions under which you can respond to it. That is, you may agree or disagree with the statement, but you must discuss certain aspects of the issue based on the accompanying instructions. The issue will be one that anyone can respond to, such as whether or not it's morally justifiable to spend resources on a pet.

This chapter describes the issue task and the possible instructions that may accompany it as well as reviewing the components of a successful issue essay. The chapter ends with a sample issue task and six models that are analyzed and scored using a rubric based on the GRE rubric for the issue task.

BASIC INFORMATION ABOUT THE ISSUE TASK

The Analytical Writing section is always first in any administration of the GRE revised General Test. For many test-takers, it is probably a relief to have it out of the way early so they no longer have to worry about it. However, reviewing the basics of the issue task, as well as the basic organization and development of a response, will help your confidence and your score.

Type of Question

The issue task presents you with one issue that you may agree or disagree with, but you must do one or the other. You can't be neutral, and you will have no choice of issues from which to choose. The purpose of the issue task is to measure how well you can stake out a position and develop your reasoning to support it. That support has to be developed according to certain conditions contained in a set of instructions that accompany the prompt. The instructions, which are described in more detail later in this chapter, may require you to

- explain how the issue might or might not hold true in some cases.
- examine examples that could be used to challenge your position on an issue.
- discuss why you disagree with a claim and the reasoning that underpins the claim.

Typically, the issue statement is very short compared to the argument prompt. The issue is usually stated in a single sentence, and it's always of a general nature that anyone could respond to. No special knowledge is required. ETS states that the claim made in the issue statement is one that can be discussed "from various perspectives" and applied "to many different situations or conditions."

Time Limit and Software

The issue task, like the argument task, has a time limit of 30 minutes. This is the same for both the computer-based version and the paper-and-pencil version.

The word processing program on the computer version allows the test-taker to insert and delete text, cut and paste text, and undo actions. A spell checker and grammar checker are not included. Similarly, those taking the paper-and-pencil version will not have access to dictionaries or grammar handbooks during the test.

Scoring

The issue task has its own rubric. You'll work through the rubric for the issue task later in this chapter. Like the argument task, issue tasks are scored on a scale from 0 to 6. The average of the two scores is taken to arrive at a combined score from 0 to 6 in half-point increments. This is the score that is reported to graduate and business schools.

UNDERSTAND THE PROMPT: THE ISSUE

The issue prompt has two parts, and you'll probably see a line of space between the two parts. The first part of the issue prompt states one side of an issue. For example, it might suggest that everyone start paying entrance fees to the public museums and institutions that are currently free in Washington, D.C. The issue will be stated briefly and simply, most likely in just one sentence.

UNDERSTAND THE PROMPT: THE WRITING INSTRUCTIONS

The second part of the prompt is the instructions that set the conditions for your response. It begins with the words "Write a response. . . ." The instructions will ask you (1) to take a position, qualifying it, as you want to or need to, by extent or degree and (2) to explain and support your position. The prompt may also ask you to explain your position in relation to one of the following:

- Conditions/circumstances under which the statement of your position might not be true
- Circumstances when the recommendation would not have the intended results
- Likely and major challenges to your position
- Views both for and against your position
- The reason on which the claim is based
- The possible consequences of taking action based on your position

The actual wording of the sets of instructions will be somewhat similar to the following:

- Discuss how much you agree or disagree with the statement and why, as well as considering how the statement might or might not always be true and how these considerations affect your point of view.
- Discuss how much you agree or disagree with the recommendation and why. Using specific examples, explain how the circumstances under which the recommendation could be adopted would or would not be advantageous. In developing and supporting your viewpoint, explain how these specific circumstances affect your point of view.
- Discuss how much you agree or disagree with the claim and include the most compelling reasons and/or examples that someone could use to dispute your point of view.
- While addressing both viewpoints provided, discuss which more closely aligns with your own. Explain your reasoning for holding this position in developing and providing evidence for your response.
- Discuss how much you agree or disagree with the claim and the reasoning used to support that claim.
- Discuss your viewpoint on the proposed policy and the reasons for your point of view. Take into consideration the potential consequences of implementing the policy and the extent to which these consequences influence your viewpoint in developing and supporting your response.

As with the argument prompt, you must take care to focus on the specific requirements in the instructions. You could present a well-reasoned and well-supported position, but if you fail to present views both for and against your position as the prompt asks, you won't earn a high score.

UNDERSTAND THE SCORING RUBRIC

Before we go any further, let's look at the scoring rubric for the issue task against which your response will be evaluated. Like your argument essay, your issue essay will be scored on a 6-point

ALERT!

The major change to the Analytical Writing section of the GRE revised General Test is in the type of response that is being measured. ETS states that the goal is to elicit "more focused responses" from test-takers, so beware of generalizing in your response.

NOTE

As you can see by the writing instructions, you'll need to be specific in presenting your response to the issue. As ETS states, you'll need to "support ideas with relevant reasons and examples" in "a well-focused, coherent discussion."

scale by two readers. These readers are your audience, and your purpose in writing this essay is to earn the best score that you can. Six is the maximum score your response can earn. The scale ranges in 1-point increments from 6 to 0.

6 Points

To earn 6 points, your response should exhibit these characteristics:

- A clear, focused position on the issue, and an overall response to the specific writing task that is thorough, cogent, and sophisticated.

- Fully developed, persuasive support for the position, including, but not limited to, particularly apt or well-chosen examples, facts, and other illustrations, as well as an explanation that clearly and effectively links the support to the specific requirements of the writing task.

- A rhetorically effective method of organization, such as one that organizes support by order of importance and saves the most effective reasons for last. Connections between and among ideas are logical and may also be as subtle as they are effective.

- A formal grace that is a product primarily of well-constructed, varied sentences and exact and rhetorically effective word choices.

- Adherence to almost all the conventions of Standard Written English, including grammar, usage, and mechanics. If there are any errors, they are minor.

5 Points

To earn 5 points, your response will likely have these characteristics, though it may exceed one or more of them yet fall short on another:

- A clear, focused position on the issue, and a thoughtful, complete response to the specific writing task.

- Persuasive support for the position, including, but not limited to, examples, facts, and other illustrations, as well as an explanation that clearly links the support to the specific requirements of the writing task.

- An effective method of organization with logical connections between and among all ideas.

- Well-constructed, varied sentences and appropriate word choices that help create clarity as well as interest.

- Adherence to almost all the conventions of Standard Written English, including grammar, usage, and mechanics. If there are any errors, they should be minor.

4 Points

To earn 4 points, a response will have these characteristics:

- A clear position on the issue, and a generally complete response to the specific writing task.

- Support for the position, as well as an explanation that links the support to the specific requirements of the writing task.

- A logical method of organization.

- Sentences and word choices that generally create clarity.

- General adherence to the conventions of Standard Written English. Some errors may occur.

3 Points

Your response will earn only 3 points if it has *one or more* of the following characteristics:

- A generally clear position and a response to the specific writing task that may be limited in scope or marred by occasional vagueness, extraneous detail, repetition, or other flaws.
- Limited or inadequate support for the position or a limited or inadequate explanation that links the support to the specific requirements of the writing task.
- Lapses in organization or confusing organization, and/or lack or misuse of transitional words and phrases.
- Sentences and word choices that occasionally interfere with clarity.
- One or more errors in the conventions of Standard Written English that are so significant that they obstruct meaning.

2 Points

Your response will earn only 2 points if it has *one or more* of the following characteristics:

- A wandering, unclear, or limited response characterized by an unclear or not fully articulated position and a response to the specific writing task that is limited or inadequate in scope or marred by vagueness, extraneous detail, repetition, or other flaws.
- Inadequate support and explanation.
- Confusing organization, and/or general lack or misuse of transitional words and phrases.
- Sentences and word choices that interfere with clarity.
- Repeated errors in the conventions of Standard Written English that are so significant that they obstruct meaning.

1 Point

Your response will earn only 1 point if it has *one or more* of the following characteristics:

- An unclear position and almost no response to, or minimal understanding of, the specific task.
- A total lack of support or only illogical or flawed support for the main point or points; a total lack of explanation or only illogical or flawed explanation of the main points of your argument in relation to the specific details of the task.
- No pattern of organization or confusing organization.
- Sentences and word choices that interfere with clarity.
- So many errors in the conventions of Standard Written English that they obstruct meaning throughout the response.

0 Points

This score is possible under the following circumstances:

- The response does not answer the task in any way.
- The response is written in a foreign language.
- The response simply copies the argument.
- The response is not legible.
- The response is nonverbal.

TIP

Much of the advice in this section can be applied to writing an argument response as well.

From these criteria, you can draw or reaffirm the following four conclusions about your task:

1. You must meet the requirements stated in the prompt completely.

2. You need a clear statement of your position; substantial, thoughtful support; and explanations that link your support to the specific task requirements.

3. You can make minor errors in grammar, usage, and mechanics without seriously jeopardizing your score, but remember that errors in these areas can affect the clarity of your writing, so be sloppy at your own peril.

4. The length of your response is in no way a deciding factor in your score. But don't assume that brevity is a virtue. According to the rubric, you'll have to produce a response of sufficient length to support your position in adequate, if not dense, detail. Although there is no magic number for success, aim to make at least three points in favor of your position—and aim to elaborate them fully.

TIP

If you're taking the paper-and-pencil version and there is enough space on the sheets of paper, write on every other line. That will leave you space to insert additions and neatly make deletions. If your handwriting isn't legible, try printing, but practice ahead of time so that you can print quickly and legibly.

REVIEW THE ANATOMY OF AN ISSUE ESSAY

In addition to keeping track of time—and using it wisely—there are some priorities that you can set and skills you can review and practice to help you write a successful response. Obviously, it takes time to develop superior—6-point—writing skills; however, staying focused on a few simple guidelines can lead to a bump up of a point or more in your score. Think about putting these recommendations to work for you.

State a Thesis, and State It Early

Don't make your reader guess what side of the issue you're on. There is nothing to be gained by being timid or staying on the middle of the fence. A thesis statement that makes your view on the issue absolutely unmistakable should appear somewhere in the first paragraph. Don't worry about being too obvious or even leading off with your thesis. You can, in fact, score a 6 if you state your point of view in the very first sentence. Of course, you must be sure that the thesis is clear and that it adequately reflects the content that follows.

Use a Standard Pattern of Organization

ETS makes it clear that test-takers don't need to employ a standard pattern of organization to succeed. But think critically about that advice. That doesn't mean that standard patterns of organization won't succeed for either the issue or the argument response. A standard pattern of organization helps to lead your reader smoothly from point to point. In addition, such patterns help create fluency.

Order Paragraphs Effectively

Now you've got your overall structure, but how do you hang your ideas on that structure so that your paragraphs flow in logical order? Possibly the best organizational model for the issue response (and the argument response, too) is order of importance. You could order the paragraphs in the body of your response either from the most important reason to the least important reason, or from the least important reason to the most important reason. The latter is the more effective technique. It often results in a strong or memorable ending.

In crafting your paragraphs, don't begin the first two body paragraphs with something like "The first reason in support of my thesis is…" and "The second reason in support of my thesis is…" Similarly, don't end with "In conclusion" or "As I have said." Use transitional words and phrases. They can provide a smooth link from one paragraph to another—and from one sentence to another—by identifying and emphasizing the relationships between ideas. In its analysis of the scoring of sample papers, as well as in its rubrics, ETS stresses the value of transitional words and phrases. In addition to helping you create coherence, transitions can help you vary the beginnings of your sentences.

TRANSITIONS

Review the following lists of transitional words and phrases and use them as you practice writing responses to the tasks in the practice tests. Then they will come more easily as you write the actual response.

Transitions to Introduce or Link Opinions and Reasons

because	evidently	indeed
besides	for this reason	on the other hand
by comparison	furthermore	since
consequently	however	therefore

Transitions that Introduce or Link Examples

for example	in this case	one type
for instance	in this situation	to illustrate this point

Transitions that Create Emphasis or Add Information

after all	furthermore	more important
again	in addition	moreover
besides	indeed	similarly
certainly	in fact	what's more

Transitions that Introduce Opposing Views

although this may be true	naturally	on the other hand
even though	nevertheless	undeniably
evidently	notwithstanding	unquestionably
it may be said	of course	without a doubt

Use a Standard Pattern of Paragraphing

Try a traditional structure for developing the paragraphs within the body of your response.

Topic Sentence: The topic sentence states the main idea of the paragraph. In an issue response, the topic sentence of each body paragraph can state a reason that supports your point of view, or a likely "challenge," or reason, against your point of view. For example, if you're arguing that it is, in fact, a reasonable policy to insist that visitors to the nation's museums in Washington, D.C., pay an entrance fee, a topic sentence might suggest that by having to pay, people will place a greater value on their visit.

Support and Development: Once you've written the topic sentence for your paragraph, you have several choices for how to develop the meat of the paragraph. You can choose restriction (a qualification or other way of narrowing and focusing the topic sentence), explanation, and/or evidence. Your job in this part of the paragraph is to make your topic sentence convincing by developing it with supporting points. In discussing paid-entry to national museums in Washington, you might talk about how families visiting for a long weekend from faraway might not come if they had to pay for two adults and several children at three museums. You could emphasize the loss of first-hand access to our nation's history for those children and how seeing, for example, the original Constitution can foster patriotism. Try to make this part of your paragraph full and dense with detail.

Final Summary or Clincher Statement: This last sentence is optional in body paragraphs, but it can give a final rhetorical punch to the paragraph. You could ask a rhetorical question or restate the idea of the paragraph in a fresh way. What you want is a way to give final emphasis to the idea developed in the paragraph. If you can't think of an original and effective clincher, don't add anything to the paragraph. Go on to the next paragraph, using a transition.

If, however, this is your final paragraph in your response, think hard for a memorable final statement. You want to end your response in way that gives closure to your thoughts and emphasizes your points. You could rephrase the thesis, summarize the main points, or direct the reader to a larger issue. The concluding paragraph should tie up all loose ends so that the reader doesn't finish with a sigh of "so what?"

Successful paragraphs can certainly deviate from this order. The important thing to keep in mind, however, is that paragraphs are themselves discrete units of discourse that require organization. It's not enough to organize the paragraphs of your essay logically. The sentences of each paragraph must be organized logically, too.

Develop Each Paragraph Fully

A huge factor in the success or relative failure of your essay will be the kinds and amount of support you provide. Never, ever write a one-sentence paragraph. If you have two-sentence paragraphs, the chances are good that they need more substance. Of course, you can't just add words for the sake of their own sake, nor should you repeat yourself. What you need is more examples, illustrations, or other evidence, as well as the explanation that relates them back to the topic sentence or to the thesis and connect them to the next ideas. If your paragraphs lack details, ask yourself if you can add any of the following:

Facts: Facts are always the best choice for support. Statistics are one kind of fact that lend credibility to an argument. You aren't expected to pull sophisticated facts and statistics out of the air on the GRE nor should you ever make up any! But you may know some general facts such as the typical miles per gallon of an SUV versus a subcompact or a domestic car brand versus a Japanese brand if you're writing a response to a policy issue on raising emissions standards. Incorporate as many facts as you can. This is one method of appealing to your reader's reason.

Authoritative Opinions or Human Interest: You may not be able to call a quote to mind, yet you may recall a famous person's idea or point of view about your topic. For example, for a response on whether government should fund the arts, you might paraphrase the chair of the National Endowment for the Arts on the value of arts to the economy or a local restaurant owner on how much the theater down the street drives business to her establishment. This kind of support is best used sparingly, especially if the quotation or opinion appeals more to emotion than to reason. In some cases, however, appeals to emotion are as effective as appeals to reason.

Observations: Your own first-hand observations about life can be useful evidence of a point of view. In fact, since you cannot use source material on the GRE, this type of evidence is extremely helpful as it is available to you in abundance. Observations may appeal to either reason or emotion.

An Anecdote: Occasionally, a brief story not only enlivens your writing, it also adds evidence. Use an anecdote to illustrate some general truth such as how schools rely on parent volunteers. This is another technique that should be used sparingly—most likely just once in a response. Like observations, anecdotes may appeal to either reason or emotion; occasionally, they appeal to both.

Examples: Multiple examples or illustrations of an idea, such as how scandals have led to government reform, will add substance and support to a position that agrees with this claim. Use examples generously to support your points; they are usually very effective appeals to reason.

Take Care with Tone and Person

ETS makes no mention of tone in its scoring rubrics. Nevertheless, you should strive to sound reasonable. You may be forceful and impassioned at the same time, but don't cross the line into harangue or diatribe. The most successful arguments rely on valid reasoning and sophisticated support, both of which can be undercut by a shrill, overly strident, or whining voice.

Similarly, ETS makes no mention of person. Using the third person is your safest bet for both types of tasks, but there may be times when you might want to, or should, incorporate the first person (*I, me, my, myself, mine*) in your essay. It's certainly better to say *I* or *me* than to try to maintain the third person by referring to yourself as "this writer" or in any other self-conscious way. That said, refer to yourself only as necessary and don't, for example, use obvious lead-ins such as "In my humble opinion."

TIP

If you think you might use the first person, brush up on when you use *I* (subject) versus *me* (object) and when using *myself* is appropriate (either as reflexive or intensive pronoun).

As Time Permits, Add Extras

Should you take time for style or craft? Yes, by all means, once you've got the substance of your ideas completely down on paper. (Of course, it's much easier for computer-based users to follow this advice than paper test-takers.) Be sure, however, to view all of the following as add-ons. You can have, for example, the most interesting and well-written introduction in the world and not do well on the task if you don't have time to develop the key points that support your opinion, or you don't have time to answer the task fully because you never deal with the key challenges to your position.

Interest-Grabbing Opening

If you have time, create an interesting lead by posing a question or offering a surprising or startling fact. Or craft a formal introduction that establishes some background or context for your position. As a review of the sample essays from ETS show, you can succeed without crafting a formal opening.

Apt Word Choice

As time permits, you should also review and revise your word choice:

- Avoid simple, overused words such as *very, really, good, bad, interesting, fun, great, awesome, incredible,* and *unbelievable.*
- Replace state of being verbs, such as *was* and *are* with active verbs.
- Edit out clichés. (For example, don't begin an essay on dogs with "A dog is man's best friend.")
- Whenever you know a more precise, forceful, or connotatively rich word that will accurately convey your meaning, use it, BUT don't go for the big word, just because it's big.

Varied Sentence Structure

If you want a 6, you have to show some style by varying your sentences. There are many ways to do this:

- Intersperse an occasional short sentence in a paragraph of long sentences.
- Vary your sentences by type by occasionally inserting a question where appropriate. (A word of caution: avoid exclamatory sentences and exclamation points. These are almost never appropriate.)
- Vary your sentences by structure, using compound, complex, and simple sentences.
- Create sentence variation by beginning sentences in different ways, that is, make sure all sentences in a paragraph don't begin with "The" followed by the subject. Begin sentences with conjunctions, prepositions, and transitions.

A Final Word of Advice

Think of the organization for your response as the box that holds your product. Although that box is absolutely necessary, chances are you won't sell that product—no matter how good it is—in a plain cardboard box. Instead, you'll need an attractive outer layer, a packaging that says "Buy me! Buy me!" That's why you must also strive for qualities such as original and sophisticated word choice, sentence variation, and rhetorical devices in your essay. ETS readers will not give a 5 or 6 to a plain cardboard box.

CREATE YOUR WRITING PLAN

You'll have just 30 minutes to read and respond to the issue prompt. But don't read the prompt and start writing. You need a plan to attack the task and that plan has three parts: prewriting, drafting, and proofreading. Of the 30 minutes, set aside 2 to 3 minutes at the end to review and proofread your response. The bulk of the 30 minutes—say 23 or so minutes—should be spent in the actual writing of your response. The first 4 to 5 minutes should be spent in planning and prewriting.

Prewriting

The prewriting part of your writing plan has three steps that will help you focus on the task, gather your ideas, and plan the development of your response. They are tailored to the issue task and are slightly different from the prewriting steps for responding to the argument task.

Because your time is so short, you may be tempted to overlook prewriting. This is inadvisable for several reasons. First, with prewriting, you're actually testing your position to see if it will work; that is, in the few minutes you spend prewriting, you will be finding out whether you have good ideas or not. Second, organization is dependent on ideas. If you have a few ideas jotted down when you start to write, it will be much easier to order your ideas effectively. It's a trick that experienced writers use because it's much easier to start writing with a short list of ideas in front of you than no ideas at all.

Restate the Prompt: Although the issue prompt is easier to read and understand than the argument prompt, don't overlook this first step. Be sure the issue is clear to you.

Think About Reasons on Both Sides of the Issue: Understanding and being able to develop both sides of the issue are necessary in crafting a successful response. There are two main reasons for this. First, you don't need—nor are you expected—to express your truest feelings. Instead, you need to choose the side of the issue for which you can present the most convincing, well-developed argument of your own. Second, to be successful with most variations of the prompt, you need to anticipate and refute the opposing point of view.

Jot a "Quick Write": Begin by briefly identifying your position on the issue and then listing reasons that support your position. Strive for the most persuasive reasons.

If the specific instructions ask for challenges, both sides of the issue, advantages or disadvantages, or other considerations related to the opposite viewpoint, list reasons that could be given to oppose your position.

The flow of ideas won't come in any particular order so reread your list and number the reasons in the order that you want to use them. You may also find that some ideas don't fit with the majority of your ideas, or that you have too many ideas, or some are weak. Don't be afraid to cross off ones that don't fit or are the least convincing.

TIP

Those taking the computer-based test will be given scrap paper for making notes, so if you're taking the computer version, consider jotting down the key requirements of the instructions. If you're taking the paper-based test, you may want to underline the key requirements.

Drafting

You'll actually be drafting and revising simultaneously because of the time limitation. To get the most of your actual writing time, keep these priorities in mind:

Answer the Task: Be sure that you answer the task. This may seem obvious, but in the hurry to write down your ideas, don't let your ideas take you on a line of thinking that doesn't respond to the issue and the task. Even though you have a "quick write" to work from, new ideas will come as you write. Be sure to go back to the last few lines of the prompt to be sure you aren't just agreeing or disagreeing with the issue, but also addressing both points of view, citing and refuting possible challenges, or doing whatever else the task specifically requires you to do.

Organize Your Response: The following pattern is a standard, or traditional, way to organize your overall response. It leads your reader smoothly through your response by eliminating confusion and guesswork. In addition, it helps to create fluency—or the illusion of it. If you're a writer who has trouble with organization, this pattern gives you a structure to develop your ideas around:

- Opening paragraph: thesis or clear statement of your position

- Body paragraph 1: Reason 1 for your position, fully explained and supported

- Body paragraph 2: Reason 2 for your position, fully explained and supported

- Body paragraph 3: A statement of the most effective counterargument, an acknowledgment of its reasonableness, and your fully explained and supported response; or any other specific and developed point needed to address the writing task instructions

- Closing paragraph: Reason 3 (another key challenge or another main point) that directly responds to the specific writing instructions; support as needed; plus a detail, statement, question, or other device that delivers closure

Suppose you use this pattern of organization. How do you decide what reason to use first, second, and third? Often, the best way to organize points for an argument is by order of importance. You could choose your most significant reason to be first or last. If you use your most powerful, that is, strongest, support as the third and final point, your readers will take away from your response your most impressive piece of argument.

Provide Ample, Thoughtful, Well-Developed Support: Developing sufficient support is the key element for success on the issue task. The most foolproof method of organization you can use in an issue essay is to begin with a clear statement of your opinion in your opening and to develop each well-chosen point of support paragraph by paragraph.

Link Ideas Clearly: Your organization doesn't have to be traditional, or based in any way on typical instruction in college writing classes, but it does have to be logical and help to create overall coherence. Based on reviewing sample analyses, ETS values transitional words and phrases, so link paragraphs and ideas appropriately as you write. Also, don't overlook the value of a topic sentence in providing an organizational boost to your essay.

Consider Style

If you're aiming for a top score, vary your sentences and word choices. Rubric criteria specify varied, well-constructed sentences; for this test, they are an important index of your sophistication as a writer. ETS readers are also looking for appropriateness, precision, and rhetorical effectiveness in word choice.

Proofreading

When you go back over your essay in the 2 or 3 minutes you may have remaining, keep the following priorities in mind, which are based on the scoring rubric:

Check Your Thesis: Make sure you've stated it and that it's clear. Make sure it also adequately reflects the content of your essay.

Look for Omitted Words: When you're writing in a hurry, it's easy to leave out words. One omitted word can, however, destroy the sense of an entire sentence, and sentence sense is an important rubric criterion.

Check for Sentence Faults: At this stage, you want to make certain that you eliminate any ineffective fragments, any run-on sentences, and any fused sentences or comma splices. Because grammar counts? No, because poor grammar can obscure your meaning and bring down your score.

Don't Spend Your Time on Spelling or Commas: Keep in mind that the rubric doesn't mention spelling. It evidently has "minor error" status for the readers. Likewise, a missing comma here or there shouldn't affect your score.

A FINAL NOTE OF CAUTION

ETS wants its computer-based users to know that their responses will be subjected to analysis by software that searches for similarities to published information. It warns that it will "cancel" a score if it contains any unacknowledged use of sources. In addition, ETS will cancel a response if an essay or any part of it has been prepared by another person. Finally, a score will be canceled if it includes language that is "substantially" similar to the language in one or more other test responses.

ISSUE PROMPT WITH SIX MODEL RESPONSES, SCORING, AND ANALYSES

Use this prompt as a practice opportunity, and compare your response with the samples, scoring, and analyses that follow.

Time yourself and follow these 6 steps. In the real test, you will have 30 minutes.

1. Read the prompt.
2. Follow the prewriting steps.
3. Stop! Compare your "quick write" plan with the sample that follows the prompt to see different ideas (perhaps more sophisticated, perhaps less) that you might have thought of.
4. Draft your response.
5. Read each model that follows the sample "quick write." Determine the positive and negative qualities of each sample response before you read its scoring analysis.
6. Score your response against the rubric on pages 128–129. Be honest in your analysis.

Issue Task

> In a world filled with significant challenges, owning pets, and especially owning costly, resource-consuming dogs, is an irresponsible use of time and money.
>
> Write a response in which you discuss how much you agree or disagree with the claim and include the most compelling reasons and/or examples that someone could use to dispute your point of view.

Sample "Quick Write"

TIP

Note how specific the "quick write" is. The writer is off to a good start for developing a response that is grounded in specific details to support any generalizations that he or she may make.

The 6-point response to this prompt began with just 3 minutes of prewriting and planning. It looked like this:

My opinion

① Dog owning <u>not</u> irresponsible

reasons

~~loveable~~

~~people's best friends~~

③ doing good for your town government or charitable org.

by getting dog off street or out of shelter—you pay for medical, food, etc.

② homeless dogs starving

②a dogs have feelings

Challenges

④b don't take care of dogs, take care of people

~~waste of $ on such things as home-made dog treats~~

④c dogs use too many resources (time? money?)

④a dogs too pampered

Making Your Plan Work

In many ways, the success of the 6-point essay based on this prewriting is due to some of the thought processes demonstrated in this plan. First, notice how the plan addresses the prompt. It has two clear parts: reasons for the position and challenges to the position. Second, notice that the writer decides not to develop all the ideas generated in the prewriting. The writer makes a judgment to develop ideas that he or she perhaps feels can be treated with deeper analysis, or are less predictable answers to the prompt.

Return to this planning guide after you read the sample 6-point model below. Notice how the prewriting does not, in fact, show the eventual order of organization. Note also that there are more details than the "quick write" includes. Once the writer began to write, ideas began to flow, affirming the idea that writing is a generative process. This should be a comforting fact to remember as you prepare to take the Analytical Writing section. You don't need to list all your ideas in a "quick write"; believe that more ideas will come as you write. However, it's also important to check your "quick write" and the task instructions to make sure that your flow of ideas isn't taking you off the track of responding accurately and adequately to the task.

Furthermore, you don't want to spend the kind of time on the prewriting process that extensive planning would require. The main goal of prewriting during a timed writing test is to be sure that you've got good points to make before you begin your writing. If you don't, quickly scratch out your first plan and make another.

Model 1: 6 points out of 6

It is not irresponsible to own a dog. In fact, the truth is quite the opposite. Owning a dog is an act of generosity and compassion—as long as the dog was once homeless or most likely would have been homeless.

There is a huge overpopulation of homeless dogs in the United States. It is estimated that some 5 million dogs and cats are euthanized each year because no one has adopted them. The reality is that the number of homeless dogs is far greater than that, because many homeless animals are not identified or counted, or they spend time in, or languish in, shelters. Dogs, like other animals, are sentient beings. Dogs without homes and proper care suffer. Some starve for food; others are starved for the love and compassion on which they thrive. As many vets and animal behaviorists have explained, dogs do have emotional lives, even if those lives are different from our own.

Of course, some will counter that if we are going to relieve the suffering of the homeless, why not relieve the suffering of homeless people? That, too, is a worthy cause. I would say that those equipped with the time, money, or inclination to deal with the suffering of homeless people should devote their resources to such a cause, and those equipped to deal with the suffering of homeless dogs, even if just by adopting a single dog, should devote their resources to that cause.

Adopting a dog is not just compassionate to the dog or gratifying to its owner, it is a generous act on behalf of society. A person who adopts a dog may be taking responsibility for an animal that might otherwise roam the streets, do damage, or spread disease. After all, shelters can only accommodate so many dogs. If people do not move existing dogs out of shelters, then more animals must wait on the streets or in the wild. A person who adopts a dog from a shelter is also taking responsibility off the public for that dog's food, medical care, spaying or neutering, or, in too many cases, euthanasia and disposal. While some people might counter that saving dogs only adds to the dog population, and perhaps the very popularity of dogs as pets, every dog that is adopted is one less dog on the public or charitable dole.

In general, of course, people may argue that there are more important ways to use private or public resources than by spending them on dogs. They are correct. There are more important uses of our time and money, such as feeding the hungry. But does one worthy cause, such as feeding the hungry, invalidate all other worthy causes, such as teaching the illiterate? Cannot some people devote themselves to some worthy causes that touch or move them personally, while others devote their resources to different worthy causes? I believe we can have compassion for the least among us, including our four-footed friends, as well as for those people who do, indeed, lay a more significant moral claim upon us.

Scoring Analysis

This essay scores 6 out of 6 because it

- **answers the task.** With care and considerable sophistication, this essay not only gives cogent reasons for disagreement, but it also responds thoughtfully to the most likely and compelling challenges.

- **is well supported.** Support for dog ownership is abundant and well explained. The writer acknowledges the validity of counterarguments, yet weakens them with provocative questions and logical reasoning or with ample and persuasive support.

- **is well organized.** The writer uses the opening paragraph to state and qualify the position and uses subsequent, discrete, and well-constructed paragraphs to counter challenges and reinforce the position. All ideas lead logically and smoothly to a satisfying conclusion.

- **is fluid, precise, and graceful.** The capable prose includes short sentences that are interspersed with longer ones for dramatic effect. Sophisticated word choices include *languish, sentient,* and *invalidate.* The tone and style help the reader form an opinion of the writer as objective and thoughtful.

- **observes the conventions of Standard Written English.**

Other observations: While the opening could create interest, or more points could be made in support of the position, the essay nevertheless meets all the criteria for a score of 6. ETS readers do not expect perfection in 30 minutes; nor do they expect you to cover the entire waterfront of your topic. What they do expect, however, are reasonably sophisticated, well-supported, well-organized, and fluent responses within the time constraints.

Write Your Observations About Model 1

_____

_____

_____

_____

_____

_____

_____

_____

_____

_____

_____

_____

_____

_____

_____

_____

_____

_____

_____

_____

_____

_____

_____

_____

_____

_____

_____

_____

_____

_____

_____

_____

_____

_____

_____

_____

Model 2: 5 points out of 6

Dogs are loveable creatures that almost no one wishes to malign. It is also true that dog owners can be responsible, morally upright human beings. Yet, it is the inescapable truth that dogs consume resources, and that we can make better use of our time, our money, and our love than by lavishing them on dogs. Coming from a family in which a pet was always like a family member, this is a statement I make with deep personal regret. Therefore, I would not go so far as to brand all dog ownership as irresponsible.

If you own a dog, you may be spending quite a lot of your time on that animal. You may exercise it two or more times a day, as well attend to its other needs to go out. You may spend time brushing it, grooming it, or taking it to be groomed, and taking it to the vet. You may have to make arrangements for it when you will be gone for a long stretch, such as more than eight hours. If you are a good dog owner, then you are also spending time training your dog and giving it the attention and love that it craves. Now think about how those hours might be spent in other ways, such as tutoring people learning English, helping an elderly person to get groceries or meet other needs, or advocating for cleaner water or air. Which is the worthiest of these causes? Of the causes mentioned, to me, the dog finishes last.

If you own a dog, you must also spend quite a bit of money on it. Sums will vary with the dog and the owner, but some dog owners report spending well over $1,000 per year on their pet. One must think about where that money could have gone, such as to homeless people, the local food pantry, or medical research aimed at finding cures for cancer. Is it really better to spend your $1,000 on Fluffy or Mitten or Max than it is to help cure cancer? I think not.

Furthermore, dogs do use up resources. The pet industry is huge in America, cranking out as it does all kinds of unnecessary items for dogs ranging from luxury dog beds to Halloween hats and costumes. Page through almost any catalog and you will find items such as luxury dog beds and designer sweaters. Furthermore, dogs soil our roads and parks. If a dog owner is responsible and cleans up, each of the nation's millions of dogs is then responsible for the use of thousands of plastic bags. A dog consumes other resources as well, such as food and water. Therefore, no matter how loveable they may be, dogs do not merit the many resources that we lavish on them.

Scoring Analysis

This essay scores 5 out of 6 because it

- **answers the task.** Both good and some excellent reasons are given for agreeing with the position. The essay also capably addresses counterarguments, such as all the hours spent on animals that might be spent more responsibly or productively.

- **is well supported.** For example, the final paragraph that bulwarks the writer's position offers capable, persuasive support. Other paragraphs also contain ample, detailed, and well-developed support.

- **is generally well organized.** A few organizational missteps mar the essay by failing to make the position as clear as possible from the outset and by articulating counterclaims or challenges (such as dogs being loveable) less clearly and centrally than they could have been. (Attention to topic sentences might have cured this problem.) For the most part, however, the flow of ideas is logical.

- **is fluid.** Words and sentences are clear; some words, such as *malign, inescapable,* and *advocating* are quite sophisticated. The sentences are, in general, more serviceable than elegant. (Compare them with the sentences in the 6-point essay.)
- **observes the conventions of Standard Written English.** There are a few minor errors that do not interfere with meaning.

Other observations: In an issue essay, be sure your position is clearly stated from the outset. If a personal statement such as the one about family might somehow obfuscate that position, leave it out. Note how the writer never really develops the qualification at the end of that final line of the first paragraph. In addition, there is no transition between that statement and the following paragraph. These failings contribute to the essay's scoring a 5 instead of a 6.

Write Your Observations About Model 2

Model 3: 4 points out of 6

Individuals and families who own dogs know what a financial drain it is to have such a pet. For a big dog, food costs alone can run $50 per month. In addition, there are vet bills for everything from routine vaccinations to heartworm medication to occassional illness or injury. There are leashes, bowls, collars, licences, whistles, and dog beds to buy. In addition, some people buy dog toys, dog sweaters and booties, and even high-end dog biscuits. Most people have to board their dogs at least from time to time, while others board them often, hire dog walkers, or send their dogs to day care. That means spending anywhere from approximately $1,000 per year to upwards of $10,000 per year, on their dog. Some of these owners pass by the homeless people on the street, or go through poor neighborhoods with children who are not eating right, with their purebred, just-groomed dog decked out in it's lovely new handnit sweater. This fabulous waste of money is common in our country, where dog ownership seems to be on the rise. Going hand in hand with that waste of money is the time they waste on caring for, walking, and toting around dogs when we might be involved in feeding the hungry, working for a cleaner enviroment or taking steps to end global warming, or addressing other really important challenges.

Pets, of course, are not useless, and they do bring joy into peoples' lives. Pets must be used as guide dogs for some people. They may also be important in mental or psychological healing. For example, when used to provide therapy to children or others who have experienced grave loss or other tramma. Also, a visit from a well-trained dog at a nursing home, children's ward, or other place where such companions are both welcome and useful has many beneficial affects. Indeed, a dog can be a light in the life of any lonely or sick person.

Those who feel their lives are not complete without a pet certainly have a right to one. But do they need a designer dog? Do they need doggie daycare? And do they need two dogs, or three, or five? Furthermore, could such people not also look outward at the world, and spend some of their energy on tasks that need doing, instead of so much energy on loving and pampering their dogs? In my humble opinion, it is far better to help the people of this world then to spend our presious time and resources on cute, but unnecessary, animal friends.

Scoring Analysis

This essay scores 4 out of 6 because it

- **answers the task.** This essay clearly takes a position and supports the position. It is less effective on responding to the possible challenges to that position.

- **supports the position well but is limited in terms of explaining and countering challenges.** Examples are appropriate and various, but responses to likely challenges are not so clearly explained or developed as they should be. In fact, the writer does a better job of agreeing with the challenges than refuting them in any way.

- **lacks strong organization.** The argument starts immediately before the position is clear; paragraph 1 needs reorganization. Paragraph 2 could also be more clearly and fluidly linked to both the paragraph that precedes it and the one that follows it.

- **is generally clear.** Most points are clear, but paragraph 2 should also be more sharply focused to reflect and specifically refute challenges to the writer's position. The tone at times verges on the harangue.

- **observes the conventions of Standard Written English.** There are several minor flaws, but they do not interfere with meaning. They do, however, help contribute to the score of 4.

Other observations: This response contains a wealth of insights, but the critical thinking outshines the writing. Because the reader almost has to remind herself or himself of the side of the question that he or she supports, the entire essay looses its persuasiveness. This problem is exemplified by the ending, where meaningful questions are raised and qualifying circumstances considered, but the level of clarity and focus is not such that the reader can be perfectly certain of where the writer is going with them. The "over-the-top" rhetoric also gets in the way of the seriousness of some of the writer's points. Notice, too, how much weaker the vocabulary (as evidenced by choices such as "really important") and sentences are in this essay than they are in the 5- and 6-point essays.

Write Your Observations About Model 3

Model 4: 3 points out of 6

Face it, America! Owning a dog is egotistical. An indulgence of the most selfish people for the most selfish reasons. Dogs are everywhere where a lot of people don't want them. There's always people who are ignoring leash laws or cleanup laws and letting their dogs run up to and frighten people and children who do not like dogs and never wanted them around in the first place. Letting their dogs make a mess in parks and on the streets, too, and just leaving that behind. Or letting their dogs use other peoples' lawns and killing bushes or green areas through repeated use. These people somehow think their dogs deserve rights, that their dog has the right to be on someone else's property as long as it is attached to their leash. There, however, being no bill of rights for dogs.

Plus, look at the money people spend on their dogs, and not just on the necessary things like a license and rabies shots but on crazy things like designer collars and bows and ribbons and special haircuts. People are making themselves, not there dogs, feel good with these things.

Some people will say that pets help you out when you are lonely and give you friend when you need one. I say why not a person for a friend instead of a dog.

Some people will also say that people should have dogs to help out blind people or to serve as guide dogs. I have no problem with that. But those dogs aren't pets. They are specially trained animals for a special service, not indulged, spoiled animals owned by selfish people.

Scoring Analysis

This essay scores 3 out of 6 because it

- **answers task in a limited way.** This essay makes its position very clear, but barely touches on the challenges to the writer's position. Only one challenge is actually dealt with—that dogs can dispel loneliness or be friends—and that challenge is treated quite simplistically and ineffectively.

- **offers inadequate support.** Support is present, especially in the first paragraph, but it could have been more effectively used in service of the writer's position had it not been presented as a laundry list of the irresponsible deeds of some dog owners. There is inadequate support to rebut the challenges to the writer's position.

- **lacks organization.** The response would benefit from a true introductory paragraph and placing much of the current paragraph 1 in a second, well-developed paragraph as support for a clearly stated topic sentence.

- **is fluid, but not precise.** Ideas flow in a variety of sentence structures, including sentence fragments, and the latter are effective in places, but the overall impression is a writer writing at break-neck speed to finish in 30 minutes.

- **observes the conventions of Standard Written English.** There are several consistent flaws, some of which interfere with meaning.

Other observations: Try to avoid the personal and name-calling approach taken here. It's fine to express passion for your point of view; you may even create a distinctive voice. But remember that an argument is most effective when it creates the appearance of objectivity. Edit out any name-calling, gratuitous judgments, or vitriol.

Write Your Observations About Model 4

Model 5: 2 points out of 6

If you want unconditional love, you need a dog. A dog will love you when no one else cares. A dog will always be there for you. A dog will help you get through the times when you are sad or lonely.

The best thing about owning a dog is coming home from a hard day and theres your dog so happy to see you and wag its tail and jump all over you like you are the greatest person in the world.

You should also own a dog because there are so many unwanted dogs in the world and some of them are going to die or be put to death in shelters and other places because no one wants them.

You should also own a dog because no animal should have to have it's life cut short when there are so many people out there who would gain so much from having a dog, even though it is expensive and takes time from you.

If someone tells you its not right to own a dog because dogs don't do anything for the world, you can tell them how much your dog does for you.

Scoring Analysis

This essay scores 2 out of 6 because it

- **answers only part of the task.** The position is clear, and, indeed, the last point is a good one, but challenges to the position are not developed.
- **lacks support.** The assertions are either not backed up or are backed up with extremely simple or inadequate support.
- **is poorly written.** Most "paragraphs" are just one sentence. No single idea is explored in depth. Variety of sentence structure and word choice are not apparent.
- **observes the conventions of Standard Written English.** There are a several minor grammatical errors that add to the overall impression that this piece was poorly conceived and written.

Other observations: This writer could probably have scored an extra point or more by paying more attention to structuring and developing paragraphs.

Write Your Observations About Model 5

Model 6: 1 point out of 6

If there's one thing people have a real, 100% right to in this nation, it's there property, and a dog is a kind of property. Therefore, no one has the right to take that property away or to say a person cannot own a dog.

It's fine for a person to own a dog because a dog meets that person's needs or wants in some way. The dog might make the person feel good or more loved. The dog might make the person feel like someone or something on this earth depends on him and would not be the same without him. The dog might even be trained to fetch the person's slippers for him or do some other job. There has even been times when dogs have saved their owner's lifes. It is not right for anyone without a dog to say that someone with a dog can't have that dog. No one has the right to do that.

Scoring Analysis

This essay scores 1 out of 6 because it

- **answers only part of the task.** This essay takes a clear position while failing to respond to challenges. The first paragraph is off task.

- **lacks support.** There is almost no support; the support that appears is simple and predictable.

Other observations: In addition to other flaws that sink the essay, the final two lines also present the reader with an example of circular reasoning—saying something is so because it is so. Avoid this kind of reasoning in your own response.

Write Your Observations About Model 6

SUMMING IT UP

- The issue task of the Analytical Writing portion of the GRE revised General Test measures how well you can develop and support your own position on an issue.

- The issue task is of a general nature, and no special knowledge is required to analyze and form an opinion about it.

- The issue will be accompanied by a set of instructions that establishes the conditions or requirements for the response.

- You will be presented with one issue to write about. You won't have a choice of issues from which to select one.

- The issue task is part of the Analytical Writing section, which is always first in an administration of the GRE. The time limit for the issue task is 30 minutes.

- If you're taking the computer version of the GRE, you'll use specially designed word processing software that allows the user to insert and delete text, cut and paste text, and undo actions. There is no spell or grammar checker.

- The issue task is scored against a rubric using a 0 to 6 range in 1-point increments. The scores for the issue task and the argument task are averaged and reported as a combined score ranging from 0 to 6 in half-point increments.

- Follow these steps when writing the issue task:
  o State the thesis early.
  o Use a standard pattern of organization, namely order of importance.
  o Order paragraphs effectively.
  o Use a standard pattern of paragraphing: topic sentence, support and development, final summary statement.
  o Develop each paragraph fully: use facts, authoritative opinions or human interest, observations, anecdote, and examples.

- While spelling is not included in the scoring rubric, transitions are, so be sure to include them as you draft your response. If time permits, you can add extras to the response such as an interest-grabbing opener, apt word choice, and varied sentence structure.

- Your writing plan should consist of:
  o Prewriting: restate the prompt, think about reasons on both sides of the issue, jot a quick write
  o Drafting: answer the task, organize your response, provide well-developed support, consider style, link ideas clearly, take care with tone and person
  o Proofreading: check your thesis, look for omitted words, check for sentence faults, don't spend time on spelling or commas

- While you shouldn't spend time on spelling or minor mechanical errors, remember that misspelled words and lack of punctuation or wrong punctuation can detract from meaning.

The Argument Task

chapter 5

OVERVIEW

- Basic information about the argument task
- Understand the prompt: the argument
- Understand the prompt: the writing instructions
- Understand the scoring rubric
- Review the basics of argumentation
- Learn the flaws in arguments
- Create your writing plan
- A final note of caution
- Argument prompt with six model responses, scoring, and analyses
- Summing it up

The Analytical Writing section of the GRE revised General Test measures both your ability to think and your ability to write in response to two kinds of prompts. The second of these prompts is the argument task. It presents you with a very brief argument and then states your task. Depending on the question, you'll have one of eight sets of directions explaining how you should construct your response. This chapter describes the prompt and sets of writing instructions and walks you through strategies that will aid you in crafting a successful response. To help you put it all together, the chapter ends with a sample argument task and six responses complete with analyses based on the GRE rubric for argument tasks.

BASIC INFORMATION ABOUT THE ARGUMENT TASK

You will find the Analytical Writing section always first in any administration of the GRE revised General Test. For many test-takers, it is probably the most stressful part of the test, so evidently the test-maker slots it first so anxious test-takers can get it out of the way.

Type of Question

For the argument task, you must write a response to an argument within certain guidelines set by the instructions that accompany the argument. The task for an argument response is not to craft your own opinion about the argument, but to analyze the argument. The instructions, which are described in more detail later in this chapter, may require that you

- explain how certain evidence would make a claim stronger or weaker.

- examine stated and unstated assumptions to explain how much the argument depends on them, as well as what the argument loses if the assumptions are not valid or correct.

- present and discuss alternative explanations that could reasonably compete with the proposed explanation.

The content of the argument will be drawn from a wide range of subject areas. You might find a prompt about funding for the fine arts, a policy to monitor employee Internet use, a health study's recommendation, or a government plan for land use. Topics are drawn from the physical and social sciences, the fine arts, and the humanities. However, no special knowledge of the subject is necessary to develop a well-reasoned and well-written response. The topics are general in nature, and the goal of the exercise is to enable test-takers to demonstrate "complex thinking and persuasive writing" ability.

Unlike other essay portions of standardized tests that you may have taken, there is only one prompt. You won't get a choice of arguments from which to choose one to write about.

Time Limit and Software

The argument task and the issue task are each allotted 30 minutes to complete. The time limit is the same on both the computer-based version and the paper-and-pencil version.

The computer version has a word processing program that allows the test-taker to edit by inserting and deleting text, cutting and pasting text, and undoing actions. There is no spell checker or grammar checker. This is similar to the restrictions placed on those taking the paper-and-pencil version. They will have no access during the test to dictionaries or grammar handbooks.

Scoring

Both the argument task and the issue task have their own rubrics. You'll work through the rubric for the argument task later in this chapter. Both tasks share the same score scale, which ranges from 0 to 6. The average of the two scores is taken to arrive at a combined score from 0 to 6 in half-point increments. This is the score that is reported to graduate and business schools.

UNDERSTAND THE PROMPT: THE ARGUMENT

All the prompts in the argument task have two parts: the argument and the specific instructions. The first part of the prompt states a brief argument, expressed completely in just a few sentences, which may end with a conclusion, a recommendation, a bit of advice, or a prediction. For example, the argument might suggest how funds are to be spent, a new policy that should be instituted, or why things would go better if a particular plan or action were implemented.

Think about this description of the first part of the prompt. An argument expressed in just a few sentences has to lack evidence—or enough evidence. Indeed, it has to be big on assertions and small on explanation and development. In short, it has to be a flawed argument.

TIP

If you're taking the paper-and-pencil version and there is enough space on the sheets of paper, write on every other line. That will leave you space to insert additions and neatly make deletions. If your handwriting isn't legible, try printing, but practice ahead of time so that you can print quickly and legibly.

Don't be fooled if the prompt has numbers, percentages, or other statistics. Their function is to support the argument—or to appear to support the argument. They may actually reveal a flaw in the argument that you can build on in your own line of reasoning.

UNDERSTAND THE PROMPT: THE WRITING INSTRUCTIONS

The second part of the prompt states the task or special instructions that define your response. These instructions will begin with the words "Write a response. . ." and then explain how that response should be shaped. Typically, you'll be told to be specific in explaining your analysis, that is, you'll need to provide examples, reasons, questions to answer, or alternative explanations, depending on the prompt. The sets of instructions for responding to an argument task will have wording similar to the following:

- Discuss the evidence needed to assess the argument. Include specific examples and an explanation of how the evidence might weaken or strengthen the argument.

- Discuss the stated and/or unstated assumptions and explain how the argument is based on these assumptions and the implications for the argument if the assumptions are shown to be unjustified.

- Discuss the questions that need to be asked and answered to determine if the recommendation and its argument are reasonable. As part of your response, describe how the answers would help in the evaluation process.

- Discuss the questions that need to be asked and answered to determine if the advice and its argument are reasonable. As part of your response, explain how the answers would help in the evaluation process.

- Discuss the questions that need to be asked and answered to determine if the recommendation is likely to result in the outcome that is projected. As part of your response, explain how the answers would help in the evaluation process.

- Discuss the questions that need to be asked and answered to determine if the prediction and its argument are reasonable. As part of your response, explain how the answers would help in the evaluation process.

- Presented with an explanation, discuss one or more alternative explanations that could reasonably compete with the proposed explanation. Explain how your explanation(s) account for the facts in the argument that is proposed.

- Discuss the questions that need to be asked and answered to determine if the conclusion and the argument it is derived from are reasonable. As part of your response, explain how the answers would help in the evaluation process.

If the task asks you to raise questions, don't fail to raise them. If it asks you to provide alternative explanations, be sure you include them. And, above all, remember that you're being asked to analyze and evaluate a flawed or, at best, an incomplete argument. That knowledge can help you focus your thinking.

NOTE

You can see by the writing instructions that you're being directed to respond in specific terms to the presented argument. In the words of ETS, you'll need to "support ideas with relevant reasons and examples" in "a well-focused, coherent discussion."

UNDERSTAND THE SCORING RUBRIC

Before we go any further, let's look at the scoring rubric for the argument task against which your response will be evaluated. Two readers will read and analyze your response using a six-point scale. The readers are your audience, and scoring high is your purpose. Scores range from 6 as the maximum to 0. Scores are whole numbers.

6 Points

To earn 6 points, your response should exhibit these characteristics:

- A logically sound, well-focused answer to the specific task that is particularly insightful, thoughtful, deep, or sophisticated.

- Fully developed, persuasive support for the main point or points of your response. At this high level of response, examples and other illustrations are particularly apt or well chosen, and their relationship to the focus of your analysis is extremely clear and/or well articulated.

- A method of organization that complements the main ideas of the analysis by effectively creating a flow of well-organized paragraphs and easing the reader's progress through the paper from first word to last. Connections between and among ideas are logical and may also be as subtle as they are effective.

- A formal grace that is a product primarily of well-constructed, varied sentences, and exact and rhetorically effective word choices.

- Adherence to almost all the conventions of Standard Written English, including grammar, usage, and mechanics. If there are any errors, they are minor.

5 Points

To earn 5 points, your response will likely have these characteristics, though it may exceed one or more of them yet fall short on another:

- A logically sound, focused answer to the specific task that reflects insight and evidences some deep thought.

- Well-developed, persuasive support for the main point or points of your response. Examples and other illustrations are well chosen, and their relationship to the focus of your analysis are clear.

- A method of organization that complements main ideas and connects ideas clearly and in a logical order.

- Well-constructed, varied sentences and appropriate word choices that help create clarity as well as interest.

- Adherence to almost all the conventions of Standard Written English, including grammar, usage, and mechanics. If there are any errors, they are minor.

4 Points

To earn 4 points, a response will have these characteristics:

- A generally focused answer to the specific task.

- Varying degrees of adequate and inadequate support.

- A logical method of organization, although some linkages may be missing or unclear.

- Sentences and word choices that generally create clarity, though some problems may exist with structure or usage.
- General adherence to the conventions of Standard Written English. Some errors may occur.

3 Points

Your response will earn only 3 points if it has *one or more* of the following characteristics:

- An inadequate answer to the specific task. It may not quite respond to the task or all aspects of it; it may be limited in its scope or number of points; or it may be vague or confusing in places.
- Inadequate support for the main point or points of your response or support that is illogical.
- A pattern of organization that does not complement the main ideas or causes confusion for the reader.
- Sentences and word choices that occasionally interfere with clarity.
- One or more errors in the conventions of Standard Written English that are so significant that they obstruct meaning, or very frequent minor errors.

2 Points

Your response will earn only 2 points if it has *one or more* of the following characteristics:

- An inadequate or unclear answer to the specific task. It may not quite respond to the task or all aspects of it; or it may be too vague or confusing to answer the task adequately.
- Little, if any, support, or support that is illogical.
- Confusing or inadequate organization.
- Sentences and word choices that interfere with clarity.
- Repeated errors in the conventions of Standard Written English that are so significant that they obstruct meaning.

1 Point

Your response will earn only 1 point if it has *one or more* of the following characteristics:

- Almost no response to, or minimal understanding of, the specific task.
- A total lack of support or only illogical or flawed support.
- No pattern of organization or confusing organization.
- Many sentences and word choices that interfere with clarity.
- So many errors in the conventions of Standard Written English that they obstruct meaning throughout the response.

0 Points

This score is possible under the following circumstances:

- The response does not answer the task in any way.
- The response is written in a foreign language.
- The response simply copies the argument.
- The response is not legible.
- The response is nonverbal.

From these criteria, you can draw or reaffirm the following four conclusions about your task:

1. You must answer the prompt completely.
2. Your ideas, support, and analysis must be in-depth, sophisticated, and well-developed to earn the highest score.
3. To dramatically affect your score, grammar, usage, and mechanics errors must be both numerous and serious. (However, that doesn't mean you can be sloppy.)
4. The quality of your ideas is far more important than the quantity. However, in order to identify significant problems or flaws and to examine them in adequate, if not dense, detail, you'll need to write a response of some length. Although there is no magic number for success, aim for well-elaborated coverage of at least three flaws in the argument.

REVIEW THE BASICS OF ARGUMENTATION

The good news about the GRE argument task is that you don't need any knowledge of formal argument. You don't have to identify an argument as deductive or inductive, or worry about syllogisms. The purpose of the argument task, according to ETS, is to assess your analytical writing skills and your informal reasoning skills. Nevertheless, a quick review of what an argument is and what it does may prove useful in helping you tease out the assumptions, supposed facts, explanations, etc., on which an argument prompt is based.

Basic Argument Facts

The following basic facts define an argument:

An Argument, or the Claim or Thesis at the Center of the Argument, Can Be Simple or Complex. In the prompts you are presented with, your job is always to find the claim, and treat it like a claim, not a fact, no matter how simple or "fact-like" it may appear.

An Argument Persuades. At the heart of an argument is the purpose of causing someone to think in a new way or adopt a new way of acting. Arguments may well inform, but if they don't also at least seek to persuade, they aren't arguments.

Arguments Rely on Evidence. Evidence can consist of everything from a simple anecdote to complex statistics. Examples, illustrations, and facts are all evidence. Evidence alone is never enough, however. The best arguments explain and interpret the evidence and successfully relate that support back to the claim. Because the arguments you will be presented with on the GRE are so brief, this kind of interpretation will be entirely missing from them. Furthermore, most arguments will lack evidence of any kind—or they will present only flawed or problematic evidence.

There is one additional fact about arguments that you won't find present in the short argument statements on the GRE, but that you can use to your advantage in writing your response:

A Successful Argument Often Depends, at Least in Part, on Rhetorical Devices to Engage and Sway the Audience. An argument may use rhetorical devices while leading into the claim, reasserting it, or explaining the evidence that supports it. Exploiting the rich connotations of words for their emotional effect, luring the reader in through an engaging opening, or using devices such as parallelism, inversion, or figures of speech to transport the reader smoothly down the road of the argument are some of the rhetorical devices that writers use. Such devices are uncommon in GRE argument prompts because they are too short. However, in developing your response, you will be framing a long analysis, which is essentially an argument for your point of view, and you can use these devices most effectively for that purpose.

Rhetorical Devices

There are a variety of rhetorical devices that you could employ in your response. The following are perhaps the most useful in this case:

- **Rhetorical question as a lead-in to your introductory paragraph:** Are libraries dead?
- **Metaphor:** A library's after-school programs are a beacon of hope for children of working parents.
- **Simile:** A library's after-school programs are like a magnet that draws the children of working parents to homework clubs and fun reading groups.
- **Understatement:** A library is home to the children of working parents.
- **Overstatement:** With fewer than 400 books a month being borrowed, the city library's circulation of books is dead!
- **Sound devices:** sssssshhhh or click-click, tap, tap—which are the sounds of the modern library?
- **Parallel structure:** I came to the library, I saw its collection of DVDs and CDs, and I was captured by the possibilities of free entertainment.

The Basic Language of Argumentation

In dissecting the argument, it will be helpful if you know what you're looking for. The following is a quick review of the parts and qualities of arguments:

The Claim: The claim is the main idea, proposition, or thesis statement of the argument. As you read the argument part of the prompt, look for the claim, that is, what the argument is about.

The Conclusion: The conclusion is the idea that is reached in the argument. Ask yourself: What's the conclusion arrived at by the end of the argument?

Premise/Assumption: The reasoning process to reach the conclusion begins with premises (or statements assumed to be true). Some people use the word "premise" as a synonym for an "assumption," which is any statement set forth as true or presumed to be true and may be stated or implied. The premises, or assumptions, are the meat of the argument. They lay out the support for the claim, proposition, or thesis. Responding to them will be the major part of your writing.

Counterargument: All argument writers should expect someone to counter their ideas, or present an opinion that opposes their own. In an extended argument, a good writer will anticipate and address counterarguments. The argument prompt is too short for any extended counterarguments; in writing your argument task you're in effect countering the argument made in the prompt.

Assessing an Argument as Sound, Valid, Logical: These are three terms that are standard ways to convey that a point is reasonable, logical, or substantiated.

Assessing an Argument as Unsound, Invalid, Illogical: Similarly, these are three terms that brand an argument as unreasonable or that identify it as untrue.

The Perspective or Point of View: As you respond to the argument task, consider the perspective or point of view from which the argument is made. As you analyze the premises, ask yourself if the information provided is one-sided, reflecting a bias, or if it presents several sides to the argument. If it's one-sided, which is likely because of space limitations and the need of item writers to provide something for test-takers to write about, what is that point of view? Then, consider what some other points of view about the topic might be and who might hold those other views. That information should help you develop your response.

LEARN THE FLAWS IN ARGUMENTS

The GRE will present you with flawed arguments. Remember that it's not your job to agree or disagree with the claim, but to expose those flaws. The most common flaws you'll find will be embedded in statements of, or references to, the following:

Unreliable Opinion Polls, Surveys, Questionnaires

You can expose the potential flaws or unreliability of an opinion poll, a survey, a questionnaire, or similar instrument by asking or speculating about the following:

- How many people took part?
- Was it a representative sample?
- Was it a random sample, self-selected, or handpicked?
- What questions were asked?
- Did the wording of the question contribute to a certain answer? (Consider that some questions are leading questions. Consider, too, that some questions do not allow for the full range of possible answers.)

In addition, instruments that are intended to measure change may not account for novelty, that is, initial responses to a change or new policy may be different over time. Also, those who design and analyze surveys, opinion polls, and questionnaires can leap to conclusions that aren't borne out by the data. They overstate or overgeneralize from the data.

Faulty Cause-and-Effect Relationships

Always examine cause-and-effect relationships in the argument. Sometimes, the prompt will confuse a correlation or an association with a cause, or propose a false cause. For example, an argument might suggest that every inch of space in a building is in use; therefore, a new building is needed. But you might be able to undercut this argument by conjecturing about how the space is being used. It may be storing useless equipment or supplies that should be discarded or recycled. You could then point out that the cause is not lack of space, but bad use of space.

False Generalizations

Even if a set of evidence does logically lead to a valid conclusion, it is possible to overgeneralize. That is, it's possible to suggest the data applies to more situations or to more people than it actually does. Another term for this is sweeping generalization.

More common, perhaps, is the hasty generalization that bases a conclusion, a recommendation, advice, or a prediction on too small a sample or an unrepresentative sample. For example, an argument might suggest that because a few public libraries in the state are failing to keep up with technology, all public libraries have the same problem and state government should fund upgrades for all libraries in the state.

False Analogies

If two or more things are alike in one or more ways, it's illogical to suggest that, on the basis of that similarity, they are alike in other ways. For example, if the city funded a new city hall last year, a good choice that met with overwhelming approval, the argument may make a false analogy by suggesting that the new public safety building will be a similarly good choice and meet with the same overwhelming approval.

Either-Or Thinking

This line of "reasoning" suggests that if one thing is true, the other cannot be true, as in "Either we build the new public safety building now, or we act with wanton disregard for the safety of every citizen in this community." Either-or thinking may be used to argue that two courses of action cannot exist at the same time or lead as effectively to the same result at the same time.

Assumptions

ETS rolls many of the specific flaws described above, as well as others, into the blanket term "assumptions." For example, ETS calls faulty cause-and-effect, or the fact that one thing is said to cause another but didn't necessarily, a flawed assumption. Therefore, feel free to use "faulty," "incorrect," or "illogical assumption" to identify most flaws you find, or expose the flaws without naming their type.

A statement such as "One problem with the argument is . . . ." is perfectly acceptable based on the models that ETS presents. What will make or break your response is not the language you use to identify flaws, but the ability to recognize flaws, explain the problems with their supposed "support" of the argument, and relate the flaws back to the specific writing instructions.

CREATE YOUR WRITING PLAN

Now that you know what to expect in an argument task, it's time to create a plan for attacking it. Think of it as three-pronged: prewriting, drafting, and proofreading. You'll have just 30 minutes to do all this, so you should plan to spend the bulk of that time—say 23 or so minutes—drafting. However, you need to know what you're going to write, so don't skip prewriting.

Prewriting

The prewriting part of your writing plan has these steps that will help you focus on the task, gather your ideas, and plan the development of your response.

TIP

Those taking the computer-based test will be given scrap paper for making notes, so if you're taking the computer version, consider jotting down the key requirements of the instructions. If you're taking the paper-based test, you may want to underline the key requirements.

Restate the Prompt: Read the entire prompt carefully and then restate it in your own words to make certain that you understand the argument and the specific instructions.

Identify the Claim/Issue and Any Statements Based on the Claim: Next, find the claim. Sometimes the word "claim" is actually used in the prompt, but most of the time it is not. Remember that the claim is the main idea or proposition. Statements based on the claim may include advice, recommendations, predictions, explanations, and conclusions. Ask:

- Is the main claim true?
- Is it true in all cases?
- Under what circumstances would it not be true?

Ask some "what if" questions about situations or circumstances in which the claim would be weakened or invalidated. Then decide whether the conclusion, recommendation, prediction, explanation, or advice logically follows from the claim. Ask yourself why.

Examine the Claim/Issue from Different Perspectives: For example, a town is deciding whether it needs a new public safety building to replace its old fire and police station.

Think about this question from the point of view of

- a person who works in the station every day.
- people who will make money from the new construction.
- people who will feel more important if a new station is built.
- taxpayers, some of whom may be burdened by high taxes, unemployment, or both.
- people who think the old building is just fine and it's better to renovate than build new.

ALERT!

The conclusion, recommendation, prediction, explanation, or advice will never be totally logical or completely unassailable!

Jot a "Quick Write": Spend 2 or 3 minutes jotting down your ideas. (Computer-based test-takers will be able to use scrap paper that is provided for this purpose.) This isn't a full outline, but just a list of flaws in the argument, main points, and few supporting ideas for each main point. Ideas won't come in any particular order, so list them as they flow. Then cross out ideas that don't seem as though they fit, and number ideas you want to use in the order in which you want to use them.

The most sophisticated ideas earn the highest scores on the analytical writing measure; therefore, don't just plan on developing the first ideas that pop into your head! Instead, use the best, least simplistic, and most original ideas for your response, ideas that you can substantiate in meaty, persuasive ways. If possible, position your best idea at the end of your essay for greatest rhetorical effect. If you can, also come up with an idea for the opening that will appeal to your audience—with drama, human interest, vivid detail.

Some Tried-and-True Sentence Starters

You can use the basic language of analyzing an argument in sentence starters such as those on the following list. You'll find fleshed-out examples of several of these starters in the sample essays later in this chapter. These sentence starters can help bring clarity to your writing, as well as give your writing an organizational boost by providing transitions between sentences and paragraphs:

- The first problem/the most fundamental problem/an obvious flaw in this argument is . . .
- The statement/prediction/conclusion that XXX is an unjustified assumption because . . .
- A problem with this reasoning is . . .
- It is arguable that . . .
- What if . . .
- The writer/author/argument implies that . . .
- Nothing in this argument actually tells/explains/supports . . .
- This argument asserts that . . .
- This assertion is illogical because . . .

Drafting

In reality, you won't just be drafting: you'll be drafting and revising simultaneously because there's no time to do them as separate steps. To get the most out of your limited time, keep these priorities in mind as you draft:

Answer the Task: Some test-takers produce competent essays that fail to answer the task and, therefore, sink them. After you write your opening or first paragraph, glance briefly back at the task to be sure you are addressing it or are on track to addressing it. (Computer-based users can do this by clicking on "Question Directions" at the top of the screen.) As you answer the task, be as thoughtful and insightful as you can be. Be sure you focused on the flaws in the argument.

Organize Your Response: The following pattern is a standard, or traditional, way to organize your overall response. It leads your reader smoothly through your response by eliminating confusion and guesswork. In addition, it helps to create fluency—or the illusion of it. If you're a writer who has trouble with organization, this pattern gives you a structure to develop your ideas around:

- Opening paragraph: Thesis or clear statement of your position
- Body paragraph 1: Reason 1 for your position, fully explained and supported
- Body paragraph 2: Reason 2 for your position, fully explained and supported
- Body paragraph 3: A statement of the most effective counterargument, an acknowledgment of its reasonableness, and your fully explained and supported response; or any other specific and developed point needed to address the writing task instructions
- Closing paragraph: Reason 3 (another key challenge or another main point) that directly responds to the specific writing instructions; provides support as needed; plus a detail, statement, question, or other device that delivers closure to your response

TIP

Using a standard pattern of organization has an added benefit. If you decide ahead of time how to set up your response, you can save time when faced with writing the actual response on test day.

Suppose you use this pattern of organization. How do you decide what reason to use first, second, and third? Often, the best way to organize points for an argument is by order of importance. You could choose your most significant reason to be first or last. If you use your most powerful, that is, strongest, support as the third and final point, your readers will take away from your response your most impressive piece of argument.

Provide Ample, Thoughtful, Well-Developed Support: As you lay out each main point of your response, be sure you support it fully with the best evidence, and be sure you explain that evidence clearly enough so that it actually does evaluate the recommendation, advice, prediction, explanation, or conclusion. All the topics are meant to be general enough that anyone can answer them. For example, a prompt may ask you to discuss the questions that would need to be asked in order to decide if a recommendation to adopt honor codes by colleges and universities is reasonable. No special knowledge is required to respond to this prompt, but if you have experience with an honor code, you could incorporate that experience. Observations, such as your own experience, facts, authoritative opinions, examples, and human interest stories can and should be used liberally to support your points.

Link Ideas Clearly: Your organization doesn't have to be traditional, or based in any way on typical instruction in college writing classes, but it does have to be logical and help to create overall coherence. Based on reviewing sample analyses, ETS values transitional words and phrases, so link paragraphs and ideas appropriately as you write. Also, don't overlook the value of a topic sentence in providing an organizational boost to your essay.

Consider Style: If you're aiming for a top score, vary your sentences and word choices. Note that transitional words and phrases not only help you create coherence, but they can help you vary the beginnings of sentences as well.

TIP

If you have enough time, look for ways to increase the style quotient of your response by making your opening more attention getting, tweaking word choice so that it's stronger or more vivid, and varying your sentences.

TRANSITIONS

Review the following lists of transitional words and phrases and use them as you practice writing responses to the tasks in the practice tests. In that way, you can integrate them into your writing style so they flow as you write your actual responses on test day.

Transitions to Introduce or Link Opinions and Reasons

because	*evidently*	*indeed*
besides	*for this reason*	*on the other hand*
by comparison	*furthermore*	*since*
consequently	*however*	*therefore*

Transitions that Introduce or Link Examples

for example	*in this case*	*one type*
for instance	*in this situation*	*to illustrate this point*

Transitions that Create Emphasis or Add Information

after all	*furthermore*	*more important*
again	*in addition*	*moreover*
besides	*indeed*	*similarly*
certainly	*in fact*	*what's more*

Transitions that Introduce Opposing Views

although this may be true	*naturally*	*on the other hand*
even though	*nevertheless*	*undeniably*
evidently	*notwithstanding*	*unquestionably*
it may be said	*of course*	*without a doubt*

Proofreading

Save 2 or 3 minutes for proofreading and fine-tuning your essay. An omitted word could invalidate a good point by making the sentence in which it appears unclear or nonsensical. Look specifically for the following:

Check Your Thesis: Make sure that you've stated it and stated it clearly. Make sure your response reflects this statement.

Look for Omitted Words: When you're writing in a hurry, it's easy to leave out what could be a crucial word.

Check for Sentence Faults: At this stage, you want to make certain that you eliminate any ineffective fragments, any run-on sentences, and any fused sentences or comma splices.

Don't Spend Time on Spelling or Commas: Keep in mind that the rubric doesn't mention spelling. Spelling evidently has "minor error" status for ETS readers. Likewise, ETS readers aren't concerned with errors such as a missing comma here or there.

> **NOTE**
>
> Correct a fused sentence by making two sentences, or, if the sentences are closely related in meaning, by replacing the comma with a semicolon.

A FINAL NOTE OF CAUTION

ETS wants its computer-based users to know that their responses will be subjected to analysis by software that searches for similarities to published information. It warns that it will "cancel" a score if it contains any unacknowledged use of sources. In addition, ETS will cancel a response if an essay or any part of it has been prepared by another person. Finally, a score will be cancelled if it includes language that is "substantially" similar to the language in one or more other test responses.

ARGUMENT PROMPT WITH SIX MODEL RESPONSES, SCORING, AND ANALYSES

Use this prompt as a practice opportunity and compare your response with the samples, scoring, and analyses that follow.

Time yourself; in the real test, you will have 30 minutes.

1. Read the prompt.
2. Follow the prewriting steps.
3. Stop! Compare your "quick write" plan with the sample that follows the prompt to see different ideas (perhaps more sophisticated, perhaps less) that you might have thought of.
4. Draft your response.
5. Read each model that follows the sample "quick write." Determine the positive and negative qualities of each sample response before you read its scoring analysis.
6. Score your response against the rubric on pages 158–159. Be honest in your analysis.

Argument Task

> In our fast-paced, digital world, the public library has long been on the way out. In Springfield, where the population voted for a library expansion in 2001, 42 percent of residents opposed the expansion at that time. One can be certain that figure has grown by leaps and bounds since then, especially now that Springfield can no longer maintain its library at its previous financial levels. Therefore, the city should accept the offer of Infogenesys to run the library with its dusty books and tattered magazines as a for-profit business. The city will divest itself of a costly burden, and residents who are still using such fast disappearing methods for getting information will retain the option of getting that information at what Infogenesys promises will be a nominal cost.
>
> Write a response in which you discuss the stated and/or unstated assumptions, and explain how the argument is based on these assumptions and the implications for the argument if the assumptions are shown to be unjustified.

Sample "Quick Write"

The 6-point response to this prompt began with a process like the one that follows. First, the writer identified flaws. Notice that not every flaw in the argument is recorded here. Notice also, however, that the writer found many flaws and, therefore, a firm basis for analysis.

Flaws

public library not on way out: library probably digital

2001 isn't now; 58% were <u>in favor</u>

"certain" that figure has grown—no evidence

dusty books/tattered magazines—true?

Who is Infogenesys? Why should city accept offer?

library is a burden?

TIP

Note how specific the "quick write" is. The writer is off to a good start for developing a response that is grounded in specific details to support any generalizations that the writer may make.

Now look at the plan the writer quickly made:

①   all? libraries digital

①b   online catalog, big variety of databases

①a   busy: meetings, tutoring, art exhibits, lectures,
          children's summer reading program, book sales

     ~~so busy can't park at Melville Library~~

③   burden—would people who use it say that?

②   2001 isn't now

②a   58% were in favor

②b   vote about expansion, not whether to have a free public
          library

Making Your Plan Work

As you'll see when you read the 6-point essay based on this prewriting activity, some of the success of the response is due directly to ideas listed here. First, notice how the plan isn't a formal outline; it doesn't need to be. There is no five-paragraph organization of intro, body, conclusion expressed in the quick write. Instead, the plan goes to the heart of the 30-minute argument task and reflects a great variety of evidence for exposing the flaws in the argument. You'll see in the response how this planning leads to a dense, richly supported analysis that effectively undermines the argument.

Notice how, even in the prewriting, the writer goes beyond the obvious ideas (that 2001 isn't now and that 58 percent of people were in favor of the expansion) to think a little more deeply about the nature of the vote and its implications.

When you read the resulting essay, you'll also see that the writer didn't use every idea here. For example, the writer left out the idea about parking, which was probably a good choice because it was one of the less thoughtful kinds of support he or she could have provided.

Furthermore, there are many more ideas in the essay than appear in this simple plan. Remember that fact when you make your plan. You don't have to come up with every possible idea during prewriting. Writing is a generative process; ideas come to writers as they write. Trust that they will come to you, too. The secrets to successful prewriting are mainly the following:

* Quickly generate more ideas than you think you need.

* Edit out the least significant, the simplest, or the most predictable ideas.

* Know when to stop: try not to spend more than 3 minutes on prewriting.

Model 1: 6 points out of 6

Someone who refers to the public library as a collection of dusty books and tattered magazines inadvertently exposes a complete ignorance of today's public libraries—of which the Springfield library may be entirely representative—whose circulation figures are now heavily comprised of digital items and whose services are as much about meeting a wide range of community needs, including job searching, as they are about making print items available. This argument needs a firmer basis in reality before it can successfully argue that the people of Springfield should hand their library over to a for-profit company.

First, it is highly arguable that the public library, or any public library, is on its way out or that it has not kept up with the changing times. In general, public libraries today have a large variety of functions that have nothing to do with print items. They provide meeting places for large groups, such as public or nonprofit committees, and small groups, such as one-on-one or one-on-two tutoring. They offer ways for new community members to learn about their town or city and its services. They provide a wide range of databases, from local and national newspapers, to encyclopedias, to health and wellness databases, to business databases that permit the user to do everything from invest wisely in a mutual fund to determine whether the refrigerator he or she is about to buy is worth the price and really does what it claims to do. Not all of this information is available to private Internet users; much of it exists in costly, subscription databases. Some public libraries hang art exhibits, offer programs on everything from gathering local grasses and herbs to the nation's history, and encourage literacy by establishing summer reading and other reading programs for children and adults. They also sponsor book groups for adults, Yet, the writer of this argument assumes that none of this is happening in the Springfield public library—when all of it and much more might be. Instead, the writer peremptorily decides that it is a place where books and magazines molder untouched.

Moreover, the prediction that people would vote overwhelmingly to rid themselves of the public library is an unjustified assumption. Even if past performance were a guarantee of future results, which it is not, the statistics do not show that people voted overwhelmingly against their library in the past; rather, they show that the people voted for it. Nor do the statistics reveal under what circumstances even 42 percent of the city voted against the new addition. Some of those people could have been in favor of expanding the library, yet waiting for a more optimal time to expand, such as when state funding might increase or during a year when Springfield was not also investing heavily in, as one possibility, its water works. Most fundamentally, a vote against expansion is not the same as a vote for no free, public library at all.

As for the library's being a costly burden to the city, a detailed cost-benefit analysis might well prove this assumption incorrect. Such an analysis might compare the cost and benefits of the Springfield Public Library with other institutions in the city; it might also more fairly and fundamentally probe the potential losses to the community if the library were no longer a free, public institution. Until such an analysis is done, the word "burden," with all its connotations of onerous, unwanted weight and responsibility, should not be used. It forms a misleading part of yet another of the unsubstantiated statements on which this illogical argument is based.

Scoring Analysis

This essay scores 6 out of 6 because it

- **answers the task.** The writer examines several statements that form the basis of the argument for their implications and for their reasonableness. In doing so, the author probes deeply to create a thoughtful analysis of several unsubstantiated statements and their implications.

- **is well supported.** The writer offers numerous examples of what today's library, and therefore, the Springfield library by inference, might be, do, and offer, thereby refuting the reasonableness of the premise that all public libraries are now a place where books gather dust. Other points are likewise well substantiated.

- **is well organized.** There is a clear opening and an effective closing, and the body paragraphs are logically organized. All ideas lead logically from one to the next.

- **is fluid, precise, and graceful.** Sentences and word choices (such as "peremptorily" and "molder") are varied and, at times, quite sophisticated and graceful. Statements are placed effectively at the ends of paragraphs for clincher effect. The tone and style are appropriate to the task.

- **observes the conventions of Standard Written English.**

Other observations: Notice how this response doesn't try to refute every statement and implication—nor does it need to in order to be successful. Notice, too, how deeply it probes. For example, it moves from the obvious flaw that 42 percent against expansion still means 58 percent for expansion (an easy problem to spot) to a more sophisticated analysis of the possible implications of that statistic. Also, examine how rich, varied, and dense the support is for the idea that public libraries are vital places.

Write Your Observations About Model 1

_____

_____

_____

_____

_____

_____

_____

_____

_____

_____

_____

_____

_____

_____

_____

_____

_____

_____

_____

_____

_____

_____

_____

_____

_____

_____

_____

_____

_____

_____

_____

Model 2: 5 points out of 6

The writer of this argument is both 100 percent certain and clear. But has s/he presented us with a reasoned, logical argument? A few questions can quickly begin to tear holes in this argument.

What if it was true that circulation rates are actually climbing at public libraries across the nation including at the Springfield Public Library? What if it was the case that the books on the shelves of the Springfield Public Library are not the least bit dusty and being read all the time instead? What if it was true that the magazines are, in fact, tattered, but they're tattered because they're being used all the time? These facts would help rip apart the argument that Springfield should give its library over to Infogenesys as a for-profit business.

Also, since when aren't libraries fast paced and digital? The writer implies that libraries in general and the Springfield library in particular aren't keeping up with the world because of not being digital or fast paced, but the argument doesn't have evidence to support that idea. Libraries across the country are filled with terminals, and usually there is a sign-up sheet for using them because every single one is occupied and so there has to be a fair way of sharing them. What if in fact many, many Springfield citizens are accessing their library catalog or databases remotely and getting services and information that way that they couldn't get on their own computers at home?

Finally, how do we know who wrote this argument. If a representative of Infogenesys, which might stand to make a very good deal by getting the library and all its assets and turning them into a business, wrote it, then many statements here might be biased or one-sided and the whole argument a lot less then valid. In fact, the argument doesn't give the background, aims, and goals of Infogenesys, and they could include buying the library, operating it short term for profit, and then selling the property it stands on (which could be prime Main Street property) for a huge redevelopment profit.

Scoring Analysis

This essay scores 5 out of 6 because it

- **answers the task.** The writer examines some statements that form the basis of the argument for their implications and for their reasonableness. The analysis raises many thoughtful points.

- **is well supported.** The writer offers competent what-if questions that expose the possible flaws in statements that form the basis of the argument. The writer also offers clear examples, although not in depth.

- **is well organized.** The ideas lead logically from one to the next.

- **is fluid and precise.** Sentences and word choices are varied, although many of the word choices are more serviceable than sophisticated. The tone and style are for the most part appropriate to the task, though a bit overwrought at times.

- **observes the conventions of Standard Written English.**

Other observations: Notice that while this response touches on many ideas, it actually examines and develops fewer statements and implications than the 6-point essay does. The opening is competent, but quite predictable. Compare the opening, as well as the body paragraphs, with the 6-point essay to see differences in the quality of both the thinking and the writing.

Write Your Observations About Model 2

Model 3: 4 points out of 6

When was the last time the writer of this arguement was really in a public library? It sounds like he never goes there at all! Public libraries I have used include Montvale Public Library, where I grew up, a branch of the New York public library where my family moved after I went to college, the Madison public library where I went to undergraduate school, and the small, but pretty busy Deansville library where I now live. All of these public libraries keep changing as the times change, they offer people the tools they need now. They are busy places with many uses. I think that many people are in them really often. I can't imagine how much people would loose if any of these libraries charged people for it's services. It would be a terrible thing if any of them had to close or be taken over by a private company like Infogenesys.

The writer of this arguement insults the users of public libraries by saying that they are people who are still using outdated methods for getting information. Implying that they are technophobes or computer illiterite. Well, what if all the people in the public library are really the smartest people in Springfield? They are in there library getting more and better information then they can get at home. Maybe they are even there getting information on Infogenesys and how it operates. All of this being left unclear by the writer who really doesn't want us knowing who Infogenesys is or what it's past is. Nevertheless, it insults the people of Springfield by saying that the people in the library are the ones who can't get information any other way.

My sense in the Montvale Public Library, where I grew up, the branch of the New York public library I used sometimes, the Madison public library and the Deansville library is that more people are using them then ever before. If the writer of this arguement ever went inside a library maybe he could see that for himself. Otherwise maybe he could get some circulation figures about these libraries or the Springfield library. The circulation figures might tell that the use of the library is going up and up and up and pretty much wreck his argument. The Springfield Library might also keep counts of how many people come thru there doors each and everyday. That would probably tell the writer that the Springfield library really is an important place in the city and not a place just to give away to some company that wants to make a profit off it.

But the writer is too busy insulting the people of Springfield, while he is actually writing an arguement that also insults the intelligence of the readers of the arguement. Being as he uses a ridiculous statistic in favor of his idea when that statistic is really against his idea. The statistic is that 42% of the people were against adding on to the library in 2001. That means that 58% of the people were for it. Last I knew 58% was a majority. So the writer is not just insulting the people of Springfield and trying to make them loose out their public library but he is also insulting the readers of this arguement.

Finally, charging people to get into their own library is a bad idea with bad consequences. It's definately going to hurt the poor people. And nobody is going to want to pay for something that use to be free. So maybe all those books and magazines and everything else that the people of Springfield paid for over all the years they had a library really is going to get dusty on the shelves. An important place for meeting and learning in the city is going to be an empty place so that some private company can profit off of it. This arguement is an insult to the people of Springfield and to the readers of the arguement.

Scoring Analysis

This essay scores 4 out of 6 because it

- **generally answers the task.** That is, it probes the argument both for what it says directly and what it implies. It identifies weaknesses in the argument that seriously undermine it.

- **is supported, but often simply and repetitively.** The examples of the writer's own libraries do form support, but that support is simple, weak, and tangential. Some ideas are repeated. Assertions about use going up and many people using the library are simplistic and vague.

- **is organized.** In general, the ideas flow in an acceptable order, though some repeated ideas should have been deleted. There is no transition between the opening paragraph and the second paragraph.

- **is sufficiently clear.** The sentences and words are mainly serviceable, though they lack sophistication. A number of sentences are convoluted and difficult to understand though they do not detract from the meaning of the paragraphs.

- **observes the conventions of Standard Written English.** There are several errors here, but, in general, they do not interfere with meaning.

Other observations: This is an example of a very long essay that doesn't succeed on the basis of its length. In fact, its length is part of its problem. The response would have been more cogent had repeated ideas and vague assertions been deleted. While ETS gives no indication in its scoring rubrics of how informal diction and a less than objective tone might undercut a score, it is probably safe to assume that the writer's choices in these regards in no way enhance this essay and may well undermine it by contributing to the scorer's sense of inadequate word choice or unconventional usage in respect to the purpose, audience, and writing occasion.

Write Your Observations About Model 3

_____
_____
_____
_____
_____
_____
_____
_____
_____
_____
_____
_____
_____
_____
_____
_____
_____
_____
_____
_____
_____
_____
_____
_____
_____
_____
_____
_____
_____
_____
_____

Model 4: 3 points out of 6

As a person who has pretty much stopped using libraries, I more or less agree that many public libraries have outworn their usefulness. They may have been a crucial nineteenth century institution. They may have even served our nation well into most of the twentieth century. But with the coming of the Internet, the public library is now an obsolete institution. If businesses can make a profit out of them while still extending some outdated services to the members of a community, that is a reasonable course of action.

There are, however, some flaws in this argument that make it less than sound. The flaws have mainly to do with things that are left out of the argument. The argument lacks evidence for most things that it says. There is no explanation and evidence for the idea that the percentage of residents who would want to vote against a public library has grown by "leaps and bounds" between 2001 and the present. Someone would actually have to do a poll to see if that were true. If it were not true, then the argument would be affected in a negative way. In addition, more explanation is needed for a reader to believe that the people who voted for expansion in 2001 would want to lose their library now. Also, what is the evidence that Springfield can "no longer maintain" its library? There might, for example, be some evidence to suggest that Springfield could actually reallocate funds from other sources for its library, if there is enough political will to do so, and that also would affect the argument in a negative way.

Scoring Analysis

This essay scores 3 out of 6 because it

- **answers the task in a very limited way.** The first paragraph is well written, but off course as it offers agreement with the argument instead of launching immediately into an analysis of it. The second paragraph does offer three acceptable insights.

- **is not well supported.** All insights in this essay are crammed into two paragraphs without much support. Sentences 2 and 3 of paragraph 2 offer more repetition than support. Statements such as "Someone would actually have to do a poll to see if that were true" begin to provide support, but only vague support.

- **lacks organization.** Paragraph 2 should have been split into separate paragraphs and each main idea developed more thoroughly.

- **is fluid and precise.** Unfortunately, good word choice and sentence construction as well as appropriate style and tone do not outrate poor critical analysis.

- **observes the conventions of Standard Written English.** Unfortunately, excellent command of the conventions of Standard Written English do not outrate poor critical analysis.

Other observations: This is an example of how a well-written response doesn't score high because the quality (or extent) of the thinking is not on the same level as the quality of the word choice or sentence construction. The writer may have run out of ideas or out of time.

Write Your Observations About Model 4

_____
_____
_____
_____
_____
_____
_____
_____
_____
_____
_____
_____
_____
_____
_____
_____
_____
_____
_____
_____
_____
_____
_____
_____
_____
_____
_____
_____
_____
_____
_____
_____
_____
_____
_____
_____
_____
_____

Model 5: 2 points out of 6

This argument suggests that Springfield and its residents would be a lot better off if its libary were in private not public hands. So the first thing to examine is the private hands. Who is Infogenesys and have they bought libaries before and what were the results in the communities where they bought the libaries? Did they really continue to provide the people of the city with a libary and was it acceptable to them and what was the nominal price they charged for using it and was the nominal price really nominal? Or did that price turn out to be pretty high for some people who didn't get the information they wanted or needed as a result? The answers affect the argument by showing that things might not go well if Infogenesys gets the library and starts charging a high price and people stop using the libary as a result.

Scoring Analysis

This essay scores 2 out of 6 because it

- **answers the task in a very limited way.** It identifies for analysis just two ideas in the argument: the motives and history of Infogenesys and the nominal price it will supposedly charge. It does, however, ask good questions.

- **is not supported.** While the writer shows some insight in the ideas selected for analysis, these ideas are, mainly, not explained and developed.

- **lacks organization.** A single paragraph is not an essay.

- **has poorly constructed sentences.** Most of the sentences coordinate one or more ideas that should be subordinated.

- **observes the conventions of Standard Written English.** While not committing obvious grammatical errors, the writer shows a lack of command of sentence construction.

Write Your Observations About Model 5

_____
_____
_____
_____
_____
_____
_____
_____
_____
_____
_____
_____
_____
_____
_____
_____
_____
_____
_____
_____
_____
_____
_____
_____
_____
_____
_____
_____
_____
_____
_____
_____

Model 6: 1 point out of 6

Selling the public libraries of our nation is a new idea that some communities are considering now, especially when their budgets are stretched. This sale may well have some validity for Springfield and its residents, especially since everyday we are getting more and more information from the Internet via our home and work computers. It is true that no one really and truly needs a library anymore, unless they don't have a computer, they are traveling and didn't bring their computer, or their computer is broken or out for repair.

Scoring Analysis

This essay scores 1 out of 6 because it

- **it does not answer the task.** Instead, it agrees with a premise in the prompt.

Write Your Observations About Model 6

SUMMING IT UP

- The argument task of the Analytical Writing portion of the GRE revised General Test measures how well test-takers can analyze an argument, including the evidence to support that argument, and then discuss their analysis using examples from the given argument.

- The argument will be of a general nature, and no special knowledge will be required to analyze and discuss it.

- The prompt will be accompanied by a set of instructions that establishes the conditions or requirements for your response.

- You will be presented with one argument. You won't have a choice from which to select.

- The argument task is part of the Analytical Writing section, which is always first in an administration of the GRE. The time limit for the argument task, like the issue task, is 30 minutes.

- Those taking the computer version of the GRE will use specially designed word processing software that allows the user to insert and delete text, cut and paste text, and undo actions. There is no spell or grammar checker.

- Like the issue task, the argument is scored against a rubric using a 0 to 6 range in 1-point increments. The scores for the argument task and the issue task are averaged and reported as a combined score ranging from 0 to 6 in half-point increments.

- The basic facts of argumentation are the following:

  o An argument can be simple or complex.

  o An argument is meant to persuade.

  o An argument relies on evidence.

  o A successful argument often depends on rhetorical devices to sway the audience.

- The basic language of argument is claim, conclusion, premise/assumption, counterargument, assessment of an argument (sound, valid, logical; unsound, invalid, illogical), perspective, or point of view.

- The flaws in an argument can be based on unreliable opinion polls, surveys, and questionnaires; faulty cause-and-effect relationships; false generalizations; false analogies; either-or thinking; or assumptions.

- Your writing plan should consist of:

  o Prewriting: restate the prompt, identify the claim/issue and any statements based on it, examine the claim/issue from different perspectives, jot a quick write

  o Drafting: answer the task, organize your response, provide well-developed support, link ideas clearly, consider style

  o Proofreading: check your thesis, look for omitted words, check for sentence faults, don't spend time on spelling or commas

- While spelling is not included in the scoring rubric, transitions are, so be sure to include them as you draft your response.

- While you shouldn't spend time on spelling or minor mechanical errors, remember that misspelled words and lack of punctuation or wrong punctuation can detract from meaning.

PART IV
VERBAL REASONING

Strategies for Reading Comprehension Questions

OVERVIEW

- Basic information about reading comprehension questions
- Active reading
- General strategies for answering multiple-choice questions
- Additional strategies for multiple-choice questions—select one or more answer choices
- Strategies for select-in-passage questions
- Practice questions
- Answer key and explanations
- Summing it up

Chapter 6 describes the reading comprehension questions on the GRE. These questions make up about half of each Verbal Reasoning section. The majority of reading comprehension questions are multiple-choice questions—select one answer choice. However, there are two other formats for reading comprehension questions: select-in-passage questions and multiple-choice questions—select one or more answer choices. In addition to basic information about the reading comprehension section, Chapter 6 offers useful strategies to help you answer reading comprehension questions in all three formats quickly and competently.

BASIC INFORMATION ABOUT READING COMPREHENSION QUESTIONS

The reading comprehension questions on the Verbal Reasoning section of the GRE assess your ability to understand, analyze, and apply information found in the types of reading you will encounter in graduate school. About half the questions on the verbal section of the GRE are reading comprehension questions.

The Passages

There are approximately ten reading comprehension passages on the GRE. They are based on information found in a wide range of scholarly and everyday sources from nonfiction books to popular periodicals to scholarly journals. The arts and humanities, physical sciences, biological sciences, social sciences, and business are all content areas that may be represented in the passages.

The passages may be from one to several paragraphs in length. Most, however, will be one paragraph; only one or two will be longer. Some passages will inform. Others will analyze. Still others will argue a point and seek to persuade. As in all real-world writing, a single passage may reflect more than one mode of exposition.

Each reading comprehension question appears on a separate screen with the passage on which it is based. If the passage is too long to display legibly on a single screen, as in the case of multi-paragraph passages, you will be able to scroll through the passage without changing screens.

Directly before the start of the passage is a statement of how many questions each passage has, for example:

QUESTIONS 1–3 ARE BASED ON THE FOLLOWING PASSAGE.

A direction line appears from time to time during the questions—not each and every time—telling you how many answers to select, for example:

> **FOR QUESTIONS 1–3, CHOOSE ONLY <u>ONE</u> ANSWER CHOICE UNLESS OTHERWISE INDICATED.**

A Word to the Wise: Put Aside Your Personal Views

When it comes to the content of the passages, ETS notes that occasionally "your own views may conflict with those presented in a passage." That is, you may have a reaction to the content of a passage that runs the gamut from mild disagreement to outrage. Don't let these reactions interfere with your analysis. To succeed, temporarily shelve any feelings and get on with answering the question(s) about the passage.

Question-and-Answer Formats

Each passage is followed by one to six questions. There are three formats that questions and answers may take for reading comprehension questions:

1. Multiple-choice questions—select one answer choice
2. Multiple-choice questions—select one or more answer choices
3. Select-in-passage

Most reading comprehension questions ask you to select *one* answer from a list of five possible answer choices. The answer choices for these questions will be preceded by *ovals*.

You will find a few multiple-choice questions that ask you to select *one or more answers* from a list of three possible choices. One, two, or all three answers may be correct. You have to select all the correct possibilities to earn credit for that question. The answer choices for these questions are preceded by *squares*.

You will find only a few questions that ask you to *select a particular sentence* in the passage as your answer. To do this, you will highlight your answer choice by clicking on the sentence. If you are working with a passage of several paragraphs, the paragraph or paragraphs that the question refers to will be marked with an arrow at the beginning and end of the subject paragraphs. Clicking on a sentence in any other part of the passage will not highlight it.

For your convenience in working through this book, we are marking answer choices as (A), (B), (C), and so on.

Skills

The purpose of the GRE is to predict success in graduate school. Therefore, the questions on the test are meant to assess the preparedness of potential graduate school students. You will find questions that ask you to use the skills and abilities that are expected of students in graduate school. To answer questions on the reading comprehension section of the GRE, you will need to be able to

- identify or infer the main idea, or major point, of a passage.

- distinguish between main and subordinate ideas (major and minor points in GRE parlance).

- summarize information.

- reason from incomplete data to infer missing information.

- determine the relationship of ideas to one another and/or to the passage in which they appear.

- analyze a text.

- draw conclusions from information.

- identify the author's assumptions or perspective.

- identify the strengths and weaknesses of a position.

- develop and assess alternative ideas.

- determine the meaning of individual words, sentences, and paragraphs, and of longer pieces of writing.

Some questions require you to use more than one skill at a time. For example, you might need the main idea to answer a question, but to find it, you might have to distinguish between main ideas and subordinate or supporting details. Or you might have to find a relationship between ideas by both inferring information about main and subordinate ideas and using structural clues to understand meaning.

Recurring Question Types

The list of skills may seem daunting, but when put in the context of actual questions, they will seem much more familiar. For example, the question "Which of the following best restates the author's point of view?" asks for the main idea of the passage. To find it, you may need to infer it, or it may be directly stated, though probably not in a graduate-level piece of writing.

You will find that certain categories of questions recur among the reading comprehension questions. The common question types are the following:

- **Main Idea Questions:** These questions require you to identify or infer the main idea (or major point), summarize the passage, draw conclusions from complete or incomplete information about the main idea, and infer relationships between the main idea and subordinating details. You will find this to be a common question type, both in this book and on the GRE. Sample questions might be:

  o   Which of the following does the passage most clearly support?

- o   What was the underlying cause of the financial crisis?
- o   What qualities of the painter's style most influenced the critic's view?
- o   The passage implies that the president's actions were based on...
- o   Select the sentence that restates the premise of the author's argument.

- **Supporting or Subordinate Details Questions:** These questions ask you to identify subordinate details, infer subordinate details, summarize the passage, draw conclusions about subordinate details, or infer relationships between two or more subordinate details.

  - o   The passage mentions financial regulations in order to...
  - o   You can infer that the president's actions were based on...
  - o   The passage notes each of the following causes EXCEPT...
  - o   Based on the passage, which of the following was excluded from the experiment?
  - o   The passage suggests that which set of data is the more compelling?
  - o   The purpose of the sentence "Yet a close look . . . continents" is to...
  - o   Select the sentence that restates the author's claim.

- **Author's Perspective Questions:** To answer these questions, you may need to infer the author's attitude or tone, or deduce the author's unstated assumptions. Not every question that mentions the author—or even the author's beliefs—is a perspective question. The question may, for example, be a main idea question such as the last example under Main Idea Questions.

  - o   What was the underlying cause of the financial crisis, according to the author?
  - o   The author attributes the early experimental results to...
  - o   It can be inferred from the passage that the author believes that...
  - o   The author of the passage most likely agrees with which historian's view as described in the passage?
  - o   Select the sentence that best describes the author's attitude toward critics of Darwin.

- **Application Questions:** These test items ask you to evaluate the strengths and weaknesses of an argument, develop alternative explanations, hypothesize about the relationship of new ideas to stated or implied ideas, and use structural clues to determine or infer meaning. As their name suggests, these questions will often require you to apply or build on what you have already identified or inferred about the main idea, supporting details, or the author's perspective in earlier questions in the set for a particular passage and then apply that information to a different idea or situation.

  - o   Which of the following, if it were true, would weaken the author's argument?
  - o   Select the sentence that best describes the opinions of the anthropologists who actually examined the skeleton.
  - o   What is the primary purpose of the two groups of words in bold type?
  - o   Which of the following is most similar in reasoning to the ideas expressed in the final sentence?
  - o   According to the passage, which is the correct sequence of events?

- **Word-Meaning Questions:** These questions are easy to spot because they're accompanied by line numbers to help you quickly pinpoint the word and the context. They require you to infer the meaning of a word from the specific context in which it appears. The phrase "specific context" is important because words have different meanings in different subject areas and as different parts of speech.
  - o "Verisimilitude" (line XX) most nearly means…
  - o In the passage, "obfuscate" means…

ACTIVE READING

This is a timed test, and you will—and should—feel the pressure of the clock. Nevertheless, you can't read a GRE reading comprehension passage at the same rate at which you read the back of a cereal box or the latest posting to your favorite blog. In general, adjust your reading rate so that you're reading every passage with concentration and active participation. This can be hard to do when the clock is ticking, but it's your best bet to improve your comprehension, and it is especially good advice when the content is unfamiliar to you.

Just slowing down as you read won't help you much. You need to focus on what you are reading and participate actively in what you're reading. Participating actively includes the following steps:

- Identify the topic, main idea, thesis, or proposition.
- Clarify your understanding.
- Summarize what you've read.

To help you understand the process, skim the following reading comprehension passage to get an idea of its topic, main idea, and details.

Passage 1

Roy Lichtenstein (born 1923) established his place in the pantheon of Pop artists through what critic Robert Hughes has called mannerism. Although his subject matter, like that of his contemporary Andy Warhol, was popular, rather than elitist in nature and most famously derived from comic strips, Lichtenstein's experiments with line, texture, and contour were formalist and had their genesis as much in creating a new relationship to old master drawings as in the abstract impressionist reaction against—and assault upon—the painterly. The most characteristic feature of Lichtenstein's work, the Benday dot, epitomizes that relationship—and that assault—through the painstakingly created mechanical repetition of form. He applied this form to works whose subject matter he branded clichéd: realistic (rather than humorous) comics; advertisements; and other contemporary mass media—to create a kind of tension. Lichtenstein's formal intensity, coupled with his pop or vernacular subject matter, distinguishes his work and gives it much of its psychological resonance and enduring appeal.

Identify the Topic, Main Idea, Thesis, or Proposition

The more unfamiliar the subject matter of the passage is, the more basic your approach must be. Furthermore, working step by step to find meaning can help you focus. Determine the main idea first. If you can't identify the main idea, then start by identifying the simple subject, or topic, of the passage. For example, the topic of Passage 1 is Pop artist Roy Lichtenstein.

TIP

If you are running out of time, you could go through remaining passages looking for word-meaning questions. To answer the sentence, read the question, the sentence referred to in the question, and the sentences immediately before and after this sentence.

To get from topic or subject to thesis, main idea, or proposition, ask yourself what the author is saying about the topic or subject. If you can establish only part of that thesis, main idea, or proposition, do as much as you can. For example, you might begin identifying the thesis of Passage 1 as:

> The author is saying that Roy Lichtenstein created something new by being formal in his work, and he used popular or Pop subject matter.

Clarify Your Understanding

There are a variety of techniques for clarifying understanding. One is to ask and answer questions as you read. For example, you might ask yourself what a concept means or the meaning of a word in the context of the passage. As you read Passage 1 on Roy Lichtenstein, you might ask yourself what mannerism is. At least one question on the reading comprehension test is almost certain to be about the meaning of a key word. Often, this word will not have the meaning most generally associated it, but will convey a meaning that is specific to the context. Again, if you can establish only part of that meaning, do at least that much. For example:

> In the test passage, the term "mannerism" seems to have a specific meaning that is related to the manner in which Lichtenstein created his art. Maybe it has something to do with his experiments with line, texture, and contour.

Another way to clarify understanding is by stopping to restate or paraphrase information. This usually involves rereading the previous sentence or perhaps a couple of sentences. For example, you might stop and ask yourself just exactly what the second sentence in the passage is saying. Restate whatever you can. Don't worry if you can't restate everything. Your thinking might be something like the following:

> The second sentence of the test passage says that Lichtenstein's subject matter was popular, like the subject matter of Andy Warhol, who was painting at the same time, but Lichtenstein's work was formal and involved experiments with line, texture, and contour that were part of a response to or attack on old master drawings and part of abstract expressionism, too.

Summarize

Quickly summarize the passage to yourself after you have read it, but before you begin answering the question(s). This strategy can also help you clarify your understanding.

GENERAL STRATEGIES FOR ANSWERING MULTIPLE-CHOICE QUESTIONS

The purposes, structures, and content of the reading comprehension passages and questions you will encounter on the GRE will vary widely, and, unfortunately, there is no single strategy and no magic bullet that can guarantee success with all. In addition to active reading, the following ten general strategies will help you answer reading comprehension multiple-choice questions, whether you need to select one answer choice or one or more answer choices:

1. Restate the question.
2. Try answering the question before you read the answer choices.

TIP

Don't forget these four test-taking strategies listed in Chapter 1: (1) anticipate and use the clock, (2) skip and return to questions, (3) eliminate answer choices that you know are incorrect, and (4) use educated guessing.

3. Read all the answers before you choose.

4. Compare answer choices to each other and the question.

5. Avoid selecting an answer you don't fully understand.

6. Choose the *best* answer.

7. Pay attention to structure and structural clues.

8. Don't select an answer just because it's true.

9. Substitute answer choices in word meaning questions.

10. Choose the answer that doesn't fit for EXCEPT questions.

There is an additional strategy later in the chapter for multiple-choice questions—select one or more answer choices. This list may seem like a huge number of strategies to remember and use on test day, but there are two things to remember about the strategies:

1. Not all strategies will work for all questions. That said, the first three strategies will work for any question. If you've taken the SAT or AP subject tests, you've used these strategies.

2. The more you practice using the strategies as you work through this book, the easier they will be to remember, to figure out which are the appropriate strategies to use for different questions, and to apply on test day.

For the first six strategies in this section, you will focus on a single reading comprehension passage and a single question. If you're reading a physical book, you will want to mark the page with the passage and the question with a sticky note or other bookmark so that you can refer to it easily. If you are using an e-book reader, you will want to mark the page for reference.

QUESTION 1 IS BASED ON THE FOLLOWING PASSAGE.

Roy Lichtenstein (born 1923) established his place in the pantheon of Pop artists through what critic Robert Hughes has called mannerism. Although his subject matter, like that of his contemporary Andy Warhol, was popular, rather than elitist in nature and most famously derived from comic strips, Lichtenstein's experiments with line, texture, and contour were
5 formalist and had their genesis as much in creating a new relationship to old master drawings as in the abstract impressionist reaction against—and assault upon—the painterly. The most characteristic feature of Lichtenstein's work, the Benday dot, epitomizes that relationship—and that assault—through the painstakingly created mechanical repetition of form. He applied this form to works whose subject matter he branded clichéd: realistic (rather than humorous)
10 comics; advertisements; and other contemporary mass media—to create a kind of tension. Lichtenstein's formal intensity, coupled with his pop or vernacular subject matter, distinguishes his work and gives it much of its psychological resonance and enduring appeal.

FOR QUESTION 1, CHOOSE ONLY <u>ONE</u> ANSWER CHOICE.

---

1. The passage suggests that Lichtenstein's work displays which of the following qualities?

(A) A return to mannerist ideals in its subject matter and execution

(B) An attempt to elevate vernacular subject matter to a painterly ideal

(C) An assault on the mechanical repetition of form

(D) A psychological resonance with the work of his contemporary Andy Warhol

(E) A contradictory and unique blend of formalism and popular culture

Time Out for Some Advice on Unfamiliar Material

If you come across a passage like this that is totally unfamiliar to you—be it fine arts, biology, economics, or whatever subject—don't mentally throw your hands up in despair certain that you'll fail. Don't leap to the conclusion that you won't be able to answer the question or questions that follow. As the GRE Web site says, "Do not be discouraged if you encounter unfamiliar material; all the questions can be answered on the basis of the information provided in the passage."

You may be tempted to "mark" a passage like this to come back to later without giving it an active reading. Although the format of the test makes it easy to mark a question and return to it, use this strategy only if you are still stumped after having given the passage a purposeful, focused reading and have at least attempted to answer one or more of the questions. This is especially true when a reading comprehension passage is accompanied by more than one question.

Think about it. If you save for later a passage with three questions, and you are doing a typical test with twenty questions, you have just delayed answering approximately 15 percent of the test. Putting off large chunks of the test until later can lead to increased anxiety. Saving, returning, and, most of all, rereading also eats into your precious time. Sometimes you may have no choice, but give the passage and its questions a good try first.

Restate the Question

Here again is the question that accompanies the passage on Roy Lichtenstein.

> **FOR QUESTION 1, CHOOSE ONLY ONE ANSWER CHOICE.**

1. The passage suggests that Lichtenstein's work displays which of the following qualities?
   - (A) A return to mannerist ideals in its subject matter and execution
   - (B) An attempt to elevate vernacular subject matter to a painterly ideal
   - (C) An assault on the mechanical repetition of form
   - (D) A psychological resonance with the work of his contemporary Andy Warhol
   - (E) A contradictory and unique blend of formalism and popular culture

Read the direction line and the question. What does the direction line ask you to do?

The direction line says to select one answer. On the computer version of the test, the ovals that precede the answer choices convey the same information.

In addition to verifying what you must select, paraphrase or restate the question to be sure that you know what you are being asked to find:

- The question asks which qualities Lichtenstein's work has.
- You need to find the characteristics or qualities of Lichtenstein's work. This may seem like you're looking for supporting details, but you're really looking for the main idea, or topic, of the passage.

Try Answering the Question Before You Read the Answer Choices

This strategy is especially useful when you feel confident that you understand the passage. But it is also a useful strategy when you feel unsure of your understanding. By trying to answer the question in your own words first, you can get part of the way toward the correct answer. When you check the answers, you'll either find an answer that's the same as your idea, but in different words, or no answer that is even close to yours, so you know you've missed the point. Coming up with your own answer or a partial answer is, in fact, a way to clarify your understanding in relation to the specific question you have to answer.

Again, returning to Question 1, come up with the best answer you can before you begin to eliminate choices. For example, you might come up with this answer:

> Lichtenstein's art is Pop art, some of it is comic books, and it has to do with a special way of drawing that uses a Benday dot. So Lichtenstein's art looks popular and simple, but it's actually painstaking and formal at the same time.

Read All the Answers Before You Choose

After you've developed some idea of the correct answer, read all the answer choices listed. Don't read the first one and, if it seems correct, choose it and go on to the next question. Keep in mind that a well-constructed test will have answers that are close approximations of the correct answer.

For example, you might jump to the conclusion that the right answer to the question about the qualities of Lichtenstein's work is choice (A). Reading carefully through all the answers, and eliminating them one by one, however, may lead you to a different choice.

Compare Answer Choices to Each Other and the Question

Suppose you eliminate three answer choices, but cannot eliminate one of the two remaining choices. If you are crunched for time, you can make your best guess at this point. If you have time, however, don't guess before you try this strategy: Compare the choices to each other and to the question. The following is based on Question 1 and assumes that you've eliminated choices (B), (C), and (D):

- Choice (A) is very different from choice (E). Choice (A) talks about "a return" to a style, but the entire paragraph is about how different Lichtenstein was and how he was doing something new. In comparison, choice (E) is all about being new. It calls Lichtenstein's work unique. It also calls it contradictory, which seems to fit with work that is unique. The terms seem correct for an artist who more or less copied comic books and other mass media, but drew them in a painstaking and "formalist" way.

- The question asks for qualities. Choice (E) describes the way Lichtenstein's work blends popular images with painstaking drawing, which is a quality of his work. In comparison, the key word in choice (A) seems to be "ideals." The ideal of mannerism does not seem like a quality. Therefore, choice (E) is correct. **The correct answer is (E).**

ALERT!

Don't rely on outside information to answer questions. Base your answers solely on the information in the passage. You may know that mannerism was a Renaissance art style, but in this passage mannerism is used in its twentieth-century sense.

ALERT!

Reading all the answers is especially important for multiple-choice questions that require you to select one or more answer choices. This question type is signaled by having squares instead of ovals and three answer choices instead of five.

Avoid Selecting an Answer You Don't Fully Understand

Again, suppose you have eliminated three choices, but you're at a loss to eliminate one of the two remaining answers. As you reread the choices, avoid selecting the one that is more confusing or unintelligible to you. You might work your way through your dilemma something like this:

- Choice (A) is hard to understand. The passage implies that mannerism is related to how Lichtenstein created his work, but the term isn't really ever defined in the passage.

- Choice (E) is easier to understand and it also clearly sums up the ideas in the paragraph. Therefore, choice (E) is more likely to be correct.

Choose the *Best* Answer

Once again, suppose you have been able to eliminate three choices, but are having trouble eliminating one of the two remaining answers. As you try to choose, remember that your goal is to select the *best* answer. Therefore, if both answers appear reasonable or possibly correct to you, your task is to choose the better—more reasonable—of the two.

- Choice (E) sums up the ideas in the paragraph. It tells what "distinguishes" Lichtenstein's work and why that work is great.

- On the other hand, choice (A) seems as if it could possibly be correct, but it definitely doesn't sum up who Lichtenstein was, what he did, or what the general qualities of his work are.

- You're looking for the main idea of the passage, so choice (E) is more likely to be correct (because it sums up the information).

For the next four strategies, you will focus on a multi-paragraph passage and four questions to learn to apply the strategies. Once again, it is probably wise to mark the passage for easy reference as you try out the various strategies.

Passage 2 differs in three significant ways from the first passage you read. First, it has four paragraphs. While most passages you encounter on the test will be a single paragraph in length, at least one passage is likely to be longer. Second, notice also that this passage contains some information in bold type. Figure that this must be important information to pay close attention to as you read. Finally, note that the passage contains two arrows. These arrows relate to the select-in-passage question type covered later in this chapter.

> **FOR QUESTIONS 2–6, CHOOSE ONLY <u>ONE</u> ANSWER CHOICE UNLESS OTHERWISE INDICATED.**

QUESTIONS 2–6 ARE BASED ON THE FOLLOWING PASSAGE.

By the mid-1970s the U.S. tailored clothing industry was foundering. In 1965, 100 percent of the average American male's wardrobe was manufactured in the United States; by the mid-1970s, 12% of all men's suits and 30% of all men's shirts and sports coats were imported, typically from low-wage countries, and the statistics were trending upward.

5   →Proactively, labor, government, and management worked together to create a nonprofit corporation in 1981 called the Tailored Clothing Technology Corporation or (TC)². Its initial goals included the development of a new system of sewing, as well the conceptualization and

engineering of equipment that would robotically manufacture men's suits. The latter goal was unrealized, although progress was made in automation during the 1980s. Nevertheless,
10   new technology failed to reverse import trends apparent in the 1970s. For example—and for a plethora of reasons—**in the years between 1994 and 1999, imports of tailored garments grew 40%.**

Research in the wake of the joint $(TC)^2$ initiative led to the development in 1991 of 3-D body scanners that make it possible to bypass traditional fittings. Once again, clothing manu-
15   facturers and retailers were placing, and some continue to place, their bets on technology—and an impressive technology it is. A single scan identifies approximately 300,000 points of data on the body and enables the reader to view the body in new and innovative ways, including as a cross section, slice area, or surface area. Knowledge of both size and shape can then be factored into a precision fit. ←
20   It is believed that the use of full-body scanners will lead to a new era of the "virtual try on" and customization of clothing. Nevertheless, the impact of these scanners, which first appeared in retail business in 1999, has yet to be translated to a growth in sales or profit for the tailored clothing industry, **suggesting that new and better technology cannot save a collapsing industry.**

Now, read Question 2.

2. What function do the two groups of words in bold type serve in this argument?
   (A) The first anticipates the argument's conclusion; the second provides support for that conclusion.
   (B) The first supports the proposition or opinion; the second states the proposition or opinion.
   (C) The first presents the proposition or opinion; the second presents the final support for the proposition or opinion.
   (D) The first serves as an intermediate conclusion; the second serves as a definitive conclusion.
   (E) The first presents the argument; the second restates and reinforces the argument.

Pay Attention to Structure and to Structural Clues

When you read actively, you should be drawing a conclusion about the author's purpose. Many passages inform, but the purpose of this particular passage is to persuade. As part of reading actively, you should also be looking for the main idea, proposition, or thesis of the passage. The point of view of this passage is that technology alone cannot save the tailored clothing industry. Once you know you are reading a persuasive piece—an argument, in other words—and once you determine the thesis or proposition, begin the work of separating main ideas from opinions or judgments and facts.

*   In the first segment in bold type, the statement about the growth of imports is a fact; it supports the idea that technology failed to reverse import trends apparent in the 1970s.

*   The second segment in bold type states an opinion.

Organizational structure for persuasive writing suggests that the conclusion may present an opinion, draw a final conclusion, or present a clincher statement that reinforces the opinion or proposition. Remember that while a proposition, or thesis, may be stated at the beginning of an argument, stating it at the end of an argument, as if it were the most logical conclusion possible, is also rhetorically effective.

Make a mental note of transitional words and phrases as you read. Transitions can show time order, add information, indicate cause and effect, and show comparisons and contrasts.

- The first segment in bold type presents a statistic that functions as supporting evidence for the idea that technology failed to reverse import trends of the 1970s.

- The transitional phrase "for example" in line 10 signals that the bold type is a supporting detail.

- The statement about import trends is itself evidence that supports the conclusion drawn by the final sentence, and the final sentence clearly states the proposition, or argument. Therefore, choice (A) is correct. **The correct answer is (A).**

Sometimes structural clues reveal the writer's thinking over the course of an entire paragraph. For example, a passage from the GRE online sample questions reveals the following structure, and clues to meaning, embedded in it:

- Sentence 1: "According to …"

- Sentence 2: "In this view …"

- Sentence 3: "… however …."

These clues tell you that you're reading one view—stated and explained in sentences 1 and 2. In sentence 3, you're reading its rebuttal or some significant qualification of it (beginning with "however") in the remainder of the paragraph.

In another sample passage, there are no structural clues until the passage's midway point. These structural clues follow:

- Sentence 4: "It follows that …"

- Sentence 6: "Therefore, …"

These clues tell you that you're most likely reading an argument.

To give you more practice with argument questions, try Question 3 also based on the same long passage as Question 2. The GRE showcases the following type of question more than once in its practice materials.

3. Which of the following, if it were true, would most seriously weaken the argument?

   (A) It is projected that imports would have increased by less than 20% from 1994 to 1999 had globalization not been a factor.

   (B) Improvements in automation resulted in increased sales in low-wage countries.

   (C) The limited use of scanners is due to the prohibitive cost of the technology.

   (D) The use of robotic arms and other technological improvements led to dramatic increases in profits in the auto industry during selected years in the same time period.

   (E) The development of a new sewing system initially led to a dramatic growth in sales in the mid-1980s.

This question asks you to find the relationship between a hypothetical or an alternative idea and the ideas in the passage. This is an application question because you're applying information from one situation to other situations. You will use a variety of reading comprehension skills to answer the question, including making inferences, drawing conclusions, and evaluating hypotheses.

Try answering Question 3 on your own before you read the following answer rationale:

The argument is that new technology alone cannot keep the U.S. clothing industry from collapsing.

- You can eliminate choice (A) because the passage makes it clear that the upward trend in imports is leading to the collapse; therefore, a 20 percent increase in imports is significant and negative, no matter how it is explained.

- You can eliminate choice (B) because the situation is different in low-wage countries; their clothing industries are, presumably, not foundering or collapsing as the U.S. clothing industry is. Furthermore, the argument is clearly relative to the U.S. clothing industry.

- Choice (C) is incorrect because it doesn't weaken the argument that technology alone cannot save the U.S. clothing industry.

- Similarly, the focus on the U.S. clothing industry, not the auto industry, means that you should eliminate choice (D).

- Choice (E) suggests that new technology did, in fact, lead (even if only initially) to the kind of sales that might save the industry. This idea contradicts the thesis, or controlling opinion. Therefore, choice (E) is correct. **The correct answer is (E).**

Don't Select an Answer Just Because It's True

You want to choose an answer because it answers the question. Some answers may be true, but that doesn't mean that they answer the question. With a question like the following, restating the question is especially useful. It will help you to anchor your thoughts before you dive into the verbiage of the answer choices.

4. The passage suggests which of the following as the reason for the formation of the Tailored Clothing Technology Corporation?
   (A) The foundering U.S.-tailored clothing industry
   (B) To promote interaction between labor, government, and management
   (C) To automate the clothing industry in the United States
   (D) To make the U.S. clothing industry more competitive through technology
   (E) The impressive efficiencies that technology could deliver

Try answering this question on your own first. Remember to read all the answer choices before you choose one.

- Choice (A) is true, but if you continued reading, you realized that this answer is too narrow, even though it is true.

- Even though it is true that labor, government, and management must have worked together to form the corporation since it was a joint endeavor, choice (B) was not their reason for forming the corporation. Working together was a by-product, not a cause.

- Automating the clothing industry, choice (C), was a goal of the corporation, but only a partial reason for the corporation's formation.

- The passage makes it clear that imports were a great concern, which means that manufacturers, labor, and government were worried about the industry's competitiveness. Choice (D) is true, but keep reading to the end of the answer choices.

- Choice (E) focuses on technology, but it doesn't include why efficiencies would be important to the tailored-clothing industry.

- Each of the five answers has some truth to it. But only choice (D) includes both the outside forces on the industry (competitiveness) and the benefit that technology would bring to the industry. Choice (D) is true, and it's the *best* answer because it's the most complete. **The correct answer is (D).**

Substitute Answer Choices in Word Meaning Questions

Word meaning questions may appear more than once on the GRE. The context in which the word is used will help you choose the correct answers. Reading the answer choices may not be enough to get you to the correct answer because often a word will have several meanings and you need to find the meaning of the word as it is used in the passage. To do this, substitute each answer choice for the word in the passage.

5. In the passage, "plethora" (line 11) most nearly means
   (A) negativity.
   (B) overabundance.
   (C) striking.
   (D) illustration.
   (E) quantifiable.

You may know that "plethora" means an overabundance, choice (B), but if you didn't, substitute each answer choice in the sentence "For example—and for a _____ of reasons—in the years between 1994 and 1999, imports of tailored garments grew 40%."

- While the reasons may have had negative effects on the domestic market, the reasons didn't have unpleasant or disagreeable features, so choice (A) is incorrect.

- Neither were the reasons vivid impressions, so choice (C) doesn't work.

- The reasons could be used to illustrate problems with the industry, but the reasons themselves weren't examples, choice (D).

- Choice (E) doesn't work because "quantifiable" means "capable of being measured." It's not the quantity itself. **The correct answer is (B).**

Choose the Answer that Doesn't Fit for EXCEPT Questions

You may find one or two EXCEPT questions. These questions ask you to find the answer choice that doesn't fit with the other answer choices. That is, you're looking for the wrong answer as your right answer. If you took the SAT or any AP subject tests, you'll remember this question type.

6. All of the following support the progress that technology made in changing the U.S.-tailor-made clothing industry EXCEPT
   (A) development of robots to construct clothing.
   (B) development of a new system of sewing.
   (C) the elimination of traditional fittings.
   (D) development of 3-D body scanners.
   (E) automation of some aspects of clothing manufacture.

The article mentions a goal to develop equipment to "robotically engineer men's suits," but the next sentence goes on to say that the goal was unrealized, so choice (A) isn't true. Choice (B) is also listed as a goal, but the article doesn't say it was unrealized, so you assume that it was realized, which makes choice (B) not the answer to the question. Choices (C), (D), and (E) are all developments that technology made possible, so they are true and not the answer to the question. Only choice (A) is untrue, and so, the correct answer to the question. **The correct answer is (A).**

ADDITIONAL STRATEGIES FOR MULTIPLE-CHOICE QUESTIONS—SELECT ONE OR MORE ANSWER CHOICES

You will find a few multiple-choice questions on the GRE that may require one or more answers to be correct. We say "may" because only one answer may be correct, or two, or all three choices. The direction for the question will state that you are to choose "all that apply." If you choose only choice (A), and choice (C) is also correct, you won't get credit for the question. To get credit, you need to select "all that apply." Half or a third of a correct answer is zero correct.

The multiple-choice questions—select one or more answer choices questions have only three choices listed as possible answers. Each choice is preceded by a square rather than an oval. For your convenience in checking answers, we have used (A), (B), and (C) to signal the answer choices.

The major strategy that you need to remember for answering questions that use the format of multiple-choice questions—select one or more answer choices is *choose an answer that answers the question on its own.*

Choose an Answer that Answers the Question on Its Own

Each answer choice has to answer the question on its own. Don't make the mistake of thinking that because there may be more than one answer, combining partial answer choices gives you a complete answer. Always assess each answer as a standalone. Is it accurate? Is it complete? Then move on to the next answer and ask yourself the same questions.

QUESTION 7 IS BASED ON THE FOLLOWING PASSAGE.

The consensus among engineers at EFG MicroDevices is that gallium arsenide (GaAs), a compound of gallium and arsenic, is a superior material to silicon (Si) in the manufacture of our leading products. GaAs has greater electron mobility and little sensitivity to heat. Devices manufactured with GaAs components also create less noise than those with silicon.
5   These qualities help bring about higher performance in several items in our product line such as smart phones. Traditionally, the sheer abundance of silicon in the Earth's crust has made it a more popular choice than gallium (Ga), which has been said to be more rare than gold and a difficult element to make. Added to this problem are potential issues related to arsenic (As), which is regulated by OSHA. EFG does not consider either of these concerns to be an
10   impediment to the design of current applications with GaAs.

FOR QUESTION 7, CONSIDER EACH ANSWER INDIVIDUALLY AND CHOOSE <u>ALL</u> THAT APPLY.

7. The second-to-last sentence "Added to . . . OSHA" (lines 8–9) serves which of the following purposes in the passage?
   (A) It counters the argument expressed in the first sentence.
   (B) It provides evidence for the effect of higher performance.
   (C) It reinforces the reasons for the popularity of silicon.

The first sentence argues that engineers at EFD MicroDevices have reasons to prefer GaAs (gallium arsenide) over silicon (Si) when they design products. The second-to-last sentence brings up a problem with the use of GaAs: there are issues and regulations related to the use of gallium arsenide because it contains arsenic. Therefore, the second-to-last sentence counters, or raises a point in opposition to, the first sentence, so choice (A) is correct. Choice (B) is incorrect because the next to the last sentence has nothing to do with higher performance. Choice (C) is, however, correct because GaAs clearly has its problems, which might lead some engineers to choose silicon over gallium arsenide. **The correct answers are (A) and (C).**

STRATEGIES FOR SELECT-IN-PASSAGE QUESTIONS

Select-in-passage questions ask you to choose a sentence within a passage as the correct answer. You will have a direction line, but no listing of multiple-choice answers (unless you're taking the paper-and-pencil test). For a passage that is a single paragraph, any sentence in the entire paragraph is fair game for the answer. For multi-paragraph passages, arrows [→] mark the beginning and end of the text from which you should select the sentence. To make your choice, click on any part of the sentence that you determine to be the answer. If you click on a sentence that is not between the arrows, it will not be highlighted and will not register as an answer.

This may seem silly, but don't lose track of where a marked section begins and ends. You don't want to waste time analyzing sentences in a part of the passage that isn't the subject of the question. If you try to click on a sentence in the unmarked portion of the passage, it won't highlight, so your answer won't be wrong, but you will have wasted precious time.

Similar to answering questions with the multiple-choice questions—select one or more answer choices format, you need to assess each sentence in the marked section of a passage as a stand-alone sentence.

The special strategy that applies to select-in-passage questions is *match the sentence to the information.*

Match the Sentence to the Information

The GRE information materials about the test note two facts about select-in-passage questions. First, a select-in-passage question contains the description of a sentence—content, tone, purpose, author's perspective, or similar aspect. In answering the question, you must look for the sentence that contains that information. However, you should not select a sentence if any part of the information in the sentence doesn't match the question.

This relates to the second caveat for select-in-passage questions: A question may not necessarily describe all aspects of the sentence for the sentence to be the correct answer. Sentences in GRE passages may be long and complicated. A question may focus on one or two aspects of a sentence. The sentence you choose just can't contradict the description in the question.

QUESTION 8 IS BASED ON THE FOLLOWING PASSAGE.

Fareed Zakaria notes in *The Post-American World* that there really is no such thing as Asia; he calls Asia a Western cultural construct. In other words, Zakaria suggests that Asia isn't really a continent, which calls for an examination of the term *continent*. If continents are defined as discrete landmasses separated by large bodies of water, then North and South
5   America should be one American continent, as the canal that separates them is neither a large nor natural body of water. Furthermore, if continents are described as large landmasses separated by large bodies of water, then Greenland, one of Earth's largest islands, is rather arbitrarily defined as an island instead of a continent.

Other problems with the historical and cultural constructs that underlie the classification
10   of continents include the classification of smaller islands, especially those located beyond the continental shelf of their so-called "continent," such as Hawaii. Clearly, political constructs also affect historical classification. Indeed, a close look at how the word *continent* is applied proves Zakaria's point and shows that the meaning of the word has more to do with the conventions long established to identify the somewhat agreed-upon number of continents
15   on Earth than it has to do with strict geographical or other criteria.

FOR QUESTION 8, CHOOSE ONLY <u>ONE</u> ANSWER CHOICE.

---

8. In which sentence does the author state the main idea of the paragraph?

(A) The first sentence ("Fareed Zakaria … construct")

(B) The second sentence ("In other words, . . . *continent*")

(C) The fifth sentence ("Other problems . . . Hawaii")

(D) The sixth sentence ("Clearly . . . classification")

(E) The last sentence ("Indeed, a close . . . criteria")

Zakaria's assertion that Asia is not a discrete or unified continent leads into the topic of continents and how they are defined. Therefore, the first sentence is not a main idea, and choice (A) should be eliminated. Whereas the second sentence does clarify the first, it doesn't yet get to the central focus of the entire passage, which goes beyond the example of Asia, so choice (B) is also incorrect. Choice (C) is incorrect because it's an example that supports the main idea. Choice (D) must also be eliminated because it supports the main idea rather than states it. Choice (E) alone provides an overview idea that encapsulates the many ideas of the paragraph. Therefore, choice (E) is the correct answer. Notice how choice (E) does a bit more than state the main idea. It also affirms Zakaria's idea. Although Zakaria's point about Asia is a minor rather than major one, the remainder of the sentence does state the main idea. **The correct answer is (E).**

PRACTICE QUESTIONS

> FOR QUESTIONS 1–15, CHOOSE <u>ONE</u> ANSWER CHOICE UNLESS OTHERWISE
> DIRECTED.

QUESTION 1 IS BASED ON THE FOLLOWING PASSAGE.

Prosopagnosia, or face blindness, was lately given a boost in long-overdue recognition as a genetic disorder when the distinguished professor of neurology and best-selling author Oliver Sacks described his own affliction with the disease. Like other proposagnosiacs, Sacks has a fundamental inability to recognize faces, and not just the faces of random strangers or
5 people he met for the first time last week. One index to the profundity of Sacks's problem is reflected in a study that found that proposagnosiacs who looked at photos of their own family members were unable to recognize 30% of the faces. Sacks himself admits that he often does not recognize a person whom he has met just five minutes before.

1. The passage achieves all of the following purposes EXCEPT

   (A) explain why prosopagnosia was given recognition as a genetic disorder.

   (B) tell or imply how prosopagnosia manifests itself.

   (C) cite research that helps define the challenges faced by prosopagnosiacs.

   (D) personalize and humanize the disorder known as prosopagnosia.

   (E) imply the severity of the challenges faced by prosopagnosiacs.

QUESTIONS 2–4 ARE BASED ON THE FOLLOWING PASSAGE.

Was ideology the leading actor in the unfinished drama that we call the Cold War? This question is endlessly disputed, often by attributing to the Soviets, as George F. Kennan was among the first to do, and to do at great length (in what became known as the "long telegram"), a messianic impulse in terms of communism. Similarly, the centrality of antipathy
5 to capitalism in Soviet policy is usually emphasized. At the same time, no such messianic impulse is routinely attributed to the United States in terms of capitalism, and if antipathy to socialism is mentioned at all, it is couched in "necessary evil" rhetoric—or the necessary evil is implied. Almost as often, the argument does not pit economic systems, but instead presents the ideological struggle as one between democracy (the forces of good) and com-
10 munism (the forces of evil).

A more reasoned way of evaluating ideology as a principal actor is to concede that ideology only partially explains the origins of the Cold War. It was, then, only contributory to the lasting struggle between U.S. and Soviet interests that continues to this day, despite the collective historical agreement that the curtain fell on the final act of the Cold War with the
15 breakup of the Soviet Union.

All such arguments, however, no matter how they express the antagonism between the United States and the Soviet Union, focus on how one or both sides concentrated its resources on a triumph over the competing ideology. Yet, this is a myopic view, as it discounts the fundamental nature and priorities of powerful states. As Mary Hampton points out in a point-
20 counterpoint on this topic, the vital interests of every state, powerful or relatively powerless, are not defined by ideology but by national security. Furthermore, a state will always seek to preserve its security, which might involve an internal shift in policy or new or shifting alliances; it will act, first and foremost, in accordance with its own power and the power distribution among states with which it is allied.

> **FOR QUESTION 2, CONSIDER EACH ANSWER INDIVIDUALLY AND CHOOSE <u>ALL</u> THAT APPLY.**

2. Which is the first sentence in this passage to clearly reflect the author's perspective on a question posed earlier in the passage?
   - (A) Sentence 5 ("Almost as often … the forces of evil.")
   - (B) Sentence 8 ("All such arguments … competing ideology.")
   - (C) Sentence 10 ("As Mary Hampton … by national security.")

3. In the passage, "discounts" (line 18) most nearly means
   - (A) reduces the price of.
   - (B) deduces.
   - (C) dismisses.
   - (D) reduces the scope of.
   - (E) conduces.

> **FOR QUESTION 4, CONSIDER EACH ANSWER INDIVIDUALLY AND CHOOSE <u>ALL</u> THAT APPLY.**

4. It can be inferred from the passage that the author believes
   - (A) the Cold War has not ended.
   - (B) those who argue that ideology was a leading cause of the Cold War have a bias toward their own ideology.
   - (C) ideology does not fully explain the origins of the Cold War.

QUESTIONS 5–7 ARE BASED ON THE FOLLOWING PASSAGE.

The precipitate rise in the incidence of type 1, or juvenile, diabetes, as well as the startling decrease in average age at onset, has led to a nearly commensurate rise in causation hypotheses. The single factor that scientists have most commonly and consistently linked with the rise of cases of type 1 diabetes is weight gain, and, indeed, children's weights are increasing
5 generation by generation, and the greater BMI (body mass index), the younger the child is likely to be at the age of onset. Other factors linked to this rise in incidence and decrease in average of age of onset and tracked with varying degrees of success in recent studies include psychological stress, the increased wealth of the homes in which the children reside, the increased levels of hygiene in the homes in which the children reside, and nourishment
10 by infant formula during the first six months of life. Some of these theories have garnered more academic support than others, but, no matter how much support they have received, correlation is not causation.

5. The writer mentions greater BMI at earlier ages in this paragraph in order to
   - (A) introduce a common causation hypothesis.
   - (B) provide support for an implied argument.
   - (C) reinforce the importance of a healthful diet for children.
   - (D) provide a possible explanation for the confusion of cause and correlation.
   - (E) cast doubt on studies that collect data on wealth and hygiene.

6. Which of the following, if it were true, would most seriously weaken the import of a specific data set suggesting a correlation?

(A) The average age at onset of type 1 diabetes decreased by one year over a period of just five years.

(B) Nourishment by baby formula has not been correlated to a rise in BMI.

(C) Among stress factors, only poor performance in school and divorce have been shown to correlate with increased incidence of type 1 diabetes.

(D) The incidence of type 1 diabetes is rising at a slower rate among children who are not overweight.

(E) There is a higher rate of type 1 diabetes in households with incomes of more than $80,000 than in households with lower incomes.

7. Which of the following statements does the passage most clearly support?

(A) The weight-gain theory originated before the other theories.

(B) There are reasons to give the stress, hygiene, wealth, and formula theories less credence than the weight-gain theory.

(C) None of the theories has shown a significant correlation with rising incidence.

(D) Only one of the theories has been linked to younger age at onset.

(E) The weight-gain theory is universally accepted by scientists.

QUESTIONS 8–9 ARE BASED ON THE FOLLOWING PASSAGE.

Robert Frost is often categorized as an anti-Romantic writer, that is, as a poet whose poetry contradicts the ideals of Romanticism as embodied in the works of Wordsworth, Keats, Shelley, and others. **Simultaneously, he is categorized as an anti-modernist, a poet who has little in common with his contemporaries, Eliot, Pound, Joyce, Woolf, and others.**
5 Nevertheless, because modernists declared that modernism was, among other things, the rejection of Romanticism, there can be only partial validity in the claim that Frost was both anti-Romantic and anti-modernist. **Instead, as the poems bear out, Frost was at once neither and a bit of both, and one does not have to look far in the poems for substantiation.** Whether the reader is "Stopping by Woods" or out among the "Birches," nature and wildness
10 are the gateways to introspection and imagination, even if emotion receives short shrift. At the same time, modernism asserts itself—albeit in traditional poetic form—in poems such as "After Apple Picking," with its evocation of a transitional state of consciousness; and in "The Death of the Hired Man," "Desert Places," and "Acquainted with the Night" with their experience of alienation, loss, and despair.

8. It can be inferred that the author judges which of the following characteristics as most clearly defining or epitomizing Romanticism?

(A) The reliance on traditional poetic forms

(B) The rejection of modernism

(C) Nature and wildness as the gateway to introspection and imagination

(D) Poems such as "Stopping by Woods" and "Birches"

(E) Poems that evoke a transitional state of consciousness

9. In the passage, what is the primary purpose of the two groups of words in boldface type?

   (A) The first provides contrast to the sentence that precedes it; the second expands upon and elucidates the sentence that precedes it.

   (B) The first provides background information that leads up to the argument; the second presents the argument.

   (C) The first reinforces the argument through contrast; the second explains the argument through explanation and expansion.

   (D) The first states a position that the argument as a whole contradicts; the second presents the argument.

   (E) The first provides contrast to the sentence that precedes it; the second provides evidence that supports the argument.

QUESTIONS 10–11 ARE BASED ON THE FOLLOWING PASSAGE.

When explaining the issues of urbanization in Africa of the late twentieth century, some textbooks conflate effects of the phenomenon with effects of urbanization in the newly industrialized cities of England in the early nineteenth century. That is, some historians restrict their analysis to the problems of overcrowding, lack of sanitation, and inadequate
5 housing that occur in the wake of rapid mass movement from rural to urban areas. Their analysis ignores arguments, such as those put forth by the 1996 UN Habitat II conference, suggesting that economies of scale are preferable for the delivery of health care, clean water, electricity, and other needs. It further overlooks the freedoms available to women in the cities, where they may escape tribal or religious practices, or find fulfillment in both traditional
10 and nontraditional roles.

10. The author of the passage would most likely consider which of the following ideas most similar to the reasoning of historians mentioned in lines 3–5?

    (A) Economies of scale is a relatively recent economic concept that suggests, not entirely accurately, that bigger is always better.

    (B) The problems of overcrowding, lack of sanitation, and inadequate housing also occurred in major U.S. cities during the Industrial Revolution.

    (C) The increased disparity in economic class in today's Mumbai cannot be attributed to globalization alone.

    (D) Urbanization has a negative effect on traditional social mores and usually proves disruptive to cultural unity.

    (E) The recent economic crises in Ireland may best be explained by examining financial crises in the United States in the late nineteenth century.

11. Which of the following, if it were true, most seriously undermines the support that the final sentence provides for the claim?

    (A) Urban women are more likely than men to have to deal directly with the problems of lack of sanitation.

    (B) Women in large urban centers often achieve a higher level of education than they achieve in rural areas.

    (C) Many rural women find fulfillment through local tribal and religious practices.

    (D) Inadequate housing in the cities often offers more advantages than adequate housing in rural areas.

    (E) Women in large urban centers often work in the marketplace.

QUESTIONS 12–14 ARE BASED ON THE FOLLOWING PASSAGE.

Andrew Dickson White famously asserted that Darwin's *Origin of the Species* came "into the theological world like a plough into an ant-hill." At all costs, the anthill had to be rebuilt with some ants reconstructing the same structure and others making only slight alterations to it. Among the many ants rebuilding the hill was Teilhard de Chardin, who, among other
5 things, posited (without so much as a wink!) that the descent of man was actually the ascent of man. His new anthill took shape in *The Phenomenon of Man,* which Julian Huxley would subsequently hail as the synthesis of the "whole of knowable reality" and a triumph of human significance. Yet, the phrase "whole of knowable reality" is, along, of course, with Teilhard's fatuous scientific arguments, a clue to just how scientifically unpalatable this
10 particular philosophically respected, yet scientifically incoherent reconstruction of the anthill was. For example, P. B. Medawar found such flowery, unscientific, and abstract language "suffocating"—and the very obfuscation of sense.

FOR QUESTION 12, CONSIDER EACH ANSWER INDIVIDUALLY AND CHOOSE ALL THAT APPLY.

---

12. The sentence "Among the many . . . the ascent of man" (lines 4–6) serves which of the following purposes in the passage?

    (A) It counters the argument expressed in the preceding sentence.

    (B) It provides evidence for the central argument or proposition of the passage.

    (C) It makes an assertion that subsequent sentences will contradict.

13. It can be inferred that P. B. Medawar took issue with all of the following aspects of *The Phenomenon of Man* EXCEPT the

    (A) blurring of scientific fact.

    (B) attempt to rebuild the anthill.

    (C) lack of concreteness and specificity.

    (D) rebuttal of Darwin's ideas in poetic language.

    (E) obfuscation of sense.

14. In the passage, "hail" (line 7) most nearly means

    (A) be a native of.

    (B) call for.

    (C) greet.

    (D) acclaim.

    (E) precipitate.

QUESTION 15 IS BASED ON THE FOLLOWING PASSAGE.

The pivotal considerations affecting the design of any stationary robotic arm are the central tasks and workspace, which will, in turn, affect the desired degrees of freedom (DOF). A relatively simple design might have just 3 DOFs—not counting any additional DOFs on the end effector or gripper. When designers create an FBD (free body diagram) for a new robotic
5 arm, other considerations reflected in that diagram will include the limitations of each DOF, which should be accounted for in the FBD by annotations showing maximum joint angles and exact arm link lengths. Engineers commonly use a coordinate system known as the Denavit-Hartenberg (D-H) Convention for this purpose.

15. According to the information in this passage, in what order would these steps in the design of a robotic arm most likely take place?

(A) Determine DOFs, plan for D-H, draw FBD.

(B) Determine maximum joint angles, draw FBD, add end effector or gripper.

(C) Draw FBD, annotate joints according to D-H system, determine DOFs.

(D) Identify robotic task(s), determine DOFs, create FBD with D-H.

(E) Create FBD, determine DOFs, add end effector DOF.

ANSWER KEY AND EXPLANATIONS

1. A	6. D	11. C
2. C	7. B	12. B
3. C	8. C	13. B
4. A, B	9. B	14. D
5. A	10. E	15. D

QUESTION 1 IS BASED ON THE FOLLOWING PASSAGE.

Prosopagnosia, or face blindness, was lately given a boost in long-overdue recognition as a genetic disorder when the distinguished professor of neurology and best-selling author Oliver Sacks described his own affliction with the disease. Like other proposagnosiacs, Sacks has a fundamental inability to recognize faces, and not just the faces of random strangers or
5 people he met for the first time last week. One index to the profundity of Sacks's problem is reflected in a study that found that proposagnosiacs who looked at photos of their own family members were unable to recognize 30% of the faces. Sacks himself admits that he often does not recognize a person whom he has met just five minutes before.

Passage Summary: The passage introduces the phenomenon of prosopagnosia to the general reader through the lens of Oliver Sacks's experience of the disease. It briefly explains what prosopagnosia, or face blindness, is.

Question

1. The passage achieves all of the following purposes EXCEPT

    (A) explain why prosopagnosia was given recognition as a genetic disorder.

    (B) tell or imply how prosopagnosia manifests itself.

    (C) cite research that helps define the challenges faced by prosopagnosiacs.

    (D) personalize and humanize the disorder known as prosopagnosia.

    (E) imply the severity of the challenges faced by prosopagnosiacs.

Answer Explanation

The correct answer is (A). This question involves main idea and supporting details. The passage briefly tells how prosopagnosia manifests itself (through the inability to recognize faces), choice (B); cites research, choice (C); personalizes and humanizes the issue by attaching a famous name to it, choice (D); and suggests the severity of the disease, choice (E), by suggesting that subjects don't recognize their own family members or people they've met five minutes earlier. Therefore, choices (B), (C), (D), and (E) are incorrect answers to the question. What the passage doesn't tell is why the disease received attention as a genetic order, choice (A). (It implies the disease has, in the past, received more attention as a disease arising from other causes.)

QUESTIONS 2–4 ARE BASED ON THE FOLLOWING PASSAGE.

Was ideology the leading actor in the unfinished drama that we call the Cold War? This question is endlessly disputed, often by attributing to the Soviets, as George F. Kennan was among the first to do, and to do at great length (in what became known as the "long telegram"), a messianic impulse in terms of communism. Similarly, the centrality of antipathy
5 to capitalism in Soviet policy is usually emphasized. At the same time, no such messianic impulse is routinely attributed to the United States in terms of capitalism, and if antipathy to socialism is mentioned at all, it is couched in "necessary evil" rhetoric—or the necessary evil is implied. Almost as often, the argument does not pit economic systems, but instead presents the ideological struggle as one between democracy (the forces of good) and com-
10 munism (the forces of evil).

A more reasoned way of evaluating ideology as a principal actor is to concede that ideology only partially explains the origins of the Cold War. It was, then, only contributory to the lasting struggle between U.S. and Soviet interests that continues to this day, despite the collective historical agreement that the curtain fell on the final act of the Cold War with the
15 breakup of the Soviet Union.

All such arguments, however, no matter how they express the antagonism between the United States and the Soviet Union, focus on how one or both sides concentrated its resources on a triumph over the competing ideology. Yet, this is a myopic view, as it discounts the fundamental nature and priorities of powerful states. As Mary Hampton points out in a point-
20 counterpoint on this topic, the vital interests of every state, powerful or relatively powerless, are not defined by ideology but by national security. Furthermore, a state will always seek to preserve its security, which might involve an internal shift in policy or new or shifting alliances; it will act, first and foremost, in accordance with its own power and the power distribution among states with which it is allied.

Passage Summary: The passage argues that ideology was not a cause of the Cold War. The ideological argument, the writer explains, typically asserts that the Soviet Union alone was messianic and that its system, unlike the capitalist system, was evil. The author acknowledges in the second paragraph that it is more rational to think of ideology as one cause, not the leading cause, of the Cold War, but then, in the third paragraph, the author calls any argument for ideology myopic, or shortsighted. Instead, the writer suggests that the Cold War occurred not because states were acting to preserve their ideology, but because states were acting to preserve their national security.

Question

2. Which is the first sentence in this passage to clearly reflect the author's perspective on a question posed earlier in the passage?

   (A) Sentence 5 ("Almost as often … the forces of evil.")

   (B) Sentence 8 ("All such arguments … competing ideology.")

   (C) Sentence 10 ("As Mary Hampton … by national security.")

Answer Explanation

The correct answer is (C). This question asks about author's perspective. The only question posed in the passage is whether ideology was a leading cause of the Cold War. Sentence 5 doesn't answer that question; instead, it helps explain the typical ideological argument, so eliminate choice (A). Sentence 8 makes a summary statement about the ideological arguments, but it doesn't answer the question, so eliminate choice (B). Sentence 10, choice (C), most clearly implies the answer, which is no: ideology was not the main cause; the vital interest of national security was.

NOTE

In the computer-version of the GRE, this would be a select-in-passage question rather than multiple choice.

Remember to read
the sentences
around the sentence
in question for its
context. Substituting
the answer choices
in the sentence may
also help.

Question

3. In the passage, "discounts" (line 18) most nearly means
    (A) reduces the price of.
    (B) deduces.
    (C) dismisses.
    (D) reduces the scope of.
    (E) conduces.

Answer Explanation

The correct answer is (C). This is an easy-to-spot word meaning question. In the context in which it appears, "discounts" has nothing to do with price—figuring out (deducing), or leading to (conducing) a price—so eliminate choices (A), (B), and (E). You can also eliminate choice (D) because the writer uses "discounts" to suggest choice (C), dismissing or failing to pay attention to, rather than reducing the scope of, states, both fundamental concepts related to the nature and priorities of powerful states.

Question

4. It can be inferred from the passage that the author believes
    (A) the Cold War has not ended.
    (B) those who argue that ideology was a leading cause of the Cold War have a bias toward their own ideology.
    (C) ideology does not fully explain the origins of the Cold War.

Answer Explanation

The correct answers are (A) and (B). This question tests your ability to understand the main idea of the passage and is also a multiple-choice question—select one or more answer choices. There are two clues that suggest that the author believes the Cold War is not over. First, in line 1, the Cold War is called "an unfinished drama." In the second paragraph, the author calls the Cold War a "lasting struggle . . . that continues to this day." Therefore, choices (A) and (B) should be selected because the author spends much of the first paragraph explaining that those who argue that ideology was a leading cause of the Cold War have a bias toward their own ideology. (Don't be thrown off by the notion that the author presents this idea through the single lens of what appears to be Western, capitalist analysis; the idea of bias is still clear in the passage.) Finally, while it is true that the author mentions the view that ideology doesn't fully explain the origins of the Cold War, it is the author's belief that ideology doesn't explain the origins at all; therefore, you should not select choice (C).

QUESTIONS 5–7 ARE BASED ON THE FOLLOWING PASSAGE.

The precipitate rise in the incidence of type 1, or juvenile, diabetes, as well as the startling decrease in average age at onset, has led to a nearly commensurate rise in causation hypotheses. The single factor that scientists have most commonly and consistently linked with the rise of cases of type 1 diabetes is weight gain, and, indeed, children's weights are increasing
5   generation by generation, and the greater BMI (body mass index), the younger the child is likely to be at the age of onset. Other factors linked to this rise in incidence and decrease in average of age of onset and tracked with varying degrees of success in recent studies

include psychological stress, the increased wealth of the homes in which the children reside, the increased levels of hygiene in the homes in which the children reside, and nourishment
10 by infant formula during the first six months of life. Some of these theories have garnered more academic support than others, but, no matter how much support they have received, correlation is not causation.

Passage Summary: This passage mentions various theories, or causation hypotheses, for the rise in incidence, or decrease in age of onset of type 1 diabetes. It begins with what has been shown to be the most common and consistent correlation with the rise of the disease, weight gain; it also presents the correlation between BMI and early onset. The writer goes on to mention other correlations, some of which have more support than others: psychological stress, household wealth, household cleanliness, and infant formula. Yet, the author warns, none of these correlations is necessarily a cause.

Question

5. The writer mentions greater BMI at earlier ages in the paragraph in order to
   (A) introduce a common causation hypothesis.
   (B) provide support for an implied argument.
   (C) reinforce the importance of a healthful diet for children.
   (D) provide a possible explanation for the confusion of cause and correlation.
   (E) cast doubt on studies that collect data on wealth and hygiene.

Answer Explanation

The correct answer is (A). Like many of the questions on the GRE, this question is about main idea and supporting details. The passage implies that scientists have most consistently explored weight gain as a cause of type 1 diabetes; weight gain is most commonly and consistently linked with the rise in incidence. While scientists have found that the increased incidence correlates with this rise, not that it causes the disease, this idea nevertheless constitutes a causation hypothesis, choice (A). Choice (B) can be eliminated because this paragraph is informational; there is no implied argument. The passage does not state or imply anything about a healthful diet, so choice (C) is incorrect. Choice (D) is also incorrect because the passage clearly states that psychological stress, increased wealth, increased levels of hygiene, and infant formula have all been linked either to the rise in incidence or to the decrease in average age of onset of the disease. The passage does not cast doubt on any studies, so choice (E) is also wrong.

Question

6. Which of the following, if it were true, would most seriously weaken the import of a specific data set suggesting a correlation?
   (A) The average age at onset of type 1 diabetes decreased by one year over a period of just five years.
   (B) Nourishment by baby formula has not been correlated to a rise in BMI.
   (C) Among stress factors, only poor performance in school and divorce have been shown to correlate with increased incidence of type 1 diabetes.
   (D) The incidence of type 1 diabetes is rising at a slower rate among children who are not overweight.
   (E) There is a higher rate of type 1 diabetes in households with incomes of more than $80,000 than in households with lower incomes.

TIP

You may have found question 5 challenging. Rather than mark it with the idea of returning to it at the end of the test, try the other two questions about this passage and then return to this question. It may seem easier after you've worked through the other questions related to the passage.

TIP

Remember "if it were true" signals that you're looking for an answer that isn't true. Think of it as another kind of "EXCEPT" or "NOT" question.

Answer Explanation

The correct answer is (D). This is an application question. Both choices (A) and (E) would strengthen the correlation, so they should be eliminated. Choice (B) should also be eliminated because, among other reasons, the question refers to a single data set. Choice (C) is also incorrect because the cited forms of stress do fall under the category of psychological stress. Even though the incidence of type 1 diabetes is rising at a slower rate among children who are not overweight, it is still rising; therefore, choice (D) undercuts or weakens the correlation between being overweight and developing the disease.

Question

7. Which of the following statements does the passage most clearly support?
    (A) The weight-gain theory originated before the other theories.
    (B) There are reasons to give the stress, hygiene, wealth, and formula theories less credence than the weight-gain theory.
    (C) None of the theories has shown a significant correlation with rising incidence.
    (D) Only one of the theories has been linked to younger age at onset.
    (E) The weight-gain theory is universally accepted by scientists.

Answer Explanation

The correct answer is (B). This is another application question. There is no evidence in the passage to suggest that the weight-gain theory arose before other theories, or that the weight-gain theory is universally accepted by scientists, so eliminate choices (A) and (E). The passage does, however, say that the weight-gain theory has been most commonly and consistently linked with the rise of type 1 diabetes. Because all of the theories have shown a significant correlation with rising incidence, choice (C) is incorrect. Choice (D) is incorrect because it's not clear which, or if only one, of the theories among the final theories discussed has been linked to the rise in incidence or the decrease in average age of onset.

QUESTIONS 8–9 ARE BASED ON THE FOLLOWING PASSAGE.

Robert Frost is often categorized as an anti-Romantic writer, that is, as a poet whose poetry contradicts the ideals of Romanticism as embodied in the works of Wordsworth, Keats, Shelley, and others. **Simultaneously, he is categorized as an anti-modernist, a poet who has little in common with his contemporaries, Eliot, Pound, Joyce, Woolf, and others.**
5 Nevertheless, because modernists declared that modernism was, among other things, the rejection of Romanticism, there can be only partial validity in the claim that Frost was both anti-Romantic and anti-modernist. **Instead, as the poems bear out, Frost was at once neither and a bit of both, and one does not have to look far in the poems for substantiation.** Whether the reader is "Stopping by Woods" or out among the "Birches," nature and wildness
10 are the gateways to introspection and imagination, even if emotion receives short shrift. At the same time, modernism asserts itself—albeit in traditional poetic form—in poems such as "After Apple Picking," with its evocation of a transitional state of consciousness; and in "The Death of the Hired Man," "Desert Places," and "Acquainted with the Night" with their experience of alienation, loss, and despair.

Passage Summary: The author argues that while some people call Frost anti-Romantic and others call him anti-modern, both labels can apply—and both labels don't apply. The author then provides evidence to show that Frost was Romantic, at least in one sense, while admitting that the poems cited are not true to all aspects of Romanticism. The writer also provides evidence that Frost was modern, at least in one sense, while also admitting that Frost was traditional in terms of poetic form.

Question

8. It can be inferred that the author judges which of the following characteristics as most clearly defining or epitomizing Romanticism?

    (A) The reliance on traditional poetic forms

    (B) The rejection of modernism

    (C) Nature and wildness as the gateway to introspection and imagination

    (D) Poems such as "Stopping by Woods" and "Birches"

    (E) Poems that evoke a transitional state of consciousness

Answer Explanation

The correct answer is (C). This question asks only about supporting details. Choices (D) and (E) can be eliminated because poems are not characteristics. The phrase about "traditional poetic forms" is couched in the discussion of what modernism is "not," so choice (A) is unlikely to be the answer. Nothing in the passage suggests that Romanticism is the rejection of modernism, so choice (B) is incorrect. The answer to this question appears in the sentence directly following the second boldfaced sentence. Here, the author is explaining why Frost "was at once neither and a bit of both." Since the second of the two sentences that follow is about modernism, it can be inferred that the first is about Romanticism. That is where the words about nature and wildness appear.

Question

9. In the passage, what is the primary purpose of the two groups of words in boldface type?

    (A) The first provides contrast to the sentence that precedes it; the second expands upon and elucidates the sentence that precedes it.

    (B) The first provides background information that leads up to the argument; the second presents the argument.

    (C) The first reinforces the argument through contrast; the second explains the argument through explanation and expansion.

    (D) The first states a position that the argument as a whole contradicts; the second presents the argument.

    (E) The first provides contrast to the sentence that precedes it; the second provides evidence that supports the argument.

Answer Explanation

The correct answer is (B). Did you notice that the question is asking you to apply information to come up with your answer? While choice (A) provides an accurate description of what the sentences do in the passage, it doesn't describe the primary purpose of the two groups of words in bold type. You can also eliminate choices (C), (D), and (E) because they don't accurately explain the purpose of the word groups. Choice (B) is the best answer—the most accurate answer—but only reading through all the answer choices will assure you of this.

QUESTIONS 10–11 ARE BASED ON THE FOLLOWING PASSAGE.

When explaining the issues of urbanization in Africa of the late twentieth century, some textbooks conflate effects of the phenomenon with effects of urbanization in the newly industrialized cities of England in the early nineteenth century. That is, some historians restrict their analysis to the problems of overcrowding, lack of sanitation, and inadequate
5 housing that occur in the wake of rapid mass movement from rural to urban areas. Their analysis ignores arguments, such as those put forth by the 1996 UN Habitat II conference, suggesting that economies of scale are preferable for the delivery of health care, clean water, electricity, and other needs. It further overlooks the freedoms available to women in the cities, where they may escape tribal or religious practices, or find fulfillment in both traditional
10 and nontraditional roles.

Passage Summary: The passage says that some textbooks mistakenly merge the issues of urbanization in late twentieth-century Africa with the issues of urbanization in the industrialized cities of England during the early nineteenth century. That is, they explain a contemporary or recent problem by providing the same explanations that have been given for a much different time and place. According to the author, these historians ignore twentieth-century ideas such as economies of scale and the changed and changing status of women.

Question

10. The author of the passage would most likely consider which of the following ideas most similar to the reasoning of historians mentioned in lines 3–5?

   (A) Economies of scale is a relatively recent economic concept that suggests, not entirely accurately, that bigger is always better.

   (B) The problems of overcrowding, lack of sanitation, and inadequate housing also occurred in major U.S. cities during the Industrial Revolution.

   (C) The increased disparity in economic class in today's Mumbai cannot be attributed to globalization alone.

   (D) Urbanization has a negative effect on traditional social mores and usually proves disruptive to cultural unity.

   (E) The recent economic crises in Ireland may best be explained by examining financial crises in the United States in the late nineteenth century.

Answer Explanation

The correct answer is (E). This is another application question. The passage makes it clear that historians don't take into account the notion of economies of scale, so choice (A) is incorrect. Choices (B), (C), and (D) take the ideas of the passage off into entirely new directions, unrelated to the reasoning specified in the question, so they should be eliminated. Only choice (E) suggests a line of reasoning in which the problems of today are explained by the events of the past.

Question

11. Which of the following, if true, most seriously undermines the support that the final sentence provides for the claim?

(A) Urban women are more likely than men to have to deal directly with the problems of lack of sanitation.

(B) Women in large urban centers often achieve a higher level of education than they achieve in rural areas.

(C) Many rural women find fulfillment through local tribal and religious practices.

(D) Inadequate housing in the cities often offers more advantages than adequate housing in rural areas.

(E) Women in large urban centers often work in the marketplace.

Answer Explanation

The correct answer is (C). How did you do with this application question? The claim is that some textbooks erroneously suggest that urbanization in Africa today leads to the same problems as it did, or is much the same phenomenon as it was, during the Industrial Revolution. The final sentence of the paragraph supports that claim by suggesting that women in particular benefit from urbanization (that is, it's not necessarily the nineteenth-century England industrial scourge) because their movement from rural areas to the cities can liberate women from tribal and religious practices, which, the passage implies, can oppress them or diminish their sphere of influence. Therefore, to undermine the claim, the correct answer has to say something about how women are not diminished by tribal life, or that city life oppresses them. Choice (D) can be immediately eliminated because it doesn't relate to women. Choices (A) and (E) neither support nor weaken the claim, whereas choice (B) strengthens it. Choice (C) is then the only correct answer because it claims that many rural women are fulfilled through local tribal and religious practices.

QUESTIONS 12–14 ARE BASED ON THE FOLLOWING PASSAGE.

Andrew Dickson White famously asserted that Darwin's *Origin of the Species* came "into the theological world like a plough into an ant-hill." At all costs, the anthill had to be rebuilt with some ants reconstructing the same structure and others making only slight alterations to it. Among the many ants rebuilding the hill was Teilhard de Chardin, who, among other
5   things, posited (without so much as a wink!) that the descent of man was actually the ascent of man. His new anthill took shape in *The Phenomenon of Man,* which Julian Huxley would subsequently hail as the synthesis of the "whole of knowable reality" and a triumph of human significance. Yet, the phrase "whole of knowable reality" is, along, of course, with Teilhard's fatuous scientific arguments, a clue to just how scientifically unpalatable this
10 particular philosophically respected, yet scientifically incoherent reconstruction of the anthill was. For example, P. B. Medawar found such flowery, unscientific, and abstract language "suffocating"—and the very obfuscation of sense.

Passage Summary: The passage begins with White's famous response to Darwin's *Origin of the Species*, which suggests that Darwin's huge, new, powerful ideas completely upset the little world of ants—that is, people who were used to thinking a certain way and simply could not accept the fundamental shift in worldview that Darwin presented. The implied claim is that ants began rebuilding the anthill, or that "little" people with little ideas began to refute Darwin's colossal ideas. One philosopher the passage maligns for "rebuilding," and, therefore, misreading or subverting Darwin, is Pierre Teilhard de Chardin. The passage also mentions responses to Teilhard de Chardin: there was Julian Huxley who lavishly praised the work, and R. P. Medawar who disliked it immensely, in large part because of Teilhard de Chardin's flowery language.

Question

12. The sentence "Among the many . . . the ascent of man" (lines 4–6) serves which of the following purposes in the passage?

   (A) It counters the argument expressed in the preceding sentence.

   (B) It provides evidence for the central argument or proposition of the passage.

   (C) It makes an assertion that subsequent sentences will contradict.

Answer Explanation

The correct answer is (B). Application question stems can take a variety of forms. This is also a multiple-choice question—select one or more answer choices. The anthill simile suggests the response to Darwin. The parenthetical "without so much as a wink" shows the attitude of the writer: he or she is stunned—and disdainful—that Teilhard de Chardin could get away with turning Darwin's ideas upside down to fit his own. Choice (A) is incorrect because the argument is not expressed in Sentence 2. Choice (C) is also incorrect because the subsequent sentences help explain and support the target sentence. On the other hand, choice (B) is correct because the target sentence does provide explanation for the central argument by providing an example of an "ant" and suggesting a response to Darwin that was, at least seemingly, illogical and something that the author clearly regards as ridiculous.

Question

13. It can be inferred that P. B. Medawar took issue with all of the following aspects of *The Phenomenon of Man* EXCEPT the

   (A) blurring of scientific fact.

   (B) attempt to rebuild the anthill.

   (C) lack of concreteness and specificity.

   (D) rebuttal of Darwin's ideas in poetic language.

   (E) obfuscation of sense.

Answer Explanation

The correct answer is (B). Supporting details are the subject of this EXCEPT question. The passage states directly that Teilhard de Chardin's *The Phenomenon of Man* contains absurd scientific arguments and is also scientifically unpalatable because of the very "flowery" way in which the work is written. When the author calls Teilhard's work an "incoherent reconstruction," he or she is stating that it lacked sense. Medawar also takes issue with how the book obfuscates sense. Eliminate both choices (A) and (E). Medawar's complaint about the flowery language eliminates choices (C) and (D) as well. Medawar does not, however, object to Teilhard's or anyone else's attempt to "rebuild the anthill"—or rebut Darwin, so choice (B) is correct.

Question

14. In the passage, "hail" (line 7) most nearly means

    (A) be a native of.

    (B) call for.

    (C) greet.

    (D) acclaim.

    (E) precipitate.

Answer Explanation

The correct answer is (D). Choice (A), "be a native of," doesn't relate to the context in any way. Because Huxley didn't "call for" Teilhard de Chardin's work (instead, he responded to it), choice (B) is also incorrect. Choice (C) should be eliminated because it doesn't suggest the positive response alluded to in the passage. Any of the meanings of "precipitate" don't make sense in the context of a critical response to a work, so choice (E) is incorrect. "Acclaim," choice (D), fits the context because it suggests a positive response.

QUESTION 15 IS BASED ON THE FOLLOWING PASSAGE.

The pivotal considerations affecting the design of any stationary robotic arm are the central tasks and workspace, which will, in turn, affect the desired degrees of freedom (DOF). A relatively simple design might have just 3 DOFs—not counting any additional DOFs on the end effector or gripper. When designers create an FBD (free body diagram) for a new robotic
5 arm, other considerations reflected in that diagram will include the limitations of each DOF, which should be accounted for in the FBD by annotations showing maximum joint angles and exact arm link lengths. Engineers commonly use a coordinate system known as the Denavit-Hartenberg (D-H) Convention for this purpose.

Passage Summary: The passage presents a few of the basic concepts in the design of a robotic arm, including identifying the central tasks and the workspace, determining the degrees of freedom, making a diagram, and labeling that diagram with coordinates.

Question

15. According to the information in this passage, in what order would these steps in the design of a robotic arm most likely take place?

    (A) Determine DOFs, plan for D-H, draw FBD.

    (B) Determine maximum joint angles, draw FBD, add end effector or gripper.

    (C) Draw FBD, annotate joints according to D-H system, determine DOFs.

    (D) Identify robotic task(s), determine DOFs, create FBD with D-H.

    (E) Create FBD, determine DOFs, add end effector DOF.

Answer Explanation

The correct answer is (D). To give you more practice, here is another application question. The passage implies that the first considerations in this design are the central tasks and the workspace; these must be known in order to determine the degrees of freedom (DOF) that the robotic arm must have. Although it may not be clear on first reading, the order of information in the paragraph is basically sequential; therefore, choices (A), (B), (C), and (E) do not follow the paragraph order, and so must be eliminated.

SUMMING IT UP

- There are approximately ten reading comprehension passages on the Verbal Reasoning sections of the GRE.

- Most passages will be one paragraph in length, though you will find one or two passages that have multiple paragraphs.

- Passages may be informational, analytical, or persuasive.

- There are three formats for questions: multiple-choice questions—select one answer choice, multiple-choice questions—select one or more answer choices, and select-in-passage answers.

- The select-in-passage questions on the computerized test will require students to choose a sentence within the passage to highlight as the answer. For international students taking the paper-and-pencil version, the select-in-passage questions will be in the form of multiple-choice questions—select one answer choice questions.

- Computer versions of the GRE will have approximately 20 questions for each of the two Verbal Reasoning sections, of which perhaps more than half will be reading comprehension questions. The time limit is 30 minutes. Students taking the paper-and-pencil version will have 25 questions to be completed in 35 minutes.

- Multiple-choice questions—select one answer choice questions are preceded by ovals. Multiple-choice questions—select one or more answer choices are preceded by squares.

- Multiple-choice questions—select one answer choice questions are followed by a list of five possible answer options. Multiple-choice questions—select one or more answer choices are followed by a list of only three answers.

- Answer all questions based only on the information contained in the passage. Don't use anything from your own experience or outside knowledge.

- Don't allow your own opinions to enter into your selection of an answer.

- You will find that certain types of questions recur among the reading comprehension questions: main idea (major point), supporting details (minor points), author's perspective, application, and word meaning.

- Remember to use the following active reading strategies when reading the passages:
  - o Identify the topic, main idea, thesis, or proposition.
  - o Clarify your understanding.
  - o Summarize what you've read.

- The following strategies can be helpful for both kinds of multiple-choice questions:
  - o Restate the question.
  - o Try answering the question before you read the answer choices.
  - o Read all the answers before you choose.
  - o Compare answer choices to each other and the question.
  - o Avoid selecting an answer you don't fully understand.
  - o Choose the *best* answer.

- o Pay attention to structure and structural clues.

- o Don't select an answer just because it's true.

- o Substitute answer choices in word meaning questions.

- o Choose the answer that doesn't fit for EXCEPT questions.

- The following strategy applies to multiple-choice questions—select more than one answer choice questions: *choose an answer that answers the question on its own.*

- In addition to choosing an answer that stands on its own, the following strategy can be helpful for answering select-in-passage questions: *match the sentence to the information.*

Strategies for Text Completion Questions

OVERVIEW

- Basic information about text completion questions
- Strategies for text completion
- Practice questions
- Answer key and explanations
- Summing it up

The GRE revised General Test has at least two Verbal Reasoning sections. Reading comprehension, text completion, and sentence equivalence questions are mixed within the Verbal Reasoning sections. This chapter describes the question formats for text completion test items and also provides a discussion of strategies to help you answer this question type.

BASIC INFORMATION ABOUT TEXT COMPLETION QUESTIONS

The text completion questions on the GRE assess your ability not only to actively interpret and evaluate what you read, but also to supply words and phrases whose meaning is consistent with the ideas that are presented. You will complete text by choosing among three to five options to fill in one, two, or three blanks in a passage. You can expect around one quarter to one third of the questions on each verbal section of the GRE to be text completion questions, that is, five to seven questions.

The text completion items (as well as the sentence equivalence items) test your vocabulary. (In some ways, they take the place of the antonyms and analogies questions that used to be on the GRE.) To do well on these questions, you need to know "big" words—words such as *refulgent, dissimulation,* and *deleterious.* Not all the words are a test of the size of one's vocabulary, however. Some items will involve words that are close in meaning or an unusual meaning of a familiar word.

As you will see in reading this chapter, the text completion items are not just about vocabulary. They also test your reading comprehension skills. Furthermore, you may also have to apply your knowledge of grammar and usage in order to choose the best answers.

Regardless of the number of blanks, each question is worth one point. All the blanks for a test item must be answered correctly in order to earn a point for that question.

Passages and Question Formats

Unlike the reading comprehension questions, the text completion items offer a predictable sameness of format. Overall, the text completion passages are much less intimidating. Generally speaking, you will need to spend less time with a text completion passage than with a reading comprehension passage, and, of course, the shorter length of a text completion passage, compared to the typical reading comprehension passage, also contributes significantly to greater ease of reading.

Text completion questions are fill-in-the-blank questions. The blanks are embedded in passages of different lengths, ranging from one sentence to approximately five sentences.

- In single sentences, you will typically be required to fill in just one blank. There are, however, exceptions.

- In passages that consist of multiple sentences, you will most likely be required to fill in two or three blanks.

Text completion items are interspersed with the other test items in the Verbal Reasoning sections. Each text completion question appears on a separate screen. All passages are short enough to display on a single screen; you won't need to scroll or change screens to answer a text completion question.

The Direction Line and Answer Choices

Text completion items have only one type of direction, which is worded something like the following:

> FOR QUESTIONS 1–10, CHOOSE <u>ONE</u> ANSWER FOR EACH BLANK. SELECT FROM THE APPROPRIATE COLUMN FOR EACH BLANK. CHOOSE THE ANSWER THAT BEST COMPLETES THE SENSE OF THE TEXT.

In most cases, you will be selecting a single word for each blank. Occasionally, you will be presented with a list of phrases or group of words from which to select the answer.

- If the sentence or passage contains only *one blank,* there will be five answer choices listed in a single column.

- If the sentence or passage contains *two blanks,* you will choose the first answer from a column of three choices (Blank (i)) and the second from a second column of three choices (Blank (ii)).

- If the sentence or passage contains *three blanks,* you will choose each answer from one of three columns—Blank (i), Blank (ii), Blank (iii)—with three choices each.

To select an answer, you will click on the cell that contains your answer choice. If you change your mind, clicking on another cell will change your answer.

Using the "Mark" Option

Depending on how the test is going for you, you might consider using the "Mark" option more readily on the text completion and sentence equivalence items than you would on reading comprehension items. Both text completion and sentence equivalence items are quicker to revisit than reading comprehension items. They're shorter and less time-consuming to read and answer.

In addition, each text completion is only one question. When you mark a text completion item to return to, no matter how many blanks it has, you're making a commitment to revisit only about 4 percent of the test section. This is not a huge task to put off until near the end and, therefore, a reasonable strategy to use when your confidence or attention wavers on a question. But be careful that you don't use it too often, or you could find yourself circling back to a quarter of the test.

STRATEGIES FOR TEXT COMPLETION

Text completion questions lend themselves to a variety of specific strategies. As you read through the following strategies, note that the first four are really commonsense reminders.

1. Try answering the question before you read the answer choice(s).
2. Focus on one blank at a time.
3. If there is more than one blank, complete the blanks in the order that makes sense to you.
4. Check your answer(s) in place.

The last four strategies ask you to make use of what you once learned in English composition classes.

1. Use structural clues.
2. Consider tone and style.
3. Consider grammar and usage.
4. Avoid selecting a word or phrase that you don't fully understand or is unfamiliar.

In addition, remember to apply the four test-taking strategies discussed in Chapter 1.

1. Anticipate and use the clock.
2. Skip and return to questions.
3. Eliminate answer choices you know are incorrect.
4. Use educated guessing.

Try Answering the Question Before You Read the Answer Choice(s)

As you read a passage, try to get a clear sense of what the passage is about. Then, before you read the answer choices, fill in the answer blank(s) in your own words. What you come up with doesn't need to be sophisticated or polysyllabic. It just needs to be a word or words that capture the meaning of the sentence. With your answer in mind, check the list of answers, and choose the one that seems to best match your idea.

Try this now with Question 1 below.

> **FOR QUESTION 1, CHOOSE <u>ONE</u> ANSWER FOR THE BLANK. CHOOSE THE ANSWER THAT BEST COMPLETES THE SENSE OF THE TEXT.**

1. Emerging African democracies of the 1960s and 1970s faced insurmountable problems that ranged from lack of infrastructure to borders that ignored ethnic conflict: in fact, these _____ governments were destined to fail.

(A) despotic
(B) ephemeral
(C) incompetent
(D) deteriorating
(E) fledgling

TIP

Remember also that there is no penalty for wrong answers. If you absolutely cannot decide on an answer even through the process of elimination, make your best guess based on what you do know.

ALERT!

If you find test time running out and you still have a number of questions to answer, go quickly through the test looking for text completion and sentence equivalence questions. They're quicker to answer than reading comprehension questions, and a point is a point, no matter what question you answer to earn it.

If you try to fill the blank before you read the answers, you might come up with either the word "new" or "democratic." You can safely eliminate "democratic" because it's highly unlikely that ETS is going to make the answer that simple. That is, the test-item writer isn't going to repeat a word, or form of a word, that already appears in the passage as the correct answer. Your next step, then, is to look for a word in the list that means the same as, or close to the same as, new. "Fledgling" means "young and inexperienced," which suggests the meaning of "new." "Fledgling" is most often applied to birds leaving the nest and trying their wings for the first time, just as the new democracies referred to in the passage were beginning to grow, develop, or "take flight" in a metaphorical sense. **The correct answer is (E).**

Focus on Only One Blank at a Time

The majority of the text completion items will present you with either two blanks or three blanks to fill. When you have multiple blanks to fill, it is best to arrive at the answers by concentrating on just one blank at a time. Try out this strategy as you read the following two-blank item.

> **FOR QUESTION 2, CHOOSE <u>ONE</u> ANSWER FOR EACH BLANK. SELECT FROM THE APPROPRIATE COLUMN FOR EACH BLANK. CHOOSE THE ANSWER THAT BEST COMPLETES THE SENSE OF THE TEXT.**

2. A major part of the body's immune system, the lymphatic system is responsible for producing, maintaining, and distributing lymphocytes (white blood cells that attack bacteria in blood and take the form of T cells and B cells) in the body, as well as for defending the body against pathogens. Besides removing waste, dead blood cells, and toxins from cells and the tissues between them, the lymphatic system also works in concert with the circulatory system to deliver oxygen, nutrients, and hormones from the blood to the cells. The (i) _____ role of the lymphatic system in fighting disease and maintaining homeostasis (ii) _____ .

Blank (i)	Blank (ii)
(A) pivotal	(D) must not be trivial
(B) autonomous	(E) cannot be gainsaid
(C) hypothetical	(F) will not be equivocated

Starting with the first blank might lead you to a word that conveys the importance or centrality of the lymphatic system. You might, for example, come up with the words "key," "major," "necessary," or "central." Reading down the list of answers for Blank (i), you find choice (A), "pivotal," which means "key" or "essential," so this is the answer for Blank (i). But read all the answer choices for Blank (i) just to be sure "pivotal" is the best choice. Once the first blank is filled, it can be easier to come up with the second answer. For example, it makes no sense to say that "the pivotal role must not be trivial." Neither does it make sense to say that "the pivotal role will not be equivocated," meaning "using vague language." Therefore, the correct answer for the second blank is choice (E), "cannot be gainsaid." "Gainsaid" means "denied." **The correct answers are (A) and (E).**

If There is More Than One Blank, Complete the Blanks in the Order That Makes Sense to You

Don't assume that you need to fill the first blank first, the second blank second, and the third blank third. Begin by filling in the blank that is easiest or most obvious to you. Try this strategy now with the following three-blank item.

> **FOR QUESTION 3, CHOOSE <u>ONE</u> ANSWER FOR EACH BLANK. SELECT FROM THE APPROPRIATE COLUMN FOR EACH BLANK. CHOOSE THE ANSWER THAT BEST COMPLETES THE SENSE OF THE TEXT.**

3. Those calling for the regulation of commodities trading are, at best, uninformed. Instead of (i) _____ traders for spikes in prices of wheat, oil, and metals, as well as for the bubbles, legislators would be wiser to consider how speculators help to create (ii) _____ by injecting cash into markets—which contributes to market efficiency. Furthermore, legislators who are gung-ho to rein in traders might bother to note that speculators have little or no effect on the production, and only (iii) _____ effect on the consumption, of goods.

Blank (i)	Blank (ii)	Blank (iii)
(A) regulating	(D) liquidity	(G) minimal
(B) scapegoating	(E) activity	(H) negative
(C) castigating	(F) inventory	(I) lasting

Suppose you read the passage and know that injecting, or moving, cash into markets creates liquidity, so you mark choice (D) for Blank (ii). With "liquidity" in place for Blank (ii), you can now move back to Blank (i) or on to Blank (iii). In either case, you can use the concept of liquidity to help you make sense of the rest of the passage. The more words you fill in, the easier it will be for you to come up with the answer that is most difficult for you. For the record, the correct answer for Blank (i) is choice (B), "scapegoating." Scapegoating means "blaming unfairly." The correct answer for Blank (iii) is choice (G), "minimal." **The correct answers are (B), (D), and (G).**

You will revisit Question 3 and read a more detailed analysis later in this chapter.

Check Your Answer(s) in Place

When you've chosen your answer(s), it's a good idea to reread the question quickly with the answers in place. All the words together should create a unified whole: that is, the meanings should all work together; everything should be grammatically correct; and the tone and style should be consistent.

Use Structural Clues

Many text completion items will take the form of organizational structures for writing that are familiar to you and that you can use to help you determine the correct answer. These structures include sentences and paragraphs that compare, contrast, restate, show causes and/or effects, and present main idea and supporting details. Some of these passages will contain what the test-maker calls "signposts," that is, trigger, signal, or transitional words and phrases to help you understand the meaning of the passage—more specifically, the relationship of ideas in that passage.

You can use the following types of structural clues to help you determine meaning and fill in the blanks of many text completion questions. As you work through various examples, you will note that, in some cases, a single sentence or passage may contain more than one type of structure and structural clue. The following clues can help you identify answers:

- Restatement
- Cause and effect
- Contrast
- Comparison or similarity structure
- Main idea and details

Restatement

Restatement is a presentation of an idea in words other than those used the first time the idea is presented; an amplification or clarification of an idea; or the presentation of an example of the idea. A sentence or passage that uses restatement will most often have two independent clauses joined by a colon, a semicolon, or a correlative conjunction such as *moreover*. Or, a restatement might take the form of two sentences, the second of which begins with a signal word for restatement. (See the box below for signal words.)

Depending on the restatement structure used, one of the following will be apparent:

- Sentence 2 or clause 2 presents in other words the meaning of sentence 1 or clause 1.
- Sentence 2 or clause 2 amplifies or clarifies sentence 1 or clause 1. This is a more likely combination than mere repetition of an idea in other words.
- Sentence 2 or clause 2 exemplifies sentence or clause 1. That is, sentence 2 or clause 2 provides a single example or illustration.

Signals for Restatement

Among the words and phrases that can signal restatement relationships are the following:

for example	*in other words*	*that is*
for instance	*in short*	*this means*
in fact	*namely*	*thus*

Often, you may have to infer the words and phrases that signal restatement, amplification, clarification, or illustration. For an example of restatement, we'll look again at Question 1. You should be able to identify a restatement signal before you read the analysis that follows the question.

> **FOR QUESTION 1, CHOOSE <u>ONE</u> ANSWER FOR THE BLANK. CHOOSE THE ANSWER THAT BEST COMPLETES THE SENSE OF THE TEXT.**

1. Emerging African democracies of the 1960s and 1970s faced insurmountable problems that ranged from lack of infrastructure to borders that ignored ethnic conflict: in fact, these _____ governments were destined to fail.

(A) despotic
(B) ephemeral
(C) incompetent
(D) deteriorating
(E) fledgling

A thought process to work through Question 1 might go something like this:

- Note that the signal phrase "in fact," along with the second clause more or less restating or amplifying the first, signals a restatement.

- Knowing that you're working with restatement, next restate, paraphrase, or summarize the item. Focus on only the parts of the passage that reflect the restatement you want to zero in on. Eliminate extraneous wording. For this passage, you would concentrate on the two main clauses and eliminate the clause that begins with "that ranged from . . . ." You might arrive at this summary: "New African governments faced huge problems; these _____ governments could do nothing but fail."

- The omission of extra words helps make it clear that the word that fits the blank must be a synonym for emerging or new, or it must in some way express a similar or close meaning.

- To arrive at the correct answer, use the process of elimination. The first four choices are not synonyms for new, nor do they evoke something new. Therefore, the correct answer is choice (E), "fledgling."

Go back to Question 1 above and drop out the words "in fact." Reread the passage without those words and you'll see that you're still dealing with restatement, even though it's not quite so apparent. **The correct answer is (E).**

Cause and Effect

A sentence or passage with a cause-and-effect structure expresses the reason(s) someone did something or something occurred, or it expresses the result(s) of an action or event. A cause-and-effect relationship can be expressed in one sentence or in a longer passage.

Cause-and-Effect Signals

Cause-and-effect relationships may or may not include signal words. Among the words and phrases that can signal cause-and-effect relationships are the following:

as a result	*in order to*	*so that*
because	*reason why*	*therefore*
consequently	*since*	*thus*
for	*so*	*why*

Sometimes, you will have to infer cause-and-effect relationships. For example, Question 4 below begins with the infinitive phrase "To defeat the English. . . ." You can and should reasonably infer that this phrase means "[In order to] defeat the English. . . . " or "[Because he wanted to] defeat the English. . . . " This is your first step.

FOR QUESTION 4, CHOOSE ONE ANSWER FOR THE BLANK. CHOOSE THE ANSWER THAT BEST COMPLETES THE SENSE OF THE TEXT.

4. To defeat the English, Metacomet, whom the English called King Philip, knew he had to bring disparate and sometimes warring groups together into a _____.

(A) battalion
(B) community
(C) legation
(D) confederation
(E) hierarchy

An analysis of Question 4 could take this shape:

- Once you know that you're working with cause and effect, begin by restating, paraphrasing, or summarizing the item in a way that reflects your understanding of the cause-and-effect relationship. For example, you might arrive at this loose paraphrase or summary: "In order to defeat the English, Metacomet had to bring together different and warring groups into a _____.

- This summary, which leaves out the clause "whom the English called King Philip" and which is extraneous to the cause-and-effect relationship, makes it clear that the reason, or cause, for bringing together the groups was defeat of the English. So the word that goes into the blank must be one that names a group that can defeat someone or something. That immediately leaves out the all-too-peaceable or scientific sounding "community," as well as the diplomatic and also peaceful "legation." It also leaves out "hierarchy": a hierarchy alone wouldn't get the job of defeating someone accomplished.

- Using cause-and-effect clues in this case quickly narrows down the possible choices to choice (A), "battalion," and choice (D), "confederation."

- To reach the correct answer, try a general strategy, such as comparing two answers against each other and against the passage. A confederation brings many different groups together, which is the point of the sentence; therefore, choice (D) is correct. **The correct answer is (D).**

Contrast

A sentence or passage with a contrast structure expresses differences. This commonly used structure is probably very familiar to you.

Contrast Signals

Like other structures, contrasts of information may or may not include signal words. Among the words and phrases that can be used to signal contrasts are the following:

although	*however*	*on the contrary*
as opposed to	*in contrast*	*on the other hand*
but	*in spite of*	*otherwise*
by contrast	*instead*	*still*
conversely	*nevertheless*	*unlike*
despite	*nonetheless*	*yet*

Most often, you will have to infer contrasts or the words and phrases that signal them. Question 5, however, does contain a contrast word.

FOR QUESTION 5, CHOOSE ONE ANSWER FOR THE BLANK. CHOOSE THE ANSWER THAT BEST COMPLETES THE SENSE OF THE TEXT.

---

5. Judging by the various glances exchanged, the statistics Mai offered during the meeting struck everyone in attendance as _____; later, however, she managed to authenticate most of them in her expansive written analysis.

(A) valid
(B) inconsequential
(C) spurious
(D) unexpurgated
(E) superfluous

An analysis of the contrast relationship in Question 5 could look something like this:

- Once you have identified the structure as a contrast, restate, paraphrase, or summarize the item in a way that reflects your understanding of the contrast relationship. For example, you might arrive at this paraphrase: "The glances showed people thought Mai's statistics were _____; later, her analysis showed they were authentic."

- This loose paraphrase makes it clear that the answer must express the opposite, or near opposite, of "authentic."
- Through the process of elimination, choices (A), (B), (D), and (E) should all be ruled out because they don't show or suggest the opposite of authentic. Choice (A), "valid," means "just, producing the desired results, or legally binding," all somewhat similar to "authentic." Choice (B), "inconsequential," is incorrect because it isn't the opposite of "authentic." Choice (D) is incorrect because "unexpurgated" refers to removing offensive material from something. Choice (E) is incorrect because "superfluous" means "unnecessary, more than what is required." Therefore, choice (C), "spurious," meaning "false," is the correct answer.

Try rereading the passage after eliminating the signal word "however" to help familiarize yourself with an alternative way in which a contrast passage might appear. **The correct answer is (C).**

Comparison or Similarity Structure

Like a sentence or passage expressing contrasting ideas, a sentence or passage expressing a comparison or similarity should also be familiar to you. Such a structure expresses how two or more things are alike.

Comparison Signals		
Among the words and phrases that can signal a comparison are the following:		
also	in comparison	moreover
and	in the same way	same
another	like	similarly
as	likewise	too
by the same token		

FOR QUESTION 6, CHOOSE <u>ONE</u> ANSWER FOR THE BLANK. CHOOSE THE ANSWER THAT BEST COMPLETES THE SENSE OF THE TEXT.

---

6. Debussy is regarded as the germinal musical impressionist who created color through the use of individual instruments in the orchestra; by the same token, Monet's use of blocks of color, in lieu of line, was a _____ influence on impressionism in art. There, however, the similarity between the two "impressionists" ends.

(A) imperative
(B) seminal
(C) discernable
(D) super
(E) formidable

An analysis of the comparison in Question 6 could look something like this:

- Note that the signal phrase "by the same token" along with the word "similarity" indicate a comparison.

- The next step is to restate, paraphrase, or summarize the item in a way that reflects your understanding of the comparison relationship, or structure. For example, you might arrive at this summary: "Debussy had great influence in music because of his use of color; likewise, Monet was a _____ influence in art because of how he used color."

- This summary significantly reduces the original in order to focus on the comparison. It makes clear that the word that belongs in the blank must be an adjective that suggests great influence.

- At this point, you might use the process of elimination. Choice (A) should be eliminated because "imperative" means "absolutely necessary." Choice (C) is also incorrect because the similarity suggests that Monet had more than a discernable, or noticeable, influence on art; he had a great influence. Choice (D) is likewise incorrect because "super," which can mean "particularly excellent," is too informal for this passage. Finally, choice (E) is incorrect because "formidable," while suggesting a meaning that fits, does not exactly match the meaning expressed by the first clause. The context makes it clear that the effect of each artist on his discipline was not only huge or formidable, it was also influential. Choice (B), "seminal," is the only word that conveys something formative or something that shaped, influenced, or decided what was to come. **The correct answer is (B).**

Now try analyzing Question 6 without the signal words in the passage.

If you look back at Question 1, you'll see that it could also be approached as a comparison, but without any signal words. Structures can be combined or overlapped in a single sentence or passage. Your task is not to identify the "right" structure, but to identify and use structures that will best help you find the answer.

Main Idea and Details

Main ideas and details as an organizing structure consist of more than one sentence. The main idea may be stated at the beginning of the passage, in the middle, or at the end. The main idea may also be implied through the details in the passage. Although passages may occasionally contain signal words and phrases such as "for example" to help you identify details, you will most likely have to infer the main idea based on the content of the passage.

Take a look again at Question 2. See if you can identify its main ideas and details before you read the analysis.

FOR QUESTION 2, CHOOSE <u>ONE</u> ANSWER FOR EACH BLANK. SELECT FROM THE APPROPRIATE COLUMN FOR EACH BLANK. CHOOSE THE ANSWER THAT BEST COMPLETES THE SENSE OF THE TEXT.

---

2. A major part of the body's immune system, the lymphatic system is responsible for producing, maintaining, and distributing lymphocytes (white blood cells that attack bacteria in blood and take the form of T cells and B cells) in the body, as well as for defending the body against pathogens. Besides removing waste, dead blood cells, and toxins from cells and the tissues between them, the lymphatic system also works in concert with the circulatory system to deliver oxygen, nutrients, and hormones from the blood to the cells. The (i) _____ role of the lymphatic system in fighting disease and maintaining homeostasis (ii) _____.

Blank (i)	Blank (ii)
(A) pivotal	(D) must not be trivial
(B) autonomous	(E) cannot be gainsaid
(C) hypothetical	(F) will not be equivocated

An analysis of the main idea and supporting details in a passage to help you answer a text completion question might look like this for Question 2:

- Begin by finding the main idea (the last sentence) and the details that support it (everything that precedes the last sentence).

- Then, once again, restate, paraphrase, or summarize the part or parts of the passage containing the blank or blanks you must fill in. For example, you might arrive at this summary: "The _____ part played by the lymphatic system in the body _____."

- This summary depends, of course, on the details for correct completion, so now reread the details. The details inform you of the various and important roles the lymphatic system plays in the body. Therefore, the first blank must have to do with importance, or being essential.

- The word that comes closest in meaning to important is "pivotal." "Pivotal," choice (A), is the correct answer for Blank (i).

- To complete Blank (ii), work with the more complete version of your summary: "The pivotal part played by the lymphatic system in the body _____." If you come up with your own answer for this blank, you might say "cannot be (or must not be or will not be) denied." Therefore, look for the answer choice that means "denied," choice (E).

If you don't know the meaning of all the words—or even if you do—remember to use the process of elimination. "Trivial" doesn't mean "denied." Neither does "equivocated." So, while you may not know that choice (E), "gainsaid," means "denied," by the process of elimination, it must be the correct answer. **The correct answers are (A) and (E).**

Consider Tone and Style

Although this strategy won't apply to every passage, some passages will carry a distinctive tone that you can use as a clue to meaning. For example, the author's attitude may be sympathetic, indignant, questioning, mournful, celebratory, or praising. If there is an obvious tone, don't overlook it as a clue to the words that belong in the blanks. Look again at Question 3 and see if you can identify the tone of the passage for Blanks (i) and (ii).

> FOR QUESTION 3, CHOOSE <u>ONE</u> ANSWER FOR EACH BLANK. SELECT FROM THE APPROPRIATE COLUMN FOR EACH BLANK. CHOOSE THE ANSWER THAT BEST COMPLETES THE SENSE OF THE TEXT.

3. Those calling for the regulation of commodities trading are, at best, uninformed. Instead of (i) _____ traders for spikes in prices of wheat, oil, and metals, as well as for the bubbles, legislators would be wiser to consider how speculators help to create (ii) _____ by injecting cash into markets—which contributes to market efficiency. Furthermore, legislators who are gung-ho to rein in traders might bother to note that speculators have little or no effect on the production, and only (iii) _____ effect on the consumption, of goods.

Blank (i)	Blank (ii)	Blank (iii)
(A) regulating	(D) liquidity	(G) minimal
(B) scapegoating	(E) activity	(H) negative
(C) castigating	(F) inventory	(I) lasting

An analysis of the question based on tone would be something like this:

- The critical, almost indignant, tone of this passage is signaled by two groups of words that denigrate legislators: "at best, uninformed" and "legislators who are gung-ho to rein in traders . . ."

- This critical tone tells you that the author is not going to choose particularly moderate or measured word choices. Instead, at least some of the words that are most consistent with the message will be words with strong negative connotations. Of all the answer choices, choice (B), "scapegoating," has the most negative connotations. It is, in fact, the correct answer for Blank (i).

- Based on this assessment of the tone and sense of the passage, the best choice for the second blank is choice (D), "liquidity."

Similarly, considering the author's style might help you arrive at a correct answer. **The correct answers are (B) and (D).**

Read Question 6 again, but this time pay attention to the writer's style.

FOR QUESTION 6, CHOOSE <u>ONE</u> ANSWER FOR THE BLANK. CHOOSE THE ANSWER THAT BEST COMPLETES THE SENSE OF THE TEXT.

---

6. Debussy is regarded as the germinal musical impressionist who created color through the use of individual instruments in the orchestra; by the same token, Monet's use of blocks of color, in lieu of line, was a _____ influence on impressionism in art. There, however, the similarity between the two "impressionists" ends.

| (A) imperative |
| (B) seminal |
| (C) discernable |
| (D) super |
| (E) formidable |

The style of the passage is formal and academic; therefore, the word that fits in the blank must be the same in order to work with that style. A quick read-through of the answer choices comes across "super." Though it means "particularly excellent" and might at first appear to be correct, "super" is an informal word appropriate to an informal context. It doesn't fit the style of this passage, so choice (D) can be eliminated. That leaves you four other choices with which to use the process of elimination.

Use Grammar and Usage

You will be able to eliminate some answer choices because they violate the rules of grammar or do not match the customary way in which a word or phrase is used. For example, look again at Question 3, Blank (iii):

FOR QUESTION 3, CHOOSE <u>ONE</u> ANSWER FOR EACH BLANK. SELECT FROM THE APPROPRIATE COLUMN FOR EACH BLANK. CHOOSE THE ANSWER THAT BEST COMPLETES THE SENSE OF THE TEXT.

---

3. Those calling for the regulation of commodities trading are, at best, uninformed. Instead of (i) _____ traders for spikes in prices of wheat, oil, and metals, as well as for the bubbles, legislators would be wiser to consider how speculators help to create (ii) _____ by injecting cash into markets—which contributes to market efficiency. Furthermore, legislators who are gung-ho to rein in traders might bother to note that speculators have little or no effect on the production, and only (iii) _____ effect on the consumption, of goods.

Blank (i)	Blank (ii)	Blank (iii)
(A) regulating	(D) liquidity	(G) minimal
(B) scapegoating	(E) activity	(H) negative
(C) castigating	(F) inventory	(I) lasting

Notice that both "negative" and "lasting" actually require the article *a* before them. Only "minimal" fits in the space as it is worded. Therefore, choice (H), "negative," and choice (I), "lasting," must both be eliminated. **The correct answer is (G).**

Avoid Selecting the Word or Phrase You Don't Fully Understand or Is Unfamiliar

Look again at Question 4 and its answer choices.

> **FOR QUESTION 4, CHOOSE ONE ANSWER FOR THE BLANK. CHOOSE THE ANSWER THAT BEST COMPLETES THE SENSE OF THE TEXT.**

4. To defeat the English, Metacomet, whom the English called King Philip, knew he had to bring disparate and sometimes warring groups together into a _____.

(A) battalion
(B) community
(C) legation
(D) confederation
(E) hierarchy

Suppose you have no idea what "legation" means. In most cases, you should not leap to choose this word or any other unfamiliar word. "Legation," which means "a permanent diplomatic mission," is incorrect in the context of Question 4. Of course, if you have clearly eliminated every other choice, then an unfamiliar word may be correct.

PRACTICE QUESTIONS

> FOR QUESTIONS 1–10, CHOOSE <u>ONE</u> ANSWER FOR EACH BLANK. SELECT FROM
> THE APPROPRIATE COLUMN FOR EACH BLANK. CHOOSE THE ANSWER THAT
> BEST COMPLETES THE SENSE OF THE TEXT.

1. The stock character known as Harlequin in commedia dell'arte invariably appeared in a diamond-patterned suit; a half-mask and a ruff were other unmistakable parts of his _____ dress.

(A) inventive
(B) flamboyant
(C) signature
(D) unusual
(E) disturbing

2. In terms of material goods, contemporary humans may well be more acquisitive than any group or society before them. Or, it may just be that contemporary patterns of acquisition are entirely consistent with the far-reaching _____ for new and different goods that characterized so many early societies.

(A) tenet
(B) grasp
(C) tussle
(D) quest
(E) yearning

3. Architects and sound engineers routinely use sound-absorbing materials on ceilings and walls. In addition, they have sometimes tried to create optimal acoustics by building the ceilings and walls of concert halls with rippled or (i) _____ surfaces, so that the sound is reflected and (ii) _____ at many angles.

Blank (i)	Blank (ii)
(A) invariably rigid	(D) distorted
(B) highly polished	(E) diffused
(C) slightly undulating	(F) auditory

4. When oblique, rather than vertical, rays of the sun pass through the atmosphere, they must (i) _____ pierce a greater part of that atmosphere, thereby lessening the (ii) _____ of their heat.

Blank (i)	Blank (ii)
(A) necessarily	(D) relativity
(B) largely	(E) delivery
(C) regularly	(F) intensity

5. The investigative panel was nothing short of outraged by the bus driver's negligence and lack of remorse. It determined that the driver had failed to follow the established (i) _____. As a result, she had compromised the safety of the passengers. More fundamentally, however, she had actually and effectively (ii) _____ at least two of her riders' rights.

Blank (i)	Blank (ii)
(A) code of conduct	(D) abrogated
(B) rules of engagement	(E) renounced
(C) terms of use	(F) negated

6. The playwright created atmosphere in part through the (i) _____ afternoon on which he set the scene. The cloying humidity seemed at once to (ii) _____ the characters' physical energy and play devil's advocate to their sense of morality.

Blank (i)	Blank (ii)
(A) sultry	(D) sap
(B) unsettled	(E) beguile
(C) bone-chilling	(F) intensify

7. Is the most spineless method of delivering the news of a breakup by means of a text message? A recent survey based on Facebook data found that 14% of those born after 1984 are likely to choose this most expedient of methods. Of course, expedience alone may not explain this choice, but the study offers no other explanation for why respondents act in such a (i) _____ manner. Readers of the study are left to infer why the perpetrators of such spineless behavior (ii) _____ the more dignified, if not relatively (iii) _____, face-to-face meeting.

Blank (i)	Blank (ii)	Blank (iii)
(A) muted	(D) disavow	(G) decorous
(B) unreliable	(E) eschew	(H) imposing
(C) craven	(F) denounce	(I) outdated

8. Is understanding your stature in relation to the universe ultimately a psychic (i) _____ of your sense of self? On the one hand, gauging your own experience of space and time in relation to the space and time of galaxies can make you feel (ii) _____ small. On the other hand, sensing you are one with this great universe, or even knowing that its cosmic rays pass through you, may in some ways (iii) _____ that sense of smallness.

Blank (i)	Blank (ii)	Blank (iii)
(A) raveling	(D) antithetically	(G) mitigate
(B) diminution	(E) debilitatingly	(H) expropriate
(C) misappropriation	(F) infinitesimally	(I) enervate

9. The peasants portrayed in Pieter Brueghel the Elder's renowned paintings performed physical labor from sunup to sundown and lived grim, short lives. In *The Wedding Dance,* Pieter Brueghel depicts a nearly frenzied release from that daily round of (i) _____ and (ii) _____ in which peasants dance and (iii) _____ to the music of the bagpipes.

Blank (i)	Blank (ii)	Blank (iii)
(A) employment	(D) inanity	(G) unwind
(B) privation	(E) woe	(H) carouse
(C) mediocrity	(F) striving	(I) sing

10. In part by personifying them, and in larger part through a selection of detail, children's books do nothing less than (i) _____ cars and trucks. The trucks are big, mighty, fearless, and friendly behemoths that happily get the job done. Cars are speedy, bright, often open conveyances that delight their drivers and passengers on similarly open roads without traffic, congestion, or exhaust fumes. Such storybook portrayals begin the process of (ii) _____ that preserves and protects the (iii) _____ of the automobile in American culture.

Blank (i)	Blank (ii)	Blank (iii)
(A) extol	(D) indoctrination	(G) desultory consequences
(B) infantilize	(E) validation	(H) eternal aggrandizement
(C) venerate	(F) vindication	(I) unquestioned dominance

ANSWER KEY AND EXPLANATIONS

1. C	6. A, D
2. D	7. C, E, G
3. C, E	8. B, F, G
4. A, F	9. B, E, H
5. A, F	10. A, D, I

Question

1. The stock character known as Harlequin in commedia dell'arte invariably appeared in a diamond-patterned suit; a half-mask and a ruff were other unmistakable parts of his _____ dress.

(A) inventive
(B) flamboyant
(C) signature
(D) unusual
(E) disturbing

Answer Explanation

The correct answer is (C). This item is structured as a restatement. The first clause tells how the Harlequin was "invariably" dressed: in a diamond-patterned suit. The second half of the sentence, or the restatement/exemplification part, further explains that invariable, or characteristic, parts of the Harlequin's dress also included a half-mask and ruff. Therefore, the multiple-meaning word "signature" is used here to mean "characteristic," or something that serves to identify. Choices (A), (B), (D), and (E) are incorrect because, while the dress of a harlequin may seem inventive, flamboyant, unusual, or even possibly disturbing to today's viewer, the sentence makes it clear that it was characteristic, as well as invariable, at the time.

Question

2. In terms of material goods, contemporary humans may well be more acquisitive than any group or society before them. Or, it may just be that contemporary patterns of acquisition are entirely consistent with the far-reaching _____ for new and different goods that characterized so many early societies.

(A) tenet
(B) grasp
(C) tussle
(D) quest
(E) yearning

Answer Explanation

The correct answer is (D). A quest is a search or pursuit that would have preceded the acquisition of goods for early societies. Choice (A) should be eliminated because "tenet," which means "opinion, belief, or principle," doesn't make sense. Choice (B) also doesn't make sense; furthermore, it can be eliminated because "grasp for" is nonstandard usage. Choice (C) is incorrect because the meaning of a scuffle, or disorderly fighting, doesn't fit the context. While choice (E) makes some sense, it's not the best answer because yearning for something is not so close to acquiring it as questing, that is, searching, for it is.

Question

3. Architects and sound engineers routinely use sound-absorbing materials on ceilings and walls. In addition, they have sometimes tried to create optimal acoustics by building the ceilings and walls of concert halls with rippled or (i) _____ surfaces, so that the sound is reflected and (ii) _____ at many angles.

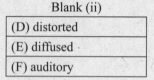

Blank (i)	Blank (ii)
(A) invariably rigid	(D) distorted
(B) highly polished	(E) diffused
(C) slightly undulating	(F) auditory

Answer Explanation

The correct answers are (C) and (E). For the first blank, the phrase with the closest meaning to "rippled" is what you're looking for. Eliminate choice (A), "invariably rigid," which means the opposite of "rippled," and choice (B), "highly polished," which makes no sense in the sentence. For the second blank, choice (E) is correct because a rippled surface would diffuse the sound "at many angles" to create the desired effect. Distortion is the opposite of the desired effect, so choice (D) is incorrect. Choice (F) should also be eliminated because "auditory" means "related to the process of hearing," not "able to be heard" or "audible."

Question

4. When oblique, rather than vertical, rays of the sun pass through the atmosphere, they must (i) _____ pierce a greater part of that atmosphere, thereby lessening the (ii) _____ of their heat.

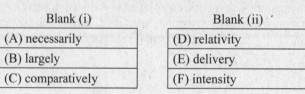

Blank (i)	Blank (ii)
(A) necessarily	(D) relativity
(B) largely	(E) delivery
(C) comparatively	(F) intensity

Answer Explanation

The correct answers are (A) and (F). Although this passage is structured as a cause-and-effect item, notice that there is also a contrast here. The contrast is between oblique and vertical rays.

Therefore, the clause with the first blank means, by inference, "oblique rays must _____ pierce a greater part of that atmosphere than vertical rays do." Choice (A), "necessarily," is correct for the first blank because it best shows this contrast. Choice (B), "largely," is incorrect because it doesn't make sense, and choice (C) is incorrect because "comparatively" creates ineffective repetition or redundancy; the comparing word "greater" already appears in the sentence. For Blank (ii), choice (D), "relativity," doesn't make sense, so eliminate it. It's a good distracter, though, because it sounds "sciency." Choice (E), "delivery," is incorrect because lessening the delivery of something doesn't make sense. Choice (F), "intensity," is the correct choice because intensity is a quality and so can be increased or decreased.

Question

5. The investigative panel was nothing short of outraged by the bus driver's negligence and lack of remorse. It determined that the driver had failed to follow the established (i) _____. As a result, she had compromised the safety of the passengers. More fundamentally, however, she had actually and effectively (ii) _____ at least two of her riders' rights.

Blank (i)	Blank (ii)
(A) code of conduct	(D) abrogated
(B) rules of engagement	(E) renounced
(C) terms of use	(F) negated

Answer Explanation

The correct answers are (A) and (F). Choice (A) is correct for Blank (i) because a "code of conduct" is a set of principles and practices outlined for an individual, group, or organization. "Rules of engagement," choice (B), generally outline when and how force should be used, and "terms of use," choice (C), often establish a relationship between a company's product and its user; therefore, choices (B) and (C) are incorrect. For Blank (ii), choice (F) is correct because this blank requires a synonym or near synonym for "denied." Choice (D), "abrogated," can be eliminated because an abrogation is an official or legislative annulment or cancellation. Eliminate choice (E) also because "renounced" makes no sense in this context.

Question

6. The playwright created atmosphere in part through the (i) _____ afternoon on which he set the scene. The cloying humidity seemed at once to (ii) _____ the characters' physical energy and play devil's advocate to their sense of morality.

Blank (i)	Blank (ii)
(A) sultry	(D) sap
(B) unsettled	(E) beguile
(C) bone-chilling	(F) intensify

Answer Explanation

The correct answers are (A) and (D). "Sultry" means "excessively hot or humid," which matches the "cloying humidity" mentioned in Sentence 2; therefore, choice (A) is correct. You can eliminate choices (B) and (C), because neither "unsettled" nor "bone-chilling" suggests excessive humidity. Choice (D) is the correct answer for the second blank, as "sap" means "to exhaust" or "to deplete." This is the only answer that makes sense in the context of lessening physical energy or moral fortitude. Choices (E) and (F), "beguile" and "intensify," make no sense.

Question

7. Is the most spineless method of delivering the news of a breakup by means of a text message? A recent survey based on Facebook data found that 14% of those born after 1984 are likely to choose this most expedient of methods. Of course, expedience alone may not explain this choice, but the study offers no other explanation for why respondents act in such a (i) _____ manner. Readers of the study are left to infer why the perpetrators of such spineless behavior (ii) _____ the more dignified, if not relatively (iii) _____, face-to-face meeting.

Blank (i)	Blank (ii)	Blank (iii)
(A) muted	(D) disavow	(G) decorous
(B) unreliable	(E) eschew	(H) imposing
(C) craven	(F) denounce	(I) outdated

Answer Explanation

The correct answers are (C), (E), and (G). For Blank (i), choice (C) is correct because "craven" can mean "cowardly," and the author clearly implies a negative judgment about the behavior that the word describes and equates it with spinelessness. Neither choices (A) nor (B), "muted" and "unreliable," make sense in the context. Although "unreliable" has a negative connotation, it's not strong enough to match the intensity of "spineless."

Choice (E) is correct for Blank (ii) because the meaning conveyed by "eschew" is "to shun" or "avoid deliberately." Choice (D), "disavow," makes no sense because, according to the passage, those who break up by text message don't disclaim knowledge or refuse to acknowledge another person. Similarly, choice (F), "denounce," must be eliminated because those who break up by text message aren't speaking out against anything.

Choice (G) is the correct choice for the third blank because "decorous" behavior is marked by propriety and dignity, which creates the correct contrast to the implied impropriety and indignity of breakup via text message. Choice (H) is incorrect because it's redundant. "Imposing" can mean "dignified," so the sentence would read "the more dignified, if not relatively dignified. . . ." While some test-takers might leap to choice (I), "outdated," it's incorrect because the passage in no way implies that the face-to-face meeting is outdated. After all, given the facts in the passage, it is possible that up to 86% of the survey respondents born after 1984 still use this method.

Question

8. Is understanding your stature in relation to the universe ultimately a psychic (i) _____ of your sense of self? On the one hand, gauging your own experience of space and time in relation to the space and time of galaxies can make you feel (ii) _____ small. On the other hand, sensing you are one with this great universe, or even knowing that its cosmic rays pass through you, may in some ways (iii) _____ that sense of smallness.

Blank (i)	Blank (ii)	Blank (iii)
(A) raveling	(D) antithetically	(G) mitigate
(B) diminution	(E) debilitatingly	(H) expropriate
(C) misappropriation	(F) infinitesimally	(I) enervate

Answer Explanation

The correct answers are (B), (F), and (G). For the first blank, choice (B) is correct because the context implies some kind of a reduction or diminishment. Choice (A) can be eliminated because "raveling" suggests an undoing rather than a decrease in size, as is clearly conveyed by Sentence 2. Choice (C), "misappropriation," makes no sense and can be eliminated. For the second blank, choice (F) is correct because "infinitesimally" conveys the sense of extreme smallness. Eliminate choice (D), "antithetically," meaning "in direct opposition," because it makes no sense, and choice (E), "debilitatingly," suggests weakening rather than diminishment and can be eliminated. Choice (G) is the correct choice for Blank (iii) because, as the signal phrase "on the other hand" suggests, this blank calls for a word that suggests a decrease or lessening of the sense of smallness. Eliminate both choices (H) and (I), "expropriate" meaning "to deprive someone of something" and "enervate" meaning "to weaken or destroy strength," because neither suggest a decrease or reduction as "mitigate" does.

Question

9. The peasants portrayed in Pieter Brueghel the Elder's renowned paintings performed physical labor from sunup to sundown and lived grim, short lives. In *The Wedding Dance,* Pieter Brueghel depicts a nearly frenzied release from that daily round of (i) _____ and (ii) _____ in which peasants dance and (iii) _____ to the music of the bagpipes.

Blank (i)	Blank (ii)	Blank (iii)
(A) employment	(D) inanity	(G) unwind
(B) privation	(E) woe	(H) carouse
(C) mediocrity	(F) striving	(I) sing

Answer Explanation

The correct answers are (B), (E), and (H). To restate the grim daily round of physical labor from sunup to sundown, choice (B) for Blank (i), "privation," and choice (E) for Blank (ii), "woe," are the best choices. For Blank (i), the words "employment" and "mediocrity," choices (A) and (C), are not only inaccurate, but they're also not negative enough. For Blank (ii), choices (D) and (F), "inanity" and "striving," are similarly insufficiently negative as well as inaccurate. For Blank (iii), choice (H), "carouse," is correct because the passage says the peasants are depicted as in "a nearly frenzied release." Neither choice (G), "unwind," nor choice (I), "sing," expresses the meaning conveyed by choice (H), "carouse": "to engage in noisy, drunken, boisterous, or even riotous merrymaking."

Question

10. In part by personifying them, and in larger part through a selection of detail, children's books do nothing less than (i) _____ cars and trucks. The trucks are big, mighty, fearless, and friendly behemoths that happily get the job done. Cars are speedy, bright, often open conveyances that delight their drivers and passengers on similarly open roads without traffic, congestion, or exhaust fumes. Such storybook portrayals begin the process of (ii) _____ that preserves and protects the (iii) _____ of the automobile in American culture.

Blank (i)	Blank (ii)	Blank (iii)
(A) extol	(D) indoctrination	(G) desultory consequences
(B) infantilize	(E) validation	(H) eternal aggrandizement
(C) venerate	(F) vindication	(I) unquestioned dominance

Answer Explanation

The correct answers are (A), (D), and (I). Choice (A), "extol," is the correct answer for Blank (i) because the author's perspective is that children's books glorify and celebrate cars and trucks. Choice (B) is incorrect because cars and trucks cannot be infantilized, or reduced to the status of an infant. Choice (C) is also incorrect because "venerate" means "to adore," and although this is close in meaning to "extol," it's not the same.

Choice (D) is the correct choice for Blank (ii) because the author suggests that the typical portrayal in children's books results in a kind of one-sided belief that cars and trucks are great. Choice (E) and choice (F), while close in meaning, are not so accurate: both a validation and a vindication (defense against criticism) fall short of an indoctrination as a way of extolling and furthering the dominance of the automobile.

For Blank (iii), choice (I), "unquestioned dominance," is the correct answer because indoctrination generally results in an unquestioning faith or loyalty in or toward something. Choice (G) should be eliminated because "desultory," which means "jumping from idea to idea," makes no sense. While choice (H) is close to the correct meaning because aggrandizement is an increase in power or the act of making something seem greater than it actually is, it's incorrect when coupled with the word "eternal." Usage can also help you eliminate this answer: there is no need to preserve and protect something eternal.

SUMMING IT UP

- Text completion questions assess your ability to interpret and evaluate what you read and supply words or phrases whose meaning is consistent with the ideas presented.

- Text completion questions have from one to three blanks to be filled in.

- Test items that have one blank offer a list of five options. Test items with two or three blanks offer lists of three options for each blank.

- Some test items will revolve around words that are close in meaning or ask for an unusual meaning of a familiar word. Some items may involve less familiar words.

- Passages for the text completion test items tend to have lighter concept loads than those for reading comprehension questions on the GRE.

- The following strategies for answering text completion questions involve both common sense and knowledge gained in English composition classes:

  o Try answering the questions before you read the answer choice(s).

  o Focus on only one blank at a time.

  o If there is more than one blank, complete the blanks in the order that makes sense to you.

  o Check your answer(s) in place.

  o Use structural clues: restatement, cause and effect, contrast, comparison, main idea, and details.

  o Consider tone and style.

  o Consider grammar and usage.

  o Avoid selecting a word or phrase that you don't fully understand or is unfamiliar.

- General test-taking strategies that are also helpful include:

  o Anticipate and use the clock.

  o Skip and return to questions.

  o Eliminate answer choices you know are incorrect.

  o Use educated guessing.

Strategies for Sentence Equivalence Questions

chapter 8

OVERVIEW

- Basic information about sentence equivalence questions
- Strategies for sentence equivalence questions
- Practice questions
- Answer keys and explanations
- Summing it up

Sentence equivalence questions ask you to determine how a sentence should be completed—in two ways. You will need to pick two words that are close in meaning. This chapter describes the purpose of the sentence equivalence test items and offers strategies to help you do well on these questions.

BASIC INFORMATION ABOUT SENTENCE EQUIVALENCE QUESTIONS

Like text completion items, sentence equivalence questions on the GRE test your ability both to interpret what you read and to supply words whose meaning is consistent with the ideas presented in the test item. Unlike text completion items, however, sentence equivalence items place more emphasis on the meaning of the completed sentence.

Also, like text completion items, sentence equivalence items test your vocabulary. Therefore, knowing "big" words—such as *dichotomous* and *prescient*—can help you do well, but that's not the only way to score points. Learning and using a few key strategies can help you as well.

Question Format

Each sentence equivalence question is a single sentence with one blank and six answer choices. This is the simplest of the verbal formats and is the same each and every time. From the list of six options, you must choose two answers for each question. You have to choose two answers that have similar (equivalent) meaning so that they both complete the sentence with a similar (equivalent) meaning.

There is only one type of direction line for the text completion items. It will be worded something like this:

> **FOR QUESTIONS 1–2, CHOOSE THE TWO ANSWERS THAT BEST FIT THE MEANING OF THE SENTENCE AS A WHOLE AND RESULT IN TWO COMPLETED SENTENCES THAT ARE ALIKE IN MEANING.**

You can expect perhaps one quarter or fewer—maybe 5 or 6—of the items on the Verbal Reasoning section to be sentence equivalence items. These items are interspersed with the other items on each of the two scored verbal sections of the test.

Each sentence equivalence item appears on a separate screen. All passages are short enough to display on a single screen, so you won't need to scroll or change screens. In fact, these short items require the least from you of any of the verbal items and should be done the most quickly.

Selecting Answers

When you have decided on an answer to a question, click on your choice. The oval preceding your selection will completely darken. Remember for sentence equivalence test items to click on two choices. Once you are satisfied with your two answers, hit the "Next" icon.

To earn credit for a sentence equivalence test item, you must choose both correct answers. Choosing only one correct answer of the pair will not gain you any credit.

Consider using the "Mark" option more readily on the sentence equivalence items than you might use it for reading comprehension items. Because sentence equivalence items are shorter and less time-consuming, they're easier to revisit than reading comprehension items. When you mark a sentence equivalence item, you are making a commitment to revisit only approximately 4 percent of the test. This is not a huge task to put off until later and, therefore, a reasonable strategy to use with challenging items.

If you're running out of time, go through the section looking for any unanswered sentence equivalence questions. You can answer them quickly and earn credit.

STRATEGIES FOR SENTENCE EQUIVALENCE QUESTIONS

You will be using many of the same strategies for sentence equivalence items that you may use for other Verbal Reasoning questions on the test. Strategies for sentence equivalence test items can be grouped into two categories: those that are general commonsense ideas and those that you learned in English composition class. The first group includes the following three strategies:

1. Read the item stem first.
2. Come up with your own answer.
3. Check your answers in place.

More specific language strategies include the following four strategies:

1. Use signal words and structural clues.
2. Avoid leaping at the first pair of synonyms.
3. Examine connotations.
4. Consider grammar and usage.

Remember to apply the following four test-taking strategies as well:

1. Anticipate and use the clock.
2. Skip and return to questions.
3. Eliminate answer choices that you know are not correct.
4. Use educated guessing.

Notice how these review strategies are integrated into the approaches for answering each of the sample items in this chapter.

Read the Item Stem First

Read through the entire sentence before you do anything else. Get a clear sense of what it's about first. The answers are deliberately structured with multiple pairs of synonyms and with close meanings that might appear correct at first glance, so you want to be sure that you understand the meaning of the incomplete sentence.

Come Up with Your Own Answer

Coming up with your own answer before you read the answer choices can be one of the most efficient methods you can use with sentence equivalence items. Try this now with Question 1 below.

> **FOR QUESTION 1, CHOOSE THE TWO ANSWERS THAT BEST FIT THE MEANING OF THE SENTENCE AS A WHOLE AND RESULT IN TWO COMPLETED SENTENCES THAT ARE ALIKE IN MEANING.**

1. Jade could not keep her negativity or aggression to herself; it seemed that everywhere she went, some kind of _____ ensued.
   - (A) kerfuffle
   - (B) insurgency
   - (C) insurrection
   - (D) rebellion
   - (E) demonstration
   - (F) disturbance

Working through the answer process might take this shape:

- Read the sentence first and try to figure out your own answer. Using this strategy, you come up with either the word "problems" or the word "difficulty."
- Step 2 is to look for a pair of words in the list that mean the same as, or close to the same as, problems or difficulty.
- "Kerfuffle" means "disturbance" or "minor outburst or tumult." It is a state of commotion rather than complete uproar like choices (B), (C), and (D). A kerfuffle is not so intense or serious as an insurgency, insurrection, or rebellion.
- In the context of the completed sentence, "disturbance" means the same thing. Therefore, the correct answers are choice (A), "kerfuffle," and choice (F), "disturbance." For the record,

"demonstration" connotes a protest, usually large in nature, so choice (E) is incorrect also. **The correct answers are (A) and (F).**

Check Your Answers in Place

You aren't finished when you select your two answer choices. Remember that the answers must create equivalence, so the last step in the process of completing this type of test item is an evaluation of meaning. To do this, read the item quickly twice, first with the first answer you have chosen in the blank, and the second time with the second answer in place. Ask yourself: Do the two sentences mean the same? Weigh the meaning of the completed sentences against each other before you click on the answer choices.

Use Signal Words and Structural Clues

Many sentence equivalence items will include transitions—signal words and phrases—such as *consequently, because, on the other hand, although, moreover, however,* and *in fact.* These words signal a relationship between ideas in the sentence. Pay close attention to them. They can help you decide whether the answer should show cause and effect, contrast, comparison, or restatement. Familiar signal words for different types of structures are included in the following boxes:

Signals for Restatement

Among the words and phrases that can signal restatement relationships are the following:

for example	in other words	that is
for instance	in short	this means
in fact	namely	thus

Cause-and-Effect Signals

Cause-and-effect relationships may or may not include signal words. Among the words and phrases that can signal cause-and-effect relationships are the following:

as a result	in order to	so that
because	reason why	therefore
consequently	since	thus
for	so	why

Contrast Signals

Like other structures, contrasts of information may or may not include signal words. Among the words and phrases that can be used to signal contrasts are the following:

although	*however*	*on the contrary*
as opposed to	*in contrast*	*on the other hand*
but	*in spite of*	*otherwise*
by contrast	*instead*	*still*
conversely	*nevertheless*	*unlike*
despite	*nonetheless*	*yet*

Comparison Signals

Among the words and phrases that can signal a comparison are the following:

also	*by the same token*	*moreover in comparison*
and	*in the same way*	*same*
another	*like*	*similarly*
as	*likewise*	*too*

Not all test items for sentence equivalence will have signal words and phrases. You will need to recognize clues to organizational structures such as restatement and cause and effect without the help of transitional words and phrases.

To practice identifying and using structural clues with sentence equivalence items, read Question 1 again and then read through the analysis that follows based on the sentence's restatement structure.

FOR QUESTION 1, CHOOSE THE TWO ANSWERS THAT BEST FIT THE MEANING OF THE SENTENCE AS A WHOLE AND RESULT IN TWO COMPLETED SENTENCES THAT ARE ALIKE IN MEANING.

---

1. Jade could not keep her negativity or aggression to herself; it seemed that everywhere she went, some kind of _____ ensued.

   (A) kerfuffle
   (B) insurgency
   (C) insurrection
   (D) rebellion
   (E) demonstration
   (F) disturbance

NOTE

A sentence or passage that uses restatement in a sentence equivalence test item will most often have two independent clauses joined by a colon, a semicolon, or a correlative conjunction, such as *moreover*.

Reading this sentence, you may decide that it has a restatement structure. The second part of the sentence (the part following the semicolon) amplifies the information in the first part of the sentence (the part preceding the semicolon). No signal word or phrase is present. Structural analysis helps you determine that the pair of words you are looking for must name something that results from negativity or aggression. Insurgency, insurrection, and rebellion are all actions that go well beyond negativity or aggression. They don't express the same minor degree of problem, commotion, or upset that is conveyed by the first part of the sentence, so eliminate choices (B), (C), and (D). Choice (E), "demonstration," is usually used in conjunction with a large group, so it is incorrect as well. Negativity and aggression might both lead to a disturbance. The only synonym or near synonym on the list for disturbance is "kerfuffle." Therefore, the correct answers are choice (A), "kerfuffle," and choice (F), "disturbance." **The correct answers are (A) and (F).**

It's also reasonable to think that this sentence is structured as a cause-and-effect relationship. The following is one way you might work through it looking for an effect of Jade's attitude:

- If you begin by restating the item with cause and effect in mind, you might arrive at this paraphrase: "Because Jade could not keep her negativity or aggression in check, she caused some kind of _____ everywhere she went."

- Structural analysis helps you determine that the pair of words you are looking for must name something that results from negativity or aggression.

- The rest of the analysis is the same as above, so the correct answers are choice (A), "kerfuffle," and choice (F), "disturbance."

Avoid Leaping at the First Pair of Synonyms

You might think it's a good idea just to find the pair of synonyms among the answer choices, wrap up an item at lightning speed, and move on to the next item. You would be wrong. First, many answer sets contain more than one set of synonyms. Second, as the test-maker warns, even if a word is a synonym for the correct choice, it doesn't necessarily lead to the same meaning in the completed sentence. Finally, two words may be synonyms, but they may have different connotations.

Take a look at Question 1 again.

FOR QUESTION 1, CHOOSE THE **TWO** ANSWERS THAT BEST FIT THE MEANING OF THE SENTENCE AS A WHOLE AND RESULT IN TWO COMPLETED SENTENCES THAT ARE ALIKE IN MEANING.

1. Jade could not keep her negativity or aggression to herself; it seemed that everywhere she went, some kind of _____ ensued.
   - (A) kerfuffle
   - (B) insurgency
   - (C) insurrection
   - (D) rebellion
   - (E) demonstration
   - (F) disturbance

The first pair of synonyms in the answer choices for Question 1 is "insurgency" and "rebellion," choices (B) and (C). The meaning of these words, however, suggests an outcome that would arise from problems that are far greater than negativity. Note also that choices (B), (C), and (D) are similar. If you chose two answers just by looking for synonym pairs in the list of answer choices, you would have a dilemma on your hands. Which two should you choose?

Examine Connotations

In choosing answers, think about the connotations that the words carry. As you read Question 2, for example, consider just exactly what kind of walking is meant.

> FOR QUESTION 2, CHOOSE THE TWO ANSWERS THAT BEST FIT THE MEANING OF THE SENTENCE AS A WHOLE AND RESULT IN TWO COMPLETED SENTENCES THAT ARE ALIKE IN MEANING.

2. Kierkegaard said that he had "walked himself into his best thoughts"; in fact, research links exercise with heightened states of _____ experience.

   (A) examining
   (B) pensive
   (C) thoughtful
   (D) meditative
   (E) generative
   (F) contemplative

The walking in this sentence led to thinking, so it was likely solitary and prolonged walking. That information may help you in considering the connotations of the answer choices. Even though "pensive" and "meditative" are synonyms, they don't quite result in equivalence in the sentence. "Pensive," choice (B), has to be eliminated because it suggests a deep or melancholy thoughtfulness, an inward kind of experience that would not likely yield the "best thoughts" or be generative. Similarly, "contemplative" and "thoughtful" are synonyms. Choice (F), "contemplative," carries connotations of prolonged thought, the kind of thought that might arise over the course of a long walk. However, "thoughtful," choice (C), doesn't have that connotation, so eliminate it. Choice (E), "generative," must be eliminated because there is no similar word that would result in equivalence. Choice (A), "examining," is also incorrect in terms of usage and has no twin. Through elimination, that leaves as the correct answers, choice (D), "meditative," and choice (F), "contemplative." They are synonyms and have similar connotations. **The correct answers are (D) and (F).**

NOTE

Two words that are often confused are "connotation" and "denotation." Connotation is an idea or meaning suggested by a word. Denotation is the literal meaning of a word.

Consider Grammar and Usage

As with the text completion items, the words you select for sentence equivalence must result in correct grammar and standard usage when inserted into the sentence. Look again at Question 2 and the first answer choice.

FOR QUESTION 2, CHOOSE THE TWO ANSWERS THAT BEST FIT THE MEANING OF THE SENTENCE AS A WHOLE AND RESULT IN TWO COMPLETED SENTENCES THAT ARE ALIKE IN MEANING.

---

2. Kierkegaard said that he had "walked himself into his best thoughts"; in fact, research links exercise with heightened states of _____ experience.
   (A) examining

You can eliminate choice (A) because, even though the form of the word "examining" makes it appear as if it could be an adjective, it results in an ambiguous and nonstandard usage in the sentence "in fact, research links exercise with heightened states of examining experience."

PRACTICE QUESTIONS

FOR QUESTIONS 1–10, CHOOSE THE <u>TWO</u> ANSWERS THAT BEST FIT THE MEANING OF THE SENTENCE AS A WHOLE AND RESULT IN TWO COMPLETED SENTENCES THAT ARE ALIKE IN MEANING.

1. Deep in credit card debt, Dylan changed his view of his grandparents, whom he had once regarded as _____, but now thought of as wise.

   (A) nitpicking

   (B) penurious

   (C) censorious

   (D) parsimonious

   (E) disingenuous

   (F) quibbling

2. Even though the senator's speeches were marked by an admirable _____, he was not always able to translate his insight into legislation.

   (A) alacrity

   (B) acuity

   (C) astuteness

   (D) perspicacity

   (E) ingenuity

   (F) erudition

3. One explanation for the nearly _____ use of the very American "okay" is that it's phonetically familiar; almost every language has sounds that approximate a long *o* followed by a quick *k* sound followed by a long *a*.

   (A) catholic

   (B) cosmic

   (C) global

   (D) pandemic

   (E) planetary

   (F) universal

4. The appetite of the venture capitalist for a quick and lucrative killing could only be described as _____.

   (A) avaricious

   (B) grasping

   (C) voracious

   (D) unslaked

   (E) indomitable

   (F) rapacious

5. While Milly conducted herself with a sort of unflappable grace even in challenging circumstances, her husband Ned could often be both _____ and petty.

(A) peevish

(B) inimical

(C) irritable

(D) despicable

(E) contemptible

(F) pusillanimous

6. The woman could scarcely have been more disparaging about her ex-husband's participation in family life and responsibilities; she accused him of both physical laziness and _____.

(A) lethargy

(B) apathy

(C) petulance

(D) decrepitude

(E) turpitude

(F) languor

7. If modern art had a personality, it might be said to be forward or fresh; it might even be said to be sassy or _____.

(A) impudent

(B) extemporaneous

(C) insolent

(D) impromptu

(E) malevolent

(F) malapropos

8. As the play progressed, Molière could see that his tragedy was falling flat, so he moved quickly to transform the developing _____ into a farce.

(A) travail

(B) flop

(C) drudgery

(D) composition

(E) fiasco

(F) creation

9. Modern monopolies or near monopolies such as Microsoft and Amazon should be embraced rather than criticized—as with earlier monopolies such as Western Union and AT&T, their universal, convenient, and _____ innovations would scarcely have been possible had there been competition.

(A) gargantuan

(B) far-reaching

(C) promethean

(D) game-changing

(E) Lilliputian

(F) sundry

10. Members of the audience practically writhed in their seats as they endured the speaker's _____.

    (A) jeremiad

    (B) oratory

    (C) exhortation

    (D) harangue

    (E) declamation

    (F) tirade

ANSWER KEY AND EXPLANATIONS

1. B, D	6. A, F
2. C, D	7. A, C
3. C, F	8. B, E
4. C, F	9. B, D
5. A, C	10. D, F

Question

1. Deep in credit card debt, Dylan changed his view of his grandparents, whom he had once regarded as _____, but now thought of as wise.
   - (A) nitpicking
   - (B) penurious
   - (C) censorious
   - (D) parsimonious
   - (E) disingenuous
   - (F) quibbling

Answer Explanation

The correct answers are (B) and (D). This item is structured as a contrast; it contains the clue "but." However, the answer is not the opposite of "wise," but the opposite of the behavior that lands a person in credit card debt. "Penurious" and "parsimonious," choices (B) and (D), meaning "extremely or excessively unwilling to spend money," fit this sentence and result in the same meaning in the two completed sentences. Choices (A) and (C), "nitpicking" and "censorious," which both mean "overly critical," don't make sense. Choices (E) and (F) are also incorrect: "disingenuous" means "fake or deceptive" and "quibbling" means "arguing over little or petty things."

Question

2. Even though the senator's speeches were marked by an admirable _____, he was not always able to translate his insight into legislation.
   - (A) alacrity
   - (B) acuteness
   - (C) astuteness
   - (D) perspicacity
   - (E) ingenuity
   - (F) erudition

Answer Explanation

The correct answers are (C) and (D). With this question, you should be looking for a comparison or similarity to "insight." Don't be fooled by the word "not." "Astuteness" and "perspicacity," choices (C) and (D), can both mean shrewdness, but they both can also mean "intellectual sharpness or keenness," depending on the context, so they are correct in this sentence. Choice (A) should be eliminated because "alacrity" means "eagerness, liveliness, or quickness" and doesn't make sense. Choice (B) is incorrect because "acuteness" refers to sensitivity, not insight. Choice (E), "ingenuity," often means "cleverness," which isn't the same as insight. Choice (F) can also be eliminated because "erudition" is scholarly or deep learning, which isn't the same as insight. It also has no twin in the list.

Question

3. One explanation for the nearly _____ use of the very American "okay" is that it's phonetically familiar; almost every language has sounds that approximate a long *o* followed by a quick *k* sound followed by a long *a*.

   (A) catholic
   (B) cosmic
   (C) global
   (D) pandemic
   (E) planetary
   (F) universal

Answer Explanation

The correct answers are (C) and (F). Whether you view this item as having a restatement or contrast structure, your analysis should hinge on the phrase "every language," because that's what makes "the very American okay" universal and global. Notice how similar all the choices are here; each could be used in a certain context to mean "universal." So try the process of elimination. Choice (A), "catholic," isn't correct. It may suggest a certain universality, but cannot be used in every context because it most often refers to a "catholicity of tastes" or to the Roman Catholic religion. You can eliminate choices (B) and (E), "cosmic" and "planetary," because these usages are generally reserved for references to the universe in the sense of the solar system or cosmos. Similarly, while choice (D), "pandemic," can mean "universal," it is mainly used only in the sense of something unwanted that is widespread, such as the outbreak of deadly disease. That leaves choices (C) and (F), "global" and "universal."

Question

4. The appetite of the venture capitalist for a quick and lucrative killing could only be described as _____.

   (A) avaricious
   (B) grasping
   (C) voracious
   (D) unslaked
   (E) indomitable
   (F) rapacious

Answer Explanation

The correct answers are (C) and (F). This is a question that hinges on word usage. "Voracious" and "rapacious" both mean "having an insatiable appetite for something," so they both match the word "appetite." Choices (A) and (B) are incorrect because even though "avaricious" and "grasping" mean "greedy," an appetite cannot be correctly described as avaricious or grasping. Choice (D) is incorrect because a thirst, not an appetite, is slaked (or left unslaked), and choice (E) is incorrect because "indomitable" is not applied to an appetite; furthermore, it doesn't fit the meaning of the sentence.

Question

5. While Milly conducted herself with a sort of unflappable grace even in challenging circumstances, her husband Ned could often be both _____ and petty.

   (A) peevish
   (B) inimical
   (C) irritable
   (D) despicable
   (E) contemptible
   (F) pusillanimous

Answer Explanation

The correct answers are (A) and (C). In this contrast item, Ned's peevish and irritable as well as petty behavior forms a loose opposite to Milly's "unflappable grace." Choice (B), "inimical," which suggests unfriendliness, provides insufficient contrast to Milly's imperturbable grace. Choices (D) and (E), "despicable" and "contemptible," which constitute a second pair of synonyms meaning "mean" or "vile," convey behavior that is too extreme to be an appropriate contrast in the sentence. "Pusillanimous," choice (F), is incorrect because cowardliness is not the opposite, or even a loose opposite, of grace.

Question

6. The woman could scarcely have been more disparaging about her ex-husband's participation
   in family life and responsibilities; she accused him of both physical laziness and _____.

   (A) lethargy
   (B) apathy
   (C) petulance
   (D) decrepitude
   (E) turpitude
   (F) languor

Answer Explanation

The correct answers are (A) and (F). Both "lethargy" and "languor" denote an extreme lack of energy or state of physical weakness or listlessness, so they match "physical laziness." You can eliminate choice (B), "apathy," which means "lack of interest"; choice (C), "petulance," which means "irritability"; choice (D), "decrepitude," which means "a state of deterioration due to old age"; and choice (E), "turpitude," which means "baseness or depravity."

Question

7. If modern art had a personality, it might be said to be forward or fresh; it might even be said to be sassy or _____.

    (A) impudent

    (B) extemporaneous

    (C) insolent

    (D) impromptu

    (E) malevolent

    (F) malapropos

Answer Explanation

The correct answers are (A) and (C). In this sentence, the second independent clause amplifies the first independent clause. Therefore, you can expect both words to be intensifications of the adjectives "forward" and "fresh," used in this sense to mean "showing a lack of restraint" or "improperly bold." Both "impudent" and "insolent," choices (A) and (C), ratchet up, or amplify, that sense of impropriety to downright rudeness. The second pair of synonyms presented by choices (B) and (D), "extemporaneous" and "impromptu," are incorrect because they mean "offhand" or "without preparation," neither of which accurately describes a personality or fits the context. Choice (E), "malevolent," meaning "displaying ill will," and choice (F), "malapropos," meaning "out of place" or "inappropriate," should also be ruled out.

Question

8. As the play progressed, Molière could see that his tragedy was falling flat, so he moved quickly to transform the developing _____ into a farce.

    (A) travail

    (B) flop

    (C) drudgery

    (D) composition

    (E) fiasco

    (F) creation

Answer Explanation

The correct answers are (B) and (E). Comparison or similarity clues in this item tip you off to the fact that what was "developing" was also falling flat, or failing to have the desired effect on the audience. Therefore, what was developing was a flop, choice (B), or a fiasco, choice (E), words that are not synonyms (a fiasco is more disastrous than a flop), but which both result in nearly the same meaning for the sentence as a whole. Choices (A) and (C), "travail" and "drudgery," which are near synonyms, make no sense in terms of usage and don't provide the proper comparison. The third set of near synonyms or possible synonyms, choices (D) and (F), "composition" and "creation," must also be eliminated because they don't convey the sense of something falling flat, or failing.

Question

9. Modern monopolies or near monopolies such as Microsoft and Amazon should be embraced rather than criticized—as with earlier monopolies such as Western Union and AT&T, their universal, convenient, and _____ innovations would scarcely have been possible had there been competition.

   (A) gargantuan
   (B) far-reaching
   (C) promethean
   (D) game-changing
   (E) Lilliputian
   (F) sundry

Answer Explanation

The correct answers are (B) and (D). Both cause and comparison ideas are at play in this item, whose answers are not synonyms; yet, the answers create equivalence in the completed sentence. Choices (A), (C), and (E) are all incorrect because the emphasis in the statement is not on the size of the innovations—"gargantuan," "promethean," "Lilliputian"—which makes no sense, but on their effect, which was both far-reaching and game-changing. Choice (F) is also incorrect because "sundry," meaning "various," doesn't express the same magnitude of greatness in relation to the innovations as the words "far-reaching" and "game-changing" do, choices (B) and (D).

Question

10. Members of the audience practically writhed in their seats as they endured the speaker's _____.

    (A) jeremiad
    (B) oratory
    (C) exhortation
    (D) harangue
    (E) declamation
    (F) tirade

Answer Explanation

The correct answers are (D) and (F). The cause in this item is the speaker's "harangue" or "tirade," and the effect is the audience's great discomfort. Choice (A) isn't so likely an answer because a "jeremiad" is often mournful; it may go on and on and may look gloomily at the future, but it is much less likely to make its listeners so physically or visibly uncomfortable as a tirade or harangue would. Mere "oratory," choice (B), or even "declamation," choice (E), which can be both pompous and excessively loud, would also not result in such great discomfort; in fact, they could as likely be uplifting, so choices (B) and (E) are also incorrect. Similarly, "exhortation" alone, no matter how forceful, is less likely to elicit the physical response of writhing with discomfort than a harangue or tirade is, so choice (C) is also incorrect.

SUMMING IT UP

- Sentence equivalence test items assess your ability to interpret what you read and to supply words whose meaning is consistent with the ideas presented in the test item.

- The emphasis is on the meaning of the complete sentence for sentence equivalence test items.

- Each sentence equivalence test item is a single sentence with one blank and six answer choices. From the six answer choices, you must select two answers for the question that will result in two sentences with a similar—equivalent—meaning.

- Both answer choices must be correct in order to earn credit for the question.

- Commonsense strategies for answering sentence equivalence questions are the following:
  - Read the item stem first.
  - Come up with your own answer.
  - Check your answers in place.

- More specific language strategies are the following:
  - Use signal words and structural clues.
  - Avoid leaping at the first pair of synonyms.
  - Examine connotations.
  - Consider grammar and usage.

- General test-taking strategies that are also helpful include:
  - Anticipate and use the clock.
  - Skip and return to questions.
  - Eliminate answer choices you know are incorrect.
  - Use educated guessing.

PART V

QUANTITATIVE REASONING

Strategies for Multiple-Choice Questions

chapter 9

OVERVIEW

- Basic information about multiple-choice question types
- Math conventions
- Strategies for selecting one answer choice
- Strategies for selecting one or more answer choices
- Strategies for multiple-choice questions in data interpretation sets
- Practice questions
- Answer key and explanations
- Summing it up

The Quantitative Reasoning section of the GRE evaluates test-takers' understanding of basic math concepts in arithmetic, algebra, geometry, and data analysis and their ability to apply these concepts to analyze and interpret real-world scenarios. This may sound daunting if you haven't had math for several years, but working through the strategies and the practice questions in this and the next two chapters should reassure you that the math on the GRE is not that difficult.

In this chapter, you will find an introduction to the two types of multiple-choice questions on the GRE and to certain strategies that will help you answer these questions correctly and quickly.

BASIC INFORMATION ABOUT MULTIPLE-CHOICE QUESTION TYPES

On the GRE revised General Test, there are two formats for multiple-choice questions:

- Multiple-choice questions—select one answer choice
- Multiple-choice questions—select one or more answer choices

You may find multiple-choice questions as stand-alone items, or they may be part of a group of questions that refer to the same tables, graphs, or other form of data presentation. In the latter case, they are known as data interpretation questions.

Most multiple-choice questions on the GRE are of the familiar multiple-choice questions—select one answer choice type. These questions are accompanied by five answer choices, each with an oval beside it. These questions have only one correct answer, as you would surmise from the name.

Multiple-choice questions—select one or more answer choices are accompanied by a varying number of answer choices. Each answer choice has a square beside it, which is a reminder that

PART V: Quantitative Reasoning

the question is a multiple-choice question that may have more than one correct answer, as the name suggests.

The following notes apply to "one or more answer choice" questions:

- The number of answer choices is not always the same—though typically you will see at least three choices.

- The number of correct answer choices is also not always the same. It may be that only one answer choice is correct, or two, or three, or all of them.

- Usually, the question asks you to select all correct answer choices. Sometimes, though, a question will instruct you to select a certain number of answer choices—in which case, of course, you should select exactly that number of choices.

- In order to answer a question correctly, you must select all the correct answer choices, and only those.

  o You do not get any credit if you select some, but not all of the correct answer choices.

  o You do not get any credit if you select the correct number of answer choices, but not all the choices you have selected are correct. (That is, if three out of five answer choices are correct, and you select two of the correct ones as well as the incorrect one, you don't get any credit.)

Although in this book we refer to answer choices as (A), (B), (C), and so on, the answer choices are not labeled on the actual GRE. The oval or square beside each answer choice is blank.

MATH CONVENTIONS

The test-maker provides the following information that applies to all questions in the Quantitative Reasoning section of the GRE:

- All numbers used are real numbers.

- All figures are assumed to lie in a plane unless otherwise indicated.

- Geometric figures, such as lines, circles, triangles, and quadrilaterals, *are not necessarily* drawn to scale. That is, you should *not* assume that quantities such as lengths and angle measures are as they appear in a figure. You should assume, however, that lines shown as straight are actually straight, points on a line are in the order shown, and more generally, all geometric objects are in the relative positions shown. For questions with geometric figures, you should base your answers on geometric reasoning, not on estimating or comparing quantities by sight or by measurement.

- Coordinate systems, such as *xy*-planes and number lines, *are* drawn to scale. Therefore, you can read, estimate, or compare quantities in such figures by sight or by measurement.

- Graphical data presentations, such as bar graphs, circle graphs, and line graphs, *are* drawn to scale. Therefore, you can read, estimate, or compare data values by sight or by measurement.

All multiple-choice questions in the computer-based test will have answer options preceded by either blank ovals or blank squares, depending on the question type. The paper-and-pencil test will follow the same format of answer choices, but it will use letters instead of ovals or squares for answer choices. For your convenience in answering questions and checking answers in this book, we use (A), (B), (C), etc. By using letters with parentheses, you will find it easy to check your answers against the answer key and explanation sections.

Remember that ovals next to answer choices mean that the correct answer consists of a single choice, whereas square boxes next to the answer choices mean that the correct answer consists of one or more answer choices.

Master the GRE® 2014

The On-Screen Calculator

The GRE revised General Test provides you with an on-screen calculator. You may use the calculator at any point during the Quantitative Reasoning sections, but you may find it particularly useful with the numeric entry questions. Before we talk about how you may use the calculator, let's discuss when you should and should not use it.

In general, you *should use* the on-screen calculator if you need to perform difficult calculations. However, most calculations on the GRE are not that complicated, so most of the time you will not need the calculator. In particular, you *should not use* it in the following cases:

- when the required calculations are simple to perform mentally or on scratch paper.

- when you need to give the answer as a fraction rather than a decimal (either in numeric entry questions or in multiple-choice ones).

- when estimating will suffice (for instance, in certain quantitative comparison or data interpretation questions).

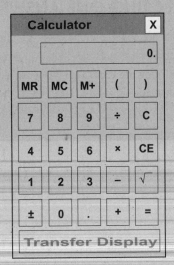

The following are a few notes on using the calculator. Learn them before test day to relieve some of the stress you may experience on that day.

- Unlike some other calculators, this one follows the order of operations. So, for instance, if you type in sequence "1", "+", "3", "×", "5", "=" the GRE calculator will yield "16" as the answer because it will perform the multiplication of 3 by 5 first and then add 1 to the result. If, however, you need to compute $(1+3)\times 5$ instead, then you must type the following sequence: "(", "1", "+", "3", ")", "×", "5", "=". Alternatively, you may type "1", "+", "3", "=", "×", "5", "=". However, it is easy to make mistakes if you try to perform a lengthy combination of operations as a single sequence on the calculator. It may be better to perform each individual computation on its own, use your scratch paper to note intermediate results, and then perform new computations on these results. In the above example, calculate $1+3$ first, note the result ("4") on your scratch paper, clear the calculator display by pressing the "C" button, and finally calculate 4×5.

- When you click the memory sum button ("M+"), the number in the calculator display is placed in the calculator's memory bank, and the letter "M" appears to the left of the display. When you later click "M+" again, the number in the calculator's display is added to the number in the memory bank. When you click the memory recall button ("MR"), the number in the calculator's memory bank at that time appears in the display area. The memory clear button ("MC") clears the memory.

- In numeric entry questions, you may click the calculator's "Transfer Display" button in order to transfer the number displayed on the calculator to the answer box. You cannot use the "Transfer Display" feature if the answer is a fraction. Note that if you click "Transfer Display" on a question that asks you to round your answer to a certain degree of accuracy, you may need to edit the number in the answer box so that it is appropriately rounded up or down.

STRATEGIES FOR SELECTING ONE ANSWER CHOICE

TIP

Don't forget these four test-taking strategies listed in Chapter 1: (1) anticipate and use the clock, (2) skip and return to questions, (3) eliminate answer choices that you know are incorrect, and (4) use educated guessing.

Reviewing the math principles that are covered in the GRE is an important part of preparing to take the test. However, using test-specific strategies can help you move through the test more quickly and with greater confidence. The following four strategies work especially well for multiple-choice questions that require only one answer:

1. Pick and plug numbers.
2. Work backwards from the answer choices.
3. Turn verbose or abstract language into concise and concrete wording.
4. Estimate.

Pick and Plug Numbers

Picking and plugging numbers can be a useful strategy IF

- a question and its answer choices contain variables, but you're not certain how to solve the question directly.

- you are dealing with a question about percents.

- you are not certain about a particular number property—such as whether the product of two odd numbers is odd or even.

Apply the strategy by

- picking simple numbers so that calculations are reasonable.

- plugging these numbers into the answer choices.

- eliminating any choices that don't produce the desired result.

> **FOR THIS QUESTION, CHOOSE <u>ONE</u> ANSWER CHOICE.**

Example 1

Susan can run $2x$ miles in y hours. In 75 minutes, how many miles will Susan run?

(A) $\dfrac{5y}{8x}$

(B) $\dfrac{2x}{75y}$

(C) $\dfrac{150x}{y}$

(D) $\dfrac{5xy}{2}$

(E) $\dfrac{5x}{2y}$

You can solve this question directly: if Susan runs $2x$ miles in y hours, then she runs $\dfrac{2x}{y}$ miles per hour. Thus, in 75 minutes, that is, in $\dfrac{5}{4}$ hours, she will run $\dfrac{2x}{y} \times \dfrac{5}{4} = \dfrac{5x}{2y}$ miles. If you don't feel comfortable solving directly, you have an alternative.

Let $x = 4$ and $y = 1$.

Susan can run 8 miles in 1 hour (60 minutes), so in 75 minutes Susan will run 10 miles: one-and-a-quarter as many miles as she can run in 1 hour. Now, plug the values $x = 4$ and $y = 1$ into the answer choices and see which of them yield(s) 10.

(A) $\dfrac{5 \times 1}{8 \times 4} = \dfrac{5}{32}$ Eliminate.

(B) $\dfrac{2 \times 4}{75 \times 1} = \dfrac{8}{75}$ Eliminate.

(C) $\dfrac{150 \times 4}{1} = 600$ Eliminate.

(D) $\dfrac{5 \times 4 \times 1}{2} = 10$ This option is a possibility. Hold on to it and choose option (E).

(E) $\dfrac{5 \times 4}{2 \times 1} = 10$ This option is also possible.

Since two answer choices produce the desired result, you need to check these choices again.

Pick different numbers—say, $x = 6$ and $y = 2$. Susan runs 12 miles every 2 hours, or 6 miles per hour. Therefore, in 75 minutes, Susan will run 7.5 miles.

(D) $\dfrac{5 \times 6 \times 2}{2} = 30$ Eliminate.

(E) $\dfrac{5 \times 6}{2 \times 2} = 7.5$ Correct.

The correct answer is (E).

Picking numbers can be a useful back-up tool if you're not confident that you can solve a question directly. However, when it comes to percentage increase/decrease problems, it is not only a good back-up, but an excellent way to find the right answer even more quickly than if you were solving directly. Consider the following example:

FOR THIS QUESTION, CHOOSE <u>ONE</u> ANSWER CHOICE.

Example 2

Mary sold her biology textbook to her friend John for a 40% discount compared with the price she paid to buy it. After completing his class, John sold the book on the Internet for 20% more than the price he paid Mary for the book. The price for which John sold the book is what percent of the price that Mary paid?

(A) 40

(B) 60

(C) 72

(D) 80

(E) 120

Pick the number $100 to represent the amount that Mary paid to buy the book. She then sold the book to John for a 40% discount of $100, or $100 − 40 = $60. John sold it for 20% more than the $60 he paid, so he sold it for $72.

What percent of $100 (the price Mary paid to buy the book) is $72 (the price John got when he sold it)?

$\dfrac{72}{100} = \dfrac{x}{100} \Rightarrow x = 72$

The correct answer is (C).

Work Backwards from the Answer Choices

In some cases, if there are numbers in the answer choices, and if, in order to solve directly, you may have to work through some complicated equations, you may choose to work backwards from the answer choices.

FOR THIS QUESTION, CHOOSE <u>ONE</u> ANSWER CHOICE.

Example 3

In city X, the first $30,000 of someone's annual income are taxed at the rate of 5%, while any income over $30,000 is taxed at the rate of 10%. If in a certain year Betty paid $2100 in city X taxes, what was her income that year?

(A) $32,000

(B) $33,000

(C) $34,000

(D) $35,000

(E) $36,000

In this example, you can turn the information in the question stem into an equation, and then solve that equation directly. Or, you can go straight to the answer choices, and, since the choices are listed from least to greatest, begin with choice (C), the middle one. If Betty's income had been $34,000, then she would have paid $\frac{5}{100}\$30,000 + \frac{10}{100}\$4000 = \$1500 + \$400 = \$1900$.

This amount is too low, so Betty must have earned more than $34,000. You can eliminate choices (A) and (B) in addition to choice (C), because they are less than choice (C). Next, check choice (D).

If Betty's income had been $35,000, then she would have paid $\frac{5}{100}\$30,000 + \frac{10}{100}\$5000 = \$2000$.

This amount, also, is too low, so you can eliminate choice (D). That leaves choice (E). **The correct answer is (E).**

Turn Verbose or Abstract Language into Concise and Concrete Wording

Sometimes it seems as though test-makers are trying to confuse you with wordy questions. Don't worry! You can always turn excessive verbiage into diagrams or mathematical expressions that are easier to understand and work with.

NOTE

Turning verbose or abstract language into concise and concrete wording is an important strategy to help you answer any math question.

Example 4

Diana prepared a certain amount of a chemical solution and stored it in 10 right-cylindrical containers, each with a diameter of 8 inches and a height of 8 inches. Alternatively, she could have stored the same amount of the solution in 40 right-cylindrical containers, all of them with the same height as one another and with a radius of 2 inches. What is the height of these containers?

(A) 4
(B) 8
(C) 10
(D) 16
(E) 40

Begin by writing down the given information, removing the clutter of any extraneous words. The dimensions of the first set of containers are $r = 4$ and $h = 8$. The dimensions of the second set of containers are $r' = 2$ and h'.

The volume of the solution equals 10 times the volume of each of the initial containers: $V_{total} = 10\pi r^2 h$. The volume also equals 40 times the volume of each of the alternate containers: $V_{total} = 40\pi r'^2 h'$. Equate these two expressions: $10\pi r^2 h = 40\pi r'^2 h'$.

Next substitute the values of r, h and r': $10\pi 4^2 \times 8 = 40\pi 2^2 h'$. Eliminate π from both sides of the equation and calculate the two squares: $10 \times 16 \times 8 = 40 \times 4h'$. Divide both sides by 160: $h' = 8$. **The correct answer is (B).**

Estimate

Estimating is a very valuable strategy for data interpretation questions as well as for quantitative comparisons. However, even in regular multiple-choice questions with a single correct answer, estimating may help, especially if you're running out of time.

Example 5

Sixty percent of the 25 professors on a certain university's engineering department are male. If two male professors retire and two female professors are hired, what percent of the department's professors will be male? (Assume no other changes in the engineering faculty.)

(A) 48
(B) 52
(C) 56.5
(D) 60
(E) 68

It's best to solve this question directly. However, you should also note that, after the changes, the engineering department will have fewer male professors than it had before, but the same total number of professors. The percentage of its faculty that's male should drop from the original 60%. Thus, you can eliminate answer choices (D) and (E) because they are greater than 60%.

For the record, to solve this directly, first find the number of male professors before the changes:

$$\frac{60}{100} = \frac{x}{25} \Rightarrow x = \frac{60 \times 25}{100} \Rightarrow x = 15$$

After the changes, the department still has 25 professors, but this time 13 of them are male. Set up a proportion in order to turn 13 into a percentage: $\frac{13}{25} = \frac{x}{100} \Rightarrow x = 52$. **The correct answer is (B).**

STRATEGIES FOR SELECTING ONE OR MORE ANSWER CHOICES

Remember that the number of answer choices is not always the same for this multiple-choice format. You might have three answers to choose from—the basic number of choices—or as many as five or more. The number of correct answers that you can be asked to choose varies as well. If you don't choose all the correct answers, you will not get credit for the correct answers that you do choose.

Of the five strategies listed for multiple-choice questions that require only one answer, the strategy of picking numbers and working backwards from the answer choices is not so useful when you aren't told how many correct answer choices there are. Estimating can be very useful, especially in data interpretation questions, as you'll see later in this chapter. As for turning verbose language into something concise and concrete: It's always a helpful strategy in mathematics! However, the following strategies and notes are specific to multiple-choice questions with one or more correct answer choices:

- Calculate the least and greatest possible values.
- Make sure you're answering the correct question.
- Think through data sufficiency questions.

NOTE

If you decide to skip a question, make sure you click the "Mark" button so you can find it quickly on the "Review" screen later. Remember: There's no wrong-answer penalty, so don't leave any questions unanswered!

Calculate the Least and Greatest Possible Values

On some questions, it is helpful to calculate what the least and greatest possible values for the answer choices are, and then eliminate any choices that do not fit within that range.

FOR THIS QUESTION, INDICATE <u>ALL</u> THE ANSWERS THAT APPLY.

Example 6

> A kiosk sells only the following snacks: cookies for $1.50 each, ice-cream bars for $2.50 each, and chips for $1.00 each. Clara bought four snacks at the kiosk. Which of the following could be the total amount that she paid?
>
> Indicate <u>all</u> such amounts.
> (A) $3.50
> (B) $4.00
> (C) $4.50
> (D) $6.50
> (E) $8.50
> (F) $10.50

You should start by calculating the least and greatest possible values, in order to limit your options. If Clara bought four bags of chips, the cheapest item, then she spent $4.00. Thus, all answer choices that are an amount less than $4.00 are incorrect. If she bought four ice-cream bars, the most expensive item, she spent $10.00. Thus, all answer choices that feature an amount greater than $10.00 are incorrect.

You're left with the middle four answer choices, and indeed, all four of them are possible: $4.00 represents a purchase of four bags of chips; $4.50 represents a purchase of three bags of chips and one cookie; $6.50 represents a purchase of two cookies, one bag of chips, and one ice-cream bar; and $8.50 represents a purchase of three ice-cream bars and one bag of chips. **The correct answers are (B), (C), (D), and (E).**

Note in which of the following questions you MUST work backwards from the answer choices. Do not start by calculating all the possible amounts that Clara could have spent. The answer choices do not have to list all of these amounts, only some of them. For instance, Clara could have spent $7.50 if she had bought two ice-cream bars, one cookie, and one bag of chips. However, $7.50 is not one of the answer choices—so you don't want to waste your time making calculations that are unnecessary.

Make Sure You're Answering the Correct Question

This is always sound advice, of course, but it is of particular importance in answering questions with one or more correct answer choices. Most of these questions ask you to select <u>all</u> the correct answer choices. However, you may also come upon a question that asks you to select a specific number of answer choices. You have to read the questions carefully to be sure of what to do.

> **FOR THIS QUESTION, INDICATE <u>ALL</u> THE ANSWERS THAT APPLY.**

Example 7

If p is a prime number, then the product of which <u>two</u> of the following numbers must be the square of an integer?

(A) $\dfrac{1}{p}$

(B) $\sqrt{p}$

(C) p^2

(D) p^3

Since you know that the product of only two of the answer choices is a perfect square, you may not need to check all the possible combinations. When you find the two answer choices that work, you can stop and move on to the next question. In this case, if you noticed early on that the product of $\dfrac{1}{p}$ and p^3 is p^2, a perfect square, you won't have to consider any other products. **The correct answers are (A) and (D).**

Think Through Data Sufficiency Questions

Example 8 is a data sufficiency question: a question that asks you to determine whether each answer choice is sufficient on its own to provide a definitive answer to the question. Sometimes, a data sufficiency question is of the yes/no variety (as is the case with this example). For such questions, an answer choice is sufficient

- if it provides a positive answer

OR

- if it provides a negative answer.

NOTE

While you're making sure you're answering the correct question, also make sure to double-check your work.

FOR THIS QUESTION, INDICATE <u>ALL</u> THE ANSWERS THAT APPLY.

Example 8

Angela is five years older than Melissa, who is two years younger than Heather. Which of the following statements <u>individually</u> provide(s) sufficient additional information to determine whether Heather is older than 23 years old?

Indicate <u>all</u> such statements.

(A) Angela is 27 year old.

(B) Melissa is younger than 21 years old.

(C) Heather is twice as old as Melissa was ten years ago.

Begin by reviewing the information in the question. If Angela is five years older than Melissa, and Melissa is two years younger than Heather, then Angela is three years older than Heather. It helps to write out these relationships as equations:

$$A = M + 5$$
$$H = M + 2$$
$$A = H + 3$$

Answer choice (A): If Angela is 27 years old, then Heather is 24 years old—in other words, she is older than 23 years old. Answer choice (A) is sufficient.

Answer choice (B): This tells you that Melissa is younger than 21 years old. Since $H = M + 2$, Heather is younger than 23 years old. Answer choice (B) is sufficient, as well.

Answer choice (C): Write out this statement as an equation:

$$H = 2(M - 10) \Rightarrow$$
$$H = 2M - 20$$

You now have two equations that relate H and M (the other one is $H = M + 2$). These two equations are distinct—that is, one is not a multiple of the other—so it is possible to solve these equations and find a unique solution for H and M. Therefore, the third answer choice is also sufficient. **The correct answers are (A), (B), and (C).**

STRATEGIES FOR MULTIPLE-CHOICE QUESTIONS IN DATA INTERPRETATION SETS

In each Quantitative Reasoning section, you should expect to see one set of questions that are grouped together and refer to the same data presentation—such as a graph or table. The questions will be either multiple-choice (both types) or numeric entry. The following strategies are helpful in solving data interpretation sets:

- Scan the data quickly.
- Make sure you're answering the correct question.
- Estimate.

The last two are useful for all types of questions in the Quantitative Reasoning section.

Quickly Scan the Data

When you first encounter a data interpretation set, scan the data in order to get a general idea of the information presented. Just as you do when reading a Reading Comprehension passage, don't waste time on the details. There will be time for the details when you look at the actual questions. Rather, note the following:

- What kind of data—such as sales figures, population trends, etc.—are presented?
- Do the graphs/tables give actual values or percentages?
- If more than one table or graph is presented, how are they related? For instance, does one table give actual values, whereas the other gives percentages?
- What units are used (for example, millions vs. billions of dollars)?
- Are there any notes above or below the data that give additional information?

The following example is a straightforward bar graph. It compares enrollment by male and female students majoring in science, engineering, and mathematics. The information is presented in real numbers.

EXAMPLES 9–10 ARE BASED ON THE FOLLOWING DATA.

NUMBER OF STUDENTS AT UNIVERSITY K MAJORING IN SCIENCE, ENGINEERING, AND MATHEMATICS

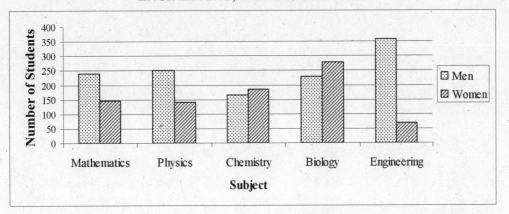

Make Sure You're Answering the Correct Question

Don't make careless mistakes when considering the questions. If a question asks about June sales figures, don't look in the July column of the table by mistake. If you're asked to find a percentage, don't look for or calculate actual values.

FOR THIS QUESTION, CHOOSE ONE ANSWER CHOICE.

Example 9

If a total of 12,049 students are enrolled in University K, approximately what percentage of these students is majoring in engineering?

(A) 0.5

(B) 3

(C) 3.5

(D) 17

(E) 20

This question is not particularly difficult, as long as you don't make any careless mistakes. Make sure you look at the bars representing the engineering majors, not any of the other four sets of bars. Also, make sure you consider both male and female engineering majors, not just male or just female students.

The number of male engineering majors is approximately 355. The number of female engineering majors is approximately 70. Thus, the total number of engineering majors is approximately 425. Solve a proportion in order to find what percent of the total student population 425 is: $\frac{425}{12,049} = \frac{x}{100} \Rightarrow x \approx 3.53$. **The correct answer is (C).**

Estimate

For some questions, you only need to find approximate values. Don't waste time performing exact calculations if you don't have to. In particular, remember that graphs are drawn to scale, so you can use them to estimate values. Consider the following:

> **FOR THIS QUESTION, INDICATE <u>ALL</u> THE ANSWERS THAT APPLY.**

Example 10

Which of the following statements about science majors at University K must be true?

Indicate <u>all</u> such statements.

(A) The absolute value of the difference of male to female physics majors was greater than the absolute value of the difference of male to female mathematics majors.

(B) More students, male and female, majored in biology than in engineering.

(C) The number of students who majored in mathematics is closer to the number of students who majored in physics than it is to the number of students who majored in biology.

Answer choice (A): From the graph you can tell that there were slightly more male physics majors than male mathematics majors, but slightly fewer female physics majors than female mathematics majors. You don't need to worry about their exact numbers. The visual evidence is sufficient to tell you that when you subtract the number of female physics majors from the number of male physics majors, you get a larger number than you do when you subtract the number of female mathematics majors from the number of male mathematics majors. Answer choice (A) is true.

Answer choice (B): The number of students who majored in biology was approximately 225 (male) + 275 (female) = 500. In example 9, you approximated the number of engineering students as 425. Again, the visual evidence is sufficient, even if your estimates are not perfect. Answer choice (B) is true.

Answer choice (C): Once again, you can estimate from the graph that the number of students who majored in mathematics is slightly less than 400, which is similar to the number of students who majored in physics. You've already estimated the number of students who majored in biology as 500. Thus, answer choice (C) is true, as well.

The correct answers are (A), (B), and (C).

PRACTICE QUESTIONS

> **FOR QUESTIONS 1–15, UNLESS THE DIRECTIONS STATE OTHERWISE, CHOOSE ONE ANSWER CHOICE.**

1. If the sum of two consecutive integers is 87 and the difference of their squares is 87, what is the larger integer?

 (A) 44

 (B) 46

 (C) 54

 (D) 69

 (E) 87

2. Each year between 2001 and 2011, an Italian winemaker in Montalcino used between 75% and 80% of his grapes to produce his Brunello di Montalcino wine, and the rest to produce his Rosso di Montalcino wine. If in 2011 he produced 2,500 cases of Brunello, which of the following could have been the total number of cases of wine he produced that year?

 Indicate all such numbers of cases.

 (A) 3,128

 (B) 3,153

 (C) 3,241

 (D) 3,308

 (E) 3,334

3. If a is a positive even integer less than 10, b is a negative even integer greater than –10, and c is a positive odd integer between 2 and 10, which of the following cannot be an integer?

 (A) $\dfrac{bc}{a}$

 (B) $\dfrac{ac}{b}$

 (C) $\dfrac{ab}{c}$

 (D) $\dfrac{ab}{c^2}$

 (E) $\dfrac{2ab}{c^3}$

4. A drawer contains 20 pairs of socks: some white, some black, and the rest brown. Picking at random, one has a 0.4 probability of removing a white pair. If 1 white pair, 1 brown pair, and 3 black pairs are added, and no pairs are removed, what is the probability that one will pick at random either a black or a brown pair?

   (A) 0.36

   (B) 0.4

   (C) 0.6

   (D) 0.64

   (E) 0.8

5. The average (arithmetic mean) weight of a football team's offensive linemen is 320 pounds, while the average weight of the team's defensive linemen is 300 pounds. If the team has at least 50% more defensive linemen than offensive linemen, which of the following could be the average weight of all of the team's offensive and defensive linemen, combined?

   Indicate all such weights.

   (A) 304

   (B) 305

   (C) 306

   (D) 307

   (E) 308

   (F) 309

6. *ABCD* is a quadrilateral, with side *AB* parallel to side *CD*. Which of the following statements individually provide(s) sufficient additional information to determine whether *ABCD* is a rectangle or not?

   Indicate all such statements.

   (A) The diagonals *AC* and *BD* are of equal length.

   (B) The diagonals *AC* and *BD* are not of equal length.

   (C) The measure of angle *CDA* is 90°, and both pairs of opposite angles are equal.

7. In a high school orchestra, 40% of the string players are violinists, 20% are violists, 25% are cellists, and 15% are bassists. If 2 violinists, 1 violist, 1 cellist, and 1 bassist are added, what will be the percentage of violinists in the orchestra? (Assume no other changes to the orchestra's string section.)

   (A) 30%

   (B) 35%

   (C) 40%

   (D) 45%

   (E) It cannot be determined.

8. If a and b are two of the solutions of the equation $x^3 - x^2 - 6x = 0$, with $a \neq 0$ and $a \neq b$, then which of the following could be the graph of $\dfrac{x}{a} > b$?

Indicate all such graphs.

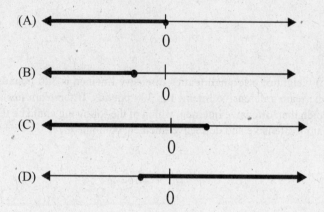

9. Each of the managers of a 20-person technical support team received $3000 as a year-end bonus, whereas each of the nonmanagers received $1200 as a year-end bonus. If the total amount that the 20 employees received was $31,200, how many of the team's members are managers?

(A) 1

(B) 2

(C) 3

(D) 4

(E) 5

QUESTIONS 10–12 ARE BASED ON THE FOLLOWING DATA.

INCOME DATA FOR TOWN X's FOUR NEIGHBORHOODS: A, B, C, and D.

Annual Income in 2011	Percent of Neighborhood Populations			
	A	B	C	D
$0–$24,999	14%	4%	17%	13%
$25,000–$49,999	30%	19%	34%	31%
$50,000–$74,999	26%	29%	27%	32%
$75,000–$99,999	19%	28%	15%	18%
$100,000–$249,999	9%	14%	6%	5%
> $250,000	2%	6%	1%	1%

10. In the neighborhood with the smallest percentage of six-figure earners in 2011, what percent of the population earned less than $50,000 that year?

    (A) 23

    (B) 31

    (C) 34

    (D) 44

    (E) 51

11. If the percentage of people who resided in neighborhood B in 2011 and earned between $0 and $24,999 was 20% less than the percentage of people who resided in neighborhood B in 2001 and earned between $0 and $24,999, and if the latter percentage was 20% less than the percentage of people who resided in neighborhood B in 1991 and earned between $0 and $24,999, what percent of the people who resided in neighborhood B in 1991 earned between $0 and $24,999 that year?

    (A) 4

    (B) 5

    (C) 6

    (D) 6.25

    (E) 6.67

12. Which of the following statements must be true?

    Indicate all such statements.

    (A) In 2011, the neighborhood with the highest average income was neighborhood B.

    (B) 12% of the people living in town X in 2011 earned less than $25,000 that year.

    (C) If in 2011 more than twice as many people lived in neighborhood A as in neighborhood B, then the number of people who lived in neighborhood A and earned $100,000 or more was greater than the number of people who lived in neighborhood B and earned $100,000 or more.

13. Which of the following graphs intersect(s) the graph of $y = x$?

    Indicate all such graphs.

    (A) The graph of $y = 2x + 2$

    (B) The graph of $y = |2x + 2|$

    (C) The graph of $y = -x + 2$

14. Streetlamps are to be placed along one side of a 1-kilometer-long road. Each streetlamp has a diameter of 50 centimeters. If the distance between streetlamps is 29.5 meters, and the first streetlamp is placed at one end of the road, how many streetlamps will be needed? (1 meter equals 100 centimeters. 1 kilometer equals 1,000 meters)

    (A) 30

    (B) 31

    (C) 32

    (D) 33

    (E) 34

15. If x and y are integers such that $|x - y| = 1$, which of the following statements individually provide(s) sufficient additional information to determine what x is?

    Indicate all such statements.

    (A) x and y are the solutions of the equation $a^2 + 7a + 12 = 0$

    (B) $y = 3$

    (C) x and y are both prime numbers, and y is odd

ANSWER KEY AND EXPLANATIONS

1. A	9. D
2. A, B, C, D	10. D
3. E	11. D
4. D	12. C
5. A, B, C, D, E	13. A, C
6. B, C	14. D
7. C	15. C
8. A, B, D	

Question

1. If the sum of two consecutive integers is 87 and the difference of their squares is 87, what is the larger integer?

   (A) 44
   (B) 46
   (C) 54
   (D) 69
   (E) 87

Answer Explanation

The correct answer is (A). Turn the abstract into an equation and solve:

$$x + (x + 1) = 87$$
$$2x + 1 = 87$$
$$2x = 86$$
$$x = 43$$
$$x + 1 = 44$$

Question

2. Each year between 2001 and 2011, an Italian winemaker in Montalcino used between 75% and 80% of his grapes to produce his Brunello di Montalcino wine, and the rest to produce his Rosso di Montalcino wine. If in 2011 he produced 2,500 cases of Brunello, which of the following could have been the total number of cases of wine he produced that year?

   Indicate <u>all</u> such numbers of cases.

   (A) 3,128
   (B) 3,153
   (C) 3,241
   (D) 3,308
   (E) 3,334

Answer Explanation

The correct answers are (A), (B), (C), and (D). For this question, the strategy "calculate the least and greatest possible values" is the most helpful. Calculate the least and greatest values and then select all the choices that fall between them. The 2,500 cases of Brunello that the winemaker produced in 2011 are between $\frac{3}{4}$ and $\frac{4}{5}$ of his total production.

If P is his total production that year, then $\frac{3}{4}P < 2,500 < \frac{4}{5}P$.

The first inequality yields $P < 3,333.\overline{3}$.

The second yields $P > 3,125$.

Any answer choice that falls between these two numbers is correct.

Question

3. If a is a positive even integer less than 10, b is a negative even integer greater than –10, and c is a positive odd integer between 2 and 10, which of the following cannot be an integer?

    (A) $\dfrac{bc}{a}$

    (B) $\dfrac{ac}{b}$

    (C) $\dfrac{ab}{c}$

    (D) $\dfrac{ab}{c^2}$

    (E) $\dfrac{2ab}{c^3}$

Answer Explanation

The correct answer is (E). "Which of the following cannot be" means that you can eliminate any answer choice for which you can find at least one example that *can* be true. In other words, it does not matter if, let's say, for choice (A), the fraction $\dfrac{bc}{a}$ is sometimes not an integer. As long as it can be an integer at least once, then (A) is not the correct answer choice.

First, turn the abstract language into more concrete wording.

- If a is a positive even integer less than 10, then a may be 2, 4, 6, or 8.
- If b is a negative even integer greater than –10, then b may be –2, –4, –6, or –8.
- If c is a positive odd integer between 2 and 10, then   may be 3, 5, 7, or 9.

Next, move on to the answer choices:

    (A) As long as $a = 2$, then $\dfrac{bc}{a}$ will be an integer, no matter what the other two numbers are.

        Eliminate it.

(B) As long as $b = -2$, then $\dfrac{ac}{b}$ will be an integer, no matter what the other two numbers are. Eliminate it.

(C) If $c = 3$ and either $a = 6$ or $b = -6$ (or both), then $\dfrac{ab}{c}$ will be an integer. Eliminate it.

(D) If $c = 3$, $a = 6$ and $b = -6$, then $\dfrac{ab}{c^2}$ will be an integer. Eliminate it.

(E) 5 and 7 are not part of the prime factorization of any of the possible values that a and b may take, so if $c = 5$ or $c = 7$, $\dfrac{2ab}{c^3}$ cannot be an integer. If $c = 3$, raising it to the third power will produce three 3s in the denominator. At best, the numerator will have two 3s as factors (if $a = 6$ and $= -$), so $\dfrac{2ab}{c^3}$ cannot be an integer if $c = 3$. Finally, if $c = 9$, the denominator will have even more 3s. Thus, $\dfrac{2ab}{c^3}$ cannot be an integer.

Question

4. A drawer contains 20 pairs of socks: some white, some black, and the rest brown. Picking at random, one has a 0.4 probability of removing a white pair. If 1 white pair, 1 brown pair, and 3 black pairs are added, and no pairs are removed, what is the probability that one will pick at random either a black or a brown pair?

   (A) 0.36
   (B) 0.4
   (C) 0.6
   (D) 0.64
   (E) 0.8

Answer Explanation

The correct answer is (D). If one has a 0.4 probability of picking a white pair out of the 20 pairs in the drawer, then there must be $0.4 \times 20 = 8$ pairs in the drawer. When the new pairs are added, the result is 9 white pairs out of 25 total pairs. Since you're asked for the probability of picking either a black or a brown pair, do not worry about the specific numbers for black and brown. You only need to treat black and brown pairs as one group: the nonwhite pairs of socks.

If there are 9 white pairs, then there are 16 nonwhite ones. Thus, the probability of picking a nonwhite pair out of the 25 is $\dfrac{16}{25} = 0.64$.

Question

5. The average (arithmetic mean) weight of a football team's offensive linemen is 320 pounds, while the average weight of the team's defensive linemen is 300 pounds. If the team has at least 50% more defensive linemen than offensive linemen, which of the following could be the average weight of all of the team's offensive and defensive linemen, combined?

Indicate <u>all</u> such weights.

(A) 304

(B) 305

(C) 306

(D) 307

(E) 308

(F) 309

Answer Explanation

The correct answers are (A), (B), (C), (D), and (E). Calculate the greatest possible value and then select all the choices that fall between it and 300. If the team has exactly 50% more defensive linemen than offensive linemen, then for every 3 defensive linemen there are 2 offensive linemen. In this scenario, the average of the weights is the following weighted average:

$$\frac{2 \times 320 + 3 \times 300}{5} = 308$$

If the team has more than 50% defensive linemen, then that average will be even lower.

ALERT!

This is a data sufficiency question— and remember that an answer statement is sufficient if it tells you that *ABCD* certainly IS a rectangle, or certainly IS NOT a rectangle.

Question

6. *ABCD* is a quadrilateral, with side *AB* parallel to side *CD*. Which of the following statements individually provide(s) sufficient additional information to determine whether *ABCD* is a rectangle or not?

Indicate <u>all</u> such statements.

(A) The diagonals *AC* and *BD* are of equal length.

(B) The diagonals *AC* and *BD* are not of equal length.

(C) The measure of angle *CDA* is 90°, and both pairs of opposite angles are equal.

Answer Explanation

The correct answers are (B) and (C). The first statement mentions a property that rectangles have: diagonals of equal length. However, rectangles are not the only quadrilaterals with this property. Isosceles trapezoids also have diagonals of equal length:

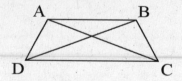

The first statement is insufficient to show whether the quadrilateral is a rectangle, so eliminate it.

The second statement, however, is sufficient to show that *ABCD* is not a rectangle: If *ABCD*'s diagonals are not equal to each other, *ABCD* cannot be a rectangle.

The final statement gives you the most information yet. Because the opposite angles are equal in pairs, *ABCD* is a parallelogram. Further, since one of the angles is a right angle, all four of them are right. Thus, *ABCD* is a rectangle, and this statement is sufficient also.

Question

7. In a high school orchestra, 40% of the string players are violinists, 20% are violists, 25% are cellists, and 15% are bassists. If 2 violinists, 1 violist, 1 cellist, and 1 bassist are added, what will be the percentage of violinists in the orchestra? (Assume no other changes to the orchestra's string section.)

    (A) 30%

    (B) 35%

    (C) 40%

    (D) 45%

    (E) It cannot be determined.

Answer Explanation

The correct answer is (C). This is a tricky question. Answer choice (E) seems correct, since you know only the starting percentages of string players but not their exact numbers. On the other hand, choice (E) may be a trap. If you don't feel confident, you can skip this question and revisit it later. However, working from what you know, you can make the information more concrete, and arrive at the correct answer. Five new string players are added, and two of them are violinists. In other words, 40% of the new players are violinists. Because 40% of the original string players were violinists, and 40% of the ones added are violinists, the percentage of violinists remains intact.

Question

8. If *a* and *b* are two of the solutions of the equation $x^3 - x^2 - 6x = 0$, with $a \neq 0$ and $a \neq b$, then which of the following could be the graph of $\dfrac{x}{a} > b$?

    Indicate <u>all</u> such graphs.

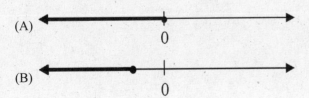

(A)

0

(B)

0

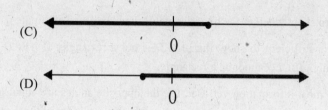

(C)

0

(D)

0

Answer Explanation

The correct answers are (A), (B), and (D). Begin by scanning the answer choices in order to see what type of answers to look for. Next, work out the math in the question, and see which answer choices fit your results.

First, manipulate the equation $x^3 - x^2 - 6x = 0$. Factor out an x from each term:

$$x(x^2 - x - 6) = 0$$

Then factor the quadratic expression, using reverse FOIL (First, Outside, Inside, Last). Remember that $x^2 - x - 6 = (x + a)(x + b)$, where $ab = -6$ and $a + b = -1$, the coefficient of x. The numbers 2 and -3 for a and b are the only ones that qualify, so the expression becomes $x(x + 2)(x - 3) = 0$.

Thus, the possible solutions of the equation are $x = 0$, $x = -2$, and $x = 3$. All three of these solutions are possible values for b and the possible values for a are -2 or 3.

Next, move on to the inequality $\dfrac{x}{a} > b$. There are four different possibilities:

1. If $a = -2$ and $b = 0$, then $x < 0$ (Remember that multiplying both sides of an inequality by a negative number reverses the direction of the inequality.) The graph of this inequality appears in answer choice (A).

2. If $a = -2$ and $b = 3$, then $x < -6$. The graph of this inequality appears in choice (B).

3. If $a = 3$ and $b = 0$, then $x > 0$. The graph of this inequality is not listed.

4. If $a = 3$ and $b = -2$, then $x > -6$. The graph of this inequality appears in choice (D).

Question

9. Each of the managers of a 20-person technical support team received \$3000 as a year-end bonus, while each of the nonmanagers received \$1200. If the total amount that the 20 employees received was \$31,200, how many of the team's members are managers?

(A) 1

(B) 2

(C) 3

(D) 4

(E) 5

TIP

When you are working backwards, start with the middle answer choice. That way, if the answer is wrong, you will know if you need to check the answers that are more or less than the middle answer.

Answer Explanation

The correct answer is (D). Work backwards, starting with choice (C). If there are 3 managers, then together they received \$9000. The remaining 17 employees received \$20,400. These two amounts add up to \$29,400, which is too low. Thus, there are more than 3 managers. Move on to choice (D).

If there are 4 managers, then together they received $12,000. The remaining 16 employees received $19,200. These two add up to $31,200.

QUESTIONS 10–12 ARE BASED ON THE FOLLOWING DATA.

INCOME DATA FOR TOWN X's FOUR NEIGHBORHOODS: A, B, C, and D.

Annual Income in 2011	Percent of Neighborhood Populations			
	A	B	C	D
$0–$24,999	14%	4%	17%	13%
$25,000–$49,999	30%	19%	34%	31%
$50,000–$74,999	26%	29%	27%	32%
$75,000–$99,999	19%	28%	15%	18%
$100,000–$249,999	9%	14%	6%	5%
> $250,000	2%	6%	1%	1%

Question

10. In the neighborhood with the smallest percentage of six-figure earners in 2011, what percent of the population earned less than $50,000 that year?

    (A) 23
    (B) 31
    (C) 34
    (D) 44
    (E) 51

Answer Explanation

The correct answer is (D). Make sure you're answering the correct question. "Six-figure earners" means that you have to look at the bottom two rows, not just the bottom row. Also, "less than $50,000" means you should add the top two rows in the appropriate column. So, first, identify the neighborhood with the smallest percentage of six-figure earners: that's neighborhood D, $5+1 = 6\%$ of its residents earn $100,000 or more. Next, add the percentages of D residents who earned between $0 and $49,999: $13+31 = 44$.

Question

11. If the percentage of people who resided in neighborhood B in 2011 and earned between $0 and $24,999 was 20% less than the percentage of people who resided in neighborhood B in 2001 and earned between $0 and $24,999, and if the latter percentage was 20% less than the percentage of people who resided in neighborhood B in 1991 and earned between $0 and $24,999, what percent of the people who resided in neighborhood B in 1991 earned between $0 and $24,999 that year?

    (A) 4
    (B) 5

(C) 6

(D) 6.25

(E) 6.67

Answer Explanation

The correct answer is (D). First, translate English into math:

The percentage of B residents who earned between $0 and $24,999 in 2011 is 4.

20% fewer B residents earned between $0 and $24,999 in 2011 than in 2001. Hence, if X is the percentage of those folks who earned between $0 and $24,999 in 2001, then $4 = \dfrac{80}{100}X \Rightarrow X = \dfrac{400}{80}$.

20% fewer B residents earned between $0 and $24,999 in 2001 than in 1991. Hence, if Y is the percentage of those folks who earned between $0 and $24,999 in 1991, then $X = \dfrac{80}{100}Y \Rightarrow \dfrac{400}{80} = \dfrac{80}{100}Y$. Solve for

Y to get $Y = 6.25$.

Question

12. Which of the following statements must be true?

    Indicate all such statements.

    (A) In 2011, the neighborhood with the highest average income was neighborhood B.

    (B) 12% of the people living in town X in 2011 earned less than $25,000 that year.

    (C) If in 2011 more than twice as many people lived in neighborhood A as in neighborhood B, then the number of people who lived in neighborhood A and earned $100,000 or more was greater than the number of people who lived in neighborhood B and earned $100,000 or more.

Answer Explanation

The correct answer is (C). Do not conclude hastily that statement 1 (A) is true. It may be, for instance, that all of the B residents earned at the lowest end of their income range (e.g., all the $250,000+ earners actually earned $250,000), while the A residents earned at the highest end of their income range. In this scenario, the residents in neighborhood A had a higher average income than the residents in neighborhood B.

Statement 2 (B) takes the straight average of the percentages of residents in the four neighborhoods who earned between $0 and $24,999. However, if all four neighborhoods did not have the same number of people in 2011, you need a weighted average—and such an average may be different from 12%. Thus, statement 2 (B) is not necessarily true.

Finally, evaluate statement 3 (C). In 2011, 11% of the residents in neighborhood A earned $100,000 or more, and 20% of the B residents did also. If P_A is the total number of A residents in 2011 and P_B is the total number of B residents in 2011, then $P_A > 2P_B$. Thus, 11% of P_A is greater than 20% of P_B and statement 3 (C) is true.

Question

13. Which of the following graphs intersect(s) the graph of $y = x$?
Indicate <u>all</u> such graphs.

(A) The graph of $y = 2x + 2$

(B) The graph of $y = |2x + 2|$

(C) The graph of $y = -x + 2$

Answer Explanation

The correct answers are (A) and (C). There are several ways to solve this question. You may treat it as a question that asks you to solve two equations simultaneously, you may choose to work with slopes and intercepts, you may pick numbers, or you may draw diagrams.

Solving a system of two equations is simple algebra, so it's an easy way to evaluate choices (A) and (C). First, choice (A), $y = 2x + 2$, solves a system of two equations.

If $y = x$ and $y = 2x + 2$ intersect, then there is an (x, y) pair that satisfies them both. Let the two ys be equal to each other, and see if that leads to a possible value of x:

$2x + 2 = x \Rightarrow x = -2$

For both equations, when x equals -2, y equals -2, so the two lines intersect.

You can evaluate choice (C) in the same way:

$-x + 2 = x \Rightarrow x = 1$

For both equations, when x equals 1, y equals 1, so the two lines intersect.

The absolute value in choice (B) makes the system of equations approach trickier. Instead, draw a diagram in order to make things more concrete:

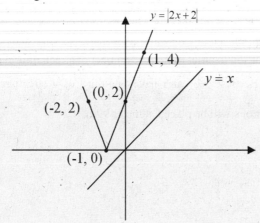

The graph of $y = x$ is easy to plot. As for the graph of $y = |2x + 2|$, four points are sufficient to plot it: when $x = 0$, $y = 2$; when $x = 1$, $y = 4$; when $x = -1$, $y = 0$; and when $x = -2$, $y = 2$. You can see from the diagram that the graphs of these two equations do not intersect.

Question

14. Streetlamps are to be placed along one side of a 1-kilometer-long road. Each streetlamp has a diameter of 50 centimeters. If the distance between streetlamps is 29.5 meters, and the first streetlamp is placed at one end of the road, how many streetlamps will be needed? (1 meter equals 100 centimeters. 1 kilometer equals 1,000 meters)

    (A) 30
    (B) 31
    (C) 32
    (D) 33
    (E) 34

Answer Explanation

The correct answer is (D). Rather than trying to work out this question in the abstract, draw a diagram in order to get a clearer picture of what's going on:

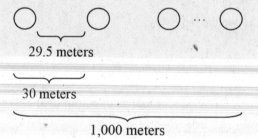

29.5 meters

30 meters

1,000 meters

So, one streetlamp will be placed at every 30-meter mark, starting with one lamp at the 0-meter mark. Now set up a proportion in order to find the number of streetlamps required for 1,000 meters: $\frac{1}{30} = \frac{x}{1000} \Rightarrow x = 33.3$. Because we can't have one-third of a streetlamp, the total number of streetlamps is 33 (the last one will be placed at meter 990).

Question

15. If x and y are integers such that $|x - y| = 1$, which of the following statements individually provide(s) sufficient additional information to determine what x is?

Indicate all such statements.

(A) x and y are the solutions of the equation $a^2 + 7a + 12 = 0$

(B) $y = 3$

(C) x and y are both prime numbers, and y is odd

Answer Explanation

The correct answer is (C). This is another data sufficiency question. First, you need to understand the question stem.

If $|x - y| = 1$, then either $x - y = 1$ or $x - y = -1$.

x and y are consecutive integers (since the absolute value of their difference is 1), but otherwise, the range of possibilities for x and y is infinite. There's nothing more you can do with the question stem alone.

Step 2 is to consider the first statement, (A). Factor the quadratic equation:

$a^2 + 7a + 12 = 0 \Rightarrow (a + 4)(a + 3) = 0$. The two solutions are $a = -4$ and $a = -3$. However, you do not know which of the two solutions is x and which is y, so this answer choice is not sufficient for you to determine what the value of x is. (Plug in $x = -4$ and $y = -3$, and then $x = -3$ and $y = -4$ into the absolute value equation in the question stem, and you'll see that both options work.)

The second statement, (B), pins down the value of y. However, that is still not sufficient: The absolute value equation is satisfied if $x = 4$ as well as if $x = 2$.

Moving on to the third statement, (C), because x and y are consecutive integers (as you determined above), and if both are prime, then they have to be the numbers 2 and 3. (All other prime numbers are odd, so the only way to get two consecutive integers that are both prime is if one of the two is the number 2.) Additionally, y is odd, which means that $x = 2$. This statement is sufficient.

SUMMING IT UP

- There are two types of multiple-choice questions on the Quantitative Reasoning section of the GRE:
  - multiple-choice—select one answer choice
  - multiple-choice—select one or more answer choices
- Multiple-choice questions may be structured separately or they may be part of a data interpretation set, which includes several questions built around presentation of data such as a table or graph.
- Multiple-choice questions that require only one answer have five answer choices to select from. Each answer choice is preceded by an oval.
- Multiple-choice questions that ask for one or more answer choices are accompanied by a varying number of answer choices. These answer choices are preceded by squares, not ovals, as a signal to choose one or more answer choices.
- Strategies that are useful for all math questions are the following:
  - Make sure you're answering the correct question.
  - Skip and come back to questions—used sparingly.
- Strategies specific to multiple-choice questions—select one answer choice are the following:
  - Pick and plug numbers.
  - Work backwards from the answer choices.
  - Turn verbose or abstract language into concise and concrete wording
  - Estimate.
- Strategies specific to multiple-choice questions—select one or more answer choices are the following:
  - Calculate the least and greatest possible values.
  - Make sure you're answering the correct question.
  - Think through data sufficiency questions.
- Strategies for data interpretation sets are the following:
  - Scan the data quickly.
  - Make sure you're answering the correct question.
  - Estimate.

Strategies for Numeric Entry Questions

chapter 10

OVERVIEW

- Answer format for numeric entry questions
- A reminder about using the on-screen calculator
- Strategies for numeric entry questions
- Practice questions
- Answer key and explanations
- Summing it up

This chapter describes the answer format for numeric entry questions and provides the following three useful strategies for solving numeric entry questions:

1. Turn verbose or abstract language into concise and concrete wording.
2. Make sure you're answering the correct question.
3. Round correctly.

Like multiple-choice questions, numeric entry questions may be stand-alone items, or they may be part of a data interpretation set: a group of questions that refer to the same tables, graphs, or other form of data presentation. Strategies for data interpretation, other than estimating, apply to numeric entry questions, as well.

Finally, remember also that you can always skip a question and return to it if you find that you're having trouble figuring out what it's asking or you think it will take too long to answer.

ANSWER FORMAT FOR NUMERIC ENTRY QUESTIONS

Numeric entry questions do not offer any answer choices from which you can choose. Rather, they present you with a question and

- one answer box, if the answer is an integer or decimal.
- two answer boxes, if the answer is a fraction.

You have to use your keyboard to input your answer in the appropriate answer box. If the answer is a fraction, type the numerator in the top box and the denominator in the bottom box.

Entering Answers

Here are a few instructions about entering answers that you should be familiar with before you take the test. Knowing how to enter answers will ease some of the stress you may experience on test day.

- To erase a numeral in the answer box, use the "backspace" key.
- To enter a negative sign, type a hyphen.
- To remove the negative sign, type the hyphen again.
- To enter a decimal point, type a period. Note that you cannot use decimal points in fractions.
- Equivalent forms of the answer, such as 2.5 and 2.50, are all correct.
- You do not need to reduce fractions to lowest terms.

A REMINDER ABOUT USING THE ON-SCREEN CALCULATOR

The on-screen calculator can be especially useful in answering numeric entry questions. One feature that can save you a few seconds—and keep you from making an entry mistake—is the "Transfer Display" function. You may click this button to transfer the number displayed on the calculator to the answer box. However, you cannot use the "Transfer Display" feature if the answer is a fraction.

Note that if you click "Transfer Display" on a question that asks you to round your answer to a certain degree of accuracy, you may need to edit the number in the answer box so that it is appropriately rounded up or down.

STRATEGIES FOR NUMERIC ENTRY QUESTIONS

Because numeric entry questions don't provide any answer choices, you will not be able to use some of the strategies—such as working backwards from the answer choices and eliminating incorrect ones—that are helpful on multiple-choice questions. On the other hand, you will not be tempted by trap answer choices, those that are the result of using incorrect processes or faulty computations. Let's review what you can—and should—do in order to answer numeric entry questions correctly.

Turn Verbose or Abstract Language into Concise and Concrete Wording

Remember to write out equations or draw diagrams when the question does not provide any, in order to get a clearer picture. In this respect, numeric entry questions are no different from multiple-choice questions.

> **FOR THIS QUESTION, ENTER YOUR ANSWER IN THE BOX.**

Example 1

Dominic bought a pair of shoes for $90, two t-shirts for $20 each, and four pairs of socks. If he paid 8% sales tax on the entire purchase, and if the total amount of the tax he paid was $12, what was the cost of each pair of socks?

Instead of trying to think this through in the abstract, write out the information you have as an equation. Let S be the cost of each pair of socks. Then, before tax, Dominic paid $\$90 + 2 \times \$20 + 4S$. The amount of tax he paid was 8% of $\$90 + 2 \times \$20 + 4S$, or

$\frac{8}{100}(\$90 + 2 \times \$20 + 4S)$. Equate this to $12 and solve for S:

$$\frac{8}{100}(\$90 + 2 \times \$20 + 4S) = \$12 \Rightarrow$$

$$\frac{2}{100}(\$90 + 2 \times \$20 + 4S) = \$3$$

$$\frac{2}{100}\$130 + \frac{2}{100}4S = \$3 \Rightarrow$$

$$\frac{2}{100}4S = \$0.4 \Rightarrow$$

$$S = \$5$$

The correct answer is \$5.

Make Sure You're Answering the Correct Question

Your worst enemy on numeric entry questions, especially if you feel you have to race against the clock, is careless mistakes—such as confusing the diameter for the radius or giving an answer in the wrong units (e.g., minutes instead of hours, or feet instead of inches). To avoid such mistakes, always read the question carefully and double-check your work.

FOR THIS QUESTION, ENTER YOUR ANSWER IN THE BOX.

Example 2

What is the median of the first ten positive integers?

This is not a hard question, but one that invites two kinds of careless mistakes. When a question asks for the mean, median, or mode, make sure you don't mistakenly calculate the wrong one. Second, don't answer hastily. In this case, don't answer "5," thinking that the middle number among the first ten positive integers will be 5. After more reasoned thinking, you would realize that because there are ten numbers—that is, an even number of numbers—the median will be the average of the middle two numbers: 5 and 6. **The correct answer is 5.5 (or equivalent).**

ALERT!

One way to be sure that you are answering the right question is to double-check your answer against the question. Did you solve for the correct variable or the proper units?

NOTE

An equivalent form of the correct answer 5.5 such as 5.50 and 5.500 will be considered correct. This is especially useful to remember when answering questions for which the answer is a fraction. You might enter this as 8/10 and someone else might enter it as 4/5. Both will be counted as correct unless you are specifically told to reduce it.

FOR THIS QUESTION, ENTER YOUR ANSWER IN THE BOXES.

Example 3

If 12 of the 20 members of Springfield's city council are male, what is the ratio of female council members to male council members?

Give your answer as a fraction.

$$\boxed{}$$
$$\boxed{}$$

Here you are asked to find a part-to-part ratio: female-to-male council members. Do not provide a part-to-whole ratio (e.g., female-to-total council members), or the wrong part-to-part ratio (male-to-female council members).

If there are 20 council members and 12 are male, the remaining 8 are female. The ratio you're looking for is $\frac{8}{12}$. Since fractions do not need to be reduced to lowest terms, you do not need to reduce $\frac{8}{12}$ to $\frac{2}{3}$. **The correct answer is $\frac{8}{12}$ (or any equivalent fraction).**

Round Correctly

Sometimes, a numeric entry question will ask you to round your answer to a certain degree of accuracy. Once you've performed the necessary calculations, don't lose sight of that instruction. For instance, if you're asked to round your answer to the nearest integer, and your calculations yield 13.6, type "14" in the answer box.

Make sure, however, that you don't round any numbers until the very end. For instance, let's say that in the process of computing the answer, you have to multiply 11.2 by 3. That product is 33.6, which, rounded to the nearest integer, is 34. However, if before performing the final calculation you had rounded 11.2 down to 11, you would have given your answer as "33," which would have been incorrect.

FOR THIS QUESTION, ENTER YOUR ANSWER IN THE BOX.

Example 4

In 2003, the sales of The Cranston Computer Company, a manufacturer of desktop and laptop computers, increased by 20% compared with 2002. In 2004, Cranston's sales decreased by 20% compared with 2003. Cranston's 2002 sales were what percent of its 2004 sales?

Give your answer to the nearest 0.1.

$$\boxed{}$$

Pick the number 100 to represent the company's sales in 2002.

Then, the 2003 sales were 120 and the 2004 sales were $120 - \frac{20}{100}(120) = 96$.

Now you need to find what percent of 96 (the 2004 sales) is 100 (the 2002 sales). Set up and solve a proportion—remembering that you need to round your answer to the nearest tenth of a percent:

$$\frac{100}{96} = \frac{x}{100} => x = \frac{10,000}{96} => x = 104.1\overline{6}$$

The correct answer is 104.2% (or equivalent).

Note that the calculator will give you the answer as 104.16667, and this is the number that will be placed into the answer box if you use the calculator's "Transfer Display" feature. In that case, you must then click onto the answer box and change "104.16667" to "104.2." If you don't, your answer will be marked incorrect.

TIP

Always read questions carefully. This plus turning confusing questions into concise and concrete wording may be the two most important strategies you can use. You need to understand what a question is asking in order to answer it correctly.

PRACTICE QUESTIONS

FOR QUESTIONS 1-10, ENTER YOUR ANSWER IN THE BOXES.

---

1. The average (arithmetic mean) of the salaries that four siblings earned last year is $50,000. If one of the siblings earned $80,000 and another earned $60,000, what is the average (arithmetic mean) of the salaries that the remaining two siblings earned last year?

   $ [   ]

2. The perimeter of a square with a side of 4 inches is equal to the perimeter of a rectangle with a height of 3 inches. What fraction of the rectangle's area is the square's area?

   Give your answer as a fraction.

   $$\frac{[\quad]}{[\quad]}$$

3. Justin bought 160 shares of company A and 50 shares of company B for a total purchase price of $2450. At the same per-share prices, Susan bought 40 shares of company A and 50 shares of company B, for a total purchase price of $1250. How much did Justin pay in total for his shares of company A?

   $ [   ]

4. Line l is perpendicular to line $2x = 3y - 6$. If the point $(0,2)$ lies on line l, what is the x-intercept of line l?

   Give your answer as a fraction.

   $$\frac{[\quad]}{[\quad]}$$

5. For all numbers a and b, $a \Diamond b = a^2 b$. What is the value of $\left[(-2) \Diamond (-3) \right] \Diamond (-2)$?

   [   ]

6. Company A, a widget manufacturer, has eight stores in town X. The average (arithmetic mean) number of widgets these stores sold in March 2006 is 150. Not including the company's flagship store in town X, the average (arithmetic mean) number of widgets the remaining seven stores sold in March 2006 is 130. How many widgets did the flagship store sell in March 2006?

   [   ]

QUESTIONS 7–8 ARE BASED ON THE FOLLOWING DATA.

SALES OF NEW CARS IN COUNTRY A,

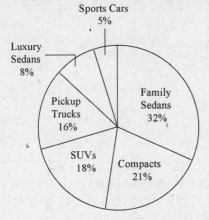

AVERAGE HIGHWAY FUEL
CONSUMPTION, BY CATEGORY, FOR
NEW CARS SOLD IN 2010

Category	Average Fuel Consumption
Compact Cars	32
Family Sedans	28
Luxury Sedans	24
Sports Cars	24
SUVs	23
Pickup Trucks	21

7. If in 2010 the total number of new cars that were sold across all categories was 1,621,018, how many categories of cars had sales of fewer than 250,000 cars?

8. What was the average fuel consumption on the highway for all cars sold in 2010?

   Give your answer to the nearest 0.1.

9. Working alone at its constant rate, Machine A produces 15 widgets every 90 minutes. Working alone at its constant rate, Machine B produces widgets twice as quickly as does Machine A. If the two machines work together at their respective constant rates, how many hours will it take them to produce 75 widgets?

   hours

10. Two of the eight lawyers who work at a law firm are partners, while the rest are associates. If a team of five lawyers is to be selected randomly from among these eight lawyers, what is the probability that more than 80% of the lawyers on the team will be associates?

    Give your answer to the nearest 0.01.

ANSWER KEY AND EXPLANATIONS

1. $30,000	6. 290
2. $\dfrac{16}{15}$	7. 2
3. $1600	8. 26.3
4. $\dfrac{4}{3}$	9. 2.5
5. −288	10. 0.11

Question

1. The average (arithmetic mean) of the salaries that four siblings earned last year is $50,000. If one of the siblings earned $80,000 and another earned $60,000, what is the average (arithmetic mean) of the salaries that the remaining two siblings earned last year?

$\boxed{}$

Answer Explanation

The correct answer is $30,000 (or equivalent). Read the question carefully and double-check your calculations along the way in order to avoid careless mistakes. If the four siblings earned $50,000 on average, then together they earned $50,000 \times 4 = $200,000.

Two of the siblings earned $140,000 of that $200,000, so the remaining two siblings together earned $200,000 − $140,000 = $60,000. Thus, the average of the salaries for these two siblings is $60,000 ÷ 2 = $30,000.

Question

2. The perimeter of a square with a side of 4 inches is equal to the perimeter of a rectangle with a height of 3 inches. What fraction of the rectangle's area is the square's area?

Give your answer as a fraction.

$\dfrac{\boxed{}}{\boxed{}}$

Answer Explanation

The correct answer is $\dfrac{16}{15}$ (or any equivalent fraction). Make sure you're answering the correct question: the rectangle's area should go in the denominator, and the square's area in the numerator. The perimeter of the square is $4 \times 4 = 16$ inches.

If the width of the rectangle is y inches, and because its perimeter is also 16 inches (equal to the square's perimeter), then $2y + 2 \times 3 = 16 \Rightarrow y = 5$.

Next, find the areas of the two shapes.

The square's area is $4 \times 4 = 16$ sq. inches.

The rectangle's area is $3 \times 5 = 15$ sq. inches.

Thus, the square's area is $\dfrac{16}{15}$ of the rectangle's area.

Question

3. Justin bought 160 shares of company A and 50 shares of company B for a total purchase price of $2450. At the same per-share prices, Susan bought 40 shares of company A and 50 shares of company B, for a total purchase price of $1250. How much did Justin pay in total for his shares of company A?

$

Answer Explanation

The correct answer is $1600 (or equivalent). Turn the question's words into concrete equations. Let A be the per-share price for company A and B be the per-share price for company B. Write out equations for Justin's and Susan's purchases.

Justin's purchase: $160A + 50B = \$2450$.

Susan's purchase: $40A + 50B = \$1250$.

Subtract the second equation from the first one and solve for A: $120A = \$1200 \Rightarrow A = \$10$.

So Justin paid $10 for each share of company A. Since he bought 160 such shares, he paid $1600 for them, in total.

Question

4. Line l is perpendicular to line $2x = 3y - 6$. If the point $(0,2)$ lies on line l, what is the x-intercept of line l?

   Give your answer as a fraction.

Answer Explanation

The correct answer is $\dfrac{4}{3}$ (or any equivalent fraction). This question requires several steps of equation manipulation, so solve carefully and double-check your work before you move on. Also make sure you do not answer the wrong question: You're looking for the x-intercept, not the y-intercept or the slope.

Perpendicular lines have slopes that are negative reciprocals of each other, that is, slopes whose product is –1. Rewrite $2x = 3y - 6$ in the slope-intercept form, $y = mx + b$, where m is the line's slope and b its y-intercept:

$$y = \frac{2}{3}x + 2$$

Therefore, the slope of $2x = 3y - 6$ is $\frac{2}{3}$, and so line l has a slope of $-\frac{3}{2}$.

Next, consider point (0,2). Because this point lies on line l, the y-intercept of line l (that is, the y-value of the point at which the line crosses the y-axis) is 2.

Now write line l in slope-intercept form: $y = -\frac{3}{2}x + 2$.

You're looking for the line's x-intercept, that is, the x-value of the point at which the line crosses the x-axis. Set $y = 0$ and solve for x:

$$0 = -\frac{3}{2}x + 2 \Rightarrow x = \frac{4}{3}$$

Question

5. For all numbers a and b, $a \lozenge b = a^2 b$. What is the value of $\left[(-2) \lozenge (-3)\right] \lozenge (-2)$?

Answer Explanation

The correct answer is –288 (or equivalent). Here, too, you should solve carefully and double-check your work before you move on. Perform the calculations, starting with the operation in brackets to the left.

$$\left[(-2) \lozenge (-3)\right] \lozenge (-2) = \left[(-2)^2 \times (-3)\right] \lozenge (-2)$$

$$= \left[4 \times (-3)\right] \lozenge (-2)$$

$$= (-12) \lozenge (-2)$$

$$= (-12)^2 \times (-2)$$

$$= 144 \times (-2)$$

$$= -288$$

Question

6. Company A, a widget manufacturer, has eight stores in town X. The average (arithmetic mean) number of widgets these stores sold in March, 2006 is 150. Not including the company's flagship store in town X, the average (arithmetic mean) number of widgets the remaining seven stores sold in March, 2006 is 130. How many widgets did the flagship store sell in March, 2006?

Answer Explanation

The correct answer is 290 (or equivalent). Turn words into equations. The eight stores together sold $150 \times 8 = 1200$ widgets.

The seven stores other than the flagship store averaged 130 widgets, so together they sold $130 \times 7 = 910$.

Thus, the flagship store sold $1200 - 910 = 290$ widgets.

QUESTIONS 7–8 ARE BASED ON THE FOLLOWING DATA.

SALES OF NEW CARS IN COUNTRY A, BY CATEGORY, IN 2010

AVERAGE HIGHWAY FUEL CONSUMPTION, BY CATEGORY, FOR NEW CARS SOLD IN 2010

Category	Average Fuel Consumption
Compact Cars	32
Family Sedans	28
Luxury Sedans	24
Sports Cars	24
SUVs	23
Pickup Trucks	21

Question

7. If in 2010 the total number of new cars that were sold across all categories was 1,621,018, how many categories of cars had sales of fewer than 250,000 cars?

Answer Explanation

The correct answer is 2 (or equivalent). Find what percent of 1,621,018 is 250,000:

$$\frac{250,000}{1,621,018} = \frac{x}{100} \Rightarrow x \approx 15.42$$

There were only two categories whose sales were less than 15.42% of the total: luxury sedans and sports cars. Make sure that you don't mistakenly answer 4, the number of categories of cars with sales of more than 15.4% of the total.

Question

8. What was the average highway fuel consumption for all cars sold in 2010?

   Give your answer to the nearest 0.1.

   [   ]

Answer Explanation

The correct answer is 26.3 (or equivalent). For this question, you need to use the two data displays together. Additionally, in the end you must remember to round correctly. The question asks you for a weighted average. Assume there were 100 cars sold, 32 of which were family sedans, 21 of which were compact cars, and so on. Then, multiply the number of cars in each category by that category's average fuel consumption. Finally, divide this product by 100, the total number of cars sold:

$$\frac{32 \times 28 + 21 \times 32 + 18 \times 23 + 16 \times 21 + 8 \times 24 + 5 \times 24}{100} = 26.3$$

Question

9. Working alone at its constant rate, Machine A produces 15 widgets every 90 minutes. Working alone at its constant rate, Machine B produces widgets twice as quickly as does Machine A. If the two machines work together at their respective constant rates, how many hours will it take them to produce 75 widgets?

   [   ] hours

Answer Explanation

The correct answer is 2.5 (or equivalent). Make the information in this question more concrete. You need to start by finding how many widgets each machine produces in an hour. If Machine A produces 15 widgets every 90 minutes, then it produces two-thirds of that number, or 10 widgets, every hour.

Machine B is twice as fast, so it produces $2 \times 10 = 20$ widgets every hour. Thus, the two machines working together produce $10 + 20 = 30$ widgets every hour. To find how many hours the two machines together will need in order to produce 75 widgets, set up and solve the proportion: $\frac{30}{1} = \frac{75}{x} \Rightarrow x = 2.5$

Question

10. Two of the eight lawyers who work at a law firm are partners, while the rest are associates. If a team of five lawyers is to be selected randomly from among these eight lawyers, what is the probability that more than 80% of the lawyers on the team will be associates?

    Give your answer to the nearest 0.01.

    [   ]

Answer Explanation

The correct answer is 0.11 (or equivalent). Make the information in the question more concrete, so that you get a better understanding of what you're looking for. If more than 80%—that is, more than four out of five—of the lawyers on the team are associates, then all five of them will be associates. To find the probability that all five of the lawyers on the team will be associates, divide the number of desirable outcomes (the total number of ways five associates can be selected from the firm's six associates) by the number of all possible outcomes (the total number of ways five lawyers can be selected from the firm's eight lawyers).

The total number of ways five associates can be selected from the firm's six associates is $_6C_5 = \dfrac{6!}{5! \times 1!}$, which equals 6.

The total number of ways five lawyers can be selected from the firm's eight lawyers is $_8C_5 = \dfrac{8!}{5! \times 3!}$.

Simplify this fraction: $_8C_5 = \dfrac{8!}{5! \times 3!} = \dfrac{8 \times 7 \times 6 \times 5!}{5! \times 3 \times 2} = 56$

Thus, the probability that more than 80% of the lawyers on the team will be associates is $\dfrac{6}{56}$. That fraction is equal to 0.107…. Make sure you round correctly: rounded to the nearest hundredth, 0.107… equals 0.11.

SUMMING IT UP

- Numeric entry questions do not offer lists of possible answers. Instead, you will be presented with a question and one or two answer boxes.

  o If the answer should be an integer or a decimal, there will be one answer box.

  o If the answer should be in the form of a fraction, there will be two answer boxes, one over the other for numerator and denominator.

- Some numeric entry questions may be part of a data interpretation set.

- The screen will show a calculator for you to use.

  o To erase numerals in an answer box, use the "backspace" key.

  o To enter a negative sign, type a hyphen, and to erase a negative sign, type the hyphen again.

  o To enter a decimal point, use a period.

- Equivalent forms of an answer are correct.

- Fractions don't need to be reduced to lowest terms, but some directions may instruct you to round decimals up or down.

- The three specific strategies to use for solving numeric entry questions are the following:

  o Turn verbose or abstract language into concise and concrete wording.

  o Make sure you're answering the correct question.

  o Round correctly.

Strategies for Quantitative Comparison Questions

chapter 11

OVERVIEW

- Basic information about quantitative comparison questions
- Strategies for quantitative comparison questions
- Practice questions
- Answer key and explanations
- Summing it up

In this chapter, you will find an introduction to the quantitative comparison questions that you will find on the GRE as well as a discussion of strategies to help you answer these questions quickly and competently. A few of these strategies will be familiar to you from the chapters on multiple-choice questions and numeric entry questions. Most, however, are specific to answering quantitative comparison questions. The strategies are:

- Pick and plug numbers.
- Simplify the quantities.
- Avoid unnecessary calculations.
- Estimate.
- Redraw the figure.
- Recognize when the answer cannot be choice (D). The relationship cannot be determined from the information given.

The one thing you won't find in the quantitative comparison section of the GRE is data sets. Each quantitative comparison question is a stand-alone item.

BASIC INFORMATION ABOUT QUANTITATIVE COMPARISON QUESTIONS

Quantitative comparisons present you with two Quantities, A and B. Your task is to compare these quantities and choose one of the following answers:

- Quantity A is greater.
- Quantity B is greater.
- The two quantities are equal.
- The relationship cannot be determined from the information given.

These answer choices, *in this exact order,* appear with all quantitative comparison questions. Memorize the answers in order, so you don't waste time reading them for each question.

On the official GRE, these answer choices are not labeled (A), (B), and so on. They are merely listed in this order, each with an oval to its left. For your convenience in this book, we've labeled the ovals (A), (B), (C), and (D).

There are two other points of information to remember.

1. Some questions feature additional information centered above the two quantities. You should use this information to help you determine the relationship between the two quantities.

2. Any symbol that appears more than once in a question (e.g., one that appears in Quantity A and in the centered information) has the same meaning throughout the question.

STRATEGIES FOR QUANTITATIVE COMPARISON QUESTIONS

In addition to the strategies explained here, remember that you can always skip and return to a question. You have to click the "Mark" button so that you can find the question quickly in the "Review" screen when you are ready to give it another try. However, you can only go back to a question in the section you are currently working on.

Pick and Plug Numbers

Picking and plugging numbers to represent variables is a powerful strategy if you are asked to compare expressions that contain variables. You pick numbers to represent the variables, and then plug these numbers into the expressions given in Quantities A and B. Work quickly, but also thoroughly. Depending on the question, you should choose

- not only positive, but also negative numbers.

- not only integers, but also fractions (in particular fractions between 0 and 1, and 0 and −1).

- the numbers 1 and 0.

> **FOR THIS QUESTION, COMPARE QUANTITY A AND QUANTITY B. THIS QUESTION HAS ADDITIONAL INFORMATION ABOVE THE TWO QUANTITIES TO USE IN DETERMINING YOUR ANSWER.**

Example 1

$$\frac{x}{y} = 3$$

$$y \neq 0$$

Quantity A	**Quantity B**
x	y

(A) Quantity A is greater.

(B) Quantity B is greater.

(C) The two quantities are equal.

(D) The relationship cannot be determined from the information given.

First, rewrite the centered information as $x = 3y$, which is easier to work with.

This question features variables in both quantities, so picking numbers is likely to get you to the right answer quickly. Choose different numbers for y, and see what results you get for x, as well as what the relationship between the two quantities is. To keep track of the results, draw a table on your scratch paper.

y		x
1	<	3
2	<	6
$\frac{1}{3}$	<	1

So, when y equals 1, x equals 3; when y equals 2, x equals 6; and when, y equals $\frac{1}{3}$, x equals 1. In all three cases x is greater than y, so you may be tempted to conclude that Quantity A will always be greater than Quantity B. However, you have not tested a sufficient variety of numbers so far, so you should not jump to a conclusion yet. (In fact, testing $y = 2$ in particular was a waste of time because there was no reason to think that it would have yielded a different result than did $y = 1$.) In order to be thorough, you should also test numbers that have some different properties.

y		x
-1	>	-3

In this example, picking a negative number for y results in y being greater than x. Because you have now found at least one instance in which x is greater than y, as well as at least one instance in which y is greater than x, you are finished. **The correct answer is (D).**

FOR THIS QUESTION, COMPARE QUANTITY A AND QUANTITY B. THIS QUESTION HAS ADDITIONAL INFORMATION ABOVE THE TWO QUANTITIES TO USE IN DETERMINING YOUR ANSWER.

Example 2

$$\frac{x}{y} = 3$$

$$y \neq 0$$

Quantity A	Quantity B
$|x|$	$|y|$

(A) Quantity A is greater.
(B) Quantity B is greater.
(C) The two quantities are equal.
(D) The relationship cannot be determined from the information given.

This question is similar to Example 1, but there is one important difference. You are now being asked to compare the absolute values of the two variables, not the variables themselves.

Again, start by rewriting the centered information in the following form: $x = 3y$

Pick numbers, again.

y	x	$|y|$		$|x|$
1	3	1	<	3
-1	-3	1	<	3
$\dfrac{1}{6}$	$\dfrac{1}{2}$	$\dfrac{1}{6}$	<	$\dfrac{1}{2}$

This time, because the absolute values eliminate the minus signs, the pattern that emerges is reliable. Because x equals 3 times y and because you're asked to compare the absolute values of x and y, no matter what value you pick for y, the absolute value of x will always be greater than the absolute value of y. **The correct answer is (A).**

When to Use Pick and Plug and When Not

Picking numbers is a useful strategy, but you should keep in mind that it doesn't always answer the question definitively.

- It is best used when it reveals quickly two different relationships between the quantities, in which case you have proved that the answer is choice (D).

- It is also helpful if the possible values that the variables may take are few, and you are able to test them all.

However, if the possible values that the variables may take are infinite—or if they are finite, but too many for you to check in any reasonable amount of time—then you cannot use this strategy alone to answer the question. Even if you test many numbers, all of which produce the same result, it's entirely possible that some other numbers, which you have not tested yet, may produce a different result.

That said, even in such a case, picking numbers may be useful if you are stuck and do not know how to proceed. After you've picked a few numbers and examined the results, you may notice a pattern that you may not have noticed previously, and that will help you compare the quantities.

Simplify the Quantities

Sometimes, test-item writers present you with expressions—either in the two quantities or in the centered information—that appear complicated, thus making your job harder. In such cases you can help yourself by

- simplifying each quantity in order to make it easier to evaluate on its own.

- manipulating one quantity in such a way as to make it easier to compare with the other quantity.

- simplifying the centered information so that you end up with a new piece of information that's easier to interpret.

TIP
Always read questions carefully. This plus turning confusing questions into concise and concrete wording may be the two most important strategies you can use. You need to understand what a question is asking in order to answer it correctly.

> **FOR THIS QUESTION, COMPARE QUANTITY A AND QUANTITY B.**

Example 3

Quantity A	**Quantity B**
$4x^2 - 8x + 4$	$(2x-2)^2$

(A) Quantity A is greater.

(B) Quantity B is greater.

(C) The two quantities are equal.

(D) The relationship cannot be determined from the information given.

As written, these quantities are hard to compare. However, you can manipulate either quantity so that it resembles the other one. For instance, if you distribute Quantity B you get:

$$(2x-2)^2 = 4x^2 - 8x + 4$$

Thus, Quantity A is the distributed form of Quantity B, so the quantities are equal. **The correct answer is (C).**

> **FOR THIS QUESTION, COMPARE QUANTITY A AND QUANTITY B. THIS QUESTION HAS ADDITIONAL INFORMATION ABOVE THE TWO QUANTITIES TO USE IN DETERMINING YOUR ANSWER.**

Example 4

$$-1 < x < y < 0$$

Quantity A	**Quantity B**
xy	$\dfrac{x}{y}$

(A) Quantity A is greater.

(B) Quantity B is greater.

(C) The two quantities are equal.

(D) The relationship cannot be determined from the information given.

In this question, you should simplify the two quantities together in order to arrive at something that's easier to compare. Start by assuming that one quantity is larger than the other, and simplify the inequality until you arrive at a statement that you can evaluate. If that statement is correct, then your initial assumption was correct. If that statement is incorrect, your initial assumption was incorrect. Let's see this process at work.

Begin by assuming that Quantity A is larger than Quantity B:

$$xy > \frac{x}{y}.$$

Next, cancel x from both sides of the inequality—that is, divide both sides by x. You can do this for two reasons: First, because $x \neq 0$, division by x is permissible; second, because $x < 0$, you know that division by x will reverse the sign of the inequality. (If you don't know whether a variable is positive or negative, you cannot multiply or divide both sides of the inequality by that variable.) So, you are left with $y < \frac{1}{y}$.

Now evaluate whether this statement is correct or not. Since y is a fraction between 0 and -1 (such as $-\frac{1}{2}$), its reciprocal will also be a negative number, but one smaller than -1 (such as -2). Thus, y is greater than $\frac{1}{y}$, and the inequality $y < \frac{1}{y}$ is incorrect. This means that the initial assumption that Quantity A is larger than Quantity B was also incorrect.

Since it turns out that $y > \frac{1}{y}$, you should reverse the sign of the inequality for each one of the prior steps, thus arriving at $xy < \frac{x}{y}$. **The correct answer is (B).**

Eliminating Terms When Simplifying Quantities

This example also illustrates another helpful tool when you simplify two expressions together: You can eliminate any term that appears on both expressions, as long as you keep the following rules in mind:

- You can add or subtract any term to or from both quantities. For instance, if both quantities feature the term $3y$, you can subtract it from both of them.

- You can multiply or divide both quantities by any nonzero term, as long as you know whether this term is positive or negative.

Avoid Unnecessary Calculations

Remember that you do not always need to find the exact value of the two quantities in order to compare them. This will save you time.

FOR THIS QUESTION, COMPARE QUANTITY A AND QUANTITY B.

Example 5

Quantity A	**Quantity B**
The average (arithmetic mean) of all odd integers between 10 and 30	The average (arithmetic mean) of all even integers between 11 and 31

(A) Quantity A is greater.

(B) Quantity B is greater.

(C) The two quantities are equal.

(D) The relationship cannot be determined from the information given.

To answer this question, you could, of course, list all the odd integers between 10 and 30, add them up, and find their average in order to determine the exact value of Quantity A. Then you could do the same for the even integers in Quantity B. However, that would be a very time-consuming process. Luckily, you don't have to do all that.

Instead, think about what the two quantities are. Quantity A is the average of ten integers, starting with the number 11 and ending with the number 29. Quantity B is also the average of ten such integers, this time starting with 12 and ending with 30. Notice that both quantities feature the same number of terms.

Next, you should note that the smallest term in Quantity B is larger than the smallest term in Quantity A; the second smallest term in Quantity B is larger than the second smallest term in Quantity A; and so on, for each of the ten terms in the two quantities, since in both cases the numbers increase by 2.

Thus, the sum of the terms in Quantity B is larger than the sum of the terms in Quantity A, and, therefore, the average of the terms in Quantity B is also larger than the average of the terms in Quantity A. No further work is needed. **The correct answer is (B).**

Estimate

One particular way of avoiding unnecessary calculations is estimating.

FOR THIS QUESTION, COMPARE QUANTITY A AND QUANTITY B.

Example 6

Quantity A	**Quantity B**
$65 \times \dfrac{6}{5}$	47% of 130

(A) Quantity A is greater.

(B) Quantity B is greater.

(C) The two quantities are equal.

(D) The relationship cannot be determined from the information given.

Avoid the temptation to use the calculator. As a quantitative comparison, the question asks you to compare the two quantities, not to evaluate them fully.

First, look at Quantity A. The fraction $\frac{6}{5}$ is greater than 1. That means that Quantity A is greater than 65. Stop there for the moment, and move on to Quantity B.

Quantity B features a number that is less than 50% of 130. 50% of 130 is 65, so Quantity B is less than 65.

In other words, Quantity A is greater than 65, whereas Quantity B is less than 65, which means that Quantity A is greater than Quantity B. **The correct answer is (A).**

TIP

Redrawing the figure can be useful in answering other question formats as well.

Redraw the Figure

Remember that geometric figures on the GRE are not necessarily drawn to scale. When in doubt, you can always redraw a figure on your scratch paper, altering any quantities such as side lengths or angle measures that have not been defined fully. Doing so may reveal additional information about the figure that may not have been obvious from the figure that the test-maker provided.

> **FOR THIS QUESTION, COMPARE QUANTITY A AND QUANTITY B. THIS QUESTION HAS ADDITIONAL INFORMATION ABOVE THE TWO QUANTITIES TO USE IN DETERMINING YOUR ANSWER.**

Example 7

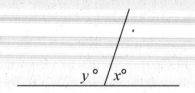

Quantity A	Quantity B
$2x$	y

(A) Quantity A is greater.

(B) Quantity B is greater.

(C) The two quantities are equal.

(D) The relationship cannot be determined from the information given.

As the figure is drawn, you may be tempted to assume that $x°$ is an acute angle and $y°$ is an obtuse angle. Further, you may be tempted to estimate the value of the two angles and try to compare the two quantities that way. Don't!

The figure is not necessarily drawn to scale, and you have no further information to help you evaluate the angles. You can redraw the figure on your scratch paper in order to see this latter point visually:

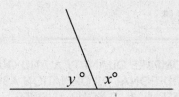

The only thing that the original figure tells you definitively is that $x°$ and $y°$ are supplementary angles—that is, that they add up to 180°. Thus, the relationship between the two quantities cannot be determined. **The correct answer is (D).**

Recognize When the Answer Cannot Be (D)

The answer in a quantitative comparison question cannot be (D) if the two quantities are defined fully. That happens

- when there are no variables in either quantity.

- when there are variables, but each of the variables may take only one value.

> **FOR THIS QUESTION, COMPARE QUANTITY A AND QUANTITY B. THIS QUESTION HAS ADDITIONAL INFORMATION ABOVE THE TWO QUANTITIES TO USE IN DETERMINING YOUR ANSWER.**

Example 8

$$x - 3 = 2$$
$$3y = x + 7$$

Quantity A	**Quantity B**
x	y

(A) Quantity A is greater.

(B) Quantity B is greater.

(C) The two quantities are equal.

(D) The relationship cannot be determined from the information given.

Even though the quantities feature variables, these variables are defined absolutely because of the two equations in the centered information. The first equation yields a unique value for x, and that value, when substituted into the second equation, yields a unique value for y. Because both quantities are fully defined, a definitive comparison between them is possible. In this case, $x = 5$ and $y = 4$. **The correct answer is (A).**

PRACTICE QUESTIONS

FOR QUESTIONS 1–15, COMPARE QUANTITY A AND QUANTITY B. SOME
QUESTIONS WILL HAVE ADDITIONAL INFORMATION ABOVE THE TWO
QUANTITIES TO USE IN DETERMINING YOUR ANSWER.

$$\frac{x}{y} - 4 = 0$$

$$x \neq 0, y \neq 0$$

1.

       <u>Quantity A</u>   <u>Quantity B</u>

        $\dfrac{1}{x}$ $\dfrac{1}{y}$

(A) Quantity A is greater.

(B) Quantity B is greater.

(C) The two quantities are equal.

(D) The relationship cannot be determined from the information given.

$$x < y$$

2.

       <u>Quantity A</u>   <u>Quantity B</u>

        $-x^2$ xy

(A) Quantity A is greater.

(B) Quantity B is greater.

(C) The two quantities are equal.

(D) The relationship cannot be determined from the information given.

3.

       <u>Quantity A</u>   <u>Quantity B</u>

The units digit of $23^8 \times 67^8 \times 89^8$ $\dfrac{4^{11} + 4^{10} + 4^9}{3 \times 4 \times 7} \times (4^{-4})^2$

(A) Quantity A is greater.

(B) Quantity B is greater.

(C) The two quantities are equal.

(D) The relationship cannot be determined from the information given.

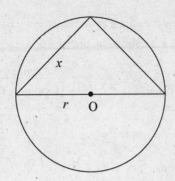

4.   Quantity A   Quantity B

The circumference of the circle $4x$
with center O and radius r

(A) Quantity A is greater.

(B) Quantity B is greater.

(C) The two quantities are equal.

(D) The relationship cannot be determined from the information given.

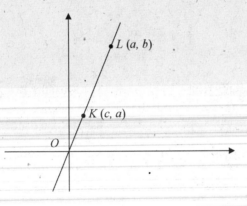

5.   Quantity A   Quantity B

$b - a$ $c - a$

(A) Quantity A is greater.

(B) Quantity B is greater.

(C) The two quantities are equal.

(D) The relationship cannot be determined from the information given.

Line l is defined by the equation $2x + y = 2$.

Line k is defined by the equation $3x + y = 4$.

6.

Quantity A	Quantity B
The x-coordinate of the point at which the two lines intersect	The slope of line l

(A) Quantity A is greater.

(B) Quantity B is greater.

(C) The two quantities are equal.

(D) The relationship cannot be determined from the information given.

7.

Quantity A	Quantity B
The sum of all multiples of 5 between 450 and 550, inclusive	The sum of all multiples of 10 between 400 and 600, inclusive

(A) Quantity A is greater.

(B) Quantity B is greater.

(C) The two quantities are equal.

(D) The relationship cannot be determined from the information given.

$$\frac{2x - xy}{3} = y - \frac{1}{3}xy$$

8.

Quantity A	Quantity B
$2x$	$2y$

(A) Quantity A is greater.

(B) Quantity B is greater.

(C) The two quantities are equal.

(D) The relationship cannot be determined from the information given.

9.

Quantity A	Quantity B
$\sqrt{230}$	The average (arithmetic mean) of all prime numbers between 10 and 20

(A) Quantity A is greater.

(B) Quantity B is greater.

(C) The two quantities are equal.

(D) The relationship cannot be determined from the information given.

10.

Quantity A	Quantity B
$\left(\dfrac{14}{42}\right)^4$	$\dfrac{1}{3} \times \dfrac{2}{9} \times \dfrac{3}{(-6)} \times \dfrac{(-1)}{3}$

(A) Quantity A is greater.

(B) Quantity B is greater.

(C) The two quantities are equal.

(D) The relationship cannot be determined from the information given.

ABC is a right triangle with legs of length $\dfrac{x}{y}$ and y.

11.

Quantity A	Quantity B
$\dfrac{x\left(5-\sqrt{17}\right)\left(\sqrt{17}+5\right)}{\sqrt{256}}$	The area of triangle ABC

(A) Quantity A is greater.

(B) Quantity B is greater.

(C) The two quantities are equal.

(D) The relationship cannot be determined from the information given.

12.

Quantity A	Quantity B
The number of prime numbers between 1 and 100	The number of multiples of 3 between 1 and 100

(A) Quantity A is greater.

(B) Quantity B is greater.

(C) The two quantities are equal.

(D) The relationship cannot be determined from the information given.

$$xy^2z^3 > 0$$
$$xyz < 0$$

13.

Quantity A	Quantity B
y	xz

(A) Quantity A is greater.

(B) Quantity B is greater.

(C) The two quantities are equal.

(D) The relationship cannot be determined from the information given.

Point $P\,(a, b)$ lies in quadrant I of the rectangular coordinate system. Point $Q\,(m,n)$ is 180° rotationally symmetric to point P about the origin O.

14.

Quantity A	Quantity B
The distance between points P and Q	$\left[\left(|a|+|n|\right)^2 - 2|bm|\right]^{\frac{1}{2}}$

(A) Quantity A is greater.

(B) Quantity B is greater.

(C) The two quantities are equal.

(D) The relationship cannot be determined from the information given.

M and N are two right cylinders, such that the height of cylinder M is 10% greater than the height of cylinder N, and the radius of cylinder M is 10% less than the radius of cylinder N.

15.

Quantity A	Quantity B
The surface area of cylinder M	The surface area of cylinder N

(A) Quantity A is greater.

(B) Quantity B is greater.

(C) The two quantities are equal.

(D) The relationship cannot be determined from the information given.

ANSWER KEY AND EXPLANATIONS

1. D	6. A	11. C
2. D	7. C	12. B
3. C	8. D	13. B
4. D	9. A	14. A
5. A	10. C	15. B

Question

$$\frac{x}{y} - 4 = 0$$
$$x \neq 0, y \neq 0$$

1.

Quantity A	Quantity B
$\dfrac{1}{x}$	$\dfrac{1}{y}$

(A) Quantity A is greater.

(B) Quantity B is greater.

(C) The two quantities are equal.

(D) The relationship cannot be determined from the information given.

Answer Explanation

The correct answer is (D). Begin by manipulating the centered information:

$$\frac{x}{y} - 4 = 0 \Rightarrow \frac{x}{y} = 4 \Rightarrow x = 4y$$

Now pick numbers for y, and see what the relationship between the two quantities is.

y	x	$\dfrac{1}{x}$		$\dfrac{1}{y}$
1	4	$\dfrac{1}{4}$	$<$	1
-1	-4	$-\dfrac{1}{4}$	$>$	-1

Clearly, the relationship between the two quantities cannot be determined from the information given.

Question

$$x < y$$

2.   Quantity A   Quantity B
                        $-x^2$ xy

(A) Quantity A is greater.

(B) Quantity B is greater.

(C) The two quantities are equal.

(D) The relationship cannot be determined from the information given.

Answer Explanation

The correct answer is (D). You cannot simplify the two quantities any more than they already are. You might be tempted to divide both quantities by x; however, that would be wrong. If x equals 0, then division by x would not be permissible. Additionally, you don't know whether x is positive or negative, so you don't know whether dividing by x would change the direction of the inequality or not. Instead, pick numbers for x and y right away.

x	y	$-x^2$		xy
2	3	-4	$<$	6
0	Any positive number	0	$=$	0

When $x = 2$ and $y = 3$, Quantity B is greater than Quantity A, whereas when $x = 0$ and $y =$ any number, then the two quantities are equal.

Question

3.   Quantity A   Quantity B

The units digit of $23^8 \times 67^8 \times 89^8$ $\dfrac{4^{11} + 4^{10} + 4^9}{3 \times 4 \times 7} \times (4^{-4})^2$

(A) Quantity A is greater.

(B) Quantity B is greater.

(C) The two quantities are equal.

(D) The relationship cannot be determined from the information given.

Answer Explanation

The correct answer is (C). Consider Quantity A first. In order to find the units digit of any number that is the product of two integers, you only need to multiply the units digits of those two integers. For instance, the units digit of 23×23 is equal to $3 \times 3 = 9$. Use this trick—albeit several times—to simplify Quantity A quickly. Calculate the units digit of the eighth power of each of the three numbers, and then multiply those three units digits together.

First, write out the units digits of the first few powers of 3, 7, and 9, to see if you can discern any pattern.

The units digit of 3^1 is 3.

The units digit of 3^2 is $3 \times 3 = 9$.

The units digit of 3^3 is the units digit of $3 \times 9 = 27$, that is, 7.

The units digit of 3^4 is the units digit of $3 \times 7 = 21$, that is, 1.

The units digit of 3^5 is $3 \times 1 = 3$.

So, the units digits of successive powers of 3 follow the pattern 3, 9, 7, 1, 3. . . . With this approach, you also find that the units digits of successive powers of 7 follow the pattern 7, 9, 3, 1, 7...; and the units digits of successive powers of 9 follow the pattern 9, 1, 9. . . .

In other words, the fourth, eighth, twelfth, and so on, powers of 3 end in 1. So do the fourth, eighth, twelfth, and so on, powers of 7, while all even powers of 9 end in 1. Therefore, Quantity A equals $1 \times 1 \times 1 = 1$.

Next, simplify Quantity B. Begin by writing the terms in the numerator as multiples of 4^9:

$$\frac{4^2 \times 4^9 + 4 \times 4^9 + 4^9}{3 \times 4 \times 7} \times (4^{-4})^2$$

Combine the terms in the numerator:

$$\frac{(4^2 + 4 + 1) \times 4^9}{3 \times 4 \times 7} \times (4^{-4})^2 = \frac{21 \times 4^9}{3 \times 4 \times 7} \times (4^{-4})^2$$

Remove the parentheses and move $(4^{-4})^2$ to the denominator:

$$\frac{21 \times 4^9}{3 \times 4 \times 7} \times 4^{-8} = \frac{21 \times 4^9}{3 \times 4 \times 7 \times 4^8}$$

Finally, combine the terms in the denominator, and eliminate:

$$\frac{21 \times 4^9}{21 \times 4 \times 4^8} = \frac{21 \times 4^9}{21 \times 4^9} = 1$$

Question

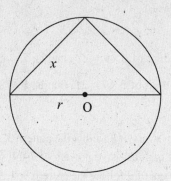

4.   Quantity A   Quantity B
        The circumference of the circle $4x$
           with center O and radius r

(A) Quantity A is greater.

(B) Quantity B is greater.

(C) The two quantities are equal.

(D) The relationship cannot be determined from the information given.

Answer Explanation

The correct answer is (D). Even though the triangle inscribed in the circle appears to be isosceles, don't assume that it is. The triangle is definitely a right one, since one of its sides is a diameter of the circle; however, you cannot tell anything about its two legs. Each of them may be of any length between (but not including) 0 and $2r$. For instance, here is one way that you may legitimately redraw the figure:

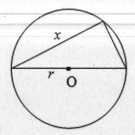

So how do we compare the two quantities? First, consider Quantity A. The circumference of the circle is $2\pi r$, and since $\pi \approx 3.14$, the circumference is approximately equal to $6.28r$.

Next, examine a couple of different possibilities for Quantity B. If the triangle were isosceles, it would be a 45–45–90 right triangle, and x would equal $r\sqrt{2}$. $\sqrt{2}$ is somewhat smaller than 1.5, so $r\sqrt{2}$ is somewhat smaller than $1.5r$, and $4x$ is somewhat smaller than $6r$. In this scenario, Quantity A is greater. However, x can be almost as large as the diameter. Therefore, $4x$ can be almost as large as $4 \times 2r$, or $8r$—so Quantity B may be greater than Quantity A.

Question

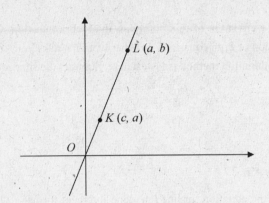

5. | Quantity A | Quantity B |
|---|---|
| $b - a$ | $c - a$ |

(A) Quantity A is greater.

(B) Quantity B is greater.

(C) The two quantities are equal.

(D) The relationship cannot be determined from the information given.

Answer Explanation

The correct answer if (A). By looking at the graph, you can estimate the relationship of the three numbers to one another—and this estimate will be enough because you don't need to find exact values in order to answer the question correctly:

b, the y-coordinate of point L, is greater than a, the y-coordinate of point K because point L is farther up than point K. That is, $b > a$, so $b - a > 0$, and Quantity A is positive.

a, the x-coordinate of point L, is greater than c, the x-coordinate of point K because point L is farther to the right than point K. That is, $a > c$, so $c - a < 0$, and Quantity B is negative.

Thus, Quantity A is larger than Quantity B.

Question

Line l is defined by the equation $2x + y = 2$.

Line k is defined by the equation $3x + y = 4$.

6. | Quantity A | Quantity B |
|---|---|
| The x-coordinate of the point at which the two lines intersect | The slope of line l |

(A) Quantity A is greater.

(B) Quantity B is greater.

(C) The two quantities are equal.

(D) The relationship cannot be determined from the information given.

Answer Explanation

The correct answer is (A). Think of this purely as an algebra question. Quantity A asks for the value of x that is a solution of both equations. In other words, it asks you to solve the simultaneous equations for x. The combination method is fastest here. Subtract the first equation from the second:

$$3x + y = 4$$

$$-(2x + y = 2)$$

$$x = 2$$

So the value of Quantity A is 2.

For Quantity B, rewrite the equation for line l in slope-intercept form:

$y = mx + b$, where m is the slope of the line.

$$y = -2x + 2$$

The coefficient of x is the slope, so Quantity B is –2.

Question

7.

Quantity A	Quantity B
The sum of all multiples of 5 between 450 and 550, inclusive	The sum of all multiples of 10 between 400 and 600, inclusive

(A) Quantity A is greater.

(B) Quantity B is greater.

(C) The two quantities are equal.

(D) The relationship cannot be determined from the information given.

Answer Explanation

The correct answer is (C). There are 21 multiples of 5 between 450 and 550, inclusive. Ten of them are less than 500, ten of them are greater than 500, and one of them is 500. Since the list consists of all multiples of a certain number, and there is an odd number of such multiples in the list, the average (arithmetic mean) of all these numbers is equal to the middle number: 500. Thus, instead of adding up all 21 numbers in order to find their sum, you should multiply their average by the number of terms in the list: The value of Quantity A is 500×21.

Similarly, there are 21 multiples of 10 between 400 and 600, inclusive, and their average is also 500. Thus, the value of Quantity B is 500×21.

Question

$$\frac{2x - xy}{3} = y - \frac{1}{3}xy$$

8.

Quantity A	Quantity B
$2x$	$2y$

(A) Quantity A is greater.

(B) Quantity B is greater.

(C) The two quantities are equal.

(D) The relationship cannot be determined from the information given.

Answer Explanation

The correct answer is (D). Begin by simplifying the centered information:

$$\frac{2x - xy}{3} = y - \frac{1}{3}xy$$

Multiply both sides by 3:

$$2x - xy = 3y - xy$$

Add xy to both sides:

$$2x = 3y$$

Finally, divide both sides by 2:

$$x = \frac{3}{2}y$$

It would be nice if the question asked you to compare $2x$ to $3y$. However, it asks you to compare $2x$ to $2y$—in other words, to compare x to y—so there's another step you have to take. Pick numbers for y and see what values these produce for x:

y		x
1	<	$\frac{3}{2}$
-1	>	$-\frac{3}{2}$

Thus, the relationship between the two quantities cannot be determined from the information given.

Question

9.

Quantity A	Quantity B
$\sqrt{230}$	The average (arithmetic mean) of all prime numbers between 10 and 20

(A) Quantity A is greater.

(B) Quantity B is greater.

(C) The two quantities are equal.

(D) The relationship cannot be determined from the information given.

Answer Explanation

The correct answer is (A). On this question, you may use the calculator or estimate. If you estimate, you should recall that 225 is the square of 15, so Quantity A is slightly larger than 15. For Quantity B, list all the primes between 10 and 20: 11, 13, 17 and 19. The average of these four numbers is exactly 15. Thus, Quantity A is larger.

Question

10.

Quantity A	Quantity B
$\left(\dfrac{14}{42}\right)^4$	$\dfrac{1}{3}\times\dfrac{2}{9}\times\dfrac{3}{(-6)}\times\dfrac{(-1)}{3}$

- (A) Quantity A is greater.
- (B) Quantity B is greater.
- (C) The two quantities are equal.
- (D) The relationship cannot be determined from the information given.

Answer Explanation

The correct answer is (C). Simplifying the two quantities is the strategy to use here. First, work on Quantity A, the simpler one of the two: $\dfrac{14}{42}=\dfrac{1}{3}$, so $\left(\dfrac{14}{42}\right)^4=\left(\dfrac{1}{3}\right)^4$. Don't calculate any further: you may not have to. If, after simplifying Quantity B, you still need to simplify Quantity A further, you can do so then. Move on to Quantity B and see what that simplifies to.

First, cancel out the minus signs from the numerator and denominator:

$$\dfrac{1}{3}\times\dfrac{2}{9}\times\dfrac{3}{6}\times\dfrac{1}{3}$$

Then, rearrange the terms:

$$\dfrac{1}{3}\times\dfrac{1}{3}\times\dfrac{2}{6}\times\dfrac{3}{9}$$

Next, simplify the last two fractions:

$$\dfrac{1}{3}\times\dfrac{1}{3}\times\dfrac{1}{3}\times\dfrac{1}{3}$$

And finally, write the product as a power of the fraction $\dfrac{1}{3}$:

$$\left(\dfrac{1}{3}\right)^4$$

The two quantities are equal.

Question

ABC is a right triangle with legs of length $\dfrac{x}{y}$ and y.

11.

Quantity A	Quantity B
$\dfrac{x\left(5-\sqrt{17}\right)\left(\sqrt{17}+5\right)}{\sqrt{256}}$	The area of triangle ABC

(A) Quantity A is greater.

(B) Quantity B is greater.

(C) The two quantities are equal.

(D) The relationship cannot be determined from the information given.

Answer Explanation

The correct answer is (C). Simplify the quantities in order to compare them more easily. Start with Quantity B, which is more straightforward. The area of this triangle is given by:

$$A = \frac{1}{2}\frac{x}{y}y = \frac{1}{2}x$$

Next, simplify Quantity A. Notice that the two terms in parentheses on the numerator are the factored form of the special product $a^2 - b^2$, where $a = 5$ and $b = \sqrt{17}$:

$$\frac{x\left(5-\sqrt{17}\right)\left(\sqrt{17}+5\right)}{\sqrt{256}} = \frac{\left(5^2 - \left(\sqrt{17}\right)^2\right)x}{\sqrt{256}} = \frac{(25-17)x}{\sqrt{256}} = \frac{8x}{\sqrt{256}}$$

As for the denominator, you should recognize that 256 is the square of 16. Thus, the fraction becomes:

$$\frac{8x}{16} = \frac{1}{2}x$$

Thus, Quantity A is equal to Quantity B.

Question

12.

Quantity A	Quantity B
The number of prime numbers between 1 and 100	The number of multiples of 3 between 1 and 100

(A) Quantity A is greater.

(B) Quantity B is greater.

(C) The two quantities are equal.

(D) The relationship cannot be determined from the information given.

Answer Explanation

The correct answer is (B). Quantity A is the harder of the two to deal with, so start with Quantity B: $99 = 33 \times 3$, so there are 33 multiples of 3 between 1 and 100.

Returning to Quantity A, you now have an easier task. You don't have to find the exact number of primes between 1 and 100. You only need to determine whether there are fewer or more prime numbers than 33. In other words, estimate! There are 98 integers between 1 and 100. Forty-nine of them are even, and none of those, other than the number 2, is prime. Thus, you are already down to $98 - 48 = 50$ numbers remaining: The number 2 and all the odd numbers in the range.

Next, you can eliminate all the odd multiples of 3 (other than 3 itself) because these are not prime. (Do not eliminate all multiples of 3 because the even ones are included in the 48 even numbers you eliminated in the previous step.) There are 33 multiples of 3 between 1 and 100, and both the first one (3) and the last one (99) are odd. Therefore, of these 33 multiples, 17 are odd and 16 are even. Subtract 16 of the 17 odd ones (that is, all of them other than 3) from the 50 remaining numbers: $50 - 16 = 34$.

At this point, if you can find at least two additional nonprime numbers, you are finished. Look for nonprime numbers that are neither even nor multiples of 3. The numbers 25 and 55 are two such numbers (not even, not multiples of 3, and not prime), so you can remove them from the list, as well. You are now left with, at most, 32 numbers; in other words, the number of primes between 1 and 100 is definitely smaller than 33. (The number is 25.)

Question

$$xy^2z^3 > 0$$
$$xyz < 0$$

13.   Quantity A   Quantity B
                           y xz

(A) Quantity A is greater.

(B) Quantity B is greater.

(C) The two quantities are equal.

(D) The relationship cannot be determined from the information given.

Answer Explanation

The correct answer is (B). On first look, this question may appear rather complicated to solve directly. If you're running out of time, or you don't feel too confident about how you should approach this question, you may wish to skip it— clicking the "Mark" button so that you can revisit the question easily at a later point.

That said, if you dissect methodically the centered information using the properties of positives and negatives, as well as those of exponents, you'll be able to find the right answer.

First, examine the first inequality: $xy^2z^3 > 0$. y^2 is positive, so the product of x and z^3 must also be positive (if xz^3 were negative, then you'd have a negative number multiplied by a positive number to produce another positive number, which is impossible).

Now, for xz^3 to be positive, x and z have to be either both positive or both negative. That's as far as you can go with this inequality alone.

Next, examine the second inequality: $xyz < 0$. Because xz^3 is positive (based on the first inequality), xz must also be positive. Therefore, for xyz to be negative, y must be negative. You can now answer the question! You have proven that Quantity A is negative, while Quantity B is positive.

Question

Point P (a,b) lies in quadrant I of the rectangular coordinate system. Point Q (m,n) is 180° rotationally symmetric to point P about the origin O.

14.	Quantity A	Quantity B
	The distance between points P and Q.	$\left[\left(|a|+|n|\right)^2 - 2|bm|\right]^{\frac{1}{2}}$

(A) Quantity A is greater.

(B) Quantity B is greater.

(C) The two quantities are equal.

(D) The relationship cannot be determined from the information given.

Answer Explanation

The correct answer is (A). This question also seems difficult at first. For one thing, Quantity B appears complicated. For another, the question tests more than one area of mathematical knowledge. So this may be another candidate for skipping and revisiting.

Nonetheless, let's see how you would solve this question. Start by interpreting the centered information. If points P and Q are symmetric about the origin, then their x- and y-coordinates are opposites of each other. In other words, $a = -m$ and $b = -n$. Also, since P lies in quadrant I, then a and b are positive numbers, while m and n are negative.

Next, examine Quantity A. Drawing a diagram helps:

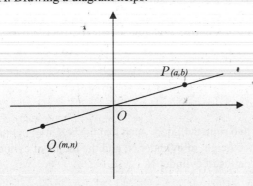

The distance between P and Q is equal to the length of line segment PO plus the length of line segment OQ. This sum is equal to two times the length of the segment PO, since $PO = OQ$.

PO is the hypotenuse of a right triangle with legs PR and OR (see the following figure). The length of PR is b (the y-coordinate of P), and the length of OR is a (the x-coordinate of R).

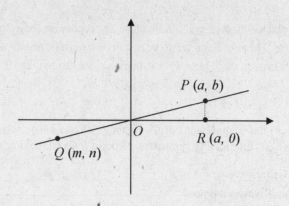

You can use the Pythagorean theorem to find the length of segment PO:

$PO = \sqrt{a^2 + b^2}$

Thus, the length of PQ is twice the length of PO: $PQ = 2\sqrt{a^2 + b^2}$.

Now, move on to Quantity B. First, tackle the absolute value signs so you can simplify the expression. Since a is positive, $|a| = a$. Additionally, since $b = -n$ and b is positive, $|n| = b$. Next, $|bm| = |b| \times |m|$, and since $m = -a$, $|bm| = |b| \times |a|$. Further, since a and b are both positive, $|bm| = a \times b$.

Now you're ready to transform the expression, so that $\left[\left(|a| + |n|\right)^2 - 2|bm|\right]^{\frac{1}{2}}$ becomes:

$\sqrt{(a+b)^2 - 2ab}$

Distribute the first term:

$\sqrt{a^2 + b^2 + 2ab - 2ab}$

Finally, cancel the two $2ab$:

$\sqrt{a^2 + b^2}$

Quantity B equals $\sqrt{a^2 + b^2}$, whereas Quantity A equals twice $\sqrt{a^2 + b^2}$. Since $\sqrt{a^2 + b^2}$ is a positive number (it's the length of a line segment), twice $\sqrt{a^2 + b^2}$ is larger than once $\sqrt{a^2 + b^2}$, so Quantity A is larger.

Question

M and N are two right cylinders, such that the height of cylinder M is 10% greater than the height of cylinder N, and the radius of cylinder M is 10% less than the radius of cylinder N.

15.

Quantity A	Quantity B
The surface area of cylinder M	The surface area of cylinder N

(A) Quantity A is greater.

(B) Quantity B is greater.

(C) The two quantities are equal.

(D) The relationship cannot be determined from the information given.

Answer Explanation

The correct answer is (B). This is a wordy question that needs translation into mathematical expressions. First, you need to recall the definition of the surface area of a cylinder: $A = 2\pi r^2 + 2\pi rh$, where r is the radius of the circular base as well as the circular top of the cylinder, while h is the height of the cylinder.

Next, write out mathematical expressions to represent the centered information:

$h_M = 1.1h_N$ and $r_M = 0.9r_N$

Now find the surface area of cylinder M with respect to r_N and h_N, in order to see whether a direct comparison with the surface area of cylinder N is possible. Start by writing the equation for the surface area of cylinder M in terms of its own radius and height:

$A_M = 2\pi r_M^2 + 2\pi r_M h_M$

Replace r_M with $0.9r_N$, and h_M with $1.1h_N$:

$A_M = 2\pi(0.9r_N)^2 + 2\pi(0.9r_N)1.1h_N$

Perform the various calculations:

$A_M = 2\pi 0.81 r_N^2 + 1.8\pi r_N 1.1h_N \Rightarrow$

$A_M = 1.62\pi r_N^2 + 1.98\pi r_N h_N$

Next, write out the expression for the surface area of cylinder N:

$A_N = 2\pi r_N^2 + 2\pi r_N h_N$

You have simplified Quantity A in such a way that you can now compare it with Quantity B. Notice that each of the two terms in the expression for Quantity B is larger than its corresponding term in the expression for Quantity A: that is, $2\pi r_N^2$ is larger than $1.62\pi r_N^2$, and $2\pi r_N h_N$ is larger than $1.98\pi r_N h_N$. Therefore, Quantity B is larger.

Alternatively, you could have determined this by subtracting Quantity A from Quantity B:

$A_N - A_M = 2\pi r_N^2 + 2\pi r_N h_N - 1.62\pi r_N^2 - 1.98\pi r_N h_N \Rightarrow$

$A_N - A_M = 0.38\pi r_N^2 + 0.02\pi r_N h_N$

The difference is a positive number, so A_N is larger than A_M.

SUMMING IT UP

- Quantitative comparison questions present two Quantities, A and B, that you must compare. To select an answer, you choose one answer from the following list:
  - o   Quantity A is greater.
  - o   Quantity B is greater.
  - o   The two quantities are equal.
  - o   The relationship cannot be determined from the information given.
- Some questions feature additional information centered above the two quantities. You should use this information to help you determine the relationship between the two quantities.
- Any symbol that appears more than once in a question (e.g., one that appears in Quantity A and in the centered information) has the same meaning throughout the question.
- Specific strategies for quantitative comparison questions are the following:
  - o   Pick and plug numbers.
  - o   Simplify the quantities.
  - o   Avoid unnecessary calculations.
  - o   Estimate.
  - o   Redraw the figure.
  - o   Recognize when the answer cannot be (D). The relationship cannot be determined from the information given.
- Data interpretation sets are not used for quantitative comparison questions.

PART VI
THREE PRACTICE TESTS

PRACTICE TEST 2 ANSWER SHEETS

Section 1: Analytical Writing

Analyze an Issue

FOR PLANNING

ANALYZE AN ISSUE RESPONSE

answer sheet

ANALYZE AN ISSUE RESPONSE

_____
_____
_____
_____
_____
_____
_____
_____
_____
_____
_____
_____
_____
_____
_____
_____
_____
_____
_____
_____
_____
_____
_____
_____
_____
_____
_____
_____
_____

ANALYZE AN ISSUE RESPONSE

_____
_____
_____
_____
_____
_____
_____
_____
_____
_____
_____
_____
_____
_____
_____
_____
_____
_____
_____
_____
_____
_____
_____
_____
_____
_____
_____
_____
_____
_____
_____
_____

ANALYZE AN ISSUE RESPONSE

_____
_____
_____
_____
_____
_____
_____
_____
_____
_____
_____
_____
_____
_____
_____
_____
_____
_____
_____
_____
_____
_____
_____
_____
_____
_____
_____

answer sheet

Analyze an Argument

FOR PLANNING

ANALYZE AN ARGUMENT RESPONSE

_____
_____
_____
_____
_____
_____
_____
_____
_____
_____
_____
_____
_____
_____
_____
_____
_____
_____
_____
_____
_____
_____
_____
_____
_____
_____
_____

answer sheet

ANALYZE AN ARGUMENT RESPONSE

ANALYZE AN ARGUMENT RESPONSE

_____
_____
_____
_____
_____
_____
_____
_____
_____
_____
_____
_____
_____
_____
_____
_____
_____
_____
_____
_____
_____
_____
_____
_____
_____
_____
_____
_____

answer sheet

ANALYZE AN ARGUMENT RESPONSE
_____
_____
_____
_____
_____
_____
_____
_____
_____
_____
_____
_____
_____
_____
_____
_____
_____
_____
_____
_____
_____
_____
_____
_____
_____
_____
_____
_____
_____
_____
_____
_____

answer sheet

Section 2: Quantitative Reasoning

1. Ⓐ Ⓑ Ⓒ Ⓓ
2. Ⓐ Ⓑ Ⓒ Ⓓ
3. Ⓐ Ⓑ Ⓒ Ⓓ
4. Ⓐ Ⓑ Ⓒ Ⓓ
5. Ⓐ Ⓑ Ⓒ Ⓓ
6. Ⓐ Ⓑ Ⓒ Ⓓ
7. Ⓐ Ⓑ Ⓒ Ⓓ
8. Ⓐ Ⓑ Ⓒ Ⓓ
9. Ⓐ Ⓑ Ⓒ Ⓓ Ⓔ
10. Ⓐ Ⓑ Ⓒ Ⓓ Ⓔ

11. Ⓐ Ⓑ Ⓒ Ⓓ Ⓔ
12. Ⓐ Ⓑ Ⓒ Ⓓ Ⓔ
13. Ⓐ Ⓑ Ⓒ Ⓓ Ⓔ
14. Ⓐ Ⓑ Ⓒ Ⓓ Ⓔ
15. Ⓐ Ⓑ Ⓒ Ⓓ Ⓔ Ⓕ Ⓖ
16. Ⓐ Ⓑ Ⓒ Ⓓ Ⓔ Ⓕ Ⓖ Ⓗ
17. ▭

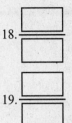

18. ▭
19. ▭
20. Ⓐ Ⓑ Ⓒ Ⓓ Ⓔ

Section 3: Quantitative Reasoning

1. Ⓐ Ⓑ Ⓒ Ⓓ
2. Ⓐ Ⓑ Ⓒ Ⓓ
3. Ⓐ Ⓑ Ⓒ Ⓓ
4. Ⓐ Ⓑ Ⓒ Ⓓ
5. Ⓐ Ⓑ Ⓒ Ⓓ
6. Ⓐ Ⓑ Ⓒ Ⓓ
7. Ⓐ Ⓑ Ⓒ Ⓓ
8. Ⓐ Ⓑ Ⓒ Ⓓ
9. Ⓐ Ⓑ Ⓒ Ⓓ
10. Ⓐ Ⓑ Ⓒ Ⓓ

11. Ⓐ Ⓑ Ⓒ Ⓓ Ⓔ
12. Ⓐ Ⓑ Ⓒ Ⓓ Ⓔ
13. Ⓐ Ⓑ Ⓒ Ⓓ Ⓔ
14. Ⓐ Ⓑ Ⓒ Ⓓ Ⓔ
15. Ⓐ Ⓑ Ⓒ Ⓓ Ⓔ

16. Ⓐ Ⓑ Ⓒ Ⓓ Ⓔ Ⓕ Ⓖ Ⓗ
17. Ⓐ Ⓑ Ⓒ Ⓓ Ⓔ Ⓕ Ⓖ Ⓗ
18. ▭
19. ▭
20. Ⓐ Ⓑ Ⓒ Ⓓ Ⓔ Ⓕ Ⓖ Ⓗ

Section 4: Verbal Reasoning

1. Ⓐ Ⓑ Ⓒ Ⓓ Ⓔ
2. Ⓐ Ⓑ Ⓒ Ⓓ Ⓔ
3. Ⓐ Ⓑ Ⓒ Ⓓ Ⓔ Ⓕ
4. Ⓐ Ⓑ Ⓒ Ⓓ Ⓔ Ⓕ
5. Ⓐ Ⓑ Ⓒ Ⓓ Ⓔ Ⓕ Ⓖ Ⓗ Ⓘ
6. Ⓐ Ⓑ Ⓒ Ⓓ Ⓔ
7. Ⓐ Ⓑ Ⓒ
8. Ⓐ Ⓑ Ⓒ Ⓓ Ⓔ
9. Ⓐ Ⓑ Ⓒ Ⓓ Ⓔ
10. Ⓐ Ⓑ Ⓒ Ⓓ Ⓔ

11. Ⓐ Ⓑ Ⓒ
12. Ⓐ Ⓑ Ⓒ Ⓓ Ⓔ
13. Ⓐ Ⓑ Ⓒ Ⓓ Ⓔ
14. Ⓐ Ⓑ Ⓒ Ⓓ Ⓔ
15. Ⓐ Ⓑ Ⓒ Ⓓ Ⓔ
16. Ⓐ Ⓑ Ⓒ Ⓓ Ⓔ Ⓕ

17. Ⓐ Ⓑ Ⓒ Ⓓ Ⓔ Ⓕ
18. Ⓐ Ⓑ Ⓒ Ⓓ Ⓔ Ⓕ
19. Ⓐ Ⓑ Ⓒ Ⓓ Ⓔ Ⓕ
20. Ⓐ Ⓑ Ⓒ Ⓓ Ⓔ

Section 5: Verbal Reasoning

1. Ⓐ Ⓑ Ⓒ Ⓓ Ⓔ
2. Ⓐ Ⓑ Ⓒ Ⓓ Ⓔ Ⓕ
3. Ⓐ Ⓑ Ⓒ Ⓓ Ⓔ Ⓕ
4. Ⓐ Ⓑ Ⓒ Ⓓ Ⓔ Ⓕ
5. Ⓐ Ⓑ Ⓒ Ⓓ Ⓔ Ⓕ Ⓖ Ⓗ Ⓘ
6. Ⓐ Ⓑ Ⓒ Ⓓ Ⓔ
7. Ⓐ Ⓑ Ⓒ
8. Ⓐ Ⓑ Ⓒ Ⓓ Ⓔ
9. Ⓐ Ⓑ Ⓒ Ⓓ Ⓔ
10. Ⓐ Ⓑ Ⓒ Ⓓ Ⓔ

11. Ⓐ Ⓑ Ⓒ Ⓓ Ⓔ
12. Ⓐ Ⓑ Ⓒ Ⓓ Ⓔ
13. Ⓐ Ⓑ Ⓒ
14. Ⓐ Ⓑ Ⓒ Ⓓ Ⓔ
15. Ⓐ Ⓑ Ⓒ Ⓓ Ⓔ
16. Ⓐ Ⓑ Ⓒ Ⓓ Ⓔ

17. Ⓐ Ⓑ Ⓒ Ⓓ Ⓔ Ⓕ
18. Ⓐ Ⓑ Ⓒ Ⓓ Ⓔ Ⓕ
19. Ⓐ Ⓑ Ⓒ Ⓓ Ⓔ Ⓕ
20. Ⓐ Ⓑ Ⓒ Ⓓ Ⓔ Ⓕ

Practice Test 2

The test begins with general information about the number of sections on the test (six for the computer version, including the unidentified unscored section or an identified research section, and five for the paper-and-pencil version) and the timing of the test (approximately 3 hours and 45 minutes including one 10-minute break after Section 3, 1-minute breaks after the other sections for the computer version, and 3 hours and 30 minutes for the paper-and-pencil version with similar breaks). The following practice test contains the five scored sections.

Each section has its own time allocation and, during that time period, you may work on only that section.

Next, you will read ETS's policy on scoring the Analytical Writing responses. Each essay is read by experienced readers, and ETS may cancel any test scores that show evidence of unacknowledged use of sources, unacknowledged collaboration with others, preparation of the response by another person, and language that is "substantially" similar to the language in one or more other test responses.

Each section has specific instructions for that section.

You will be told when to begin.

SECTION 1: ANALYTICAL WRITING

Analyze an Issue

30 minutes

The time for this task is 30 minutes. You must plan and draft a response that evaluates the issue given below. If you do not respond to the specific issue, your score will be zero. Your response must be based on the accompanying instructions, and you must provide evidence for your position. You may use support from reading, experience, observations, and/or course work.

> Some people believe that a world leader, such as a president, premier, or prime minister, must, in general, act so decisively that he or she is a lightning rod for controversy. Others argue that the best world leaders are, in general, consensus builders who can bring about change through compromise.
>
> Write an essay identifying which view most accurately reflects your own view and explain why. Address both of the views above.

Your response will be read by experienced readers who will assess your ability to do the following:

- Follow the set of task instructions.
- Analyze the complexities involved.
- Organize, develop, and explain ideas.
- Use pertinent reasons and/or illustrations to support ideas.
- Adhere to the conventions of Standard Written English.

You will be advised to take some time to plan your response and to leave time to reread it before the time is over. Those taking the paper-and-pencil version of the GRE will find a blank page in their answer booklet for making notes and then four ruled pages for writing their actual response. Those taking the computer version will be given scrap paper for making notes.

STOP

> If you finish before the time is up, you may check your work in this section only.

Analyze an Argument
30 minutes

The time for this task is 30 minutes. You must plan and draft a response that evaluates the argument given below. If you do not respond to the given argument, your score will be zero. Your response must be based on the accompanying instructions, and you must provide evidence in support of your analysis.

You should not present your views on the subject of the argument but on the strengths or weakness of the argument.

> The constant use by children of computers, computer games, and devices such as smart phones that integrate computer technology is perilously diminishing the attention spans of the students at Medville Elementary. A coalition of concerned parents and teachers hereby recommends the banning of computers, computer games, and cell phones in Medville School (except when a phone must be used for necessary communication with parents/guardians or other caregivers at designated times and in designated areas), and the judicious use of computers only when necessary to teach fundamental skills, such as searching for information. All of us want to educate children who can maintain the kind of sustained, focused attention that will be necessary for success in the 21st-century workplace.
>
> Write an essay that raises questions that would have to be answered in order to evaluate the reasonableness of the recommendation and the argument on which it is based. Be sure to explain how the answers to the questions would help to determine whether the argument and recommendation are reasonable.

Your response will be read by experienced readers who will assess your ability to do the following:

- Follow the set of task instructions.
- Analyze the complexities involved.
- Organize, develop, and explain ideas.
- Use pertinent reasons and/or illustrations to support ideas.
- Adhere to the conventions of Standard Written English.

You will be advised to take some time to plan your response and to leave time to reread it before the time is over. Those taking the paper-and-pencil version of the GRE will find a blank page in their answer booklet for making notes and then four ruled pages for writing their actual response. Those taking the computer version will be given scrap paper for making notes.

STOP

> If you finish before the time is up, you may check your work in this section only.

INSTRUCTIONS FOR THE VERBAL REASONING AND QUANTITATIVE REASONING SECTIONS

You will find information here on the question formats for the Verbal Reasoning and Quantitative Reasoning sections as well as information about how to use the software program, or, if you're taking the paper-and-pencil version, how to mark your answers in the answer booklet.

Perhaps the most important information is a reminder about how these two sections are scored. Every correct answer earns a point, but wrong answers don't subtract any points. The advice from ETS is to guess if you aren't sure of an answer. ETS says that this is better than not answering a question.

All multiple-choice questions in the computer-based test will have answer options preceded by either blank ovals or blank squares, depending on the question type. The paper-and-pencil test will follow the same format of answer choices, but it will use letters instead of ovals or squares for answer choices.

For your convenience in answering questions and checking answers in this book, we use (A), (B), (C), etc. By using letters with parentheses, you will find it easy to check your answers against the answer key and explanation sections.

SECTION 2: QUANTITATIVE REASONING

35 minutes • 20 questions

(The paper-and-pencil version will have 25 questions to be completed in 40 minutes.)

For each question, follow the specific directions and choose the best answer.

The test-maker provides the following information that applies to all questions in the Quantitative Reasoning section of the GRE:

- All numbers used are real numbers.

- All figures are assumed to lie in a plane unless otherwise indicated.

- Geometric figures, such as lines, circles, triangles, and quadrilaterals, *are not necessarily* drawn to scale. That is, you should *not* assume that quantities such as lengths and angle measures are as they appear in a figure. You should assume, however, that lines shown as straight are actually straight, points on a line are in the order shown, and more generally, all geometric objects are in the relative positions shown. For questions with geometric figures, you should base your answers on geometric reasoning, not on estimating or comparing quantities by sight or by measurement.

- Coordinate systems, such as *xy*-planes and number lines, *are* drawn to scale. Therefore, you can read, estimate, or compare quantities in such figures by sight or by measurement.

- Graphical data presentations, such as bar graphs, circle graphs, and line graphs, *are* drawn to scale. Therefore, you can read, estimate, or compare data values by sight or by measurement.

FOR QUESTIONS 1–8, COMPARE QUANTITY A AND QUANTITY B. SOME QUESTIONS WILL HAVE ADDITIONAL INFORMATION ABOVE THE TWO QUANTITIES TO USE IN DETERMINING YOUR ANSWER.

1.

Quantity A	Quantity B
$6(4)\left(\dfrac{1}{2}\right)^2$	6

(A) Quantity A is greater.

(B) Quantity B is greater.

(C) The two quantities are equal.

(D) The relationship cannot be determined from the information given.

$$xy = 12$$

2.

Quantity A	Quantity B
$(3x)(2y)$	**60**

(A) Quantity A is greater.

(B) Quantity B is greater.

(C) The two quantities are equal.

(D) The relationship cannot be determined from the information given.

3.

Quantity A	Quantity B
40% of $\frac{5}{8}$	60% of $\frac{3}{4}$

(A) Quantity A is greater.

(B) Quantity B is greater.

(C) The two quantities are equal.

(D) The relationship cannot be determined from the information given.

$$x \neq 0$$

4.

Quantity A	Quantity B
$\dfrac{5}{x}$	$5x$

(A) Quantity A is greater.

(B) Quantity B is greater.

(C) The two quantities are equal.

(D) The relationship cannot be determined from the information given.

$$x + 3 = 4x - 2$$
$$5y - 2 = 2y + 1$$

5.
Quantity A	Quantity B
$3x$	$6y$

(A) Quantity A is greater.

(B) Quantity B is greater.

(C) The two quantities are equal.

(D) The relationship cannot be determined from the information given.

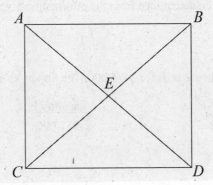

6.
Quantity A	Quantity B
The area of AEC	The area of CED

(A) Quantity A is greater.

(B) Quantity B is greater.

(C) The two quantities are equal.

(D) The relationship cannot be determined from the information given.

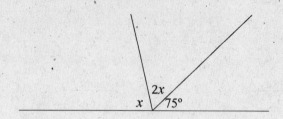

7.   <u>Quantity A</u>   <u>Quantity B</u>
                     5x   180

(A) Quantity A is greater.

(B) Quantity B is greater.

(C) The two quantities are equal.

(D) The relationship cannot be determined from the information given.

A 2,475-square-foot house sells for $475,000. The broker's fee is 6%.

8.   <u>Quantity A</u>   <u>Quantity B</u>
               The broker's fee $31,000

(A) Quantity A is greater.

(B) Quantity B is greater.

(C) The two quantities are equal.

(D) The relationship cannot be determined from the information given.

Questions 9–20 have several formats. Unless the directions state otherwise, choose one answer choice. For Numeric Entry questions, follow the instructions below.

Numeric Entry Questions

The following items are the same for both the computer-based version of the test and the paper-and-pencil version. However, those taking the computer-based version will have additional information about entering answers in decimal and fraction boxes on the computer screen. Those taking the paper-and-pencil version will have information about entering answers on answer grids.

- Your answer may be an integer, a decimal, or a fraction, and it may be negative.

- If a question asks for a fraction, there will be two boxes. One box will be for the numerator and one will be for the denominator.

- Equivalent forms of the correct answer, such as 2.5 and 2.50, are all correct.

- Enter the exact answer unless the question asks you to round your answers.

QUESTIONS 9–11 REFER TO THE CHART BELOW.

Sales by type 2010

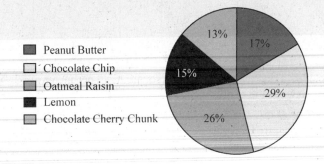

- ■ Peanut Butter
- ☐ Chocolate Chip
- ■ Oatmeal Raisin
- ■ Lemon
- ■ Chocolate Cherry Chunk

9. The two most popular types of cookies were what percentage of sales?

(A) 26

(B) 29

(C) 42

(D) 44

(E) 55

10. How many different types of cookies do NOT have chocolate in them?

    (A) 1

    (B) 2

    (C) 3

    (D) 4

    (E) 5

11. If total sales for the year were $94,480, what was the total amount sold of the third most popular cookie?

    (A) $12,543

    (B) $16,062

    (C) $17,727

    (D) $24,980

    (E) $27,589

12. The above circle has a diameter of 8, and the square has a perimeter of 32. What is the difference in the area between the two?

    (A) 11.82

    (B) 12.96

    (C) 13.33

    (D) 13.76

    (E) 15.97

13. Lacy receives 45% of the commission of every painting she sells. If she recently sold a painting for $256,000 and received a commission of $7,488, what was the total rate of commission?

    (A) 0.016

    (B) 0.029

    (C) 0.065

    (D) 0.067

    (E) 0.076

14. The expression $(4x+7y)^2 - (2x-3y)^2$ is equivalent to

    (A) $4(3x^2 + 17xy + 10y^2)$

    (B) $16x^2 + 10y^2$

    (C) $12x^2 + 12xy - 9y^2$

    (D) $x^2 + 12xy + 40y^2$

    (E) None of the above

FOR QUESTIONS 15–16, INDICATE <u>ALL</u> THE ANSWERS THAT APPLY.

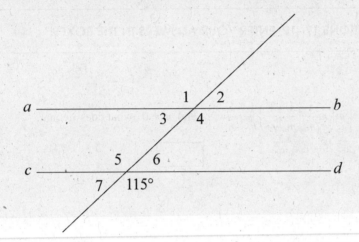

15. If ab and cd are parallel, what other angles are equal to 115°?

    (A) 1

    (B) 2

    (C) 3

    (D) 4

    (E) 5

    (F) 6

    (G) 7

16. What are the next three numbers in the sequence 0, 1, 3, 7, 15, 31,...

(A) 57

(B) 63

(C) 72

(D) 111

(E) 127

(F) 295

(G) 255

(H) 511

FOR QUESTIONS 17–19, ENTER YOUR ANSWERS IN THE BOXES.

---

17. If $m\left(m\left(m\left(m\left(m\frac{1}{m}\right)\frac{1}{m}\right)\frac{1}{m}\right)\frac{1}{m}\right)\frac{1}{m} = x$, and $m \neq 0$, what does x equal?

☐

18. $\dfrac{1}{2} + \dfrac{1}{3} + \dfrac{3}{4} + \dfrac{5}{6} =$

Give your answer as a fraction.

$\dfrac{\Box}{\Box}$

19. On a rugby team of 15 players, the ratio of forwards to backs is $\dfrac{8}{7}$. What is the ratio of backs to total number of players?

Give your answer as a fraction.

$\dfrac{\Box}{\Box}$

20. If an acre is equal to 43,560 square feet, how many acres are there in 362,985 square feet?

(A) 6.33

(B) 7.33

(C) 8.33

(D) 9.33

(E) 10.33

STOP

If you finish before the time is up, you may check your work in this section only.

SECTION 3: QUANTITATIVE REASONING

35 minutes • 20 questions

(The paper-and-pencil version will have 25 questions to be completed in 40 minutes.)

For each question, follow the specific directions and choose the best answer.

> The test-maker provides the following information that applies to all questions in the Quantitative Reasoning section of the GRE:
>
> - All numbers used are real numbers.
>
> - All figures are assumed to lie in a plane unless otherwise indicated.
>
> - Geometric figures, such as lines, circles, triangles, and quadrilaterals, *are not necessarily* drawn to scale. That is, you should *not* assume that quantities such as lengths and angle measures are as they appear in a figure. You should assume, however, that lines shown as straight are actually straight, points on a line are in the order shown, and more generally, all geometric objects are in the relative positions shown. For questions with geometric figures, you should base your answers on geometric reasoning, not on estimating or comparing quantities by sight or by measurement.
>
> - Coordinate systems, such as *xy*-planes and number lines, *are* drawn to scale. Therefore, you can read, estimate, or compare quantities in such figures by sight or by measurement.
>
> - Graphical data presentations, such as bar graphs, circle graphs, and line graphs, *are* drawn to scale. Therefore, you can read, estimate, or compare data values by sight or by measurement.

FOR QUESTIONS 1–10, COMPARE QUANTITY A AND QUANTITY B. SOME QUESTIONS WILL HAVE ADDITIONAL INFORMATION ABOVE THE TWO QUANTITIES TO USE IN DETERMINING YOUR ANSWER.

$$\frac{5}{8}x = \frac{1}{12}$$

1.   **Quantity A**   **Quantity B**

          x $\dfrac{2}{15}$

(A) Quantity A is greater.

(B) Quantity B is greater.

(C) The two quantities are equal.

(D) The relationship cannot be determined from the information given.

2.

Quantity A	Quantity B
$\dfrac{0.00008}{0.00006}$	0.75

(A) Quantity A is greater.
(B) Quantity B is greater.
(C) The two quantities are equal.
(D) The relationship cannot be determined from the information given.

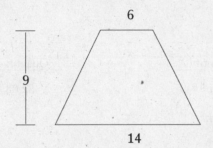

3.

Quantity A	Quantity B
The area of the trapezoid	80

(A) Quantity A is greater.
(B) Quantity B is greater.
(C) The two quantities are equal.
(D) The relationship cannot be determined from the information given.

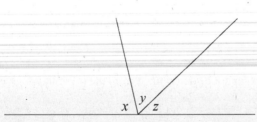

4.

Quantity A	Quantity B
The mean of angles x, y, z	60

(A) Quantity A is greater.
(B) Quantity B is greater.
(C) The two quantities are equal.
(D) The relationship cannot be determined from the information given.

5.

Quantity A	Quantity B
$\sqrt{(66)(27)}$	$(8)(4.9)$

(A) Quantity A is greater.

(B) Quantity B is greater.

(C) The two quantities are equal.

(D) The relationship cannot be determined from the information given.

$$xy = 3.2$$

6.

Quantity A	Quantity B
$1.5x(4.6y)$	22.08

(A) Quantity A is greater.

(B) Quantity B is greater.

(C) The two quantities are equal.

(D) The relationship cannot be determined from the information given.

7.

Quantity A	**Quantity B**
Time it takes a bicycle to travel 15 miles	Time it takes a car to travel 60 miles

(A) Quantity A is greater.

(B) Quantity B is greater.

(C) The two quantities are equal.

(D) The relationship cannot be determined from the information given.

An apple costs \$0.25. An orange costs \$0.35. A pear costs $\frac{1}{2}$ of the sum of an apple and an orange.

8.   Quantity A   Quantity B
         5 apples and 5 oranges   12 pears

(A) Quantity A is greater.

(B) Quantity B is greater.

(C) The two quantities are equal.

(D) The relationship cannot be determined from the information given.

There were x iPads in the Apple store. After $\frac{1}{10}$ of them were sold, 6 more were brought into the store, giving them 51 in stock.

9.   Quantity A   Quantity B
                    x 54

(A) Quantity A is greater.

(B) Quantity B is greater.

(C) The two quantities are equal.

(D) The relationship cannot be determined from the information given.

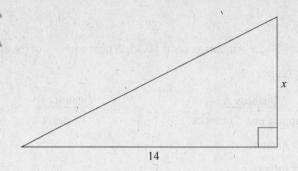

the area of the triangle is 70

10.

Quantity A	Quantity B
x	10

(A) Quantity A is greater.

(B) Quantity B is greater.

(C) The two quantities are equal.

(D) The relationship cannot be determined from the information given.

Questions 11–20 have several formats. Unless the directions state otherwise, choose one answer choice. For Numeric Entry questions, follow the instructions below.

Numeric Entry Questions

The following items are the same for both the computer-based version of the test and the paper-and-pencil version. However, those taking the computer-based version will have additional information about entering answers in decimal and fraction boxes on the computer screen. Those taking the paper-and-pencil version will have information about entering answers on answer grids.

- Your answer may be an integer, a decimal, or a fraction, and it may be negative.

- If a question asks for a fraction, there will be two boxes. One box will be for the numerator and one will be for the denominator.

- Equivalent forms of the correct answer, such as 2.5 and 2.50, are all correct.

- Enter the exact answer unless the question asks you to round your answers.

QUESTIONS 11–13 REFER TO THE GRAPH BELOW.

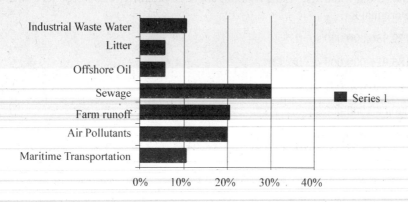

Pollutants Entering the Ocean

11. What is the percentage of offshore oil compared to all pollutants?

   (A) 5%

   (B) 10%

   (C) 15%

   (D) 20%

   (E) 30%

12. Sewage, litter, and air pollution make up what percentage of the whole?

   (A) 5%

   (B) 15%

   (C) 30%

   (D) 45%

   (E) 55%

13. If air pollution is eliminated from the graph, what percentage would sewage be of the new graph "Water-Born Pollutants Entering the Ocean"?

(A) 24%

(B) 28%

(C) 37.5%

(D) 40%

(E) 44.5%

14. A receptionist greeted the following numbers of people during one work week: 4, 19, 21, 18, 23. What is the mean of the number of people she greeted?

(A) 17

(B) 19

(C) 20

(D) 21

(E) 85

15. A farmer owns a square property and wants to sell a lot formed by dividing the lot in half, both lengthwise and widthwise. If the resulting lot has a perimeter of 888,000 feet, what is the area of the original lot?

(A) 179,936,000,000 sq. ft.

(B) 185,926,000,000 sq. ft.

(C) 197,136,000,000 sq. ft.

(D) 200,000,000,000 sq. ft.

(E) 212,386,000,000 sq. ft.

FOR QUESTION 16, CHOOSE THE <u>TWO</u> ANSWERS THAT APPLY.

---

16. What are the two factors of $x^2 + 9x + 18$?

(A) $x + 3$

(B) $x - 3$

(C) $x + 2$

(D) $x - 2$

(E) $x + 9$

(F) $x - 9$

(G) $x + 6$

(H) $x - 6$

FOR QUESTION 17, INDICATE <u>ALL</u> THE ANSWERS THAT APPLY.

17. The local baseball team employs at least 3 times as many pitchers as catchers, but never more than 11 players total. Pitchers make an average of $45,000, and catchers make an average of $30,000. Which of the following amounts are the possible averages for all the pitchers and catchers, rounded to the nearest dollar?

   (A) 30,000

   (B) 35,899

   (C) 40,375

   (D) 41,250

   (E) 41,956

   (F) 42,273

   (G) 43,743

   (H) 45,000

FOR QUESTIONS 18–19, ENTER YOUR ANSWERS IN THE BOXES.

18. $\dfrac{\left(\left(2^3\right)^2\right)^2}{\left(2^2\right)^3} =$

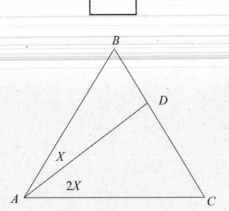

19. If ABC is an equilateral triangle, what is the measure of angle BAD?

FOR QUESTION 20, INDICATE **ALL** THE ANSWERS THAT APPLY.

20. Which of the following numbers have factors of 2, 5, 6?

    (A) 60

    (B) 84

    (C) 95

    (D) 110

    (E) 125

    (F) 166

    (G) 247

    (H) 300

STOP

If you finish before the time is up, you may check your work in this section only.

SECTION 4: VERBAL REASONING

30 minutes • 20 questions

(The paper-and-pencil version will have 25 questions to be completed in 35 minutes.)

For each question, follow the specific directions and choose the best answer.

FOR QUESTIONS 1–5, CHOOSE <u>ONE</u> ANSWER FOR EACH BLANK. SELECT FROM THE APPROPRIATE COLUMN FOR EACH BLANK. CHOOSE THE ANSWER THAT BEST COMPLETES THE SENSE OF THE TEXT.

---

1. Myanmar's path to unity is complicated by its physical geography. Mountains and plateaus _____ contacts among different regions within the nation and with its neighbors, making commerce, communication, and human movement difficult.

(A) bar
(B) exhaust
(C) hamper
(D) blockade
(E) harm

2. Although there is much talk about the value of entrepreneurship, less is said about intrapreneurship, or entrepreneurial activity within an existing business. The creation of the iPhone by Apple is an example of intrapreneurship. The innovative spirit within Apple has produced a number of such _____ products.

(A) similar
(B) exceptional
(C) innovative
(D) excellent
(E) breakthrough

3. Although the scientific evidence for human activity as the cause of climate change appears (i) _____, many remain (ii) _____ that it's simply part of the natural climate cycle. One wonders in that case if they have considered the possibility of an Ice Age.

Blank (i)	Blank (ii)
(A) urgent	(D) implacable
(B) irrefutable	(E) inflexible
(C) uncontrollable	(F) adamant

4. Setting an eighteenth-century opera in the twenty-first century can make the opera seem both (i) _____ in some ways and (ii) _____ at the same time. How many modern households have servants popping out of closets singing?

Blank (i)	Blank (ii)
(A) strangely mundane	(D) humorous
(B) really interesting	(E) diverting
(C) definitively secular	(F) farcical

5. The (i) _____ nature of modern pop culture makes it easy to think of it as throwaway culture, here today and gone in "15 minutes," in a(n) (ii) _____ to Andy Warhol. However, it is possible that some elements of it may indeed be (iii) _____.

Blank (i)	Blank (ii)	Blank (iii)
(A) imperceptible	(D) illusion	(G) memorable
(B) discernible	(E) allusion	(H) prestigious
(C) inconsequential	(F) paraphrase	(I) prominent

FOR QUESTIONS 6–20, CHOOSE ONLY ONE ANSWER CHOICE UNLESS OTHERWISE INDICATED.

QUESTIONS 6–8 ARE BASED ON THE FOLLOWING PASSAGE.

In a *Washington Post* column, Abigail Trafford raised a question about the reportage of the health of presidents and presidential candidates. She noted that the past has made us cautious about White House cover-ups regarding presidents' illnesses. Yet she pointed to an interesting dilemma: that of the confidentiality of the doctor–patient relationship. How
5 can we reconcile the public's right to know with a public figure's right to this confidential relationship? Trafford brings up a suggestion posed by historian Robert H. Ferrell that "the personal physicians of the president be scrutinized by Congress." Ferrell believes that this would deter physicians from saying anything untruthful regarding the president's health. But Trafford points out that this would cause many doctors to reconsider becoming the
10 president's doctor if it meant being questioned by Congress. Robert S. Robins, a professor of political science at Tulane University, is quoted in the column as believing that this could result in the president's ending up with a choice he doesn't want. Robins says, "This could lead a president to forgo treatment rather than see his doctor or to secretly consult people he trusts." Trafford herself believes that some information from medical reports can also be
15 misleading if they are not followed up on.

6. This passage implies that if Congress were involved in the choice of the president's doctor, the

   (A) president would no longer be able to consult Congress on certain crucial issues.

   (B) American public would no longer need to know so many specific details about the health of the president.

   (C) White House could no longer need to cover up incriminating details about the health of the president.

   (D) president's doctor would totally respect the confidentiality of the president.

   (E) president would not agree to accept the choice of doctor.

FOR QUESTION 7, CONSIDER EACH ANSWER CHOICE SEPARATELY AND SELECT
<u>ALL</u> ANSWER CHOICES THAT APPLY.

7. Select the sentence in the passage that expresses an opinion of Abigail Trafford.

   (A) Yet she pointed to an interesting dilemma: that of the confidentiality of the doctor–
       patient relationship.

   (B) Trafford brings up a suggestion posed by historian Robert H. Ferrell that "the personal
       physicians of the president be scrutinized by Congress."

   (C) But Trafford points out that this would cause many doctors to reconsider becoming the
       president's doctor if it meant being questioned by Congress.

8. The author of the passage most likely agrees with which view as described in the passage?

   (A) Personal physicians of the president should be scrutinized by Congress.

   (B) The current system of choosing a doctor for the president is flawed.

   (C) The White House no longer covers up the health of the president quite so much as it
       used to.

   (D) There would probably be a smaller pool of doctors to choose from if Congress had a say
       in the choice of doctors for the president.

   (E) The press publishes too much information about the health of the president.

QUESTIONS 9–10 ARE BASED ON THE FOLLOWING PASSAGE.

A new generation of artists emerged in the United States at the beginning of the twentieth century. They distinguished themselves from the conventional American Impressionist artists of the period because instead of painting genteel portraits, they painted scenes of everyday urban life, specifically that of New York City. The most famous group of the period, the
5   Eight, as they were later known, were inspired and led by the artist Robert Henri. Henri believed that art should not be separated from life and thus, he encouraged his followers to paint exactly what they observed of urban life. This included scenes of drunks, prostitutes, slum dwellers, alleys, tenements, and bars. This type of painting later became known as the "Ashcan School," referring to the ever-present garbage cans of the city. The Eight exhibited
10 together only once in 1908 at New York's Macbeth Gallery. It was the first exhibition staged by a group of artists, and it caused a sensation, both shocking and thrilling their audience. However, despite their focus on slum life, these Ashcan School of artists can now be seen as far less radical than they imagined themselves to be. They were most interested in the aesthetic qualities of their paintings and did not address the social problems their works
15 represented. It was not until the Great Depression of the 1930s that American artists began to tackle these issues in their works.

9. Which of the following, if it were true, would weaken the author's argument?

(A) Other American artists in the early 1900s pointed to the paintings of the Ashcan School as inspiration for their own paintings.

(B) The Ashcan School artists did not find their own paintings aesthetically pleasing.

(C) Robert Henri discouraged his group from painting pictures of wealthy New Yorkers.

(D) New York City was not the only city to be depicted by the Ashcan School artists.

(E) The Ashcan School artists continued to paint in the 1930s.

10. In the passage, "genteel" (line 3) means

(A) infamous.

(B) notorious.

(C) wholesome.

(D) decent.

(E) refined.

QUESTIONS 11-13 ARE BASED ON THE FOLLOWING PASSAGE.

The Human Genome Project was an international research project that sought to find the sequence of the human genome and to identify the genes that it contains. A genome is the complete set of DNA, or hereditary material, found in the cells of nearly all living organisms. In humans, a copy of the entire genome is contained in all cells that have a nucleus.

5   To begin the human genome project, researchers identified thousands of DNA sequences in blood cells that had been anonymously donated. Then scientists created a collection of DNA clones, in which each clone contained a small fragment of human DNA. These clones were stored in *E. Coli,* which are bacteria that normally live in human intestines. Each *E. Coli* cell contained a single segment of human DNA.

10 When scientists needed to retrieve DNA for sequencing, the *E. Coli* cells were taken out of storage freezers and brought up to 37 degrees Centigrade, the temperature of the intestines. *E. Coli* cells containing the same bit of human DNA were then released into a warm broth. The cells were shaken vigorously, which caused them to divide rapidly. In a few hours, the broth contained billions of *E. Coli* cells, which meant billions of copies of the particular

15 fragment of human DNA each contained. The *E. Coli* cells were broken open to release their DNA, which allowed enough copies of the DNA fragment to set up a sequencing reaction. In 2003, after sequencing the 3 billion parts of the human genome over and over again, the Human Genome Project was considered complete, with a DNA sequence for 99 percent of the genome.

FOR QUESTION 11, CONSIDER EACH ANSWER CHOICE SEPARATELY AND SELECT ALL ANSWER CHOICES THAT APPLY.

---

11. What was significant about the use of *E. Coli* cells specifically in helping to sequence human DNA?

   (A) *E. Coli* could be stored in freezers and brought back up to room temperature.

   (B) Fragments of human DNA could be stored in *E. Coli.*

   (C) *E. Coli* is normally found in human intestines.

12. The point of this passage is to

   (A) convince the reader that if it were not an international effort, the Human Genome Project could never have been accomplished.

   (B) describe to the reader how scientists sequenced DNA.

   (C) encourage the reader to support the Human Genome Project.

   (D) inform the reader about the purpose of the Human Genome Project.

   (E) explain the significance of *E. Coli* in scientific experiments.

13. Select the sentence in the passage that does NOT add to the support for the main idea.

(A) Then scientists created a collection of DNA clones, in which each clone contained a small fragment of human DNA.

(B) *E. Coli* cells containing the same bit of human DNA were then released into a warm broth.

(C) In 2003, after sequencing the 3 billion parts of the human genome over and over again, the Human Genome Project was considered complete, with a DNA sequence for 99 percent of the genome.

(D) A genome is the complete set of DNA, or hereditary material, found in the cells of nearly all living organisms.

(E) Each *E. Coli* cell contained a single segment of human DNA.

QUESTIONS 14–15 ARE BASED ON THE FOLLOWING PASSAGE.

Historians are often drawn to studies of African American migration as a way of understanding the black urban experience, both past and present. But as Gretchen Lemke-Santangelo points out in her book *Abiding Courage*, black urban migration studies frequently focus on just the first two decades of the twentieth century and most often on the experiences of men.
5 Lemke-Santangelo sets out to generate "new perspectives on where and how social change takes place." Therefore, the subjects of her study are black Southern women who migrated to California's East Bay community during World War II. In this way, Lemke-Santangelo introduces the reader to a much lesser known (but no less important) aspect of African American migration history, namely the move from the South to the West, which occurred
10 with increasing frequency during the 1940s. Also, by underscoring the experience of women, Lemke-Santangelo demonstrates the importance of female participation in the migration process and the subsequent organization of the new community.

14. "Underscoring" (line 10) most nearly means

(A) overrating.
(B) accentuating.
(C) facilitating.
(D) recommending.
(E) obfuscating.

15. Select the sentence that restates the premise of the author's argument.

(A) African American women in the 1940s migrated in much greater numbers to the West than was previously understood.

(B) The experience of African American men in the Great Migration is entirely limited.

(C) Urban migration studies are not complete if they only focus on certain experiences.

(D) The first two decades of the twentieth century saw the greatest movement of African Americans out of the South.

(E) African American women were instrumental in organizing new communities in the West.

16. Because of _____ wording in the press release, some people thought that the CEO was being ousted because of irregularities in accounting when it was the CFO who was fired.

    (A) explicit
    (B) mystifying
    (C) inscrutable
    (D) ambiguous
    (E) impressionable
    (F) equivocal

17. The particularly _____ caricature done by the artist's wife showed her intense, though subconscious, dislike of her husband.

    (A) amateurish
    (B) grotesque
    (C) imitative
    (D) bizarre
    (E) incompetent
    (F) mocking

18. The brainstorming activity resulted in _____ ideas for how to improve morale and boost productivity—but in the evaluative process, most were found not to be viable.

    (A) satisfactory
    (B) sufficient
    (C) requisite
    (D) elective
    (E) abundant
    (F) copious

19. The team's proposal was still in its early stages, but one could see from the _____ ideas how the study would take shape and probably result in useful conclusions.

    (A) inchoate
    (B) incipient
    (C) incoherent
    (D) incongruous
    (E) immutable
    (F) obtuse

QUESTION 20 IS BASED ON THE FOLLOWING PASSAGE.

Despite the seeming benefits to the environment that electric cars provide, there are still several challenges that need to be addressed if fully electric vehicles can be realistically expected to replace fuel-powered cars or hybrids in the foreseeable future. Currently, electric cars are limited by the output of their batteries and the current technology that uses energy produced
5 while braking to partly recharge the batteries. This technology would have to be improved in order to allow drivers to travel long distances. In addition, most plug-in electric cars take hours to recharge, which is another serious hindrance to their long-term use. Finally, in order for electric cars to become a truly workable option, charging and battery-exchange stations will have to be put in place everywhere cars are driven. These stations will also have to be
10 designed in such a way that their operation would not drain the power from municipal power grids. There is also the question of electricity production. As long as electric power plants continue to run on nonrenewable fossil fuels, such as coal, recharging electric cars will still release carbon emissions into the atmosphere, which is not a benefit to the environment.

20. What is the author's opinion about the future of electric cars?

(A) There are serious pros and cons to this issue.

(B) It is probably not a realistic option.

(C) Technology simply needs to improve.

(D) Electric cars do not solve the problem of carbon emissions in the atmosphere.

(E) The production of electricity will continue to rely on fossil fuels.

STOP

If you finish before the time is up, you may check your work in this section only.

SECTION 5: VERBAL REASONING

30 minutes • 20 questions

(The paper-and-pencil version will have 25 questions to be completed in 35 minutes.)

For each question, follow the specific directions and choose the best answer.

FOR QUESTIONS 1–5, CHOOSE <u>ONE</u> ANSWER FOR EACH BLANK. SELECT FROM THE APPROPRIATE COLUMN FOR EACH BLANK. CHOOSE THE ANSWER THAT BEST COMPLETES THE SENSE OF THE TEXT.

1. The _____ nature of the prototype site was apparent in that it kept crashing.

| (A) immature |
| (B) rudimentary |
| (C) sophisticated |
| (D) elemental |
| (E) primal |

2. Though (i) _____, the conclusions are based on actual economic activities as surveyed by a(n) (ii) _____ outside research team.

Blank (i)	Blank (ii)
(A) certainly credible	(D) impartial
(B) actually impervious	(E) interested
(C) seemingly implausible	(F) nonpartisan

3. In 1961, putting a man on the moon by 1970 seemed not only (i) _____, but also not (ii) _____ in the time frame.

Blank (i)	Blank (ii)
(A) improbable	(D) serviceable
(B) unusual	(E) feasible
(C) fortuitous	(F) durable

4. The (i) _____ of ideas for reforming the pension system was matched only by the (ii) _____ promises to do something—at some point.

Blank (i)	Blank (ii)
(A) sparsity	(D) keen
(B) derisory	(E) fatuous
(C) paucity	(F) vacuous

5. The success of the show's previews (i) _____ the need for reworking the script. However, the male lead (ii) _____ the playwright to expand his role, but the playwright (iii) _____ and nothing happened.

Blank (i)	Blank (ii)	Blank (iii)
(A) reduced	(D) taunted	(G) condescended
(B) obviated	(E) persisted	(H) demurred
(C) discarded	(F) importuned	(I) patronized

FOR QUESTIONS 6–20, CHOOSE ONLY <u>ONE</u> ANSWER CHOICE UNLESS OTHERWISE INDICATED.

QUESTIONS 6–8 ARE BASED ON THE FOLLOWING PASSAGE.

Winston Churchill is often regarded as the greatest British leader of the twentieth century. His achievements reached their peak when he became the Prime Minister of the United Kingdom in 1940, after Neville Chamberlain resigned. Churchill's refusal to surrender to the Germans helped inspire the British resistance, especially when England was at first the only
5 country to oppose Adolf Hitler. Churchill's powerful speeches and radio broadcasts to boost the morale of the British made him a hero in his own country and ultimately to the Allied forces. Yet despite the tremendous support for Churchill during the war, he was defeated in the 1945 election that followed the end of the war.

There are a number of reasons given for his defeat, among them that the Labour Party had
10 a tightly organized campaign that spoke directly to the needs of post-war Britain. In addition, though Churchill was viewed as an outsider by the Conservative Party, many of the British who liked Churchill were simply unwilling to vote for a Conservative Party candidate. But ironically Churchill's leadership during the war may have also been a cause for his defeat in the election. Once the war ended, the British public began to look toward national recovery.
15 Many people were concerned that Churchill might not be well equipped for handling domestic problems and felt that a good war leader could not also be a good peacetime leader.

6. Select the sentence in the passage that is extraneous to the main idea.

(A) Once the war ended, the British public began to look toward national recovery.

(B) There are a number of reasons given for his defeat, among them that the Labour Party had a tightly organized campaign that spoke directly to the needs of post-war Britain.

(C) Yet despite the tremendous support for Churchill during the war, he was defeated in the 1945 election that followed the end of the war.

(D) Winston Churchill is often regarded as the greatest British leader of the twentieth century.

(E) Churchill's powerful speeches and radio broadcasts to boost the morale of the British made him a hero in his own country and ultimately to the Allied forces.

> **FOR QUESTION 7, CONSIDER EACH ANSWER INDIVIDUALLY AND CHOOSE <u>ALL</u> THAT APPLY.**

7. Which of the following, if it were true, would weaken the author's argument?

   (A) Churchill was known to be a strong ally of Russia.

   (B) Churchill's health was declining at this time.

   (C) Churchill and his party had a concrete peacetime plan.

8. The passage implies that Churchill's defeat in the 1945 election was because

   (A) he was such a good leader during the war.

   (B) the British people could not accept him in a different role.

   (C) the British people wanted to erase the memory of the war and Churchill was too much of a reminder.

   (D) the Conservative Party did not do enough to promote Churchill during the election.

   (E) the British people reconsidered Churchill's role in the war.

QUESTIONS 9–10 ARE BASED ON THE FOLLOWING PASSAGE.

More than half of all people diagnosed with cancer are prescribed chemotherapy, which is a term to describe drugs used to stop cancer cells from growing. The advantage of chemotherapy over surgery and radiation is that drugs can attack cancer cells wherever they are in the body. Unfortunately, older chemotherapy drugs caused many terrible side effects because
5 they could not distinguish between healthy and cancerous cells and so attacked other fast-growing cells in the body, **such as those in the lining of the intestines or in the mouth or in the bloodstream.** However, some newer chemotherapy drugs are specifically designed to target cancer cells. One new drug contains antibody molecules that are engineered in a laboratory to attach to specific defects in cancer cells. The antibody makes cancer cells more
10 noticeable to the immune system and allows anti-cancer drugs to penetrate into cancer cells. The drug also impedes the vessels delivering blood to cancer cells, **which makes it harder for tumors to grow.**

9. Based on the passage, the author evidently believes that

   (A) there needs to be more funding for cancer research.

   (B) only the newest kinds of cancer drugs should be used to treat cancer.

   (C) chemotherapy is not the only option for treating cancer.

   (D) new cancer drugs can target specific cancers.

   (E) the future for cancer treatment is improving.

10. What function do the two groups of words in bold type serve in this argument?

   (A) The first provides an explanation of evidence; the second provides an example of an argument.

   (B) The first supports an argument; the second provides an example of evidence.

   (C) The first provides support for the author's conclusion; the second confirms the support for the conclusion.

   (D) The first provides an example of evidence; the second provides an explanation of evidence.

   (E) The first presents an argument; the second provides evidence to support the argument.

QUESTIONS 11–13 ARE BASED ON THE FOLLOWING PASSAGE.

According to its own Web site, Wikipedia is "a free, web-based, collaborative, multilingual encyclopedia project." The obvious advantage of an online encyclopedia is that it can instantly produce articles on up-to-the-minute topics. However, unlike traditional encyclopedias, the millions of articles on Wikipedia can be edited by anyone who visits the Web site. Not
5 surprisingly, this means that a lot of information on Wikipedia is incorrect or biased, or has no other sources to back it up.

If you use Wikipedia for research, you must proceed with caution. Some articles may contain serious factual errors, and some may be in the process of being edited. Some articles are deficient, presenting only one side of a controversial issue or detailing only certain parts
10 of a person's life. In addition, many contributors to Wikipedia do not cite their sources, which can make it difficult to judge the credibility of what is written. Sometimes Wikipedia articles reference other resources, such as news articles, which can be helpful, but these should be verified. In many cases, Wikipedia can provide a good starting point from which to begin your research, but it should never be your only source of information.

11. Select the sentence from the passage that best exemplifies the main point of the author.

   (A) Not surprisingly, this means that a lot of information on Wikipedia is incorrect, or biased, or has no other sources to back it up.

   (B) The obvious advantage of an online encyclopedia is that it can instantly produce articles on up-to-the-minute topics.

   (C) In many cases, Wikipedia can provide a good starting point from which to begin your research, but it should never be your only source of information.

   (D) In addition, many contributors to Wikipedia do not cite their sources, which makes it difficult to judge the credibility of what is written.

   (E) Some articles are deficient, presenting only one side of a controversial issue or detailing only certain parts of a person's life.

12. The passage implies all of the following statements EXCEPT

(A) Wikipedia articles can contain useful information.

(B) Wikipedia articles never provide backup source material.

(C) you should not write a paper using only Wikipedia research.

(D) contributors to Wikipedia articles may or may not cite their sources.

(E) if sources are cited on Wikipedia, you might still not be able to tell who wrote each article.

FOR QUESTION 13, CONSIDER EACH ANSWER CHOICE INDIVIDUALLY AND CHOOSE ALL THAT APPLY.

---

13. Based on the article, how should a person use Wikipedia when doing research on a particular topic?

(A) Start with Wikipedia and then move on to more academic sources.

(B) Not use Wikipedia unless there is no other information to be found on the topic.

(C) Should only use those Wikipedia articles that contain citations.

QUESTIONS 14–16 ARE BASED ON THE FOLLOWING PASSAGE.

Of the novels published in the late eighteenth and early nineteenth centuries, Jane Austen's are among the few to survive to the present day. However, during her lifetime, Austen's novels were not read widely and were noted by just a few critics who reviewed them, mostly favorably. Not long after Austen died in 1817, most of her novels were all but forgotten.
5 This changed in 1870 with the publication of *Memoir of Jane Austen*, written by her nephew James Edward Austen-Leigh. Although his portrayal of Austen was somewhat misleading, the biography marked the beginning of a new appreciation of Jane Austen's works, both in scholarly and popular circles. Austen-Leigh portrayed his Aunt Jane as a woman who recorded the domestic rural life she lived in just as she saw it—with all its domestic crises
10 and affairs of the heart. This memoir had an immeasurable effect on the public perception of Jane Austen, and it dramatically increased her popularity. The publication of the memoir also spurred the reissue of Austen's novels, which became popular classics and in the twentieth century, popular movies and television programs.

14. Without publication of the *Memoir of Jane Austen*, which of the following would likely be true?

(A) Modern readers would not still be reading the works of Jane Austen.

(B) People's opinions of Jane Austen would not be based on misleading information.

(C) Jane Austen's books would not have been reissued.

(D) People would not know much about the lives of women in the nineteenth century.

(E) Modern readers would know much less about Jane Austen's life.

15. Based on the passage, what was the most significant result of the publication of the memoir?

   (A) It introduced the reading public to the works of Jane Austen.

   (B) It changed the public's perception of Jane Austen.

   (C) It made her works a critical and popular success.

   (D) It gave Austen's fans a glimpse into the real life of their beloved author.

   (E) It recorded the details of late eighteenth-century rural life.

16. In the passage, "immeasurable" (line 10) means

   (A) incalculable.

   (B) monstrous.

   (C) infinitesimal.

   (D) intricate.

   (E) convoluted.

FOR QUESTIONS 17–20, CHOOSE THE TWO ANSWERS THAT BEST FIT THE MEANING OF THE SENTENCE AS A WHOLE AND RESULT IN TWO COMPLETED SENTENCES THAT ARE ALIKE IN MEANING.

---

17. The sales revenue lost during the economic downturn can be _____ if every sales representative contacts one former or current customer and three new customers every day.

   (A) redeemed

   (B) returned

   (C) remediable

   (D) recovered

   (E) remediated

   (F) rectified

18. Wildlife in urban areas includes such non-typical city creatures as foxes that have increased as restaurants with their treat-filled garbage bags have _____.

   (A) gotten along

   (B) proliferated

   (C) progressed

   (D) advanced

   (E) multiplied

   (F) thrive

19. Big box stores cause anxiety among small towns and cities because they appear to be the harbingers of the _____ of the downtown business area as shoppers forsake local small businesses for the big discounters.

    (A) decline

    (B) degradation

    (C) depreciation

    (D) obsolescence

    (E) deterioration

    (F) retrogression

20. Some of the more unforgettable characters in literature are _____. Who can forget the servile, groveling, and fawning Uriah Heep or the Reverend Collins?

    (A) enthralling

    (B) curmudgeonly

    (C) surly

    (D) gruff

    (E) sycophantic

    (F) obsequious

STOP

> If you finish before the time is up, you may check your work in this section only.

ANSWER KEY AND EXPLANATIONS

Section 1: Analytical Writing

Analyze an Issue

Model: 6 points out of 6

A great leader has many important qualities, only one of which is the ability to build consensus and bring about change through compromise. This crucial quality is far more important than the need to act decisively; it is certainly far more important than creating controversy.

Great world leaders of the past have built consensus. For example, Gandhi led the Indian people to independence through a number of important leadership skills, including wisdom and courage, but also through building consensus. Through his nonviolent protests, he drew more and more people into the movement for independence and put more and more pressure on the British rulers, by using nonviolent methods that people admired and were drawn to, such as fasting and marching. A process of compromise ensued as the British gave in on several fronts, including representation for untouchables in government and the lifting of the tax on salt. Each step brought India closer to independence, which was Gandhi's ultimate goal for his people.

President Abraham Lincoln was also a consensus builder. His sense of fairness led him to include people who had run against him for president to serve in his cabinet. That is, he not only sought the advice of people who held views opposite to his own, but he included them in his day-to-day decision-making. He knew that in a deeply divided nation he had to represent opposing views as well as his own. He relied on other views to enrich his knowledge and broaden his perspectives. Lincoln, who was against slavery, also preferred consensus building and compromise on this most important issue. He engaged the North in war on the basis of union, rather than on the basis of the unfairness of slavery. Although it cannot be said with certainty, it is possible that the lack of decisiveness—that slowly building toward consensus on a deeply divisive issue—helped Lincoln achieve his goals and helped the nation return to union.

Decisiveness also has value, and certainly both Gandhi and Lincoln acted decisively when they had to, but decisiveness also has extremely negative consequences, especially when it leads to wars, violence, and injustice. One could certainly say that President Andrew Jackson acted decisively when he ordered the removal of the Cherokee against the orders of the U.S. Supreme Court, a decision that resulted in the tragic, forced migration called the "Trail of Tears." Hitler also acted decisively when he ordered various invasions, including the invasion of Poland in 1939. These actions made both leaders into "lightning rod[s] for controversy"—with extremely tragic consequences for their victims.

In the end, of course, leadership is a complex issue and not reducible to either consensus building or decisiveness. Qualities such as integrity (as evidenced by George Washington) and even confidence, enthusiasm, and a sense of humor (as evidenced by both Presidents Bill Clinton and George W. Bush) are also important. Certainly we want our leaders to be dedicated and intelligent as well. In a complex world with the ability to destroy itself in a second, however, the time, thought, and respect necessary to build consensus will always be preferable to go-it-alone, swift-acting, and potentially tragic, decisiveness.

This essay scores 6 out of 6 because it

- **answers the task.** This essay takes a thoughtful position (that consensus building is better, although it is only one of many important skills), explains the position, and addresses both sides of the issue.

- **is well supported.** Notice how effectively the writer uses a series of examples of world leaders, from Gandhi to Lincoln to Andrew Jackson to Hitler, to exemplify the positions taken. Notice how the support is explained and elaborated upon logically, clearly, and convincingly. Part of this support appears in the acknowledgment and explanation of the issue's complexity.

- **is well organized.** Paragraph 1 clearly takes a position; paragraphs 2 and 3 each develop distinct examples in support of the position; paragraph 4 focuses on the other side of the issue by providing and explaining persuasive examples; and the final paragraph brings thoughtful closure to the essay. Throughout, ideas are connected logically with transitional words and phrases and the type of effective repetition that creates coherence.

- **is fluid, precise, and graceful.** Precise word choices include nouns such as *confidence* and *decisiveness,* and adjectives such as *go-it-alone.* Sentences are varied in their structure, type, length, and openings.

- **observes the conventions of Standard Written English.**

Model: 1 point out of 6

What is democracy if not for being a matter for compromise and consensus? The very fabric of the Constitution having been weaved from the cloth of compromise. Compromise, not one person making up their mind and demanding, also being how we pass laws in this nation. Decisiveness is fine for an authoritarian or totalitarian leader, it worked fine for Communist Russia and works fine now for Communist China, it is anti-democratic even in just a leader and therefore undesirable. So if you want to be a democratic leader you're most important skill is compromise. Not making controversy or acting as if you are the one and the only one with all the answers. Not going off in a huff either because you cannot get your own way. That kind of leadership is for a dictator—like Fidel Castro. Even though there are sometimes when a leader has to lead in order to be respected and make his or her people follow and do the right thing, most times it is better to reach a compromise in this complex world with the ability to destroy itself in a second.

This essay scores 1 out of 6 because it

- **barely answers the task.** While the position (that consensus building is better) is clear, the essay does not address both sides of the issue.

- **lacks support.** Even though the writer offers a few examples, they are vague and undeveloped. The essay does not support its position.

- **has major problems with the conventions of Standard Written English.** The problems with lack of sentence structure are significant enough to obscure meaning.

Analyze an Argument

Model: 6 points out of 6

Many questions would have to be answered before this argument could be considered even vaguely reasonable. The first of these questions relates to the nature of an attention span. For example, what is an attention span? Has anyone ever measured one? How can the parents and teachers make a recommendation based on something that no one has the first idea of how to quantify or track? Even if attention span were quantifiable or trackable, wouldn't the school have to have conducted baseline studies and then have collected statistics suggesting diminishment for students before drawing the conclusion that attention spans are diminishing? This fundamental question of what, actually, constitutes an attention span, and its so-called diminishment, is a fundamental problem with the argument, which undercuts the recommendation based on it. It is also just the first of the argument's multiple problems.

An almost equally fundamental problem with this argument is the assumption of a cause-and-effect relationship between "computers, computer games, and devices such as smart phones that integrate computer technology" and a perilous drop in attention spans. Again, just exactly who has measured this? More fundamentally, is such a cause and effect even measurable? Educators and parents may so dislike computer games or so gravely suspect them to be impediments to learning that they leap to the conclusion that one thing causes the other. Yet, is there actual evidence that this is the case? The question of actual cause and effect must also be answered before this recommendation can be logically evaluated.

In addition, the argument asserts that the parents and teachers who are making the recommendation to ban computers are motivated by the desire to prepare children for the serious work of the 21st century workplace. This part of the argument, too, leaves many questions unanswered. The parents and teachers seem to assume that workers will need to sustain a single focus to do the jobs of the future, but isn't it possible that the best skill set for the jobs ahead in a fast-changing world will include skills that allow workers to instantly switch their focus from one task to the next, to switch rapidly from idea to idea or situation to situation? Could it be possible that instead of intense concentration, or perhaps in addition to it, a certain distractibility or willingness to follow new links and ideas to wherever they lead will also be crucial for success? In other words, what is the evidence that the skills learned by playing computer games or communicating almost instantly are not going to be the necessary skills, or among the necessary skills, for success in future employment? The answers to these questions may completely contradict the recommendation or render it totally illogical.

In fact, nowhere does this argument actually tell what the effects of using computers actually are. Instead, the argument implies that this behavior is negative and rushes to the conclusion that it is putting students at risk. The argument then suggests banning certain computer technology under almost all circumstances. Thus the argument remains unreasonable even after questions of what constitutes an attention span are answered.

This essay scores 6 out of 6 because it

- **answers the task.** The writer poses and discusses many important questions that would have to be answered to decide whether the recommendation and the argument on which it is based are reasonable. The essay also explains how the answers to these questions will help to evaluate the argument.

- **is well supported.** Questions of what an attention span is, and the inability to measure it, are insightful, logical, and effective. The reader clearly sees how this central problem with the argument devalues the recommendation based on it. Other cogent discussion is offered throughout the essay. Particularly insightful are supporting details and explanation related to twenty-first-century workplace skills.

- **is well organized.** All four substantial paragraphs are logically organized and lead smoothly one to the next. The essay concludes as sure-footedly as it begins. Transitions and other elements of coherence ease the reader's passage through the essay.

- **is fluid and precise.** The writing is clear and direct; the voice is clear and assertive; the tone is appropriate. Word choices are apt and sentences are varied.

- **observes the conventions of Standard Written English.**

Model: 1 point out of 6

I am in complete agreement that attention spans are going down and educaters and parents need to do something drastic about it as soon as possible and not just in one school but across our hole nation. My main reason for agreeing with this view point is that I have a little brother who has been taking medication for attention deficit disorder for sevral years now. He was playing computer games before he was two years old and is totally obsessed with computers and technology now. But he is very antisocial and shows behaviors that are concerning to my parents and to his teachers, such as occasional outbursts that have harmed other kids he played with. Even his placement in the public school is in jepardy being due to his attention deficit disorder. I believe strongly that technology brung on his problems and therefore it should be banned. Not completely, but definitely in the classroom if it isn't absolutely necessary, such as in teaching search skills.

Their are so many students just like my little brother! When I went to elementry school, maybe one out of every five or six kids at least were taking some kind of medicine to un-hyper them. I recently read that now about 25% of all students in U.S. elementry schools take a drug for there attention deficit disorder. It is troubling to think of young children on these meds. When all we really need to do is pull the plug on the computer games and get back to traditional reading and other focused things in our classrooms. Kids will still get plenty of exposure to technology, such as computers, computer games, and cellphones, at home, and they will still keep up with there world. I'm not saying that technology isn't important or shouldn't be used. I'm not saying computer games aren't fun. But school should be a place, instead, for concentration on just one thing at a time. That being learning the skills needed for success in the 21st century workplace.

This essay scores 1 out of 6 because it

- **does not answer the task.** While an issue task requires you to agree or disagree, with or without qualification, an argument task requires you to evaluate the argument in some way. This essay does not do that. It ignores the instructions accompanying the prompt by raising no questions about the validity of the position. A response that does not answer the task completely cannot be successful no matter what other qualities it may demonstrate. This writer does show a certain fluency with the written word, but his or her lack of complete compliance with the instructions cannot earn more than a 1.

Section 2: Quantitative Reasoning

1. C	11. B	16. B, E, G
2. A	12. D	17. 1
3. B	13. C	18. $\dfrac{29}{12}$
4. D	14. A	
5. B	15. A, D, E	19. $\dfrac{7}{15}$
6. D		20. C
7. B		
8. B		
9. E		
10. C		

Question

1.

Quantity A	Quantity B
$6(4)\left(\dfrac{1}{2}\right)^2$	6

(A) Quantity A is greater.

(B) Quantity B is greater.

(C) The two quantities are equal.

(D) The relationship cannot be determined from the information given.

Answer Explanation

The correct answer is (C). Simplify $6(4)\left(\dfrac{1}{2}\right)^2$.

$$6(4)\left(\dfrac{1}{2}\right)^2$$

$$= 6(4)\left(\dfrac{1}{4}\right)$$

$$= 6$$

So, both quantities are the same, 6.

Question

$$xy = 12$$

2.   **Quantity A**   **Quantity B**
                  $(3x)(2y)$ **60**

(A) Quantity A is greater.

(B) Quantity B is greater.

(C) The two quantities are equal.

(D) The relationship cannot be determined from the information given.

Answer Explanation

The correct answer is (A). Simplify and substitute.

$(3x)(2y)$

$= 6xy$

$= 6(12)$

$= 72$

So, 72 is greater than 60.

Question

3.   Quantity A   Quantity B

              40% of $\dfrac{5}{8}$ 60% of $\dfrac{3}{4}$

(A) Quantity A is greater.

(B) Quantity B is greater.

(C) The two quantities are equal.

(D) The relationship cannot be determined from the information given.

Answer Explanation

The correct answer is (B). Evaluate:

$\left(\dfrac{2}{5}\right)\left(\dfrac{5}{8}\right) = \dfrac{10}{40} = \dfrac{1}{4}$

$\left(\dfrac{3}{5}\right)\left(\dfrac{3}{4}\right) = \dfrac{9}{20}$

Question

$$x \neq 0$$

4.   <u>Quantity A</u>   <u>Quantity B</u>

                    $\dfrac{5}{x}$ $5x$

(A) Quantity A is greater.

(B) Quantity B is greater.

(C) The two quantities are equal.

(D) The relationship cannot be determined from the information given.

Answer Explanation

The correct answer is (D). Pick numbers to find the answer. Be sure to pick a positive, a negative, and a fraction to test all possibilities.

$x = 1$

$\dfrac{5}{1} = 5$ and $5(1) = 5$, which are equal.

$x = -1$

$\dfrac{5}{-1} = -5$ and $5(-1) = -5$, which are equal.

$x = \dfrac{1}{5}$

$\dfrac{5}{\frac{1}{5}} = 25$ and $5\left(\dfrac{1}{5}\right) = 5$, which are not equal.

Question

$$x + 3 = 4x - 2$$
$$5y - 2 = 2y + 1$$

5.   <u>Quantity A</u>   <u>Quantity B</u>

                    $3x$ $6y$

(A) Quantity A is greater.

(B) Quantity B is greater.

(C) The two quantities are equal.

(D) The relationship cannot be determined from the information given.

Answer Explanation

The correct answer is (B). Solve the equations:

$$x + 3 = 4x - 2$$
$$-3x = -5$$
$$x = \frac{5}{3}$$
$$5y - 2 = 2y + 1$$
$$3y = 3$$
$$y = 1$$

$$3x = 3\left(\frac{5}{3}\right) = 5$$
$$6y = 6(1) = 6$$

Question

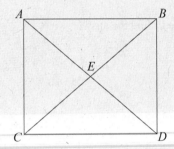

6.

Quantity A	Quantity B
The area of *AEC*	The area of *CED*

(A) Quantity A is greater.

(B) Quantity B is greater.

(C) The two quantities are equal.

(D) The relationship cannot be determined from the information given.

Answer Explanation

The correct answer is (D). Because there are no parameters given for the shape *ABCD*, the areas can't be determined.

Question

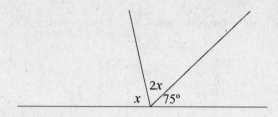

7.   <u>Quantity A</u>   <u>Quantity B</u>
                        $5x$ 180

(A) Quantity A is greater.

(B) Quantity B is greater.

(C) The two quantities are equal.

(D) The relationship cannot be determined from the information given.

Answer Explanation

The correct answer is (B). Solve to find the answer:

$$x + 2x + 75 = 180$$
$$3x + 75 = 180$$
$$3x = 105$$
$$x = 35$$

$$5x = 5(35) = 175$$

Question

A 2,475-square-foot house sells for $475,000. The broker's fee is 6%.

8.   <u>Quantity A</u>   <u>Quantity B</u>
                    The broker's fee $31,000

(A) Quantity A is greater.

(B) Quantity B is greater.

(C) The two quantities are equal.

(D) The relationship cannot be determined from the information given.

Answer Explanation

The correct answer is (B). Estimate 6% of $475,000 which will be a little less than 6% of $500,000, which is $30,000 which is less than $31,000.

QUESTIONS 9–11 REFER TO THE GRAPH BELOW.

Sales by type 2010

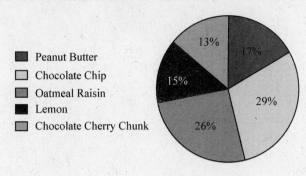

- Peanut Butter
- Chocolate Chip
- Oatmeal Raisin
- Lemon
- Chocolate Cherry Chunk

Question

9. The two most popular types of cookies were what percentage of sales?

(A) 26

(B) 29

(C) 42

(D) 44

(E) 55

Answer Explanation

The correct answer is (E). Evaluate:

$$29 + 26 = 55$$

Question

10. How many different types of cookies do NOT have chocolate in them?

(A) 1

(B) 2

(C) 3

(D) 4

(E) 5

Answer Explanation

The correct answer is (C). Peanut butter, oatmeal raisin, and lemon are chocolate-less. This may seem like a simple question, but some people will try to figure out the shadings on the graph so they can work out percentages before they realize what the question is asking; others will look for the cookies with chocolate chips and select "2" as the answer.

Question

11. If total sales for the year were $94,480, what was the total amount sold of the third most popular cookie?

(A) $12,543

(B) $16,062

(C) $17,727

(D) $24,980

(E) $27,589

Answer Explanation

The correct answer is (B). Turn the words into equations, using the information from the pie chart.

17% of $94,480 = 0.17(94,480) = $16,062

Question

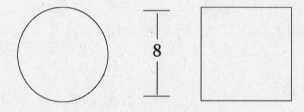

12. The above circle has a diameter of 8, and the square has a perimeter of 32. What is the difference in the area between the two?

(A) 11.82

(B) 12.96

(C) 13.33

(D) 13.76

(E) 15.97

Answer Explanation

The correct answer is (D). Find the areas of the two figures and subtract.

Area of a square $h(w)$:

$8(8) = 64$

Area of a circle πr^2:

$3.14(4)^2$

$3.14(16) = 50.24$

$64 - 50.24 = 13.76$

Question

13. Lacy receives 45% of the commission of every painting she sells. If she recently sold a painting for $256,000 and received a commission of $7,488, what was the total rate of commission?

(A) 0.016

(B) 0.029

(C) 0.065

(D) 0.067

(E) 0.076

Answer Explanation

The correct answer is (C). Turn the problem into equations and solve:

$$7488 \div 0.45 = 16,640$$
$$16,640 \div 256,000 = 0.065$$

Question

14. The expression $(4x+7y)^2 - (2x-3y)^2$ is equivalent to

(A) $4(3x^2 + 17xy + 10y^2)$

(B) $16x^2 + 10y^2$

(C) $12x^2 + 12xy - 9y^2$

(D) $x^2 + 12xy + 40y^2$

(E) None of the above

Answer Explanation

The correct answer is (A). You can simplify the expression:

$$(4x+7y)^2 - (2x-3y)^2$$
$$= 16x^2 + 56xy + 49y^2 - (4x^2 - 12xy + 9y^2)$$
$$= 16x^2 + 56xy + 49y^2 - 4x^2 + 12xy - 9y^2$$
$$= 12x^2 + 68xy + 40y^2$$
$$= 4(3x^2 + 17xy + 10y^2)$$

Or do small parts of the math and check the answers:

$$16x^2 - 4x^2 = 12x^2 = 4(3x^2)$$

Choices (A) and (C) have this. Now do another part of the math:

$$48y^2 - 9y^2 = 40y^2 = 4(10y^2)$$

Of choices (A) and (C), only choice (A) has this.

Question

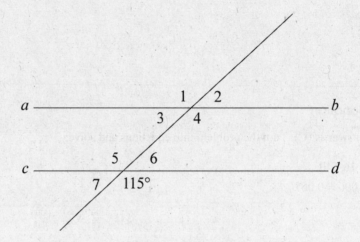

15. If *ab* and *cd* are parallel, what other angles are equal to 115°?

    (A) 1

    (B) 2

    (C) 3

    (D) 4

    (E) 5

    (F) 6

    (G) 7

Answer Explanation

The correct answers are (A), (D), and (E). The other angles equal to 115° are 1, 4, 5.

Question

16. What are the next three numbers in the sequence 0, 1, 3, 7, 15, 31,…

(A) 57

(B) 63

(C) 72

(D) 111

(E) 127

(F) 295

(G) 255

(H) 511

Answer Explanation

The correct answers are (B), (E), and (G). Determine the relationship of the sequence:

$2^{n-1} - 1$

$2^{7-1} - 1 = 2^6 - 1 = 64 - 1 = 63$

$2^{8-1} - 1 = 2^7 - 1 = 128 - 1 = 127$

$2^{9-1} - 1 = 2^8 - 1 = 256 - 1 = 255$

Question

17. If $m\left(m\left(m\left(m\left(m\frac{1}{m}\right)\frac{1}{m}\right)\frac{1}{m}\right)\frac{1}{m}\right)\frac{1}{m} = x$, and $m \neq 0$, what does x equal?

Answer Explanation

The correct answer is 1. Any number times its inverse equals 1.

Question

18. $\dfrac{1}{2}+\dfrac{1}{3}+\dfrac{3}{4}+\dfrac{5}{6}=$

Give your answer as a fraction.

Answer Explanation

The correct answer is $\dfrac{29}{12}$. Solve: $\dfrac{1}{2}+\dfrac{1}{3}+\dfrac{3}{4}+\dfrac{5}{6}=\dfrac{6}{12}+\dfrac{4}{12}+\dfrac{9}{12}+\dfrac{10}{12}=\dfrac{29}{12}$

Question

19. On a rugby team of 15 players, the ratio of forwards to backs is $\dfrac{8}{7}$. What is the ratio of backs to total number of players?

Give your answer as a fraction.

Answer Explanation

The correct answer is $\dfrac{7}{15}$. The ratio is 7 backs to 15 players.

Question

20. If an acre is equal to 43,560 square feet, how many acres are there in 362,985 square feet?

(A) 6.33

(B) 7.33

(C) 8.33

(D) 9.33

(E) 10.33

Answer Explanation

The correct answer is (C). $362,985 \div 43,560 = 8.33$

Section 3: Quantitative Reasoning

1. C	11. A	16. A, G
2. A	12. E	17. D
3. A	13. C	18. 64
4. C	14. A	19. 20
5. A	15. C	20. A, H
6. C		
7. D		
8. B		
9. B		
10. C		

Question

$$\frac{5}{8}x = \frac{1}{12}$$

1.

Quantity A	Quantity B
x	$\dfrac{2}{15}$

(A) Quantity A is greater.

(B) Quantity B is greater.

(C) The two quantities are equal.

(D) The relationship cannot be determined from the information given.

Answer Explanation

The correct answer is (C). Work backwards to find the answer.

$$x = \frac{5}{8}\left(\frac{2}{15}\right) = \frac{10}{120} = \frac{1}{12}$$

Question

2.

Quantity A	Quantity B
$\dfrac{0.00008}{0.00006}$	0.75

(A) Quantity A is greater.

(B) Quantity B is greater.

(C) The two quantities are equal.

(D) The relationship cannot be determined from the information given.

Answer Explanation

The correct answer is (A). Evaluate to find the answer.

$$\frac{0.00008}{0.00006} = 1.333$$

Question

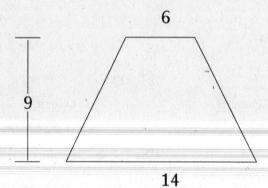

3.

Quantity A	Quantity B
The area of the trapezoid	80

(A) Quantity A is greater.

(B) Quantity B is greater.

(C) The two quantities are equal.

(D) The relationship cannot be determined from the information given.

Answer Explanation

The correct answer is (A). Calculate the area:

$$area = h\left(\frac{b_1 + b_2}{2}\right)$$

$$= 9\left(\frac{6 + 14}{2}\right) = 9(10) = 90$$

Question

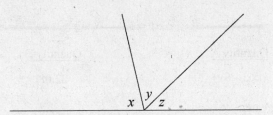

4. | Quantity A | Quantity B |
    |---|---|
    | The mean of angles x, y, z | 60 |

(A) Quantity A is greater.

(B) Quantity B is greater.

(C) The two quantities are equal.

(D) The relationship cannot be determined from the information given.

Answer Explanation

The correct answer is (C). Work backwards:

$$180 = x + y = z$$

$$\frac{180}{3} = 60$$

Question

5. | Quantity A | Quantity B |
    |---|---|
    | $\sqrt{(66)(27)}$ | $(8)(4.9)$ |

(A) Quantity A is greater.

(B) Quantity B is greater.

(C) The two quantities are equal.

(D) The relationship cannot be determined from the information given.

Answer Explanation

The correct answer is (A). Use your calculator:

$$\sqrt{(66)(27)} > \sqrt{(64)(25)}$$
$$\sqrt{(64)(25)} = (8)(5)$$
$$(8)(5) > (8)(4.9)$$

Question

$$xy = 3.2$$

6.

Quantity A	Quantity B
$1.5x(4.6y)$	22.08

(A) Quantity A is greater.

(B) Quantity B is greater.

(C) The two quantities are equal.

(D) The relationship cannot be determined from the information given.

Answer Explanation

The correct answer is (C). Simplify and substitute:

$xy = 3.2$

$1.5x(4.6y) =$

$\quad 6.9xy =$

$\quad 6.9(3.2) = 22.08$

Question

7.

Quantity A	Quantity B
Time it takes a bicycle to travel 15 miles	Time it takes a car to travel 60 miles

(A) Quantity A is greater.

(B) Quantity B is greater.

(C) The two quantities are equal.

(D) The relationship cannot be determined from the information given.

Answer Explanation

The correct answer is (D). Because there are no parameters given for the problem, no relationship can be determined.

Question

An apple costs $0.25. An orange costs $0.35. A pear costs $\frac{1}{2}$ of the sum of an apple and an orange.

8.   Quantity A   Quantity B
          5 apples and 5 oranges   12 pears

(A) Quantity A is greater.

(B) Quantity B is greater.

(C) The two quantities are equal.

(D) The relationship cannot be determined from the information given.

Answer Explanation

The correct answer is (B). Set up expressions and evaluate:

A pear costs $\frac{0.25 + 0.35}{2} = \$0.30$

5 apples and 5 oranges cost $5(.25) + 5(.35) = \$3.00$

12 pears cost $12(.30) = \$3.60$

Question

There were x iPads in the Apple store. After $\frac{1}{10}$ of them were sold, 6 more were brought into the store, giving them 51 in stock.

9.   Quantity A   Quantity B
                   x 54

(A) Quantity A is greater.

(B) Quantity B is greater.

(C) The two quantities are equal.

(D) The relationship cannot be determined from the information given.

Answer Explanation

The correct answer is (B). Turn the words into equations and solve:

$$x - 0.1x + 6 = 51$$
$$0.9x = 45$$
$$x = 50$$

Question

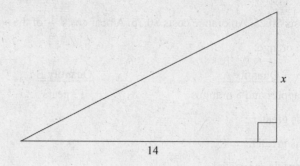

the area of the triangle is 70

10.   <u>Quantity A</u>   <u>Quantity B</u>
                x 10

(A) Quantity A is greater.

(B) Quantity B is greater.

(C) The two quantities are equal.

(D) The relationship cannot be determined from the information given.

Answer Explanation

The correct answer is (C). Solve:

$$area = \frac{1}{2}(b)(h)$$

$$70 = \frac{1}{2}(14)(x)$$

$$70 = 7x$$

$$10 = x$$

QUESTIONS 11–13 REFER TO THE BAR GRAPH BELOW.

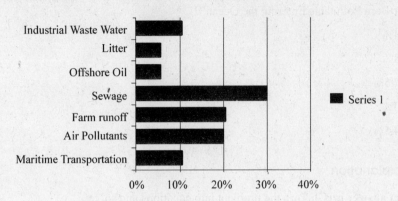

Pollutants Entering the Ocean

Question

11. What is the percentage of offshore oil compared to all pollutants?

(A) 5%

(B) 10%

(C) 15%

(D) 20%

(E) 30%

Answer Explanation

The correct answer is (A). To find the answer, read the graph: 5%.

Question

12. Sewage, litter, and air pollution make up what percentage of the whole?

(A) 5%

(B) 15%

(C) 30%

(D) 45%

(E) 55%

Answer Explanation

The correct answer is (E).

30% + 5% + 20% = 55%

Question

13. If air pollution is eliminated from the graph, what percentage would sewage be of the new graph "Water-Born Pollutants Entering the Ocean"?

    (A) 24%

    (B) 28%

    (C) 37.5%

    (D) 40%

    (E) 44.5%

Answer Explanation

The correct answer is (C). Turn the problem into equations and solve:

$$\frac{x}{100} = \frac{30}{80}$$
$$x = \frac{3000}{80}$$
$$x = 37.5$$

Question

14. A receptionist greeted the following numbers of people during one work week: 4, 19, 21, 18, 23. What is the mean of the number of people she greeted?

    (A) 17

    (B) 19

    (C) 20

    (D) 21

    (E) 85

Answer Explanation

The correct answer is (A). The mean is the average. The sum of the numbers is 85. There are 5 data points. Dividing the sum by the number of data points results in 17.

Question

15. A farmer owns a square property and wants to sell a lot formed by dividing the lot in half, both lengthwise and widthwise. If the resulting lot has a perimeter of 888,000 feet, what is the area of the original lot?

(A) 179,936,000,000 sq. ft.

(B) 185,926,000,000 sq. ft.

(C) 197,136,000,000 sq. ft.

(D) 200,000,000,000 sq. ft.

(E) 212,386,000,000 sq. ft.

Answer Explanation

The correct answer is (C). Drawing a diagram will help you to visualize the problem. Then calculate:

$888,000 \div 4 = 222,000$

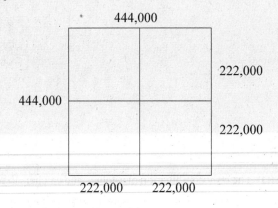

$444,000 \times 444,000 = 197,136,000,000$ or 197.136 billion

Question

16. What are the two factors of $x^2 + 9x + 18$?

(A) $x + 3$

(B) $x - 3$

(C) $x + 2$

(D) $x - 2$

(E) $x + 9$

(F) $x - 9$

(G) $x + 6$

(H) $x - 6$

Answer Explanation

The correct answers are (A) and (G). You could use the quadratic formula, or you could estimate which is faster. The factors of 18 are (1,18) (3,6) (2,9). The only ones when added together or subtracted from each other to equal 9 are 3 and 6. Since both $6x$ and 18 are positive, then both 3 and 6 are positive.

Question

17. The local baseball team employs at least 3 times as many pitchers as catchers, but never more than 11 players total. Pitchers make an average of $45,000, and catchers make an average of $30,000. Which of the following amounts are the possible averages for all the pitchers and catchers, rounded to the nearest dollar?

    (A) 30,000

    (B) 35,899

    (C) 40,375

    (D) 41,250

    (E) 41,956

    (F) 42,273

    (G) 43,743

    (H) 45,000

Answer Explanation

The correct answer is (D). The only combination of pitchers and catchers that apply are 3 pitchers/1 catcher and 6 pitchers/2 catchers. Both combinations leave you with the same answer: 41,250.

$$\frac{3(45,000)+30,000}{3+1}$$

$$=\frac{135,000+30,000}{4}$$

$$=\frac{165,000}{4}$$

$$=41,250$$

$$\frac{6(45,000)+2(30,000)}{6+2}$$

$$=\frac{270,000+60,000}{8}$$

$$=\frac{330,000}{8}$$

$$=41,250$$

The answer must be 41,250.

Question

18. $\dfrac{\left(\left(2^3\right)^2\right)^2}{\left(2^2\right)^3} =$

☐

Answer Explanation

The correct answer is 64. Calculate:

$$\frac{\left(\left(2^3\right)^2\right)^2}{\left(2^2\right)^3}$$

$$= \frac{\left(8^2\right)^2}{\left(4\right)^3}$$

$$= \frac{64^2}{64}$$

$$= 64$$

Question

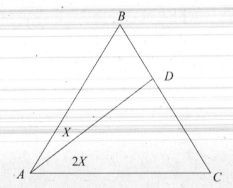

19. If ABC is an equilateral triangle, what is the measure of angle BAD?

☐

Answer Explanation

The correct answer is 20. Turn the information into an equation and solve.

The angles in an equilateral triangle are equal to 60, so:

$60 = 2x + x$

$60 = 3x$

$x = 20$

Question

20. Which of the following numbers have factors of 2, 5, 6?

(A) 60

(B) 84

(C) 95

(D) 110

(E) 125

(F) 166

(G) 247

(H) 300

Answer Explanation

The correct answers are (A) and (H). First, find all the numbers with a factor of 5: 60, 95, 110, 125, 300. Then, of those six numbers, find all those with a factor of 2: 60, 110, 300. Of those three, find the numbers with a factor of 6: 60, 300.

Section 4: Verbal Reasoning

1. C	11. B, C	16. D, F
2. E	12. B	17. B, D
3. A, F	13. D	18. E, F
4. A, F	14. B	19. A, B
5. C, E, G	15. C	20. A
6. C		
7. C		
8. D		
9. A		
10. E		

Question

1. Myanmar's path to unity is complicated by its physical geography. Mountains and plateaus
_____ contacts among different regions within the nation and with its neighbors, making
commerce, communication, and human movement difficult.

(A) bar
(B) exhaust
(C) hamper
(D) blockade
(E) harm

Answer Explanation

The correct answer is (C). Choice (A), "bar," is incorrect because the final part of the second sentence indicates that carrying on commerce, communication, and human movement is difficult, but not impossible, which it would be if they were barred, or blocked, from occurring. For this reason, choice (D), "blockade" is also incorrect; it means "to block, to keep from passing" and often has a legal or quasi-legal meaning. Choice (B), "exhaust," may be true about trekking over mountains, but it doesn't fit the context, so eliminate it. Choice (E) is incorrect because "harm" means "to injure in some way, physically, morally, or mentally," and that doesn't fit with the effects of geography.

Question

2. Although there is much talk about the value of entrepreneurship, less is said about intrapreneur-ship, or entrepreneurial activity within an existing business. The creation of the iPhone by Apple is an example of intrapreneurship. The innovative spirit within Apple has produced a number of such _____ products.

(A) similar
(B) exceptional
(C) innovative
(D) excellent
(E) breakthrough

Answer Explanation

The correct answer is (E). Tone will help you answer this question. While choice (A), "similar," makes sense, it doesn't fit with the tone of the phrase "innovative spirit" or the idea of entrepreneurship. Choice (B), "exceptional," also makes sense and is closer to the sense of "innovative spirit," so it might work. However, choice (E), "breakthrough," meaning "a major achievement," better fits the tone of the sentence. Choice (C), "innovative," might work to create parallelism, but breakthrough indicates a higher level of creativity and importance. Choice (D), "excellent," indicates quality, but not necessarily inventiveness.

Question

3. Although the scientific evidence for human activity as the cause of climate change appears (i) _____, many remain (ii) _____ that it's simply part of the natural climate cycle. One wonders in that case if they have considered the possibility of an Ice Age.

Blank (i)	Blank (ii)
(A) urgent	(D) implacable
(B) irrefutable	(E) inflexible
(C) uncontrollable	(F) adamant

Answer Explanation

The correct answers are (A) and (F). Answer Blank (i): When you consider the two blanks, it becomes apparent that choice (A), "urgent," meaning "requiring immediate action" fits the sense of the sentence, which is about differences in opinion, not the need for action. Choice (B), "irrefutable," which means "impossible to disprove, unassailable," doesn't fit the sense. Climate change may or may not be "uncontrollable," but that's not the point of the sentence.

Answer Blank (ii): Choice (F), "adamant," meaning "firm, stubbornly unyielding, not open to reason or persuasion" fits the sense. Choice (D), "implacable," means "not capable of pleasing, unforgiving" and doesn't fit the sense. "Inflexible," choice (E), is a synonym of "implacable" and, therefore, can be eliminated. Note also that choices (D) and (E) don't sound "right" to the ear; both are usually followed by a preposition, not a clause.

Question

4. Setting an eighteenth-century opera in the twenty-first century can make the opera seem both (i) _____ in some ways and (ii) _____ at the same time. How many modern households have servants popping out of closets singing?

Blank (i)	Blank (ii)
(A) strangely mundane	(D) humorous
(B) really interesting	(E) diverting
(C) definitively secular	(F) farcical

Answer Explanation

The correct answers are (A) and (F). Answer Blank (i): This is a question where it may make more sense to complete the second blank first to help you figure out the first. In that case, you would be able to eliminate "really interesting" because it doesn't counterbalance choice (F), "farcical," the answer for the second blank. Choice (C), "definitively secular," meaning "worldly, earthly," doesn't make sense.

Answer Blank (ii): While choice (D), "humorous," might fit the sense, choice (F), "farcical," is a better answer considering the next sentence, which describes a situation that you might find in a farce; a farce tells its story through exaggerated situations and characters, improbable plot lines, and slapstick. Choice (E) is incorrect because "diverting" indicates something that might be only mildly humorous, and the context indicates something much funnier.

Question

5. The (i) _____ nature of modern pop culture makes it easy to think of it as throwaway culture, here today and gone in "15 minutes," in a(n) (ii) _____ to Andy Warhol. However, it is possible that some elements of it may indeed be (iii) _____.

Blank (i)	Blank (ii)	Blank (iii)
(A) imperceptible	(D) illusion	(G) memorable
(B) discernible	(E) allusion	(H) prestigious
(C) inconsequential	(F) paraphrase	(I) prominent

Answer Explanation

The correct answers are (C), (E), and (G). Answer Blank (i): Choices (A) and (B) are opposites, so either both are incorrect, or one is correct. In this case both are incorrect. Choice (A), "imperceptible," means "difficult to perceive or subtle" and choice (B), "discernible," means "able to perceive." Neither fits the sense that modern pop culture is so insubstantial that it can be easily forgotten. Choice (C), "inconsequential," fits this sense.

Answer Blank (ii): Choice (E), "allusion," is "an indirect reference to someone or something." An "illusion," choice (D), is "a mistaken perception of reality" and doesn't make sense in the sentence. Choice (F), a "paraphrase," is a restating in your own words of what someone else said and is incorrect because the phrase "15 minutes" is quoted.

Answer Blank (iii): Because of the reference to time in the first sentence, choice (G), "memorable," meaning "lasting, worth remembering," matches the sense. Neither choices (H) nor (I) include the sense of time. Choice (H), "prestigious," means "being esteemed or honored," and choice (I), "prominent," means "to stand out, be widely known."

QUESTIONS 6–8 ARE BASED ON THE FOLLOWING PASSAGE.

In a *Washington Post* column, Abigail Trafford raised a question about the reportage of the health of presidents and presidential candidates. She noted that the past has made us cautious about White House cover-ups regarding presidents' illnesses. Yet she pointed to an interesting dilemma: that of the confidentiality of the doctor–patient relationship. How
5 can we reconcile the public's right to know with a public figure's right to this confidential relationship? Trafford brings up a suggestion posed by historian Robert H. Ferrell that "the personal physicians of the president be scrutinized by Congress." Ferrell believes that this would deter physicians from saying anything untruthful regarding the president's health. But Trafford points out that this would cause many doctors to reconsider becoming the
10 president's doctor if it meant being questioned by Congress. Robert S. Robins, a professor of political science at Tulane University, is quoted in the column as believing that this could result in the president's ending up with a choice he doesn't want. Robins says, "This could lead a president to forgo treatment rather than see his doctor or to secretly consult people he trusts." Trafford herself believes that some information from medical reports can also be
15 misleading if they are not followed up on.

Question

6. This passage implies that if Congress were involved in the choice of the president's doctor, the

(A) president would no longer be able to consult Congress on certain crucial issues.

(B) American public would no longer need to know so many specific details about the health of the president.

(C) White House would no longer need to cover up incriminating details about the health of the president.

(D) president's doctor would totally respect the confidentiality of the president.

(E) president would not agree to accept the choice of doctor.

Answer Explanation

The correct answer is (C). The passage implies that if Congress chose the president's doctor, the doctor would tell the truth about the president's health so the White House would not be able to cover up serious health issues. Choice (A) is incorrect because nowhere in the passage does it discuss how the president would consult with Congress on other issues. Choice (B) is incorrect because this is not implied in the passage and actually contradicts its main point. Choice (D) might seem correct because it is very likely true, but it is not what is implied by the statement presented in the question. Choice (E) is incorrect because the passage neither says nor implies that the president's doctor would be chosen by any one other than the president. The passage only says Congress would question the doctor, not confirm him.

Question

7. Select the sentence in the passage that expresses an opinion of Abigail Trafford.

(A) Yet she pointed to an interesting dilemma: that of the confidentiality of the doctor–patient relationship.

(B) Trafford brings up a suggestion posed by historian Robert H. Ferrell that "the personal physicians of the president be scrutinized by Congress."

(C) But Trafford points out that this would cause many doctors to reconsider becoming the president's doctor if it meant being questioned by Congress.

Answer Explanation

The correct answer is (C). Trafford expresses an opinion by presuming that doctors would reconsider becoming the president's doctor. This cannot be proven. Choices (A) and (B) are incorrect because they are merely pointing out information, not stating her opinion.

Question

8. The author of the passage most likely agrees with which view as described in the passage?

(A) Personal physicians of the president should be scrutinized by Congress.

(B) The current system of choosing a doctor for the president is flawed.

(C) The White House no longer covers up the health of the president quite so much as it used to.

(D) There would probably be a smaller pool of doctors to choose from if Congress had a say in the choice of doctors for the president.

(E) The press publishes too much information about the health of the president.

Answer Explanation

The correct answer is (D). Based on the opinions of the people quoted in the article, we can draw the conclusion that the author feels that if Congress could question the president's doctor, fewer doctors would want the job. Choice (A) is incorrect because though this is presented as an opinion in the passage, there is no indication that the author agrees with it. Choice (B) seems correct, except that nowhere in the passage does it suggest that at this time doctors are *chosen* for the president. Choice (C) is not addressed in the passage, and choice (E) is incorrect because this is not implied in the passage.

QUESTIONS 9–10 ARE BASED ON THE FOLLOWING PASSAGE.

A new generation of artists emerged in the United States at the beginning of the twentieth century. They distinguished themselves from the conventional American Impressionist artists of the period because instead of painting genteel portraits, they painted scenes of everyday urban life, specifically that of New York City. The most famous group of the period, the
5   Eight, as they were later known, were inspired and led by the artist Robert Henri. Henri believed that art should not be separated from life and thus, he encouraged his followers to paint exactly what they observed of urban life. This included scenes of drunks, prostitutes, slum dwellers, alleys, tenements, and bars. This type of painting later became known as the "Ashcan School," referring to the ever-present garbage cans of the city. The Eight exhibited
10   together only once in 1908 at New York's Macbeth Gallery. It was the first exhibition staged by a group of artists, and it caused a sensation, both shocking and thrilling their audience. However, despite their focus on slum life, these Ashcan School of artists can now be seen as far less radical than they imagined themselves to be. They were most interested in the aesthetic qualities of their paintings and did not address the social problems their works
15   represented. It was not until the Great Depression of the 1930s that American artists began to tackle these issues in their works.

Question

9. Which of the following, if it were true, would weaken the author's argument?

   (A) Other American artists in the early 1900s pointed to the paintings of the Ashcan School as inspiration for their own paintings.

   (B) The Ashcan School artists did not find their own paintings aesthetically pleasing.

   (C) Robert Henri discouraged his group from painting pictures of wealthy New Yorkers.

   (D) New York City was not the only city to be depicted by the Ashcan School artists.

   (E) The Ashcan School artists continued to paint in the 1930s.

Answer Explanation

The correct answer is (A). If other painters in the early 1900s were inspired by the Ashcan School of artists, it would not be true to say that it was only in the 1930s that artists began to tackle social issues in their work, the assumption being that the paintings of the Ashcan School influenced the painters of the 1930s. Choice (B) is incorrect because even if the artists didn't find their paintings aesthetically pleasing, it doesn't necessarily follow that their work wasn't radical. Choice (C) has nothing to do with the author's argument, so eliminate it. Choice (E), if it were true, would not weaken the author's argument, but strengthen it.

Question

10. In the passage, "genteel" (line 3) means

(A) infamous.

(B) notorious.

(C) wholesome.

(D) decent.

(E) refined.

Answer Explanation

The correct answer is (E). "Genteel" means about the same as "refined, polite, well-brought up," choice (E). Choices (A) and (B) both mean "well-known in a bad way, having a bad reputation," the opposite of "genteel." Choices (C) and (D) are incorrect because "wholesome" and "decent" are synonyms for each other, but they don't mean the same as "refined or polite."

QUESTIONS 11–13 ARE BASED ON THE FOLLOWING PASSAGE.

The Human Genome Project was an international research project that sought to find the sequence of the human genome and to identify the genes that it contains. A genome is the complete set of DNA, or hereditary material, found in the cells of nearly all living organisms. In humans, a copy of the entire genome is contained in all cells that have a nucleus.

5   To begin the human genome project, researchers identified thousands of DNA sequences in blood cells that had been anonymously donated. Then scientists created a collection of DNA clones, in which each clone contained a small fragment of human DNA. These clones were stored in *E. Coli,* which is bacteria that normally live in human intestines. Each *E. Coli* cell contained a single segment of human DNA.

10   When scientists needed to retrieve DNA for sequencing, the *E. Coli* cells were taken out of storage freezers and brought up to 37 degrees Centigrade, the temperature of the intestines. *E. Coli* cells containing the same bit of human DNA were then released into a warm broth. The cells were shaken vigorously, which caused them to divide rapidly. In a few hours, the broth contained billions of *E. Coli* cells, which meant billions of copies of the particular

15   fragment of human DNA each contained. The *E. Coli* cells were broken open to release their DNA, which allowed enough copies of the DNA fragment to set up a sequencing reaction. In 2003, after sequencing the 3 billion parts of the human genome over and over again, the Human Genome Project was considered complete, with a DNA sequence for 99 percent of the genome.

Question

11. What was significant about the use of *E. Coli* cells specifically in helping to sequence human DNA?

(A) *E. Coli* could be stored in freezers and brought back up to room temperature.

(B) Fragments of human DNA could be stored in *E. Coli.*

(C) *E. Coli* is normally found in human intestines.

Answer Explanation

The correct answers are (B) and (C). It is significant that human DNA could be stored in *E. Coli* because it enabled scientists to work with it easily during sequencing experiments. The fact that *E. Coli* is normally found in human intestines is also significant because it allowed the DNA to be stored in a workable environment. Choice (A) is incorrect because though it is true, it is true for other bacteria as well, not specifically *E. Coli*. The word "specifically" is an important qualifier and in this question the clue to the correct answers.

Question

12. The point of this passage is to

    (A) convince the reader that if it were not an international effort, the Human Genome Project could never have been accomplished.

    (B) describe to the reader how scientists sequenced DNA.

    (C) encourage the reader to support the Human Genome Project.

    (D) inform the reader about the purpose of the Human Genome Project.

    (E) explain the significance of *E. Coli* in scientific experiments.

Answer Explanation

The correct answer is (B). This passage gives a step-by-step description of how scientists went about sequencing DNA for the Human Genome Project. Choices (A) and (C) are incorrect because the author doesn't try to persuade or encourage the reader about anything in the passage. Choice (D) is incorrect because although the purpose of the Human Genome Project is addressed, the passage is really about what scientists involved in the project actually did. Choice (E) is incorrect because the use of *E. Coli* is only addressed in this one particular project.

Question

13. Select the sentence in the passage that does NOT add to the support for the main idea.

    (A) Then scientists created a collection of DNA clones, in which each clone contained a small fragment of human DNA.

    (B) *E. Coli* cells containing the same bit of human DNA were then released into a warm broth.

    (C) In 2003, after sequencing the 3 billion parts of the human genome over and over again, the Human Genome Project was considered complete, with a DNA sequence for 99 percent of the genome.

    (D) A genome is the complete set of DNA, or hereditary material, found in the cells of nearly all living organisms.

    (E) Each *E. Coli* cell contained a single segment of human DNA.

Answer Explanation

The correct answer is (D). All the other choices are significant details that support the thesis of the passage. But choice (D), though true, is not significant in the description of how human DNA was sequenced during the Human Genome Project.

QUESTIONS 14–15 ARE BASED ON THE FOLLOWING PASSAGE.

Historians are often drawn to studies of African American migration as a way of understanding the black urban experience, both past and present. But as Gretchen Lemke-Santangelo points out in her book *Abiding Courage*, black urban migration studies frequently focus on just the first two decades of the twentieth century and most often on the experiences of men.
5 Lemke-Santangelo sets out to generate "new perspectives on where and how social change takes place." Therefore, the subjects of her study are black Southern women who migrated to California's East Bay community during World War II. In this way, Lemke-Santangelo introduces the reader to a much lesser known (but no less important) aspect of African American migration history, namely the move from the South to the West, which occurred
10 with increasing frequency during the 1940s. Also, by underscoring the experience of women, Lemke-Santangelo demonstrates the importance of female participation in the migration process and the subsequent organization of the new community.

Question

14. "Underscoring" (line 10) most nearly means

 (A) overrating.

 (B) accentuating.

 (C) facilitating.

 (D) recommending.

 (E) obfuscating.

Answer Explanation

The correct answer is (B). "Underscoring" means the same as "accentuating," meaning "emphasizing." Choice (A) is incorrect because "overrating" means "overvaluing," and that is the opposite of the author's opinion of Lemke-Santangelo's work. Choice (C) is incorrect because "facilitating" means "helping," which is not the same as emphasizing. Choice (D) is incorrect because "recommending" means "praising," which is not the same as emphasizing. Choice (E) is incorrect because "obfuscating" means "disguising or making something confused," which is the opposite of emphasizing.

Question

15. Select the sentence that restates the premise of the author's argument.

    (A) African American women in the 1940s migrated in much greater numbers to the West than was previously understood.

    (B) The experience of African American men in the Great Migration is entirely limited.

    (C) Urban migration studies are not complete, if they only focus on certain experiences.

    (D) The first two decades of the twentieth century saw the greatest movement of African Americans out of the South.

    (E) African American women were instrumental in organizing new communities in the West.

Answer Explanation

The correct answer is (C). The author's thesis is that African American urban migration studies tend to focus on the experience of only one group (men) and only during a certain time period (first two decades of the twentieth century) and are, therefore, incomplete. Choices (A), (D), and (E) may all be true statements, but these points are not what the author is arguing in the passage. Choice (B) is incorrect because this point is not raised in the passage.

Question

16. Because of _____ wording in the press release, some people thought that the CEO was being ousted because of irregularities in accounting when it was the CFO who was fired.

    (A) explicit

    (B) mystifying

    (C) inscrutable

    (D) ambiguous

    (E) impressionable

    (F) equivocal

Answer Explanation

The correct answers are (D) and (F). Lack of clarity caused confusion, so choice (D), "ambiguous," and choice (F), "equivocal," are the correct answers. They mean "unclear, open to different interpretations." Had the wording been explicit, choice (A), that is, clearly stated, there would have been no confusion. Choices (B) and (C), "mystifying" and "inscrutable," are synonyms; "inscrutable" means "unclear, difficult to understand," "mystifying" means to involve in mystery or obscurity which doesn't apply in this sentence. The ambiguous press release may have made an impression, but it wasn't impressionable, choice (E), that is, nothing made an impression or influenced the press release.

Question

17. The particularly _____ caricature done by the artist's wife showed her intense, though sub-conscious, dislike of her husband.

(A) amateurish

(B) grotesque

(C) imitative

(D) bizarre

(E) incompetent

(F) mocking

Answer Explanation

The correct answers are (B) and (D). "Grotesque," choice (B), describes something that is mis-shapen or distorted in a strange or horrifying way, which could indicate intense dislike. Choice (D), "bizarre," means something "grotesquely strange." Choices (A) and (E), "amateurish" and "incom-petent," are synonyms but don't fit the sense of intense dislike the way grotesque and bizarre do. Nor does choice (F), "mocking," meaning "to make fun of." Choice (C), "imitative," might work except that it doesn't fit the sense either.

Question

18. The brainstorming activity resulted in _____ ideas for how to improve morale and boost productivity—but in the evaluative process, most were found not to be viable.

(A) satisfactory

(B) sufficient

(C) requisite

(D) elective

(E) abundant

(F) copious

Answer Explanation

The correct answers are (E) and (F). Choices (E) and (F), "abundant" and "copious," mean "plen-tiful, ample" and fit within the context. Choice (A), "satisfactory," might seem like a reasonable answer on a quick read, but it doesn't fit with the fact that the ideas weren't viable; if they weren't viable, they couldn't have been satisfactory. Choice (B),"sufficient," meaning "enough," could fit the sense, but it has no synonym in the list of answers. Neither do choice (C), "requisite," meaning "required," nor choice (D), "elective," meaning "optional."

Question

19. The team's proposal was still in its early stages, but one could see from the _____ ideas how the study would take shape and probably result in useful conclusions.

    (A) inchoate

    (B) incipient

    (C) incoherent

    (D) incongruous

    (E) immutable

    (F) obtuse

Answer Explanation

The correct answers are (A) and (B). "Inchoate," choice (A), means "at an early stage," similar to the meaning of "incipient," choice (B), meaning "emerging, coming into being." Choice (C), "incoherent," means "muddled, confused" and doesn't fit the context of ideas taking shape. Choice (D), "incongruous," means "conflicting, contradictory, or even inappropriate" and doesn't fit the sense of ideas coming together. Choice (E), "immutable," means "unchanging." Choice (F), "obtuse," means "slow to understand, lacking in intelligence or quickness." Both have to do with ideas or concepts but are neither appropriate in this sentence nor synonymous.

QUESTION 20 IS BASED ON THE FOLLOWING PASSAGE.

Despite the seeming benefits to the environment that electric cars provide, there are still several challenges that need to be addressed if fully electric vehicles can be realistically expected to replace fuel-powered cars or hybrids in the foreseeable future. Currently, electric cars are limited by the output of their batteries and the current technology that uses energy produced
5 while braking to partly recharge the batteries. This technology would have to be improved in order to allow drivers to travel long distances. In addition, most plug-in electric cars take hours to recharge, which is another serious hindrance to their long-term use. Finally, in order for electric cars to become a truly workable option, charging and battery-exchange stations will have to be put in place everywhere cars are driven. These stations will also have to be
10 designed in such a way that their operation would not drain the power from municipal power grids. There is also the question of electricity production. As long as electric power plants continue to run on nonrenewable fossil fuels, such as coal, recharging electric cars will still release carbon emissions into the atmosphere, which is not a benefit to the environment.

Question

20. What is the author's opinion about the future of electric cars?

    (A) There are serious pros and cons to this issue.

    (B) It is probably not a realistic option.

    (C) Technology simply needs to improve.

    (D) Electric cars do not solve the problem of carbon emissions in the atmosphere.

    (E) The production of electricity will continue to rely on fossil fuels.

Answer Explanation

The correct answer is (A). We can infer from the passage that the author thinks there are serious issues to be worked out to determine the future of electric cars. Choice (B) is incorrect because the author never implies this. Choice (C) is incorrect because the author does not conclude that technology is the only solution. Choice (D) is incorrect because the author never implies this. Instead the author says that at the current time, this is true. Choice (E) is incorrect because the author does not make any conclusions about this fact.

Section 5: Verbal Reasoning

1. B	11. C	16. A
2. C, D	12. B	17. A, D
3. A, E	13. A	18. B, E
4. C, F	14. E	19. A, E
5. B, F, H	15. B	20. E, F
6. A		
7. C		
8. B		
9. E		
10. D		

Question

1. The _____ nature of the prototype site was apparent in that it kept crashing.

(A) immature
(B) rudimentary
(C) sophisticated
(D) elemental
(E) primal

Answer Explanation

The correct answer is (B). "Rudimentary," choice (B), means "at the earliest stages of development" and fits the sense of the sentence. Choice (A), "immature," means "not fully developed," but usage will help you decide that it's not the correct answer. "Immature" is typically used to describe an animate being, not an inanimate object. Choice (C) is incorrect because "sophisticated" doesn't fit the prototype as described, though it might describe the concept of the site. Choice (D), "elemental," means "basic or essential" and doesn't make sense; had the choice been "elementary," that would fit the context. Choice (E), "primal," is similar in meaning to "elemental" so it's incorrect, too.

Question

2. Though (i) _____, the conclusions are based on actual economic activities as surveyed by a(n) (ii) _____ outside research team.

Blank (i)	Blank (ii)
(A) certainly credible	(D) impartial
(B) actually impervious	(E) interested
(C) seemingly implausible	(F) nonpartisan

Answer Explanation

The correct answers are (C) and (D). Answer Blank (i): This set of answers is a good reason to read the sentence and all the answer choices carefully. "Certainly credible," choice (A), could be the answer except that it doesn't fit the sense. The sentence needs the opposite of "credible" because the word "though" sets up a contrast relationship. Choice (B), "actually impervious," means "unaffected, invulnerable, unmoved" and makes no sense. Choice (C), "seemingly implausible," means "difficult to believe, unlikely" and fulfills the contrast relationship in the sentence.

Answer Blank (ii): It might have been easier to fill the second blank first to help you identify the contrast relationship. The clue for this part of the sentence is the word "outside." Choice (D) is correct because "impartial" means "unbiased, unprejudiced, fair." Choice (E), "interested," doesn't fit the sense because an interested party would be one that showed some interest or connection to the survey. Choice (F), "nonpartisan," is incorrect because it refers to political parties, and no parties are mentioned in the sentence.

Question

3. In 1961, putting a man on the moon by 1970 seemed not only (i) _____, but also not (ii) _____ in the time frame.

Blank (i)	Blank (ii)
(A) improbable	(D) serviceable
(B) unusual	(E) feasible
(C) fortuitous	(F) durable

Answer Explanation

The correct answers are (A) and (E). Answer Blank (i): Once you figure out all the negatives in the sentence, you'll see that you need two words that balance each other. Choice (A), "improbable," means "unlikely to happen." Choice (B), "unusual," meaning "out of the ordinary, odd" doesn't strike the right significance in describing putting a human on the moon. Choice (C) is incorrect because "fortuitous" means "happening by chance, unplanned," the opposite of requirements for the space program.

Answer Blank (ii): Choice (E), "feasible," meaning "possible, viable" balances "improbable" when you add the "not" from the sentence in front of "feasible." Choice (D), "serviceable," means "usable, capable of lasting for a long time." The latter definition makes it a synonym for choice (F), "durable," but you're not looking for synonyms, and those words don't make sense in the context.

Question

4. The (i) _____ of ideas for reforming the pension system was matched only by the (ii) _____ promises to do something—at some point.

Blank (i)	Blank (ii)
(A) sparsity	(D) keen
(B) derisory	(E) fatuous
(C) paucity	(F) vacuous

Answer Explanation

The correct answers are (C) and (F). Answer Blank (i): You're looking for two words that balance each other. Choice (A) is incorrect because "sparsity" refers to "thinly scattered, not densely populated or crowded," so it doesn't make sense in the context of ideas. Choice (B) is incorrect because "derisory" is an adjective meaning "laughable, ridiculous," and while the ideas might be that, the word doesn't make sense in the construction (it has no noun to modify). Choice (C), "paucity" meaning "scarcity, small number" makes sense.

Answer Blank (ii): The phrase "to do something—at some point" indicates an unwillingness or inability to act and coupled with "paucity" in the first part of the sentence makes choice (F), "vacuous," meaning "lacking in substance or meaning or ideas" the correct choice. Choice (D), "keen," means "intellectually sharp, quick-witted" and is the opposite of the sense that the phrase plus the word "paucity" create. "Fatuous," choice (E), means "foolish, silly in a self-satisfied way" and doesn't fit the sense of the sentence.

Question

5. The success of the show's previews (i) _____ the need for reworking the script. However, the male lead (ii) _____ the playwright to expand his role, but the playwright (iii) _____ and nothing happened.

Blank (i)	Blank (ii)	Blank (iii)
(A) reduced	(D) taunted	(G) condescended
(B) obviated	(E) persisted	(H) demurred
(C) discarded	(F) importuned	(I) patronized

Answer Explanation

The correct answers are (B), (F), and (H). Answer Blank (i): Choice (B), "obviated," means "to have made unnecessary," and presumably successful preview performances would have made any rewrites unnecessary. Choice (A), "reduced," is incorrect based on the sense that if something was successful, no changes would be necessary, not just fewer. Choice (C), "discarded," means "to have thrown out, to have gotten rid of," and doesn't quite fit the sense of the sentence.

Answer Blank (ii): This is another instance where usage can help you determine the answer. Choice (E), "persisted," means "to have been insistent, to have held firm to a purpose"; however, "persisted" doesn't take an object, so "persisted him" doesn't make sense (the clause would need to read "persisted in asking the playwright . . ."). If the actor wanted the playwright to rewrite his role, he would hardly taunt him, that is, try to provoke him by mocking him or criticizing him, so eliminate choice (D). Choice (F), "importuned," means "to have repeatedly asked for, to plead," so it's the correct answer.

Answer Blank (iii): "To demur" is "to object to something that a person doesn't want to do, to be reluctant" so choice (H) is the best answer. Choice (G), "condescended," means "to patronize someone, to act graciously toward someone considered beneath one's social or economic level" and there is no indication of that in the passage. Choice (I), "patronized," is similar to "condescended" and is, therefore, incorrect.

QUESTIONS 6–8 ARE BASED ON THE FOLLOWING PASSAGE.

Winston Churchill is often regarded as the greatest British leader of the twentieth century. His achievements reached their peak when he became the Prime Minister of the United Kingdom in 1940, after Neville Chamberlain resigned. Churchill's refusal to surrender to the Germans helped inspire the British resistance, especially when England was at first the only
5 country to oppose Adolf Hitler. Churchill's powerful speeches and radio broadcasts to boost the morale of the British made him a hero in his own country and ultimately to the Allied forces. Yet despite the tremendous support for Churchill during the war, he was defeated in the 1945 election that followed the end of the war.

There are a number of reasons given for his defeat, among them that the Labour Party had
10 a tightly organized campaign that spoke directly to the needs of post-war Britain. In addition, though Churchill was viewed as an outsider by the Conservative Party, many of the British who liked Churchill were simply unwilling to vote for a Conservative Party candidate. But ironically Churchill's leadership during the war may have also been a cause for his defeat in the election. Once the war ended, the British public began to look toward national recovery.
15 Many people were concerned that Churchill might not be well equipped for handling domestic problems and felt that a good war leader could not also be a good peacetime leader.

Question

6. Select the sentence in the passage that is extraneous to the main idea.

(A) Once the war ended, the British public began to look toward national recovery.

(B) There are a number of reasons given for his defeat, among them that the Labour Party had a tightly organized campaign that spoke directly to the needs of post-war Britain.

(C) Yet despite the tremendous support for Churchill during the war, he was defeated in the 1945 election that followed the end of the war.

(D) Winston Churchill is often regarded as the greatest British leader of the twentieth century.

(E) Churchill's powerful speeches and radio broadcasts to boost the morale of the British made him a hero in his own country and ultimately to the Allied forces.

Answer Explanation

The correct answer is (A). All the other choices are significant points that explain both why Winston Churchill was so popular during the war and why he was defeated in the 1945 election. Although choice (A) is true, it is not entirely necessary to support the main idea of the passage, which is about how Churchill, although a hero to the British during the war, was defeated in the election after the war.

Question

7. Which of the following, if it were true, would weaken the author's argument?

(A) Churchill was known to be a strong ally of Russia.

(B) Churchill's health was declining at this time.

(C) Churchill and his party had a concrete peacetime plan.

Answer Explanation

The correct answer is (C). If Churchill and his party had a concrete peacetime plan, it would weaken the argument that the British didn't believe Churchill would be a good peacetime leader. Choices (A) and (B) are both irrelevant details, which, if true, would neither strengthen nor weaken the author's argument that the British felt Churchill would not be a good leader during peacetime.

Question

8. The passage implies that Churchill's defeat in the 1945 election was because

    (A) he was such a good leader during the war.

    (B) the British people could not accept him in a different role.

    (C) the British people wanted to erase the memory of the war and Churchill was too much of a reminder.

    (D) the Conservative Party did not do enough to promote Churchill during the election.

    (E) the British people reconsidered Churchill's role in the war.

Answer Explanation

The correct answer is (B). The author's main point is that despite, and ironically, because of, Churchill's great leadership during the war, the British could not accept him as a leader during peacetime. Choice (A) might seem correct, but it doesn't explain the whole picture. It wasn't just that Churchill was such a good leader during the war; it was that the British could not see him in a different leadership role. Choice (C) might also seem correct, but this was never implied in the passage. Choices (D) and (E), while possibly true statements, are not addressed in the passage.

QUESTIONS 9–10 ARE BASED ON THE FOLLOWING PASSAGE.

More than half of all people diagnosed with cancer are prescribed chemotherapy, which is a term to describe drugs used to stop cancer cells from growing. The advantage of chemotherapy over surgery and radiation is that drugs can attack cancer cells wherever they are in the body. Unfortunately, older chemotherapy drugs caused many terrible side effects because
5 they could not distinguish between healthy and cancerous cells and so attacked other fast-growing cells in the body, **such as those in the lining of the intestines or in the mouth or in the bloodstream.** However, some newer chemotherapy drugs are specifically designed to target cancer cells. One new drug contains antibody molecules that are engineered in a laboratory to attach to specific defects in cancer cells. The antibody makes cancer cells more
10 noticeable to the immune system and allows anti-cancer drugs to penetrate into cancer cells. The drug also impedes the vessels delivering blood to cancer cells, **which makes it harder for tumors to grow.**

Question

9. Based on the passage, the author evidently believes that

(A) there needs to be more funding for cancer research.

(B) only the newest kinds of cancer drugs should be used to treat cancer.

(C) chemotherapy is not the only option for treating cancer.

(D) new cancer drugs can target specific cancers.

(E) the future for cancer treatment is improving.

Answer Explanation

The correct answer is (E). The author does not present much of an opinion in this passage, but we can infer, based on the details presented, that the author sees an improvement for the future of cancer treatment. Choice (A) is incorrect because this funding isn't addressed in the passage. Choice (B) might seem correct because the author discusses the new drugs; however, the author might also favor older drugs for certain treatments. There is no information to determine if this is true or not. Choices (C) and (D) are both true statements and would not be considered merely the beliefs of an author.

Question

10. What function do the two groups of words in bold type serve in this argument?

(A) The first provides an explanation of evidence; the second provides an example of an argument.

(B) The first supports an argument; the second provides an example of evidence.

(C) The first provides support for the author's conclusion; the second confirms the support for the conclusion.

(D) The first provides an example of evidence; the second provides an explanation of evidence.

(E) The first presents an argument; the second provides evidence to support the argument.

Answer Explanation

The correct answer is (D). Choice (A) is incorrect because the first section in bold is an example of evidence, and the second bold portion is an explanation of evidence; choice (A) has these reversed. Choice (B) is incorrect because although the first section supports an argument, the second section explains evidence but does not provide a piece of evidence. Choice (C) is incorrect because neither portion in bold type deals with the author's conclusion. Choice (E) is incorrect because neither portion in bold presents or supports the author's argument.

QUESTIONS 11–13 ARE BASED ON THE FOLLOWING PASSAGE.

According to its own Web site, Wikipedia is "a free, web-based, collaborative, multilingual encyclopedia project." The obvious advantage of an online encyclopedia is that it can instantly produce articles on up-to-the-minute topics. However, unlike traditional encyclopedias, the millions of articles on Wikipedia can be edited by anyone who visits the Web site. Not
5 surprisingly, this means that a lot of information on Wikipedia is incorrect or biased, or has no other sources to back it up.

If you use Wikipedia for research, you must proceed with caution. Some articles may contain serious factual errors, and some may be in the process of being edited. Some articles are deficient, presenting only one side of a controversial issue or detailing only certain parts
10 of a person's life. In addition, many contributors to Wikipedia do not cite their sources, which can make it difficult to judge the credibility of what is written. Sometimes Wikipedia articles reference other resources, such as news articles, which can be helpful, but these should be verified. In many cases, Wikipedia can provide a good starting point from which to begin your research, but it should never be your only source of information.

Question

11. Select the sentence from the passage that best exemplifies the main point of the author.

(A) Not surprisingly, this means that a lot of information on Wikipedia is incorrect, or biased, or has no other sources to back it up.

(B) The obvious advantage of an online encyclopedia is that it can instantly produce articles on up-to-the-minute topics.

(C) In many cases, Wikipedia can provide a good starting point from which to begin your research, but it should never be your only source of information.

(D) In addition, many contributors to Wikipedia do not cite their sources, which makes it difficult to judge the credibility of what is written.

(E) Some articles are deficient, presenting only one side of a controversial issue or detailing only certain parts of a person's life.

Answer Explanation

The correct answer is (C). This is the main point of the passage. The other choices are all important details about Wikipedia, but only choice (C) clearly states the thesis that Wikipedia, while useful as a starting point for research, should never be the only source of information.

Question

12. The passage implies all of the following statements EXCEPT

(A) Wikipedia articles can contain useful information.

(B) Wikipedia articles never provide backup source material.

(C) you should not write a paper using only Wikipedia research.

(D) contributors to Wikipedia articles may or may not cite their sources.

(E) if sources are cited on Wikipedia, you might still not be able to tell who wrote each article.

Answer Explanation

The correct answer is (B). The passage implies that *sometimes* Wikipedia articles do not provide valid backup source material, but it does not imply that this is always the case. The other choices are all incorrect because each one is true and can be proven using the details of the passage.

Question

13. Based on the article, how should a person use Wikipedia when doing research on a particular topic?

    (A) Start with Wikipedia and then move on to more academic sources.

    (B) Not use Wikipedia unless there is no other information to be found on the topic.

    (C) Should only use those Wikipedia articles that contain citations.

Answer Explanation

The correct answer is (A). The passage suggests you can start with Wikipedia at first, but always move on to other sources. Choice (B) is incorrect because the point of the article is that Wikipedia should never be the only source to use. Choice (C) is incorrect because the passage points out that Wikipedia articles are a good starting point as long as other sources are used.

QUESTIONS 14–16 ARE BASED ON THE FOLLOWING PASSAGE.

Of the novels published in the late eighteenth and early nineteenth centuries, Jane Austen's are among the few to survive to the present day. However, during her lifetime, Austen's novels were not read widely and were noted by just a few critics who reviewed them, mostly favorably. Not long after Austen died in 1817, most of her novels were all but forgotten.
5 This changed in 1870 with the publication of *Memoir of Jane Austen*, written by her nephew James Edward Austen-Leigh. Although his portrayal of Austen was somewhat misleading, the biography marked the beginning of a new appreciation of Jane Austen's works, both in scholarly and popular circles. Austen-Leigh portrayed his Aunt Jane as a woman who recorded the domestic rural life she lived in just as she saw it—with all its domestic crises
10 and affairs of the heart. This memoir had an immeasurable effect on the public perception of Jane Austen, and it dramatically increased her popularity. The publication of the memoir also spurred the reissue of Austen's novels, which became popular classics and in the twentieth century, popular movies and television programs.

Question

14. Without publication of the *Memoir of Jane Austen*, which of the following would likely be true?

    (A) Modern readers would not still be reading the works of Jane Austen.

    (B) People's opinions of Jane Austen would not be based on misleading information.

    (C) Jane Austen's books would not have been reissued.

    (D) People would not know much about the lives of women in the nineteenth century.

    (E) Modern readers would know much less about Jane Austen's life.

Answer Explanation

The correct answer is (E). The *Memoir* gave details about Austen's life, and it is likely that without this material from her nephew we would not know so much about Austen. Choices (A) and (C) are incorrect because there is no way of knowing if other events would have sparked a renewed interest in Jane Austen. Choice (B) is incorrect because it is impossible to know what precisely people's opinions of Jane Austen would be based on. Choice (D) is incorrect because there are other works that would have told us about women's lives in the nineteenth century.

Question

15. Based on the passage, what was the most significant result of the publication of the memoir?

    (A) It introduced the reading public to the works of Jane Austen.

    (B) It changed the public's perception of Jane Austen.

    (C) It made her works a critical and popular success.

    (D) It gave Austen's fans a glimpse into the real life of their beloved author.

    (E) It recorded the details of late eighteenth-century rural life.

Answer Explanation

The correct answer is (B). The change in the public's perception of Austen was the most *significant* result of the publication of the memoir, which, in turn, made them more interested in reading her work. Choices (A) and (C) are incorrect because although true, these were effects of the change in the public's perception and their consequent reading of her novels. Choice (D) is incorrect because the passage suggests that the memoir was somewhat misleading and also assumes that her fans read the *Memoir*, whereas the passage indicates that the *Memoir* created her fans. Choice (E) is incorrect because the memoir recorded details of Jane Austen's life, which may have touched on eighteenth-century rural life, but that was not the topic of the work.

Question

16. In the passage, "immeasurable" (line 10) means

    (A) incalculable.

    (B) monstrous.

    (C) infinitesimal.

    (D) intricate.

    (E) convoluted.

Answer Explanation

The correct answer is (A). "Immeasurable" means about the same as "incalculable," meaning "limitless." Choice (B) is incorrect because "monstrous," meaning in this case "huge, colossal," is not the same as "limitless." Choice (C) is incorrect because "infinitesimal" means "insignificant," the opposite of "immeasurable." Choices (D) and (E) are incorrect because "intricate" and "convoluted" mean "complicated," which is not the same as "limitless."

Question

17. The sales revenue lost during the economic downturn can be _____ if every sales representative contacts one former or current customer and three new customers every day.

   (A) redeemed

   (B) returned

   (C) remediable

   (D) recovered

   (E) remediated

   (F) rectified

Answer Explanation

The correct answers are (A) and (D). Choice (A), "redeemed," may mean "made up for," and choice (D), "recovered," may mean "returned to or regained a previous state or condition." Both fit the idea that the revenue that was lost, that is, not generated, can be made up by hard work. Choice (B), "returned," doesn't fit because the money was not lost in the sense of "being mislaid or misplaced." Choices (C) and (D) are similar and incorrect. "Remediable," choice (C), means "capable of being remedied or redressed" and doesn't fit the sense. Choice (E), "remediated," meaning "correcting a fault or a flaw" doesn't fit the sense because lost revenue isn't a flaw. Choice (F), "rectified," meaning "having set right or corrected something," is similar to choices (C) and (E) and incorrect for the same reason.

Question

18. Wildlife in urban areas includes such non-typical city creatures as foxes that have increased as restaurants with their treat-filled garbage bags have _____.

   (A) gotten along

   (B) proliferated

   (C) progressed

   (D) advanced

   (E) multiplied

   (F) thrive

Answer Explanation

The correct answers are (B) and (E). "Proliferated" means "to grow in number rapidly" and is similar to "multiplied," meaning "to increase in number," so choices (B) and (E) are synonyms and the correct answers. Choice (A), "gotten along," means "make progress" and is similar to "thrive," choice (F), meaning "to make progress, to succeed," but neither includes the idea of increasing in number implicit in the balance set up by the phrase "increase as restaurants . . . have . . ." Choices (C) and (D), "progressed" and "advanced," are also synonym pairs and mean "to move forward, to improve," but they lack the idea of increasing in number.

Question

19. Big box stores cause anxiety among small towns and cities because they appear to be the harbingers of the _____ of the downtown business area as shoppers forsake local small businesses for the big discounters.

   (A) decline

   (B) degradation

   (C) depreciation

   (D) obsolescence

   (E) deterioration

   (F) retrogression

Answer Explanation

The correct answers are (A) and (E). Choice (E), "deterioration," is a synonym for choice (A), "decline," and also means "a lessening in value, a weakening." Choice (D), "obsolescence," meaning "falling into disuse, becoming outdated," would also be a good choice, but it has no synonym among the answer options. Choice (B), "degradation," means "to move to a lower level, or a state of dishonor or disgrace," neither of which fit the sense. Choice (C), "depreciation," means "a decrease in worth" and is an economics term. Choice (F), "retrogression," means "returning to a former state, regression," and doesn't make sense.

Question

20. Some of the more unforgettable characters in literature are _____. Who can forget the servile, groveling, and fawning Uriah Heep or the Reverend Collins?

   (A) enthralling

   (B) curmudgeonly

   (C) surly

   (D) gruff

   (E) sycophantic

   (F) obsequious

Answer Explanation

The correct answers are (E) and (F). "Servile, groveling, and fawning" actually describe choices (E) and (F), "sycophantic" and "obsequious." Choice (A), "enthralling," which means "appealing, beguiling, enchanting," doesn't fit the description. Choice (B), "curmudgeonly," is another type of obnoxious character, but one who is ill-tempered, stubborn, and resentful, which is similar to "surly," choice (C), and "gruff," choice (D).

PRACTICE TEST 3 ANSWER SHEETS

Section 1: Analytical Writing

Analyze an Issue

FOR PLANNING

ANALYZE AN ISSUE RESPONSE

_____
_____
_____
_____
_____
_____
_____
_____
_____
_____
_____
_____
_____
_____
_____
_____
_____
_____
_____
_____
_____
_____
_____
_____
_____
_____
_____
_____
_____
_____
_____
_____
_____
_____
_____
_____

ANALYZE AN ISSUE RESPONSE

_____
_____
_____
_____
_____
_____
_____
_____
_____
_____
_____
_____
_____
_____
_____
_____
_____
_____
_____
_____
_____
_____
_____
_____
_____
_____
_____
_____

answer sheet

ANALYZE AN ISSUE RESPONSE

_____
_____
_____
_____
_____
_____
_____
_____
_____
_____
_____
_____
_____
_____
_____
_____
_____
_____
_____
_____
_____
_____
_____
_____
_____
_____
_____
_____
_____
_____
_____
_____
_____
_____
_____
_____
_____

ANALYZE AN ISSUE RESPONSE

_____
_____
_____
_____
_____
_____
_____
_____
_____
_____
_____
_____
_____
_____
_____
_____
_____
_____
_____
_____
_____
_____
_____
_____
_____
_____
_____
_____
_____

Analyze an Argument

FOR PLANNING

ANALYZE AN ARGUMENT RESPONSE

_____
_____
_____
_____
_____
_____
_____
_____
_____
_____
_____
_____
_____
_____
_____
_____
_____
_____
_____
_____
_____
_____
_____
_____
_____
_____
_____
_____
_____
_____
_____

answer sheet

ANALYZE AN ARGUMENT RESPONSE

ANALYZE AN ARGUMENT RESPONSE

answer sheet

ANALYZE AN ARGUMENT RESPONSE

_____

_____

_____

_____

_____

_____

_____

_____

_____

_____

_____

_____

_____

_____

_____

_____

_____

_____

_____

_____

_____

_____

_____

_____

_____

_____

_____

_____

_____

_____

_____

_____

_____

_____

Section 2: Verbal Reasoning

1. Ⓐ Ⓑ Ⓒ Ⓓ Ⓔ
2. Ⓐ Ⓑ Ⓒ Ⓓ Ⓔ
3. Ⓐ Ⓑ Ⓒ Ⓓ Ⓔ Ⓕ
4. Ⓐ Ⓑ Ⓒ Ⓓ Ⓔ Ⓕ Ⓖ Ⓗ Ⓘ
5. Ⓐ Ⓑ Ⓒ Ⓓ Ⓔ Ⓕ Ⓖ Ⓗ Ⓘ
6. Ⓐ Ⓑ Ⓒ Ⓓ Ⓔ
7. Ⓐ Ⓑ Ⓒ Ⓓ Ⓔ
8. Ⓐ Ⓑ Ⓒ
9. Ⓐ Ⓑ Ⓒ Ⓓ Ⓔ
10. Ⓐ Ⓑ Ⓒ Ⓓ Ⓔ

11. Ⓐ Ⓑ Ⓒ Ⓓ Ⓔ
12. Ⓐ Ⓑ Ⓒ Ⓓ Ⓔ
13. Ⓐ Ⓑ Ⓒ Ⓓ Ⓔ
14. Ⓐ Ⓑ Ⓒ
15. Ⓐ Ⓑ Ⓒ Ⓓ Ⓔ

16. Ⓐ Ⓑ Ⓒ Ⓓ Ⓔ Ⓕ
17. Ⓐ Ⓑ Ⓒ Ⓓ Ⓔ Ⓕ
18. Ⓐ Ⓑ Ⓒ Ⓓ Ⓔ Ⓕ
19. Ⓐ Ⓑ Ⓒ Ⓓ Ⓔ Ⓕ
20. Ⓐ Ⓑ Ⓒ Ⓓ Ⓔ

Section 3: Verbal Reasoning

1. Ⓐ Ⓑ Ⓒ Ⓓ Ⓔ
2. Ⓐ Ⓑ Ⓒ Ⓓ Ⓔ
3. Ⓐ Ⓑ Ⓒ Ⓓ Ⓔ Ⓕ
4. Ⓐ Ⓑ Ⓒ Ⓓ Ⓔ Ⓕ Ⓖ Ⓗ Ⓘ
5. Ⓐ Ⓑ Ⓒ Ⓓ Ⓔ Ⓕ Ⓖ Ⓗ Ⓘ
6. Ⓐ Ⓑ Ⓒ Ⓓ Ⓔ
7. Ⓐ Ⓑ Ⓒ Ⓓ Ⓔ
8. Ⓐ Ⓑ Ⓒ Ⓓ Ⓔ
9. Ⓐ Ⓑ Ⓒ Ⓓ Ⓔ
10. Ⓐ Ⓑ Ⓒ Ⓓ Ⓔ

11. Ⓐ Ⓑ Ⓒ Ⓓ Ⓔ
12. Ⓐ Ⓑ Ⓒ
13. Ⓐ Ⓑ Ⓒ Ⓓ Ⓔ
14. Ⓐ Ⓑ Ⓒ Ⓓ Ⓔ
15. Ⓐ Ⓑ Ⓒ

16. Ⓐ Ⓑ Ⓒ Ⓓ Ⓔ Ⓕ
17. Ⓐ Ⓑ Ⓒ Ⓓ Ⓔ Ⓕ
18. Ⓐ Ⓑ Ⓒ Ⓓ Ⓔ Ⓕ
19. Ⓐ Ⓑ Ⓒ Ⓓ Ⓔ Ⓕ
20. Ⓐ Ⓑ Ⓒ Ⓓ Ⓔ

Section 4: Quantitative Reasoning

1. Ⓐ Ⓑ Ⓒ Ⓓ
2. Ⓐ Ⓑ Ⓒ Ⓓ
3. Ⓐ Ⓑ Ⓒ Ⓓ
4. Ⓐ Ⓑ Ⓒ Ⓓ
5. Ⓐ Ⓑ Ⓒ Ⓓ
6. Ⓐ Ⓑ Ⓒ Ⓓ
7. Ⓐ Ⓑ Ⓒ Ⓓ
8. Ⓐ Ⓑ Ⓒ Ⓓ
9. Ⓐ Ⓑ Ⓒ Ⓓ Ⓔ
10. Ⓐ Ⓑ Ⓒ Ⓓ Ⓔ

11. Ⓐ Ⓑ Ⓒ Ⓓ Ⓔ
12. Ⓐ Ⓑ Ⓒ Ⓓ Ⓔ
13. Ⓐ Ⓑ Ⓒ Ⓓ Ⓔ
14. Ⓐ Ⓑ Ⓒ Ⓓ Ⓔ
15. Ⓐ Ⓑ Ⓒ Ⓓ Ⓔ

16. Ⓐ Ⓑ Ⓒ Ⓓ Ⓔ
17. Ⓐ Ⓑ Ⓒ Ⓓ Ⓔ Ⓕ
18. Ⓐ Ⓑ Ⓒ Ⓓ Ⓔ
19. ☐
20. ☐

answer sheet

Section 5: Quantitative Reasoning

1. Ⓐ Ⓑ Ⓒ Ⓓ
2. Ⓐ Ⓑ Ⓒ Ⓓ
3. Ⓐ Ⓑ Ⓒ Ⓓ
4. Ⓐ Ⓑ Ⓒ Ⓓ
5. Ⓐ Ⓑ Ⓒ Ⓓ
6. Ⓐ Ⓑ Ⓒ Ⓓ
7. Ⓐ Ⓑ Ⓒ Ⓓ
8. Ⓐ Ⓑ Ⓒ Ⓓ
9. Ⓐ Ⓑ Ⓒ Ⓓ Ⓔ
10. Ⓐ Ⓑ Ⓒ Ⓓ Ⓔ Ⓕ Ⓖ Ⓗ

11. ☐
12. Ⓐ Ⓑ Ⓒ Ⓓ Ⓔ
13. Ⓐ Ⓑ Ⓒ Ⓓ Ⓔ
14. Ⓐ Ⓑ Ⓒ Ⓓ Ⓔ
15. Ⓐ Ⓑ Ⓒ Ⓓ Ⓔ

16. Ⓐ Ⓑ Ⓒ Ⓓ Ⓔ
17. Ⓐ Ⓑ Ⓒ Ⓓ
18. Ⓐ Ⓑ Ⓒ Ⓓ Ⓔ Ⓕ Ⓖ Ⓗ
19. ☐
20. ☐

Practice Test 3

The test begins with general information about the number of sections on the test (six for the computer version, including the unidentified unscored section or an identified research section, and five for the paper-and-pencil version) and the timing of the test (approximately 3 hours and 45 minutes including one 10-minute break after Section 3, 1-minute breaks after the other sections for the computer version, and 3 hours and 30 minutes for the paper-and-pencil version with similar breaks). The following practice test contains the five scored sections.

Each section has its own time allocation and, during that time period, you may work on only that section.

Next, you will read ETS's policy on scoring the Analytical Writing responses. Each essay is read by experienced readers, and ETS may cancel any test scores that show evidence of unacknowledged use of sources, unacknowledged collaboration with others, preparation of the response by another person, and language that is "substantially" similar to the language in one or more other test responses.

Each section has specific instructions for that section.

You will be told when to begin.

practice test 3

SECTION 1: ANALYTICAL WRITING

Analyze an Issue
30 minutes

The time for this task is 30 minutes. You must plan and draft a response that evaluates the issue given below. If you do not respond to the specific issue, your score will be zero. Your response must be based on the accompanying instructions, and you must provide evidence for your position. You may use support from reading, experience, observations, and/or course work.

> The American public education system is broken and only drastic changes can save it.
>
> Write an essay that takes and explains a position on this issue. As you present, develop, and explain your position, discuss when and how the statement might or might not hold true. Explain how those possibilities provide support for your own point of view.

Your response will be read by experienced readers who will assess your ability to do the following:

- Follow the set of task instructions.
- Analyze the complexities involved.
- Organize, develop, and explain ideas.
- Use pertinent reasons and/or illustrations to support ideas.
- Adhere to the conventions of Standard Written English.

You will be advised to take some time to plan your response and to leave time to reread it before the time is over. Those taking the paper-and-pencil version of the GRE will find a blank page in their answer booklet for making notes and then four ruled pages for writing their actual response. Those taking the computer version will be given scrap paper for making notes.

STOP

> If you finish before the time is up, you may check your work in this section only.

Analyze an Argument
30 minutes

The time for this task is 30 minutes. You must plan and draft a response that evaluates the argument given below. If you do not respond to the given argument, your score will be zero. Your response must be based on the accompanying instructions, and you must provide evidence in support of your analysis.

You should not present your views on the subject of the argument but on the strength or weakness of the argument.

During a recent opinion poll, citizens of our town noted that one of the town's most pressing needs was a new public safety building. The old building was erected in 1961 and was, at the time, merely a police and fire station. It is now overcrowded and unable to accommodate the additional and necessary functions of a 911 communications center, an emergency management center, and an emergency management office; it also cannot accommodate the new environmental safety team. Furthermore, there are insufficient garages for all the police vehicles, and the latest-model ambulances do not fit in the station bays. For all these reasons, a new building, which residents clearly support, and which will help ensure a greater level of safety in our town, must be constructed.

Write an essay that identifies and explains the specific evidence required to determine whether the argument is reasonable. Discuss how that evidence would weaken or strengthen the argument.

Your response will be read by experienced readers who will assess your ability to do the following:

- Follow the set of task instructions.
- Analyze the complexities involved.
- Organize, develop, and explain ideas.
- Use pertinent reasons and/or illustrations to support ideas.
- Adhere to the conventions of Standard Written English.

You will be advised to take some time to plan your response and to leave time to reread it before the time is over. Those taking the paper-and-pencil version of the GRE will find a blank page in their answer booklet for making notes and then four ruled pages for writing their actual response. Those taking the computer version will be given scrap paper for making notes.

STOP

If you finish before the time is up, you may check your work in this section only.

INSTRUCTIONS FOR THE VERBAL REASONING AND QUANTITATIVE REASONING SECTIONS

You will find information here on the question formats for the Verbal Reasoning and Quantitative Reasoning sections as well as information about how to use the software program, or, if you're taking the paper-and-pencil version, how to mark your answers in the answer booklet.

Perhaps the most important information is a reminder about how these two sections are scored. Every correct answer earns a point, but wrong answers don't subtract any points. The advice from ETS is to guess if you aren't sure of an answer. ETS says that this is better than not answering a question.

All multiple-choice questions in the computer-based test will have answer options preceded by either blank ovals or blank squares, depending on the question type. The paper-and-pencil test will follow the same format of answer choices, but it will use letters instead of ovals or squares for answer choices.

For your convenience in answering questions and checking answers in this book, we use (A), (B), (C), etc. By using letters with parentheses, you will find it easy to check your answers against the answer key and explanation sections.

SECTION 2: VERBAL REASONING

30 minutes • 20 questions

(The paper-and-pencil version will have 25 questions to be completed in 35 minutes.)

For each question, follow the specific directions and choose the best answer.

> FOR QUESTIONS 1–5, CHOOSE <u>ONE</u> ANSWER FOR EACH BLANK. SELECT FROM THE APPROPRIATE COLUMN FOR EACH BLANK. CHOOSE THE ANSWER THAT BEST COMPLETES THE SENSE OF THE TEXT.

1. One of the major concerns as States pulled themselves out of the deficits created during the Great Recession was whether they would return to their _____ spending habits once the good times began to roll again.

(A) decadent
(B) profligate
(C) parsimonious
(D) immoral
(E) licentious

2. To the board of directors, it appeared that the only way to placate _____ stockholders was to remove the CEO.

(A) seditious
(B) subversive
(C) insubordinate
(D) disobedient
(E) disgruntled

3. In discussing the vanishing ecosystem of the Grand Canyon, the speaker spoke (i) _____ and passionately about his subject. It was obvious that the (ii) _____ of the natural environment caused him grave concern.

Blank (i)	Blank (ii)
(A) eloquently	(D) mutilation
(B) emotionally	(E) reparation
(C) prominently	(F) destruction

4. The epic heroes who undergo a series of (i) _____ challenges to attain a goal are (ii) _____ feature of many national cultural identities. Many of the challenges involve some (iii) _____ feat of daring.

Blank (i)	Blank (ii)	Blank (iii)
(A) extraordinary	(D) an underlying	(G) intrepid
(B) copious	(E) an external	(H) steadfast
(C) massive	(F) a conventional	(I) resolute

5. Among the health scams that the FDA warns the (i) _____ public about are (ii) _____ cancer-treatment products and weight-loss programs with FDA (iii) _____ ingredients.

Blank (i)	Blank (ii)	Blank (iii)
(A) wary	(D) trick	(G) unsanctioned
(B) circumspect	(E) mock	(H) unmeasured
(C) credulous	(F) deceptive	(I) characteristic

FOR QUESTIONS 6–20, CHOOSE ONLY <u>ONE</u> ANSWER CHOICE UNLESS OTHERWISE INDICATED.

QUESTIONS 6–8 ARE BASED ON THE FOLLOWING PASSAGE.

In the year 1901, Spanish painter Pablo Picasso entered what is now referred to as his Blue Period. At the time Picasso was just 20 years old, living in Paris as a relatively unknown artist. Up to this point, the paintings Picasso produced were vibrantly colored, expressing the decadent life he and his friend Carlos Casagemas had been leading together in Paris. But
5 the suicide of Casagemas in 1901 was a major trigger for Picasso's Blue Period, in which Picasso began to paint in various shades of blue, giving the paintings a haunting and melancholy feel. The recurring theme of the Blue Period paintings is the desolation of outsiders, which included beggars, prisoners, and circus people. By 1904, Picasso had emerged from the Blue Period and began what is known as the Rose Period, characterized by bright colors,
10 and featuring acrobats and harlequins. A few years later, Picasso began to explore Cubism, which broke completely from the traditional three-dimensional representation of objects, and for which he became famous. The Blue and Rose Periods can be viewed as transitional times for Picasso in which he moved from the traditional art of his youth to the iconoclastic art of his adulthood.

6. Based on the passage the author evidently believes that

   (A) the Rose Period is less significant a time period than the Blue Period in the artistic development of Picasso.

   (B) the suicide of Casagemas had an effect on Picasso that would haunt him for the rest of his life.

   (C) if Picasso had not gone through the Blue and Rose Periods he would have never been ready to explore a new form of art.

   (D) there is no way to understand Cubism without seeing the artistic road that led Picasso to it over the course of his work.

   (E) the Blue Period was how Picasso expressed himself artistically during a difficult time of his life.

7. In this passage, "iconoclastic" (line 13) means

   (A) eclectic.

   (B) eccentric.

   (C) consequential.

   (D) revolutionary.

   (E) conservative.

> FOR QUESTION 8, CONSIDER EACH ANSWER INDIVIDUALLY AND SELECT <u>ALL</u> CHOICES THAT APPLY.

8. Which of the following ideas are clearly supported in this passage?

(A) After the Blue Period, Picasso no longer painted pictures of desolation.

(B) Picasso is best known for his Cubist works.

(C) The Rose Period was just as significant as the Blue Period in terms of Picasso's growth as an artist.

QUESTIONS 9–10 ARE BASED ON THE FOLLOWING PASSAGE.

Most professional photographers today cannot imagine using anything but a digital camera for their work. With a digital camera, you can take thousands of pictures using just one memory card, and you can instantly see the results, while checking for exposure, focus, and sharpness all at the same time. The traditional film camera involves much more thought to
5 ensure that every image has the correct exposure, composition, and lighting. In addition, film photographers spend hours processing their film and printing it in a darkroom, whereas only a very small percentage of the images taken on a digital camera are processed and printed. Photographers who use digital cameras simply take raw images, edit them on their computers, and upload them online. Because so much of the guesswork is eliminated, digital cameras
10 are simply better than film cameras for learning the art of photography.

9. All of the following are implied in this passage EXCEPT

(A) digital photography takes less time to learn than film photography.

(B) more professional photographers today use digital cameras as opposed to film cameras.

(C) photographs taken with film cameras are harder to process than those taken with digital cameras.

(D) people tend to make more mistakes with film cameras than digital cameras.

(E) digital cameras have changed the way people share photographs with each other.

10. Which of the following statements expresses the author's opinion about film cameras?

(A) Film cameras take higher quality photographs, but they are harder to use.

(B) You cannot take many photographs with a film camera.

(C) If you are learning photography, you should use a digital camera.

(D) Film cameras are bulky and difficult to use for that reason.

(E) The differences between the two types of cameras are so great as to make any comparison worthless.

QUESTIONS 11–12 ARE BASED ON THE FOLLOWING PASSAGE.

The use of solar energy to produce electricity can be an excellent alternative to using fossil fuels. Solar panels give off no pollution, and, unlike other alternative energy sources like wind turbines, are silent. One big advantage of solar energy is that it can harness electricity in remote locations that are not connected to a national grid. One example of this is in space,
5 where high-efficiency solar cells are used to power satellites. Although the initial investment for solar cells is high, once they are installed, they provide free electricity. Yet unfortunately this initial cost is one reason people are hesitant to embrace solar energy as an alternative energy source. Currently, a single solar cell can cost more than $1000, and some households

may need more than one. Also, solar cells do not generate electricity 24 hours a day, so
10 excess electricity needs to be captured during daylight time for later use. The weather and
pollution levels can also affect a solar cell's efficiency, which could have a huge impact on
solar panels installed in cities. However, cost is still considered the main deterrent. Because
fossil fuels still cost less than the initial investment for solar panels, it will likely be some
time before we see a significant shift toward solar energy use.

11. Select the sentence that is NOT a major detail that supports the author's opinion.

(A) One example of this is in space, where high-efficiency solar cells are used to power
satellites.

(B) The weather and pollution levels can also affect a solar cell's efficiency, which could
have a huge impact on solar panels installed in cities.

(C) Currently, a single solar cell can cost more than $1000, and some households may need
more than one.

(D) Because fossil fuels still cost less than the initial investment for solar panels, it will
likely be some time before we see a significant shift toward solar energy use.

(E) The use of solar energy to produce electricity can be an excellent alternative to using
fossil fuels.

12. Which of the following, if it were true, would weaken the author's conclusion?

(A) Fossil fuels and solar energy cost about the same.

(B) Solar panels will eventually be able to run 24 hours a day.

(C) Solar panels can sometimes create more noise than wind turbines.

(D) Many people who use solar panels are disappointed with the results.

(E) There are many alternatives to solar energy that are much cheaper.

QUESTIONS 13–15 ARE BASED ON THE FOLLOWING PASSAGE.

The story of Phineas Gage is one of the earliest documented cases of a person whose personality changed after brain trauma. In 1848, twenty-five-year-old Gage was foreman of a
crew of railroad construction workers who were excavating rocks to make way for railroad
track near Cavendish, Vermont. The work involved drilling holes into the rocks and filling
5 them with dynamite. While Gage was using a tool called a tamping iron to pack explosive
powder into a hole, a spark ignited the powder, and propelled the tamping iron into the air,
sending it straight through Gage's skull. Gage was treated by Dr. John Martyn Harlow, and
he remarkably survived the accident.

Soon after, Harlow wrote a case report of Gage's injuries that was published in the *Boston
10 Medical and Surgical Journal*. The report was met with skepticism, however, because it
seemed unlikely that anyone could survive such a terrible injury. Yet twenty years later, in
1868, Harlow further documented Gage's brain injuries in a report published in the *Bulletin
of the Massachusetts Medical Society*. For the first time, his report described changes to
Gage's personality: "He is fitful, irreverent, indulging at times in the grossest profanity (which
15 was not previously his custom), manifesting but little deference for his fellows, impatient of
restraint of advice when it conflicts with his desires. . . In this regard, his mind was radically
changed, so decidedly that his friends and acquaintances said he was 'no longer Gage'."

This publication of Gage's personality changes was significant because it coincided with
reports from other scientists of the effects of brain damage on behavior. Gage's case confirmed
20 other findings that damage to the prefrontal cortex could result in personality changes while
leaving other functions intact. Gage's case is likely one of the first cases to demonstrate that
the frontal cortex is involved in personality.

13. What is the most significant detail about the case of Phineas Gage?

(A) Gage survived a brain injury from which most people would have died.

(B) Gage became more aggressive after his accident.

(C) The tamping iron went straight through his skull.

(D) Dr. Harlow published a detailed report of Gage's accident twenty years after it occurred.

(E) People did not believe Dr. Harlow's initial report about Gage's accident.

FOR QUESTION 14, CONSIDER EACH ANSWER INDIVIDUALLY AND SELECT <u>ALL</u> CHOICES THAT APPLY.

---

14. If Dr. Harlow had not published a second report about Phineas Gage twenty years after the accident, which of the following would most likely have occurred?

(A) The case of Phineas Gage would have been eventually described by someone else.

(B) There would be no record of Phineas Gage's accident.

(C) Scientists would have used a different case to support the connection between the prefrontal cortex and personality.

15. "Deference" (line 15) most nearly means

(A) respect.

(B) insolence.

(C) impudence.

(D) detriment.

(E) presumption.

FOR QUESTIONS 16–19, CHOOSE THE <u>TWO</u> ANSWERS THAT BEST FIT THE MEANING OF THE SENTENCE AS A WHOLE AND RESULT IN TWO COMPLETED SENTENCES THAT ARE ALIKE IN MEANING.

---

16. The gallery owner has a(n) _____ eye and an amazing ability to select the next hot artist from all the new artists who show him their portfolios.

(A) discerning

(B) discriminating

(C) detecting

(D) investigative

(E) observant

(F) understanding

17. _____ data from the traffic safety survey shows a 17 percent increase in nonfatal pedestrian accidents due to texting drivers. The final report will be available next year.
    (A) Improvised
    (B) Acting
    (C) Interim
    (D) Permanent
    (E) Terminal
    (F) Provisional

18. Scrooge has come to be considered the _____ miser from whom all similar characters are drawn.
    (A) pattern
    (B) eccentric
    (C) archetypal
    (D) unusual
    (E) alternate
    (F) classic

19. While economics may be exciting to some, the yawning student in the back of the room thought it _____.
    (A) tedious
    (B) sundry
    (C) repetitive
    (D) soporific
    (E) disingenuous
    (F) monotonous

QUESTION 20 IS BASED ON THE FOLLOWING PASSAGE.

For years astronomers could not figure out why the Sun's outer atmosphere, or corona, is millions of degrees hotter than its surface, but recently NASA scientists came up with an answer. The corona consists of loops of hot gas that are thousands of miles high, but from the Earth, the corona can only be seen during a total solar eclipse, which has made it difficult
5 to study. However, NASA scientists recently determined that nanoflares, tiny bursts of heat and energy, are what make the temperature so much hotter in the corona. The loops of gas are made up of bundles of smaller magnetic strands that can reach temperatures of several million degrees Kelvin, which is significantly hotter than the surface of the Sun. NASA scientists created a simulation to see how nanoflares might occur and determined that the
10 million-degree temperatures in the corona could only be produced by impulsive energy bursts. However, the magnetic strands cool very quickly, which explains why this phenomenon had been so difficult to detect.

20. Select the sentence that best explains the recent discovery about the Sun's corona.

   (A) However, the magnetic strands cool very quickly, which explains why this phenomenon had been so difficult to detect.

   (B) The corona consists of loops of hot gas that are thousands of miles high, but from the Earth, the corona can only be seen during a total solar eclipse, which has made it difficult to study.

   (C) For years astronomers could not figure out why the Sun's outer atmosphere, or corona, is millions of degrees hotter than its surface, but recently NASA scientists came up with an answer.

   (D) The loops of gas are made up of bundles of smaller magnetic strands that can reach temperatures of several million degrees Kelvin, which is significantly hotter than the surface of the Sun.

   (E) However, NASA scientists recently determined that nanoflares, tiny bursts of heat and energy, are what make the temperature so much hotter in the corona.

STOP

> If you finish before the time is up, you may check your work in this section only.

SECTION 3: VERBAL REASONING

30 minutes • 20 questions

(The paper-and-pencil version will have 25 questions to be completed in 35 minutes.)

For each question, follow the specific directions and choose the best answer.

> **FOR QUESTIONS 1–5, CHOOSE ONE ANSWER FOR EACH BLANK. SELECT FROM THE APPROPRIATE COLUMN FOR EACH BLANK. CHOOSE THE ANSWER THAT BEST COMPLETES THE SENSE OF THE TEXT.**

1. Even though technology has vastly improved the accuracy of weather forecasts, it is unlikely that technology will enhance forecasting enough to enable accurate forecasts for more than two weeks because weather is too _____.

(A) unpredictable
(B) subjective
(C) arbitrary
(D) unreliable
(E) elusive

2. The Library of Congress recordings of American African folk songs recorded on location in the Deep South are considered the _____ versions against which musicologists evaluate all other versions.

(A) indispensable
(B) momentous
(C) explicit
(D) definitive
(E) scholarly

3. At one end of the spectrum is Van Gogh's (i) _____ life driven by the demons of madness and at the other end is Monet's (ii) _____ life in his beloved garden at Giverny.

Blank (i)	Blank (ii)
(A) turbulent	(D) stoical
(B) rowdy	(E) tranquil
(C) boisterous	(F) bucolic

4. Ernest Hemingway was (i) _____ storyteller—an artist with words. He could paint (ii) _____ portrait of a proud young man locked in deadly combat with a ferocious bull and an equally (iii) _____ picture of a proud old man in his epic struggle with a giant fish.

Blank (i)	Blank (ii)	Blank (iii)
(A) an accomplished	(D) an impressive	(G) glittering
(B) a consummate	(E) an interesting	(H) riveting
(C) a perfect	(F) a stunning	(I) conspicuous

5. The anthropologist's explanation for the difference in cultural traits had always seemed (i) _____, but they were later deemed (ii) _____ after new discoveries. His entire life's work was (iii) _____ by the academic community and his career was in ruins.

Blank (i)	Blank (ii)	Blank (iii)
(A) desirable	(D) delusory	(G) reneged
(B) tenable	(E) deceptive	(H) annulled
(C) worthwhile	(F) specious	(I) repudiated

FOR QUESTIONS 6–20, CHOOSE ONLY ONE ANSWER CHOICE UNLESS OTHERWISE INDICATED.

QUESTIONS 6–8 ARE BASED ON THE FOLLOWING PASSAGE.

Although it still faces many challenges, India is on the verge of becoming a world superpower. With 1.1 billion residents, India is the second largest country on Earth in population and the seventh largest country in geographical area. India's economy has grown an average of 6 percent annually over the past decade, which is among the fastest rates in the world. Yet what makes India's growth especially striking is that it is driven only by a very small fraction of its population. The majority of people live in rural poverty, with poor infrastructure and high illiteracy rates. Yet the nation is a world leader in the high-tech service sector, which accounts for one half of the country's gross national product, even though this industry is made up of less than 1 percent of the population.

6. Select the sentence that restates the author's opinion.

(A) India's economy is dominated by the high-tech service industry.

(B) India's economy is growing faster than most other countries, although its main economic industry employs less than 1 percent of its population.

(C) Due to its untapped potential in the high-tech service industry, India will one day have a larger economy than the United States.

(D) India is divided between a large majority of people living in rural poverty and a small percent who are wealthy.

(E) India is becoming a world superpower despite the fact that so much of its population lives in rural poverty.

7. Which of the following sentences from the passage is irrelevant to the author's main point?

(A) Although it still faces many challenges, India is on the verge of becoming a world superpower.

(B) The majority of people live in rural poverty, with poor infrastructure and high illiteracy rates.

(C) With 1.1 billion residents, India is the second largest country on Earth in population and the seventh largest country in geographical area.

(D) India's economy has grown an average of 6 percent annually over the past decade, which is among the fastest rates in the world.

(E) Yet the nation is a world leader in the high-tech service sector, which accounts for one half of the country's gross national product, even though this industry is made up of less than 1 percent of the population.

8. What is most significant about the growth of India's economy over the past decade?

   (A) It shows that India's economy has not always grown that quickly.

   (B) It shows that India's economy is growing faster than many other economies around the world.

   (C) It shows that despite the problems many of its citizens face, India's economy is growing.

   (D) It shows that the high-tech service sector is what makes the economy grow.

   (E) It shows that India can become a world superpower within the next decade.

QUESTIONS 9–11 ARE BASED ON THE FOLLOWING PASSAGE.

Until the late nineteenth century, a loophole in U.S. copyright law allowed publishers to reprint British books without paying royalties to the authors. Charles Dickens was among the many authors who were affected. Dickens was even more popular in the United States than he was in England, partly because of the availability of his works and their low prices in the
5   United States. When Dickens travelled to America for the first time in 1841, he wrote that "there never was a king or Emperor upon the Earth, so cheered, and followed by crowds." Even so, during this visit he gave speeches calling for an international copyright law. The U.S. press, whose papers readily took advantage of free British content, were outraged. Editors took up their pens in an effort to convince the public that Dickens was ungrateful and greedy.
10   When he returned to England, Dickens published a critical book about his travels called *American Notes,* which included his outrage over his experience with the press. He also began a new novel, *Martin Chuzzlewit,* that details the adventures of a young man seeking his fortune in the United States. Dickens used the novel to seek revenge on the U.S. press. It satirized U.S. customs as well as the press, which ironically ran serialized installments of
15   the novel without compensating Dickens. *Martin Chuzzlewit* sold poorly in England, perhaps because it was so obviously aimed at the U.S. audience.

9. "Compensating" (line 15) most nearly means

   (A) remunerating.

   (B) resolving.

   (C) equivocating.

   (D) extrapolating.

   (E) ingratiating.

10. Based on the passage, what was Dickens's probable attitude toward Americans in general during his visit to the United States?

   (A) indebtedness

   (B) belligerence

   (C) dislike

   (D) merciful

   (E) ingratitude

11. According to the passage, what was Dickens's main reason for writing *Martin Chuzzlewit*?

   (A) To write a book that would sell well in the United States

   (B) To make the United States change its existing copyright laws

   (C) To force U.S. publishers to sell his book in the United States

   (D) To attack Americans for their love of his novels

   (E) To show how he felt about the U.S. press

QUESTIONS 12–13 ARE BASED ON THE FOLLOWING PASSAGE.

Isadora Duncan is credited with inventing what came to be known as Modern Dance. She was the first American dancer to compare dance to other arts, defending it as "high art" as much as painting or poetry was. In 1903 she delivered a speech in Berlin called "The Dance of the Future," in which she stated that "the dance of the future will have to become again
5 a high religious art as it was with the Greeks. **For art which is not religious is not art, is mere merchandise."** The dances that Duncan created consisted of movements inspired by nature and folk dances. They involved simple free-flowing costumes, bare feet, and loose hair. **Her point was that the dancer should be the focus.**

FOR QUESTION 12, CONSIDER EACH ANSWER INDIVIDUALLY AND SELECT ALL CHOICES THAT APPLY.

---

12. What does Isadora Duncan's quote about the "dance of the future" mean?
    (A) That dance will be considered a valuable art in the future
    (B) That dance in the future would resemble the dances of the ancient Greeks
    (C) That dance in the future should be a form of religion

13. What function do the two groups of words in bold type serve in this passage?
    (A) The first presents an argument; the second presents support for the argument.
    (B) The first anticipates a conclusion; the second provides support for that conclusion.
    (C) The first presents an opinion; the second provides an additional opinion that supports the first.
    (D) The first serves as an intermediate conclusion; the second serves as the final conclusion.
    (E) The first supports an opinion; the second states the opinion.

QUESTIONS 14–15 ARE BASED ON THE FOLLOWING PASSAGE.

The American electoral system is commonly called a "two-party system" because there have historically been only two major political parties dominating electoral politics. Today, the Republican and Democratic Parties are the major two, but there are more than 30 other political parties active in the United States. One major role of third parties in the United States
5 has been to refocus the two major parties on issues they may have not dealt with effectively. Sometimes this happens when one of the major parties fears that a third party is going to become a viable alternative to a major party candidate, or will at least siphon off votes from that candidate during an election. At that point, what often happens is that the major party that feels threatened will take on certain policy positions of the third party in order to lure
10 more voters to it or keep voters from abandoning it. Third parties may also strengthen the government by giving those unhappy with the status quo a legitimate platform for demanding reform. In addition, third parties can simply be a welcoming place for people who want to belong to a group of like-minded people.

14. The author's primary purpose in this passage is to

(A) encourage Americans to vote for third-party candidates in elections.

(B) explain how third parties affect the U.S. electoral system.

(C) emphasize the importance of third parties to the electoral process.

(D) suggest that the U.S. electoral system could not function without third parties.

(E) analyze various platforms of third parties in the United States.

FOR QUESTION 15, CONSIDER EACH ANSWER INDIVIDUALLY AND SELECT ALL CHOICES THAT APPLY.

---

15. The author of the passage implies that third parties in the United States function in the electoral system by

(A) allowing people to vote for the candidate they believe in.

(B) giving people a platform for radical ideas.

(C) making the major parties rethink some of their policies.

FOR QUESTIONS 16–19, CHOOSE THE TWO ANSWERS THAT BEST FIT THE MEANING OF THE SENTENCE AS A WHOLE AND RESULT IN TWO COMPLETED SENTENCES THAT ARE ALIKE IN MEANING.

---

16. The _____ doctor of internal medicine received an honorary degree from his alma mater in further recognition of his humanitarian work in Zambia.

(A) humble

(B) illustrious

(C) brilliant

(D) illustrative

(E) celebrated

(F) dignified

17. The Director of Marketing's _____ assistant kept making suggestions about how to shoot the product launch until the photographer finally told him to sit down and be quiet, which he did.

(A) officious

(B) overbearing

(C) condescending

(D) supercilious

(E) meddlesome

(F) diligent

18. The young people were not so _____ as their elders when it came to accepting the imposition of martial law including curfews beginning at 5 p.m.

(A) alterable

(B) resilient

(C) amenable

(D) adaptable

(E) tractable

(F) movable

19. At the end of the meeting, the participants released a joint statement pledging to continue their dialogue in an effort to improve the _____ relations over trade differences.

(A) taut

(B) stressed

(C) tense

(D) strained

(E) difficult

(F) demanding

QUESTION 20 IS BASED ON THE FOLLOWING PASSAGE.

Many of the basic ideas that comprise contemporary American journalism can be traced back to seventeenth- and eighteenth-century English and French philosophers. John Locke expressed the idea that press freedom was an inimitable right and that journalists had a social responsibility to seek morality. David Hume, a skeptic, believed that we can never know
5 anything for certain and the best we can do is to draw probable conclusions from what we perceive. He rejected the idea that a single truth could be uncovered; journalists were to look for a probable truth. French philosopher Jean Jacques Rousseau also argued that journalists had a social responsibility to society; they should give the public not just what it wants but what it needs. He believed that journalists should provide the context for a story in addition
10 to the facts. Voltaire, who was a journalist himself, preached a credo of toleration: "I don't agree with what you have to say but I will fight to the death for your right to say it." Voltaire believed that history should not consist only of kings and wars, but of the common people's experiences. He stressed attention to detail of individual behavior and in his stories used a single person to tell a larger truth.

20. Which of the following can be implied from this passage?

(A) Journalists today must provide the public with not just what it wants, but what it needs.

(B) Journalists today should acknowledge that their basic journalistic principles come from English and French philosophers of the past.

(C) Though they might not know it, journalists today operate under principles spelled out several hundred years ago by English and French philosophers.

(D) Journalists today should follow basic principles spelled out by English and French philosophers, such as looking for a probable truth.

(E) English and French philosophers of several hundred years ago made it possible for journalism to function the way it does today.

STOP

If you finish before the time is up, you may check your work in this section only.

SECTION 4: QUANTITATIVE REASONING

35 minutes • 20 questions

(The paper-and-pencil version will have 25 questions to be completed in 40 minutes.)

For each question, follow the specific directions and choose the best answer.

The test-maker provides the following information that applies to all questions in the Quantitative Reasoning section of the GRE:

- All numbers used are real numbers.

- All figures are assumed to lie in a plane unless otherwise indicated.

- Geometric figures, such as lines, circles, triangles, and quadrilaterals, *are not necessarily* drawn to scale. That is, you should *not* assume that quantities such as lengths and angle measures are as they appear in a figure. You should assume, however, that lines shown as straight are actually straight, points on a line are in the order shown, and more generally, all geometric objects are in the relative positions shown. For questions with geometric figures, you should base your answers on geometric reasoning, not on estimating or comparing quantities by sight or by measurement.

- Coordinate systems, such as *xy*-planes and number lines, *are* drawn to scale. Therefore, you can read, estimate, or compare quantities in such figures by sight or by measurement.

- Graphical data presentations, such as bar graphs, circle graphs, and line graphs, *are* drawn to scale. Therefore, you can read, estimate, or compare data values by sight or by measurement.

FOR QUESTIONS 1–8, COMPARE QUANTITY A AND QUANTITY B. SOME QUESTIONS WILL HAVE ADDITIONAL INFORMATION ABOVE THE TWO QUANTITIES TO USE IN DETERMINING YOUR ANSWER.

1.

Quantity A	Quantity B
$\dfrac{5}{\left(\frac{1}{5}\right)^2}$	125

(A) Quantity A is greater.

(B) Quantity B is greater.

(C) The two quantities are equal.

(D) The relationship cannot be determined from the information given.

2.

Quantity A	Quantity B
$\dfrac{1}{2}+\dfrac{1}{3}+\dfrac{1}{4}+\dfrac{1}{5}$	1

(A) Quantity A is greater.
(B) Quantity B is greater.
(C) The two quantities are equal.
(D) The relationship cannot be determined from the information given.

$$y \neq 0$$

3.

Quantity A	Quantity B
$\dfrac{5}{y}$	$5y$

(A) Quantity A is greater.
(B) Quantity B is greater.
(C) The two quantities are equal.
(D) The relationship cannot be determined from the information given.

$$a > b > 0 > c > d$$

4.

Quantity A	Quantity B
$a+d$	$b+c$

(A) Quantity A is greater.
(B) Quantity B is greater.
(C) The two quantities are equal.
(D) The relationship cannot be determined from the information given.

$$x > 0$$

5.

Quantity A	Quantity B
$x^3 (x-1)$	$x^4 + x^3$

(A) Quantity A is greater.
(B) Quantity B is greater.
(C) The two quantities are equal.
(D) The relationship cannot be determined from the information given.

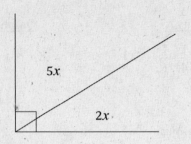

6.   Quantity A   Quantity B
                         x 15

(A) Quantity A is greater.

(B) Quantity B is greater.

(C) The two quantities are equal.

(D) The relationship cannot be determined from the information given.

$$x \neq 0$$

7.   Quantity A   Quantity B

                      $x^{-3}(x^3)$ $\dfrac{1}{x^{-3}(x^3)}$

(A) Quantity A is greater.

(B) Quantity B is greater.

(C) The two quantities are equal.

(D) The relationship cannot be determined from the information given.

Sam is 3 times as old as Sue. In 5 years Sam will be 12 years older than twice Sue's age.

8.   Quantity A   Quantity B
                      Sue's age   22

(A) Quantity A is greater.

(B) Quantity B is greater.

(C) The two quantities are equal.

(D) The relationship cannot be determined from the information given.

Questions 9–20 have several formats. Unless the directions state otherwise, choose one answer choice. For Numeric Entry questions, follow the instructions below.

Numeric Entry Questions

The following items are the same for both the computer-based version of the test and the paper-and-pencil version. However, those taking the computer-based version will have additional information about entering answers in decimal and fraction boxes on the computer screen. Those taking the paper-and-pencil version will have information about entering answers on answer grids.

- Your answer may be an integer, a decimal, or a fraction, and it may be negative.
- If a question asks for a fraction, there will be two boxes. One box will be for the numerator and one will be for the denominator.
- Equivalent forms of the correct answer, such as 2.5 and 2.50, are all correct.
- Enter the exact answer unless the question asks you to round your answers.

QUESTIONS 9–11 REFER TO THE BAR GRAPH BELOW.

Average Daily Use Per Salesperson
(rounded to the nearest dollar)

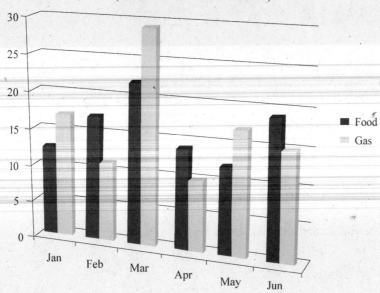

9. If there are 33 salespeople in the company, what was the approximate total spent on food and gas for January?

(A) $24,765

(B) $25,575

(C) $29,865

(D) $35,805

(E) $36,905

10. In February, the company had an outlay of $21,056 for food. How many salespeople did the company employ for the month?

    (A) 28
    (B) 47
    (C) 56
    (D) 73
    (E) 75

11. The projections for the coming year indicate an increase of 10 percent in the average cost of gas. How much more per day will the company pay out on average for gas for the first 6 months of next year?

    (A) $9
    (B) $12
    (C) $15
    (D) $18
    (E) $21

12. The frame shop has a rectangular mat 36" by 22". If a mat is cut from it that is 2" less all the way around, what is the area of the new mat?

    (A) 576
    (B) 680
    (C) 648
    (D) 792
    (E) 822

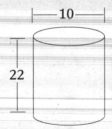

13. What is the volume of the given cylinder?

    (A) 345.5
    (B) 690.8
    (C) 1727
    (D) 3799.4
    (E) 6908

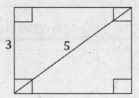

14. Find the perimeter of the figure.

    (A) 7

    (B) 8

    (C) 14

    (D) 16

    (E) 30

15. The original price of a shirt was $40. It was marked down twice before it was sold. First it was marked down 20%, and then it was marked down 15% of its discounted price. What percentage of the original price did it sell for?

    (A) 68%

    (B) 48%

    (C) 32%

    (D) 85%

    (E) 80%

16. What is the mean salary of 5 potters when two make $15.50 per hour, one makes $12 per hour, and the other two make $13.50 per hour?

    (A) $10

    (B) $12

    (C) $14

    (D) $16

    (E) $17

FOR QUESTION 17, CHOOSE THE <u>TWO</u> ANSWERS THAT APPLY.

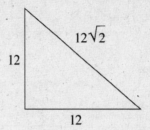

17. In the given triangle, what are the measures of the three angles?
    (A) 30°
    (B) 45°
    (C) 60°
    (D) 90°
    (E) 110°
    (F) 115°

FOR QUESTION 18, INDICATE <u>ALL</u> THE ANSWERS THAT APPLY.

18. If $x^2 - 11x - 12 = 0$, what are the two possible values for x?
    (A) −12
    (B) −1
    (C) 0
    (D) 1
    (E) 12

FOR QUESTIONS 19–20, ENTER YOUR ANSWERS IN THE BOXES.

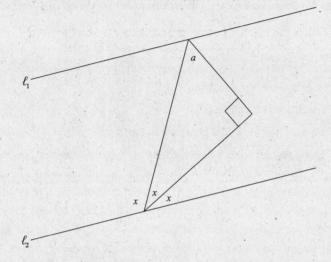

19. Lines 1 and 2 are parallel. What is the value of a?

20. In the barber shop, a haircut costs $22.50. How many haircuts must be done to cover the monthly rent of $1,276? Round the answer up to the nearest haircut.

STOP

If you finish before the time is up, you may check your work in this section only.

SECTION 5: QUANTITATIVE REASONING

35 minutes • 20 questions

(The paper-and-pencil version will have 25 questions to be completed in 40 minutes.)

For each question, follow the specific directions and choose the best answer.

The test-maker provides the following information that applies to all questions in the Quantitative Reasoning section of the GRE:

- All numbers used are real numbers.

- All figures are assumed to lie in a plane unless otherwise indicated.

- Geometric figures, such as lines, circles, triangles, and quadrilaterals, *are not necessarily* drawn to scale. That is, you should *not* assume that quantities such as lengths and angle measures are as they appear in a figure. You should assume, however, that lines shown as straight are actually straight, points on a line are in the order shown, and more generally, all geometric objects are in the relative positions shown. For questions with geometric figures, you should base your answers on geometric reasoning, not on estimating or comparing quantities by sight or by measurement.

- Coordinate systems, such as *xy*-planes and number lines, *are* drawn to scale. Therefore, you can read, estimate, or compare quantities in such figures by sight or by measurement.

- Graphical data presentations, such as bar graphs, circle graphs, and line graphs, *are* drawn to scale. Therefore, you can read, estimate, or compare data values by sight or by measurement.

FOR QUESTIONS 1–8, COMPARE QUANTITY A AND QUANTITY B. SOME QUESTIONS WILL HAVE ADDITIONAL INFORMATION ABOVE THE TWO QUANTITIES TO USE IN DETERMINING YOUR ANSWER.

$$w < x < y < z$$

1.

Quantity A	Quantity B
$w + y$	$x + z$

(A) Quantity A is greater.

(B) Quantity B is greater.

(C) The two quantities are equal.

(D) The relationship cannot be determined from the information given.

2.

Quantity A	Quantity B
The number of dimes in $5.10	The number of pennies in 2 quarters

(A) Quantity A is greater.

(B) Quantity B is greater.

(C) The two quantities are equal.

(D) The relationship cannot be determined from the information given.

3.

Quantity A	Quantity B
$\frac{4}{3}\left(\frac{1}{2}\right)\left(\frac{11}{9}\right)$	$\frac{3}{4}\left(\frac{15}{16}\right)\left(\frac{15}{12}\right)$

(A) Quantity A is greater.

(B) Quantity B is greater.

(C) The two quantities are equal.

(D) The relationship cannot be determined from the information given.

$$\frac{x}{y} = 12$$

4.

Quantity A	Quantity B
x	y

(A) Quantity A is greater.

(B) Quantity B is greater.

(C) The two quantities are equal.

(D) The relationship cannot be determined from the information given.

Given triangle ABC
Where $AB = BC = CA$

5.

Quantity A	Quantity B
Value of an interior angle	60°

(A) Quantity A is greater.

(B) Quantity B is greater.

(C) The two quantities are equal.

(D) The relationship cannot be determined from the information given.

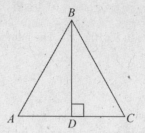

6.

Quantity A	Quantity B
$\angle A$	$\angle C$

(A) Quantity A is greater.

(B) Quantity B is greater.

(C) The two quantities are equal.

(D) The relationship cannot be determined from the information given.

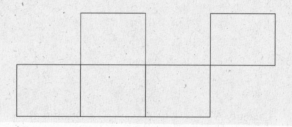

The above shape is made up of 5 congruent squares. The area of the shape is 180.

7.

Quantity A	Quantity B
84	The perimeter of the shape

(A) Quantity A is greater.

(B) Quantity B is greater.

(C) The two quantities are equal.

(D) The relationship cannot be determined from the information given.

8.

Quantity A	Quantity B
$11^4 \times 11^5$	11^9

(A) Quantity A is greater.

(B) Quantity B is greater.

(C) The two quantities are equal.

(D) The relationship cannot be determined from the information given.

Questions 9–20 have several formats. Unless the directions state otherwise, choose one answer choice. For Numeric Entry questions, follow the instructions below.

Numeric Entry Questions

The following items are the same for both the computer-based version of the test and the paper-and-pencil version. However, those taking the computer-based version will have additional information about entering answers in decimal and fraction boxes on the computer screen. Those taking the paper-and-pencil version will have information about entering answers on answer grids.

- Your answer may be an integer, a decimal, or a fraction, and it may be negative.
- If a question asks for a fraction, there will be two boxes. One box will be for the numerator and one will be for the denominator.
- Equivalent forms of the correct answer, such as 2.5 and 2.50, are all correct.
- Enter the exact answer unless the question asks you to round your answers.

9. If the salesperson receives a $5,500 commission on the sale of a yacht, how much did the yacht sell for if the commission rate is 5%?

(A) $110
(B) $1,100
(C) $11,000
(D) $110,000
(E) $1,100,000

FOR QUESTION 10, CHOOSE <u>ALL</u> THE ANSWERS THAT APPLY.

---

10. Find all the prime numbers between 20 and 29.

(A) 21
(B) 22
(C) 23
(D) 24
(E) 25
(F) 26
(G) 27
(H) 28

11. If a square mile is equal to 640 acres and an acre is equal to 43,560 square feet, how many square feet are there in $\frac{1}{17}$ of a square mile? Round your answers to two decimal places.

☐ square feet

12. Evaluate $27^{\frac{2}{3}}$.

   (A) 3
   (B) 9
   (C) 18
   (D) 27
   (E) 81

QUESTIONS 13–14 REFER TO THE FIGURE BELOW.

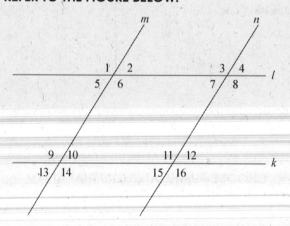

m is parallel to n and k is parallel to l

13. If $m\angle 3 = 2x$, and $m\angle 10 = 63$, find the value of x.

   (A) 58.5
   (B) 63
   (C) 72
   (D) 117
   (E) 119.5

14. In the parallelogram formed by the intersection of the lines, what is the sum of the measures of the interior angles?

   (A) < 270
   (B) < 360
   (C)   360
   (D) > 360
   (E) > 540

QUESTION 15 REFERS TO THE TABLE BELOW.

PURCHASING-POWER PARITY (PPP)

Rank	Country	PPP Total (billion)	PPP/capita ($)	Population (million)
1.	European Union	10,840	28,600	379
2.	USA	10,400	37,600	290
3.	China	5,700	4,400	1,287
4.	Japan	3,550	28,000	127
5.	India	2,660	2,540	1,049
6.	Germany	2,180	26,600	82
7.	France	1,540	25,700	60
8.	Britain	1,520	25,300	60
9.	Italy	1,440	25,000	57
10.	Russia	1,350	9,300	144
11.	Brazil	1,340	7,600	182

15. Which country in the bottom 5 of population has the highest PPP Total?

   (A) Italy
   (B) Britain
   (C) France
   (D) Germany
   (E) Japan

16. What is the first month's interest payment on a 1-year loan of $34,000 at 8.28%?

   (A) $2346.00
   (B) $281.52
   (C) $234.60
   (D) $2815.20
   (E) $242.90

FOR QUESTIONS 17–18, CHOOSE ALL THE ANSWERS THAT APPLY.

17. If m, n, and p are positive integers, and m is a factor of n, and n is a factor of p, which of the following statements are true?
   (A) m is a factor of p
   (B) n is a factor of p^3
   (C) p is the product of $m(n)$
   (D) n is a factor of $m(p)$

18. Find the numbers in the sequence from t_5 to t_7, using the formula $t_n = n(n-2)$.
   (A) –1
   (B) 0
   (C) 3
   (D) 8
   (E) 15
   (F) 24
   (G) 35
   (H) 48

FOR QUESTIONS 19–20, ENTER YOUR ANSWERS IN THE BOXES.

19. It takes 3 electricians four 8-hour days to wire a house. If the general contractor wanted the house wired in three 8-hour days, how many electricians should he have hired?

20. In a random bag of candy, there are 7 more caramels than lollipops. If lollipops cost a quarter and caramels cost a nickel, and the total cost of the bag is $2.75, how many caramels are in the bag?

STOP

If you finish before the time is up, you may check your work in this section only.

ANSWER KEY AND EXPLANATIONS

Section 1: Analytical Writing

Analyze an Issue

Model: 6 points out of 6

Who has not expressed their dissatisfaction with the American public school system? Every disappointment in American society is regularly laid at the doorstep of the public schools, which surely have gotten everything wrong from methods used to teach reading to policies related to discipline and detention. American public schools, it seems, don't just provide miserable educations. They also serve the wrong lunches, cannot teach math, provide inadequate preparation for the world of work, betray students who aspire to the best colleges and universities, have got it all wrong when it comes to physical education, and have turned the U.S. population into morons who neither understand simple scientific facts such as the seasons nor know simple civic facts such as the name of the current chief justice of the Supreme Court. Or so the story goes.

Are these the actual facts, however? The United States is one of the great powers of the world, one of the world leaders in everything from goods produced to standards of living to basic human rights. Was it our failing, inadequate, "broken" schools that produced this leadership? Perhaps it was schools that work, despite inevitable flaws, that helped propel the United States to the top over more than two centuries of remarkable achievement and progress.

The creation of a universal public education system is one of the great achievements of American democracy. Education isn't guaranteed by the Constitution; instead, this great right and privilege is based on abiding beliefs in fundamental equality: the right of everyone to achieve. And in that noble goal and commitment lie its flaws: if you are committed to democracy, truly committed to educating everyone, including children who may not speak English or are so severely handicapped that they perhaps need a year to develop skills that other children develop over the course of days or weeks, then it is difficult to also maintain the highest standards of achievement. This fundamental contradiction is at the heart of American education: we are committed both to democracy and high standards. No wonder that we sometimes don't quite make it on either count.

Yet, the relatively occasional failings are so often centerpieced, while the achievements of our system are overlooked or denigrated. Instead of thinking about all the constituencies that American education serves, and how many capable citizens it creates (are you, my reader, not one of them?) people focus instead on the shortcomings and inadequacies of our system. They then posit some kind of magic bullet, such as charter schools, as a cure for all the system's supposed ills. I do not argue here that charter schools are wrong or cannot be beneficial to students; what I do argue, however, is that it is not necessarily the case, as many statistics have shown, that even radically new schools and approaches end up producing better results than our American public schools do.

Furthermore, I do not argue that schools could not do better. There is no question that some populations remain underserved, such those as in areas in which a kind of de facto segregation exists—not by race but by income level. Again, however, what sprawling, many-faceted, complex institution could not do better? An admission that the American school system could make improvements is not an admission that is broken. Far from it. Over time, the American public school system has served more and more students and educated them at higher and higher levels. Yesterday's high school graduation rates are today's college graduation rates. Those who succeed in American society, and their numbers are legion, may credit their colleges or universities, their parents, and their own talents and drive, but surely the American public school system also played a key role in so many of those successes.

This essay scores 6 out of 6 because it

- **answers the task.** It follows specific instructions by disagreeing with the statement and supporting that disagreement; simultaneously, it thoughtfully reveals some of the complexities of the issue and how they help shape the writer's position.

- **is well supported.** The complex approach to the issue is best reflected in the clear and satisfying support, which draws on issues related to our Constitution and our democracy, as well as the problems of serving many constituencies. Examples are persuasive and developed.

- **is well organized.** The formal introduction creates interest; the body paragraphs provide thoughtful, focused support; and the essay concludes appropriately. Effective transitions between and within the paragraphs connect ideas.

- **is fluid.** Sentences are richly varied; constructions range from effective fragments to complex ideas linked by conjunctive adverbs to a sentence that uses a parenthetical element for rhetorical effect. Powerful, precise words characterize the writing throughout.

- **observes the conventions of Standard Written English.**

Model: 1 point out of 6

You have got that right. At Martindale High only a few kids ending up graduated. The numbers gone down each year, from freshmen year when maybe 1000 kids are in the school and then by sophmore year theres only 500 left and then by junior year theres only 250 till you get to senior year and a handful of kids get out with a diploma but then only some of them go on to college, or they can't afford to go anyway.

This essay scores 1 out of 6 because it

- **barely answers the task.** While the essay does take a position that agrees with the prompt, it could scarcely be more simple or inappropriate in the way it states that agreement.

- **is not supported.** The writer does offer one bit of evidence, but it is presented as a single run-on sentence. Furthermore, the evidence, based on one school, is not explained or broadened to support the position.

- **has no sense of sentence construction.** Of the three sentences in the paragraph, one is a very long series of unpunctuated ideas that are combined in one run-on sentence.

- **contains major errors in the conventions of Standard Written English.**

Analyze an Argument

Model: 6 points out of 6

The person who penned this argument clearly wants a new public safety building. But is this building truly needed and wanted?

Several types of evidence would be useful in evaluating whether a new building is necessary, including exact facts and figures of what the current building now accommodates and exact facts and figures relating to ideal or acceptable amounts of space required to integrate capacities that were never planned for in the 1961 building. For example, one would need to know how much space the current building has, and how much of that space is currently used, and for what. One might also ask whether the space in the 1961 building could be used better to accommodate more functions. In addition, one absolutely needs to know how much space, and what kind of space, is needed, either in ideal or baseline-acceptable terms, to accommodate the new environmental team, the 911 communications center, the emergency management center, and an emergency management office. One presumes, for instance, that the 1961 building already has some kind of arrangement and space allotment for dealing with 911 calls as well as for dealing with emergencies in general. After all, it currently performs these functions every day. Therefore, it is necessary to know if more space is actually needed for those functions, and if it is needed, how much more space, and why.

If evidence shows that the current building is too cramped or space is so inadequate that emergency calls cannot be met, or if current statistics point to a date in the near future when emergency calls cannot be met because of reasons of space, that evidence would seriously strengthen the argument. On the other hand, if data suggest that calls are being met, and trends suggest that they will continue to be met, that evidence would weaken the argument. In the same manner, if the facts show that emergency management computers, monitors, desks, and other equipment could be installed in spaces now crammed with items that could be discarded, or that the use of space in the 1961 building could be effectively redesigned at an acceptable cost, that would seriously weaken the argument for a new building.

The issue of public support for this building project also requires more evidence to strengthen the argument. No facts are given about the opinion poll, which may have listed 20 projects of importance to the town and which may not have limited the number that residents could list as important, high priority, or "pressing." This means that some residents could have marked all 20. Furthermore, the opinion poll may have been conducted only among a small group or among supporters of the project. If the evidence shows that only people who work in the current police and fire facility were polled, then the results are dramatically biased. If the evidence shows that only 3 percent of the town's population was polled, and of that number, only 51 percent identified a new public safety building as a "pressing need," then the results of that poll are not especially valid or credible. These results would, of course, seriously weaken the argument.

A final idea in the argument that is crying out for evidence or substantiation is the conclusion that the town will be safer once a new public safety building is built. To strengthen this argument, the writer could supply many types of evidence related to unsafe conditions that are a result, perhaps, of groups being unable to perform their jobs as well as they might perform them due to lack of proper facilities or adequate space. For example, if the environmental team cannot meet, or has no central or adequate office equipment available to each member, perhaps it cannot as carefully monitor water quality or toxic waste sites that do present a real and quantifiable threat to public health. These and other similar facts would seriously strengthen the conclusion of increased safety.

This essay scores 6 out of 6 because it

- **answers the task.** It discusses thoughtfully and logically the specific evidence that is needed to evaluate the argument, and it clearly explains how that evidence might strengthen or weaken the argument.

- **is well supported.** The explanation of evidence is specific and persuasive and drills down to key issues such as square footage, redesign of existing space, and possible percentages that might have constituted the opinion poll.

- **is well organized.** Paragraph 1 clearly states the focus, while the next paragraph begins with a clear and cogent topic sentence that is logically and coherently developed through the paragraph. Ideas for the ensuing paragraphs follow logically, and all the paragraphs are characterized by coherence and unity.

- **is fluid.** The sentences are sophisticated; no run-ons interfere with meaning or precision. There are a variety of sentence types and openers. Word choices are precise and appropriate.

- **observes the conventions of Standard Written English.**

Model: 1 point out of 6

This argument for a new public safety building lacks evidence. The argument says that theres not enough space for the police cars now or for the latest-model ambulance but it doesn't say how much space these cars need or how much bigger the new public safety building has to be. There should also be evidence about why the town needs all those new "functions of a 911 communications center, emergency management center, an emergency management office, and the new environmental safety team." What is the purpose of these teams and are they really needed has to be answered but isn't. This is not stated and it should be, including the evidence for needing these offices, centers, and teams. Many people in the town think that the new public safety building is necessary. That is not evidence to prove that the public safety building should be built. You have to do more than have the opinion that it is necessary, you have to have the facts that tell clearly why it is necessary. That is, what is concluded at the end does not necessarily follow from what is stated.

This essay scores 1 out of 6 because it

- **does not answer the task.** While this essay refers to the need for evidence, it provides no concrete examples of evidence that would actually weaken or strengthen the argument.

- **lacks organization.** The single paragraph lacks clear focus. The response fails to divide the main ideas into separate, cogent units of discourse.

- **offers illogical support.** The writer does try to say something specific about how much space the vehicles require, but this "evidence" would neither weaken nor strengthen the argument, as it is already a matter of fact stated in the argument that, for instance, the ambulance does not fit in its bay.

- **has poorly constructed sentences.** Run-on sentences and convoluted sentences interfere with coherence.

- **contains some errors in the conventions of Standard Written English.** In a better organized and written response, they would have stood out less.

Section 2: Verbal Reasoning

1. B	11. A	16. A, B
2. E	12. A	17. C, F
3. A, F	13. B	18. C, F
4. A, D, G	14. C	19. A, D
5. C, E, G	15. A	20. E
6. E		
7. D		
8. B, C		
9. D		
10. C		

Question

1. One of the major concerns as States pulled themselves out of the deficits created during the Great Recession was whether they would return to their _____ spending habits once the good times began to roll again.

(A) decadent
(B) profligate
(C) parsimonious
(D) immoral
(E) licentious

Answer Explanation

The correct answer is (B). "Profligate," choice (B), means "wildly extravagant, recklessly wasteful" as well as "dissolute." In this case, the first meanings fit the sense of the sentence. Usage will help you eliminate "decadent," choice (A), meaning "characterized by decay or decline" or "self-indulgent," because it is usually used to refer to persons. Choice (C), "parsimonious," means "frugal, penny-pinching" and the opposite of what is required by the context. Choice (D), "immoral," means "corrupt, against moral principles," and there is nothing to suggest that in the context. "Licentious," choice (E), can be eliminated for the same reason; it means "lacking moral discipline" and is usually used in reference to sexual promiscuity.

Question

2. To the board of directors, it appeared that the only way to placate _____ stockholders was to remove the CEO.

| (A) seditious |
| (B) subversive |
| (C) insubordinate |
| (D) disobedient |
| (E) disgruntled |

Answer Explanation

The correct answer is (E). Choice (E), "disgruntled," means "feeling or showing discontent or anger." Choice (A), "seditious," usually refers to inciting rebellion against civil authority, not a board of directors, so eliminate it. Choice (B), "subversive," might be applicable, but there is nothing to indicate that the stockholders were working to overthrow the governance of the company. Also, the word is usually used in reference to overthrowing a civil government. Choice (C), "insubordinate," is a synonym of "subversive" and means "refusal to submit to authority, disobedient." A person may be insubordinate to a boss, but stockholders don't answer to the board; it's the other way around, so eliminate choice (C). Choice (D), "disobedient," can also be eliminated because stockholders don't answer to the board.

Question

3. In discussing the vanishing ecosystem of the Grand Canyon, the speaker spoke (i) _____ and passionately about his subject. It was obvious that the (ii) _____ of the natural environment caused him grave concern.

Blank (i)	Blank (ii)
(A) eloquently	(D) mutilation
(B) emotionally	(E) reparation
(C) prominently	(F) destruction

Answer Explanation

The correct answers are (A) and (F). Answer Blank (i): You need to find the answer that balances the word "passionately." You can eliminate choice (B) because "emotionally" is similar to "passionately" so choice (B) would be redundant. Choice (C) is incorrect because "prominently" means "noticeably, remarkably" and doesn't fit the sense or usage so well as choice (A), "eloquently," meaning "articulately, vividly, movingly."

Answer Blank (ii): Sometimes, the simplest answer is the best answer. Choice (F), "destruction," means "destroying, or having been destroyed." Choice (D), "mutilation," means "to remove some essential part of a body, or to disfigure by damaging" and is usually used to refer to human disfigurement or something like a statute." Choice (E), "reparation," makes no sense because it means "making repairs or amends, or paying compensation."

Question

4. The epic heroes who undergo a series of (i) _____ challenges to attain a goal are (ii) _____ feature of many national cultural identities. Many of the challenges involve some (iii) _____ feat of daring.

Blank (i)	Blank (ii)	Blank (iii)
(A) extraordinary	(D) an underlying	(G) intrepid
(B) copious	(E) an external	(H) steadfast
(C) massive	(F) a conventional	(I) resolute

Answer Explanation

The correct answers are (A), (D), and (G). Answer Blank (i): Choice (A), "extraordinary," is the best answer. Choice (B), "copious," means "abundant, large quantity" and could fit the sense, but "series" implies "many," so to say "abundant" would be redundant. Choice (C), "massive," meaning "extremely large in amount, or large and heavy," doesn't make sense.

Answer Blank (ii): Choice (D), "underlying," means "lying beneath" literally, but it also means "hidden and significant, or essential," the appropriate meaning in this context. Choice (E), "external," means "coming from the outside, or suitable for use on the outside, or something outside the scope," and doesn't fit the sense. Choice (F), "conventional," means "socially accepted, customary, or established by general use or agreement," which doesn't fit the sense.

Answer Blank (iii): Choice (G), "intrepid," means "courageous" and fits the sense of daring feats. Choice (H), "steadfast," meaning "persistent, loyal, unwavering" may be true about epic heroes, but doesn't fit the sense. Nor does choice (I), "resolute," which means "firm in belief or purpose, or quickness."

Question

5. Among the health scams that the FDA warns the (i) _____ public about are (ii) _____ cancer-treatment products and weight-loss programs with FDA (iii) _____ ingredients.

Blank (i)	Blank (ii)	Blank (iii)
(A) wary	(D) trick	(G) unsanctioned
(B) circumspect	(E) mock	(H) unmeasured
(C) credulous	(F) deceptive	(I) characteristic

Answer Explanation

The correct answers are (C), (E), and (G). Answer Blank (i): If the public was "wary," choice (A), meaning "cautious, suspicious," the FDA might not need to warn it. Choice (B), "circumspect," is similar to "wary" in meaning and so doesn't fit. Choice (C), "credulous," meaning "gullible, trusting, naïve," fits the sense.

Answer Blank (ii): "Trick," choice (D), can mean "weak, defective, liable to fail; or designed for doing tricks," none of which fit the sense. Choice (E), "mock," as an adjective means "false, sham, imitative" and fits the context. Choice (F), "deceptive," might seem correct, but "deceptive" means "misleading," and these products are more than misleading—they're fake!

Answer Blank (iii): Choice (G), "unsanctioned," means "unapproved, unendorsed, unauthorized." The inclusion of "FDA" before the word is a clue. Choice (H), "unmeasured," might seem correct, but sense tips the answer toward "unsanctioned" as stronger and making better sense. Choice (I), "characteristic," doesn't make sense.

QUESTIONS 6–8 ARE BASED ON THE FOLLOWING PASSAGE.

In the year 1901, Spanish painter Pablo Picasso entered what is now referred to as his Blue Period. At the time Picasso was just 20 years old, living in Paris as a relatively unknown artist. Up to this point, the paintings Picasso produced were vibrantly colored, expressing the decadent life he and his friend Carlos Casagemas had been leading together in Paris. But
5 the suicide of Casagemas in 1901 was a major trigger for Picasso's Blue Period, in which Picasso began to paint in various shades of blue, giving the paintings a haunting and melancholy feel. The recurring theme of the Blue Period paintings is the desolation of outsiders, which included beggars, prisoners, and circus people. By 1904, Picasso had emerged from the Blue Period and began what is known as the Rose Period, characterized by bright colors,
10 and featuring acrobats and harlequins. A few years later, Picasso began to explore Cubism, which broke completely from the traditional three-dimensional representation of objects, and for which he became famous. The Blue and Rose Periods can be viewed as transitional times for Picasso in which he moved from the traditional art of his youth to the iconoclastic art of his adulthood.

Question

6. Based on the passage the author evidently believes that

(A) the Rose Period is less significant a time period than the Blue Period in the artistic development of Picasso.

(B) the suicide of Casagemas had an effect on Picasso that would haunt him for the rest of his life.

(C) if Picasso had not gone through the Blue and Rose Periods he would have never been ready to explore a new form of art.

(D) there is no way to understand Cubism without seeing the artistic road that led Picasso to it over the course of his work.

(E) the Blue Period was how Picasso expressed himself artistically during a difficult time of his life.

Answer Explanation

The correct answer is (E). The author explains that during Picasso's Blue Period he painted scenes of desolation because he was so affected by his friend's suicide. Choice (A) is incorrect because the author never states or implies that either period is more significant than the other. Choice (B) is incorrect because the author only implies that Casamegas's suicide affected Picasso during his Blue Period. Choice (C) is incorrect because although this might be a conclusion that could be drawn, the author of the passage doesn't draw this conclusion. Choice (D) is incorrect because although it might seem true, the author does not imply this in the passage.

Question

7. In this passage, "iconoclastic" (line 13) means

    (A) eclectic.

    (B) eccentric.

    (C) consequential.

    (D) revolutionary.

    (E) conservative.

Answer Explanation

The correct answer is (D). "Iconoclastic" means "revolutionary, one who attacks the status quo." Choice (A) is incorrect because "eclectic" means "diverse." Choice (B) is incorrect because "eccentric" means "unconventional," which is not so close in meaning as "revolutionary." Choice (C) is incorrect because "consequential" means "significant," which doesn't express the degree or quality of difference that "revolutionary" does. Choice (E) is incorrect because "conservative" means about the opposite of revolutionary.

Question

8. Which of the following ideas are clearly supported in this passage?

    (A) After the Blue Period, Picasso no longer painted pictures of desolation.

    (B) Picasso is best known for his Cubist works.

    (C) The Rose Period was just as significant as the Blue Period in terms of Picasso's growth as an artist.

Answer Explanation

The correct answers are (B) and (C). The passage states that Cubism made Picasso famous, and we can infer that he is best known for these works. The Rose and Blue Periods are both cited as artistic expressions Picasso explored in his youth. Choice (A) is incorrect because even if it were true, we have no way of knowing this from the details of the passage.

QUESTIONS 9–10 ARE BASED ON THE FOLLOWING PASSAGE.

Most professional photographers today cannot imagine using anything but a digital camera for their work. With a digital camera, you can take thousands of pictures using just one memory card, and you can instantly see the results, while checking for exposure, focus, and sharpness all at the same time. The traditional film camera involves much more thought to
5 ensure that every image has the correct exposure, composition, and lighting. In addition, film photographers spend hours processing their film and printing it in a darkroom, whereas only a very small percentage of the images taken on a digital camera are processed and printed. Photographers who use digital cameras simply take raw images, edit them on their computers, and upload them online. Because so much of the guesswork is eliminated, digital cameras
10 are simply better than film cameras for learning the art of photography.

Question

9. All of the following are implied in this passage EXCEPT
   (A) digital photography takes less time to learn than film photography.
   (B) more professional photographers today use digital cameras as opposed to film cameras.
   (C) photographs taken with film cameras are harder to process than those taken with digital cameras.
   (D) people tend to make more mistakes with film cameras than digital cameras.
   (E) digital cameras have changed the way people share photographs with each other.

Answer Explanation

The correct answer is (D). All the statements except choice (D) are supported by information in the passage. Although the passage implies that it's easier to correct mistakes with a digital camera, it doesn't state or imply that people make more mistakes using film cameras.

Question

10. Which of the following statements expresses the author's opinion about film cameras?
    (A) Film cameras take higher quality photographs, but they are harder to use.
    (B) You cannot take many photographs with a film camera.
    (C) If you are learning photography, you should use a digital camera.
    (D) Film cameras are bulky and difficult to use for that reason.
    (E) The differences between the two types of cameras are so great as to make any comparison worthless.

Answer Explanation

The correct answer is (C). The last sentence of the passage clearly supports the idea that anyone learning photography should use a digital camera. Choice (A) is incorrect because though this statement may be true, there is no indication that the author believes this. Choice (B) may seem correct, but the author states only that it's easier to take more pictures with a digital camera. If you have enough film, you might be able to take many pictures with a film camera. Choice (D) is neither stated nor implied in the passage. Choice (E) is a vague space holder. The passage sets up a series of contrasts between the two types of cameras, but doesn't discuss how they are alike, so there is no way of knowing whether comparisons can be made and what the analysis might show.

QUESTIONS 11–12 ARE BASED ON THE FOLLOWING PASSAGE.

The use of solar energy to produce electricity can be an excellent alternative to using fossil fuels. Solar panels give off no pollution, and, unlike other alternative energy sources like wind turbines, are silent. One big advantage of solar energy is that it can harness electricity in remote locations that are not connected to a national grid. One example of this is in space,

5 where high-efficiency solar cells are used to power satellites. Although the initial investment for solar cells is high, once they are installed, they provide free electricity. Yet unfortunately this initial cost is one reason people are hesitant to embrace solar energy as an alternative energy source. Currently, a single solar cell can cost more than $1000, and some households may need more than one. Also, solar cells do not generate electricity 24 hours a day, so

10 excess electricity needs to be captured during daylight time for later use. The weather and pollution levels can also affect a solar cell's efficiency, which could have a huge impact on solar panels installed in cities. However, cost is still considered the main deterrent. Because fossil fuels still cost less than the initial investment for solar panels, it will likely be some time before we see a significant shift toward solar energy use.

Question

11. Select the sentence that is NOT a major detail that supports the author's opinion.

(A) One example of this is in space, where high-efficiency solar cells are used to power satellites.

(B) The weather and pollution levels can also affect a solar cell's efficiency, which could have a huge impact on solar panels installed in cities.

(C) Currently, a single solar cell can cost more than $1000, and some households may need more than one.

(D) Because fossil fuels still cost less than the initial investment for solar panels, it will likely be some time before we see a significant shift toward solar energy use.

(E) The use of solar energy to produce electricity can be an excellent alternative to using fossil fuels.

Answer Explanation

The correct answer is (A). This is the only sentence that is a minor point in the discussion of the author's topic: There are pros and cons that are weighed in choosing solar energy. That solar cells power satellites in space is a specialized use of no relevance to the average consumer of power.

Question

12. Which of the following, if it were true, would weaken the author's conclusion?

(A) Fossil fuels and solar energy cost about the same.

(B) Solar panels will eventually be able to run 24 hours a day.

(C) Solar panels can sometimes create more noise than wind turbines.

(D) Many people who use solar panels are disappointed with the results.

(E) There are many alternatives to solar energy that are much cheaper.

Answer Explanation

The correct answer is (A). The author concludes the passage by stating that the main deterrent to widespread use of solar energy is cost and that fossil fuels cost less than the initial investment for solar panels. So, if they cost about the same, this would weaken the author's conclusion. Choices (B) and (C) are incorrect because even if they were true, they don't address the conclusion, which is the cost of solar panels. Choice (D) is incorrect because if it were true, it still doesn't address the cost of the solar panels. Choice (E) is incorrect because if it were true it would actually strengthen, not weaken, the author's argument.

QUESTIONS 13–15 ARE BASED ON THE FOLLOWING PASSAGE.

The story of Phineas Gage is one of the earliest documented cases of a person whose personality changed after brain trauma. In 1848, twenty-five-year-old Gage was foreman of a crew of railroad construction workers who were excavating rocks to make way for railroad track near Cavendish, Vermont. The work involved drilling holes into the rocks and filling
5   them with dynamite. While Gage was using a tool called a tamping iron to pack explosive powder into a hole, a spark ignited the powder, and propelled the tamping iron into the air, sending it straight through Gage's skull. Gage was treated by Dr. John Martyn Harlow, and he remarkably survived the accident.

Soon after, Harlow wrote a case report of Gage's injuries that was published in the *Boston*
10 *Medical and Surgical Journal*. The report was met with skepticism, however, because it seemed unlikely that anyone could survive such a terrible injury. Yet twenty years later, in 1868, Harlow further documented Gage's brain injuries in a report published in the *Bulletin of the Massachusetts Medical Society*. For the first time, his report described changes to Gage's personality: "He is fitful, irreverent, indulging at times in the grossest profanity (which
15 was not previously his custom), manifesting but little deference for his fellows, impatient of restraint of advice when it conflicts with his desires. . . In this regard, his mind was radically changed, so decidedly that his friends and acquaintances said he was 'no longer Gage'."

This publication of Gage's personality changes was significant because it coincided with reports from other scientists of the effects of brain damage on behavior. Gage's case confirmed
20 other findings that damage to the prefrontal cortex could result in personality changes while leaving other functions intact. Gage's case is likely one of the first cases to demonstrate that the frontal cortex is involved in personality.

Question

13. What is the most significant detail about the case of Phineas Gage?

(A) Gage survived a brain injury from which most people would have died.

(B) Gage became more aggressive after his accident.

(C) The tamping iron went straight through his skull.

(D) Dr. Harlow published a detailed report of Gage's accident twenty years after it occurred.

(E) People did not believe Dr. Harlow's initial report about Gage's accident.

Answer Explanation

The correct answer is (B). That Gage became more aggressive after his accident is the most significant detail about his case because it points directly to the connection between the brain injury and his change in personality. Choices (A) and (C) are incorrect because even though they are important details of the case, they are not so significant as the connection between his injury and his change in personality. Choice (D) is incorrect because this is only significant in that people took more notice of Gage's accident at that time. Choice (E) is incorrect because this detail doesn't really explain anything about the accident, but more importantly is not true, because the passage says that people were skeptical, not that they didn't take notice of the report.

Question

14. If Dr. Harlow had not published a second report about Phineas Gage twenty years after the accident, which of the following would most likely have occurred?

    (A) The case of Phineas Gage would have been eventually described by someone else.

    (B) There would be no record of Phineas Gage's accident.

    (C) Scientists would have used a different case to support the connection between the prefrontal cortex and personality.

Answer Explanation

The correct answer is (C). We can conclude that eventually another brain injury case might have resulted in similar conclusions, though it is unknown when this would have occurred. Choice (A) is incorrect because it is very likely that Gage's case would have been forgotten considering the skepticism that met it when Dr. Harlow's first report was published. Choice (B) is incorrect because there would still be Harlow's initial published report shortly after the accident.

Question

15. "Deference" (line 15) most nearly means

    (A) respect.

    (B) insolence.

    (C) impudence.

    (D) detriment.

    (E) presumption.

Answer Explanation

The correct answer is (A). "Deference" means about the same as "respect." Choices (B) and (C) are incorrect because "insolence" and "impudence" both mean "disrespect," the opposite of "deference." Choice (D) is incorrect because "detriment" means "disadvantage," having nothing to do with respect. Choice (E) is incorrect because "presumption" means a "belief or guess."

Question

16. The gallery owner has a(n) _____ eye and an amazing ability to select the next hot artist from all the new artists who show him their portfolios.

    (A) discerning

    (B) discriminating

    (C) detecting

    (D) investigative

    (E) observant

    (F) understanding

Answer Explanation

The correct answers are (A) and (B). Choice (A), "discerning," means "good judgment, perceptive," and choice (B), "discriminating," also means "perceptive, showing careful judgment or good taste." Choice (C), "detecting," and choice (D), "investigative," are synonyms, but don't fit the sense. There is no indication that the gallery owner looks for these artists; they come to him. Choice (E), "observant," might work in the sentence, but it has no synonym in the list. The same is true for choice (F), "understanding," but that's not typically used to describe eyes.

Question

17. _____ data from the traffic safety survey shows a 17 percent increase in nonfatal pedestrian accidents due to texting drivers. The final report will be available next year.

   (A) Improvised
   (B) Acting
   (C) Interim
   (D) Permanent
   (E) Terminal
   (F) Provisional

Answer Explanation

The correct answers are (C) and (F). Choice (C), "interim," and choice (F), "provisional," mean "temporary, short-term," which counterbalance the second sentence discussing a "final" report. Choice (A), "improvised," means "invented, used what was available," and is not consistent with data from a survey; there also is no synonym for it in the list. Although choice (B), "acting," is sometimes a synonym for "interim," in this case, it doesn't make sense to say "acting data." "Acting" is typically used to describe a person, such as "acting head of the department." Choice (D), "permanent," is the opposite of "interim" and doesn't make sense in the sentence. Choice (E), "terminal," on a quick read might be confused with "temporary," but the choice is "terminal" and is incorrect. It means "an ending point or place or part."

Question

18. Scrooge has come to be considered the _____ miser from whom all similar characters are drawn.

   (A) pattern
   (B) eccentric
   (C) archetypal
   (D) unusual
   (E) alternate
   (F) classic

Answer Explanation

The correct answers are (C) and (F). Choice (C), "archetypal," means "original model from which others are patterned or an ideal example of something." In this case, the first meaning works. Choice

(F), "classic," means "serving as a model or standard" and is, therefore, a synonym for "archetypal." Choice (A), "pattern," doesn't work based on usage; the construction would have to be "pattern for a miser" to be correct. Choice (B), "eccentric," is incorrect because "eccentric" means "not conventional, departing from the usual pattern," and although Scrooge might be eccentric in his views, that doesn't fit the context. "Unusual," choice (D), doesn't fit the context either. Choice (E), "alternate," meaning "other," doesn't make sense either.

Question

19. While economics may be exciting to some, the yawning student in the back of the room thought it _____.
    (A) tedious
    (B) sundry
    (C) repetitive
    (D) soporific
    (E) disingenuous
    (F) monotonous

Answer Explanation

The correct answers are (A) and (D). The context clue is "yawning." Choice (A), "tedious," means "causing mental fatigue, monotonous" and choice (D), "soporific," means "sleep inducing." Choice (B) is less likely to put someone to sleep because "sundry" means "varied" as well as "miscellaneous." Choice (C), "repetitive," could work with "tedious" because it means "characterized by repetition," which may be tedious and boring, but doesn't include the idea of sleep. On first reading, choice (F), "monotonous," also could seem as though it might work because it means "spoken in the same tone, lacking in variety, tedious," but "monotonous" doesn't have the element of sleep inducing, so it doesn't fit the context so well as "soporific." Choice (E), "disingenuous," means "insincere, calculating, not straightforward," which doesn't relate to the context.

QUESTION 20 IS BASED ON THE FOLLOWING PASSAGE.

For years astronomers could not figure out why the Sun's outer atmosphere, or corona, is millions of degrees hotter than its surface, but recently NASA scientists came up with an answer. The corona consists of loops of hot gas that are thousands of miles high, but from the Earth, the corona can only be seen during a total solar eclipse, which has made it difficult
5   to study. However, NASA scientists recently determined that nanoflares, tiny bursts of heat and energy, are what make the temperature so much hotter in the corona. The loops of gas are made up of bundles of smaller magnetic strands that can reach temperatures of several million degrees Kelvin, which is significantly hotter than the surface of the Sun. NASA scientists created a simulation to see how nanoflares might occur and determined that the
10 million-degree temperatures in the corona could only be produced by impulsive energy bursts. However, the magnetic strands cool very quickly, which explains why this phenomenon had been so difficult to detect.

Question

20. Select the sentence that best explains the recent discovery about the Sun's corona.

(A) However, the magnetic strands cool very quickly, which explains why this phenomenon had been so difficult to detect.

(B) The corona consists of loops of hot gas that are thousands of miles high, but from the Earth, the corona can only be seen during a total solar eclipse, which has made it difficult to study.

(C) For years astronomers could not figure out why the Sun's outer atmosphere, or corona, is millions of degrees hotter than its surface, but recently NASA scientists came up with an answer.

(D) The loops of gas are made up of bundles of smaller magnetic strands that can reach temperatures of several million degrees Kelvin, which is significantly hotter than the surface of the Sun.

(E) However, NASA scientists recently determined that nanoflares, tiny bursts of heat and energy, are what make the temperature so much hotter in the corona.

Answer Explanation

The correct answer is (E). This sentence sums up why the corona is so much hotter than the surface of the Sun. Choice (A) is incorrect because it only explains why the phenomenon was difficult to detect, but not what the phenomenon is. Choice (B) is incorrect because it describes what the corona consists of, but it doesn't explain why the corona is hotter than the Sun's surface. Choice (C) is incorrect because though it poses the problem, it doesn't answer it. Choice (D) is incorrect because although it explains an important detail about the phenomenon, it doesn't fully explain the phenomenon.

Section 3: Verbal Reasoning

1. A	11. E	16. B, E
2. D	12. A	17. A, E
3. A, E	13. A	18. C, E
4. B, F, H	14. B	19. C, D
5. B, F, I	15. A, B, C	20. C
6. E		
7. C		
8. B		
9. A		
10. A		

Question

1. Even though technology has vastly improved the accuracy of weather forecasts, it is unlikely that technology will enhance forecasting enough to enable accurate forecasts for more than two weeks because weather is too _____.

(A) unpredictable
(B) subjective
(C) arbitrary
(D) unreliable
(E) elusive

Answer Explanation

The correct answer is (A). "Unpredictable," choice (A), means "not able to be foretold or foreseen," so it fits the context of not being able to forecast the weather. Choice (B), "subjective," meaning "based on or influenced by attitudes, opinions, or beliefs instead of on verifiable evidence," is incorrect; weather is not subjective—it's objective. Choice (C), "arbitrary," is incorrect because it means "determined or founded on personal whim or impulse, not reasoned" and is used in reference to people or actions of people. Choice (D), "unreliable," is incorrect because it means "not trustworthy, not to be relied on," which doesn't make sense. Choice (E), "elusive," means "difficult to describe, detect, or analyze," which may seem correct, but it doesn't have the idea of seeing into the future that "unpredictable" includes, so eliminate choice (E).

Question

2. The Library of Congress recordings of American African folk songs recorded on location in the Deep South are considered the _____ versions against which musicologists evaluate all other versions.

(A) indispensable
(B) momentous
(C) explicit
(D) definitive
(E) scholarly

Answer Explanation

The correct answer is (D). Choice (D), "definitive," means "the recognized authority, authoritative" and best fits the context. Choice (A), "indispensable," meaning "necessary, very useful," is a good candidate for the answer, but it doesn't quite fit with the context: that these versions are the ones against which other versions are evaluated. This implies they're the standard—the authoritative versions. Choice (B), "momentous," meaning "very important, significant," though another near choice, doesn't include the idea of being the standard. Choice (C), "explicit," means "clearly expressed or defined" and doesn't fit the sense. Choice (E), "scholarly," may on a fast read be the answer by default, but it doesn't fit the context: these are recordings of actual folk songs that were made on location. They're not scholarly works, so choice (E) is incorrect.

Question

3. At one end of the spectrum is Van Gogh's (i) _____ life driven by the demons of madness and at the other end is Monet's (ii) _____ life in his beloved garden at Giverny.

Blank (i)	Blank (ii)
(A) turbulent	(D) stoical
(B) rowdy	(E) tranquil
(C) boisterous	(F) bucolic

Answer Explanation

The correct answers are (A) and (E). Answer Blank (i): Choices (B) and (C) are similar. Although both "rowdy" and "boisterous" have other meanings, they mean "loud," so their similarity makes either suspect as the correct answer. Choice (A), "turbulent," meaning "having a chaotic or restless nature, agitated, disturbed," fits the idea of mental illness best.

Answer Blank (ii): Choice (D), "stoical," is incorrect because it means "unemotional, indifferent," and the clause states that Monet loved his garden, so he wasn't indifferent. Choice (F), "bucolic," means "pastoral, relating to the countryside," which describes where Monet lived, but choice (E) is a better answer. You need an answer that counterbalances the emotionalism of Van Gogh, and that's "tranquil," meaning "free of disturbance, not agitated," choice (E).

Question

4. Ernest Hemingway was (i) _____ storyteller—an artist with words. He could paint (ii) _____ portrait of a proud young man locked in deadly combat with a ferocious bull and an equally (iii) _____ picture of a proud old man in his epic struggle with a giant fish.

Blank (i)	Blank (ii)	Blank (iii)
(A) an accomplished	(D) an impressive	(G) glittering
(B) a consummate	(E) an interesting	(H) riveting
(C) a perfect	(F) a stunning	(I) conspicuous

Answer Explanation

The correct answers are (B), (F), and (H). Answer Blank (i): Choice (A), "accomplished," meaning "skilled," is true, but choice (B), "consummate," meaning "masterful, highly skilled," captures the sense of the sentence better. It's a matter of degree: Hemingway isn't just a good storyteller, he's also great at his craft. Choice (C) is incorrect because "perfect" means "without defect, complete" and doesn't quite make sense.

Answer Blank (ii): To answer the second and third blanks, you need to consider the choices together because the phrase "and an equally" indicates that you need to look for two words that balance each other (are equal). Choices (D), "impressive," and (E), "interesting," are somewhat similar, and based on the style of the passage, which is slightly ornate, not intense enough, so eliminate them. Choice (F), "stunning," meaning "commanding attention, or shocking, astonishing," fits the context.

Answer Blank (iii): In choosing your third answer, look for a word that is similar to "stunning." Choice (H), "riveting," means "holding attention," so it's the correct answer. Choice (G), "glittering," means "showy, dazzling," and may be true of the portrait, but doesn't balance "stunning." As a double-check, it doesn't balance "impressive" or "interesting": it's of a more intense degree than either word. Choice (I), "conspicuous," means "obvious, without attempting to hide anything" and doesn't fit the context.

Question

5. The anthropologist's explanation for the difference in cultural traits had always seemed (i) _____, but they were later deemed (ii) _____ after new discoveries. His entire life's work was (iii) _____ by the academic community and his career was in ruins.

Blank (i)	Blank (ii)	Blank (iii)
(A) desirable	(D) delusory	(G) reneged
(B) tenable	(E) deceptive	(H) annulled
(C) worthwhile	(F) specious	(I) repudiated

Answer Explanation

The correct answers are (B), (F), and (I). Answer Blank (i): Choice (B), "tenable," means "based on reasoning and evidence, believable, defensible." It's the only option that contains the idea of credibility and defensibility, which would be necessary in a scientific field. Choice (A), "desirable," means "worth having or valuable," and choice (C), "worthwhile," means "valuable, useful, rewarding."

Answer Blank (ii): Choice (F), "specious," means "seemingly true, but actually false; not true" and fits the context. Both choice (D), "delusory," and choice (E), "deceptive," include an element of "intending to mislead" or "likely to mislead," which is not borne out in the passage.

Answer Blank (iii): Choice (I), "repudiated," means "to reject something as untrue" and fits the context. Choice (G), "reneged," means "to fail to act on a promise" and doesn't make sense. Choice (H), "annulled," means "to declare invalid in a legal sense" and doesn't make sense.

QUESTIONS 6–8 ARE BASED ON THE FOLLOWING PASSAGE.

Although it still faces many challenges, India is on the verge of becoming a world superpower. With 1.1 billion residents, India is the second largest country on Earth in population and the seventh largest country in geographical area. India's economy has grown an average of 6 percent annually over the past decade, which is among the fastest rates in the world. Yet
5   what makes India's growth especially striking is that it is driven only by a very small fraction of its population. The majority of people live in rural poverty, with poor infrastructure and high illiteracy rates. Yet the nation is a world leader in the high-tech service sector, which accounts for one half of the country's gross national product, even though this industry is made up of less than 1 percent of the population.

Question

6. Select the sentence that restates the author's opinion.
   (A) India's economy is dominated by the high-tech service industry.
   (B) India's economy is growing faster than most other countries, although its main economic industry employs less than 1 percent of its population.
   (C) Due to its untapped potential in the high-tech service industry, India will one day have a larger economy than the United States.
   (D) India is divided between a large majority of people living in rural poverty and a small percent who are wealthy.
   (E) India is becoming a world superpower despite the fact that so much of its population lives in rural poverty.

Answer Explanation

The correct answer is (E). The author notes that despite India's becoming a world superpower, much of India's population lives in rural poverty, which is a striking phenomenon. Choices (A), (B), and (D) are all incorrect because even though they're facts stated in the passage, they don't sum up the point the author is trying to make. Choice (C) is incorrect because the information is neither stated nor implied in the passage.

Question

7. Which of the following sentences from the passage is irrelevant to the author's main point?

(A) Although it still faces many challenges, India is on the verge of becoming a world superpower.

(B The majority of people live in rural poverty, with poor infrastructure and high illiteracy rates.

(C) With 1.1 billion residents, India is the second largest country on Earth in population and the seventh largest country in geographical area.

(D) India's economy has grown an average of 6 percent annually over the past decade, which is among the fastest rates in the world.

(E) Yet the nation is a world leader in the high-tech service sector, which accounts for one half of the country's gross national product, even though this industry is made up of less than 1 percent of the population.

Answer Explanation

The correct answer is (C). That India's population and land area are both large is factual and interesting, but are not major points in support of the author's thesis, which has to do with the discrepancy between India's rise as a superpower and the poverty of the majority of its population. Choices (A), (B), (D), and (E) relate to India's economy and its population more directly and help to support the main idea.

Question

8. What is most significant about the growth of India's economy over the past decade?

(A) It shows that India's economy has not always grown that quickly.

(B) It shows that India's economy is growing faster than many other economies around the world.

(C) It shows that despite the problems many of its citizens face, India's economy is growing.

(D) It shows that the high-tech service sector is what makes the economy grow.

(E) It shows that India can become a world superpower within the next decade.

Answer Explanation

The correct answer is (B). The passage points out that India's growth is "among the fastest rates in the world," which indicates it is growing faster than many other economies. Choice (A) is incorrect because the passage doesn't indicate how fast India's economy was growing previously. Choice (C) is incorrect because the rate of economic growth doesn't address the problems many of India's citizens face. Choice (D) is incorrect because the statistic describes the economy in general, not just the high-tech sector. Choice (E) is incorrect because this single, isolated statistic doesn't contain enough information to draw this conclusion.

QUESTIONS 9–11 ARE BASED ON THE FOLLOWING PASSAGE.

Until the late nineteenth century, a loophole in U.S. copyright law allowed publishers to reprint British books without paying royalties to the authors. Charles Dickens was among the many authors who were affected. Dickens was even more popular in the United States than he was in England, partly because of the availability of his works and their low prices in the
5 United States. When Dickens travelled to America for the first time in 1841, he wrote that "there never was a king or Emperor upon the Earth, so cheered, and followed by crowds." Even so, during this visit he gave speeches calling for an international copyright law. The U.S. press, whose papers readily took advantage of free British content, were outraged. Editors took up their pens in an effort to convince the public that Dickens was ungrateful and greedy.
10   When he returned to England, Dickens published a critical book about his travels called *American Notes,* which included his outrage over his experience with the press. He also began a new novel, *Martin Chuzzlewit,* that details the adventures of a young man seeking his fortune in the United States. Dickens used the novel to seek revenge on the U.S. press. It satirized U.S. customs as well as the press, which ironically ran serialized installments of
15 the novel without compensating Dickens. *Martin Chuzzlewit* sold poorly in England, perhaps because it was so obviously aimed at the U.S. audience.

Question

9. "Compensating" (line 15) most nearly means
   (A) remunerating.
   (B) resolving.
   (C) equivocating.
   (D) extrapolating.
   (E) ingratiating.

Answer Explanation

The correct answer is (A). "Remunerating," choice (A), means "paying." Choice (B) is incorrect because "resolving" means "finding a solution," and the solution may be paying someone, but it's not the same as compensating someone. Choice (C) is incorrect because "equivocating" means "vacillating, being unclear," which doesn't make sense. Choice (D) is incorrect because "extrapolating" means "inferring, drawing a conclusion" and makes no sense. Choice (E) is incorrect because "ingratiating" means "gaining favor" and makes no sense.

Question

10. Based on the passage, what was Dickens's probable attitude toward Americans in general during his visit to the United States?
    (A) indebtedness
    (B) belligerence
    (C) dislike
    (D) merciful
    (E) ingratitude

Answer Explanation

The correct answer is (A). The passage explains that Dickens enjoyed the crowds that he received during his visit and he likely felt indebtedness, or gratitude, for that. For the same reason, choice (C), "dislike," is incorrect. Choice (B) is incorrect because "belligerence" means "aggression," and though the passage explains that Dickens was upset about the copyright laws, "belligerence" seems too strong to describe how he felt about the press, and in addition, the question asks about Americans in general, not the press. Choice (D) is incorrect because there is nothing to indicate he would have had any reason to feel merciful toward the American audience. Choice (E) is incorrect because it was implied that he was, in fact, grateful to his U.S. audiences.

Question

11. According to the passage, what was Dickens's main reason for writing *Martin Chuzzlewit*?
    - (A) To write a book that would sell well in the United States
    - (B) To make the United States change its existing copyright laws
    - (C) To force U.S. publishers to sell his book in the United States
    - (D) To attack Americans for their love of his novels
    - (E) To show how he felt about the U.S. press

Answer Explanation

The correct answer is (E). Dickens seemed to want to take out his anger on the U.S. press and writing the book was a way for him to do it. Choice (A) is incorrect because even if the book sold well, this apparently wasn't Dickens's motivation for writing it. Choice (B) is incorrect because although Dickens wanted the copyright laws changed, this is not mentioned as a motivation for writing the book. Choice (C) is incorrect because publishers were already printing his works. Choice (D) is incorrect because Dickens was not angered by Americans' love of his novels, but rather by attacks from the press.

QUESTIONS 12–13 ARE BASED ON THE FOLLOWING PASSAGE.

Isadora Duncan is credited with inventing what came to be known as Modern Dance. She was the first American dancer to compare dance to other arts, defending it as "high art" as much as painting or poetry was. In 1903 she delivered a speech in Berlin called "The Dance of the Future," in which she stated that "the dance of the future will have to become again
5 a high religious art as it was with the Greeks. **For art which is not religious is not art, is mere merchandise."** The dances that Duncan created consisted of movements inspired by nature and folk dances. They involved simple free-flowing costumes, bare feet, and loose hair. **Her point was that the dancer should be the focus.**

Question

12. What does Isadora Duncan's quote about the "dance of the future" mean?
    - (A) That dance will be considered a valuable art in the future
    - (B) That dance in the future would resemble the dances of the ancient Greeks
    - (C) That dance in the future should be a form of religion

Answer Explanation

The correct answer is (A). By stating that the dance of the future would again be "a high religious art," Duncan was implying that dance would be considered an important and valuable art form. Choice (B) is incorrect because Duncan doesn't indicate that the new dances will be like dances of the ancient Greeks, but that they will be considered as important art as they were in ancient Greece. Choice (C) is incorrect because though Duncan calls the dance of the future "a high religious art," she doesn't mean that dance should become literally a form of religion, but that it should be held in high regard.

Question

13. What function do the two groups of words in bold type serve in this passage?
    (A) The first presents an argument; the second presents support for the argument.
    (B) The first anticipates a conclusion; the second provides support for that conclusion.
    (C) The first presents an opinion; the second provides an additional opinion that supports the first.
    (D) The first serves as an intermediate conclusion; the second serves as the final conclusion.
    (E) The first supports an opinion; the second states the opinion.

Answer Explanation

The correct answer is (A). The first statement is Duncan's argument that dance should be considered "a high art"; the second sentence supports this argument by explaining that this art would have the dancer—an artist—as the focal point. Choices (B) and (D) are incorrect because there are no conclusions to be drawn from these statements. Choice (C) is incorrect because the first statement is Duncan's thesis, and the second statement is not an opinion, but an explanation of support for the opinion. Choice (E) is incorrect because neither is an opinion.

QUESTIONS 14–15 ARE BASED ON THE FOLLOWING PASSAGE.

The American electoral system is commonly called a "two-party system" because there have historically been only two major political parties dominating electoral politics. Today, the Republican and Democratic Parties are the major two, but there are more than 30 other political parties active in the United States. One major role of third parties in the United States
5   has been to refocus the two major parties on issues they may have not dealt with effectively. Sometimes this happens when one of the major parties fears that a third party is going to become a viable alternative to a major party candidate, or will at least siphon off votes from that candidate during an election. At that point, what often happens is that the major party that feels threatened will take on certain policy positions of the third party in order to lure
10 more voters to it or keep voters from abandoning it. Third parties may also strengthen the government by giving those unhappy with the status quo a legitimate platform for demanding reform. In addition, third parties can simply be a welcoming place for people who want to belong to a group of like-minded people.

Question

14. The author's primary purpose in this passage is to
    (A) encourage Americans to vote for third-party candidates in elections.
    (B) explain how third parties affect the U.S. electoral system.
    (C) emphasize the importance of third parties to the electoral process.
    (D) suggest that the U.S. electoral system could not function without third parties.
    (E) analyze various platforms of third parties in the United States.

Answer Explanation

The correct answer is (B). The author's purpose is to explain how third parties work in the U.S. electoral system. Choice (A) is incorrect because the author doesn't encourage or discourage anyone's vote. Choice (C) may seem correct, but the point of the passage is less to show how important third parties are than to explain how they work. Choice (D) is incorrect because the author assumes third parties as a given and doesn't consider what it would be like without them. Choice (E) is incorrect because no platforms are analyzed in this passage.

Question

15. The author of the passage implies that third parties in the United States function in the electoral system by
    (A) allowing people to vote for the candidate they believe in.
    (B) giving people a platform for radical ideas.
    (C) making the major parties rethink some of their policies.

Answer Explanation

The correct answers are (A), (B), and (C). All three answer choices are presented in the passage as functions of third parties in the U.S. electoral system.

Question

16. The _____ doctor of internal medicine received an honorary degree from his alma mater in further recognition of his humanitarian work in Zambia.
    (A) humble
    (B) illustrious
    (C) brilliant
    (D) illustrative
    (E) celebrated
    (F) dignified

Answer Explanation

The correct answers are (B) and (E). Choices (B) and (E) are synonymous and fit the sense of the sentence. While the doctor may be choice (A), humble; choice (D), brilliant; and choice (F), dignified, there are no synonyms for any of them in the list and so can't be correct answers. Choice

(C), illustrative, might confuse you on a quick read of the answers because it means "exemplifying, instructive."

Question

17. The Director of Marketing's _____ assistant kept making suggestions about how to shoot the product launch until the photographer finally told him to sit down and be quiet, which he did.
    (A) officious
    (B) overbearing
    (C) condescending
    (D) supercilious
    (E) meddlesome
    (F) diligent

Answer Explanation

The correct answers are (A) and (E). Choices (A) and (E), "officious" and "meddlesome," mean "interfering, excessively eager to help." Depending on the context, it can also be "overbearing, condescending, and supercilious," choices (B), (C), and (D). However, the context doesn't seem to fit these three words because the assistant was "making suggestions" and sat down when told to. Choice (F), "diligent," means "hardworking, earnest, and busy," but it has no synonym in the list.

Question

18. The young people were not so _____ as their elders when it came to accepting the imposition of martial law including curfews beginning at 5 p.m.
    (A) alterable
    (B) resilient
    (C) amenable
    (D) adaptable
    (E) tractable
    (F) movable

Answer Explanation

The correct answers are (C) and (E). "Amenable," choice (C), and "tractable," choice (E), include the idea of authority that the other choices don't, so they are the best answers. "Amenable" means "willing to comply, willing to listen to authority," and "tractable" means "governable, easily managed." Choice (A), "alterable," means "able to be changed or altered in some way," whereas "adaptable," choice (D), means "capable of changing," so they are synonyms and might fit, except they don't include the idea of authority or governance. Choice (B),"resilient," means "able to recover from adversity" and doesn't fit the sense; nor does choice (F), "movable," meaning "able to be rearranged, impermanent."

Question

19. At the end of the meeting, the participants released a joint statement pledging to continue their dialogue in an effort to improve the _____ relations over trade differences.

    (A) taut

    (B) stressed

    (C) tense

    (D) strained

    (E) difficult

    (F) demanding

Answer Explanation

The correct answers are (C) and (D). Choices (C), "tense," and choice (D), "strained," are synonyms. Although choice (A), "taut," may seem as though it should be a synonym because it means "subject to tension, stretched tight," it is used in reference to people and objects, not to ideas. Choice (B), "stressed," might also seem like a plausible option, but it means "physical, mental, or emotional strain, worry, anxiety." Choice (E), "difficult," meaning "not easy to do, troublesome," might seem to work, but it has no synonym in the list. "Demanding," choice (F), might seem like a synonym, but substitute it in the sentence and it doesn't make sense.

QUESTION 20 IS BASED ON THE FOLLOWING PASSAGE.

Many of the basic ideas that comprise contemporary American journalism can be traced back to seventeenth- and eighteenth-century English and French philosophers. John Locke expressed the idea that press freedom was an inimitable right and that journalists had a social responsibility to seek morality. David Hume, a skeptic, believed that we can never know

5   anything for certain and the best we can do is to draw probable conclusions from what we perceive. He rejected the idea that a single truth could be uncovered; journalists were to look for a probable truth. French philosopher Jean Jacques Rousseau also argued that journalists had a social responsibility to society; they should give the public not just what it wants but what it needs. He believed that journalists should provide the context for a story in addition

10   to the facts. Voltaire, who was a journalist himself, preached a credo of toleration: "I don't agree with what you have to say but I will fight to the death for your right to say it." Voltaire believed that history should not consist only of kings and wars, but of the common people's experiences. He stressed attention to detail of individual behavior and in his stories used a single person to tell a larger truth.

Question

20. Which of the following can be implied from this passage?

    (A) Journalists today must provide the public with not just what it wants, but what it needs.

    (B) Journalists today should acknowledge that their basic journalistic principles come from English and French philosophers of the past.

    (C) Though they might not know it, journalists today operate under principles spelled out several hundred years ago by English and French philosophers.

    (D) Journalists today should follow basic principles spelled out by English and French philosophers, such as looking for a probable truth.

    (E) English and French philosophers of several hundred years ago made it possible for journalism to function the way it does today.

Answer Explanation

The correct answer is (C). The author points out that many of the basic journalistic ideas practiced today come from earlier philosophers, but the author doesn't claim that journalists are aware of this. Choice (A) is incorrect because this philosophy is stated in the passage, not implied. Choices (B) and (D) are incorrect because the author never indicates that journalists should acknowledge the origins of these principles nor continue to follow them. Choice (E) might be a conclusion that could be drawn from the information in this passage, but it's not implied.

Section 4: Quantitative Reasoning

1. C	11. A	16. C
2. A	12. A	17. B, D
3. D	13. C	18. B, E
4. D	14. C	19. 30
5. B	15. A	20. 57
6. B		
7. C		
8. B		
9. C		
10. B		

Question

1.

Quantity A	Quantity B
$\dfrac{5}{\left(\dfrac{1}{5}\right)^2}$	125

(A) Quantity A is greater.

(B) Quantity B is greater.

(C) The two quantities are equal.

(D) The relationship cannot be determined from the information given.

Answer Explanation

The correct answer is (C).

$$\frac{5}{\left(\frac{1}{5}\right)^2} = \frac{5}{\frac{1}{25}} = 125$$

Question

2.   Quantity A   Quantity B

$$\frac{1}{2}+\frac{1}{3}+\frac{1}{4}+\frac{1}{5}$$ 1

(A) Quantity A is greater.
(B) Quantity B is greater.
(C) The two quantities are equal.
(D) The relationship cannot be determined from the information given.

Answer Explanation

The correct answer is (A). Convert to decimals and calculate:

$$\frac{1}{2}+\frac{1}{3}+\frac{1}{4}+\frac{1}{5} = 0.5+0.33+0.25+0.20 = 1.28$$

$1.28 > 1$

Question

$$y \neq 0$$

3.   Quantity A   Quantity B

$$\frac{5}{y}$$ $5y$

(A) Quantity A is greater.
(B) Quantity B is greater.
(C) The two quantities are equal.
(D) The relationship cannot be determined from the information given.

Answer Explanation

The correct answer is (D). Pick numbers:

If $y = 5$, then the result is 1, 25; $1 < 25$

If $y = -5$, then the result is -1, -25; $-1 > -25$

Question

$$a > b > 0 > c > d$$

4.　　　　　　Quantity A　　　　　　　　　Quantity B

　　　　　　　　$a + d$　　　　　　　　　　　　$b + c$

(A) Quantity A is greater.

(B) Quantity B is greater.

(C) The two quantities are equal.

(D) The relationship cannot be determined from the information given.

Answer Explanation

The correct answer is (D). Pick numbers: $a + d$, $b + c$

$-3 + 4 = 1$, $-1 + 1 = 0$, so not equal and A > B

$-4 + 2 = -2$, $-1 + 1 = 0$, so not equal and B > A

Question

$$x > 0$$

5.　　　　　　Quantity A　　　　　　　　　Quantity B

　　　　　　　　$x^3 (x - 1)$　　　　　　　　　$x^4 + x^3$

(A) Quantity A is greater.

(B) Quantity B is greater.

(C) The two quantities are equal.

(D) The relationship cannot be determined from the information given.

Answer Explanation

The correct answer is (B). Simplify:

$x^3 (x - 1) = x^4 - x^3$

$x^4 - x^3 \neq x^4 + x^3$

Since $x \neq 0$, all the numbers will be positives:

So, $x^4 - x^3 < x^4 + x^3$.

So, A < B.

Question

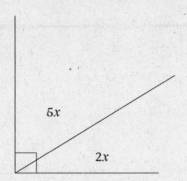

$5x$

$2x$

6.   Quantity A   Quantity B

                          x 15

(A) Quantity A is greater.

(B) Quantity B is greater.

(C) The two quantities are equal.

(D) The relationship cannot be determined from the information given.

Answer Explanation

The correct answer is (B). Set up an equation and solve:

$$5x + 2x = 90$$
$$7x = 90$$
$$x = 12\frac{6}{7}$$

Question

$$x \neq 0$$

7.   Quantity A   Quantity B

               $x^{-3}(x^3)$ $\dfrac{1}{x^{-3}(x^3)}$

(A) Quantity A is greater.

(B) Quantity B is greater.

(C) The two quantities are equal.

(D) The relationship cannot be determined from the information given.

Answer Explanation

The correct answer is (C). Simplify:

$$x^{-3}(x^3) = \frac{x^3}{x^{-3}} = 1$$

$$\frac{1}{x^{-3}(x^3)} = \frac{1}{\frac{1}{x^{-3}}(x^3)} = \frac{1}{\frac{x^3}{x^{-3}}} = \frac{1}{1} = 1$$

Question

Sam is 3 times as old as Sue. In 5 years Sam will be 12 years older than twice Sue's age.

8.

	Quantity A	Quantity B
	Sue's age	22

(A) Quantity A is greater.

(B) Quantity B is greater.

(C) The two quantities are equal.

(D) The relationship cannot be determined from the information given.

Answer Explanation

The correct answer is (B). Turn the problems into equations:

	now	in 5 years
Sue	x	$x+5$
Sam	$3x$	$3x+5$

In 5 years Sam $(3x + 5)$ is 12 more than twice Sue's age $(x + 5)$, so that is $2(x + 5) + 12$.

Calculate: $3x + 5 = 2(x + 5) + 12$

$3x + 5 = 2x + 10 + 12$

$x = 17$ Sue now

$3x = 51$ Sam now

22 is greater than 17.

QUESTIONS 9–11 REFER TO THE BAR GRAPH BELOW.

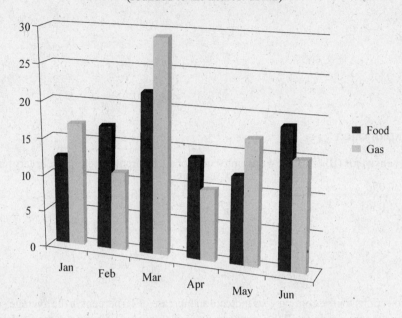

Average Daily Use Per Salesperson
(rounded to the nearest dollar)

Question

9. If there are 33 salespeople in the company, what was the approximate total spent on food and gas for January?

   (A) $24,765
   (B) $25,575
   (C) $29,865
   (D) $35,805
   (E) $36,905

Answer Explanation

The correct answer is (C). Remember there are 31 days in January. Estimate to find a highest and lowest possible number:

Lowest: food > 10, gas > 15

$$(10+15)(31)(33) = 25(31)(33) = 25,575$$

Highest: food < 15, gas < 20

$$(15+20)(31)(33) = 35(31)(33) = 35,805$$

$25,575 > answer > 35,805$, so the answer is 29,865

Question

10. In February, the company had an outlay of $21,056 for food. How many salespeople did the company employ for the month?

(A) 28

(B) 47

(C) 56

(D) 73

(E) 75

Answer Explanation

The correct answer is (B). Turn the words into equations—and remember that February has 28 days:

$$16(28)x = 21,056$$
$$448x = 21,056$$
$$x = 47$$

Question

11. The projections for the coming year indicate an increase of 10 percent in the average cost of gas. How much more per day will the company pay out on average for gas for the first 6 months of next year?

(A) $9

(B) $12

(C) $15

(D) $18

(E) $21

Answer Explanation

The correct answer is (A).

$$16+10+29+9+16+14 = 94$$
$$94 \times 1.10 = 103$$
$$103 - 94 = 9$$

Question

12. The frame shop has a rectangular mat 36" by 22". If a mat is cut from it that is 2" less all the way around, what is the area of the new mat?

(A) 576

(B) 680

(C) 648

(D) 792

(E) 822

Answer Explanation

The correct answer is (A). Drawing a figure will help you solve this problem:

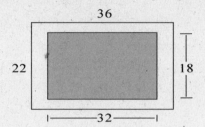

$32 \times 18 = 576$

Question

13. What is the volume of the given cylinder?
   (A) 345.5
   (B) 690.8
   (C) 1727
   (D) 3799.4
   (E) 6908

Answer Explanation

The correct answer is (C).

The volume of a cube is $\pi(r^2)(h)$.

$3.14(5^2)(22) = 3.14(25)(22) = 1727$

Question

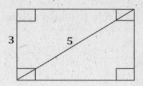

14. Find the perimeter of the figure.
    (A) 7
    (B) 8
    (C) 14
    (D) 16
    (E) 30

Answer Explanation

The correct answer is (C). Using the Pythagorean theorem:

$$a^2 + b^2 = c^2$$
$$3^2 + b^2 = 5^2$$
$$9 + b^2 = 25$$
$$b^2 = 16$$
$$b = 4$$

$$3 + 4 + 3 + 4 = 14$$

Question

15. The original price of a shirt was $40. It was marked down twice before it was sold. First it was marked down 20%, and then it was marked down 15% of its discounted price. What percentage of the original price did it sell for?
    (A) 68%
    (B) 48%
    (C) 32%
    (D) 85%
    (E) 80%

Answer Explanation

The correct answer is (A). Turn the words into equations:

$$40(1 - 0.20) = 40(0.80) = 32$$

$$32(1 - 0.15) = 32(0.85) = 27.20$$

$$\frac{27.2}{40} = 0.68 \text{ or } 68\%$$

Question

16. What is the mean salary of 5 potters when two make $15.50 per hour, one makes $12 per hour, and the other two make $13.50 per hour?

    (A) $10
    (B) $12
    (C) $14
    (D) $16
    (E) $17

Answer Explanation

The correct answer is (C). Calculate the mean salary:

$$\frac{2(15.50) + 12 + 2(13.50)}{5}$$

$$= \frac{31 + 12 + 27}{5}$$

$$= \frac{70}{5} = 14$$

Question

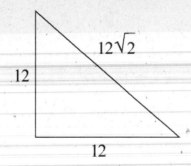

17. In the given triangle, what are the measures of the three angles?

    (A) 30°
    (B) 45°
    (C) 60°
    (D) 90°
    (E) 110°
    (F) 115°

Answer Explanation

The correct answers are (B) and (D). This is a special right triangle: a 45° right triangle. The measures of the three angles are 45°(2) and 90°.

Question

18. If $x^2 - 11x - 12 = 0$, what are the two possible values for x?

(A) -12

(B) -1

(C) 0

(D) 1

(E) 12

Answer Explanation

The correct answers are (B) and (E). Factor:

$$x^2 - 11x - 12 = 0$$

$$(x - 12)(x + 1) = 0$$

$$x = 12 \text{ or } x = -1$$

Question

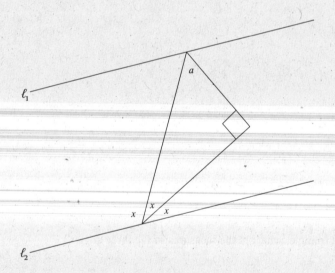

19. Lines 1 and 2 are parallel. What is the value of a?

Answer Explanation

The correct answer is 30.

$$3x = 180$$

$$x = 60$$

$$60 + 90 = 150$$

$$180 - 150 = 30$$

Question

20. In the barber shop, a haircut costs $22.50. How many haircuts must be done to cover the monthly rent of $1,276? Round the answer up to the nearest haircut.

[   ]

Answer Explanation

The correct answer is 57. Calculate:

$1,276 \div 22.50 = 56.71 = \$57$

Section 5: Quantitative Reasoning

1. B	11. 1,639,905.88	16. C
2. A	12. B	17. A, B, D
3. B	13. A	18. E, F, G
4. D	14. C	19. 4
5. C	15. E	20. 15
6. D		
7. C		
8. C		
9. D		
10. C		

Question

$$w < x < y < z$$

1.

Quantity A	Quantity B
$w + y$	$x + z$

(A) Quantity A is greater.

(B) Quantity B is greater.

(C) The two quantities are equal.

(D) The relationship cannot be determined from the information given.

Answer Explanation

The correct answer is (B). Compare:

$w < x < y < z$

$w < x, y < z$

$w + y < x + z$

Question

2.

Quantity A	Quantity B
The number of dimes in $5.10	The number of pennies in 2 quarters

(A) Quantity A is greater.

(B) Quantity B is greater.

(C) The two quantities are equal.

(D) The relationship cannot be determined from the information given.

Answer Explanation

The correct answer is (A). Calculate:

$5.10 \div 0.10 = 51$

$0.50 \div 0.01 = 50$

Question

3.

Quantity A	Quantity B
$\dfrac{4}{3}\left(\dfrac{1}{2}\right)\left(\dfrac{11}{9}\right)$	$\dfrac{3}{4}\left(\dfrac{15}{16}\right)\left(\dfrac{15}{12}\right)$

- (A) Quantity A is greater.
- (B) Quantity B is greater.
- (C) The two quantities are equal.
- (D) The relationship cannot be determined from the information given.

Answer Explanation

The correct answer is (B). Estimate:

$1 + \left(\dfrac{1}{2}\right)(1+) \approx \dfrac{1^{+}}{2}$

$\dfrac{3}{4}\left(1^{-}\right)\left(1^{+}\right) = \dfrac{3}{4}$

Question

$$\frac{x}{y} = 12$$

4.

Quantity A	Quantity B
x	y

- (A) Quantity A is greater.
- (B) Quantity B is greater.
- (C) The two quantities are equal.
- (D) The relationship cannot be determined from the information given.

Answer Explanation

The correct answer is (D). Pick numbers. Be sure to pick a positive, a negative, and a fraction to test all possibilities.

$\dfrac{144}{12} = 12$

$\dfrac{-144}{-12} = 12$

$-144 < -12 < 12 < 144$

Question

Given triangle <i>ABC</i>
Where <i>AB</i> = <i>BC</i> = <i>CA</i>

5.   Quantity A   Quantity B
                   Value of an interior angle   60°

(A) Quantity A is greater.

(B) Quantity B is greater.

(C) The two quantities are equal.

(D) The relationship cannot be determined from the information given.

Answer Explanation

The correct answer is (C). Draw a figure if needed to help you determine the answer. If the three sides are equal, it is an equilateral triangle, and the three angles are equal to:

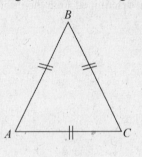

$3x = 180$

$x = 60$

Question

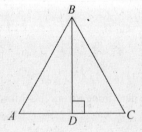

6.   Quantity A   Quantity B
                              $\angle A$ $\angle C$

(A) Quantity A is greater.

(B) Quantity B is greater.

(C) The two quantities are equal.

(D) The relationship cannot be determined from the information given.

Answer Explanation

The correct answer is (D). It is not possible to determine a relationship.

Question

The above shape is made up of 5 congruent squares. The area of the shape is 180.

7.
Quantity A	Quantity B
84	The perimeter of the shape

(A) Quantity A is greater.
(B) Quantity B is greater.
(C) The two quantities are equal.
(D) The relationship cannot be determined from the information given.

Answer Explanation

The correct answer is (C).

$180 \div 5 = 36$

$\sqrt{36} = 6$

$14 \times 6 = 84$

Question

8.
Quantity A	Quantity B
$(11^4)(11^5)$	11^9

(A) Quantity A is greater.
(B) Quantity B is greater.
(C) The two quantities are equal.
(D) The relationship cannot be determined from the information given.

Answer Explanation

The correct answer is (C). Calculate:

$(11^4)(11^5) = 11^9$

Question

9. If the salesperson receives a $5,500 commission on the sale of a yacht, how much did the yacht sell for if the commission rate is 5%?

(A) $110

(B) $1,100

(C) $11,000

(D) $110,000

(E) $1,100,000

Answer Explanation

The correct answer is (D). Calculate:

$$\frac{\$5,500}{0.05} = \$110,000$$

Question

10. Find all the prime numbers between 20 and 29.

(A) 21

(B) 22

(C) 23

(D) 24

(E) 25

(F) 26

(G) 27

(H) 28

Answer Explanation

The correct answer is (C). Factor the numbers:

$21 = 1, 3, 7, 21$

$22 = 1, 2, 11, 21$

$23 = 1, 23$

$24 = 1, 2, 3, 4, 6, 8, 12, 24$

$25 = 1, 5, 25$

$26 = 1, 2, 13, 23$

$27 = 1, 3, 9, 27$

$28 = 1, 2, 4, 7, 14, 28$

Question

11. If a square mile is equal to 640 acres and an acre is equal to 43,560 square feet, how many square feet are there in $\frac{1}{17}$ of a square mile? Round your answer to two decimal places.

[   ] square feet

Answer Explanation

The correct answer is 1,639,905.88. Calculate:

$$\frac{1}{17}(640)(43,560) = 1,639,905.88$$

Question

12. Evaluate $27^{\frac{2}{3}}$.

(A) 3
(B) 9
(C) 18
(D) 27
(E) 81

Answer Explanation

The correct answer is (B). Simplify and evaluate:

$$27^{\frac{2}{3}} = \left(\sqrt[3]{27}\right)^2 = 3^2 = 9$$

QUESTIONS 13–14 REFER TO THE FIGURE BELOW.

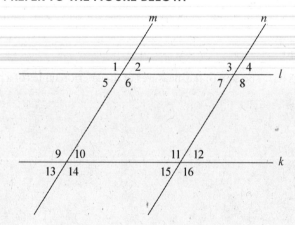

m is parallel to n and k is parallel to l

Question

13. If $m\angle 3 = 2x$, and $m\angle 10 = 63$, find the value of x.

(A) 58.5

(B) 63

(C) 72

(D) 117

(E) 119.5

Answer Explanation

The correct answer is (A).

$m\angle 3 = m\angle 9$

$$m\angle 9 + m\angle 10 = 180$$
$$2x + 63 = 180$$
$$2x = 117$$
$$x = 58.5$$

Question

14. In the parallelogram formed by the intersection of the lines, what is the sum of the measures of the interior angles?

(A) < 270

(B) < 360

(C) 360

(D) > 360

(E) > 540

Answer Explanation

The correct answer is (C). The sum of the measures of the interior angles of a parallelogram $= 360$.

QUESTION 15 REFERS TO THE TABLE BELOW.

PURCHASING-POWER PARITY

Rank	Country	PPP Total (billion)	PPP/capita ($)	Population (million)
1.	European Union	10,840	28,600	379
2.	USA	10,400	37,600	290
3.	China	5,700	4,400	1,287
4.	Japan	3,550	28,000	127
5.	India	2,660	2,540	1,049
6.	Germany	2,180	26,600	82
7.	France	1,540	25,700	60
8.	Britain	1,520	25,300	60
9.	Italy	1,440	25,000	57
10.	Russia	1,350	9,300	144
11.	Brazil	1,340	7,600	182

Question

15. Which country in the bottom 5 of population has the highest PPP Total?

   (A) Italy

   (B) Britain

   (C) France

   (D) Germany

   (E) Japan

Answer Explanation

The correct answer is (E). Reading the PPP total for these five nations, Japan at $3,550 billion has the highest PPP total.

Question

16. What is the first month's interest payment on a 1-year loan of $34,000 at 8.28%?

   (A) $2346.00

   (B) $281.52

   (C) $234.60

   (D) $2815.20

   (E) $242.90

Answer Explanation

The correct answer is (C). Calculate:

$$\frac{34,000(0.0828)}{12} = \frac{2815.20}{12} = 234.60$$

Question

17. If m, n, and p are positive integers, and m is a factor of n, and n is a factor of p, which of the following statements are true?

(A) m is a factor of p

(B) n is a factor of p^3

(C) p is the product of $m(n)$

(D) n is a factor of $m(p)$

Answer Explanation

The correct answers are (A), (B), and (D). Pick numbers:

n	m	p	Statement
8	16	32	8 is a factor of 32
2	4	8	2 is a factor of 512
4	8	16	16 is not the product of (4)(8)
10	20	40	10 is a factor of 80

Question

18. Find the numbers in the sequence from t_5 to t_7, using the formula $t_n = n(n-2)$.

(A) −1

(B) 0

(C) 3

(D) 8

(E) 15

(F) 24

(G) 35

(H) 48

Answer Explanation

The correct answers are (E), (F), and (G). Calculate:

$5(5-2) = 15$

$6(6-2) = 24$

$7(7-2) = 35$

Question

19. It takes 3 electricians four 8-hour days to wire a house. If the general contractor wanted the house wired in three 8-hour days, how many electricians should he have hired?

$$\boxed{}$$

Answer Explanation

The correct answer is 4. Set up an equation:

$$(32)(3) = 24x$$

$$4 = x$$

Question

20. In a random bag of candy, there are 7 more caramels than lollipops. If lollipops cost a quarter and caramels cost a nickel, and the total cost of the bag is $2.75, how many caramels are in the bag?

$$\boxed{}$$

Answer Explanation

The correct answer is 15. Turn the words into equations:

$$C = L + 7$$
$$25L + 5C = 275$$
$$25L + 5(L + 7) = 275$$
$$25L + 5L + 35 = 275$$
$$30L = 240$$
$$L = 8$$
$$C = 8 + 7$$
$$C = 15$$

PRACTICE TEST 4 ANSWER SHEETS

Section 1: Analytical Writing

Analyze an Issue

FOR PLANNING

ANALYZE AN ISSUE RESPONSE

_____

_____

_____

_____

_____

_____

_____

_____

_____

_____

_____

_____

_____

_____

_____

_____

_____

_____

_____

_____

_____

_____

_____

_____

_____

_____

_____

_____

_____

_____

_____

_____

_____

ANALYZE AN ISSUE RESPONSE

_____

_____

_____

_____

_____

_____

_____

_____

_____

_____

_____

_____

_____

_____

_____

_____

_____

_____

_____

_____

_____

_____

_____

_____

_____

answer sheet

ANALYZE AN ISSUE RESPONSE

ANALYZE AN ISSUE RESPONSE

_____

_____

_____

_____

_____

_____

_____

_____

_____

_____

_____

_____

_____

_____

_____

_____

_____

_____

_____

_____

_____

_____

_____

_____

_____

answer sheet

Analyze an Argument

FOR PLANNING

ANALYZE AN ARGUMENT RESPONSE

_____
_____
_____
_____
_____
_____
_____
_____
_____
_____
_____
_____
_____
_____
_____
_____
_____
_____
_____
_____
_____
_____
_____
_____
_____
_____
_____

answer sheet

ANALYZE AN ARGUMENT RESPONSE

ANALYZE AN ARGUMENT RESPONSE

_____

_____

_____

_____

_____

_____

ANALYZE AN ARGUMENT RESPONSE

Section 2: Verbal Reasoning

1. Ⓐ Ⓑ Ⓒ Ⓓ Ⓔ
2. Ⓐ Ⓑ Ⓒ Ⓓ Ⓔ
3. Ⓐ Ⓑ Ⓒ Ⓓ Ⓔ Ⓕ
4. Ⓐ Ⓑ Ⓒ Ⓓ Ⓔ Ⓕ
5. Ⓐ Ⓑ Ⓒ Ⓓ Ⓔ Ⓕ Ⓖ Ⓗ Ⓘ
6. Ⓐ Ⓑ Ⓒ Ⓓ Ⓔ
7. Ⓐ Ⓑ Ⓒ Ⓓ Ⓔ
8. Ⓐ Ⓑ Ⓒ Ⓓ Ⓔ
9. Ⓐ Ⓑ Ⓒ
10. Ⓐ Ⓑ Ⓒ Ⓓ Ⓔ

11. Ⓐ Ⓑ Ⓒ Ⓓ Ⓔ
12. Ⓐ Ⓑ Ⓒ Ⓓ Ⓔ
13. Ⓐ Ⓑ Ⓒ Ⓓ Ⓔ
14. Ⓐ Ⓑ Ⓒ Ⓓ Ⓔ
15. Ⓐ Ⓑ Ⓒ Ⓓ Ⓔ Ⓕ

16. Ⓐ Ⓑ Ⓒ Ⓓ Ⓔ Ⓕ
17. Ⓐ Ⓑ Ⓒ Ⓓ Ⓔ Ⓕ
18. Ⓐ Ⓑ Ⓒ Ⓓ Ⓔ Ⓕ
19. Ⓐ Ⓑ Ⓒ
20. Ⓐ Ⓑ Ⓒ Ⓓ Ⓔ

Section 3: Quantitative Reasoning

1. Ⓐ Ⓑ Ⓒ Ⓓ
2. Ⓐ Ⓑ Ⓒ Ⓓ
3. Ⓐ Ⓑ Ⓒ Ⓓ
4. Ⓐ Ⓑ Ⓒ Ⓓ
5. Ⓐ Ⓑ Ⓒ Ⓓ
6. Ⓐ Ⓑ Ⓒ Ⓓ
7. Ⓐ Ⓑ Ⓒ Ⓓ
8. Ⓐ Ⓑ Ⓒ Ⓓ
9. Ⓐ Ⓑ Ⓒ Ⓓ Ⓔ
10. Ⓐ Ⓑ Ⓒ Ⓓ Ⓔ

11. Ⓐ Ⓑ Ⓒ Ⓓ Ⓔ
12. Ⓐ Ⓑ Ⓒ Ⓓ Ⓔ
13. Ⓐ Ⓑ Ⓒ Ⓓ Ⓔ
14. Ⓐ Ⓑ Ⓒ Ⓓ Ⓔ
15. Ⓐ Ⓑ Ⓒ Ⓓ Ⓔ

16. Ⓐ Ⓑ Ⓒ Ⓓ Ⓔ
17. Ⓐ Ⓑ Ⓒ Ⓓ Ⓔ Ⓕ
18. Ⓐ Ⓑ Ⓒ Ⓓ Ⓔ Ⓕ Ⓖ
19. ☐
20. ☐

Section 4: Quantitative Reasoning

1. Ⓐ Ⓑ Ⓒ Ⓓ
2. Ⓐ Ⓑ Ⓒ Ⓓ
3. Ⓐ Ⓑ Ⓒ Ⓓ
4. Ⓐ Ⓑ Ⓒ Ⓓ
5. Ⓐ Ⓑ Ⓒ Ⓓ
6. Ⓐ Ⓑ Ⓒ Ⓓ
7. Ⓐ Ⓑ Ⓒ Ⓓ
8. Ⓐ Ⓑ Ⓒ Ⓓ
9. Ⓐ Ⓑ Ⓒ Ⓓ
10. Ⓐ Ⓑ Ⓒ Ⓓ Ⓔ

11. Ⓐ Ⓑ Ⓒ Ⓓ Ⓔ
12. Ⓐ Ⓑ Ⓒ Ⓓ Ⓔ
13. Ⓐ Ⓑ Ⓒ Ⓓ Ⓔ
14. Ⓐ Ⓑ Ⓒ Ⓓ Ⓔ
15. Ⓐ Ⓑ Ⓒ Ⓓ Ⓔ

16. Ⓐ Ⓑ Ⓒ Ⓓ Ⓔ Ⓕ
17. Ⓐ Ⓑ Ⓒ Ⓓ Ⓔ
18. ☐
19. ☐/☐
20. Ⓐ Ⓑ Ⓒ Ⓓ Ⓔ

Section 5: Verbal Reasoning

1. Ⓐ Ⓑ Ⓒ Ⓓ Ⓔ
2. Ⓐ Ⓑ Ⓒ Ⓓ Ⓔ
3. Ⓐ Ⓑ Ⓒ Ⓓ Ⓔ Ⓕ
4. Ⓐ Ⓑ Ⓒ Ⓓ Ⓔ Ⓕ Ⓖ Ⓗ Ⓘ
5. Ⓐ Ⓑ Ⓒ Ⓓ Ⓔ Ⓕ Ⓖ Ⓗ Ⓘ
6. Ⓐ Ⓑ Ⓒ Ⓓ Ⓔ
7. Ⓐ Ⓑ Ⓒ Ⓓ Ⓔ
8. Ⓐ Ⓑ Ⓒ
9. Ⓐ Ⓑ Ⓒ Ⓓ Ⓔ
10. Ⓐ Ⓑ Ⓒ Ⓓ Ⓔ

11. Ⓐ Ⓑ Ⓒ Ⓓ Ⓔ
12. Ⓐ Ⓑ Ⓒ
13. Ⓐ Ⓑ Ⓒ Ⓓ Ⓔ
14. Ⓐ Ⓑ Ⓒ Ⓓ Ⓔ
15. Ⓐ Ⓑ Ⓒ Ⓓ Ⓔ

16. Ⓐ Ⓑ Ⓒ Ⓓ Ⓔ Ⓕ
17. Ⓐ Ⓑ Ⓒ Ⓓ Ⓔ Ⓕ
18. Ⓐ Ⓑ Ⓒ Ⓓ Ⓔ Ⓕ
19. Ⓐ Ⓑ Ⓒ Ⓓ Ⓔ Ⓕ
20. Ⓐ Ⓑ Ⓒ

Practice Test 4

The test begins with general information about the number of sections on the test (six for the computer version, including the unidentified unscored section or an identified research section, and five for the paper-and-pencil version) and the timing of the test (approximately 3 hours and 45 minutes, including one 10-minute break after Section 3, 1-minute breaks after the other sections for the computer version, and 3 hours and 30 minutes for the paper-and-pencil version with similar breaks). The following practice test contains the five scored sections.

Each section has its own time allocation and, during that time period, you may work on only that section.

Next, you will read ETS's policy on scoring the Analytical Writing responses. Each essay is read by experienced readers, and ETS may cancel any test scores that show evidence of unacknowledged use of sources, unacknowledged collaboration with others, preparation of the response by another person, and language that is "substantially" similar to the language in one or more other test responses.

Each section has specific instructions for that section.

You will be told when to begin.

SECTION 1: ANALYTICAL WRITING

Analyze an Issue
30 minutes

The time for this task is 30 minutes. You must plan and draft a response that evaluates the issue given below. If you do not respond to the specific issue, your score will be zero. Your response must be based on the accompanying instructions, and you must provide evidence for your position. You may use support from reading, experience, observations, and/or course work.

> In an era of increased fiscal responsibility, we must institute a policy of charging entrance fees to all museums and other public buildings in our nation's capital, such as the U.S. Mint, the Library of Congress, and the White House.
>
> Write an essay that takes a position on this proposed policy. As you explain and support your position, also discuss how the likely results or consequences of the policy help to shape your position.

Your response will be read by experienced readers who will assess your ability to do the following:

- Follow the set of task instructions.
- Analyze the complexities involved.
- Organize, develop, and explain ideas.
- Use pertinent reasons and/or illustrations to support ideas.
- Adhere to the conventions of Standard Written English.

You will be advised to take some time to plan your response and to leave time to reread it before the time is over. Those taking the paper-and-pencil version of the GRE will find a blank page in their answer booklet for making notes and then four ruled pages for writing their actual response. Those taking the computer version will be given scrap paper for making notes.

STOP

> If you finish before the time is up, you may check your work in this section only.

Analyze an Argument
30 minutes

The time for this task is 30 minutes. You must plan and draft a response that evaluates the argument given below. If you do not respond to the given argument, your score will be zero. Your response must be based on the accompanying instructions and you must provide evidence in support of your analysis.

You should not present your views on the subject of the argument but on the strength or weakness of the argument.

Alzheimer's disease is not only causing much pain and suffering, but is also bankrupting our nation. The federal allocation of research dollars aimed at understanding and curing disease is more important than ever before. James Watson, co-winner of the Nobel Prize for the discovery of the molecular structure of DNA, understands this problem well. As he has suggested, the National Institutes of Health should immediately stop spreading research dollars around to second- and third-rate institutions and fund only the scientific elite. This action would help to bring about more rapid advances in our knowledge of disease-causing mechanisms and end the scourge of deadly and debilitating diseases sooner. It could even result, as Watson hopes, in a cure for cancer within the next ten years.

Write an essay that raises the questions required to evaluate this argument and the prediction it makes. Be sure to explain how the answers to these questions would help to decide whether the prediction and the argument on which it is based are reasonable.

Your response will be read by experienced readers who will assess your ability to do the following:

- Follow the set of task instructions.
- Analyze the complexities involved.
- Organize, develop, and explain ideas.
- Use pertinent reasons and/or illustrations to support ideas.
- Adhere to the conventions of Standard Written English.

You will be advised to take some time to plan your response and to leave time to reread it before the time is over. Those taking the paper-and-pencil version of the GRE will find a blank page in their answer booklet for making notes and then four ruled pages for writing their actual response. Those taking the computer version will be given scrap paper for making notes.

STOP

If you finish before the time is up, you may check your work in this section only.

INSTRUCTIONS FOR THE VERBAL REASONING AND QUANTITATIVE REASONING SECTIONS

You will find information here on the question formats for the Verbal Reasoning and Quantitative Reasoning sections as well as information about how to use the software program, or, if you're taking the paper-and-pencil version, how to mark your answers in the answer booklet.

Perhaps the most important information is a reminder about how these two sections are scored. Every correct answer earns a point, but wrong answers don't subtract any points. The advice from ETS is to guess if you aren't sure of an answer. ETS says that this is better than not answering a question.

All multiple-choice questions in the computer-based test will have answer options preceded by either blank ovals or blank squares, depending on the question type. The paper-and-pencil test will follow the same format of answer choices, but it will use letters instead of ovals or squares for answer choices.

For your convenience in answering questions and checking answers in this book, we use (A), (B), (C), etc. By using letters with parentheses, you will find it easy to check your answers against the answer key and explanation sections.

SECTION 2: VERBAL REASONING

30 minutes • 20 questions

(The paper-and-pencil version will have 25 questions to be completed in 35 minutes.)

For each question, follow the specific directions and choose the best answer.

> FOR QUESTIONS 1–5, CHOOSE ONE ANSWER FOR EACH BLANK. SELECT FROM
> THE APPROPRIATE COLUMN FOR EACH BLANK. CHOOSE THE ANSWER THAT
> BEST COMPLETES THE SENSE OF THE TEXT.

1. The managing partner of the investment company _____ its yearly earnings in a speech broadcast by satellite to financial analysts around the world. He was ebullient over the results.

(A) announced
(B) boasted about
(C) declared
(D) stated
(E) took satisfaction in

2. Lacking in new or interesting ideas, the conference presentations seemed _____.

(A) unrelenting
(B) continuous
(C) interminable
(D) assiduous
(E) persistent

3. Motivated by the (i) _____ national debt, lawmakers after years of discussion, agreed to eliminate earmarks for local programs from the budget. The consequences touched a (ii) _____ of projects from sewer treatment plants to widening of roadways.

Blank (i)	Blank (ii)
(A) burgeoning	(D) panoply
(B) emerging	(E) plethora
(C) sprouting	(F) diversity

4. In recent recessions economists have noted (i) _____ known as a jobless recovery. A comparison of data shows that the economy begins to grow before the number of jobs increases. This is a(n) (ii) _____ divergence from previous recoveries.

Blank (i)	Blank (ii)
(A) a phenomenon	(D) imperceptible
(B) an episode	(E) precise
(C) an omen	(F) pronounced

5. Recently passed and more (i) _____ regulations related to energy efficiency are putting pressure on vehicle manufacturers to produce more energy-efficient vehicles. This means new designs for cars, trucks, and buses to meet (ii)_____ emission standards. Another (iii) _____ to change is the growing demand for vehicles powered by alternative fuels.

Blank (i)	Blank (ii)	Blank (iii)
(A) stringent	(D) stricter	(G) force
(B) compliant	(E) disciplined	(H) movement
(C) adaptable	(F) sterner	(I) impetus

FOR QUESTIONS 6–20, CHOOSE ONLY <u>ONE</u> ANSWER CHOICE UNLESS OTHERWISE INDICATED.

QUESTIONS 6–8 ARE BASED ON THE FOLLOWING PASSAGE.

Luigi Pirandello's 1921 play *Six Characters in Search of an Author* may be considered the first existentialist drama. The play explores the relationship between imaginary characters and the writer who has created them. The premise of the play is that six characters have taken on a life of their own because their author has failed to complete their story. The characters
5 invade a rehearsal of another play by Pirandello and insist on acting out their lives. Somehow there is an immutable reality for these six characters, despite the fact that they are merely the fabrications of a writer. As the play's structure begins to break down, the characters begin to question how anyone can tell when reality ends and pretense begins. Pirandello leaves his audience wondering the same thing.

6. The passage is primarily concerned with
   (A) contrasting the difference between reality and pretense in Pirandello's play.
   (B) comparing how Pirandello's play differed from most others of its time.
   (C) explaining how the structure of Pirandello's play mirrored real life.
   (D) demonstrating how Pirandello challenged his audience's perception of reality.
   (E) showing how the characters in Pirandello's play interacted with one another.

7. "Immutable" (line 6) most nearly means
   (A) variable.
   (B) enclosed.
   (C) unsure.
   (D) flexible.
   (E) enduring.

8. Select the sentence in the passage in which the author provides a succinct description of Pirandello's play.
   (A) Luigi Pirandello's 1921 play *Six Characters in Search of an Author* may be considered the first existentialist drama.
   (B) The characters invade a rehearsal of another play by Pirandello and insist on acting out their lives.

(C) Somehow there is an immutable reality for these six characters, despite the fact that they are merely the fabrications of a writer.

(D) The premise of the play is that six characters have taken on a life of their own because their author has failed to complete their story.

(E) As the play's structure begins to break down, the characters begin to question how anyone can tell when reality ends and pretense begins.

QUESTIONS 9–10 ARE BASED ON THE FOLLOWING PASSAGE.

The Bialystoker Synagogue in New York City is one of the known stops on the Underground Railroad in New York City and is preserved today as a monument to its "conductors" and the escaping blacks who found safety there. In a corner of what is now the synagogue's women's gallery, there is a small hidden door in the wall. Behind this door is a wooden ladder that
5 leads to an attic with two small windows that dimly light the room. It was here that runaway enslaved blacks were hidden from the authorities until they could make their way to freedom.

Although slavery was abolished in New York State in 1827, the Fugitive Slave Law of 1850 made it illegal to help those fleeing slavery. Therefore, New York City was not typically a final destination, but a way-station on the route to Canada. Many safe places in New
10 York City were in neighborhoods that had communities of free blacks, but they also included homes of Quakers, other white abolitionists, and others willing to help blacks on their way to freedom.

Because the punishment for helping escaping slaves was severe, there are few records of the secret passageways and safe houses associated with the Underground Railroad. This
15 means that many stops along the Underground Railroad are only speculative and many other stops have yet to be uncovered.

FOR QUESTION 9, CONSIDER EACH ANSWER INDIVIDUALLY AND SELECT ALL CHOICES THAT APPLY.

---

9. Which of the following statements are supported by the passage?

(A) The Bialystoker Synagogue was one of the most important stops on the Underground Railroad.

(B) There may have been other Underground Railroad stops in places of worship.

(C) All escaping slaves passing through New York City would have stopped at the Bialystoker Synagogue.

10. The author mentions the Fugitive Slave Act in this passage in order to

(A) introduce an important concept to the reader.

(B) provide support for an earlier argument.

(C) provide a possible explanation for other details in the passage.

(D) reinforce the main point the author is trying to make.

(E) contrast this detail with earlier information in the passage.

QUESTIONS 11–12 ARE BASED ON THE FOLLOWING PASSAGE.

Recycled plastic bottles can be turned into a soft and durable fiber used to make fleece and other clothing fabrics. The process begins at a recycling plant, where plastic bottles (made of polyethylene terephthalate, or PET) are separated from other materials and sorted. The plastic is chopped coarsely and then crushed into tiny flakes, which are melted in large vats,
5 and the resulting liquid is pushed through a strainer to create fibrous strands. The strands are stretched to make them thinner and stronger, and then cut into short thread-like pieces that can be woven into fabric. Recycling plastic bottles into fiber is an excellent "green" solution because it both keeps them out of landfills and saves the energy that would be needed to manufacture new plastics.

11. The passage provides information on each of the following EXCEPT

(A) reasons to recycle plastic bottles.

(B) what recycled plastic bottles can become.

(C) how plastic can be stretched into fibers.

(D) the type of plastic bottles used for making fabrics.

(E) the way different plastics are sorted.

12. The author suggests that recycling old plastic bottles into fiber

(A) is the best use for them.

(B) may be only one option out of many.

(C) saves both time and money.

(D) is an efficient way to save resources.

(E) is a time-consuming use of resources.

QUESTIONS 13–14 ARE BASED ON THE FOLLOWING PASSAGE.

By the end of World War II, European countries were eager to pursue an economic and political amalgamation in order both to increase prosperity in the region and to foster a sense of unity. The European Union, whose origins began in the 1950s, was officially established in 1993. The creation of the Eurozone in 1999 further solidified economic ties between certain
5 European countries. The Eurozone originally consisted of 11 countries, but now includes 17, both in Western and Eastern Europe. Every country that is in the Eurozone must use the euro as its sole legal currency. Monetary rules for the Eurozone are created and maintained by the European Central Bank. Currently, member states have to abide by the rules of the Stability and Growth Pact that was first adopted in 1997. They cannot exceed an annual
10 budget deficit of 3 percent of the gross domestic project or have an inflation rate over 2 percent. Plus all Eurozone countries must maintain a national debt lower than 60% of their gross domestic product.

13. The author's primary purpose in the passage is to

(A) present an overview of the Eurozone.

(B) analyze the rules of the Stability and Growth Pact of the Eurozone.

(C) suggest alternatives to some of the Stability and Growth Pact's rules.

(D) emphasize the importance of the Eurozone.

(E) show why other countries should join the Eurozone.

14. "Amalgamation" (line 2) most nearly means
   (A) combination.
   (B) severance.
   (C) melting.
   (D) variance.
   (E) anomaly.

FOR QUESTIONS 15–18, CHOOSE THE <u>TWO</u> ANSWERS THAT BEST FIT THE MEANING OF THE SENTENCE AS A WHOLE AND RESULT IN TWO COMPLETED SENTENCES THAT ARE ALIKE IN MEANING.

---

15. The job applicant was _____ in his interview by not telling the interviewer about his lack of credentials.
   (A) invidious
   (B) disingenuous
   (C) artless
   (D) clandestine
   (E) devious
   (F) indirect

16. Studies of the age-old _____ of nature versus nurture have resulted in some interesting results. Studies of identical and fraternal twins have indicated that a sense of humor is the result of nurture rather than nature.
   (A) paradox
   (B) provocation
   (C) enigma
   (D) challenge
   (E) conundrum
   (F) paradigm

17. Mulling over the various plans for the reorganization of the sales department, the vice president and the HR director finally and _____ chose the plan that laid off the most salespeople but kept the benefits at the same level for those who were left.
   (A) timidly
   (B) diffidently
   (C) reticently
   (D) stingily
   (E) hesitantly
   (F) reluctantly

18. The audience sat in rapt attention as the poet read his poetry with _____ in his deep, rich baritone voice.
    (A) confidence
    (B) grace
    (C) fluency
    (D) panache
    (E) ease
    (F) flair

QUESTIONS 19–20 ARE BASED ON THE FOLLOWING PASSAGE.

Groundwater contamination arises when groundwater becomes polluted by various substances, including chemicals, medications, bacteria, viruses, fertilizer, and fuel. Groundwater contamination can also come from polluted runoff from farms or when factories dump manufacturing wastes in waterways. Once groundwater becomes contaminated, it can be
5 very difficult to remove the contaminants. Sometimes filtration systems can be used, but in other cases, the groundwater may be so polluted as to be rendered undrinkable. Since much of the world's supply of drinking water comes from groundwater, contamination is a serious issue. In communities in some places in the world that cannot afford other sources of water, people may have no other choice than to drink contaminated groundwater with its
10 consequent serious side effects.

FOR QUESTION 19, CONSIDER EACH ANSWER INDIVIDUALLY AND SELECT ALL CHOICES THAT APPLY.

19. It can be inferred from the passage that the author would agree with which of the following statements?
    (A) Groundwater contamination should be an important consideration of municipal governments.
    (B) People should consider using alternate sources of water whenever possible.
    (C) Once groundwater contamination is detected, it must be addressed.

20. Select the sentence in the passage that best establishes the author's position.
    (A) Groundwater contamination can also come from polluted runoff from farms or when factories dump manufacturing wastes in waterways.
    (B) Since much of the world's supply of drinking water comes from groundwater, contamination is a serious issue.
    (C) Once groundwater becomes contaminated, it can be very difficult to remove the contaminants.
    (D) Sometimes filtration systems can be used, but in other cases, the groundwater may be so polluted as to be rendered unpotable.
    (E) In communities in some places in the world that cannot afford other sources of water, people may have no other choice than to drink contaminated groundwater with its consequent serious side effects.

STOP

If you finish before the time is up, you may check your work in this section only.

SECTION 3: QUANTITATIVE REASONING

35 minutes • 20 questions

(The paper-and-pencil version will have 25 questions to be completed in 40 minutes.)

For each question, follow the specific directions and choose the best answer.

> The test-maker provides the following information that applies to all questions in the Quantitative Reasoning section of the GRE:
>
> - All numbers used are real numbers.
> - All figures are assumed to lie in a plane unless otherwise indicated.
> - Geometric figures, such as lines, circles, triangles, and quadrilaterals, *are not necessarily* drawn to scale. That is, you should *not* assume that quantities such as lengths and angle measures are as they appear in a figure. You should assume, however, that lines shown as straight are actually straight, points on a line are in the order shown, and more generally, all geometric objects are in the relative positions shown. For questions with geometric figures, you should base your answers on geometric reasoning, not on estimating or comparing quantities by sight or by measurement.
> - Coordinate systems, such as *xy*-planes and number lines, *are* drawn to scale. Therefore, you can read, estimate, or compare quantities in such figures by sight or by measurement.
> - Graphical data presentations, such as bar graphs, circle graphs, and line graphs, *are* drawn to scale. Therefore, you can read, estimate, or compare data values by sight or by measurement.

FOR QUESTIONS 1–8, COMPARE QUANTITY A AND QUANTITY B. SOME QUESTIONS WILL HAVE ADDITIONAL INFORMATION ABOVE THE TWO QUANTITIES TO USE IN DETERMINING YOUR ANSWER.

1.

Quantity A	Quantity B
(12)(5)(9)(107)	(8)(104)(5)(12)

(A) Quantity A is greater.
(B) Quantity B is greater.
(C) The two quantities are equal.
(D) The relationship cannot be determined from the information given.

$$a \neq 0$$

a is the reciprocal of B.

2.
Quantity A	Quantity B
B	a

(A) Quantity A is greater.

(B) Quantity B is greater.

(C) The two quantities are equal.

(D) The relationship cannot be determined from the information given.

3.
Quantity A	Quantity B
$\left(\sqrt[3]{86}\right)^2$	9

(A) Quantity A is greater.

(B) Quantity B is greater.

(C) The two quantities are equal.

(D) The relationship cannot be determined from the information given.

$$\frac{12z}{y} = \frac{x}{2}$$

4.
Quantity A	Quantity B
$8z$	$3xy$

(A) Quantity A is greater.

(B) Quantity B is greater.

(C) The two quantities are equal.

(D) The relationship cannot be determined from the information given.

Mary is twice as old as Jay was 5 years ago. Jay is twice as old as Sue.
All together they are 15 years older than Mary is now.

5.
Quantity A	Quantity B
Mary	Jay

(A) Quantity A is greater.

(B) Quantity B is greater.

(C) The two quantities are equal.

(D) The relationship cannot be determined from the information given.

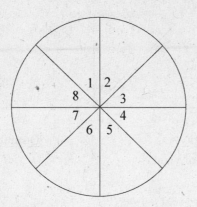

6.

Quantity A	Quantity B
m∠1 + m∠2 + m∠3 + m∠4	m∠3 + m∠4 + m∠5 + m∠6

(A) Quantity A is greater.

(B) Quantity B is greater.

(C) The two quantities are equal.

(D) The relationship cannot be determined from the information given.

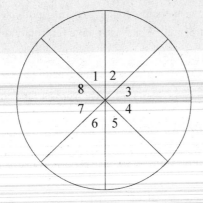

7.

Quantity A	Quantity B
m∠3 + m∠4 + m∠5	m∠1 + m∠8 + m∠7

(A) Quantity A is greater.

(B) Quantity B is greater.

(C) The two quantities are equal.

(D) The relationship cannot be determined from the information given.

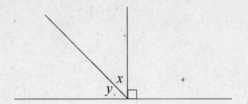

8.   Quantity A   Quantity B
        The mean of x and y 60

(A) Quantity A is greater.

(B) Quantity B is greater.

(C) The two quantities are equal.

(D) The relationship cannot be determined from the information given.

Questions 9–20 have several formats. Unless the directions state otherwise, choose one answer choice. For Numeric Entry questions, follow the instructions below.

Numeric Entry Questions

The following items are the same for both the computer-based version of the test and the paper-and-pencil version. However, those taking the computer-based version will have additional information about entering answers in decimal and fraction boxes on the computer screen. Those taking the paper-and-pencil version will have information about entering answers on answer grids.

- Your answer may be an integer, a decimal, or a fraction, and it may be negative.

- If a question asks for a fraction, there will be two boxes. One box will be for the numerator and one will be for the denominator.

- Equivalent forms of the correct answer, such as 2.5 and 2.50, are all correct.

- Enter the exact answer unless the question asks you to round your answers.

9. What is the area of a circle with a diameter of 12?

(A) 6π

(B) 12π

(C) 24π

(D) 36π

(E) 144π

10. A bag of cement weighs 94 pounds and a bag of lime weighs 50 pounds. How many pounds does a shipment of 18 bags of cement and 5 bags of lime weigh?

(A) 250

(B) 1,370

(C) 1,442

(D) 1,692

(E) 1,942

11. Given $4f + 4g = 14$ and $15h + 15i = 60$, what is the mean of f, g, h, and i?

(A) $1\frac{7}{8}$

(B) $2\frac{1}{4}$

(C) $8\frac{3}{5}$

(D) $12\frac{3}{4}$

(E) $18\frac{1}{2}$

12. From a well-shuffled deck of cards, what is the probability of drawing a red 8?

(A) $\frac{1}{4}$

(B) $\frac{1}{13}$

(C) $\frac{2}{13}$

(D) $\frac{1}{26}$

(E) $\frac{1}{52}$

13. A right triangle has a base of 12 and a hypotenuse of 13. What is the height of the remaining leg?

(A) 4

(B) 5

(C) 15

(D) 20

(E) 25

14. To manufacture soft pretzels, there is a built-in cost of $320 to start the machines and an additional cost for materials of $0.05 per pretzel. If the pretzels sell for 4 for $1.00, how many have to be sold to break even for the day?

(A) 100

(B) 160

(C) 320

(D) 1,600

(E) 3,200

QUESTIONS 15–17 REFER TO THE TABLE BELOW.

Tahoe and Suburban Sales
1995–2009

	Tahoe	Suburban
1995	72,000	70,000
1996	127,000	92,000
1997	127,000	101,000
1998	131,000	110,000
1999	126,000	137,000
2000	150,000	132,000
2001	201,000	152,000
2002	209,000	150,000
2003	197,000	132,000
2004	188,000	118,000
2005	151,000	88,000
2006	160,000	76,000
2007	148,000	83,000
2008	90,000	52,000
2009	71,000	42,000

15. What is the range of vehicles sold between 1995 and 2009?

(A) 42,000

(B) 194,000

(C) 167,000

(D) 280,000

(E) 290,000

16. If the average price of a Tahoe in 2006 was $35,600 and the average price of a Suburban in 2006 was $57,700, what was the total sales number in dollars for both vehicles that year?

(A) 1.00812×10^{10}

(B) 1.65712×10^{10}

(C) 2.65712×10^{10}

(D) 2.98112×10^{10}

(E) 3.12912×10^{10}

FOR QUESTIONS 17–18, CHOOSE **ALL** THAT APPLY.

17. What are the mode and the median of the number of Tahoes sold between 1995 and 2009?

(A) 71,000

(B) 127,000

(C) 131,000

(D) 148,000

(E) 151,000

(F) 180,000

18. What are the two answers to the equation $x^2 + 3x - 4 = 0$?

    (A) −4

    (B) −3

    (C) −1

    (D) 0

    (E) 1

    (F) 3

    (G) 4

FOR QUESTIONS 19–20, ENTER YOUR ANSWERS IN THE BOXES.

---

19. Jack Rosato pays a flat rate business tax in his township of 0.438% on all invoices. He had invoices totaling $297,849.00 last year. What was his township tax bill? (Round your answer to two decimal places.)

    $ [   ]

20. Justin is twice as old as Deven. In 5 years, twice the sum of their ages will be 104. How old is Justin now?

    [   ]

STOP

If you finish before the time is up, you may check your work in this section only.

SECTION 4: QUANTITATIVE REASONING

35 minutes • 20 questions

(The paper-and-pencil version will have 25 questions to be completed in 40 minutes.)

For each question, follow the specific directions and choose the best answer.

The test-maker provides the following information that applies to all questions in the Quantitative Reasoning section of the GRE:

- All numbers used are real numbers.

- All figures are assumed to lie in a plane unless otherwise indicated.

- Geometric figures, such as lines, circles, triangles, and quadrilaterals, *are not necessarily* drawn to scale. That is, you should *not* assume that quantities such as lengths and angle measures are as they appear in a figure. You should assume, however, that lines shown as straight are actually straight, points on a line are in the order shown, and more generally, all geometric objects are in the relative positions shown. For questions with geometric figures, you should base your answers on geometric reasoning, not on estimating or comparing quantities by sight or by measurement.

- Coordinate systems, such as *xy*-planes and number lines, *are* drawn to scale. Therefore, you can read, estimate, or compare quantities in such figures by sight or by measurement.

- Graphical data presentations, such as bar graphs, circle graphs, and line graphs, *are* drawn to scale. Therefore, you can read, estimate, or compare data values by sight or by measurement.

FOR QUESTIONS 1–9, COMPARE QUANTITY A AND QUANTITY B. SOME QUESTIONS WILL HAVE ADDITIONAL INFORMATION ABOVE THE TWO QUANTITIES TO USE IN DETERMINING YOUR ANSWER.

$$x > 0$$
$$y > 0$$

1.
Quantity A	Quantity B
x	y

(A) Quantity A is greater.

(B) Quantity B is greater.

(C) The two quantities are equal.

(D) The relationship cannot be determined from the information given.

2.

Quantity A	Quantity B
$\frac{1}{3}$ of 12	$\frac{1}{4}$ of 16

(A) Quantity A is greater.
(B) Quantity B is greater.
(C) The two quantities are equal.
(D) The relationship cannot be determined from the information given.

3.

Quantity A	Quantity B
$\frac{1}{5} + \frac{1}{5}$	0.04

(A) Quantity A is greater.
(B) Quantity B is greater.
(C) The two quantities are equal.
(D) The relationship cannot be determined from the information given.

$$x^7 = -128$$

4.

Quantity A	Quantity B
x^5	$8x^2$

(A) Quantity A is greater.
(B) Quantity B is greater.
(C) The two quantities are equal.
(D) The relationship cannot be determined from the information given.

$$\frac{5}{16}m = \frac{1}{8}$$

5.

Quantity A	Quantity B
m	$\frac{2}{5}$

(A) Quantity A is greater.
(B) Quantity B is greater.
(C) The two quantities are equal.
(D) The relationship cannot be determined from the information given.

Triangle ABC lies on the xy-plane with A at $(0,0)$, B at $(4,0)$, and C at (x,y).

$$x,y > 0$$
$$area = 24$$

6.   Quantity A   Quantity B
                 x 6

(A) Quantity A is greater.
(B) Quantity B is greater.
(C) The two quantities are equal.
(D) The relationship cannot be determined from the information given.

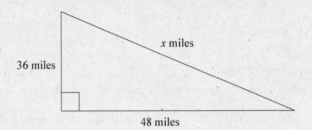

7.   Quantity A   Quantity B
                 x 72

(A) Quantity A is greater.
(B) Quantity B is greater.
(C) The two quantities are equal.
(D) The relationship cannot be determined from the information given.

$$x + y = 16$$

8.   Quantity A   Quantity B
        Maximum value of xy 63

(A) Quantity A is greater.
(B) Quantity B is greater.
(C) The two quantities are equal.
(D) The relationship cannot be determined from the information given.

$$8x = 3.2$$
$$y = 4x - 1$$

9.   Quantity A   Quantity B
                       x y

(A) Quantity A is greater.

(B) Quantity B is greater.

(C) The two quantities are equal.

(D) The relationship cannot be determined from the information given.

Questions 10–20 have several formats. Unless the directions state otherwise, choose one answer choice. For Numeric Entry questions, follow the instructions below.

Numeric Entry Questions

The following items are the same for both the computer-based version of the test and the paper-and-pencil version. However, those taking the computer-based version will have additional information about entering answers in decimal and fraction boxes on the computer screen. Those taking the paper-and-pencil version will have information about entering answers on answer grids.

*   Your answer may be an integer, a decimal, or a fraction, and it may be negative.

*   If a question asks for a fraction, there will be two boxes. One box will be for the numerator and one will be for the denominator.

*   Equivalent forms of the correct answer, such as 2.5 and 2.50, are all correct.

*   Enter the exact answer unless the question asks you to round your answers.

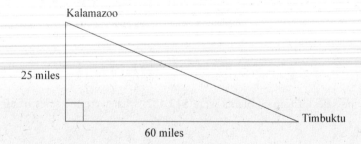

10. How many miles is it from Kalamazoo to Timbuktu?

(A) 68

(B) 65

(C) 66

(D) 63

(E) 64

11. The local football booster club sells food at all home games. To make the accounting equal, they sell all products for the same price of $1.00. If over the course of the season they sold 4 times as many hot dogs as candy bars, and half as many drinks as hot dogs, and they sold a total of $1,400 worth of food, how many drinks did they sell?

    (A) 200

    (B) 400

    (C) 600

    (D) 800

    (E) 1,400

12. Solve for x: $x^{\frac{3}{2}} = 125$

    (A) −25

    (B) −5

    (C) 5

    (D) 25

    (E) 125

QUESTIONS 13–15 REFER TO THE GRAPH BELOW.

Vegetable Plant Sales in May

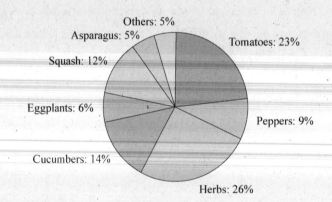

Others: 5%
Asparagus: 5%
Squash: 12%
Tomatoes: 23%
Eggplants: 6%
Peppers: 9%
Cucumbers: 14%
Herbs: 26%

13. If in May the sales of tomato plants were $13,482, what were the sales of all the vegetable plants?

    (A) $58,617.39

    (B) $59,871.09

    (C) $60,740.87

    (D) $62,137.83

    (E) $63,820.31

14. Total vegetation sales in May were $124,717.85. What were the total sales of cucumbers and herbs combined?

    (A) $34,675.93

    (B) $37,897.02

    (C) $40,320.04

    (D) $42,739.84

    (E) $49,887.14

15. What is the ratio of squash sales to eggplant sales?

    (A) $\dfrac{2}{9}$

    (B) $\dfrac{2}{1}$

    (C) $\dfrac{5}{4}$

    (D) $\dfrac{4}{7}$

    (E) $\dfrac{6}{11}$

FOR QUESTION 16, CHOOSE ALL THAT APPLY.

---

16. Find the next three numbers in the sequence: 1, –4, 16, –64, …

    (A) –4,096

    (B) –1,024

    (C) –256

    (D) 256

    (E) 1,024

    (F) 4,096

FOR QUESTION 17, CHOOSE THE <u>TWO</u> ANSWERS THAT APPLY.

---

17. Find the two values for x, where $x^2 + 9x + 11 = 0$.

    (A) $x = \dfrac{-9 - \sqrt{37}}{2}$

    (B) 11

    (C) 1

    (D) 9

    (E) $x = \dfrac{-9 + \sqrt{37}}{2}$

FOR QUESTIONS 18–19, ENTER YOUR ANSWERS IN THE BOXES.

---

18. Jeff is 3 times as old as Billy, who is 2 times as old as Joe. In 7 years, their combined age will be 3 times Jeff's age now, plus 3. How old is Billy now?

19. $\left(\dfrac{1}{3} - 2 \right)\left(\dfrac{1}{4} - 2 \right) =$

Give answer as a fraction.

20. A cookie-cutting machine can cut 134 cookies a minute. How many cookies will it cut in an hour and a half?

    (A) 90

    (B) 201

    (C) 8,040

    (D) 12,060

    (E) 15,080

STOP

If you finish before the time is up, you may check your work in this section only.

SECTION 5: VERBAL REASONING
30 minutes • 20 questions

(The paper-and-pencil version will have 25 questions to be completed in 35 minutes.)

For each question, follow the specific directions and choose the best answer.

> **FOR QUESTIONS 1–5, CHOOSE <u>ONE</u> ANSWER FOR EACH BLANK. SELECT FROM THE APPROPRIATE COLUMN FOR EACH BLANK. CHOOSE THE ANSWER THAT BEST COMPLETES THE SENSE OF THE TEXT.**

1. Research on school improvement has found that instruction must convey information _____ to be effective. Lessons that don't proceed logically from A to B to C, confuse, rather than inform.

| (A) coherently |
| (B) smoothly |
| (C) articulately |
| (D) cogently |
| (E) eloquently |

2. Mechanical weathering, which breaks down rock, includes a number of processes. One is caused by the _____ quality of rock particles. The particles rushing by in water or carried by the wind break down the rocks with which they come in contact.

| (A) coarse |
| (B) rough |
| (C) rasping |
| (D) grating |
| (E) abrasive |

3. Critics may consider his style (i)_____ of the worst in advertising art, but he charges (ii)_____ prices for his representational paintings and makes a fortune.

Blank (i)	Blank (ii)
(A) derivative	(D) munificent
(B) a by-product	(E) magnanimous
(C) a complement	(F) exorbitant

4. The (i)_____ view of many Americans for years was that the 1950s were a time of peace and prosperity. However, this (ii)_____ version of the time period is (iii)_____ by the racial unrest that erupted in the latter part of the decade.

Blank (i)	Blank (ii)	Blank (iii)
(A) prevailing	(D) implied	(G) concealed
(B) hypothetical	(E) epic	(H) misrepresented
(C) academic	(F) fictional	(I) belied

5. His grades in school never seemed (i) _____ with his intelligence, and this (ii) _____ assessment was borne out in his later work life. Known for his (iii) _____ ability to penetrate to the core issues, he rose to become CEO of a Fortune 1000 company.

Blank (i)	Blank (ii)	Blank (iii)
(A) congenial	(D) astute	(G) laser-like
(B) commensurate	(E) practiced	(H) discerning
(C) complaisant	(F) adroit	(I) caustic

FOR QUESTIONS 6–20, CHOOSE ONLY <u>ONE</u> ANSWER CHOICE UNLESS OTHERWISE INDICATED.

QUESTIONS 6–8 ARE BASED ON THE FOLLOWING PASSAGE.

American artist Mary Cassatt (1845–1926) is noteworthy for being one of the few women artists to succeed professionally during the late nineteenth century. Because of her friendship with Edgar Degas, she was the only American to take part in the 1879 exhibition of French Impressionist artists in Paris. Though Cassatt's style was influenced by the Impressionists,
5 she developed her own unique style and subject matter. It is easy to see the influence of Degas in her paintings, but her interest in Japanese prints is also reflected in many of her paintings. Much of her earliest work portrays women engaging in home activities, such as reading, sewing, or writing letters. After the French exhibition, Cassatt began to explore what she eventually became famous for: paintings of women caring for children. It is through these
10 paintings that Cassatt highlights the often overlooked role in painting of women as mothers.

6. Select the sentence in the passage in which the author notes influences on Cassatt's style.

(A) After the French exhibition, Cassatt began to explore what she eventually became famous for: paintings of women caring for children.

(B) It is easy to see the influence of Degas in her paintings, but her interest in Japanese prints is also reflected in many of her paintings.

(C) Much of her earliest work portrays women engaging in home activities, such as reading, sewing, or writing letters.

(D) It is through these paintings that Cassatt highlights the often overlooked role in painting of women as mothers.

(E) Because of her friendship with Edgar Degas, she was the only American to take part in an 1879 exhibition of French Impressionist artists in Paris.

7. The author's primary purpose in the passage is to

(A) explain why Mary Cassatt began painting women and children.

(B) argue that Mary Cassatt was a huge influence on later female painters.

(C) suggest reasons that Mary Cassatt's art began to change after the Impressionist exhibition.

(D) analyze the ways that Mary Cassatt was influenced by the Impressionists.

(E) describe the development of Mary Cassatt's artistic style and themes.

FOR QUESTION 8, CONSIDER EACH ANSWER INDIVIDUALLY AND SELECT <u>ALL</u> CHOICES THAT APPLY.

8. Which of the following statements is supported by the passage?

  (A) Mary Cassatt began to paint women and children as a way to express her frustration with contemporary male artists.

  (B) Mary Cassatt was inspired by several artistic styles from different parts of the world.

  (C) Mary Cassatt expressed a unique perspective through her art.

QUESTIONS 9–10 ARE BASED ON THE FOLLOWING PASSAGE.

Modest Mussorgsky was one of a group of Russian composers known as "The Five" or "The Mighty Handful," whose goal in the late 1800s was to create Russian nationalist music. Mussorgsky's most famous work, the opera *Boris Godunov*, completed in 1873, is the story of the powerful, though flawed Russian tsar who ruled in the early seventeenth century. The
5 opera met with negative criticism from some of Mussorgsky's contemporaries. Another member of "The Five," Nicolai Rimsky-Korsakov, said of *Boris Godunov* that "I adore it for its originality, power, boldness, distinctiveness, and beauty; I abhor it for its lack of polish, the roughness of its harmonies, and, in some places, the sheer awkwardness of the music." Because of this, Rimsky-Korsakov revised the opera after Mussorgsky's death at age forty-
10 one in 1881, correcting what he believed were technical weaknesses in the original score. Rimsky-Korsakov's revised version of *Boris Gudonov* became the preferred edition of the opera. In recent years, however, Mussorgsky's unique style and orchestration have come to be appreciated, even celebrated, and his is the version that opera-goers are more likely to see performed.

9. "Nationalist" (line 2) most nearly means

  (A) loyalty to one's country.

  (B) dedicated to the interests or culture of a nation.

  (C) love of one's country.

  (D) isolationist.

  (E) separatist.

10. The author suggests that Mussorgsky's work

  (A) lacked polish and technique.

  (B) was well-respected by his contemporaries.

  (C) covered complex themes that were far ahead of their time.

  (D) was too technically challenging to perform in the original.

  (E) was not fully appreciated in his own lifetime.

QUESTIONS 11–13 ARE BASED ON THE FOLLOWING PASSAGE.

Despite advances in medicine and technology, the demand for organ transplants remains much greater than the number of organ donors available. Ironically, this is mainly because of the increasing success rate of organ transplant operations over the years. Early transplant operations often failed because patients' immune systems rejected the foreign organ. However, the introduction of the drug cyclosporine in the 1980s helped solve this problem, and organ transplants subsequently became much more routine, which, in turn, resulted in the need for more organ donations.

Researchers looking for a way to solve this problem have begun to work on developing artificial organs, **though this is still in a highly experimental phase.** So far, laboratories around the world have developed artificial hearts, lungs, livers, and other organs, but with only limited success. Other scientists are working on techniques to grow organs from a patient's own cells, **which could ultimately eliminate the need for organ donors.** Yet because this involves cloning and stem cell research, it also raises ethical questions that make this a much more complicated issue than developing artificial organs.

11. What function do the two groups of words in bold type serve in this passage?
    (A) The first presents an argument; the second reinforces the argument.
    (B) The first presents an opinion; the second presents final support for the opinion.
    (C) The first serves as an intermediate conclusion; the second serves as a definitive conclusion.
    (D) The first anticipates the argument's conclusion; the second supports the conclusion.
    (E) The first qualifies a fact; the second states a conclusion.

12. It can be inferred from the passage that the author would agree with which of the following statements?
    (A) The discovery of the drug cyclosporine made it much harder for people who needed organs to get them.
    (B) Scientists should continue to experiment trying to develop organs in order to solve the problem of the organ donor shortage.
    (C) The technique of growing organs from patients' own cells is so potentially divisive that it should be discontinued.

13. If the information in this passage is true, which of the following must also be true?
    (A) Some people who need organ transplants today will not receive them in time.
    (B) Artificial organs will never be a viable option for people needing organ transplants.
    (C) Because of use of the drug cyclosporine, the human body no longer rejects foreign organs.
    (D) Creating organs from patients' own cells will become much easier over time.
    (E) In the future, people will no longer need organ transplants from donor organs.

QUESTIONS 14–15 ARE BASED ON THE FOLLOWING PASSAGE.

The British Commonwealth is composed of fifty-four member countries, most former colonies
of Great Britain, with a combined population of nearly 1.8 billion people, or about 30 percent
of the world's population. The term "commonwealth" was eventually settled on to describe
this collective group of former colonies because many of the older, established colonies of
5 Britain were already self-governing, and it was felt that this "community of nations" could
ultimately become a federation of equal nation states. However, this is not how the British
Commonwealth developed. Although it has a secretary-general, a position first established
in 1965, it has no united policy or principles and no shared institutions. The only feature that
all member states share is that they acknowledge the British monarch as symbolic head of
10 the Commonwealth, but fewer than half recognize the monarch as the head of their countries.
Even so, the British Commonwealth does serve a purpose: its biennial meetings allow an
opportunity for nations of disparate cultures to get together and share their ideas.

14. "Disparate" (line 12) most nearly means

(A) incongruent.
(B) analogous.
(C) homogeneous.
(D) tantamount.
(E) acclaimed.

15. The passage provides information on each of the following EXCEPT

(A) how the term "commonwealth" came to be used to describe the mostly former British
colonies.
(B) what the British Commonwealth nations share in common.
(C) the number of people who belong to the British Commonwealth.
(D) the most important countries of the British Commonwealth.
(E) the general purpose of the British Commonwealth.

**FOR QUESTIONS 16–19, CHOOSE THE TWO ANSWERS THAT BEST FIT THE
MEANING OF THE SENTENCE AS A WHOLE AND RESULT IN TWO COMPLETED
SENTENCES THAT ARE ALIKE IN MEANING.**

---

16. Government economists released a report showing how the _____ housing market was depressing prices across a number of areas in the construction industry.

(A) obsolescent
(B) outmoded
(C) superseded
(D) moribund
(E) motionless
(F) stagnant

17. Many doctors are still _____ digitizing their patients' records. They see the process as expensive and time-consuming and are not convinced of its value.

(A) wary of

(B) scrupulous about

(C) meticulous about

(D) skeptical about

(E) dubious about

(F) critical about

18. Delivered in a defiant tone, the leader's _____ denial of any wrongdoing in his cabinet failed to quell calls for an investigation into the allegations of malfeasance in office.

(A) qualified

(B) eligible

(C) blunt

(D) intransigent

(E) intractable

(F) stark

19. The critic applauded the novel for its wit but decried the one-dimensional nature of its characters. Upon reading the review, the novelist railed against the _____ of critics who can't tell that these characters are supposed to be one-dimensional.

(A) perfidy

(B) obtuseness

(C) treachery

(D) ignorance

(E) denseness

(F) inexorableness

QUESTION 20 IS BASED ON THE FOLLOWING PASSAGE.

Although there are many serious consequences resulting from the destruction of tropical rainforests, perhaps the most significant is that of climate change. Tropical rainforests can absorb about 20 percent of the world's carbon dioxide emissions from the atmosphere, but as rainforests are cut down, less carbon dioxide is absorbed. In addition, by slashing and
5 burning the rainforests, human activities are adding huge amounts of carbon dioxide to the atmosphere, even more than is emitted by factories, planes, and automobiles all over the world. Ultimately, as deforestation continues, the amount of carbon dioxide and other greenhouse gas levels in the atmosphere will rise. This will, in turn, lead to an increase in temperature, eventually resulting in a change in weather patterns and sea levels.

FOR QUESTION 20, CONSIDER EACH ANSWER INDIVIDUALLY AND SELECT <u>ALL</u> CHOICES THAT APPLY.

---

20. The author suggests which of the following will happen in the future if deforestation continues?

   (A) There will be no tropical rainforests left in the world.

   (B) The Earth's temperature will rise each year.

   (C) Less carbon dioxide will be absorbed from the atmosphere.

STOP

If you finish before the time is up, you may check your work in this section only.

ANSWER KEY AND EXPLANATIONS

Section 1: Analytical Writing

Analyze an Issue

Model: 6 points out of 6

Washington, D.C., is the seat of our nation's democracy and a symbol of democratic and egalitarian ideals around the world. Unlike other U.S. cities, it offers visitors a chance to visit, without paying a penny of admission, some of the finest and most important institutions in the world. This is a glorious policy, which should excite our pride, not our parsimony. Certainly, the United States, the richest nation in the world, can afford to extend an open hand to visitors to its own capital.

That open hand must be extended, minimally, to all American visitors. Americans should not have to pay to see the treasures in the Smithsonian museums or to visit the living repositories of their own nation's government and history. Besides the fact that it seems most undignified to ask them to do so, haven't Americans paid for all these things already through their taxes? These museums and their treasures as well as the other free institutions of learning and government in our nation's capital are already the rightful possesions of the American people.

Some possibly unforeseen consequences of a new policy of payment could also prove quite negative. Washington, D.C., earns a substantial amount of money each year through tourism. It seems almost inevitable that tourism and the revenues earned from it would decrease if admission fees were suddenly charged. The school group from Chicago or the senior citizens group from Omaha might still come, but spend fewer days. Other groups and families might decide, given the other costs involved in vacationing in a big city, that it is just as cost effective to go elsewhere. Furthermore, a new policy of payment would mean fewer visitors, and that would probably result in a decrease in the ways in which some of the institutions involved, such as museums that operate restaurants and shops, earn money. Thus, some of the gains in revenue achieved through admission could well be offset by a decrease in revenue at these businesses.

The largest losses, of course, would be to the American public, especially to those who are least able to pay. What resides in their nation's capital is their rightful patrimony, yet they would be disenfranchised from it. Those with the ability to make choices about where and how to spend their money might decide that with the museums and other sites charging a fee, why not take the children to that theme park where they really want to go? In that way, opportunities for enrichment, for learning, and for participating in one's American heritage would all be lost.

This essay scores 6 out of 6 because it

- **answers the task.** With considerable insight, it discusses and explains the writer's views on the policy and considers the consequences of implementing the policy.

- **is well supported.** The writer offers perceptive and persuasive support, beginning with the idea that the United States is the world's richest nation ending with the ideas about rightful patrimony.

- **is well organized.** From the engaging opening to the dramatic placement of the most important ideas last, the essay provides a logical and smooth progression of ideas. Clear, appropriate connections help unify the ideas and ease the reader's passage through the response.

- **is fluid.** Word choices are sophisticated and effective, while sentences demonstrate qualities of directness and variety as well as parallelism.
- **observes the conventions of Standard Written English.**

Model: 1 point out of 6

Its time to face reality and be fiscaly responsable and begin asking visitor's to our nations capitol to pay for going to the many fine places in Washington, D.C. that they don't pay for now. Visitors are use to such fees for almost every other museum they go to and for historical sights across the country. The only place where it would be hard to get use to paying a fee would be for visiting the library.

This essay scores 1 out of 6 because it

- **does not answer the task.** While the writer does state a position, it is not fully explained, and the consequences of implementing the policy are omitted.
- **lacks support and development.** There is only one simple idea that might be categorized as support.
- **has multiple errors in Standard Written English.** While a few errors matter little in a well-organized and well-developed essay, the errors in this piece greatly hinder comprehension.

Analyze an Argument

Model: 6 points out of 6

This unreasonable argument makes an unreasonable prediction. Among its many assumptions is the idea that James Watson fully understands, or is an expert on, the issues related to allocation of research dollars. Because the argument gives Watson's main credentials as a scientist, and a very great scientist indeed, one would have to ask if science were not Watson's main area of expertise, rather than the understanding of how best to allocate funds. One would also have to ask whether Watson truly understands all the workings of how funds are allocated, or has simply leapt to the conclusion that the National Institutes of Health have it all wrong.

The main claim of this argument, that the National Institutes of Health should fund only the scientific elite, and the idea that this will bring about advances and cures faster, is open to many questions. First, the argument does not specify exactly who the scientific elite is. Anyone could rapidly come to reasonable conclusions here, perhaps by naming the most prestigious institutions in, for example, cancer research and treatment. But no matter what data a reader might base a list of "elite" institutions on, the problem still remains that he or she may not define the word *elite* in the same way that the argument writer or James Watson does. So one must ask which institutions are covered under the term *elite,* as well as which ones are covered under the terms *second-rate* or *third-rate.* Once those questions are answered, further questions arise about these institutions. Most prominent of these is elite or second- or third-rate in what sense? And do the institutions then deserve more or less research dollars as a result?

One would also have to ask how it is that scientific and medical breakthroughs and cures arise. Cannot a cure, or a theory that might lead the way to an advance that is important in identifying a cure, arise at any institution at any time? Furthermore, is it not possible that so-called elite institutions are already among the best-funded institutions in the nation? If that is the case, are they now producing all or even most of the breakthroughs and advances while so-called second- and third-rate institutions are producing none at all? Logic would seem to suggest that the information in the application for the NIH grant or research dollars would be a more important criteria in the allocation of funds than the prestige of the originating institution would be.

As for the prediction of cures, who can say when that will be? Unless advances are so close as to clearly point to the next very probable steps, no one can predict a cure within ten years or any other number of years. It is illogical, if not laughable, to think that a simple shift in funding can do what decades of intense, concentrated, dedicated research have been unable to do.

This essay scores 6 out of 6 because it

- **answers the task.** It offers many probing and thoughtful questions that would have to be answered before the reasonableness of the argument and the prediction could be evaluated. It also clearly relates the answers to those questions, stated or implied, to the prediction.

- **is well supported.** Ample reasons and examples include the question of Watson's main area of expertise and his ability to make recommendations on matters of research funding; the question of who the elite are and who defines them; whether such institutions necessarily deserve a greater allocation of funds—or aren't already receiving the lion's share.

- **is well organized.** Paragraph 1 launches directly into the issue of Watson's credibility and sticks to that issue; paragraph 2 treats the main claim of the argument and does a good job of raveling it; paragraph 3 suggests that scientific breakthroughs may occur at any institution; and paragraph 4 focuses on the prediction of a cure while also bringing closure to the essay. Ideas are clearly linked throughout the essay to create coherence without self-conscious transitions or unnecessary repetition.

- **is fluid.** There is a mixture of sentence types, including simple, compound, and complex constructions. Questions are interspersed effectively in paragraph 3. The final sentence is more dramatic and rhetorically effective because of its parallelism.

- **observes the conventions of Standard Written English.**

Model: 1 point out of 6

Cancer, Parkinson's disease, and Alzheimer's disease are terrible problems. They are causing great suffering and bankrupting our nation.

For this reason, research into these diseases is of paramount importance. It is especially important that federal dollars reach the right institutions, so that the money can be spent on curing these diseases as quickly and efficiently as possible. Although it is an idea that will prove unpopular, it is better to send research dollars aimed at curing such diseases to elite institutions than to send those same dollars to second- or third-rate institutions. As James Watson, winner of the Nobel Prize, notes, these institutions have a far better chance of using the money well and actually making rapid advances in our knowledge of disease causing mechanisms than second- and third-rate institutions have. For this reason, these institutions have a better probability of ending the scourge of deadly and debilitating disease sooner. They might even come up with a cure for cancer within the next ten years.

This essay scores 1 out of 6 because it

- **does not answer the task.** This essay does not present a single question that would have to be answered in order to decide whether the prediction and argument on which it is based are reasonable.

- **mainly copies the task.** Although this is not a word-for-word copy of the topic section of the prompt, the response says little more than the prompt itself does.

- **is fluid.** The writer uses varied sentences and appropriate word choices. The writer has a fluid, interesting, and appropriate style.

- **adheres to the conventions of Standard Written English.** Notice that the writer's perfect adherence to the conventions of Standard Written English, as well as the writer's varied sentences and appropriate word choices, cannot save an essay that does not answer the task.

Section 2: Verbal Reasoning

1. B	11. E	16. D, E
2. C	12. D	17. C, F
3. A, F	13. A	18. D, F
4. A, F	14. A	19. A, C
5. A, D, I	15. B, E	20. B
6. D		
7. E		
8. D		
9. B		
10. C		

Question

1. The managing partner of the investment company _____ its yearly earnings in a speech broadcast by satellite to financial analysts around the world. He was ebullient over the results.

(A) announced
(B) boasted about
(C) declared
(D) stated
(E) took satisfaction in

Answer Explanation

The correct answer is (B). Knowing the meaning of the word "ebullient," which is a clue to the answer, would have helped you, but if you don't know that it means "cheerful, happy, jovial," you can still figure out the answer from the context. Holding a global call with financial analysts indicates that the earnings must have been very good. Choice (B), "boasted about," has this element of intensity more so than choices (A) and (C), "announced" and "declared," which do mean "made known publicly." Choice (D), "stated," also lacks any emotional intensity. Choice (E), "took satisfaction in," might work, but "boasted" fits the mood better with "ebullient."

Question

2. Lacking in new or interesting ideas, the conference presentations seemed _____.

(A) unrelenting
(B) continuous
(C) interminable
(D) assiduous
(E) persistent

Answer Explanation

The correct answer is (C). Choice (C), "interminable," means "very long, seemingly endless" and undoubtedly describes the conference attendees' feelings. Choice (A), "unrelenting," means "unyielding, persistent, not diminishing in intensity," which doesn't fit the sense of the sentence or include the idea of time. Choice (B), "continuous," means "uninterrupted, unceasing," and doesn't fit the sense. The problem wasn't that the presentations weren't interrupted, but that they went on and on. Choice (D), "assiduous," meaning "hardworking, done with care and perseverance" may be true of the presenters making the presentations, but it doesn't fit the context. Choice (E), "persistent," is a synonym for "unrelenting," but it also means "not giving up." The presentations didn't persist, only the presenters, so "persistent" wouldn't be good usage in this sentence.

Question

3. Motivated by the (i) _____ national debt, lawmakers after years of discussion, agreed to eliminate earmarks for local programs from the budget. The consequences touched a (ii) _____ of projects from sewer treatment plants to widening of roadways.

Blank (i)	Blank (ii)
(A) burgeoning	(D) panoply
(B) emerging	(E) plethora
(C) sprouting	(F) diversity

Answer Explanation

The correct answers are (A) and (F). Answer Blank (i): The correct answer is "burgeoning," choice (A), which means "growing or developing rapidly." Choice (C), "sprouting," meaning "emerging and developing rapidly," is a close synonym for "burgeoning," but "sprouting" would sound strange in this sentence. Based on the sentence, you can infer that the budget problem has been around for years, so choice (C) doesn't truly fit the context. For this same reason, choice (B), "emerging," is incorrect.

Answer Blank (ii): Choice (F), "diversity," means "variety" as well as "range" and fits the context. Choice (D), "panoply," means "splendid or magnificent collection" and based on the examples in the sentence, this doesn't fit. Choice (E), "plethora," means "overabundance, excessive in number," and while this may be objectively true, the sentence doesn't indicate this, so choice (E) has to be eliminated.

Question

4. In recent recessions economists have noted (i) _____ known as a jobless recovery. A comparison of data shows that the economy begins to grow before the number of jobs increases. This is a(n) (ii) _____ divergence from previous recoveries.

Blank (i)	Blank (ii)
(A) a phenomenon	(D) imperceptible
(B) an episode	(E) precise
(C) an omen	(F) pronounced

Answer Explanation

The correct answers are (A) and (F). Answer Blank (i): Choice (A), "a phenomenon," best fits the context. It means "an unusual or significant fact or occurrence." Choice (B), "an episode," refers to "a single event in a series or sequence," which doesn't fit the context. Choice (C), "an omen," meaning "an indicator of a future event," doesn't fit the context either.

Answer Blank (ii): Choice (F), "pronounced," meaning "distinct, noticeable," fits with the context of a significant difference. Choice (D), "imperceptible," means "difficult to perceive, subtle" and doesn't fit with the idea that a jobless recovery is a phenomenon, which is a significant difference. Choice (E), "precise," means "sharply exact, designating a certain thing and nothing else" and doesn't make sense in the context.

Question

5. Recently passed and more (i) _____ regulations related to energy efficiency are putting pressure on vehicle manufacturers to produce more energy-efficient vehicles. This means new designs for cars, trucks, and buses to meet (ii)_____ emission standards. Another (iii) _____ to change is the growing demand for vehicles powered by alternative fuels.

Blank (i)	Blank (ii)	Blank (iii)
(A) stringent	(D) stricter	(G) force
(B) compliant	(E) disciplined	(H) movement
(C) adaptable	(F) sterner	(I) impetus

Answer Explanation

The correct answers are (A), (D), and (I). Answer Blank (i): "Stringent," choice (A), means "severe, imposing rigorous standards of performance" and fits the context. Choice (B), "compliant," means "willing to comply, obedient" and doesn't make sense in the sentence. Choice (C), "adaptable," means "able to be adapted, changing easily" and may seem like a possible answer, but reading further in the passage, you'll find that "easily changed regulations" don't fit with the answer for the second blank.

Answer Blank (ii): Choice (D), "stricter," meaning "tougher, enforced rigorously" fits the context (and helps you answer the first blank). Choice (E), "disciplined," meaning "obeying the rules" doesn't make sense; the emission standards are the rules. Choice (F), "sterner," doesn't fit because it means "harsh" as applied to a person or "grim or unyielding or relentless," none of which describe emission standards.

Answer Blank (iii): Choice (I), "impetus," means "a force moving forward, an incentive, a stimulus" and fits the context. Choice (G), "force," might work except that usage dictates the phrasing would need to read "another force for change" and the actual wording is "another force to change," radically altering the meaning of the sentence. Choice (H), "movement," might seem correct, but if you read it in the sentence, it doesn't make sense either.

QUESTIONS 6–8 ARE BASED ON THE FOLLOWING PASSAGE.

Luigi Pirandello's 1921 play *Six Characters in Search of an Author* may be considered the first existentialist drama. The play explores the relationship between imaginary characters and the writer who has created them. The premise of the play is that six characters have taken on a life of their own because their author has failed to complete their story. The characters
5   invade a rehearsal of another play by Pirandello and insist on acting out their lives. Somehow there is an immutable reality for these six characters, despite the fact that they are merely the fabrications of a writer. As the play's structure begins to break down, the characters begin to question how anyone can tell when reality ends and pretense begins. Pirandello leaves his audience wondering the same thing.

Question

6. The passage is primarily concerned with
   (A) contrasting the difference between reality and pretense in Pirandello's play.
   (B) comparing how Pirandello's play differed from most others of its time.
   (C) explaining how the structure of Pirandello's play mirrored real life.
   (D) demonstrating how Pirandello challenged his audience's perception of reality.
   (E) showing how the characters in Pirandello's play interacted with one another.

Answer Explanation

The correct answer is (D). The passage describes the way that Pirandello set up characters to question reality and pretense within the play and used this device to challenge the audience similarly. Choice (A) is incorrect because the passage itself doesn't contrast the difference between reality and pretense in the play but describes how it was done. Choice (B) is incorrect because the passage doesn't discuss other plays of the same time period. Choice (C) is incorrect because the play doesn't mirror real life, but in fact questions the difference between real life and pretense. Choice (E) is incorrect because the passage doesn't describe how the characters in the play interacted.

Question

7. "Immutable" (line 6) most nearly means
   (A) variable.
   (B) enclosed.
   (C) unsure.
   (D) flexible.
   (E) enduring.

Answer Explanation

The correct answer is (E). "Immutable "means "enduring or permanent." Choice (A) is incorrect because "variable" means "changeable," which is the opposite of "enduring." Choice (B) is incorrect because "enclosed" means "surrounded on all sides" and doesn't make sense. Choice (C), "unsure," might seem correct, but the rest of the sentence indicates that a meaning that is somehow the opposite of "fabrications" is needed. Choice (D) is incorrect because "flexible" means "adaptable," and in the context of the passage, the characters have nothing to adapt to because they have no play.

Question

8. Select the sentence in the passage in which the author provides a succinct description of Pirandello's play.

(A) Luigi Pirandello's 1921 play *Six Characters in Search of an Author* may be considered the first existentialist drama.

(B) The characters invade a rehearsal of another play by Pirandello and insist on acting out their lives.

(C) Somehow there is an immutable reality for these six characters, despite the fact that they are merely the fabrications of a writer.

(D) The premise of the play is that six characters have taken on a life of their own because their author has failed to complete their story.

(E) As the play's structure begins to break down, the characters begin to question how anyone can tell when reality ends and pretense begins.

Answer Explanation

The correct answer is (D). This sentence offers a short description of the play: six characters take on a life of their own when their author fails to complete their story. Choice (A) is incorrect because this sentence doesn't describe the plot of the play but categorizes it as the first existentialist drama. Choices (B), (C), and (E) are incorrect because these sentences only give details about the play, not a summary.

QUESTIONS 9–10 ARE BASED ON THE FOLLOWING PASSAGE.

The Bialystoker Synagogue in New York City is one of the known stops on the Underground Railroad in New York City and is preserved today as a monument to its "conductors" and the escaping blacks who found safety there. In a corner of what is now the synagogue's women's gallery, there is a small hidden door in the wall. Behind this door is a wooden ladder that
5　leads to an attic with two small windows that dimly light the room. It was here that runaway enslaved blacks were hidden from the authorities until they could make their way to freedom.

　　Although slavery was abolished in New York State in 1827, the Fugitive Slave Law of 1850 made it illegal to help those fleeing slavery. Therefore, New York City was not typically a final destination, but a way-station on the route to Canada. Many safe places in New
10　York City were in neighborhoods that had communities of free blacks, but they also included homes of Quakers, other white abolitionists, and others willing to help blacks on their way to freedom.

　　Because the punishment for helping escaping slaves was severe, there are few records of the secret passageways and safe houses associated with the Underground Railroad. This
15　means that many stops along the Underground Railroad are only speculative and many other stops have yet to be uncovered.

Question

9. Which of the following statements are supported by the passage?

(A) The Bialystoker Synagogue was one of the most important stops on the Underground Railroad.

(B) There may have been other Underground Railroad stops in places of worship.

(C) All escaping slaves passing through New York City would have stopped at the Bialystoker Synagogue.

Answer Explanation

The correct answer is (B). The passage states lists of the variety of places that served as safe houses in New York City and also states that not all Underground Railroad stops have been uncovered. This implies that there may have been other stops in New York City, and some might have been places of worship as well. Choice (A) is incorrect because the Bialystoker Synagogue is not described as an important stop but simply a known stop on the Underground Railroad. Choice (C) is incorrect because though some runaway slaves stopped at the Bialystoker Synagogue, there is nothing to indicate and much to contradict the idea that all escaping slaves stopped at the synagogue. In a hurry to move through the test, don't overlook qualifiers such as "all," "many," "some," and similar words.

Question

10. The author mentions the Fugitive Slave Act in this passage in order to
    (A) introduce an important concept to the reader.
    (B) provide support for an earlier argument.
    (C) provide a possible explanation for other details in the passage.
    (D) reinforce the main point the author is trying to make.
    (E) contrast this detail with earlier information in the passage.

Answer Explanation

The correct answer is (C). Mentioning the Fugitive Slave Act helps explain why runaway slaves needed to hide when they came to New York City on their way to Canada. Choice (A) is incorrect because the Fugitive Slave Act is not a concept that needs to be explained; it's a law. Choice (B) is incorrect because there is no argument earlier in the passage. Choice (D) is incorrect because the Fugitive Slave Act doesn't reinforce the point of the passage; it simply supplies an additional detail. Choice (E) is incorrect because there is no information that contrasts with the mention of the Fugitive Slave Act.

QUESTIONS 11–12 ARE BASED ON THE FOLLOWING PASSAGE.

Recycled plastic bottles can be turned into a soft and durable fiber used to make fleece and other clothing fabrics. The process begins at a recycling plant, where plastic bottles (made of polyethylene terephthalate, or PET) are separated from other materials and sorted. The plastic is chopped coarsely and then crushed into tiny flakes, which are melted in large vats,
5   and the resulting liquid is pushed through a strainer to create fibrous strands. The strands are stretched to make them thinner and stronger, and then cut into short thread-like pieces that can be woven into fabric. Recycling plastic bottles into fiber is an excellent "green" solution because it both keeps them out of landfills and saves the energy that would be needed to manufacture new plastics.

Question

11. The passage provides information on each of the following EXCEPT
    (A) reasons to recycle plastic bottles.
    (B) what recycled plastic bottles can become.
    (C) how plastic can be stretched into fibers.
    (D) the type of plastic bottles used for making fabrics.
    (E) the way different plastics are sorted.

Answer Explanation

The correct answer is (E). Although the passage does mention that plastics are sorted, it doesn't explain the process. Choices (A), (B), (C), and (D) are mentioned in the passage, so they are not the correct answer to the question. For an EXCEPT or a NOT question, you're looking for the answer that doesn't match the passage.

Question

12. The author suggests that recycling old plastic bottles into fiber
    (A) is the best use for them.
    (B) may be only one option out of many.
    (C) saves both time and money.
    (D) is an efficient way to save resources.
    (E) is a time-consuming use of resources.

Answer Explanation

The correct answer is (D). The author explains that recycling old plastic bottles into fiber keeps them out of landfills and saves energy, which ultimately saves resources. Choice (A) is incorrect because the author never suggests that the best use for old plastic bottles is to recycle them into fiber. Choice (B) is incorrect because we are never told about other ways that recycled plastic bottles can be used. Choice (C) is incorrect because neither time nor money is mentioned in this passage. Choice (E) is incorrect because the amount of time involved in the process is not introduced.

QUESTIONS 13–14 ARE BASED ON THE FOLLOWING PASSAGE.

By the end of World War II, European countries were eager to pursue an economic and political amalgamation in order both to increase prosperity in the region and to foster a sense of unity. The European Union, whose origins began in the 1950s, was officially established in 1993. The creation of the Eurozone in 1999 further solidified economic ties between certain
5   European countries. The Eurozone originally consisted of 11 countries, but now includes 17, both in Western and Eastern Europe. Every country that is in the Eurozone must use the euro as its sole legal currency. Monetary rules for the Eurozone are created and maintained by the European Central Bank. Currently, member states have to abide by the rules of the Stability and Growth Pact that was first adopted in 1997. They cannot exceed an annual
10 budget deficit of 3 percent of the gross domestic project or have an inflation rate over 2 percent. Plus all Eurozone countries must maintain a national debt lower than 60% of their gross domestic product.

Question

13. The author's primary purpose in the passage is to

(A) present an overview of the Eurozone.

(B) analyze the rules of the Stability and Growth Pact of the Eurozone.

(C) suggest alternatives to some of the Stability and Growth Pact's rules.

(D) emphasize the importance of the Eurozone.

(E) show why other countries should join the Eurozone.

Answer Explanation

The correct answer is (A). The passage focuses on the formation of the Eurozone and some of its basic rules—an overview, in other words. Choices (B) and (C) are incorrect because the author doesn't attempt to analyze the rules of the Stability and Growth Pact, but only presents some of them, nor does the author suggest any alternatives. Choice (D) is incorrect because the importance of the Eurozone is never suggested. Choice (E) is incorrect because the author doesn't suggest or even imply that other countries should join the Eurozone.

Question

14. "Amalgamation" (line 2) most nearly means

(A) combination.

(B) severance.

(C) melting.

(D) variance.

(E) anomaly.

Answer Explanation

The correct answer is (A). "Amalgamation" means "a combining or uniting." Choice (B) is incorrect because "severance" is a breaking apart, and the second part of the sentence indicates that the nations wanted to foster unity. Choice (C), "melting," means "blending, becoming less visible or distinguishable," which doesn't quite fit the sense of the passage. Choice (D), "variance," means "discord, disagreement, divergence" and is contrary to the facts of the passage. Choice (E), an "anomaly," is something that is different from the usual, and while integration of economic and political interests was an anomaly in Europe at the time, you need to answer the question based solely on the content of the passage, and there is nothing in the passage to indicate this. Therefore, choice (A) is the best choice.

Question

15. The job applicant was _____ in his interview by not telling the interviewer about his lack of credentials.

(A) invidious

(B) disingenuous

(C) artless

(D) clandestine

(E) devious

(F) indirect

Answer Explanation

The correct answers are (B) and (E). "Disingenuous" and "devious," choices (B) and (E), mean "not straightforward, lacking in candor" and fit the context. Choice (A), "invidious," means "unpleasant, offensive, difficult," and there is nothing in the sentence to indicate this. Choice (C), "artless," is the opposite of "disingenuous" and "devious." Choice (D), "clandestine," means "done in secret" and doesn't fit the sense. Choice (F), "indirect" means "roundabout, hinted at," and there is nothing in the sentence to indicate the applicant was hinting at the truth.

Question

16. Studies of the age-old _____ of nature versus nurture have resulted in some interesting results. Studies of identical and fraternal twins have indicated that a sense of humor is the result of nurture rather than nature.

(A) paradox

(B) provocation

(C) enigma

(D) challenge

(E) conundrum

(F) paradigm

Answer Explanation

The correct answers are (D) and (E). Choice (D), "challenge," means "a demanding or stimulating situation or question" and "conundrum," choice (E), is a "puzzling question or problem" and are the better pair of synonyms for the context. Choices (A) and (C), "paradox" and "enigma," are close synonyms, meaning "a seemingly contradictory statement that may be true" and "something seemingly inexplicable, baffling," respectively. Choice (B), "provocation," means "something that provokes or incites, stirring to action" and doesn't fit the context. Choice (F), "paradigm," means "typical example or a relationship of ideas to one another" and doesn't fit, nor does it or choice (B) have synonyms on the list.

Question

17. Mulling over the various plans for the reorganization of the sales department, the vice president and the HR director finally and _____ chose the plan that laid off the most salespeople but kept the benefits at the same level for those who were left.

(A) timidly
(B) diffidently
(C) reticently
(D) stingily
(E) hesitantly
(F) reluctantly

Answer Explanation

The correct answers are (C) and (F). "Reticently" means "reluctantly, unwillingly" and is a synonym for choice (F), "reluctantly." Choices (A) and (B), "timidly" and "diffidently," are synonyms meaning "lacking in self-confidence, shyly." "Timidly" can also mean "hesitantly," choice (E). The fact that there are three similar words should signal that none is correct. There is also nothing to indicate that the two acted timidly. In context, acting reluctantly makes better sense. Choice (D), "stingily," doesn't make sense in the context.

Question

18. The audience sat in rapt attention as the poet read his poetry with _____ in his deep, rich baritone voice.

(A) confidence
(B) grace
(C) fluency
(D) panache
(E) ease
(F) flair

Answer Explanation

The correct answers are (D) and (F). All the choices could fit the sense of the sentence, but there is only one pair of synonyms. Both choice (D), "panache," and choice (F), "flair," mean "distinctive and stylish elegance." Choice (A), "confidence," means "self-assurance." Choice (B), "grace," means "elegance of movement; pleasing, charming." Choice (C), "fluency," means "eloquence." Choice (E), "ease," means "comfortable."

QUESTIONS 19–20 ARE BASED ON THE FOLLOWING PASSAGE.

Groundwater contamination arises when groundwater becomes polluted by various substances, including chemicals, medications, bacteria, viruses, fertilizer, and fuel. Groundwater contamination can also come from polluted runoff from farms or when factories dump manufacturing wastes in waterways. Once groundwater becomes contaminated, it can be
5 very difficult to remove the contaminants. Sometimes filtration systems can be used, but in other cases, the groundwater may be so polluted as to be rendered undrinkable. Since

much of the world's supply of drinking water comes from groundwater, contamination is a serious issue. In communities in some places in the world that cannot afford other sources of water, people may have no other choice than to drink contaminated groundwater with its
10 consequent serious side effects.

Question

19. It can be inferred from the passage that the author would agree with which of the following statements?

(A) Groundwater contamination should be an important consideration of municipal governments.

(B) People should consider using alternate sources of water whenever possible.

(C) Once groundwater contamination is detected, it must be addressed.

Answer Explanation

The correct answers are (A) and (C). The author of the passage makes it clear that groundwater contamination is a serious issue and so it would be important for municipal governments to take it seriously and to address the problem once detected. Choice (B) is incorrect because the author doesn't suggest that groundwater shouldn't be used, only that groundwater contamination should be taken care of, and even says that in some areas people have no alternative.

Question

20. Select the sentence in the passage that best establishes the author's position.

(A) Groundwater contamination can also come from polluted runoff from farms or when factories dump manufacturing wastes in waterways.

(B) Since much of the world's supply of drinking water comes from groundwater, contamination is a serious issue.

(C) Once groundwater becomes contaminated, it can be very difficult to remove the contaminants.

(D) Sometimes filtration systems can be used, but in other cases, the groundwater may be so polluted as to be rendered unpotable.

(E) In communities in some places in the world that cannot afford other sources of water, people may have no other choice than to drink contaminated groundwater with its consequent serious side effects.

Answer Explanation

The correct answer is (B). This statement succinctly establishes the author's position: groundwater contamination is a serious issue. Choices (A), (C), (D), and (E) explain details about groundwater contamination that support the author's position, but they don't state the author's position.

Section 3: Quantitative Reasoning

1. A	11. A	16. A
2. D	12. D	17. B, D
3. A	13. B	18. A, E
4. B	14. D	19. $1304.58
5. C	15. C	20. 28
6. C		
7. C		
8. B		
9. D		
10. E		

Question

1.

Quantity A	Quantity B
$(12)(5)(9)(107)$	$(8)(104)(5)(12)$

(A) Quantity A is greater.

(B) Quantity B is greater.

(C) The two quantities are equal.

(D) The relationship cannot be determined from the information given.

Answer Explanation

The correct answer is (A). Calculate:

$(12)(5)(9)(107) = 57,780$

$(8)(104)(5)(12) = 49,920$

Question

$$a \neq 0$$

a is the reciprocal of B.

2.

Quantity A	Quantity B
B	a

(A) Quantity A is greater.

(B) Quantity B is greater.

(C) The two quantities are equal.

(D) The relationship cannot be determined from the information given.

Answer Explanation

The correct answer is (D). Pick numbers:

If a is $\dfrac{1}{1}$, then B is 1.

If a is 2, then B is $\dfrac{1}{2}$.

If a is $-\dfrac{1}{2}$, then B is -2.

Question

3.   Quantity A   Quantity B

$$\left(\sqrt[3]{86}\right)^2 \qquad\qquad 9$$

(A) Quantity A is greater.
(B) Quantity B is greater.
(C) The two quantities are equal.
(D) The relationship cannot be determined from the information given.

Answer Explanation

The correct answer is (A). Simplify and evaluate:

$$\left(\sqrt[3]{86}\right)^2 > \left(\sqrt[3]{64}\right)^2$$

$$\left(\sqrt[3]{64}\right)^2 = 4^2 = 16$$

$$\left(\sqrt[3]{86}\right)^2 > 9$$

Question

$$\frac{12z}{y} = \frac{x}{2}$$

4.   Quantity A   Quantity B
     $8z$ $3xy$

(A) Quantity A is greater.
(B) Quantity B is greater.
(C) The two quantities are equal.
(D) The relationship cannot be determined from the information given.

Answer Explanation

The correct answer is (B). Simplify and evaluate:

$$\frac{12z}{y} = \frac{x}{2}$$
$$24z = xy$$
$$3xy = 3(24z)$$
$$3xy = 72z$$

Question

Mary is twice as old as Jay was 5 years ago. Jay is twice as old as Sue.
All together they are 15 years older than Mary is now.

5.

	Quantity A		Quantity B
	Mary		Jay

(A) Quantity A is greater.
(B) Quantity B is greater.
(C) The two quantities are equal.
(D) The relationship cannot be determined from the information given.

Answer Explanation

The correct answer is (C). Draw a table and turn words into an equation and solve:

		$x = 5$
Mary	$2(2x-5)$	10
Jay	$2x$	10
Sue	x	5
Total	$2(2x-5)+2x+x$	

$$2(2x-5)+2x+x = 2(2x-5)+15$$
$$2x+x = 15$$
$$3x = 15$$
$$x = 5$$

Question

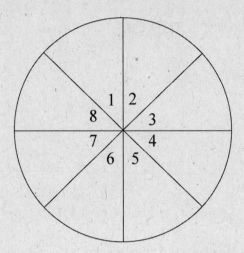

6.
Quantity A	Quantity B
m∠1 + m∠2 + m∠3 + m∠4	m∠3 + m∠4 + m∠5 + m∠6

(A) Quantity A is greater.

(B) Quantity B is greater.

(C) The two quantities are equal.

(D) The relationship cannot be determined from the information given.

Answer Explanation

The correct answer is (C). Calculate:

Supplementary angles sum to = 180

m∠1 + m∠2 + m∠3 + m∠4 = 180

m∠3 + m∠4 + m∠5 + m∠6 = 180

Question

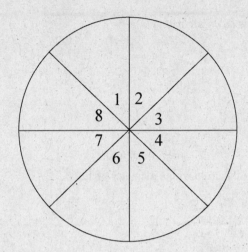

7.   Quantity A   Quantity B
        m∠3 + m∠4 + m∠5   m∠1 + m∠8 + m∠7

   (A) Quantity A is greater.

   (B) Quantity B is greater.

   (C) The two quantities are equal.

   (D) The relationship cannot be determined from the information given.

Answer Explanation

The correct answer is (C). Compare vertical angles:

m∠1 = m∠5
m∠3 = m∠7
m∠4 = m∠8

Question

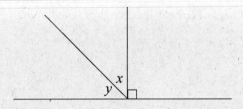

8.   Quantity A   Quantity B
        The mean of x and y 60

   (A) Quantity A is greater.

   (B) Quantity B is greater.

   (C) The two quantities are equal.

   (D) The relationship cannot be determined from the information given.

Answer Explanation

The correct answer is (B). Calculate:

$$x + y = 90$$
$$\frac{x+y}{2} = 45$$

Question

9. What is the area of a circle with a diameter of 12?

    (A) 6π

    (B) 12π

    (C) 24π

    (D) 36π

    (E) 144π

Answer Explanation

The correct answer is (D). Evaluate:

$$d = 2r$$
$$12 = 2r$$
$$6 = r$$

$$area = \pi r^2$$
$$area = \pi 6^2$$
$$area = 36\pi$$

Question

10. A bag of cement weighs 94 pounds and a bag of lime weighs 50 pounds. How many pounds does a shipment of 18 bags of cement and 5 bags of lime weigh?

    (A) 250

    (B) 1,370

    (C) 1,442

    (D) 1,692

    (E) 1,942

Answer Explanation

The correct answer is (E). Turn the words into equations and solve:

$$total = 18(94) + 5(50)$$
$$total = 1,692 + 250$$
$$total = 1,942$$

Question

11. Given $4f + 4g = 14$ and $15h + 15i = 60$, what is the mean of f, g, h, and i?

(A) $1\dfrac{7}{8}$

(B) $2\dfrac{1}{4}$

(C) $8\dfrac{3}{5}$

(D) $12\dfrac{3}{4}$

(E) $18\dfrac{1}{2}$

Answer Explanation

The correct answer is (A). Simplify and evaluate:

$$4f + 4g = 14$$
$$f + g = \frac{7}{2}$$
$$f + g = 3.5$$

$$15h + 15i = 60$$
$$h + i = 4$$

$$f + g + h + i = 4 + 3.5$$
$$f + g + h + i = 7.5$$

$$mean = \frac{f + g + h + i}{4} = \frac{7.5}{4} = 1.875 = 1\frac{7}{8}$$

Question

12. From a well-shuffled deck of cards, what is the probability of drawing a red 8?

(A) $\dfrac{1}{4}$

(B) $\dfrac{1}{13}$

(C) $\dfrac{2}{13}$

(D) $\dfrac{1}{26}$

(E) $\dfrac{1}{52}$

Answer Explanation

The correct answer is (D). Evaluate:

2 ways to draw a red 8

52 total outcomes

$$\frac{2}{52} = \frac{1}{26}$$

Question

13. A right triangle has a base of 12 and a hypotenuse of 13. What is the height of the remaining leg?

    (A) 4
    (B) 5
    (C) 15
    (D) 20
    (E) 25

Answer Explanation

The correct answer is (B). Draw a figure:

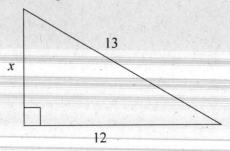

$$x^2 + 12^2 = 13^2$$
$$x^2 + 144 = 169$$
$$x^2 = 25$$
$$x = 5$$

Question

14. To manufacture soft pretzels, there is a built-in cost of $320 to start the machines and an additional cost for materials of $0.05 per pretzel. If the pretzels sell for 4 for $1.00, how many have to be sold to break even for the day?

    (A) 100
    (B) 160
    (C) 320
    (D) 1,600
    (E) 3,200

Answer Explanation

The correct answer is (D). Turn the words into equations and solve:

$0.25p = 320 + 0.05p$

$0.20p = 320$

$p = 1,600$

QUESTIONS 15–17 REFER TO THE TABLE BELOW.

Tahoe and Suburban Sales (number sold)

1995–2009

	Tahoe	Suburban
1995	72,000	70,000
1996	127,000	92,000
1997	127,000	101,000
1998	131,000	110,000
1999	126,000	137,000
2000	150,000	132,000
2001	201,000	152,000
2002	209,000	150,000
2003	197,000	132,000
2004	188,000	118,000
2005	151,000	88,000
2006	160,000	76,000
2007	148,000	83,000
2008	90,000	52,000
2009	71,000	42,000

Question

15. What is the range of vehicles sold between 1995 and 2009?

    (A) 42,000

    (B) 194,000

    (C) 167,000

    (D) 280,000

    (E) 290,000

Answer Explanation

The correct answer is (C). Range is the difference from highest to lowest:

$209,000 - 42,000 = 167,000$

Question

16. If the average price of a Tahoe in 2006 was \$35,600 and the average price of a Suburban in 2006 was \$57,700, what was the total sales number (in dollars) for both vehicles that year?

(A) 1.00812×10^{10}

(B) 1.65712×10^{10}

(C) 2.65712×10^{10}

(D) 2.98112×10^{10}

(E) 3.12912×10^{10}

Answer Explanation

The correct answer is (A). Turn the words into equations and solve:

$$total = 160,000(35,600) + 76,000(57,700)$$
$$total = 5,696,000,000 + 4,385,200,000$$
$$total = 1.00812 \times 10^{10}$$

Question

17. What are the mode and the median of the number of Tahoes sold between 1995 and 2009?

(A) 71,000

(B) 127,000

(C) 131,000

(D) 148,000

(E) 151,000

(F) 180,000

Answer Explanation

The correct answers are (B) and (D). Create a table to help you visualize the information:

71
72
90
126
127
127
131
148
150
151
160
188
197
201
209

Mode is the most repeated number: 127,000.

Median is the middle value: 148,000.

Question

18. What are the two solutions to the equation $x^2 + 3x - 4 = 0$?

(A) -4
(B) -3
(C) -1
(D) 0
(E) 1
(F) 3
(G) 4

Answer Explanation

The correct answers are (A) and (E). Factor:

$x^2 + 3x - 4 = 0$

$(x + 4)(x - 1) = 0$

$x = -4$ or $x = 1$

Question

19. Jack Rosato pays a flat rate business tax in his township of 0.438% on all invoices. He had invoices totaling $297,849.00 last year. What was his township tax bill? (Round your answer to two decimal places.)

$

Answer Explanation

The correct answer is $1304.58. Turn the words into equations and solve:

$0.00438(\$297,849) = \$1304.58$

Question

20. Justin is twice as old as Deven. In 5 years, twice the sum of their ages will be 104. How old is Justin now?

Answer Explanation

The correct answer is 28. Turn the words into equations and solve:

$$J = 2D$$
$$2(J+5+D+5) = 104$$
$$2(2D+5+D+5) = 104$$
$$2(3D+10) = 104$$
$$6D+20 = 104$$
$$6D = 84$$
$$D = 14$$
$$J = 28$$

Section 4: Quantitative Reasoning

1. D	11. B	16. B, D, F
2. C	12. D	17. A, E
3. A	13. A	18. 4
4. B	14. E	19. $\dfrac{35}{12}$
5. C	15. B	20. D
6. D		
7. B		
8. A		
9. B		
10. B		

Question

$$x > 0$$
$$y > 0$$

1.   Quantity A   Quantity B
                    x y

(A) Quantity A is greater.

(B) Quantity B is greater.

(C) The two quantities are equal.

(D) The relationship cannot be determined from the information given.

Answer Explanation

The correct answer is (D). Pick numbers:

x	y
1	2
2	1

Question

2.   Quantity A   Quantity B

$\frac{1}{3}$ of 12 $\frac{1}{4}$ of 16

(A) Quantity A is greater.

(B) Quantity B is greater.

(C) The two quantities are equal.

(D) The relationship cannot be determined from the information given.

Answer Explanation

The correct answer is (C). Evaluate:

$$\frac{1}{3}(12) = 4$$

$$\frac{1}{4}(16) = 4$$

Question

3.   Quantity A   Quantity B

$\frac{1}{5} + \frac{1}{5}$ 0.04

(A) Quantity A is greater.

(B) Quantity B is greater.

(C) The two quantities are equal.

(D) The relationship cannot be determined from the information given.

Answer Explanation

The correct answer is (A). Calculate:

$$\frac{1}{5} + \frac{1}{5} = \frac{2}{5} = 0.4$$

Question

$$x^7 = -128$$

4.   Quantity A   Quantity B
                    x^5 $8x^2$

(A) Quantity A is greater.

(B) Quantity B is greater.

(C) The two quantities are equal.

(D) The relationship cannot be determined from the information given.

Answer Explanation

The correct answer is (B). Evaluate:

$$x^7 = -128$$
$$x = -2$$

$$8x^2 = 8(-2)^2 = 8(4) = 32$$
$$x^5 = -2^5 = -32$$

Question

$$\frac{5}{16}m = \frac{1}{8}$$

5.   Quantity A   Quantity B
                    m $\frac{2}{5}$

(A) Quantity A is greater.

(B) Quantity B is greater.

(C) The two quantities are equal.

(D) The relationship cannot be determined from the information given.

Answer Explanation

The correct answer is (C). Evaluate:

$$\frac{5}{16}m = \frac{1}{8}$$
$$m = \frac{1}{8}\left(\frac{16}{5}\right) = \frac{2}{5}$$

Question

Triangle *ABC* lies on the *xy*-plane with *A* at (0,0), *B* at (4,0), and *C* at (*x,y*).

$$x, y > 0$$
$$area = 24$$

6.   <u>Quantity A</u>   <u>Quantity B</u>

                       x   **6**

(A) Quantity A is greater.

(B) Quantity B is greater.

(C) The two quantities are equal.

(D) The relationship cannot be determined from the information given.

Answer Explanation

The correct answer is (D). Draw a figure:

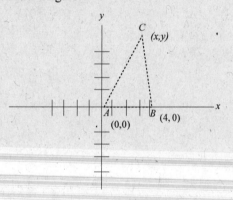

$$area = \frac{1}{2}bh$$

$$24 = \frac{1}{2}4h$$

$$12 = h$$

Therefore, *y* = 12. However, that still does not tell us what *x* equals. *x* could be any positive number, since we don't know anything else about this triangle.

Question

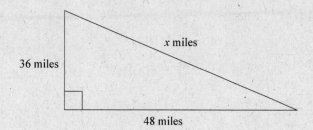

7.   Quantity A   Quantity B
                            x 72

(A) Quantity A is greater.

(B) Quantity B is greater.

(C) The two quantities are equal.

(D) The relationship cannot be determined from the information given.

Answer Explanation

The correct answer is (B). Evaluate:

$$36^2 + 48^2 = x^2$$
$$3600 = x^2$$
$$60 = x$$

Question

$$x + y = 16$$

8.   Quantity A   Quantity B
              Maximum value of xy 63

(A) Quantity A is greater.

(B) Quantity B is greater.

(C) The two quantities are equal.

(D) The relationship cannot be determined from the information given.

Answer Explanation

The correct answer is (A). Evaluate:

x	y	xy
1	15	15
2	14	28
3	13	39
4	12	48
5	11	55
6	10	60
7	9	63
8	8	64

Question

$$8x = 3.2$$
$$y = 4x - 1$$

9.

Quantity A	Quantity B
x	y

(A) Quantity A is greater.

(B) Quantity B is greater.

(C) The two quantities are equal.

(D) The relationship cannot be determined from the information given.

Answer Explanation

The correct answer is (B). Evaluate:

$$x = \frac{3.2}{8} = 0.4$$

$$y = 4x - 1$$
$$y = 4(0.4) - 1$$
$$y = 1.6 - 1 = 0.6$$

Question

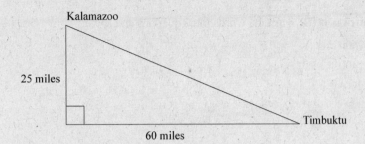

10. How many miles is it from Kalamazoo to Timbuktu?

(A) 68

(B) 65

(C) 66

(D) 63

(E) 64

Answer Explanation

The correct answer is (B). Calculate:

$$25^2 + 60^2 = c^2$$
$$625 + 3600 = c^2$$
$$4225 = c^2$$
$$c = 65$$

Question

11. The local football booster club sells food at all home games. To make the accounting equal, they sell all products for the same price of $1.00. If over the course of the season they sold 4 times as many hot dogs as candy bars, and half as many drinks as hot dogs, and they sold a total of $1400 worth of food, how many drinks did they sell?

(A) 200

(B) 400

(C) 600

(D) 800

(E) 1400

Answer Explanation

The correct answer is (B). Turn the words into equations and solve:

$$x + 4x + 2x = 1400$$
$$7x = 1400$$
$$x = 200$$
$$2x = 400$$

Question

12. Solve for x: $x^{\frac{3}{2}} = 125$

   (A) -25
   (B) -5
   (C) 5
   (D) 25
   (E) 125

Answer Explanation

The correct answer is (D).

$$x^{\frac{3}{2}} = 125$$
$$\left(\sqrt{x}\right)^3 = 125$$
$$x = 25$$

QUESTIONS 13–15 REFER TO·THE GRAPH BELOW.

Vegetable Plant Sales in May

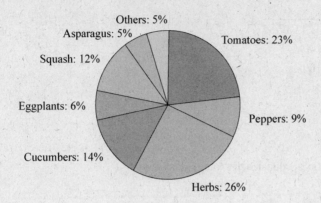

Question

13. If in May the sales of tomato plants were $13,482, what were the sales of all the vegetable plants?

(A) $58,617.39

(B) $59,871.09

(C) $60,740.87

(D) $62,137.83

(E) $63,820.31

Answer Explanation

The correct answer is (A). Turn the words into equations and solve:

$$\frac{23}{100} = \frac{13,482}{x}$$

$$23x = 13,482(100)$$

$$23x = 1,348,200$$

$$x = 58,617.39$$

Question

14. Total vegetation sales in May were $124,717.85. What were the total sales of cucumbers and herbs combined?

(A) $34,675.93

(B) $37,897.02

(C) $40,320.04

(D) $42,739.84

(E) $49,887.14

Answer Explanation

The correct answer is (E). Turn the words into equations and solve:

$$\frac{14+26}{100} = \frac{x}{124,717.85}$$

$$40(124,717.85) = 100x$$

$$4,988,714 = 100x$$

$$49,887.14 = x$$

Question

15. What is the ratio of squash sales to eggplant sales?

(A) $\dfrac{2}{9}$

(B) $\dfrac{2}{1}$

(C) $\dfrac{5}{4}$

(D) $\dfrac{4}{7}$

(E) $\dfrac{6}{11}$

Answer Explanation

The correct answer is (B). Evaluate:

$$\frac{12\%}{6\%} = \frac{2}{1}$$

Question

16. Find the next three numbers in the sequence: 1, –4, 16, –64, …

(A) –4,096

(B) –1,024

(C) –256

(D) 256

(E) 1,024

(F) 4,096

Answer Explanation

The correct answers are (B), (D), and **(F).** Evaluate:

The sequence is formed by multiplying the previous term by (–4)

$1(-4) = -4$
$-4(-4) = 16$
$16(-4) = -64$
$-64(-4) = 256$
$256(-4) = -1,024$
$-1,024(-4) = 4,096$

Question

17. Find the two values for x, where $x^2 + 9x + 11 = 0$.

(A) $x = \dfrac{-9 - \sqrt{37}}{2}$

(B) 11

(C) 1

(D) 9

(E) $x = \dfrac{-9 + \sqrt{37}}{2}$

Answer Explanation

The correct answers are (A) and (E). Evaluate using the quadratic formula:

$$x = \frac{-b \pm \sqrt{b^2 - 4ac}}{2a}$$

$$x = \frac{-9 \pm \sqrt{9^2 - 4(1)(11)}}{2(1)}$$

$$x = \frac{-9 \pm \sqrt{81 - 44}}{2}$$

$$x = \frac{-9 \pm \sqrt{37}}{2}$$

$$x = \frac{-9 - \sqrt{37}}{2}$$

or

$$x = \frac{-9 + \sqrt{37}}{2}$$

Question

18. Jeff is 3 times as old as Billy, who is 2 times as old as Joe. In 7 years, their combined age will be 3 times Jeff's age now, plus 3. How old is Billy now?

Answer Explanation

The correct answer is 4. Turn the words into equations and solve:

	now	+7
Jeff	3(2x)	6x + 7
Billy	2x	2x + 7
Joe	x	x + 7
combined		x + 7 + 2x + 7 + 6x + 7

$$x+7+2x+7+6x+7 = 3(6x)+3$$
$$9x+21 = 18x+3$$
$$18 = 9x$$
$$2 = x$$
$$2(2) = 4$$

Question

19. $\left(\dfrac{1}{3}-2\right)\left(\dfrac{1}{4}-2\right) =$

Give answer as a fraction.

Answer Explanation

The correct answer is $\dfrac{35}{12}$. Evaluate:

$$\left(\frac{1}{3}-2\right)\left(\frac{1}{4}-2\right)$$
$$\left(\frac{1}{3}-\frac{6}{3}\right)\left(\frac{1}{4}-\frac{8}{4}\right)$$
$$\left(-\frac{5}{3}\right)\left(-\frac{7}{4}\right)$$
$$\frac{35}{12}$$

Question

20. A cookie-cutting machine can cut 134 cookies a minute. How many cookies will it cut in an hour and a half?

(A) 90

(B) 201

(C) 8,040

(D) 12,060

(E) 15,080

Answer Explanation

The correct answer is (D). Turn the words into equations and solve:

$1.5(60) = 90$

$90(134) = 12,060$

Section 5: Verbal Reasoning

1. A	11. E	16. D, F
2. E	12. B	17. D, E
3. A, F	13. A	18. C, F
4. A, F, I	14. A	19. B, E
5. B, D, G	15. D	20. C
6. B		
7. E		
8. B, C		
9. B		
10. E		

Question

1. Research on school improvement has found that instruction must convey information _____ to be effective. Lessons that don't proceed logically from A to B to C, confuse, rather than inform.

(A) coherently
(B) smoothly
(C) articulately
(D) cogently
(E) eloquently

Answer Explanation

The correct answer is (A). The context indicates that instruction must be logical, and only choice (A), "coherently," includes the idea of logic; the word means "orderly and logically consistent." Choice (B), "smoothly," means "having no problems or difficulties." Choice (C), "articulately," means "using clear language," which undoubtedly helps instruction, but doesn't fit the context. Choice (D), "cogently," means "appealing to reason, convincing." Choice (E), "eloquently," means "expressing something vividly or movingly."

Question

2. Mechanical weathering, which breaks down rock, includes a number of processes. One is caused by the _____ quality of rock particles. The particles rushing by in water or carried by the wind break down the rocks with which they come in contact.

(A) coarse
(B) rough
(C) rasping
(D) grating
(E) abrasive

Answer Explanation

The correct answer is (E). "Abrasive," choice (E), means "wearing something down." Choice (A), "coarse," meaning "rough," and choice (B), "rough," can be eliminated because all rocks are not rough; some are smooth. Choice (C), "rasping," means "filing or scraping with a file" and can also mean "making a grating sound," so it's a synonym for choice (D), "grating," an annoying sound." Neither fits the context.

Question

3. Critics may consider his style (i)_____ of the worst in advertising art, but he charges (ii) _____ prices for his representational paintings and makes a fortune.

Blank (i)	Blank (ii)
(A) derivative	(D) munificent
(B) a by-product	(E) magnanimous
(C) a complement	(F) exorbitant

Answer Explanation

The correct answers are (A) and (F). Answer Blank (i): "Derivative," choice (A), means "based on something else." Choice (B), "a by-product," is something produced in the making of something else and doesn't fit the sense. Choice (C), a "complement," means "something that completes, making a whole" and doesn't make sense (nor would "compliment").

Answer Blank (ii): "Exorbitant," choice (F), means "excessive, overpriced" and matches the context. Choice (D), "munificent," means "generous, philanthropic, benevolent" and makes no sense in the context. Nor does choice (E), "magnanimous," meaning "generous and understanding, noble."

Question

4. The (i) _____ view of many Americans for years was that the 1950s were a time of peace and prosperity. However, this (ii)_____ version of the time period is (iii)_____ by the racial unrest that erupted in the latter part of the decade.

Blank (i)	Blank (ii)	Blank (iii)
(A) prevailing	(D) implied	(G) concealed
(B) hypothetical	(E) epic	(H) misrepresented
(C) academic	(F) fictional	(I) belied

Answer Explanation

The correct answers are (A), (F), and (I). Answer Blank (i): Choice (A), "prevailing," means "current," and for years that was the current view. Choice (B), "hypothetical," means "possible, theoretical," but based on the passage, the view was accepted as true, so it wasn't hypothetical or theoretical. "Academic," choice (C), also means "theoretical" as well as "speculative" and is incorrect for the same reason.

Answer Blank (ii): Choice (F), "fictional," means "creation of the imagination, invented reality" and fits the context. Choice (D), "implied," is incorrect because the passage doesn't indicate that the view was only hinted at or suggested. Choice (E), "epic," is incorrect because it means "very large or heroic" and doesn't fit the context.

Answer Blank (iii): Choice (I), "belied," means "shown to be false" and matches the sense. Choice (G), "concealed," means "hidden" and would make the sentence read that the racial unrest hid the fictional version of the period. Choice (H), "misrepresented," meaning "falsely represented" is incorrect because it, too, would reverse the meaning of the sentence.

Question

5. His grades in school never seemed (i) _____ with his intelligence, and this (ii) _____ assessment was borne out in his later work life. Known for his (iii) _____ ability to penetrate to the core issues, he rose to become CEO of a Fortune 1000 company.

Blank (i)	Blank (ii)	Blank (iii)
(A) congenial	(D) astute	(G) laser-like
(B) commensurate	(E) practiced	(H) discerning
(C) complaisant	(F) adroit	(I) caustic

Answer Explanation

The correct answers are (B), (D), and (G). Answer Blank (i): Choice (B), "commensurate," means "in proportion to." Choice (A), "congenial," means "agreeable, or similar, compatible" and is used in reference to people, so it doesn't make sense. Choice (C), "complaisant," means "obliging, willing to please" and doesn't make sense either.

Answer Blank (ii): Choice (D), "astute," means "perceptive" and fits the context. Choice (E), "practiced," means "expert because of long experience" and doesn't make sense in the context. Choice (F), "adroit," means "quick or skillful in action or thought," but doesn't quite fit the sense, which requires perception, rather than quickness.

Answer Blank (iii): Choice (H), "discerning," might seem like the correct answer because it means "showing good judgment," but choice (G), "laser-like," meaning "highly focused," better fits with "penetrate." Choice (I), "caustic," means "harsh in tone," and nothing suggests this about the person.

QUESTIONS 6–8 ARE BASED ON THE FOLLOWING PASSAGE.

American artist Mary Cassatt (1845–1926) is noteworthy for being one of the few women artists to succeed professionally during the late nineteenth century. Because of her friendship with Edgar Degas, she was the only American to take part in the 1879 exhibition of French Impressionist artists in Paris. Though Cassatt's style was influenced by the Impressionists,
5   she developed her own unique style and subject matter. It is easy to see the influence of Degas in her paintings, but her interest in Japanese prints is also reflected in many of her paintings. Much of her earliest work portrays women engaging in home activities, such as reading, sewing, or writing letters. After the French exhibition, Cassatt began to explore what she eventually became famous for: paintings of women caring for children. It is through these
10   paintings that Cassatt highlights the often overlooked role in painting of women as mothers.

Question

6. Select the sentence in the passage in which the author notes influences on Cassatt's style.

(A) After the French exhibition, Cassatt began to explore what she eventually became famous for: paintings of women caring for children.

(B) It is easy to see the influence of Degas in her paintings, but her interest in Japanese prints is also reflected in many of her paintings.

(C) Much of her earliest work portrays women engaging in home activities, such as reading, sewing, or writing letters.

(D) It is through these paintings that Cassatt highlights the often overlooked role in painting of women as mothers.

(E) Because of her friendship with Edgar Degas, she was the only American to take part in an 1879 exhibition of French Impressionist artists in Paris.

Answer Explanation

The correct answer is (B). Cassatt's stylistic inspirations were both Degas's paintings and Japanese prints as this statement clearly points out. Choices (A) and (C) are incorrect because these statements explain the themes of Cassatt's later and early paintings but not influences on her style. Choice (D) is incorrect because this statement describes what Cassatt highlighted in her work but not her influencers. Choice (E) is incorrect because this statement describes Cassatt's participation in the Impressionist exhibition, but it doesn't explain influences on her.

Question

7. The author's primary purpose in the passage is to

(A) explain why Mary Cassatt began painting women and children.

(B) argue that Mary Cassatt was a huge influence on later female painters.

(C) suggest reasons that Mary Cassatt's art began to change after the Impressionist exhibition.

(D) analyze the ways that Mary Cassatt was influenced by the Impressionists.

(E) describe the development of Mary Cassatt's artistic style and themes.

Answer Explanation

The correct answer is (E). The passage describes how Mary Cassatt was influenced by Impressionists and Japanese prints but developed her own style and subject matter; in other words, it provides a brief overview. Choice (A) is incorrect because though this information is touched on, the passage doesn't go into any detail about it, so it can't be the primary purpose of the piece. Choice (B) is incorrect because though this might be true, the author neither argues nor mentions this point. Choice (C) is incorrect because although the passage describes how Cassatt's art changed, it doesn't give reasons for the changes. Choice (D) is incorrect because the author never addresses how exactly Cassatt was influenced by the Impressionists.

Question

8. Which of the following statements is supported by the passage?
   (A) Mary Cassatt began to paint women and children as a way to express her frustration with contemporary male artists.
   (B) Mary Cassatt was inspired by several artistic styles from different parts of the world.
   (C) Mary Cassatt expressed a unique perspective through her art.

Answer Explanation

The correct answers are (B) and (C). The passage points out that Cassatt was influenced by the French Impressionists and by Japanese prints. The passage also explores how Cassatt's own style and subject matter were unique. Choice (A) is incorrect because there is nothing in the passage to suggest this.

QUESTIONS 9–10 ARE BASED ON THE FOLLOWING PASSAGE.

Modest Mussorgsky was one of a group of Russian composers known as "The Five" or "The Mighty Handful," whose goal in the late 1800s was to create Russian nationalist music. Mussorgsky's most famous work, the opera *Boris Godunov,* completed in 1873, is the story of the powerful, though flawed Russian tsar who ruled in the early seventeenth century. The
5 opera met with negative criticism from some of Mussorgsky's contemporaries. Another member of "The Five," Nicolai Rimsky-Korsakov, said of *Boris Godunov* that "I adore it for its originality, power, boldness, distinctiveness, and beauty; I abhor it for its lack of polish, the roughness of its harmonies, and, in some places, the sheer awkwardness of the music." Because of this, Rimsky-Korsakov revised the opera after Mussorgsky's death at age forty-
10 one in 1881, correcting what he believed were technical weaknesses in the original score. Rimsky-Korsakov's revised version of *Boris Gudonov* became the preferred edition of the opera. In recent years, however, Mussorgsky's unique style and orchestration have come to be appreciated, even celebrated, and his is the version that opera-goers are more likely to see performed.

Question

9. "Nationalist" (line 2) most nearly means
   (A) loyalty to one's country.
   (B) dedicated to the interests or culture of a nation.
   (C) love of one's country.
   (D) isolationist.
   (E) separatist.

Answer Explanation

The correct answer is (B). Choice (B), "dedicated to the interests or culture of a nation," is the definition of "nationalist." "Loyalty to one's country," choice (A), may prompt nationalism, but it's not the same. Choice (C), "love of one's country," is the definition of "patriotism." Choice (D), "isolationist," is "one who supports a nation's policy of having no political or economic contacts with other nations." Choice (E), "separatist," is "one who advocates breaking ties with a larger political entity."

Question

10. The author suggests that Mussorgsky's work
    (A) lacked polish and technique.
    (B) was well-respected by his contemporaries.
    (C) covered complex themes that were far ahead of their time.
    (D) was too technically challenging to perform in the original.
    (E) was not fully appreciated in his own lifetime.

Answer Explanation

The correct answer is (E). The author points out that it is only recently that audiences have been able to hear Mussorgsky's opera as he wrote it and not in its revised version. Choice (A) is incorrect because the author implies that Mussorgsky's contemporaries may have felt this, but this was in fact not true. Choice (B) is incorrect because the author points out that Mussorgsky's contemporaries had negative criticisms and even revised his work. Choice (C) is incorrect because although this might be true, the passage doesn't mention this issue. Choice (D) is incorrect because this is never implied; the author states simply that Rimsky-Korsakov felt that Mussorgsky's work needed revision.

QUESTIONS 11–13 ARE BASED ON THE FOLLOWING PASSAGE.

Despite advances in medicine and technology, the demand for organ transplants remains much greater than the number of organ donors available. Ironically, this is mainly because of the increasing success rate of organ transplant operations over the years. Early transplant operations often failed because patients' immune systems rejected the foreign organ. However,
5   the introduction of the drug cyclosporine in the 1980s helped solve this problem, and organ transplants subsequently became much more routine, which, in turn, resulted in the need for more organ donations.

Researchers looking for a way to solve this problem have begun to work on developing artificial organs, **though this is still in a highly experimental phase**. So far, laboratories
10   around the world have developed artificial hearts, lungs, livers, and other organs, but with only limited success. Other scientists are working on techniques to grow organs from a patient's own cells, **which could ultimately eliminate the need for organ donors.** Yet because this involves cloning and stem cell research, it also raises ethical questions that make this a much more complicated issue than developing artificial organs.

Question

11. What function do the two groups of words in bold type serve in this passage?

(A) The first presents an argument; the second reinforces the argument.

(B) The first presents an opinion; the second presents final support for the opinion.

(C) The first serves as an intermediate conclusion; the second serves as a definitive conclusion.

(D) The first anticipates the argument's conclusion; the second supports the conclusion.

(E) The first qualifies a fact; the second states a conclusion.

Answer Explanation

The correct answer is (E). The first part sets up the fact that artificial organs are still in the experimental phase, and the second part concludes that organs grown from a patient's own cells could eliminate the need for donors altogether. Choice (A) is incorrect because no argument is presented in the passage. Choice (B) is incorrect because the two statements are not opinions; they can be proven. Choice (C) is incorrect because the first statement is not a conclusion. Choice (D) is incorrect because the passage doesn't set up an argument.

Question

12. It can be inferred from the passage that the author would agree with which of the following statements?

(A) The discovery of the drug cyclosporine made it much harder for people who needed organs to get them.

(B) Scientists should continue to experiment trying to develop organs in order to solve the problem of the organ donor shortage.

(C) The technique of growing organs from patients' own cells is so potentially divisive that it should be discontinued.

Answer Explanation

The correct answer is (B). The point of the passage is to explain that because there is an organ donor shortage, scientists should explore other options for organ transplants. Choice (A) is incorrect because the author points out that the drug cyclosporine made organ transplants easier, not that it made it harder for people to get organs. Choice (C) is incorrect because although the author brings up the ethical questions involved, at no point does the author imply that these experiments should be discontinued because of the issues.

Question

13. If the information in this passage is true, which of the following must also be true?
    (A) Some people who need organ transplants today will not receive them in time.
    (B) Artificial organs will never be a viable option for people needing organ transplants.
    (C) Because of use of the drug cyclosporine, the human body no longer rejects foreign organs.
    (D) Creating organs from patients' own cells will become much easier over time.
    (E) In the future, people will no longer need organ transplants from donor organs.

Answer Explanation

The correct answer is (A). If there is a shortage of organ donations, then it's likely that some people who need organ transplants will not get them. Choice (B) is incorrect because the passage actually implies that artificial organs could be a real option in the future. Choice (C) is incorrect because we can imply that cyclosporine might not work in every case. Choices (D) and (E) are incorrect because although these statements could be true, it is not definite that they must be true.

QUESTIONS 14–15 ARE BASED ON THE FOLLOWING PASSAGE.

The British Commonwealth is composed of fifty-four member countries, most former colonies of Great Britain, with a combined population of nearly 1.8 billion people, or about 30 percent of the world's population. The term "commonwealth" was eventually settled on to describe this collective group of former colonies because many of the older, established colonies of
5 Britain were already self-governing, and it was felt that this "community of nations" could ultimately become a federation of equal nation states. However, this is not how the British Commonwealth developed. Although it has a secretary-general, a position first established in 1965, it has no united policy or principles and no shared institutions. The only feature that all member states share is that they acknowledge the British monarch as symbolic head of
10 the Commonwealth, but fewer than half recognize the monarch as the head of their countries. Even so, the British Commonwealth does serve a purpose: its biennial meetings allow an opportunity for nations of disparate cultures to get together and share their ideas.

Question

14. "Disparate" (line 12) most nearly means
    - (A) incongruent.
    - (B) analogous.
    - (C) homogeneous.
    - (D) tantamount.
    - (E) acclaimed.

Answer Explanation

The correct answer is (A). "Disparate" most nearly means "incongruent, dissimilar, fundamentally different." Choice (B) is incorrect because "analogous" means "similar," as does "homogeneous," choice (C). Choice (D) is incorrect because "tantamount" means "equivalent in some way to another," which is undoubtedly true of the cultures, but doesn't answer the question. Choice (E) is incorrect because "acclaimed" means "respected," which may describe the cultures, but doesn't answer the question.

Question

15. The passage provides information on each of the following EXCEPT
    - (A) how the term "commonwealth" came to be used to describe the mostly former British colonies.
    - (B) what the British Commonwealth nations share in common.
    - (C) the number of people who belong to the British Commonwealth.
    - (D) the most important countries of the British Commonwealth.
    - (E) the general purpose of the British Commonwealth.

Answer Explanation

The correct answer is (D). There is no mention of any of the countries in the British Commonwealth, so choice (D) is the correct answer. Choices (A), (B), (C), and (E) contain information that is found in the passages, so they are incorrect answers to this question.

Question

16. Government economists released a report showing how the _____ housing market was depressing prices across a number of areas in the construction industry.
    - (A) obsolescent
    - (B) outmoded
    - (C) superseded
    - (D) moribund
    - (E) motionless
    - (F) stagnant

Answer Explanation

The correct answers are (D) and (F). "Moribund" means "near death," but it also means "stagnant," choice (F). Choice (A), "obsolescent," means "becoming out of date, obsolete," and is a synonym of "outmoded," choice (B), meaning "unfashionable, no longer useful." The two don't fit the sense of the sentence. Choice (C), "superseded," means "supplanted, set aside" and doesn't fit the sense, nor does choice (E), "motionless," meaning "inactive, not in motion."

Question

17. Many doctors are still _____ digitizing their patients' records. They see the process as expensive and time-consuming and are not convinced of its value.

    (A) wary of
    (B) scrupulous about
    (C) meticulous about
    (D) skeptical about
    (E) dubious about
    (F) critical about

Answer Explanation

The correct answers are (D) and (E). Choices (D) and (E), "skeptical about" and "dubious about," both mean "doubtful." Choice (A), "wary of," meaning "cautious," could fit the sense of the sentence, but there is no synonym for it among the answer choices. Choices (B) and (C), "scrupulous about" and "meticulous about," are near synonyms, but they mean "conscientious, using great care" and "very careful and precise," respectively. While doctors would undoubtedly be careful about entering patient information, that's not the context for the answers. Choice (F), "critical about," means both "being negative about" and "making a careful evaluation" and, whereas the latter definition might work, there is no synonym for the word.

Question

18. Delivered in a defiant tone, the leader's _____ denial of any wrongdoing in his cabinet failed to quell calls for an investigation into the allegations of malfeasance in office.

    (A) qualified
    (B) eligible
    (C) blunt
    (D) intransigent
    (E) intractable
    (F) stark

Answer Explanation

The correct answers are (C) and (F). "Blunt" and "stark," choices (C) and (F), mean "lacking in qualifications or disguise, frank." The opening phrase sets the tone for the sentence, and these are the best choices based on that tone. Choice (A), "qualified," means "limited or modified." Choice (B), "eligible," means "qualified" also, but a "denial" may not be "eligible." Choice (D), "intransigent," might seem like a good choice because it means "uncompromising," but in the sense of "refusing to give in to persuasion," it doesn't fit the context. Choice (E), "intractable," also means "not giving in to persuasion," so it and "intransigent" are synonyms, but they don't fit the sense.

Question

19. The critic applauded the novel for its wit but decried the one-dimensional nature of its characters. Upon reading the review, the novelist railed against the _____ of critics who can't tell that these characters are supposed to be one-dimensional.

   (A) perfidy
   (B) obtuseness
   (C) treachery
   (D) ignorance
   (E) denseness
   (F) inexorableness

Answer Explanation

The correct answers are (B) and (E). The writer is criticizing the critic for his obtuseness and denseness. Choice (B), "obtuseness," means "lacking in perception or intelligence," and choice (E), "denseness," means "the quality or state of lacking intelligence or quickness of mind." Choice (A), "perfidy," means "treachery" and is a synonym of choice (C), "treachery." Although they are a synonym pair, there is no evidence in the passage that the critic betrayed the novelist in any way, so eliminate them. Choice (D), "ignorance," means "lacking in education," and that's unlikely for someone who is a critic by profession. Choice (F), "inexorableness," means "not able to be persuaded," and there is no evidence that the novelist has tried to persuade the critic.

QUESTION 20 IS BASED ON THE FOLLOWING PASSAGE.

Although there are many serious consequences resulting from the destruction of tropical rainforests, perhaps the most significant is that of climate change. Tropical rainforests can absorb about 20 percent of the world's carbon dioxide emissions from the atmosphere, but as rainforests are cut down, less carbon dioxide is absorbed. In addition, by slashing and
5 burning the rainforests, human activities are adding huge amounts of carbon dioxide to the atmosphere, even more than is emitted by factories, planes, and automobiles all over the world. Ultimately, as deforestation continues, the amount of carbon dioxide and other greenhouse gas levels in the atmosphere will rise. This will, in turn, lead to an increase in temperature, eventually resulting in a change in weather patterns and sea levels.

Question

20. The author suggests which of the following will happen in the future if deforestation continues?
    (A) There will be no tropical rainforests left in the world.
    (B) The Earth's temperature will rise each year.
    (C) Less carbon dioxide will be absorbed from the atmosphere.

Answer Explanation

The correct answer is (C). The relationship between carbon dioxide and rainforests is clearly spelled out in the passage, and a reader could accurately infer this idea from the passage. Choice (A) might seem correct, but the author doesn't imply that all the rainforests will be cut down. Choice (B) might also seem correct, but a conclusion this specific is neither stated nor implied.

APPENDIXES

Common Errors
in Grammar and
Mechanics

The rubrics for both the argument task and the issue task have expectations in regard to both grammar and mechanics. One of the ways a writer can gain a score of 6 is to "demonstrate facility with the conventions of Standard English (i.e., grammar, usage, and mechanics), but [the essay] may have minor errors." The question is: How "minor" are minor errors? The rubric goes on to indicate that errors "in grammar, usage or mechanics . . . can interfere with meaning." That's the real problem with errors in grammar and mechanics—no matter how minor, they can hinder the reader's understanding of your ideas. Certain errors can stop a reader dead and, thus, interrupt the flow of the ideas that you want to get across. Certain "minor errors" can force the reader to reread the sentence or even a couple of sentences to try to figure out what you mean.

Common Errors in Grammar and Mechanics is neither extensive nor exhaustive, but it focuses on those common problems with sentence construction that trip up many writers, including the best ones occasionally. This information should help you avoid some of the errors that can throw your meaning into question and detract from your analysis. It also highlights some problems with pronouns that, if consistently present, may detract from your score. You won't have much time to edit your response, so concentrate on possible problems in the order that you see here:

- Sentence Faults
- Misplaced Modifiers
- Subject-Verb Agreement
- Pronoun Problems
- A Few Additional Words of Advice

SENTENCE FAULTS

The most important idea to take away from this section on sentence faults is that fixing these problems is not just a matter of cleaning up grammar; it's a matter of making decisions that will make it easier for your reader to understand your ideas. There are three sentence faults, or problems with sentence constructions, that you should be aware of as you write and proofread your responses. You won't have time to do much editing, so concentrate on finding and correcting these three problems first as you review your responses. They can seriously detract from meaning and hinder your reader's understanding of your thesis.

Comma Splice

A comma splice occurs when two or more independent clauses are joined only by a comma.

Sam decided to go back for his <u>umbrella, Jack</u> thought he would get his, too.

641

You can fix a comma fault by separating the two clauses completely with a period, or by separately them less completely with a semicolon. In the example sentence, the ideas are so closely related that a semicolon could be considered the better choice.

> Sam decided to go back for his umbrella; Jack thought he would get his, too.

You can also fix a comma fault by using a coordinating or a subordinating conjunction to join the two clauses.

- With a coordinating conjunction, the two clauses remain equal in importance.
- With a subordinating conjunction, one clause becomes subordinate to the other.

This decision isn't just a matter of grammar; it's a matter of meaning. It's a choice that you, as the writer, need to make. Are the ideas equally important? Or, is there one idea that you want to emphasize over the other? Perhaps you decide that the two ideas are equally important, and you choose to use a coordinating conjunction to connect the two ideas/clauses.

Coordinating Conjunctions

The coordinating conjunctions are:

and	for	so
but	nor	yet
or		

With a coordinating conjunction:

> Sam decided to go back for his umbrella, **and** Jack thought he would get his, too.

If you decide that one idea is more important than the other, then you need to emphasize that idea. That idea becomes the main clause of the new sentence, and the second idea becomes the dependent, or subordinate, clause. Then you need to use a subordinating conjunction to fix the comma fault.

With subordinating conjunction:

> **When** Sam decided to go back for his umbrella, Jack thought he would get his, too.

Subordinating Conjunctions

The following are commonly used subordinating conjunctions:

after	if	until
although	in case that	unless
as far as	no matter how	when
as soon as	now that	whenever
as if	once	where
as though	provided that	whereas
because	rather than	wherever
before	since	whether
even if	so that	while
even though	though	why
how		

Run-on Sentence

A run-on sentence has two or more independent clauses that are not connected by either punctuation or a conjunction.

> Sam took his wife's yellow <u>umbrella he</u> couldn't find his when he left for work.

Like comma splices, you can fix a run-on sentence by separating the two clauses with a period if the ideas are equal in importance. If the ideas are equal in importance and closely related, then use a semicolon between the two clauses.

> Sam took his wife's yellow umbrella; he couldn't find his when he left for work.

If the sentences are not equal in importance, the easiest way to correct the problem is with a subordinating conjunction.

> Sam took his wife's yellow umbrella *because* he couldn't find his when he left for work.

However, there are additional ways to solve the problem with a run-on sentence. You could use a conjunctive adverb or a transitional phrase. Both may require some rewriting of the original sentence.

With a conjunctive adverb:

> Sam couldn't find his umbrella when he left for work; *consequently,* he had his wife's yellow umbrella.

With a transitional phrase:

> Sam couldn't find his umbrella when he left for work. *As a result,* he had his wife's yellow umbrella.

There are a variety of conjunctive adverbs and transitional phrases you can use to solve run-on sentence problems.

TIP

Often in trying to get thoughts down in a timed situation like answering the Analytical Writing tasks, some writers tend to write a series of simple sentences. As you review your responses, if you have a number of simpler sentences in a row, try to combine some of them into a variety of sentences such as compound (using coordinating conjunctions), complex (using subordinating conjunctions, conjunctive adverbs, and transitional phrases), and compound-complex sentences (using both coordinating conjunctions and the other connectors listed in this section).

Conjunctive Adverbs

also	incidentally	now
anyhow	indeed	otherwise
anyway	likewise	similarly
besides	meanwhile	still
consequently	moreover	then
finally	nevertheless	therefore
furthermore	next	thus
however	nonetheless	

Transitional Phrases

after all	by the way	in other words
as a consequence	even so	in the first place, in the second
as a result	for example	place, etc.
at any rate	in addition	on the contrary
at the same time	in fact	on the other hand

Like fixing comma splices; fixing run-on sentences is not just a matter of cleaning up a grammar problem. It's a matter of deciding what you want to say—what's important—and choosing the best solution to make your meaning clear.

Sentence Fragment

A sentence fragment is a group of words that has a period at the end, but does not express a complete thought. It may have a verb form, that is, a verbal such as a participle, but that's not the same as a verb.

Sam *carrying* a yellow umbrella to the office.

The following are possible corrections of the problem depending on time:

Sam *is carrying* a yellow umbrella to the office.

Sam *carries* a yellow umbrella to the office.

Sam *was carrying* a yellow umbrella to the office.

Sam *carried* a yellow umbrella to the office.

There are several types of sentence fragments in addition to the example above and several ways to correct them.

A subordinate clause alone:

Because he thought it would rain. Sam was carrying his umbrella.

Rewritten as a subordinate clause:

Because he thought it would rain, Sam was carrying his umbrella.

A phrase:

> Sam was ready for rain. *First, his umbrella and then his raincoat.*

Rewritten as a sentence:

> Sam was ready for rain. ***First, he took out his umbrella and then his raincoat.***

A prepositional phrase:

> Sam was impatient for the bus to come. *Kept looking up the street for it.*

Combined and rewritten as a single new sentence:

> ***Sam, impatient for the bus to come, kept looking up the street for it.***

This is an example of a writer's judgment. The writer decided that being impatient was less important to the context of what he or she wanted to say than looking up the street for the bus.

About Using Dashes

Use dashes sparingly. They often mark the work of writers who don't have a command of standard English, don't know how to develop ideas clearly, or have little to say. Use dashes if you want to show a break in thought, or to emphasize a parenthetical idea, for example, ". . . would be a sufficient reason—unless you are a dog owner."

Misplaced Modifiers

A misplaced modifier is any word, phrase, or clause that does not refer clearly and logically to other words or phrases in the sentence. There are two problems involving misplace modifiers.

The first occurs when a word, phrase, or clause is not close to the part of the sentence that it refers to, thus confusing the reader.

> Sam *wrote* that he was taking her umbrella *in the note he left his wife.*

A clearer version is:

> Sam ***wrote in the note*** he left his wife that he was taking her umbrella.

> Sam's *wife* was annoyed because now she didn't have an umbrella *who is usually very easy-going*.

A clearer version is:

> Sam's ***wife who is usually very easy-going*** was annoyed because now she didn't have an umbrella.

> At the bus stop, Sam didn't see the *bus trying to stay dry under his umbrella.*

The bus was trying to stay dry under the umbrella? Interesting mental picture, but try:

> At the bus stop, ***Sam trying to stay dry under his umbrella*** didn't see the bus.

NOTE

It's worth repeating again that the names of the parts of speech are irrelevant. What you need to remember are the different problems you might run into in your writing and how to solve them.

An easy way to rec-
ognize a participle is
by the *-ing* ending.
Not all participles end
in *-ing* in English, but
many do.

The second and more major problem with misplaced modifiers occurs when a phrase introduced by
a verbal (a word formed from a verb but functioning as a different part of speech) such as a participle
doesn't relate clearly to another word or phrase in the sentence. The problem is often the lack of a
clear relationship between the subject of the sentence and the phrase.

> *Holding the umbrella sideways, the car* splashed him anyway.

In this sentence, the true subject is missing. It seems that the car was holding the umbrella sideways
when the writer meant:

> ***Holding the umbrella sideways, Sam*** was splashed by the car anyway.

> *On entering the bus, there* were no seats.

Who entered the bus?

> ***On entering the bus, Sam saw*** there were no seats

> *Hot and tired, that* was the perfect end to a perfect day thought Sam ironically.

What? Try instead:

> Hot and tired, Sam thought ironically it was the perfect end to a perfect day.

The above examples are all simple so that you can easily see the problem and the correction. But
the following example shows what can happen when a writer writes quickly to get thoughts down.
See if you can spot the errors in this excerpt from a response to an issue task and how you think
they should be fixed.

> The arts make an important contribution to the economy of communities
> across the nation this is true. Even when the economy is in trouble.
> Governments should fund arts programs. When arts programs thrive,
> tax receipts flow into government coffers. It's not just the artists who
> make money. But people who work in allied businesses. For example,
> my small city has a live theater company that produces three plays a year
> plus has several concerts and dance programs. Having no other theater
> for a 75-mile radius, it brings in people from the region. These people
> go to dinner at local restaurants they park in a garage near the theater if
> they come early, they shop in local stores. All this brings in money to
> stores and restaurant that have to hire people to serve these theatergoers.
> Every sale means sales tax for the city and for the state, jobs and income
> taxes for the state and the federal government.

A revised version might read like this:

> The arts make an important contribution to the economy of <u>communities.</u>
> <u>Across</u> the nation this is true. Even when the economy is in <u>trouble,</u>
> <u>governments</u> should fund arts programs. When arts programs thrive, tax
> receipts flow into government coffers. It's not just the artists who make
> <u>money, but</u> also people who work in allied businesses. For example, my
> small city has a live theater company that produces three plays a year
> plus has several concerts and dance programs. <u>Having no other theater</u>

for a 75-mile radius, people come to my city from across the region. These people go to dinner at local restaurants and park in a garage near the theater. If they come early, they shop in local stores. All this brings in money to stores and restaurants that have to hire people to serve these theatergoers. Every sale means sales tax for the city and the state and jobs and income taxes for the state and the federal government.

As you can see from the examples in this section, it is often necessary to rework sentences to establish the clear relationship between the misplace word, phrase, or clause and the word it modifies. Keep this in mind as you revise your practice drafts so that on test day, you'll be able to spot problems quickly and know a range of options for correcting them.

Subject-Verb Agreement Problems

The following are probably two rules that you've heard a thousand times:

- A singular subject takes a singular verb.
- A plural subject takes a plural verb.

However, the correct subject-verb agreement can still elude a writer when several words, phrases, or even a subordinate clause comes between the subject and the verb. This is especially true when the subject is singular, but a plural noun ends a prepositional phrase just before the verb, or vice versa. Such an error usually doesn't impede understanding and one or two won't hurt your score, but try for as few of these problems as possible.

Sam's *umbrella* along with his briefcase and gym *shoes were* under his desk.

The correct version may sound odd to your ear, but the verb should be *was*.

Sam's *umbrella* along with his briefcase and gym shoes *was* under his desk.

Here's a plural subject-verb agreement problem:

The *umbrellas*, which belonged to Sam and Jack and were a riot of color, *was* a welcome sight on the gray day.

In this example, the comma after "color" should clue you that "color" can't be the subject of the verb.

The *umbrellas,* which belonged to Sam and Jack and were a riot of color, *were* a welcome sight on the gray day.

Pronoun Problems

There are a variety of pronouns and a variety of problems you can get into when using them. The most common problems involve using incorrect forms, having unclear antecedents, and confusing pronouns with other words. One or two or even three mistakes with pronouns shouldn't be reflected in your score, but consistent mistakes throughout your response could cause you to lose a point. Unclear antecedents are a meaning issue; if the reader can't tell to whom or to what you're referring, that can affect meaning.

Unclear Antecedents for Pronouns

The antecedent is the word that the pronoun refers to, or stands in for, in the sentence. When you review your essays, check for any problems with clarity so that the reader will have no difficulty in telling to whom or to what pronouns refer.

> Jack and Sam went back to their offices to get their umbrellas because it was starting to rain. They were gone for a few minutes because ***theirs*** were across the floor from the elevator.

A clearer version is:

> Jack and Sam went back to their offices to get their umbrellas because it was starting to rain. They were gone for a few minutes because ***their offices*** were across the floor from the elevator.

Incorrect Forms

Is it *I* or *me, she* or *her, he* or *him, we* or *them*? Most people don't have trouble figuring out which pronoun to use when the subject of a sentence or clause is singular. The trouble comes when the subject is plural.

> *Her* and I went. *Him* and I went. We and *them* went, or even, *us* and *them* went.

The sentences should read:

> ***She*** and I went. ***He*** and I went. ***We*** and they went.

Objects of verbs and prepositions (*of, for, in, on,* etc.) are another problem area for pronoun forms.

> The umbrellas belong to him and *I*, or even, to *he* and *I*.

> The umbrellas belong to her and *I*, or even, to s*he* and *I*.

> The umbrellas belong to them and *I*, or even, to *they* and *I*.

The correct sentences are:

> The umbrellas belong to ***him*** and ***me***.

> The umbrellas belong to ***her*** and ***me***.

> The umbrellas belong to ***them*** and ***me***.

Confusing Pronoun Forms with Other Words

You've probably heard these rules in every English/language arts class you've ever taken, but they're worth repeating because many writers still make these errors.

- **it's or its**

It's is a contraction that stands for *it is: **It's*** raining. (***It is*** raining.)

Its is an adjective that modifies a noun: The dog got ***its*** coat wet because ***it's*** raining.

An easy way to test which word you should use is to substitute *it is* in the sentence: The dog got ***it is*** coat wet because ***it is*** raining. "It is coat" doesn't make sense, so it must be "***its*** coat."

- **who's or whose**

This pair of often confused words is similar to the problem—and the solution—with *it's* and *its*. *Who's* is a contraction that stands for *who is*: **Who's** going to take an umbrella? (**Who is** going to take an umbrella?)

Whose is an interrogative pronoun that shows possession: **Whose** umbrella will we take?

Like testing out *it's* and *its*, substitute *who* and *whose* into the sentence: **Who is** going to take **who is** umbrella? "Who is umbrella" doesn't make sense, so it must be "*whose* umbrella."

- **they're, their, or there**

They're is a contraction that stands for *they are*: **They're** going to take umbrellas. (**They are** going to take umbrellas.)

Their is a possessive adjective that shows possession or ownership: Jack and Sam are taking **their** own umbrellas.

There is a pronoun that is used to introduce a clause or a sentence when the subject comes after the verb: **There** were no umbrellas in the closet.

Substitute *they are* in a sentence to see if the substitution makes sense: **They are** looking in **they are** desks for umbrellas. "They are desks" makes no sense, so it must be "*their* desks."

Knowing the difference between *there* and the other two forms is something you must learn; there's no easy solution, which brings up the issue of *there's* and *theirs*.

Theirs is a form of the personal pronoun that shows ownership in the third person (as opposed to the first person [*mine, ours*] or the second person [*yours*]): Those umbrellas are **theirs.** (The umbrellas belong to certain people.)

There's is a contraction that stands for *there is*: **There's** no umbrella in the closet. (**There is** no umbrella in the closet.)

Substitute *there is* in the sentence: **There is** one umbrella, but I doubt that it's either one of *there is*. "There is" at the end of the sentence doesn't make sense, so it must be *theirs,* meaning something belonging to two or more.

A Few Additional Words of Advice

Please keep these ideas in mind as you write and revise your responses:

- **Use Active Voice Whenever Possible.** Passive voice (the parts of the verb *to be*) can weaken your writing. Instead of "Ticket sales were underwritten by a grant," try "a grant underwrote ticket sales."

- **Get Rid of Redundancies.** Avoid wordiness and redundancies just to fill up space. It's the quality of your thoughts that counts toward your score, not the length. Repetition and wordiness can mask a good analysis.

- **Don't Use Jargon, Clichés, and Slang.** Jargon (a strange, outlandish, or barbarous language or dialect) doesn't fit the tone and style required to answer either an issue or an argument task. The use of clichés (trite or overused expressions or ideas) can indicate that the writer is (1) not a very original thinker or (2) trying to fill up space. Slang doesn't fit the tone or style either.

FOUR STEPS TO HELP YOU PRACTICE YOUR GRAMMAR SKILLS

1. To practice what you've learned about correcting common errors that can affect your comprehension, choose four pieces of writing that you've done recently that are about the same length as the Analytical Writing tasks on the GRE. Review each one to see if you have any of the errors that are described in this section. Revise any errors that you find.

2. Review the two tasks on the Diagnostic Test and any of the Practice Tests (if you have already taken them). Correct any errors that you find.

3. Keep the concepts from this feature in mind as you write any of the remaining writing tasks on the Practice Tests. After you evaluate and score each one, go back and correct any errors. The fewer the errors in Standard English, the better the chance of a score of 5 or 6 on the GRE and the better presentation you'll make in any written document in your professional life.

4. **Remember:** Errors like the ones described in these pages can make it difficult for the reader to understand your ideas, and that can affect your score.

Often Confused and Confusing Words

The confusion with these words may not come from a misunderstanding of their meaning, but rather from a problem of misspelling. As you review the word pairs in this section, pay special attention to the spelling of each word as well as its meaning.

A

accept: (verb) to receive
except: (preposition) excluding or omitting
    (conjunction) other than, but
He bought all the tulips *except* the white ones.
He would have *accepted* the award in person *except* he was in Hong Kong.

accuse: (verb) to blame
allege: (verb) to state as a fact something that has yet to be proven
He was *accused* of white collar theft and was *alleged* to have stolen $5 million.

adopt: (verb) to take as one's own
adapt: (verb) to change
adept: (adjective) very skilled
Adept at organizational design, she *adopted* the plan and then *adapted* it to her unit's needs.

advice: (noun) opinion
advise: (verb) to express an opinion
He *advised* the accused on his rights, but his *advice* was ignored.

affect: (verb) to influence; to pretend
effect: (noun) result or outcome
   (verb) to bring about (less common usage)
He was able to *affect* her decision, but the *effect* was minimal.
Her downfall was *effected* by her arrogance.

aggregate: (noun) collection of separate parts into a whole
    (verb) to combine into one
total: (noun) a whole without regard to its parts
  (verb) to add up
The *aggregate* budget deficits for the five largest cities *totaled* more than $100 billion; the *total* was staggering.

alternate: (adjective) happening in turns, first one and then the other
    (verb) to take turns
alternative: (noun) choice between two mutually exclusive options
Rather than always meeting on the third Thursday of the month, the *alternative* was to *alternate* between third Thursdays and Tuesdays.

allude: (verb) to refer indirectly to a person, object, or event
elude: (verb) to evade or slip away from
The candidate *alluded* to her opponent by mimicking his answer that "the nuances of the Iran policy *elude*" some who would serve on the foreign affairs committee.

allusion: (noun) reference or mention of something or someone
illusion: (noun) mistaken perception of reality
In an effort to create the *illusion* of erudition in his paper, the student used many *allusions* to Shakespearian characters and themes.

ambivalent: (adjective) holding conflicting wishes, unable to decide, unsure
ambiguous: (adjective) difficult to understand, having more than one interpretation
He was *ambivalent* about the promotion because the new job description was *ambiguous* about to whom he actually reported: the CFO or the COO.

anachronism: (noun) person or object placed in the wrong time
anomaly: (noun) departure from the norm; peculiar, irregular, abnormal
The play had a number of *anachronisms*, but the worst was the presence of a telephone in an 1850s parlor; then there was the greatest *anomaly:* a zombie as the house maid.

arbitrate: (verb) to settle a dispute in a legal sense
mediate: (verb) to act as a go-between, to negotiate between parties
Jack was called in to *arbitrate* between management and the union when the judge ordered an injunction against the strikers.
Will had to *mediate* a dispute between his sons over whose turn it was to have the car.

authoritarian: (adjective) having complete power, expecting complete obedience
authoritative: (adjective) official, very reliable; exercising power
The president was *authoritarian* in his manner because the military backed him up.
The president had a very *authoritative* manner in dealing with his ministers.
This edition of the play is the *authoritative* version; no scholar questions that it represents the author's complete changes.

C

condemn: (verb) to express disapproval
condone: (verb) to excuse, to overlook; to forgive
The dictator *condemned* the protesters as criminals, but he *condoned* the methods his soldiers used to suppress the protesters.

complaisant: (adjective) desirous of pleasing an other
complacent: (adjective) pleased with one's self
The members up for re-election were *complacent,* thinking their record in office was sufficient for re-election. They saw no need to be *complaisant* toward the voters and were soundly defeated as a result.

complement: (noun) completing a whole, satisfying a need
       (verb) to complete a whole, to satisfy a need
compliment: (noun) praise
       (verb) to praise
The full *complement* of engineers who worked on the project was *complimented* on their diligence. The work of the engineers *complemented* the work of the programmers—all of whom received *compliments* on their work.

contention: (noun) point made in an argument; dispute, controversy, quarrel
contentious: (adjective) quarrelsome, always ready to argue
The board meeting turned *contentious* with the *contention* by the new member that the director was out of order.

continual: (adjective) recurring regularly or frequently
continuous: (adjective) occurring without interruption
constantly: (adverb) regularly recurring
The faucet was leaking constantly, and I couldn't stand the *continual* drip-drip; it was worse than the sound of a *continuous* stream of water would have been.

credible: (adjective) believable, plausible
credulous: (adjective) too ready to believe, gullible
The plaintiff's testimony that she had bought drugs on the street thinking they were incense was *credible* only to the *credulous* member of the jury who had recently moved to the city.

D

defective: adjective: faulty, flawed
deficient: adjective: lacking some essential part, inadequate
The *defective* part didn't work; it was *deficient*.

deterrent: (noun) something that keeps another from doing something
detriment: (noun) something that causes harm or loss
Star Wars was supposed to be a *deterrent* to war with the Soviet Union, but it was considered by many to be a *detriment* to increased funding for the conventional army.

disinterested: (adjective) impartial
uninterested: (adjective) bored
The mediator was a *disinterested* party to the dispute between the couple, one of whom yawned constantly and seemed *uninterested* in the proceedings.

distinct: (adjective) unmistakable, clear
distinctive: (adjective) something that sets a person or thing apart from everything else, characteristic
I had the *distinct* impression that she wore a red scarf with every outfit so she would be *distinctive* in a roomful of her peers.

discrete: (adjective) separate, distinct, unconnected
discreet: (adjective) prudent, unobtrusive, diplomatic
The scientist was examining *discrete* bits of evidence and finding that they did not support his colleague's theory, but he was *discreet* about his findings until he was sure.

E

elicit: verb: to draw out, to call forth
illicit: adjective: unlawful
The lawyer was able to *elicit* from the witness information about the *illicit* bank transactions.

endemic: (adjective) prevalent in a particular area or among a particular group or region
epidemic: (adjective) spreading rapidly
          (noun) outbreak of a contagious disease
With the availability of air travel, an *epidemic* has the potential to spread quickly from being *endemic* to a country to being global.

energize: (verb) to give energy to, to invigorate
enervate: (verb) to weaken
I find that exercise *energizes* me rather than *enervates* me; I find that I am more alert and ready to tackle work after a good run.

expatiate: (verb) to enlarge on, to speak or write at length
expiate: (verb) to make amends for, to make up for
The professor *expatiated* on his favorite poet oblivious to the growing restlessness in his class. In an effort to *expiate* for his digression, the professor dismissed the class early.

expedient: (adjective) suitable, appropriate
          (noun) means to an end
expeditiously: (adjective) acting quickly and efficiently
The *expedient* thing to do was to process the woman's visa request as *expeditiously* as possible so she could visit her ill mother.

F

fortuitous: (adjective) occurring by chance or accident; happening by a lucky chance
fortunate: (adjective) being lucky, having good luck
Jack's winning the lottery was *fortuitous* because it means he'll be *fortunate* enough to begin his career with no debt.

H

humane: (adjective) marked by mercy, kindness, or compassion
humanitarian: (adjective) having the best interests of humankind at heart
          (noun) philanthropist
Mother Theresa was a great *humanitarian*; she believed that everyone, even the poorest of the poor, deserved *humane* care.

hypercritical: (adjective) excessively critical, overcritical
hypocritical: (adjective) insincere, expressing feelings or virtues that one doesn't have
The review panel's analysis was *hypercritical,* finding fault even with the feeding times used. The chief reviewer expressed sympathy with the lead researcher who thought him *hypocritical* because the two often competed for the same grants.

I

imply: (verb) to suggest indirectly
infer: (verb) to draw a conclusion from
The report *implied* that the deal was fraudulent, and I *inferred* from the details that the executive was the culprit.

incipient: (adjective) beginning to appear, emergent
insipid: (adjective) lacking spirit, dull boring; lacking taste or flavor
The *incipient* revolt was quashed by the army before it could attract many followers.
Lacking in flavor, the tea was as *insipid* as the dull host's conversation was boring.

ingenious: (adjective) inventive, skillful; clever; shrewd
ingenuous: (adjective) candid, frank, straightforward
ingénue: (noun) naïve young woman or girl
Casting the college student as the *ingénue* was *ingenious*; she is perfect for the part of an *ingenuous* newcomer to Broadway.

insoluble: (adjective) unable to dissolve; unable to solve
insolvent: (adjective) unable to pay debts, bankrupt
Why two chemicals when mixed together were *insoluble* in water was an *insoluble* (also spelled *unsolvable*) problem for the chemistry class.
The company was *insolvent* and filed for Chapter 11 bankruptcy.

intense: (adjective) extreme, using great effort
intensive: (adjective) concentrated, making heavy use of something
The six-week immersion course in Spanish was *intensive* and was a very *intense* experience.

J

judicial: (adjective) relating to the courts
judicious: (adjective) showing good judgment
Certain *judicial* appointments below the Supreme Court require Senate confirmation, and presidents attempt to be *judicious* in selecting nominees who will win confirmation without heated debate.

M

marshal: (verb) to arrange in order; to solicit, to guide
martial: (adjective) relating to war or a fighter
Before applying for a license, the businessman *marshaled* support for his *martial* arts studio from the other storefront businesses.

N

negligible: (adjective) insignificant, unimportant
negligent: (adjective) lacking attention to something, careless
The attorney was *negligent* in not telling his witness of the change in court dates. However, the effect on the case was *negligible*.

P

populace: (noun) general public, population
populous: (adjective) having a large population
Much of the *populace* lived in the *populous* suburbs of the three major cities.

precede: (verb) to go before
proceed: (verb) to continue
He waved for the woman to *precede* him through the door, and then they *proceeded* down the hall together.

precipitate: (verb) to cause to happen sooner than expected
precipitous: (adjective) hasty, acting without thinking
The prime minister's refusal to fire his cabinet secretary *precipitated* a call for elections in June rather than September. The opposition may find that the move was *precipitous* because its poll numbers are falling steadily.

prescribe: (verb) to establish a rule or guide; to order medicine
proscribe: (verb) to forbid, to prohibit
The doctor *prescribed* an antibiotic for the infection.
The judge *proscribed* any further contact between the two parties to the lawsuit.

proceeding: (noun) course of action, sequence of events, legal action
preceding: (adjective) coming before
The juvenile *proceeding* took place in the judge's chamber, *preceding* the regular court cases for the day.

R

reversal: (noun) turning around
reversion: (noun) turning back
The *reversal* of the appeal required a *reversion* of the patent to the company's former employee.

S

simple: (adjective) not involved or complicated; unpretentious; humble
simplistic: (adjective) making complex problems overly simple
The explanation of the motivations of the antagonist was *simplistic*, but then the critic tended to look at most motivations as *simple* issues of right and wrong.

stultify: (verb) to make useless or worthless; to take away strength or efficiency
stupefy: (verb) to make dull or stupid; to confuse or astound
Many experts fear that the hours of television that children watch every day *stultifies* their brains. A woman born in 1900 would be *stupefied* by the gadgets available today in most U.S. kitchens.

subtitle: (noun) second part of a title, often an explanation of the title
subtle: (adjective) not obvious, difficult to detect or understand
The *subtitle* of the report was not *subtle* in describing the author's opinion.

PRACTICE

After you finish reading the list once, go back and check off each word that you have difficulty with or are unfamiliar with. Write a sentence of your own that will help you remember the word.

NOTES

NOTES

NOTES

NOTES